CONSUMER AND COMMERCIAL CREDIT MANAGEMENT

The Irwin Series in Marketing

Consulting Editor   Gilbert A. Churchill, Jr.
                       University of Wisconsin, Madison

CONSUMER AND COMMERCIAL CREDIT MANAGEMENT

Ninth Edition

Robert H. Cole, Ph.D.
Professor Emeritus of Marketing
University of Nebraska—Lincoln

IRWIN

Homewood, IL 60430
Boston, MA 02116

This symbol indicates that the paper in this book is made from recycled paper. Its fiber content exceeds the recommended minimum of 50% waste paper fibers as specified by the EPA.

© RICHARD D. IRWIN, INC., 1960, 1964, 1968, 1972, 1976, 1980, 1984, 1988, and 1992

Sponsoring editor: Elizabeth S. MacDonell
Developmental editor: Kate Perez
Project editor: Karen Smith
Production manager: Ann Cassady
Interior designer: Larry J. Cope
Cover designer: Ivy I. Snider
Compositor: Weimer Typesetting Co., Inc.
Typeface: 10/12 Century Schoolbook
Printer: R. R. Donnelley & Sons Company

Library of Congress Cataloging-in-Publication Data

Cole, Robert Hartzell.
    Consumer and commercial credit management / Robert H. Cole. — 9th ed.
       p.   cm.—(The Irwin series in marketing)
    Includes bibliographical references and index.
    ISBN 0-256-09187-0
    1. Credit—Management.   2. Consumer credit.   I. Title.
II. Series.
HG3751.C64   1991
658.8'8—dc20   91–9218

Printed in the United States of America
1 2 3 4 5 6 7 8 9 0 DOC 8 7 6 5 4 3 2 1

To the Family

PREFACE

We live in a world of credit. Thus it is important for everyone to know and to understand the many advantages and benefits of credit, as well as the possible limitations arising from the use of credit. With such knowledge and experience, we are in a position to use credit more wisely.

The reader is encouraged to recognize that credit has enabled millions of American consumers to enjoy the happiness and opportunities of our material standard of living and has enabled American business firms to expand and profit.

It is equally important that we have a clear understanding of the legal framework—federal, state, and local—within which credit and collections operations are conducted. Thus even more space is devoted in this edition to the legal aspects of the field of credit.

The Suggested Readings at the end of the chapters have been expanded, in the hope that the reader will have a better knowledge of the large array of articles being prepared on the various credit topics.

The opening sentence of the 1960 preface, 32 years ago in the *first* edition of this book, was, "Credit is an increasingly important force in the lives of all of us today." This sentence is even more true today, as credit has become an increasingly important part of all phases of American life. And its importance will continue to grow in the years to come.

In this ninth edition, coverage of the vital consumer and commercial credit activities has been expanded and updated. Credit is not a static field; rather, it is dynamic and ever-changing. Keeping up with these changes was made possible by the recommendations and suggestions of the reviewers whose ideas are incorporated into this edition: Lon L. Mishler, Northeast Wisconsin Technical Institute; Louis Firenze, Northwood Institute; Alan R. Hamlin, South Utah State College; James W. Marco, Wake Technical College; Dennis L. Varin, Southern Oregon State College; and Jason K. Yee, National University.

Special thanks go to the following executives who gave their unlimited help and cooperation in the revising and updating of this ninth edition. It could not have been written without them.

- David B. Williams of the Dun & Bradstreet Business Credit Services.
- William H. Detlefsen of the Associated Credit Bureaus, Inc.
- Paul J. Mignini, Jr., of the National Association of Credit Management.
- Richard L. Cole of Cole Enterprises, Inc.
- William Bohmer of Credit Bureau Reports, Inc.
- Don Harrison of International Business Machines Corporation.

- Lucy H. Harr and Jack E. Blake of the Credit Union National Association.
- Mary Ann Armour of the International Credit Association.
- Jenifer Neu Sanchez of TRW Credit Data.
- Liz Rittler of Trans Union.
- John Ford of Equifax Inc.
- Debra Ciskey of the American Collectors Association, Inc.

As in all previous editions, any and all suggestions from the readers of this book will be most welcome, so the complete story of the management of consumer and commercial credit and collection activities can continue to be told.

Robert H. Cole

CONTENTS

Background to the Field of Credits and Collections

Credit in the Economy

The Objectives or Goals of Chapter 1 Are:

1. To give an overall view of the entire field of credit.
2. To define the term *credit* and to set up a classification of credit.
3. To point out what credit does for the consumer, for the retailer and service business operator, for the manufacturer and the wholesaler, for the financial institution, and for various government agencies.
4. To explain why all types of credit should be considered productive.
5. To discuss the interrelationship between public and private credit.
6. To illustrate the need for more education in the credit field.

We live in a world of credit. Every day, in every way, we become more and more involved in various aspects of this credit world.

Credit is an integral part of all phases of American life, and its importance will continue to grow into the 21st century. It has contributed to the development of the American economy and to the high standard of living enjoyed by most Americans. Credit helped the United States change from an agrarian, rural economy to a highly industrialized, urbanized one.

Credit is a familiar social invention that we use freely. As a result, it is essential for individual consumers, retailers, service business operators, wholesalers, manufacturers, financial executives, and government officials to have a clear understanding of what credit is, what it does, what it can do, and what it cannot do. To help meet this challenge, it is necessary to examine the current role of credit, look at the changes in the various types of credit plans and the factors that encourage or inhibit growth, and identify the social and economic goals served by credit and how these goals can best be reached by industry and government. Likewise, it is important that we understand the legal framework in which our credit and collection operations are conducted.

During the past five decades, the federal government, state and local governments, and business enterprises have greatly expanded their use of credit. Likewise, American consumers used credit extensively to purchase homes, buy cars and other consumer goods, repair and improve their residences, and obtain the services they need and want. Thus the terms *installment credit, revolving credit, open charge credit, service credit, credit card and charge card credit, cash loan credit, commercial credit, financial credit,* and *public credit* have become familiar to most of us.

The consumer's attitude toward credit has changed substantially over the years; today individual debt has attained respectability. More and more consumers have the financial security to satisfy wants and desires far in excess of their basic needs. While such financial security does not always suffice for cash purchases, it normally covers payments and interest charges for credit purchases.

Retailers and service business operators have increasingly favorable attitudes toward the use of consumer credit, as they discover that credit can be a powerful competitive device to expand sales, profits, and market share. This attitude, reflected backward through the channels of distribution, also has a favorable effect on wholesalers, manufacturers, and financial institutions.

Many people, however, continue to be disturbed when they hear the word *credit*. Some individuals condemn all types of credit, particularly installment credit, without stopping to analyze what our nation would be like without credit. The simple fact is that the United States runs on credit. If all credit activities stopped right now, business and government would come to a screeching stop. Few manufacturers, wholesalers, retailers, and service business operators would be able to stay in business without credit. Few individuals would be able to buy homes, cars, and appliances without some form of credit. And few people would be willing to pay cash for each newspaper delivery or for their gas, electricity, water, and telephone.

Thus we are using credit more and more, whether we are consumers, retailers, wholesalers, financial institutions, manufacturers, government, or other institutions engaged in marketing of goods, services, and money.

WHAT CREDIT IS

The term *credit* has been defined in many ways and by many writers. When analyzed, however, many of the proposed definitions are simply descriptions of credit or statements as to the use of credit, rather than definitions of credit itself. To contribute to an understanding of what credit is and what it does, the following definition will be followed throughout this book: *credit is a medium of exchange of limited acceptance.* Figure 1–1 illustrates this definition.

Medium of Exchange

Figure 1–1 shows that credit acts as a medium of exchange by facilitating the passage of goods or services from seller to buyer—just like money.

FIGURE 1–1 **How Credit Works**

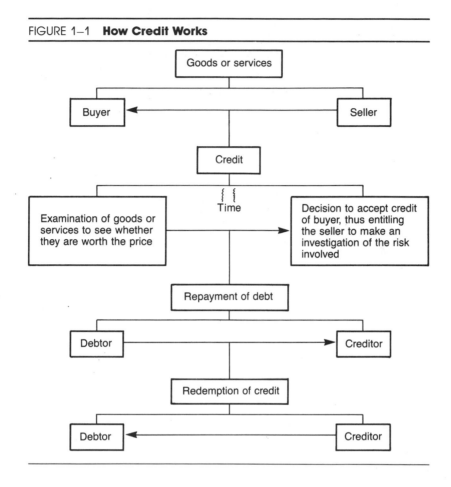

But credit does have particular characteristics. It is a medium of ex-change that is created at the time of the transaction and that arises for the purpose of facilitating that transaction. It is a medium of exchange that, after being issued, does not close the transaction; at some future time a further step must be taken—the credit must be redeemed by the process known as payment.

This medium of exchange creates certain rights and privileges. Credit is given by the buyer to the seller; the seller exchanges goods or services for the buyer's credit. Only after agreeing to accept the buyer's credit does the seller transfer the goods or services. In practice it is common to say that "Store X offers credit to its customers," but, in fact, Store X is simply accepting (or refusing) its customers' credit for the goods and services it has for sale.

Limited Acceptance

When a customer offers a merchant $20 today in exchange for a $20 sport shirt, the retailer doesn't stop to analyze whether to accept the $20 (except perhaps for caution against counterfeiting). Metal and paper money have a characteristic called *unlimited acceptance*. This is the main difference between credit, which has limited acceptance, and money, which has unlimited acceptance.

This limited-acceptance concept of credit is more clearly understood by looking at the definition diagramed in Figure 1–1. Although the buyer has the option of examining the goods or services to see whether they are worth the asking price and whether to offer credit, the seller also has the right to investigate the buyer and decide whether to accept the individual as a credit risk. Every credit transaction involves passage of time before the debt is repaid. Because of these two elements—"risk" and "time"— credit has limited acceptance.

When two parties to a transaction exchange goods or services for credit, we call them *buyer* and *seller,* but after the exchange we use the legal terms *debtor* and *creditor.* The exchange does not end their relationship, which continues until the credit is redeemed by the exchange of money. Upon payment, the buyer's credit is returned. The buyer can reuse this credit to purchase other goods or services if he or she can find another willing seller.

Credit as an Act versus Credit as a Power

Credit as an act can be measured in dollars. When a person offers credit to a retailer for a new suit and the retailer accepts the person as a credit risk, a credit act has taken place and a dollar amount can be placed on the indebtedness incurred.

Credit, however, can also be thought of as a power inherent in all of us—the power to create a medium of exchange. The quantity of this power that each of us can issue depends on the acceptance we can obtain for it— how many people we can induce to accept our credit and in what amount. Everyone has a quantity limit, but we can raise this limit by convincing others to accept additional credit. Thus credit as a power cannot be measured.

The power to issue credit is thus limited by the extent to which we can convince others of its acceptability. The credit record we make as consumers or business executives is the most significant contribution to our power to issue acceptable credit. Another important factor is our future ability to adhere to our promises. No matter how good our record may be, we still have to persuade others to validate it by accepting our credit. This willingness to accept our credit power rests on confidence.

Credit as a Right

Is credit a privilege or a right? Traditionally, those in the credit industry accepted the viewpoint that personal credit is a privilege and not a right. However, during the late 1960s and early 1970s, a trend emerged called the *galloping psychology of entitlement*. In this psychological process, an individual's wants or desires are converted into a set of presumed social rights—for example, from "I would like to be able to buy a home and to finance it with a 95 percent mortgage" to "I have the *right* to buy a home and to finance it with a 95 percent mortgage." This process of converting desires into rights, part of a worldwide revolution of rising expectations, is being applied to the field of credit.

Closely associated with this question of whether credit is a privilege or a right is the growing importance of the consumerism movement. While consumerism means a lot of things to a lot of people—mostly dissatisfaction with the marketplace and remedial efforts—it also has resulted in consumers becoming more conscious of what rights they really have.

Consumerism is a powerful force in America and has caused many social changes. Every industry has been influenced by consumers' outcries, and consumer testimony is a strong force in hearings on credit and charge card fraud.

Effect on Purchasing Power

Does credit increase or decrease purchasing power? To get an answer, we must determine whether the question involves an individual consumer or a business. The time frame is also involved.

If consumers' money runs out before the end of the month and they make purchases on credit, purchasing power for the short run is increased. However, at the end of the month payment is due, and if consumers are faced with an interest charge too, their purchasing power is correspondingly less than it would have been if they had delayed buying.

Alternatively, in their efforts to obtain material possessions quickly, many people agree to installment payments too large to be met out of their regular paychecks. Thus the family needs more income and family members begin moonlighting (holding second jobs) to meet the monthly payments. In a sense, then, the need to meet installment payments necessitates harder work and, as a result, the family gains more purchasing power. This larger purchasing power is reduced, however, by the amount of the interest charged.

Business concerns' use of credit facilitates the production of goods and services at a hoped-for profit, which in turn can be used to liquidate the indebtedness and to increase the firms' purchasing power.

Is Credit Productive?

Despite the close relationship between government credit, business credit, and consumer credit, there is no agreement as to the economic significance of each type. These differences in opinion are partly the result of regarding business credit and government credit as essentially *productive* in use and consumer credit as essentially *consumptive*. Attempts to classify credit into *productive* and *consumptive* categories and to regard only productive credit as beneficial to the economic welfare of the nation often lead to fallacious reasoning. Unfortunately, this approach to credit is still practiced in a few circles.

Some people hold the following views: business credit is productive because it facilitates the production of goods and services at a profit, which in turn liquidates the indebtedness; government credit, which is not self-liquidating, does, however, encourage production of goods and services and sets the wheels in motion to produce the conditions for debt liquidation; and consumer credit is used only to acquire items for consumption. In fact, some people regard consumers' use of credit with reservation and even as ill-advised.

But *all* credit—government, business, and consumer—is productive, and to view it otherwise is an economic fallacy. Consumer credit has helped raise our standard of living, afforded a host of consumer satisfactions, and resulted in the creation of utility. Consumer credit serves American consumers' needs and stimulates the economy in many ways.

Only recently have economists realized the importance of credit in our economy. The reason is that certain types of credit had little or no economic impact until the middle or late 1920s. For example, consumer credit is a phenomenon of the last four or five decades, with enormous growth since World War II. The broadened credit activities of financial institutions is of quite recent origin. Despite the prolonged use of some types of credit throughout the history of commerce and the importance of credit as a device for financing governments, few types of credit were used widely enough to affect business and consumer life.

Credit and Invasion of Privacy

Since the Fair Credit Reporting Act (FCRA) passed in 1971, a clear and definable definition of privacy has eluded governmental and private organizations.[1]

The report and recommendations of the Privacy Protection Study Commission (1977) attempted to reach a "thoughtful and reasonable point

---

[1]See Chapter 6 for details of the Fair Credit Reporting Act. Also see Peter J. Gray, "Federal Privacy Legislation," *The Credit World,* March–April 1990, p. 18, and "Is Nothing Private?" *Business Week,* September 4, 1989, p. 74.

FIGURE 1–2 **Major Federal Laws on Privacy**

Fair Credit Reporting Act of 1971. This law prevents credit agencies from sharing credit information with anyone but authorized customers. Consumers have the right to review their credit records under certain circumstances and to be notified of insurance and employment credit investigations.

Privacy Act of 1974. Federal agencies are prevented from allowing information collected for one purpose to be used for another.

Right to Financial Privacy Act of 1978. Federal agencies must follow strict procedures in going through banks' customer records.

Video Privacy Protection Act of 1988. Retailers cannot disclose video-rental records without customers' consent or a court order, nor can they sell such records.

Computer Matching and Privacy Protection Act of 1988. Computer matching of federal data to verify federal benefits eligibility or to claim delinquent debts is forbidden.

---

of balance with the amount and type of information that a person is expected to disclose and the good that a person can expect from such disclosure." The commission directed its efforts toward strengthening the individual consumer's desire to augment three basic principles:

1. The principle of maximizing fairness.
2. The principle of legitimizing expectations of confidentiality.
3. The principle of minimizing intrusiveness.

Figure 1–2 summarizes the major federal laws on privacy.

In early 1990, Equifax Inc. commissioned Louis Harris & Associates, a marketing research firm, to conduct a nationwide survey to canvass the views of the public and selected business executives about access to and use of consumer data, the safeguarding of such data, and the information trade-offs consumers would consider.

The survey sought public attitudes about issues such as:

1. Personal privacy, concern over revealing personal information, and the collection and use of individual information by organizations.
2. Engaging in what some consider immoral or illegal practices.
3. The trade-offs consumers are willing to make between use of individual information and desire/need for goods and services.
4. Level of confidence for responsible use of individual information by government and privacy-intensive industries.
5. Relationship between consumers' attitudes about direct marketers and their perception of the industry.
6. Collection of information for pre-employment purposes.
7. Use of credit reports for lending evaluation; and use of claims information as basis for health insurance rates.
8. View of executives of privacy-intensive industries toward information necessary to make decisions about job applicants, credit and

insurance, and their attitude about their own company's privacy protection policies.

9. Attitudes about Caller ID.
10. Attitudes toward capabilities of computers.[2]

Equifax's long-range commitment included plans for testing a program designed to increase consumer participation in direct marketing and for annual supplemental surveys.

CLASSIFICATION OF CREDIT

Credit is a medium of exchange of limited acceptance. We have explained how credit differs from money and have pointed out that credit also may be viewed as a potential power in the hands of users as well as a debt once the credit is accepted. But throughout this entire introduction, credit has been viewed primarily as one concept; no clear distinction has been made among the diverse types of credit that appears in our economy today. Yet the specific aims and results of the different types of credit are multifold. While many classifications are possible, the following permits a workable examination of credit in our present economy.

Note that credit is divided into two main classifications according to the form of the debtors' responsibility—private credit and public credit. Private credit concerns individual consumers and private businesses. This book is primarily concerned with the field of private credit.

> *Private credit*
> Consumer credit
> Merchandise (retail)
> Revolving
> Installment
> Open charge
> Service
> Open charge
> Revolving
> Installment
> Cash (banks, personal finance companies, etc.)
> Conventional installment
> Other types of installment
> Single payment
> Real estate credit

---

[2] "Equifax Report on Consumers in the Information Age," *The Credit World,* July–August 1990, p. 18.

Business credit
Merchandise and services (commercial or mercantile)
Cash (financial) (banks, finance companies, factors, insurance companies, etc.)
Long-term borrowing
Intermediate-term borrowing
Short-term borrowing
Public credit (federal, state, and other governmental units)

Public credit involves credit activities of the federal, state, and other governmental units. Private credit does not operate completely separate from public credit. The use of credit by the various governmental units and by the institutions established to administer public credit has an important influence on the amount and type of private credit. The United States has numerous governmental bodies—federal, state, and local—including such units as municipalities, school districts, sanitary districts, park boards, counties, and townships. A common characteristic of public credit is that it is generally not self-liquidating but is expected to be retired from payments made by the citizens. The quality of this credit and its acceptance by the citizens ultimately rest on the ability of the governing body to pay off the debt by collecting taxes; in other words, they rest on the income of the citizens.

Consumer Credit

While the study of credit as a vital function of business was begun early in the 1900s, attention to consumer credit[3] is a present-day development. This phase of credit is defined as the medium of exchange that an individual consumer may offer to a seller of goods or services or to a lender of money in order to obtain these items in the present and repay at some future time. At times, the study of consumer credit was relegated to a secondary position, with business credit, and in particular commercial credit, occupying the top position. Yet almost every person in America eventually has contact with some phase of consumer credit. The extent to which consumers use credit varies, of course. Some individuals buy only the bare minimum on credit, such as gas, water, electricity, and telephone. Others start using credit early and remain in a state of indebtedness throughout their lifetime.

MERCHANDISE (RETAIL) CREDIT.   This type of credit concerns retail sales to consumers. The sale may take place as a revolving credit, an installment, or an open charge transaction.

---

[3]See Suggested Readings at the end of the chapter.

Retail Revolving Credit. In this plan, the most common type, a customer buys goods and agrees to pay for them without a finance charge within 25 to 30 days after the statement closing date. However, if total payment is not made, the customer agrees to make a monthly payment that includes an interest charge for the privilege of using this type of credit. As long as the balance due is below the amount that the retail store believes the customer should not exceed, the customer is automatically eligible to make additional purchases on his or her account without any further investigation by the store.

The various credit card plans found in the economy today are one way of financing revolving credit purchases. In recent years the acceptance and collection of revolving credit transactions has been transferred from retail firms (where the transactions originate) to commercial banks and the private credit card companies. In statistical data on consumer credit (as reported by the Federal Reserve System), consumer revolving credit transactions usually are reported as part of consumer installment credit.

Retail Installment Credit. The type of consumer credit that has received the greatest praise and criticism over the years is retail installment credit. In this form of credit, payment for goods is extended over a considerable period of time and a carrying charge is levied on the customer for the privilege of delayed payment. Retail installment credit generally involves the purchase of only one item (such as a car), and the installment account may be secured by some additional legal agreement.

Commercial banks are closely connected with the retail installment field and are the largest holders of installment paper sold by retail dealers. Sales finance companies have also appeared in response to the growing demand for installment credit and to the financial needs of retailers making installment sales.

Retail Open Charge Credit. Until the advent and growth of revolving credit, open charge (or, as it is sometimes called, 30-day or regular or normal) credit was the type that the average customer would think of first when asked what the term *credit* meant. Today, however, this type of credit has become almost universally restricted to small retail establishments serving a limited clientele. This type of account enables customers to purchase goods now and pay for them usually 30 days later without any carrying charge or other expense. Any number of purchases may be made, provided that the combined dollar total does not exceed the credit limit that the store has set for that individual.

SERVICE CREDIT. Service credit is often neglected or overlooked in any discussion of consumer credit, but it is rapidly becoming a customary method of doing business between consumers and businesses dealing in services. Doctors, dentists, and lawyers—to name only a few—

are becoming accustomed to billing their customers for services rendered. The use of credit for utilities (gas, electricity, water, and telephone) is accepted almost without thought by most consumers. The three arrangements of open charge, revolving, and installment credit are found in service credit.

CASH CREDIT. Another whole field of credit activity involves lending *money* directly to consumers. This money may be repaid under one of three arrangements: (1) conventional installment, (2) other types of installment, and (3) single payment. Although borrowing for personal use has occurred throughout history, cash loan credit as we know it today is a development of the past 50 years. Today consumer finance companies (sometimes called personal finance companies or small loan companies), commercial or industrial banks (personal or consumer loan departments), credit unions, savings and loan associations, insurance companies, and other types of lenders serve the needs of their customers by lending money that consumers agree to repay. Also, cash advances through credit and charge card plans have been expanding in importance in recent years.

REAL ESTATE CREDIT. Although home mortgage loans used to be controversial, home mortgage credit is now readily accepted as a form of consumer credit. The amount borrowed to purchase a home generally is the largest amount for which the family will offer its credit, and the repayment period is much longer.

Business Credit

The second major field of credit is business credit. Business credit is one of the principal means by which business executives can translate opportunities into productive ventures. It gives them a valuable means of obtaining goods and services (or money with which to purchase goods and services) vital to the successful performance of their business activities. Business executives then try to sell their products for a profit, thus enabling them to repay the debts created. Thus, business credit is self-liquidating.

Business credit can be broken into two components: (1) commercial (or mercantile) credit and (2) cash (or financial) credit.

COMMERCIAL CREDIT. This form of credit enables a business to buy goods and services from another business and to pay for these items at some future time. If a firm sells both to consumers and to other business firms, only credit sales to other firms are considered commercial credit transactions. Commercial credit is an outstanding example of how the economy operates on a self-liquidating credit basis; an estimated 90 to 95 percent of transactions between commercial and industrial concerns are handled on credit.

CASH (FINANCIAL) CREDIT. Just like consumers, businesses also need to borrow money to be repaid at some future time. Most businesses borrow cash to acquire both current and fixed assets and agree to repay the amounts borrowed on a long-term (over five years), an intermediate-term (one to five years), or a short-term (less than one year) basis. Principal sources of business loans are commercial banks, investment companies, insurance companies, factors, commercial finance companies, and individuals. Bond and stock issues and commercial paper also should be considered.

Government Use of Credit

Public credit, which includes credit used by all governmental bodies and units, completes the structure of credit in the U.S. economy. Federal, state, and municipal governments find it increasingly necessary to use credit to meet their expenditures. In recent decades, governments' increased reliance on credit to finance their operations stems from (1) greatly increased costs and (2) the expansion of public programs in the areas of national defense, education, highways, and health and welfare. Governments borrow money for the same reason that businesses borrow money; their financing needs exceed their incomes. When governments borrow money, they usually issue a credit instrument. State and municipal governments often issue bonds; the federal government, on the other hand, may issue bonds or the shorter term Treasury notes, Treasury bills, and Treasury certificates. Each of these instruments represents government's promise to pay at some future date in exchange for the credit used to acquire money, goods, or services for government use. Such instruments typically result in the creation of checking accounts in the banking system against which government draws to meet its needs.

The credit capacity of any government is based on the sustained confidence it enjoys and its ability to levy and collect taxes from the public. The federal government's credit involves little risk on the part of lenders.[4] Some other political bodies enjoy this same high rating among lenders, but a number of local governments have difficulty in fulfilling their credit needs. In recent years, it has become increasingly difficult to raise revenue from existing tax sources and even more difficult to find additional tax sources. As this problem worsens, local governmental units will be able to provide fewer services. This problem is eased by the fact that most

---

[4]However, changes occur in interest rates and have corresponding effects on the prices of government securities. Purchasers of government securities may find themselves "tied in" until maturity of these securities if they buy when interest rates are low and these rates experience a substantial upward movement. Of course, the purchasers may secure the face value of the securities by waiting until maturity, but at the same time they lose possible interest return because of the low interest rate established at the time of purchase.

municipal bond issues are exempt from federal income tax. Because taxation is the local government's principal source of income, which is partly used to meet its credit obligations, a close relationship must exist between the two. Except for the federal government (because it can actually create money), the creditworthiness of political subdivisions rests more on their tax revenue potential than on the degree of confidence they enjoy. In this respect local government is like a business that must assure creditors of its income possibilities relative to its actual and planned expenditures. While governmental use of credit is not of major interest in this volume, it takes on significance when considered in relation to business and consumer credit.

INTERRELATIONSHIP BETWEEN PUBLIC, BUSINESS, AND CONSUMER CREDIT

To fully appreciate their part in the credit economy, credit executives must familiarize themselves with the close relationship between public credit, business credit, and consumer credit. Expansion and contraction of any form of credit influence each of the other major types of credit, and hence affect the conditions under which credit management must operate and formulate policies. Monetary and credit conditions help to explain the general level of prices and the overall price-making processes that influence the creditworthiness of credit risks. To serve their companies with the greatest effectiveness, credit managers must be knowledgeable of monetary matters and how their employers' and their customers' activities are affected.

A brief summary of the workings of our monetary system will illustrate the close relationship between public and private credit.

Credit Expansion and Contraction

The monetary system of the United States is a complex mechanism founded on credit transactions. The Constitution of the United States, in Section 8 of Article I, allocates to Congress the power "to coin Money" and "regulate the Value thereof." With the establishment of the Federal Reserve System in 1913, Congress delegated to the Federal Reserve Board a large portion of its authority to manage the nation's money supply and determine credit conditions.[5] In addition, the board has broad supervisory and regulatory controls over commercial banks that are members of the

---

[5]For a complete and detailed discussion of the operations of the Federal Reserve System, see *The Federal Reserve System, Purposes and Functions,* 6th ed. (Washington, D.C.: Board of Governors of the Federal Reserve System, 1974). Also see *A Guide to Federal Reserve Regulations,* rev. ed. (Washington, D.C.: Board of Governors of the Federal Reserve System, 1986). In addition, see Suggested Readings at the end of the chapter.

Federal Reserve System, bank holding companies, bank mergers, international banking facilities in the United States, the Edge Act and agreement corporations, foreign activities of member banks, and activities of the U.S. branches and agencies of foreign banks. Also, the board plays a vital role in maintaining the smooth functioning and continued development of the vast payment system of the nation and is responsible for implementing the major federal laws governing consumer credit. Although the Federal Reserve was structured in a way that made it both a part of and independent of government, the system has undergone many changes.

Under the Federal Reserve System, one key to expansion and contraction of bank credit is the fact that each bank is required to maintain a fractional cash reserve sufficient to support the bank's deposit liabilities. This reserve must be kept at a specified percentage of its demand, savings, and time deposits; the percentage is set by law and regulation. Whenever the bank's reserves exceed the minimum requirements, it can loan or invest the excess.

Credit expansion and contraction arise from the lending activities of individual banks, operating within the framework of the entire banking system. An individual bank can lend only the money that it acquires (from its depositors, the Federal Reserve, or other sources) in excess of its reserve requirements. After leaving the hands of the first bank, the money continues to do business as it passes into the banking system from bank to bank (in the form of deposits) or from person to person. Each loan or investment results in a series of events that permits a multiple expansion of credit.

Contraction of credit in the commercial banking system can result when the same processes work in reverse. Hence, credit contraction can occur as a result of actions taken by the Treasury or by businesses. As businesses need less credit from the banking system, loan repayments occur faster than the making of new loans, and a contraction of deposit credit takes place. Credit contraction is cumulative, as is credit expansion.

In practice, however, the processes frequently take place in different ways. The important thing is that checking account money (credit) is used to settle the bulk of all business transactions.

THE ROLE OF CREDIT IN OUR ECONOMY

Figure 1–3 shows the flow of goods and services from manufacturers to consumers. Money and credit are exchanged for goods and services as they progress through the channels and are finally purchased by consumers. The chart shows the interdependence that exists between consumer credit and much of the business credit used in producing and distributing the nation's goods and services.

Although economists disagree as to the particular forces that generate economic activity, for the purpose of our discussion, the chain of events shown in Figure 1–3 begins when consumer demand is stimulated and

FIGURE 1–3 **The Flow of Goods and Services versus the Flow of Money and Credit**

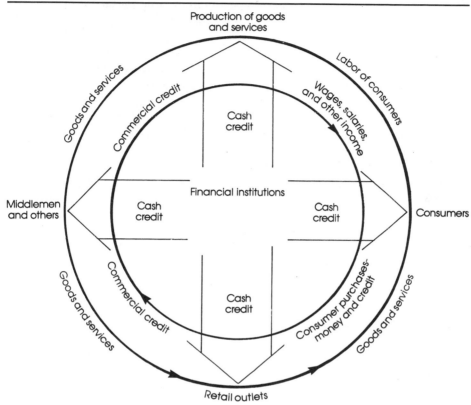

consumers make purchases. Rather than pay cash, either because of greater convenience or because of necessity, many consumers use their credit, or, in other words, exchange their credit for goods and services. Retailers of goods and services then are *holders* of consumer credit, and they in turn finance their inventories and other working capital needs by using their business credit. Retailers' inventories are usually financed by middlemen and manufacturers, who hold the retailers' credit. This chain of events repeats itself throughout the entire production, distribution, and consumption process.

Financial institutions feed cash credit into the production and distribution systems. This is also shown in Figure 1–3. Funds loaned to either businesses or consumers are used in a number of ways. Businesses may require additional cash for long-term needs (such as financing plant and equipment) or for short-term needs (such as financing inventories and other current assets). Likewise, consumers have similar long-term and short-term cash needs (for example, financing real estate and purchases of durable goods such as automobiles and major appliances). Channeling cash or cash credit into various segments of the economy affects each using segment. Economic segments are affected by cash credit supplied by financial institutions as well as merchandise credit resulting from the flow of goods and services in the distribution channel. This "broadbroom" analysis indicates the interrelationships and interdependence of the various kinds of credit. The simple fact is that if credit were not available for mass distribution of consumer goods, mass production of these goods would not occur.

In 1946 the federal government passed the Employment Act, which dealt with government responsibility in promoting economic stability and so-called full employment. But the definition of full employment changes periodically according to the wishes and beliefs of current government officials.[6]

Credit is an important factor in both government and private business efforts to provide full employment, despite the different interpretations of this term. The employment of labor to produce goods and services largely depends on business executives' forecasts of future market expectations, which are in turn importantly influenced by consumers' desires and their ability to fulfill these desires. Consumer credit is a vital link between mass production and mass distribution because it gives consumers the power to buy more goods and services. Likewise, business credit helps increase employment because it lets businesses expand their operations and thus employ more labor.

What Credit Does for Consumers

Individual consumers basically use credit for one of the following reasons: (1) because they want to raise their standard of living or increase their enjoyment, (2) because credit is convenient, or (3) because of the pressure of necessity.

TO RAISE STANDARD OF LIVING.   Human nature being what it is, consumers want to raise their standard of living and gain more enjoyment from life by having more of those goods and services that contribute to these ends.

Because consumers can use credit as a means of payment rather than having to save and accumulate funds, they considerably increase the range of goods available to them. Certain commodities have a high unit value, and only rarely are consumers able to accumulate the cash to pay for them immediately. Most homes are purchased through credit and paid for over

---

[6]Full employment does not actually mean that everyone should have a job; a certain percentage of unemployment is accepted as a fact of life. It is this accepted unemployment figure that has varied from time to time.

a long period. A number of other commodities with high unit value are now common in today's lifestyles. Frequently, these items (generally durable goods) are purchased on the installment plan. If this credit device were not available, few lower- and middle-income individuals would be able to use and enjoy such goods. Once consumers commit themselves to the purchase, they are impelled to make regular payment by terms of the contract. If they tried to save in advance of the purchase, it is doubtful that they would be able to accumulate the necessary funds. It is more likely that day-to-day temptations would arise, and they would dissipate their funds on "nonlasting" purchases.

CONVENIENCE OFFERED. Convenience is a vital reason why consumer credit has become so generally accepted. It is far more convenient to say, "Charge it, please," than to carry cash. Also, when credit is available at local stores, other members of the family can charge too. It may also facilitate household budgeting to have retailers assume part of the responsibility. Many people pay their bills only once a month, although their bank account is ample throughout the month, so that they could well pay cash.

PRESSURE OF NECESSITY. Necessity is a third reason why many consumers use credit. Some circumstances—birth, death, sickness, and similar events—demand a large immediate outlay. Not having sufficient reserves for the occasion, individuals secure a loan or use their credit for goods and services. Occasionally, of course, opinions differ as to what constitutes an emergency. The use of credit to pay off other bills may be classified as an emergency need. Frequently, consumers' installment payments are higher than they can handle out of current income.

What Credit Does for Retailers and Service Business Operators

Credit for retailers or service businesses serves a threefold purpose. First, it enables them to sell more goods or services by allowing customers to purchase on credit. Second, it permits them to purchase goods on credit. Third, cash loans from commercial banks or other financial institutions enable them to meet expenses and even expand their operations.

Why do retailers or service operators use credit as a medium of exchange when it may be more risky than other mediums? One obvious explanation is the desire to sell more goods or services. Buyers prefer this medium, so it is advantageous for business to accept it. In fact, the extent to which merchants lower their standard of credit acceptability often determines the extent to which they can enlarge their market opportunity. By accepting credit, merchants get a larger volume of business from customers with limited financial resources who would not be able to buy without it.

Credit also enables retailers and service operators to purchase their goods and services and pay for them at some future date. When they are able to buy additional goods on credit, they can stock more merchandise. By deferring payment, they can obtain funds from the sale of these goods, either in part or in total, before the time of payment. This, of course, enables them to do more business than they could do if their transactions were limited to present cash resources.

What Credit Does for Manufacturers and Wholesalers

Manufacturers and wholesalers depend on credit arrangements to sell their goods to their customers. Over the years this has become the customary way of doing business, although credit terms vary widely, depending on the character of the goods, the nature of the credit risk, the class of customer, competition, the financial resources of the manufacturer or wholesaler, economic conditions, and many other factors.

With many manufacturers and wholesalers, the problem is to make certain that their merchandise has the maximum exposure to consumers—more sales result if goods are offered in a large number of outlets. Thus a device that enlarges the number of sellers who stock the line will increase sales. Also, manufacturers seeking entry into a market in which they are unknown have to overcome a lack of confidence in their merchandise and in themselves. Since confidence is likely to generate confidence, their offer to accept the buyer's credit is more likely to develop acceptance of themselves and of their line. Acceptance of credit usually generates a series of transactions rather than a single sale. Thus credit relations are more likely to be continuing relations.

Competition with other manufacturers is another major reason why manufacturers accept credit. Companies that believe they are undisputed leaders in their particular industries or fields occasionally attempt to tighten credit terms. Unless competitors follow suit, they usually lose business and must return to their former, longer credit terms.

Both manufacturers and wholesalers use commercial credit when buying from their own sources of supply. Likewise, they are concerned with the availability of all types of cash (financial) credit. However, manufacturers and wholesalers are not directly involved with consumer credit unless they distribute goods to the ultimate consumer.

What Credit Does for Financial Institutions

Financial concerns—commercial banks, consumer and commercial finance companies, industrial banks, credit unions, savings and loan institutions, sales finance companies, insurance companies—all fill the vital need of providing cash to consumers and businesses. This may involve long-term or short-term borrowing or something in between. It may involve buying accounts receivable and notes receivable, thus providing needed capital to various types of businesses. Financial institutions are credit institutions. They accept their customers' credit so customers can use the cash received to buy goods and services and to carry on their own personal and business transactions. Interest income from credit transactions is the leading source of revenue to financial institutions.

Dangers in Using Credit

Properly used, credit is an efficient medium of exchange and an aid to the productive use of wealth and capital. But credit has its dangers. Sometimes the use of credit permits savers' capital to be allocated to nonproductive rather than productive uses. Thus accumulation of savings may be lost by unwise acceptance of credit.

Credit may overstimulate business activity, leading to inflation and boom followed by corrective action. Such errors of judgment have widespread repercussions. Because credit joins all units of the economy, the entire economy suffers as a result of those who make mistakes in their use of credit. Just as credit benefits all members of the economic community, it can cause all to suffer.

Because dangers result from abuses and excesses in the use of credit, this device must be used with care. Buyers and sellers, borrowers and lenders, debtors and creditors, credit managers and sales managers should all strive to use rather than abuse the services that credit offers.

THE CHANGING ROLE OF CREDIT AND THE NEED FOR EDUCATION

Despite the important role credit plays in our economy, some disagree as to its effects and its desirability. Some consumers still view the use of credit as dangerous and imprudent. A few writers hold the same attitudes and beliefs because they refuse to regard the consumption function as the dominant objective of economic activity. Furthermore, commercial credit, which is emphasized in the last half of this book, is often overlooked as an important device for financing businesses' short-term needs.

In the future both consumer and commercial credit should gain in emphasis and economic significance.

And credit will play an increasingly important role in our economy. Credit is replacing cash as a medium of exchange for government, business, and consumer transactions. New techniques will expand the opportunities for consumers to buy on credit almost every conceivable line of merchandise and most consumer services.

In view of the increased and changing use of consumer credit, an interest has arisen in education to help consumers understand credit and use it more intelligently and judiciously. While some observers feel that consumer education should be taught in the home, some favor consumer education in schools. Many young marriages break up due to financial problems, and overextended credit is a contributing factor.

Associations are expanding educational programs for those considering credit as a career field. For example, the 1989 International Credit Conference (ICC) was concerned mainly with "new directions" in consumer credit education.[7] The conference emphasized the partnership between the U.S. Office of Consumer Affairs (USOCA) and the American Association of Community and Junior Colleges (AACJC), the only national organization devoted solely to serving community, technical, and junior colleges.

In a recent national survey of some 1,200 colleges, the AACJC found that about one third of the 408 responding colleges have used Consumer Credit Counseling Services. Three-fourths of the respondents said they offer consumer-related courses. About 71 percent attached some importance to consumer courses, but only 8 percent believed community colleges should prepare citizens to be competent consumers.

The credit profession has long been involved in consumer education. One notable method used over the years is the National Credit Education Week in April. Many high schools offer credit subjects and personal finance as an elective. It is hoped this will reduce the personal and professional problems later associated with poor personal financial management. Educational programs in both the consumer and business credit fields will be discussed in detail in subsequent chapters.

DISCUSSION QUESTIONS

1. Explain why we live in a credit world.
2. What is meant by the statement that credit is a medium of exchange?
3. Why is credit considered to have limited acceptance, while money is said to have unlimited acceptance?
4. What is the difficulty involved in defining credit as a power?
5. What problems are involved if credit is considered a right rather than a privilege?
6. Does credit increase or decrease a person's purchasing power? Explain your answer.
7. Explain how the necessity of meeting credit payments may result in a family taking action to increase its purchasing power. Is this viewpoint realistic or theoretical? Why?
8. Is credit productive? Why or why not? Explain.

---

[7]For more on the conference, see Geraldine Bower, "Partnerships: New Directions," *The Credit World,* September–October 1989, p. 24. Also see Gale Burbach, "Education: A Never-Ending Task," *Business Credit,* April 1990, p. 17.

9. What are the two main subdivisions of private credit?

10. Distinguish between consumer credit and business credit.

11. What types of activities does public credit involve?

12. Explain why retail open charge credit has become less important in recent years and why revolving credit has become more important.

13. Explain why some people oppose the use of retail installment credit.

14. Distinguish between short-term, intermediate-term, and long-term borrowing of business concerns.

15. How do consumers use credit to raise their standard of living?

16. As a business executive, what advantages do you see in the use of business credit? What disadvantages?

17. Explain how credit functions as an aid to mass production, to mass distribution, to full employment, and to a higher standard of living.

18. Discuss the connection between a consumer's use of credit and an invasion of his or her privacy.

19. What is the nature of the demand for business credit?

20. What is the role of commercial credit in the financial scheme of most businesses?

21. What is meant by the statement "The monetary system of the United States is founded on credit transactions"?

22. What considerations lead some to regard consumer credit as *consumptive* in character, whereas business credit is more often regarded as *productive*?

23. What was the basic purpose of the Employment Act of 1946?

24. Why don't credit managers attempt to expand credit during the recession phase of a business cycle when it is perhaps most needed?

25. Do you believe that the present level of consumer credit is excessive? Why or why not?

26. What educational courses in credit are given in the public school system of your community?

27. Why was the Federal Reserve Board chosen to implement the major federal laws governing consumer credit?

28. What actions are taken in your community to celebrate National Credit Education Week?

SUGGESTED READINGS

Credit Expansion and Contraction

AVERY, ROBERT B., GREGORY E. ELLIEHAUSEN, and ARTHUR B. KENNICKELL. "Changes in Consumer Installment Debt: Evidence from the 1983 and 1986 Surveys of Consumer Finances." *Federal Reserve Bulletin,* October 1987, p. 761.

BERNANKE, BEN. "Monetary Policy Transmission: Through Money or Credit?" Federal Reserve Bank of Philadelphia *Business Review,* November–December 1988, p. 3.

BRYAN, LOWELL L. "The Credit Bomb in Our Financial System." *Harvard Business Review,* January–February 1987, p. 45.

FACKLER, JAMES S. "Should the Federal Reserve Continue to Monitor Credit?" Federal Reserve Bank of Kansas City *Economic Review,* June 1988, p. 39.

PARTHEMOS, JAMES. "The Federal Reserve Act of 1913 in the Stream of U.S. Monetary History." Federal Reserve Bank of Richmond *Economic Review,* July–August 1988, p. 19.

SIMPSON, THOMAS D. "Developments in the U.S. Financial System Since the Mid-1970s." *Federal Reserve Bulletin,* January 1988, p. 1.

Understanding
Consumer Credit

Types of Consumer Credit—Retail and Service

The Objectives or Goals of Chapter 2 Are:

1. To distinguish between "consumer retail and service" credit and "consumer cash" credit.
2. To explain the factors that influence a business manager's decision to sell on credit.
3. To explain the characteristics, benefits, and pitfalls of revolving credit plans.
4. To discuss the variations in computing finance charges in these revolving credit plans.
5. To trace the development and explain the principles of retail installment credit.
6. To show how to compute the annual percentage rate (APR) of finance charges in installment transactions.
7. To trace the development and changing importance of retail charge account credit.
8. To explain the growing importance of service credit.

Contrary to common belief, consumer credit dates back to ancient times. But most of our modern-day credit institutions are of fairly recent origin. Likewise, the story of consumer credit, like that of so many other business phenomena, is one of dramatic change and growth. Accompanying this change and growth has been the changing attitude of government, both federal and state, toward controlling the use of consumer credit.

Table 2–1 shows the growth of consumer credit from 1970 to 1988 broken down into installment and noninstallment categories. Installment credit is further broken down into automobile paper, revolving, mobile home paper, and all other loans. Noninstallment credit is subdivided into single-payment loans and charge accounts.

To put the volume of consumer credit in proper perspective, Table 2–1 also gives the ratio of consumer credit to disposable personal income (personal income less taxes). Figure 2–1 gives the same information in chart form.

TABLE 2–1 **Consumer Credit Outstanding: 1970 to 1988** (in $ billions, except percent. Estimated amounts of credit outstanding as of end of year. Seasonally adjusted.)

Type of Credit	1970	1975	1978	1979	1980	1981	1982	1983	1984	1985	1986	1987	1988
Credit outstanding	**131.6**	**204.9**	**308.3**	**347.5**	**349.4**	**366.6**	**381.1**	**430.4**	**511.8**	**592.4**	**647.2**	**679.2**	**728.9**
Ratio to disposable personal income (percent)*	18.3	17.9	19.8	20.0	18.2	17.2	16.9	17.7	19.1	20.8	21.4	21.2	21.0
Installment	103.9	167.0	262.0	296.5	297.6	310.7	323.5	367.9	442.5	517.8	572.0	607.7	659.5
Automobile paper	36.3	56.9	98.7	112.4	111.9	118.9	124.2	143.7	173.7	209.6	247.3	266.0	281.2
Revolving	4.9	14.5	45.2	53.3	54.8	60.8	66.2	78.6	100.2	122.0	137.0	153.9	174.8
Mobile home paper	2.4	15.3	16.9	18.2	18.6	20.3	22.8	23.7	25.7	26.8	27.4	26.4	25.7
All other loans	60.2	80.1	101.1	112.4	112.1	110.5	110.2	121.6	142.8	159.2	160.4	161.5	177.8
Commercial banks	48.6	82.9	135.5	152.7	145.5	146.0	149.1	169.3	209.1	241.6	263.0	282.9	318.9
Finance companies	27.2	32.7	45.7	57.1	61.9	69.7	74.9	82.9	89.5	111.0	133.9	140.3	145.2
Credit unions	12.8	25.4	43.9	46.1	43.6	45.5	46.8	52.9	65.5	71.9	76.2	80.1	86.1
Retailers†	12.9	16.6	23.6	25.5	26.1	28.4	29.4	34.1	37.2	39.1	39.4	41.0	43.5
Other‡	2.3	9.2	13.0	14.9	20.3	20.8	23.2	28.4	41.1	53.9	59.4	63.5	65.8
Noninstallment	27.7	37.9	46.3	51.0	51.8	56.0	57.6	62.5	69.2	74.7	75.1	71.4	69.4
Single-payment loans	18.9	26.8	35.1	39.1	39.6	43.8	45.5	48.8	54.6	59.1	58.4	53.0	49.0
Charge accounts	8.7	11.0	11.2	11.8	12.1	12.1	12.0	13.6	14.6	15.6	16.7	18.5	20.4

*Based on fourth-quarter, seasonally adjusted disposable personal income at annual rates as published by the U.S. Bureau of Economic Analysis.

†Excludes 30-day charge credit held by travel and entertainment companies.

‡Comprises savings institutions and gasoline companies.

Source: Board of Governors of the Federal Reserve System.

FACTORS AFFECTING A DECISION TO SELL ON CREDIT[1]

In their decision to adopt some type of consumer credit plan, merchants or service business operators must consider many factors including effects on sales and on profits, costs of operation, customer desires, amount of capital available, competition, type of goods, reliability of credit information, availability of credit card plans, and legal restrictions.

Effect on Sales and on Profits

Whether to introduce or expand consumer credit activities depends primarily on how such actions will affect sales and profits. Despite all other factors, unless merchants or service business operators believe that increased sales and profits will result, or unless they are forced to offer or expand consumer credit activities to maintain their present profit level, they should not do so.

---

[1]Consideration should be given to the differences between consumer retail and service credit (as discussed in this chapter) and consumer cash credit (as discussed in Chapter 4) where loan proceeds are used to purchase a retail item or to pay for some service.

FIGURE 2–1 **Consumer Credit, 1970 to 1988**

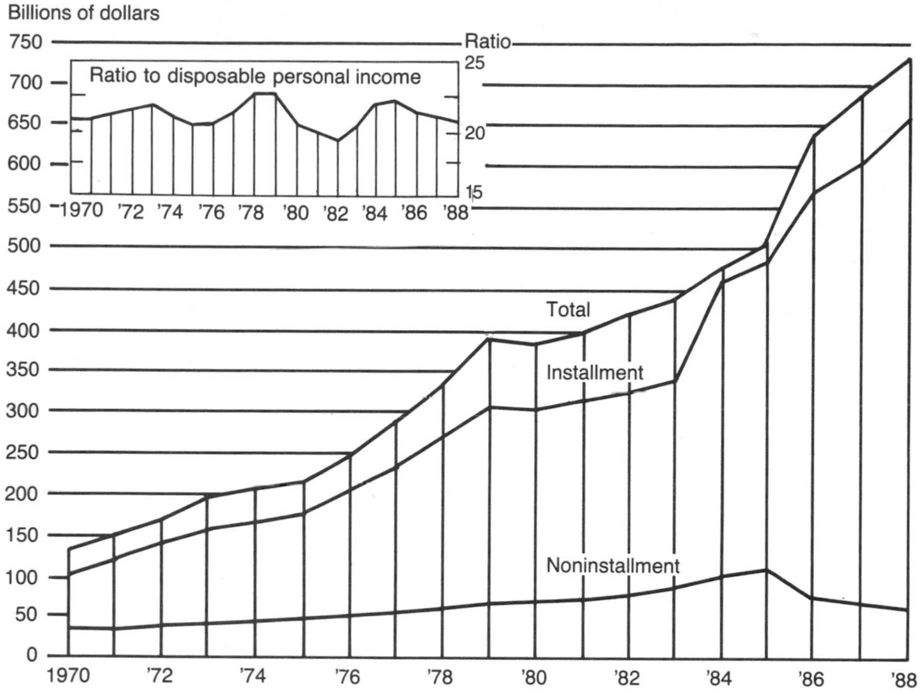

Source: Based on data in Table 2–1.

Costs of Operation

Credit activities incur costs in soliciting new accounts, investigating credit applications, making decisions on whether to accept or reject, preparing and issuing identification cards, preparing and handling monthly statements, receiving payments from customers, tracing and contacting delinquent accounts, investing capital in accounts receivable, and bad debts. Other costs involve equipment, supplies, space, and utilities. Offsetting these expenses, the business can increase its sales and profits and earn income from finance charges.

Customer Desires

Simply installing a consumer credit plan doesn't guarantee higher sales and profits, unless customers actually want to buy on credit or can be persuaded to do so.

Customers of smaller stores often ask to be trusted for a few days until they have the money to pay for their goods. And some firms claiming to be cash stores carry the accounts of their "privileged" customers. Such practices and requests encourage stores to offer or expand credit operations.

Amount of Capital Available

A consumer credit plan automatically increases a store's capital needs. No longer does the business receive immediate cash for every item sold. In fact, increased credit sales call for a larger capital investment. Business executives don't get longer terms from a supplier simply because they operate on a credit basis. As a result they often have to borrow money to pay their own bills or invest more of their own capital (if available) before customers pay for goods bought on credit.

As an alternative, some credit plans allow merchants to sell their accounts receivable to an organization operating such a plan. Merchants thus continue to work on a "cash" basis but pay a fee or discount for this privilege. This type of plan will be discussed in a later chapter.

Competition

Competitors' policies influence other vendors' decisions. Credit is one of the most important services retailers provide their customers. Retailers without credit services are in a weakened competitive position. For example, durable goods are commonly purchased on credit. American consumers *expect* this arrangement, and the chances are that they will buy high-unit-valued items from those firms that can satisfy this requirement.

Type of Goods

This factor plays an important role in the decision to adopt a consumer credit plan and the type of plan to adopt. If a store handles primarily big-ticket items (such as appliances, furniture, and similar consumer durables), a successful plan must provide a long enough repayment period to permit reasonable monthly payments. With these types of goods, regular recurring purchases are not customary. However, goods that would be consumed before they are completely paid for, such as groceries, are not usually good candidates for credit plans. Yet some firms use extended payment plans even for the purchase of groceries.

Changes do occur. In 1989, some movie chains started accepting credit cards. Now customers at hundreds of theaters charge both tickets and concessions on credit cards. The second-largest U.S. movie chain, Cineplex Odeon, began taking American Express credit cards at its 502 theaters on May 1, 1989. Some chains allow moviegoers to charge by phone ahead of time and pick up tickets at the box office the day of the show. Charging at the movies started in Europe and is an accepted method of payment there.

Reliability of Credit Information

To make sound credit decisions, businesses need accurate and up-to-date credit information. Traditionally local retail credit bureaus have been the main source of such information. However, today other sources are competing with local credit bureaus. This topic will be discussed in a subsequent chapter.

Use of Credit Card and Charge Card Plans

Some firms want to adopt a credit plan but don't have or can't obtain the necessary capital. Others don't want to deal with all the details, procedures, and paperwork. As a result, they decide to sell part or all of their credit activities to a consumer financing institution. See Chapter 3 for a detailed discussion of the financing of credit transactions.

Legal Restrictions

In addition to federal law, consumer credit transactions are also regulated by state laws. Most states stipulate the maximum interest rate allowed on various types of credit plans, the maximum length of time such plans are allowed to run, and other details of the credit contract.

RETAIL OPTION-TERMS REVOLVING CREDIT

One of the most popular credit plans is the retail option-terms revolving credit plan. Revolving credit is a hybrid of installment credit and open charge credit, two types that will be discussed later in this chapter.

In May 1956, J. L. Hudson's Department Store in Detroit introduced its "30-Day Account with Optional Terms." Under this plan customers could pay in full in 30 days without a finance charge, or they could pay as little as one-fourth of the balance each month with a minimum monthly payment of $10 if the balance was $50 or less. If customers chose to extend their payments past 30 days, the store added a finance charge.

The most important features of a typical, present-day option-terms revolving credit plan are listed here.

- Customers ordinarily make a series of purchases—in fact, retail stores consider their sales promotion programs faulty if this doesn't happen.
- There is no down payment.
- If the account is not paid within the prescribed time, a series of recurring payments are made.
- There is a finance charge if the account is not paid within the prescribed time.
- In most states, revolving credit transactions are governed by state law.[2]

---

[2]New York was the first state to pass such a law. The New York law, which went into effect October 1, 1957, recognized that retail stores have different problems in handling revolving credit accounts, as opposed to other types of credit plans. Today almost all states have passed special legislation to regulate revolving credit transactions.

FIGURE 2–2

SEARSCHARGE CREDIT ACCOUNT APPLICATION ID 63

STORE NO.

Please indicate below name in which account is to be carried. Applicant, if married, may apply for a separate account.

INFORMATION ABOUT YOURSELF

Form fields: (COURTESY TITLES ARE OPTIONAL) FIRST NAME, MIDDLE INITIAL, LAST NAME; ☐ MR. ☐ MRS. ☐ MISS ☐ MS.; ADDRESS (TO WHICH YOU WANT YOUR BILLING MAILED), APT., CITY, STATE, ZIP CODE; RESIDENCE ADDRESS, APT., CITY, STATE, ZIP CODE; HOME TELEPHONE, BUSINESS TELEPHONE, SOCIAL SECURITY NUMBER, AGE, NO. OF DEPENDENTS (EXCLUDE YOURSELF); ARE YOU A U.S. CITIZEN? ☐ YES ☐ NO (IF NO, EXPLAIN IMMIGRATION STATUS); ARE YOU A PERMANENT RESIDENT? ☐ YES ☐ NO; HOW LONG AT PRESENT ADDRESS ☐ YEARS ☐ MOS.; DO YOU: ☐ OWN ☐ RENT ☐ OTHER ☐ BOARD ☐ L/W PARENTS; MONTHLY RENT OR MORTGAGE $; PREVIOUS ADDRESS (IF LESS THAN 2 YEARS AT PRESENT ADDRESS), APT., CITY, STATE, ZIP CODE, HOW LONG? ☐ YEARS ☐ MOS.; EMPLOYER (RETIRED/STUDENT, INDICATE: HOW LONG/YEAR IN SCHOOL), ADDRESS, CITY, STATE, ZIP CODE, HOW LONG? ☐ YEARS ☐ MOS.; OCCUPATION (FORMER OCCUPATION IF RETIRED), NET INCOME (TAKE HOME PAY) ☐ PER MONTH ☐ PER WEEK, PREVIOUS EMPLOYER (IF LESS THAN 1 YEAR WITH PRESENT.), HOW LONG? ☐ YEARS ☐ MOS.; OTHER INCOME✱ $ ☐ PER MONTH ☐ PER WEEK, SOURCE OTHER INCOME, ✱Note: Alimony, child support or separate maintenance income need not be disclosed if you do not wish to have it considered as a basis for paying this obligation.

FINANCIAL INFORMATION

Form fields: MAJOR CREDIT CARDS (VISA, MASTERCARD, ETC.), ACCOUNT NUMBER, MO. PAYMENT $, AUTO LOAN? NAME OF LENDER ☐ YES ☐ NO, MO. PAYMENT $; OTHER CREDIT CARDS (DEPT. STORES, ETC.), ACCOUNT NUMBER, MO. PAYMENT $, PREVIOUS SEARS ACCOUNT? ☐ YES ☐ NO, ACCOUNT NUMBER; DO YOU HAVE A: CHECKING ACCOUNT? ☐ YES ☐ NO, NAME OF BANK/FINANCIAL INSTITUTION, ACCOUNT NO. (OPTIONAL), IS THIS AN INTEREST PAYING OR NOW ACCOUNT? ☐ YES ☐ NO; DO YOU HAVE A: ☐ SAVINGS ACCOUNT ☐ CD ☐ MONEY MARKET ☐ OTHER, NAME OF BANK/FINANCIAL INSTITUTION, ACCOUNT NO. (OPTIONAL); RELATIVE OR PERSONAL REFERENCE NOT LIVING WITH YOU, ADDRESS, CITY, STATE, RELATIONSHIP.

Complete this section if you want cards issued to additional buyers on your account.

Form fields: 1. FIRST NAME, LAST, RELATIONSHIP; 2. FIRST NAME, LAST, RELATIONSHIP.

SPOUSE INFORMATION

Complete this section if: (1) your spouse is an authorized buyer, (2) you reside in a community property state (AZ, CA, ID, LA, NV, NM, TX, WA, WI), or (3) you are relying on the income or assets of a spouse as a source for payment.

Form fields: SPOUSE, FIRST NAME, MIDDLE INITIAL, LAST NAME, AGE; EMPLOYER, ADDRESS, CITY, STATE, ZIP CODE; HOW LONG? ☐ YEARS ☐ MOS., OCCUPATION, SOCIAL SECURITY NUMBER, NET INCOME (TAKE HOME PAY) $ ☐ PER MONTH.

I agree to pay Sears in accordance with the credit terms disclosed to me and to comply with all terms of the SearsCharge Agreement. A copy of the SearsCharge Agreement will be given to me to keep when my application is approved. Sears will retain a security interest under the Uniform Commercial Code on all merchandise charged to the account. Sears is authorized to investigate my credit, employment, and income references and to report to proper persons and credit bureaus my performance of the account. Finance charges not in excess of those permitted by law will be charged on the outstanding balance from month to month.

X_____ APPLICANT'S SIGNATURE _____ DATE

- Under the federal Truth in Lending Act, disclosure procedures are spelled out for open-end (including revolving credit) credit transactions.[3]

Figure 2–2 shows the credit account application form used by one of the larger retail chains for its revolving credit plan.

Under the option-terms revolving credit plan commonly found today, customers usually have the option of paying their bills within 25 to 30 days (from billing date) without any finance charge. The plan provides a schedule of payments for amounts carried beyond the prescribed time. For each range of unpaid balances—for example, $10.01–$200—a specific monthly payment such as $10 or $11 is due. In the example shown in Table 2–2,

---

[3]For details of the federal Truth in Lending Act, see Chapter 6.

FIGURE 2–2   (concluded)

IMPORTANT SEARSCHARGE CREDIT TERMS

The information below includes the costs associated with a SearsCharge Account. It is accurate as of October 1989, but may change after that date. To find out what may have changed write to: Sears Telemarketing Center, 2269 Village Mall Dr., Mansfield, OH 44906. A copy of the entire SearsCharge agreement for you to keep, with all terms applicable to your state of residence, will be sent to you with the credit card(s). You need not accept the card and are not required to pay any fee or charge disclosed unless the card is used.

Annual Percentage Rate	The annual percentage rate is 21% unless you reside in a state shown below:	Balance Calculation Method For Purchases	The Average Daily Balance method (including new transactions) is used in all states except Maine, Massachusetts, Minnesota, Mississippi, Montana, New Mexico and North Dakota where the Average Daily Balance method (excluding new transactions) is used.

	Alabama .... 21% Massachusetts 18%
	  to $750, 18% on excess Michigan 20%
	Alaska .... 18% Minnesota 18%
	  to $1000, 10.5% on excess Missouri 20.04%
	Arkansas .... 12% Nebraska 21%
	  (See Variable Rate Information) to $500, 18% on excess
	California ....19.2% No. Carolina 18%
	Connecticut .... 18% No. Dakota 18%
	Florida .... 18% Pennsylvania 18%
	Hawaii .... 18% Puerto Rico 20.4%
	Iowa .... 19.8% Rhode Island 18%
	Kansas .... 21% Texas 18%
	  to $1000, 14.4% on excess Washington 18%
	Louisiana .... 18% W. Virginia 18%
	Maine .... 18% Wisconsin 18%
		Minimum Finance Charge	A minimum monthly finance charge of 50¢ applies in all states except Arkansas, Connecticut, Hawaii, Maryland, Nebraska, Nevada, No. Carolina, No. Dakota, Rhode Island, Virginia, Dist. of Columbia, and Puerto Rico.

		Late Payment Fees	Late payment fees vary from state to state. They range from zero to the lesser of $5 or 5% with a minimum of $1 on payments more than 10 days late.
Variable Rate Information	(Arkansas Residents Only) Your Annual Percentage Rate may vary. The rate is determined by adding 5% per annum to the Federal Reserve Discount Rate on 90 day commercial paper in Arkansas.	Annual Fees	None
		Over-The-Credit-Limit Fees	None
Grace Period To Repay Balance	You have 30 days from your billing date to repay your balance before being charged a finance charge.	Transaction Fees	None

Source: Reprinted with permission of Sears, Roebuck and Co.

TABLE 2–2 **An Option-Terms Revolving Credit Plan**

Schedule of minimum monthly payments. The required minimum monthly payment is based on the highest New Balance on the account.

When the Highest New Balance Reaches:	The Minimum Monthly Payment will be:	
$ .01 to $ 10.00	Balance	You may always pay more than the required minimum monthly payment. The minimum payment will change only if charges to the account increase the balance to a new high. The minimum payment will not decrease until the New Balance is paid in full.
10.01 to 200.00	$10.00	
200.01 to 240.00	11.00	
240.01 to 280.00	12.00	
280.01 to 320.00	13.00	
320.01 to 360.00	14.00	
360.01 to 400.00	15.00	
400.01 to 440.00	16.00	
440.01 to 470.00	17.00	
470.01 to 500.00	18.00	

Over $500.00: 1/28th of highest account balance rounded to next higher whole dollar amount.

---

when the account balance is over $500, the monthly payment is 1/28th of the account balance, which includes the finance charge. Payment due is predicated on the balance owed, providing for reduced monthly payments as the balance outstanding declines. Repayment schedules vary among retail organizations.

Variations in Computing Finance Charges

Different stores use different methods to compute finance charges on re-volving credit accounts: the previous or opening balance method, the average daily balance method, and the adjusted balance method.

In the oldest of the three methods, the previous balance method, the finance charge is based on the previous month's balance without deducting payments or credits made during the month if the account is not paid in full. This method was formulated under the cash price–time price doctrine, prior to the time when retail credit rates were controlled by state laws.

In the average daily balance method, the finance charge varies according to the point in the billing cycle when the customer makes a payment. A fairly recent development, this method is a by-product of the computerization of retail accounts receivable. The average daily balance is the sum of the actual amounts owing each day of the monthly billing period, including charges made during the current monthly billing period but excluding unpaid finance or insurance charges, if any, divided by the number of days in the billing period. All payments and other credits are subtracted from the previous day's balance.[4]

The adjusted balance method bases the finance charge on the previous month's ending balance less any payments or credits. Few stores use this method although it may be best for the customer.

The following table compares the three revolving credit card billing systems. APR stands for annual percentage rate, which will be explained in detail later in the chapter.

	Adjusted Balance	Previous Balance	Average Daily Balance
Monthly rate	1½%	1½%	1½%
APR	18%	18%	18%
Previous balance	$400	$400	$400
Payments	$300	$300	$300 on 15th day
Finance charge	**$1.50** (1½% × $100)	**$6.00** (1½% × $400)	**$3.75** (1½% × average balance of $250)

---

[4]Professor E. Ray McAlister of North Texas State University extensively researched the methods of assessing finance charges on revolving credit accounts. He points out that the average daily balance method is not a single method; there are at least three or four different variations of this method, each with a different impact on the finance charge yield to the creditor and cost to the consumer.

As the example shows, the finance charge may vary considerably for the same pattern of purchases and payments on a revolving credit card account. Even when the annual percentage rate is the same, the amount of the finance charge depends on how the creditor treats payments. Most creditors also charge a flat annual membership fee for the use of their card.

Since customers can avoid finance charges on revolving credit card accounts by paying within a certain time, it is important that they receive the bill promptly and get credit for paying promptly. Customers should also check the payment date on the statement; in most instances creditors must credit payments on the day received. And customers should also follow the creditor's instructions as to where, how, and when to make payments in order to avoid delays that may result in finance charges.

Other Important Characteristics

It is illegal for a revolving charge creditor (this also applies to credit cards as discussed in Chapter 3) to send a customer a credit card unless the customer asks or applies for one. However, a card issuer may send a customer, without request, a new card to replace an expired one. The customer also may be sent an application for a card in the mail or be asked to apply by phone.[5]

The customer's risk for unauthorized charges on lost or stolen cards is limited to $50 on each card, even if someone charges hundreds of dollars before the card is reported missing.[6] The customer does not have to pay for any unauthorized charges made after the customer notifies the issuer of the loss or theft of the card.

Customers may withhold payment on any damaged or shoddy goods or unsatisfactory services purchased with a credit card, as long as they make an effort to solve the problem with the merchant.[7]

Discounts for Cash or Surcharges on Credit

In 1974, Congress amended the Consumer Credit Protection Act[8] to encourage merchants to offer discounts to customers who pay with cash instead of credit cards. The amendments prohibited card issuers from contractually forbidding merchants to offer cash discounts and exempted cash discounts of up to 5 percent from the requirement of disclosure as finance charges under the federal law. The surcharge prohibition was

---

[5]See the Credit Card Issuance Act in Chapter 6.
[6]Ibid.
[7]See the Fair Credit Reporting Act in Chapter 6.
[8]See Chapter 6.

extended in 1978 for an additional two years, until February 27, 1981, without change.

Under the Cash Discount Act of 1981, the surcharge prohibition was extended until February 27, 1984, but only after considerable debate and the additional requirement that the Federal Reserve Board prepare a study on credit cards. Such a study was prepared,[9] but the surcharge ban expired without further congressional action and surcharges on credit card use are currently valid.

Benefits and Pitfalls of Revolving Credit

A revolving credit plan doesn't automatically assure higher profits. And many of the advantages for the store are disadvantages for the customers.

TO THE CUSTOMER.   Customers who use a revolving credit plan can usually charge more than under a 30-day plan because they have more time to pay. They are free to buy any time (usually up to a limit set by the store) without having their credit rechecked with each purchase, as is the case with the usual installment buying. In addition, customers can pay the entire amount due with no finance charge or pay the amount owed in a series of payments with a finance charge added.

Despite the advantages, customers encounter certain pitfalls. Because it is so easy to buy, some people find themselves continually in debt to the store. In fact, some customers look on revolving credit payments in the same way as income tax and other types of payroll deductions.

Another factor is the finance charge. The most commonly used finance charge, 1½ percent per month on the unpaid balance, results in a true annual rate of approximately 18 percent.

On their 1989 federal income tax forms, consumers could deduct only 20 percent of the personal interest they paid on their revolving credit accounts. The Tax Reform Act of 1986 phased out the tax deduction on personal borrowing. As of 1991, the consumer could not write off any interest.

Some customers don't understand the finance charges they are paying or certain provisions in the contract they sign. For example, a store usually claims title to merchandise purchased under its revolving credit agreement until paid in full. Each payment is applied to merchandise and services as follows: first, to unpaid finance charges; then, if items are purchased on different dates, the first purchased is the first paid; if items are purchased on the same date, the lowest priced is first paid. Different contracts have different provisions as to title.

---

[9]*Credit Cards in the U.S. Economy* (Washington, D.C.: Board of Governors of the Federal Reserve System, 1983).

TO THE STORE. A store's primary purpose in introducing revolving credit is to increase sales and, in turn, profits. In addition the store gains added income from finance charges.

By offering a revolving credit plan, a store can meet its competition, attract new customers, and encourage current customers to make more purchases. Many stores adopt a revolving credit plan to decrease bad-debt losses; customers not only purchase more but also can pay off the amount they owe much more easily through small but regular monthly payments.

Revolving credit plans require more capital investment because customers pay over an extended period of time. Some stores incur more bad-debt losses due to "skips." The type of clientele, which may change with the introduction of revolving credit, may call for more careful and costly credit investigation. But "calling for" a different type of investigation and actually "making it" are two different things. Revolving credit also involves additional bookkeeping, billing, and other related tasks, thus adding to the store's operating expenses.

Current Status of Retail Revolving Credit

In the 1970s and early 1980s, retail chains and oil companies pushed their retail revolving credit plans. At the close of 1988, Sears reported 66 million credit cards outstanding with annual charges of $88.9 billion; J.C. Penney, 36 million credit cards with annual charges of $7.3 billion; and Amoco, Shell, and Mobil Oil had a combined total of 45 million credit cards outstanding.

In addition to its own store credit card, Sears, Roebuck and Co. issues and promotes the Discover card, which can be used in Sears stores and other retail stores. Discover card is discussed in Chapter 3.

Table 2–3 reflects the number of credit card holders, the number of cards outstanding, the dollar amount spent by consumers using credit cards, and the dollar amount of credit card debt from 1980 to 1987.

Major Oil Company Plans

Major oil companies were initially very strict in their acceptance of individuals as credit risks. And customers were allowed to charge only items normally asked for in a service station (gas, oil, tires, repairs). A company consolidated a customer's purchases over a period of time (generally 30 days) on one bill to be paid as a regular 30-day open account with no finance charge, even for late payment. This situation changed, however, when the major oil companies adopted the revolving credit type of plan. Interest rates are determined by the law in the consumer's home state, not the state where the card-issuing company is located or the state in which the purchase is made.

TABLE 2–3   **Credit Cards—Holders, Numbers, Spending, and Debt, 1980–1988**

Type of Credit Card	Cardholders (millions)			Number of Cards (millions)			Credit Card Spending ($ billions)			Credit Card Debt ($ billions)		
	1980	1985	1988	1980	1985	1988	1980	1985	1988	1980	1985	1988
Total	(NA)	(NA)	**108.4***	(NA)	(NA)	**859.5**	**205.4**	**322.7**	**397.1**	**81.2**	**128.0**	**180.0**
Bank	63.3	73.3	83.1	110.6	161.4	197.8	52.9	125.9	189.9	25.0	65.6	113.5
Travel and entertainment	10.5	15.5	20.2	10.3	18.8	24.2	21.2	51.0	84.6	2.7	6.4	12.3
Retail store	83.0	91.0	93.5	290.5	341.0	400.9	74.4	90.0	64.9	47.3	50.5	41.8
Oil company marketers	68.5	78.0	80.1	109.6	117.0	118.6	28.9	28.8	21.9	2.2	2.7	2.5
Other†	(NA)	(NA)	89.0	(NA)	(NA)	118.0	28.0	27.0	35.8	4.0	2.8	9.9

NA = Not available.

*Cardholders may hold more than one type of card.

†Includes airline, automobile rental, telephone company, hotel, motel, and other miscellaneous credit cards.

Source: *Statistical Abstract of the United States* (Washington, D.C.: U.S. Department of Commerce, Bureau of the Census, 1990), p. 500; Board of Governors, Federal Reserve System.

Service stations also honor bank credit cards, although some major oil company stations manage their own credit plans in addition to the bank card plan. Such an arrangement, they believe, encourages customer loyalty. In fact, several major oil companies recently decided to accept only their own company cards, to the exclusion of all other credit plans.

The top six oil company card issuers are Shell, Chevron, Mobil, Amoco, Exxon, and Texaco. Only a small percentage of these cards carry an annual fee, typically $20 per year. In addition to providing revolving credit on oil station purchases, Amoco and Shell provide credit at certain restaurants and hotels.

RETAIL INSTALLMENT CREDIT

Retail installment credit has been the subject of more praise and more criticism than any other type of consumer credit. Since most American families use installment credit, often to purchase the more expensive items in the family budget, it is important to these families, to the business and financial institutions concerned, and to society in general that installment credit be used wisely and correctly.

Increasing Frequency of Use

Table 2–1, which breaks down consumer installment credit by type, indicates its increasing frequency of use. To what factors can we attribute this rapid growth in installment credit? First, an expanding variety of consumer products is adaptable to installment selling. Second, consumer attitudes changed with respect to this type of credit. And third, retailers changed their attitudes over the years with respect to this powerful selling tool.[10]

CHANGING ATTITUDE OF CONSUMERS. In the early days of installment credit, the sales techniques used by some vendors damaged customer goodwill. Exaggerated claims, misunderstandings between vendor and customer, and threats of force to collect overdue accounts contributed to the stigma associated with this type of selling. Not until this stigma was removed did installment buying become commonplace. Fortunately, the early abuses were short-lived, and the industry recognized that customer goodwill was essential to its success.

CHANGING ATTITUDE OF RETAILERS. Many retailers built up the same prejudice against installment selling as consumers had against installment buying. Retailers shunned this type of selling because of the industry's prevailing low standards and because they failed to recognize it as a productive merchandising tool. However, as consumers' attitudes changed, so did retailers'. The adoption of high standards by the sales finance industry soon convinced retailers of the sales possibilities of installment selling.[11]

PRINCIPLES OF RETAIL INSTALLMENT CREDIT

The following installment credit principles successfully serve both vendors and customers.

Type of Goods

The best items to sell on an installment basis are durable and high-unit-value goods. In fact, installment sales should be confined to high-value lines. In general, goods of high unit value are consumed over a relatively long period, and consumers have many months or years of enjoyment from them. Consumers tend to feel more responsibility to pay a debt when they are still using and enjoying the merchandise. Goods that are consumed immediately place a creditor in a more difficult position from the collection standpoint.

---

[10]While many retail firms today use revolving credit plans in place of the older type of installment credit plans for the purchase of durable appliances, installment credit plans are still the primary devices used to purchase cars, mobile homes, and so on.

[11]The sales finance industry is discussed in Chapter 3.

Down Payment

The down payment should be sufficient to create a sense of ownership. A sense of ownership creates pride of possession in the customer's mind and provides a safety margin for the vendor. If customers have no sense of ownership, they may face their debts with discouragement and spite.

The amount of down payment varies with the type of goods financed. For years, the customary down payment on new cars ranged from one-fifth to one-third of the original purchase price. Customers with excellent credit standing or with large equity in their cars being traded in were generally allowed to make lower down payments. In recent years, however, automobile manufacturers have fallen on hard times, largely because of intense foreign competition. As a result, factory rebates to the consumer have become customary. Car advertising often uses promotional gimmicks such as "factory rebates up to $3,000 on selected models"; "up to $4,000 off any new last year's models"; "6.9% APR financing on selected models"; "no down payment or 2.3% APR financing"; "use your factory rebate as your down payment."

Although such policies violate good business practice, automobile manufacturers and dealers have to play "follow the leader" in order to meet competition and to remain profitable.

The Amount and Schedule of Payments

The amount and schedule of payments are important to the consumer. The amount to be paid must be relative to the customer's income and other outstanding obligations. Second, payments should be, but are not always, set up so that the unpaid balance is no greater than the resale value of the goods. The amount of the payments should not exceed what is judged to be reasonable and possible for the customer to meet, and payments should be timed to correlate with the receipt of income. If the customer gets paid twice a month and must pay a home mortgage and other obligations on the first, additional installments should coincide with the second paycheck. The same procedure holds when the purchaser is paid weekly. When a customer gets paid once a month, a date in the week following the receipt of income is the best choice.

Installment Terms

Installment terms and the amount and schedule of payments are closely related. The principle that *the unpaid balance should not be more than the resale value of the goods* is also a function of installment terms. This principle is affected by the amount of payments and by the item's useful life. When a vendor extends terms too far into the future, the owner's equity in the purchase may be too small and the item worth less than the amount owed on it. In this case, customers may want to relieve their obligations by simply surrendering the item to the retailer.[12] To avoid this risk vendors should adjust their terms to the item's useful life.

In general, the terms of an installment contract should be as short as possible. When installment contracts run for long periods, even though the customer could pay in a shorter time, the customer pays more finance charges than necessary. Each installment contract should be adjusted to the characteristics of the customer.

Finance Charges

Finance charges should be adequate to defray the costs of installment transactions. The cost of an installment business varies according to the size of the average sale and the volume transacted; in general, the greater the volume, the less the unit cost.

To avoid misunderstandings, vendors should spell out all finance charges to their installment customers. This is covered under the Truth in Lending Act (as amended), discussed in Chapter 6.

Note that a finance charge may be called a service charge, a carrying charge, or an interest charge.

For years businesses could sell goods and services at one price for cash and at a higher price on time without violating the interest and usury laws. This situation arose from the generally accepted idea that such sales did not involve the loaning of money. Interest and usury laws were interpreted over the years as applicable only to the lending of money. Carried one step further, a business firm did not violate the interest and usury laws by selling an installment contract to a financial institution.

The first deviation from this time-price doctrine occurred in the 1957 *Sloan v. Sears, Roebuck & Co.* case. The Arkansas supreme court decided that the state usury law was not limited to finance charges on loans or forbearances but covered credit sales as well. Commenting on this, Professor Richardson of Arizona State University pointed out:

> In this state and in all other states, except Arkansas, installment sellers of automobiles, home appliances, boats, furniture, jewelry and a multitude of other goods, charge service or finance fees which, if they were converted to an annual interest rate, would exceed state usury laws. Yet, in no state, except Hawaii, are merchants licensed under small loan laws or subject to small finance charge limitations. This is because sellers of merchandise on time are not considered by the court to be making a cash loan and, therefore, there can be no forbearance or illegal interest. This ruling, called the time sale doctrine, which goes back to English Common Law, states that sellers may offer their wares for a time price which is

---

[12]Many people believe that surrendering an article relieves them of the obligation to meet any balance remaining on their installment purchase. Wrong! If the repossessed article does not have sufficient resale value to cover the indebtedness, the buyer is liable for the remaining balance.

greater than the cash price. The difference between the cash price and the time price, the time price differential or finance charge, in a *bona fide* time sale, is a matter for individual bargaining and not subject to usury restrictions.[13]

In 1935 Indiana became the first state to pass this type of special legislation; five other states had enacted similar legislation by 1945. Today almost all of the states and the District of Columbia regulate the time sales of motor vehicles, other durable goods, or both. Although provisions vary, common basic points provide:

1. State licensing of everyone in the business of buying time sale contracts.
2. Maximum limit on the time-price differential, or finance charge.
3. Complete disclosure of all the contract terms, and signing of blank contracts prohibited.
4. Specific methods of refunding to customers who prepay their contract.
5. Penalties for violations.

TRUTH IN LENDING ACT. The federal Truth in Lending Act became effective July 1, 1969. The main purpose of this law was to assure meaningful disclosure of credit terms (primarily the finance charge and the true annual percentage rate) so that consumers would be able to compare credit terms more readily and use credit more wisely. Legally, installment transactions are considered closed-end credit transactions and revolving credit transactions are considered open-end credit transactions.

Consumers seldom understand interest charges and the actual cost of credit. The cost of credit is significant for both consumers and vendors, but for different reasons. Consumers should know the cost of credit so they

---

[13]Barrie Richardson, "Regulation of Retail Revolving Credit Transactions," *Arizona Business Bulletin* 9, no. 4 (April 1962), p. 3. Author's note: The supreme court of Arkansas, in a decision on December 23, 1957, held that an installment sale contract by Sears, Roebuck and Co. was usurious and void. This *Sears* case put Arkansas in a unique position. Arkansas merchants had to restrict their time price of goods to no more than the legal rate of interest above their cash price. In this particular case the contract showed "Total cash price $393.98" plus "Carrying charge $37.17." The total of $431.15 was payable in monthly installments of $22, and the carrying charge exceeded the maximum interest rate of 10 percent established by the Arkansas constitution, which provided that "all contracts for a greater rate of interest than 10 percent per annum shall be void." In its decision the court noted that Sears has "a splendid reputation for its dealings with the public; . . . but if we should hold that this contract is not usurious, it would be a precedent by which all the sellers of merchandise of every kind and description could add any amount to the cash price as interest, carrying charge, differential or what not, that those whom the Constitution and statutes were designed to protect would of necessity agree to pay. And Art. 19, par. 13, of the Constitution, prohibiting usury, would amount to nothing more than a scrap of paper."

can evaluate alternatives—i.e., accept or reject the installment credit or seek alternate ways to make their purchase. Vendors, on the other hand, must know the yield of their finance charge so they can cover their costs and earn a profit.

CONVERTING CHARGES INTO ANNUAL RATES. Three terms are important in the process of converting charges into annual rates: *nominal rate, nominal annual rate,* and *annual percentage rate (APR).*

The nominal rate, sometimes known as the quoted rate, is simply the dollar amount of interest charged divided by the dollar amount of credit. Since finance charges are normally thought of on a yearly basis, the nominal rate must be converted to a nominal annual rate if the period of time is less or more than one year. Since the consumer makes periodic payments in a retail installment transaction and thus does not have full use of the credit during the entire period, the nominal annual rate must be converted to an annual percentage rate (sometimes called a simple annual rate or a true annual rate). The finance charge in a retail installment transaction is figured on the total amount of credit granted.

For example, a person borrows $100 from a friend at 10 percent interest for one year and agrees to pay back $110 in a lump sum at the end of 12 months. In this example, the nominal rate is 10 percent, the nominal annual rate is 10 percent since the time period involved is 12 months or one year, and the annual percentage rate is also 10 percent, since the person had full use of the money during the entire credit period. This example, used for purposes of simplicity, involves the loaning of money and not a retail installment sale.

However, when consumers make a retail purchase on an installment plan and agree to repay the principal at stated intervals, they are paying an annual percentage rate of interest higher than the nominal rate or the nominal annual rate. The nominal annual rate doesn't account for the fact that the debtor doesn't have use of the total principal for the entire duration of the contract. The formula for determining this is simply $n + 1 \div 2$, where n represents the number of installments needed to discharge the debt. Hence, an installment account repaid in 10 payments means that the debtor has full use of the principal amount for 5½ months on the average. This explains the need for computing the annual percentage rate on installment purchases. The debtor has full use of the creditor's principal for slightly more than half of the total installment period, so the annual percentage rate is approximately twice the nominal annual rate. For many years in the finance field, the nominal rate per year times two was a rule-of-thumb method for computing the annual percentage rate.

Today, under the provisions of the Truth in Lending Act as amended (see Chapter 6), computers are used to determine accurate annual percentage rates. Table 2–4 shows a manual method for computing approximate annual percentage rates for level monthly payment plans.

TABLE 2–4 Table for Computing Approximate Annual Percentage Rate for Level Monthly Payment Plans

EXAMPLE:

Finance charge = $38 (Finance charge is per $100 of balance to be financed.)
Total amount to be financed = $250
Number of monthly payments = 24

Number of Level Monthly Payments :	: 5% :	5½% :	6% :	6½% :	7% :	7½% :	8% :	9% :	10% :	11% :	12% :	13% :
1	$0.40	$0.44	$0.48	$0.52	$0.56	$0.60	$0.65	$0.71	$0.79	$0.88	$0.96	$1.04
2	.59	.66	.72	.78	.84	.91	.97	1.06	1.19	1.31	1.44	1.57
3	.79	.88	.96	1.04	1.13	1.21	1.29	1.42	1.59	1.76	1.92	2.09
4	.99	1.10	1.20	1.31	1.41	1.51	1.62	1.78	1.99	2.20	2.41	2.62
5	1.19	1.32	1.44	1.57	1.69	1.82	1.95	2.13	2.39	2.64	2.89	3.15
6	1.39	1.54	1.68	1.83	1.98	2.13	2.27	2.49	2.79	3.08	3.38	3.68
7	1.59	1.76	1.93	2.09	2.26	2.43	2.60	2.85	3.19	3.53	3.87	4.21
8	1.79	1.98	2.17	2.36	2.55	2.74	2.93	3.21	3.60	3.98	4.36	4.74
9	1.99	2.20	2.41	2.62	2.83	3.05	3.26	3.57	4.00	4.43	4.85	5.28
10	2.19	2.42	2.65	2.89	3.12	3.35	3.59	3.94	4.41	4.88	5.35	5.82
11	2.39	2.64	2.90	3.15	3.41	3.66	3.92	4.30	4.81	5.33	5.84	6.36
12	2.59	2.87	3.14	3.42	3.69	3.97	4.25	4.66	5.22	5.78	6.34	6.90
13	2.79	3.09	3.39	3.68	3.98	4.28	4.58	5.03	5.63	6.23	6.84	7.44
14	2.99	3.31	3.63	3.95	4.27	4.59	4.91	5.39	6.04	6.69	7.34	7.99
15	3.20	3.54	3.88	4.22	4.56	4.90	5.24	5.76	6.45	7.14	7.84	8.53
16	3.40	3.76	4.12	4.48	4.85	5.21	5.58	6.13	6.86	7.60	8.34	9.08
17	3.60	3.98	4.37	4.75	5.14	5.52	5.91	6.49	7.27	8.06	8.84	9.63
18	3.80	4.21	4.61	5.02	5.43	5.84	6.25	6.86	7.69	8.52	9.35	10.19
19	4.01	4.43	4.86	5.29	5.72	6.15	6.58	7.23	8.10	8.98	9.86	10.74
20	4.21	4.66	5.11	5.56	6.01	6.46	6.92	7.60	8.52	9.44	10.37	11.30
21	4.41	4.88	5.35	5.83	6.30	6.78	7.26	7.97	8.94	9.90	10.88	11.85
22	4.62	5.11	5.60	6.10	6.60	7.09	7.59	8.35	9.36	10.37	11.39	12.41
23	4.82	5.33	5.85	6.37	6.89	7.41	7.93	8.72	9.77	10.84	11.90	12.97
24	5.02	5.56	6.10	6.64	7.18	7.73	8.27	9.09	10.19	11.30	12.42	13.54
25	5.23	5.79	6.35	6.91	7.48	8.04	8.61	9.47	10.62	11.77	12.93	14.10
26	5.43	6.01	6.60	7.18	7.77	8.36	8.95	9.84	11.04	12.24	13.45	14.67
27	5.64	6.24	6.85	7.46	8.07	8.68	9.29	10.22	11.46	12.71	13.97	15.24
28	5.84	6.47	7.10	7.73	8.36	9.00	9.64	10.60	11.89	13.18	14.49	15.81
29	6.05	6.70	7.35	8.00	8.66	9.32	9.98	10.97	12.31	13.66	15.01	16.38
30	6.25	6.92	7.60	8.28	8.96	9.64	10.32	11.35	12.74	14.13	15.54	16.95
31	6.46	7.15	7.85	8.55	9.25	9.96	10.67	11.73	13.17	14.61	16.06	17.53
32	6.66	7.38	8.10	8.82	9.55	10.28	11.01	12.11	13.59	15.09	16.59	18.11
33	6.87	7.61	8.35	9.10	9.85	10.60	11.36	12.49	14.02	15.57	17.12	18.69
34	7.08	7.84	8.61	9.37	10.15	10.92	11.70	12.88	14.45	16.05	17.65	19.27
35	7.28	8.07	8.86	9.65	10.45	11.25	12.05	13.26	14.89	16.53	18.18	19.85
36	7.49	8.30	9.11	9.93	10.75	11.57	12.40	13.64	15.32	17.01	18.71	20.43
37	7.70	8.53	9.37	10.20	11.05	11.89	12.74	14.03	15.75	17.49	19.25	21.02
38	7.91	8.76	9.62	10.48	11.35	12.22	13.09	14.41	16.19	17.98	19.78	21.61
39	8.11	8.99	9.87	10.76	11.65	12.54	13.44	14.80	16.62	18.46	20.32	22.20
40	8.32	9.22	10.13	11.04	11.95	12.87	13.79	15.19	17.06	18.95	20.86	22.79
41	8.53	9.45	10.38	11.32	12.25	13.20	14.14	15.57	17.50	19.44	21.40	23.38
42	8.74	9.69	10.64	11.60	12.56	13.52	14.50	15.96	17.94	19.93	21.94	23.98
43	8.95	9.92	10.89	11.87	12.86	13.85	14.85	16.35	18.38	20.42	22.49	24.57
44	9.16	10.15	11.15	12.15	13.16	14.18	15.20	16.74	18.82	20.91	23.03	25.17
45	9.37	10.38	11.41	12.44	13.47	14.51	15.55	17.13	19.26	21.41	23.58	25.77
46	9.58	10.62	11.66	12.72	13.77	14.84	15.91	17.53	19.70	21.90	24.13	26.37
47	9.79	10.85	11.92	13.00	14.08	15.17	16.26	17.92	20.15	22.40	24.68	26.98
48	10.00	11.09	12.18	13.28	14.39	15.50	16.62	18.31	20.59	22.90	25.23	27.58
49	10.21	11.32	12.44	13.56	14.69	15.83	16.98	18.71	21.04	23.39	25.70	28.19
50	10.42	11.55	12.70	13.84	15.00	16.16	17.33	19.10	21.48	23.89	26.33	28.80
51	10.63	11.79	12.95	14.13	15.31	16.50	17.69	19.50	21.93	24.40	26.89	29.41
52	10.84	12.02	13.21	14.41	15.62	16.83	18.05	19.89	22.38	24.90	27.45	30.02
53	11.05	12.26	13.47	14.69	15.92	17.16	18.41	20.29	22.83	25.40	28.00	30.64
54	11.26	12.49	13.73	14.98	16.23	17.50	18.77	20.69	23.28	25.91	28.56	31.25
55	11.48	12.73	13.99	15.26	16.54	17.83	19.13	21.09	23.73	26.41	29.13	31.87
56	11.69	12.97	14.25	15.55	16.85	18.17	19.49	21.49	24.19	26.92	29.69	32.49
57	11.90	13.20	14.52	15.84	17.17	18.50	19.85	21.89	24.64	27.43	30.25	33.11
58	12.11	13.44	14.78	16.12	17.48	18.84	20.21	22.29	25.10	27.94	30.82	33.74
59	12.33	13.68	15.04	16.41	17.79	19.18	20.58	22.70	25.55	28.45	31.39	34.36
60	12.54	13.92	15.30	16.70	18.10	19.52	20.94	23.10	26.01	28.96	31.96	34.99

Note: The values in this table have been computed by the actuarial or annuity method, which conforms to the U.S. rule.

TABLE 2–4 (concluded)

SOLUTION: *Step 1:* Divide the finance charge by the total amount to be financed and multiply by $100. This gives the finance charge per $100 of amount to be financed. That is, $38 ÷ $250 × $100 = $15.20. (Alternative method: Find the number of $100 units in the amount to be financed by setting the decimal two places to the left, for example, 2.50 units. Then, $38 ÷ 2.50 = $15.20.)

Step 2: Follow down the left-hand column of the table to the line for 24 months. Follow across this line until you find the two numbers between which the finance charge of $15.20 falls. In this example, $15.20 falls between $14.66 and $15.80. Read up between the two columns of figures to find the annual percentage rate. In this example, it is 14 percent.

: 14% :	15% :	16% :	18% :	20% :	22% :	24% :	26% :	28% :	30% :	33% :	36% :
$1.12	$1.21	$1.29	$1.42	$1.58	$1.75	$1.92	$2.08	$2.25	$2.42	$2.62	$2.88	$3.12
1.69	1.82	1.94	2.13	2.38	2.63	2.88	3.14	3.39	3.64	3.95	4.33	4.71
2.26	2.43	2.59	2.85	3.18	3.52	3.86	4.20	4.53	4.87	5.30	5.80	6.31
2.83	3.04	3.25	3.57	3.99	4.41	4.84	5.26	5.69	6.11	6.65	7.29	7.93
3.40	3.65	3.91	4.29	4.80	5.31	5.82	6.34	6.85	7.37	8.01	8.79	9.57
3.97	4.27	4.57	5.02	5.61	6.21	6.81	7.42	8.02	8.63	9.39	10.30	11.22
4.55	4.89	5.23	5.75	6.43	7.12	7.81	8.51	9.20	9.90	10.77	11.83	12.88
5.13	5.51	5.90	6.48	7.26	8.03	8.82	9.60	10.39	11.18	12.17	13.36	14.57
5.71	6.14	6.57	7.22	8.08	8.95	9.83	10.70	11.58	12.47	13.58	14.92	16.27
6.29	6.77	7.24	7.96	8.91	9.88	10.84	11.81	12.79	13.77	15.00	16.48	17.89
6.88	7.40	7.92	8.70	9.75	10.80	11.86	12.93	14.00	15.08	16.43	18.06	19.71
7.46	8.03	8.59	9.45	10.59	11.74	12.89	14.05	15.22	16.40	17.87	19.66	21.46
8.05	8.66	9.27	10.20	11.43	12.67	13.93	15.18	16.45	17.72	19.33	21.26	23.22
8.64	9.30	9.96	10.95	12.28	13.62	14.97	16.32	17.69	19.06	20.79	22.88	25.00
9.23	9.94	10.64	11.71	13.13	14.57	16.01	17.47	18.93	20.41	22.27	24.52	26.79
9.83	10.58	11.33	12.46	13.99	15.52	17.06	18.62	20.19	21.76	23.75	26.16	28.60
10.43	11.22	12.02	13.23	14.85	16.48	18.12	19.78	21.45	23.13	25.25	27.82	30.42
11.03	11.87	12.72	13.99	15.71	17.44	19.19	20.95	22.72	24.51	26.76	29.50	32.26
11.63	12.52	13.41	14.76	16.58	18.41	20.26	22.12	24.00	25.89	28.28	31.18	34.12
12.23	13.17	14.11	15.54	17.45	19.38	21.33	23.30	25.28	27.29	29.81	32.88	35.99
12.84	13.82	14.82	16.31	18.33	20.36	22.41	24.49	26.58	28.69	31.36	34.60	37.88
13.44	14.48	15.52	17.09	19.21	21.34	23.50	25.68	27.88	30.10	32.91	36.32	39.78
14.05	15.14	16.23	17.88	20.09	22.33	24.60	26.88	29.19	31.53	34.48	38.06	41.70
14.66	15.80	16.94	18.66	20.98	23.33	25.70	28.09	30.51	32.96	36.05	39.81	43.63
15.28	16.46	17.65	19.45	21.87	24.32	26.80	29.31	31.84	34.40	37.64	41.58	45.58
15.89	17.13	18.37	20.24	22.77	25.33	27.91	30.53	33.18	35.85	39.23	43.36	47.54
16.51	17.80	19.09	21.04	23.67	26.34	29.03	31.76	34.52	37.31	40.84	45.15	49.52
17.13	18.47	19.81	21.84	24.58	27.35	30.15	33.00	35.87	38.78	42.46	46.95	51.51
17.75	19.14	20.53	22.64	25.49	28.37	31.28	34.24	37.23	40.26	44.09	48.77	53.52
18.38	19.81	21.26	23.45	26.40	29.39	32.42	35.49	38.60	41.75	45.73	50.60	55.54
19.00	20.49	21.99	24.26	27.32	30.42	33.56	36.75	39.97	43.24	47.38	52.44	57.58
19.63	21.17	22.72	25.07	28.24	31.45	34.71	38.01	41.36	44.75	49.05	54.29	59.63
20.26	21.85	23.46	25.88	29.16	32.49	35.86	39.28	42.75	46.26	50.72	56.16	61.70
20.90	22.54	24.19	26.70	30.09	33.53	37.02	40.56	44.15	47.79	52.40	58.04	63.78
21.53	23.23	24.94	27.52	31.02	34.58	38.18	41.84	45.56	49.32	54.09	59.93	65.87
22.17	23.92	25.68	28.35	31.96	35.63	39.35	43.14	46.97	50.86	55.80	61.83	67.98
22.81	24.61	26.42	29.18	32.90	36.69	40.53	44.43	48.39	52.41	57.51	63.75	70.11
23.45	25.30	27.17	30.01	33.85	37.75	41.71	45.74	49.82	53.97	59.24	65.68	72.25
24.09	26.00	27.92	30.85	34.80	38.82	42.90	47.05	51.26	55.54	60.97	67.62	74.40
24.73	26.70	28.68	31.68	35.75	39.89	44.09	48.37	52.71	57.12	62.72	69.57	76.56
25.38	27.40	29.44	32.52	36.71	40.96	45.29	49.69	54.16	58.70	64.47	71.53	78.74
26.03	28.10	30.19	33.37	37.67	42.05	46.50	51.03	55.63	60.30	66.24	73.51	80.94
26.68	28.81	30.96	34.22	38.63	43.13	47.71	52.36	57.09	61.90	68.01	75.50	83.14
27.33	29.52	31.72	35.07	39.60	44.22	48.93	53.71	58.57	63.51	69.80	77.50	85.36
27.99	30.23	32.49	35.92	40.58	45.32	50.15	55.06	60.06	65.13	71.60	79.51	87.60
28.65	30.94	33.26	36.78	41.55	46.42	51.38	56.42	61.55	66.76	73.40	81.53	89.85
29.31	31.66	34.03	37.64	42.54	47.53	52.61	57.78	63.05	68.40	75.22	83.57	92.11
29.97	32.37	34.81	38.50	43.52	48.64	53.85	59.15	64.56	70.05	77.04	85.61	94.38
30.63	33.09	35.59	39.37	44.51	49.75	55.09	60.53	66.07	71.70	78.88	87.67	96.67
31.29	33.82	36.37	40.24	45.50	50.87	56.34	61.92	67.59	73.37	80.72	89.74	98.96
31.96	34.54	37.15	41.11	46.50	51.99	57.60	63.31	69.12	75.04	82.58	91.82	101.28
32.63	35.27	37.94	41.99	47.50	53.12	58.86	64.70	70.66	76.72	84.44	93.91	103.60
33.30	36.00	38.72	42.87	48.50	54.26	60.12	66.11	72.20	78.41	86.31	96.01	105.94
33.98	36.73	39.52	43.75	49.51	55.39	61.40	67.52	73.75	80.10	88.19	98.13	108.29
34.65	37.46	40.31	44.64	50.52	56.54	62.67	68.93	75.31	81.81	90.09	100.25	110.65
35.33	38.20	41.11	45.53	51.54	57.68	63.96	70.36	76.88	83.52	91.99	102.38	113.02
36.01	38.94	41.91	46.42	52.56	58.84	65.25	71.78	78.45	85.24	93.90	104.53	115.41
36.69	39.68	42.71	47.32	53.58	59.99	66.54	73.22	80.03	86.97	95.82	106.68	117.81
37.37	40.42	43.51	48.21	54.61	61.15	67.84	74.66	81.62	88.71	97.75	108.85	120.22
38.06	41.17	44.32	49.12	55.64	62.32	69.14	76.11	83.21	90.45	99.68	111.03	122.64

Source: The table was issued with Department of Defense Directive 1344-7.

The following model (with an outlined step-by-step discussion) may be modified to fit simple or complex installment cases.

a.	Cash price	$_____
b.	Less: Down Payment or trade-in	$_____
	Equals: Remaining balance	$_____
c.	Plus: Insurance, other purchases etc.	$_____
	Equals: Balance to finance	$_____
d.	Plus: Finance charge	$_____
e.	Equals: Total amount of obligation	$_____

a. Determine the cash price. The cash price of an article is the total amount a consumer needs to buy the item outright.

b. Deduct the cash down payment or an allowance for a trade-in if any. The down payment or trade-in reduces the amount of the cash price to a remaining balance; if no other additions are made, it becomes the balance to finance.

c. Add any insurance, other purchases, or "add-ons" that increase the balance remaining to arrive at the total balance to finance. Most financing institutions require insurance on an automobile installment account. Other purchases are anything the customer selects as an additional item to finance, such as accessory items and other small purchases. These, added to the former balance, result in the total amount to be financed.

d. Arrive at the finance charge. If the charge is quoted as an annual rate, multiply this figure by the balance to finance. The finance charge applies to the amount of credit sought.

e. The total amount of the obligation is the balance financed plus the total finance charge. Creditors use this figure to set the amount of each installment payment. When the amount is not divisible into equal installments, the first or last payment may differ. In this way there is less risk of customer confusion.

To illustrate a complete installment transaction, suppose Fred's Appliances sells an automatic washer and dryer for the combined cash price of $565. The customer makes a 10 percent down payment, and the installment payments are extended over 18 months. Fred adds a carrying charge of $61.02. What is the annual percentage rate of interest involved? What are the customer's monthly installment payments?

Cash price	$565.00
Less: Down payment	56.50
Balance to finance	$508.50
Plus: Finance charge	61.02
Total obligation	$569.52

Following the instructions shown at the top of Table 2–4, divide the finance charge by the total amount to be financed and multiply by $100. This gives the finance charge per $100 of the amount to be financed. For the washer-dryer: $61.02 ÷ $508.50 × $100 = $12. As shown in step 2 of Table 2–4, follow down the left-hand column of the table to the line for 18 months. Follow across this line until you find the two numbers between which the finance charge of $12 falls. Reading up between the two columns, you find that the annual percentage rate is 15 percent.[14] Thus the 18 monthly installment payments are $31.64 each.

Repossession

Sellers under an installment arrangement have an added protection: if the customer doesn't comply with the terms of the agreement, the article can be repossessed. However, this is the last action most sellers want to take. And repossession is difficult to accomplish, particularly in articles that can be easily moved.

Rebates for Prepayment

A customer should always be allowed to prepay in full the unpaid balance of any installment obligation at any time without penalty. In such instances the customer may receive a rebate of the unearned portion of the finance charge computed according to the balance-of-the-digits method (also known as the sum-of-the-digits or the rule-of-78s method)[15] or the actuarial method. In the case of credit for defective goods, the customer should be entitled to the same rebate as if payment in full had been made on the day the defect was reported to the creditor or merchant.

Both the rule-of-78s method and the actuarial method of rebate computation take into account the amount of credit available to the debtor and the time the debtor has had use of the credit. For example, if a customer obtains $1,200 of credit under an installment credit transaction with a finance charge of $72 repayable in 12 monthly installments of $106, the customer used the credit as follows:

---

[14]In using Table 2–4, it isn't necessary to convert the nominal rate into a nominal annual rate. This is done automatically by selecting the correct number of level monthly payments shown in the left-hand column.

Remember, the annual percentage rate just computed is only approximate.

[15]Some people consider the rule of 78s a misnomer because the sum of the digits is 78 only if the period of installment payments is 12 months. The rule of 78s is rapidly declining in use, as more and more states limit its application in installment transactions or use other methods of quoting finance charges.

Month	Dollar Months of Use
1st	1,200
2nd	1,100
3rd	1,000
4th	900
5th	800
6th	700
7th	600
8th	500
9th	400
10th	300
11th	200
12th	100
	7,800

If the customer prepays the indebtedness at the end of the fourth month, the debtor would have had the use of 4,200 dollar months (1,200 + 1,100 + 1,000 + 900) out of a total of 7,800 dollar months. Under the rule-of-78s method, the creditor would be entitled to retain $^{42}/_{78}$ of the initial finance charge, and the debtor would receive a refund of $^{36}/_{78}$ of that charge. In this example, the refund to the debtor would be $^{36}/_{78} \times \$72$, or $33.23.

Credit Investigation

The credit investigation is uniquely important in installment credit trans-actions. Installment credit accounts usually represent a high average sale and extend over a relatively long time. In the sale of cars, for example, the sum to be financed is quite large. These factors present a risk peculiar to this type of credit. The principle created by these conditions is that the credit investigation should be thorough enough to diminish the inherent risk. Even though the right of repossession may offer the creditor consid-erable protection, profit in installment sales really depends on completion of the payments. Repossessions can be costly and even disastrous if they occur too frequently. Creditors should rely on the quality of the risk as revealed by the credit investigation rather than on other contingent factors.

BENEFITS AND PITFALLS OF INSTALLMENT CREDIT

Installment credit has been a profitable and effective sales-building tool for retailers and created much enjoyment and satisfaction for consumers. The real danger in installment credit, as in so many other things, is not in its use but in its abuse. Consumers can easily overextend themselves with this type of credit, and a few have installment debts out of proportion to their ability to pay. Such a situation is damaging to the credit industry and presents a problem of consumer education in the use of credit.

Retailers must be aware that the customer's credit qualities are more crucial elements to the risk than the lien retained. Retailers must accept credit wisely. Some customers are imprudent or impetuous, and others are dishonest. By adhering to sound principles of credit management, retailers can do much to avoid individuals who don't have the ability or character to pay.

RETAIL CHARGE ACCOUNT CREDIT

The generic term *charge account* includes numerous types of plans. All have the same objective—to sell merchandise at a profit; each, however, represents some variation in the merchant's ability to meet competition and to carry the account until the customer pays the amount due.

Some firms use divided payment accounts. It is debatable whether divided payment accounts should be classified as charge accounts or as installment accounts. Most retail merchants recognize the fact that although their charge account terms are 30 days, in practice customers may take longer to pay. Some retailers use this situation as a sales promotion device. They allow customers to charge higher priced goods (such as furniture, appliances, and carpeting) and make payments of one-third in 30 days, one-third in 60 days, and one-third in 90 days, usually with no finance charge.

Retail firms in a few areas of the country honor a club membership "cash" card and allow discounts from their stated prices for cash payments. In effect, then, their quoted price is actually the credit price.

Under the retail charge account credit plan, the customer usually purchases a series of lower priced soft goods with no down payment. Title passes to the customer at the time of the sale so the retailer has no right of repossession.

Retail charge accounts normally run 30 days. However, in practice bills may be outstanding for a longer period, depending on general economic conditions, the season of the year, the type of store involved, and the type of customers. Retailers expect that customers will pay their bills out of their normal recurring income.

Delayed payments have troubled retail merchants for years, and they continue to present a problem—whether to charge a fee on accounts that are not paid by the end of the normal 30-day period. Most stores undoubtedly prefer to do so, but they are restrained by competition. Also, simply because a store threatens to add a carrying charge if accounts are not paid within a specified time—often 60 days after receipt of the statement—there is no guarantee that such a policy will be indiscriminately enforced. Many stores screen their overdue accounts and are very careful not to offend their "good but slow" customers by imposing charges and writing collection letters. If a store decides to place a charge on late accounts, it must decide on the amount.

Retail charge accounts involve several types of costs not found in cash sales. Bad-debt losses occur despite merchants' best efforts to weigh the risks involved. Retailers who accept credit thus walk a tightrope; a new account may increase profits through increased sales or expand the store's uncollectible accounts. In many stores, however, and in smaller stores in particular, pressure of personal friendship, lack of knowledge of general and local economic conditions, inadequate facilities for obtaining credit information and even lack of knowledge of how to obtain it, pressure of other duties, and lack of adequate record-keeping all combine to make retail credit acceptance a somewhat careless operation. Another cost factor involved is payment for personnel, equipment, and space to carry on the credit activities. If proprietors devote time to this function, they limit the time they can devote to buying, selling, and other administrative duties. Another factor is the additional cost of merchandise returns, which charge account customers look on as a special privilege. In addition, if the store decides to carry the account for a period of time to secure full payment, the interest on the money tied up for this period is another cost item.

For some smaller firms, charge accounts are still a factor in credit policies and practices. But retail charge account credit has declined rapidly in importance in the expanding consumer credit picture. Today, retail charge account credit accounts for an estimated 2 to 3 percent of total consumer credit outstanding.

SERVICE CREDIT

Although service credit is an important segment of the total consumer credit picture, it has been practically ignored in consumer credit literature. Service credit has been defined by the Federal Reserve Board as "the amount owed by individuals to professional practitioners and service establishments." In the past decade, the amount of noninstallment service credit has increased an estimated three to four times.

Problems of Professional Credit

Credit is a customary method of doing business with physicians and dentists.[16] Private practitioners and clinics accept some credit from their patients, and most of them expect to collect most of the amount due. However, some patients' fees are entered as receivables on the books, even though the practitioner knows that the recipients will be unable to pay at any time in the future.

---

[16]Susan E. Crawford, "Healthy Alternative to Cash," *The Credit World,* July–August 1990, p. 31.

Thirty-day accounts are the most common type of credit in the medical and dental professions. But professionals should encourage patients who prefer to arrange installment payments for protracted treatments or services.

Credit arrangements also are found in the legal profession; services are rendered for a client, who is billed at some later date.

The vast growth of hospital, medical, and surgical insurance plans has permitted millions of people to take care of their health needs on a "cash basis" by shifting the financial burden—or a large part of it—to insurance companies. Medicare and Medicaid plans play a similar role for senior citizens.

Credit in Service Establishments

Basically, credit in a service establishment is like credit in a retail establishment. In many instances, it is difficult to separate the two because thousands of retailers offer repair and other services that may be purchased on credit.

Note that the word *service* does not mean the various devices a store uses to attract and hold customers—e.g., free delivery, credit arrangements, parking lots, and so on. A *service* establishment fills some need or performs some operation or task on a customer's goods. The term *service* may also apply to individuals who don't have a so-called place of business but who are handy with tools and have an ability to fix things. These service people may operate from their car or truck, have regular customers for whom they perform certain services, and send bills at the end of the month.

The number of service establishments has increased rapidly over the years, and a large segment conducts business on credit. When people heat their homes with gas and receive a bill for this utility service, credit is involved just as much as if they had walked into a department store, bought a suit of clothes, and charged it. Again, as in the medical and dental professions, credit is a customary method of doing business, although the time involved is usually short, and the installment method of repayment is not as commonly used. The cost of services continues to take a larger share of the American consumer's budget and will continue to do so in the years to come.

DISCUSSION QUESTIONS

1. In their decision to adopt a credit plan, merchants must take many factors into consideration. What are these factors? Which one or ones do you believe are the most important? Why?
2. Should groceries be sold on a revolving credit plan? Why or why not?

3. What is the option-terms revolving credit plan? What are its most important characteristics?

4. What are the advantages of the option-terms plan to the store and to the customer? The disadvantages?

5. Discuss the various methods used to compute finance charges under an option-terms revolving credit account.

6. Why would a merchant decide to use an installment credit plan rather than a revolving credit plan?

7. Why would a merchant decide to use a revolving credit plan rather than an installment credit plan?

8. Discuss the factors that affect a retailer's decision to sell on installment credit. Which factor is the most important? Why?

9. What is meant by the "changing attitude of consumers" toward installment credit? The "changing attitude of retailers"?

10. Explain the provisions of the Truth in Lending Act in connection with retail installment transactions.

11. What is the annual percentage rate of interest in a retail installment transaction?

12. Why should you, as a consumer, be interested in knowing the annual percentage rate of interest you are paying?

Use Table 2–4 to compute the approximate annual percentage rate of interest in the following problems:

13. An appliance store sold Mr. Lynn a stereo for $495. A down payment of 10 percent of the sale price was required, and the payment period was set to cover 24 months. The store added an interest charge of $60. What is the approximate annual percentage rate of interest paid by Mr. Lynn? Would this rate be legal in your state?

14. The Tyler family has just purchased a new television set. The cash price of the TV set is $300. The set was bought under the following arrangement: $30 down and a carrying charge of 12 percent of the balance. The payment period is 12 months. What is the amount of the contract, and what are the monthly payments? What is the approximate annual percentage rate of interest?

15. Mr. Gibbons purchased a five-year-old automobile for $950. He paid $325 down and made arrangements to finance the balance by signing a contract for $750 to be repaid in 18 monthly installments. The insurance premium was paid in cash directly to the insurance company. What approximate annual percentage rate is involved in this transaction?

16. Distinguish carefully between a retail charge account and a retail installment account. Between a retail charge account and a retail revolving account.

17. What factors should retailers consider in deciding whether to adopt retail charge accounts? Which factor is the most important? Why?

18. How do you account for the changing importance of retail charge account credit?

19. When should finance charges be used with regular retail charge accounts?
20. Distinguish between divided payment accounts and regular 30-day charge plans.
21. What is service credit, and why should it be recognized and fully understood?
22. Discuss the problems of professional credit.
23. Discuss the possible differences between discounts for cash and surcharges on credit in revolving credit transactions.

Financing Retail and Service Credit Transactions

The Objectives or Goals of Chapter 3 Are:
1. To trace the development and to set forth the benefits and problem areas of bank credit card plans.
2. To compare the Discover credit card and the Optima credit card.
3. To explain developments in electronic banking services.
4. To discuss the activities of charge card plans, such as American Express, Diners Club, and Carte Blanche.
5. To explain the methods available to a commercial bank for acquiring installment business.
6. To spell out the variety of financing plans for installment transactions available to the retail dealer.
7. To trace the development of sales finance companies and to illustrate how such companies operate.

American consumers are actively buying cars, appliances, and a wide variety of other consumer goods and services. For some of these, they pay cash that they have earned or inherited. For others, they borrow the money directly from some financial institution and pay "cash." For still others, they will make a credit arrangement with the sellers. In turn, the sellers may decide to carry their own credit plan until maturity or to sell it (or part of it) to some type of consumer financing institution.

FINANCING RETAIL AND SERVICE CREDIT PLANS

To introduce and expand a credit plan, a store needs additional capital. This capital may be furnished by the store's own reinvested earnings or by loans from commercial banks or other types of financial institutions. Either of these methods may enable retail merchants to carry their own accounts until they receive payments from customers. Loans may be based solely on the store's unsecured credit position, but the store usually has to put up certain assets as collateral.

In recent years, however, most retail and service concerns have sold part or all of their credit activities and have used credit card plans, such as Visa, MasterCard, Discover, and Optima, and charge card plans, such as American Express, Diners Club, and Carte Blanche. The distinction between credit card plans and charge card plans appeared in the Fair Credit and Charge Card Disclosure Act of 1988. Under this act, a charge card is defined as "a card, plate, or other single credit device that may be used from time to time to obtain credit which is not subject to a finance charge." A credit card is subject to a finance charge. This distinction will be explained in detail in Chapter 6.

Bank Credit Card Plans

Bank credit card plans evolved largely because of greatly increased demand for consumer credit after World War II. Very little was heard about these types of plans before 1950.[1] The need for some type of plan to aid retail merchants had been voiced for years by many people and numerous organizations. Some felt that, since the majority of specialty shops and other types of small independent retailers couldn't afford a full-fledged credit operation, they had a distinct disadvantage with their competitors— local department stores and other large retail and service concerns financially able to conduct credit operations. As a result, in 1947 the first community credit plan, called "Charg-It," began serving a two-square-block area in Brooklyn, New York.

The early 1950s saw a sporadic development of bank card plans, with a rapid increase from 1951 to 1952 followed by a rapid decline by 1955. Profits did not live up to bankers' expectations, and high administrative start-up and processing costs coupled with low volume caused many of them to abandon their plans. During the latter 1950s and the early 1960s, banks again entered the credit card arena.

In July 1967, the California Bankcard Association created Master Charge. Also in 1967, 11 banks in the state of New York instigated another joint effort in bank credit cards. This plan, called "Interbank Card," was an arrangement for coordinating banks throughout the country in the credit card field. On each member bank's card, an imprinted "I" indicated that it was an "Interbank Card." By January 1968, Master Charge ownership had passed to the Interbank Card Association. In early 1981, the name was changed to MasterCard International and Master Charge cards were replaced.

The Bank of America introduced its program in 1958 and began licensing its card in 1966 through Bank of America Service Corporation. This led to the formation of National BankAmericard, Inc. (NBI), in July

---

[1]Robert H. Cole, *Financing Retail Credit Sales through Charge Account Bank Plans* (Urbana: University of Illinois, Bureau of Business Management, 1955).

1970. NBI was formed as an independent, nonstock membership corporation to administer, promote, and develop the BankAmericard system throughout the United States. The name Bank Americard was changed to Visa on January 1, 1977.

Bank credit cards are issued to individual consumers, who may or may not be depositors of the issuing bank. Initially and for many years, there was no charge for the card itself, but today most banks charge an issuance and renewal fee. Before passage of the Credit Card Issuance Act of October 1970 (see Chapter 6), larger banks introduced their cards by an unsolicited—but not indiscriminate—mailing of cards and/or applications (see Figure 3–1) to individuals selected usually on the basis of their deposit or loan relationship with the card-issuing bank. The owner's signature is required on the card, which normally expires within a given period, usually one year. The cardholder is usually assigned a credit line—the maximum amount of credit the bank will extend through the card. At times the bank may allow cardholders to exceed their stated credit line. The Credit Card Issuance Act requires that no credit card be issued except in response to a request or application. This requirement, however, does not apply to renewals or substitutions for previously accepted cards. The law limits cardholders' liability to $50 in cases where the card is used without their permission; the cardholder is not even liable for the $50 if the card issuer has not provided the customer with a self-addressed, prestamped notification to be mailed in the event the card is lost or stolen.

The bank credit card permits the holder to charge purchases at firms (this can include retail outlets, service dispensers, medical facilities, educational institutions, and tax-collecting agencies) that are participating members. The bank bills the cardholder for all purchases made during a month. Cardholders can pay the full amount due within a specified grace period[2]—usually 25 to 30 days after the billing date—without any finance charge; or the account is placed on a revolving basis, which carries a finance charge that varies from state to state. Note that the state in which the card-issuing bank is located determines the interest rate charged, regardless of where the consumer resides or where the purchase is made. Most card-issuing banks also require a minimum repayment.

The card plays a dual role. It gives the merchant evidence that a consumer has been granted a line of credit, and it is a convenient, accurate means of imprinting sales drafts. The merchant deposits these sales slips with the card-issuing bank or one of its agents. In either case merchants receive an immediate deposit, less a discount, in their own bank accounts. The discount is theoretically determined by the potential profitability of the relationship between the bank and the merchant. And this profitability is determined by the dollar volume of credit purchases the merchant generates, the average ticket size, the competitive anxiety in the

---

[2]Some banks do not allow this grace period.

FIGURE 3–1

Application For MasterCard/Visa

I would prefer MasterCard ☐   or Visa ☐   or Both ☐
Yes, I'm interested in your Auto Pay service ☐

☐ NEW ACCOUNT ☐ REISSUE REQUEST ☐ REQUEST LIMIT INCREASE

ACCOUNT NUMBER ☐☐☐☐☐☐☐☐☐☐☐☐☐☐☐☐☐

IMPORTANT		
Read these Directions before completing this Application and Check Appropriate Box.	☐ If you are applying for an individual account in your own name and are relying on your own income or assets and not the income or assets of another person as the basis for repayment of the credit requested, complete only Sections A and C. ☐ If you are applying for a joint account or an account that you and another person will use, complete all Sections, providing information in B about the joint applicant or user. ☐ If you are applying for an individual account, but are relying on income from alimony, child support, or separate maintenance or on the income or assets of another person as the basis for repayment of the credit requested, complete all Sections to the extent possible, providing information in B about the person on whose alimony, support, or maintenance payments or income or assets you are relying.	

SECTION A—APPLICANT

FIRST NAME	MIDDLE NAME	LAST NAME	SOCIAL SECURITY NUMBER	BIRTHDATE MO/DAY/YR

STREET ADDRESS APT. NO.	CITY	STATE	ZIP	HOW LONG?	HOME PHONE NO. ( )

☐ OWN ☐ RENT ☐ BUYING ☐ LIVE W/RELATIVES	PREVIOUS STREET ADDRESS CITY	STATE ZIP	HOW LONG?	NO. DEPENDENTS AGES:

EMPLOYED BY	HOW LONG?	ADDRESS	MONTHLY SALARY $

BUSINESS PHONE POSITION ( )	PREVIOUS EMPLOYER	ADDRESS	CITY	STATE	HOW LONG?

NAME OF NEAREST RELATIVE NOT LIVING WITH YOU	STREET ADDRESS	CITY	STATE	PHONE NO. ( )	RELATION

BANK WITH	BRANCH	☐ CHECKING ACCOUNT NO.	☐ LOAN
		☐ SAVINGS ACCOUNT NO.	☐ CREDIT CARD

Alimony, child support, or separate maintenance income need not be revealed if you do not wish to have it considered as a basis for repaying this obligation.

OTHER INCOME $	SOURCE(S) OF OTHER INCOME	ALIMONY, CHILD SUPPORT, SEPARATE MAINTENANCE, RECEIVED UNDER: ☐ COURT ORDER ☐ WRITTEN AGREEMENT ☐ ORAL UNDERSTANDING

SECTION B—JOINT APPLICANT

FIRST NAME	MIDDLE NAME	LAST NAME	SOCIAL SECURITY NUMBER	BIRTHDATE MO/DAY/YR	HOME PHONE NO. ( )

STREET ADDRESS APT. NO.	CITY	STATE	ZIP	HOW LONG?	NO. DEPENDENTS AGES:

☐ OWN ☐ RENT ☐ BUYING ☐ LIVE W/RELATIVES	PREVIOUS STREET ADDRESS	CITY	STATE ZIP	HOW LONG?	RELATION TO APPLICANT IF ANY

EMPLOYED BY	HOW LONG?	ADDRESS	MONTHLY SALARY $

BUSINESS PHONE POSITION ( )	PREVIOUS EMPLOYER	ADDRESS	HOW LONG?

NAME OF NEAREST RELATIVE NOT LIVING WITH YOU	STREET ADDRESS	CITY	STATE	PHONE NO. ( )	RELATION

BANK WITH	BRANCH	☐ CHECKING ACCOUNT NO.	☐ LOAN
		☐ SAVINGS ACCOUNT NO.	☐ CREDIT CARD

Alimony, child support, or separate maintenance income need not be revealed if you do not wish to have it considered as a basis for repaying this obligation.

OTHER INCOME $	SOURCE(S) OF OTHER INCOME	ALIMONY, CHILD SUPPORT, SEPARATE MAINTENANCE, RECEIVED UNDER: ☐ COURT ORDER ☐ WRITTEN AGREEMENT ☐ ORAL UNDERSTANDING

community, the coverage of the community by the cardholders, and the types of participating merchants. Variations in discounts should be avoided among merchants selling the same types of merchandise. The range of this discount is usually between 2 and 5 percent. Discounts on airline ticket sales usually are lower than discounts at retail and service establishments, and public service transactions frequently carry a very low discount or none at all.

PRESENT-DAY BENEFITS. Although the present-day benefits of bank credit card plans are similar to those of earlier bank plans, there are some significant differences.

FIGURE 3–1 *(concluded)*

SECTION C—OBLIGATIONS AND REFERENCES						
PLEASE LIST BELOW ALL DEBTS, INCLUDING ANY ALIMONY OR CHILD SUPPORT. YOU MAY ALSO LIST ANY ACCOUNTS (PAID OUT OR OPEN) WHICH YOU WISH THE BANK TO CONSIDER AS A CREDIT REFERENCE. USE SEPARATE SHEET IF NECESSARY.						
NAME OF COMPANY OR BANK		ACCOUNT NUMBER	PRESENT BALANCE	MONTHLY PAYMENT	ACCOUNT IN NAME OF	
RENT OR MORTGAGE PAYABLE TO					☐ APPLICANT ☐ JOINT APPLICANT ☐ OTHER	
AUTOMOBILE FINANCED BY	YEAR MAKE				☐ APPLICANT ☐ JOINT APPLICANT ☐ OTHER	
	YEAR MAKE				☐ APPLICANT ☐ JOINT APPLICANT ☐ OTHER	
					☐ APPLICANT ☐ JOINT APPLICANT ☐ OTHER	
					☐ APPLICANT ☐ JOINT APPLICANT ☐ OTHER	
					☐ APPLICANT ☐ JOINT APPLICANT ☐ OTHER	

Are you a co-maker, endorser, or guarantor on any loan or contract? Yes ☐ No ☐ If yes

For whom? _____ To whom? _____

Are there any unsatisfied judgements against you? Yes ☐ No ☐ If yes to whom owed? _____

Have you been declared bankrupt in the last 10 years? Yes ☐ No ☐ If Yes where? _____ Year _____

FOR ARMED FORCES PERSONNEL ONLY-HOME OF RECORD Service Member is ☐ Applicant ☐ Joint Applicant

Address of Home of Record	City, State, Zip	Expiration of Category	Rank

CREDIT LIMIT REQUESTED: _____

The applicant and joint applicant, if any, hereby request a MasterCard/Visa, affirm that everything stated in this application is true and correct, understanding that the Bank will retain this application whether or not it is approved, authorize the Bank to check the above credit and employment history and to answer questions about the credit experience with the account, and agree to be obligated by the terms and conditions of the MasterCard/Visa Agreement and Disclosure required by Federal Law as amended from time to time delivered to them. Should a MasterCard/Visa be issued and without limiting the generality of said agreement they specifically agree, jointly and severally to pay for credit extended through the use of the card and all costs incurred in collecting that indebtedness, including a reasonable attorney's fee.

_____ _____   _____ _____
Applicant's Signature   Date   Other Signature (where Applicable)   Date

FIRST FLORIDA BANK

Member FDIC   Please fold and tape securely; postage is paid. Or, bring into your local First Florida Bank branch.

1. To Customers. As more and more firms participate in these plans, customers can use their cards at an ever-widening assortment of firms. An increasing number of service establishments accept bank credit cards. Some educational institutions accept them for tuition payments and governmental agencies for tax payments. With the cash-advance feature customers can obtain cash loans quickly and conveniently.[3] More businesses are installing unattended 24-hour terminals (cash dispensers and automated tellers) for cash-advance loans.

2. To Participating Merchants. The advantages of increased sales and profits, improved cash position, and freedom from credit department detail continue to benefit participating merchants. As credit becomes a way of life in this country, many merchants who had a cash-only policy are finding credit a necessity for survival. Bank credit card plans provide the means for such merchants to switch to a cash-credit policy.

Participating merchants also receive the benefit of a declining discount rate, based on the volume of sales slips routed to the bank.

---

[3]This topic will be discussed in Chapter 4.

In fact, some merchants permit their banks to handle all their credit operations.

Merchants also get point-of-purchase promotional material from card-issuing banks and benefit from bank cards' widespread national advertising. Cooperative advertising by banks and merchants has virtually disappeared.

3. To Banks.   Credit card plans continue to help banks develop new business from participating merchants, "cross-sell" bank services to cardholders, and create a progressive image. Bankers contend that credit cards allow them to offer a new service to existing customers, provide a means of penetrating new consumer and merchant markets, and increase the opportunities for promoting other bank services.

Dual issuance of bank credit cards was made possible in May 1976 by a major shift in the membership policy of National BankAmericard, Inc., due to threatened antitrust action. Prior to this date, banks handled only one card plan, and most consumers had only one bank credit card—either MasterCard (then Master Charge) or Visa (then BankAmericard), depending on where they banked. (Some customers dealt with two banks in order to carry both cards.) Today commercial banks commonly issue both cards to the same customer.

Present-day bank credit cards also provide banks with an important source of income. Participating merchants pay a discount on sales slips sent to the bank, and customers who extend their payments make a monthly interest payment for this privilege.

PRESENT-DAY PROBLEM AREAS.   While bank credit card plans have experienced outstanding growth, certain problem areas remain.

1. To Customers.   Consumers who don't understand their financial position can overbuy. Also, they extend their payments, and the finance charge results in a substantial additional expense. Early disadvantages—loss of private dealings between merchant and customer, limited merchant participation, low credit limits—have substantially decreased in importance.

2. To Participating Merchants.   Early disadvantages—obligations of the merchant to the bank, loss of store traffic, loss of merchant individuality have declined in importance. Some large, well-known retail establishments add bank credit card plans to their own credit arrangements. By doing so, they recognize consumer demand but they also earn interest income by carrying a substantial portion of their own revolving credit accounts. Under such a combination of plans, merchants can no longer claim that a bank sets its credit limits too low or its credit standards too high. Merchants can simply accept the questionable transaction themselves.

3. To Banks.   A bank contemplating the adoption of such a plan has a number of decisions to make, including: (1) how many cardholders are necessary to make the plan a success; (2) what criteria should be used to define an acceptable cardholder; (3) how should potential customers be induced to apply for a card; (4) how many merchants are necessary for successful operation (this factor is declining in importance in today's saturated market); (5) what procedures should be used to select desirable merchants; and (6) how should the schedule of discounts be established?

Banks want to make a profit from their credit card operations. The costs of introducing and operating a credit card plan vary greatly from bank to bank depending on the type of credit card service offered, management's schedule for market penetration, size and composition of the market, availability of personnel and equipment within the bank, extent and cost of new personnel and equipment, and type and strength of the competition. In making its decision to implement a credit card plan, a bank must also consider the procedures it wishes to follow with regard to interchange privileges.

The Fair Credit Billing Act (see Chapter 6) makes credit card issuers subject to all claims (other than tort claims) and defenses arising out of any transaction in which the credit card is used for payment. This presents another complication for the bank credit card issuer. For example, a consumer may charge car repairs on a bank credit card. If the repair job is defective, the bank as well as the dealer may be held responsible. This regulation requires better policing of merchants who join bank credit card plans.

RECENT DEVELOPMENTS IN BANK PLANS.   Bank credit card operations have changed recently and are continuing to change.

1. Independent Sales Organizations (ISOs).[4]   Recently, some banks used outside assistance to sign up additional cardholders and retail and service concerns to expand their bank credit card programs. In some instances, very small banks gained nationwide coverage through this arrangement.

While the majority of bank-ISO relationships have worked satisfactorily, problems have arisen. When a bank uses an ISO as an intermediary with a potential cardholder and/or merchant, the ISO becomes an agent of the bank. This ordinarily makes the bank liable for the acts the ISO performs on the bank's behalf. Bank employees also are agents, but they are under the direct supervision and control of the bank. The ISO, however, is not under the direct control of the bank and has great discretion in carrying out its activities.

Banks have discovered it is smart to check the ISO's background and qualifications. Banks also are learning to protect themselves from risk by

---

[4]See Suggested Readings at the end of the chapter.

following the procedures recommended by Visa and MasterCard headquarters in selecting ISOs. For example, Visa members must:

- Conduct background investigation.
- Conduct on-site inspection.
- Contact agent reference file.
- Register the ISO.
- Notify Visa of any changes or termination.
- Have a written agreement with each ISO, signed by an officer or member.
- Keep records for two years.
- Indemnify Visa against losses.
- Warrant that the ISO will comply with operating regulations.

2. Prestige Cards.   In recent years, both MasterCard and Visa have experienced record growth in their gold card or premium card programs. These associations consolidated the wide array of bank products (such as higher credit card limits, personal check cashing services, travel-accident insurance, emergency cash, free traveler's checks, car rental discounts, and so on) into a single prestige product.

Previously, each bank credit card plan designed its own prestige card with its own attractive features, thus preventing the promotion of the cards through national marketing campaigns. Once their cards were launched, Visa and MasterCard encouraged growth by subsidizing issuers' direct mail, print advertising material, and TV and radio spots.

Prestige cards are profitable for banks because many customers pay fees that average 50 percent higher than those on so-called standard cards; customers charge more per purchase than regular cardholders; and customers maintain considerably higher-than-standard account balances and thus pay more in deferred payment charges.

3. Affinity Credit Cards.[5]   Marketing bank credit cards to organizations or looser groupings of people with common interests—affinity groups—is a valuable tool in building market share. Many banks keep their name off the face of the card; most people choose an affinity card because of the identity of the group and the card's overall appeal, not because a certain bank issued it.

The groupings of people vary widely. One of the most important pioneer groups in this field is the nation's credit unions (see Chapter 4) to whom affinity group marketing is old stuff. Traditionally, credit union members feel part of a family concerning financial services, and this has carried over to credit card programs.

---

[5]See Suggested Readings at the end of the chapter.

In 1985, the AFL-CIO sponsored a labor-related affinity credit card that provided members with favorable interest rates while promoting organized labor's image. Today this card is one of the most successful in the affinity card market.

Other successful groupings include public service employees, clothing and textile workers, steelworkers, mail handlers, letter carriers, electrical workers, hotel and restaurant employees, golfers and tennis players, and church organizations. Affinity Group Marketing, Inc., a New York-based marketing firm, actively promotes such programs.

4. Interest Rates on Bank Credit Cards.[6]   During the 1980s, most interest rates fell substantially, but those on bank credit debt changed relatively little. Several bills Congress considered in 1986 would have imposed a nationwide rate ceiling on credit card accounts, but none of these was enacted into law.

While Visa and MasterCard dominate the credit card industry, they control only the fees that members pay. Each bank sets the interest rates and membership fees that consumers pay. Thus banks are free to compete on price, which includes interest rates, annual fees, and grace periods.

5. Competition from Nonbank Corporations and Credit Card Banks.[7]   Visa and MasterCard face competition not only from each other but also from many other outside sources. Since 1980 when nonbanks discovered a loophole in the Bank Holding Act that allowed them to enter the banking system, some 160 nonbanks have been formed to operate outside the restrictions limiting bank holding companies.

When Congress passed the Competitive Equality Banking Act of 1987 (CEBA), bankers viewed it as a means to restore competitive balance in the industry by curbing the growing influence of banks owned by nonbank companies. However, CEBA authorized a new type of bank—the credit card bank—and limited its functions to credit card lending.

Nonbank banks and credit card banks are powerful opponents to their full-service bank counterparts. Sears, Roebuck and Co., ITT Corp., and General Electric Co. have obtained charters for credit card banks. Many of the companies applying for credit card banks already operate nonbanks grandfathered by CEBA. At the close of 1988, five nonbanks ranked among the top 25 issuers: Greenwood Trust (Discover), Centurion Bank (American Express), Associates National Bank (Ford Motor Co.), Lomas Bank (partly owned by Merrill Lynch Capital Partners), and Household Bank.

6. Bank Credit Card Fraud.   Bank credit card fraud is a growing problem. Any business that accepts bank credit cards is a potential target for credit

---

[6]See Suggested Readings at the end of the chapter.

[7]For excellent coverage of this topic, see Linda Punch, "The Nonbanks Are Back," *Credit Card Management,* October 1989, p. 36.

card fraud. Major credit card issuers at times fail to provide adequate security for their cards, thus permitting the stealing of credit card numbers without detection. To complicate matters, merchants often fail to secure proper identification to prove that the customer who presents the card is the card owner.

Visa and MasterCard estimated that bank credit card losses in 1988 totaled almost $1 billion. This included application fraud; telemarketing fraud; lost, stolen, and counterfeit cards; and bankruptcy fraud. Bankruptcy fraud was the main contributor to this total.[8]

7. Secured-Card Programs. Traditionally, bank credit card accounts have been structured as unsecured lines of credit available through the use of plastic cards. Recently, however, a few bank card issuers have begun offering credit cards to consumers considered uncreditworthy. The consumers, who pay higher-than-normal interest rates and fees, supply a deposit to secure the card.[9] These programs generally require the cardholder to give the bank a form of security, generally a deposit account or a certificate of deposit, that equals the line of credit issued.

If not properly structured, however, secured-card programs can expose issuers to new liabilities and to federal and state legal problems.

8. Collection by Federal Agencies. Many U.S. government agencies are joining the federal government's credit card collection efforts. At the beginning of 1990, some 40 agencies planned to accept credit cards to collect funds.[10]

The bank credit card business has changed drastically over the past 30 years; and as the number of potential eligible cardholders hits saturation, credit card companies are reaching into new markets and are trying to improve service to cardholders and to retail and service concerns.[11] The key word is profitability, and the bank credit card companies are striving for this by stressing improvements in existing activities and by coming up with new and consumer-oriented services. Both Visa and MasterCard realize that the 1990s will be a battle decade.

Recent Developments in Retail Electronic Banking

More and more financial institutions now use retail electronic banking in the form of automated clearing house (ACH) services, automated teller machines (ATM), and on-line authorization and off-line clearing and

---

[8]John Stewart, "Going to the Cleaners," *Credit Card Management,* January 1990, p. 40.

[9]Anita Boomstein, "Reducing the Risk of Secured-Card Programs," *Credit Card Management,* March 1990, p. 24.

[10]"Federal Agencies' Credit Card Activity," *Credit Card Management,* July–August 1988, p. 62.

[11]See Suggested Readings at the end of the chapter.

deferred settlement arrangements. The debit cards are regulated by the Electronic Funds Transfer Act, as described in Chapter 6.

In today's marketplace, there are three types of debit cards:

The Automated Clearing House Model. In this model, the transaction flows from the merchant to the merchant bank to an ACH facility, and then to the customer's bank. The merchant enrolls customers—sometimes issuing its own cards—provides off-line authorizations, and creates an ACH file. The merchant's bank receives the transactions from the merchant, separates "on-us" transactions—those made by a bank's cardholders at one of that bank's merchants—and sends the rest to the ACH facility. The customer's bank receives the transaction and posts it against the customer's demand-deposit account. There is generally a one-to-two day delay between date of settlement and merchant settlement.

* * * * *

The ATM Model. In this model, which has on-line authorization and settlement, merchants accept cards with personal identification number (PIN) at the point of sale and send transactions to the merchant bank, which separates on-us transactions and enters the others into the network. The bank issues cards, receives the transactions, and posts them the same day.

* * * * *

The issuer and merchant also face increased exposure to fraud and bad debt. Unlike credit cards, ATM debit cards are mass-issued with little concern for the customer's creditworthiness. The customer's identity and availability of funds are verified for the salesperson. There are greater fraud implications for the ATM debit cards than for ATM cards used solely for deposit or cash withdrawal because debit cards at the point of sale are used to purchase goods and services as well as to withdraw cash.

* * * * *

The Credit Card Model. This model, with its on-line authorizations and off-line clearing and deferred settlement, is typified by Master Debit and Visa Debit. It has the same kind of guarantees and similar loss potential as a credit card. Such cards are selectively issued, as are credit cards, typically with a line of credit for overdraft protection.

* * * * *

The ACH model, the ATM model, and the credit card model, each with its own characteristics, have a role in consumer payments. But for the debit product to successfully play a role, risk issues must be carefully balanced against service and technology.[12]

Sears' Discover Credit Card

Sears introduced its Discover credit card in a direct-mail nationwide campaign early in 1986 by offering the card to the 25 million active users of

---

[12]William D. Neumann, "Making the Debit Card Fraud-Resistant," *Credit Card Management,* March 1990, p. 77. Also see Suggested Readings at the end of this chapter.

TABLE 3–1   **Financial Services of Discover Card**

No Annual Fee—Unlike most other major credit cards, Discover[SM] Card does not charge a membership fee. It costs nothing to receive a generous line of credit and all the benefits and services that are designed especially for Discover Cardmembers.

Money Back—With every Discover Card purchase, you earn a yearly Cashback Bonus of up to 1% of your total purchases based on your annual level of spending. So the more you use the Discover Card, the more money you earn.

Instant Cash Advances—Discover Cardmembers can get cash advances instantly at more than 700 full-line Sears stores, at participating Automated Teller Machines (ATMs) nationwide, and by writing Discover Card Checks.

Save on Travel—Discover Cardmembers can enroll in Discover Card Travel Services and save time and money on all domestic travel. Benefits include guaranteed lowest airfares and 5% money back on all qualified travel.

Money-Saving Discounts—Discover Cardmembers receive ValueFinders[SM] coupons which offer discounts on an assortment of brand name products and services.

Cardmember Protection Services—Discover Cardmembers have access to a wealth of protection services. Protection for all your valuables and credit card registration with The Register.[SM] Term Life Insurance at group rates from Allstate. And Automatic $100,000 Travel Accidental Death Insurance, offered at no cost to Discover Cardmembers.

Specially Designed Financial Services—Discover Cardmembers can also take advantage of unique personal financial opportunities which include the high interest Discover Savers' Account and convenient Discover Card Auto Financing through Sears Consumer Financial Corporation and Subsidiaries.

CreditSafe[SM] Plus—Valuable credit insurance when you need it most. Financial protection that's what credit insurance is all about. What kind of insurance should you have? Life? Disability? Unemployment? . . . CreditSafe Plus protects your credit against all three, and it can help to ensure that when you can't make your payments, Allstate will.

Accepted Nationwide—The Discover Card is welcomed at leading stores, restaurants, hotels, airlines, car rentals, and service stations coast to coast.

Apply Today—The Discover Card has been designed like no other credit card. It is a personal financial resource issued by Greenwood Trust Company, a member of the Sears Financial Network. Apply for it today! **No annual fee!**

Source: Sears, Roebuck and Co.

its Sears' store credit card.[13] Sears described its new general-purpose credit card as a multifeature, family financial services card offering revolving credit, savings instruments, electronic services, insurance, and other financial planning services.

Sears is relying on two factors to give it an advantage in the competitive card market: first, a broad base of consumers already familiar with Sears' assortment packages; and second, an assortment of financial services not available through any other single card. Table 3–1 lists Discover's financial services.

---

[13]See Suggested Readings at the end of the chapter.

Discover is market testing a premium credit card in several areas of the United States. The card being tested offers a higher credit line, bigger cash rebates at a $40 annual fee, and a travel assistance package including collision damage waivers on rental cars. For Discover, the most attractive feature of the new card is the annual fee—there is none!

American Express' Optima Credit Card

In March 1987, American Express launched its Optima credit card plan. This new product varied from the American Express green charge card (to be explained later in this chapter) by including a revolving credit feature, a 13.5 percent APR, and a $15 annual fee. When it was introduced, American Express officials said Optima would be offered only to existing American Express cardholders in the United States who had been customers in good standing for at least one year. Optima was characterized as "a new extended payment service available only to American Express Cardmembers."

Changes since the introduction include the following: marketing Optima to American Express gold cardholders (to be explained later in the chapter); using a variable APR figured at 1.8 times prime; launching Optima in Canada, the United Kingdom, and France; and increasing the variable APR to 16.75 percent.

Although Optima accounted for only approximately 1 percent[14] of the credit cards issued in the United States as of June 30, 1989, many bankers resent American Express' entry into the revolving credit area. In addition, Optima has raised friction between American Express and the banks selling its traveler's checks, which command worldwide acceptance. Banks earn a commission based on the volume of traveler's checks sold.

Retail Private-Label Credit Cards

Retail private-label credit cards are typically issued by banks or finance companies. While the card carries the name of the retailer, the card issuer is responsible for making the credit decisions, collecting the balances, and financing the receivables.

The Nilson Report estimated private-label card outstandings for 1988 at approximately $14 billion, with the five largest holders being GE Capital Corp., Citicorp Retail Services, Household Retail Services, First Data Resources, and Sears Payment System.[15]

---

[14]"The Optima Story," *Credit Card Management,* January 1990, p. 51. Also see "Is Optima a Threat or Not?" *ABA Banking Journal,* September 1987, p. 88, and Andrea Gordon, "The Banks' Beef with AmEx," *Credit Card Management,* September–October 1988, p. 58.

[15]See the Suggested Readings at the end of the chapter.

In studies conducted in 1987 and 1988, Elrick and Lavidge Inc. of Atlanta discovered that customers with a department store credit card spend roughly twice as much and rate the store higher in all aspects of customer service than customers who do not have the card.[16] Some retail organizations believe that private-label cards are a weapon in establishing and maintaining store loyalty.

TELEPHONE CREDIT CARDS. The battle for the telephone card business began in 1982 when U.S. District Judge Harold Greene approved a consent agreement proposed by American Telephone & Telegraph Co. and the Justice Department. In the 1984 settlement, AT&T was allowed to keep its long distance service and phone card operations. The phone card business at that time was about $4 billion a year and growing.[17]

MCI Communications Corp. entered the telephone card business in 1984. In 1988 Judge Greene ruled the card validation system and the monopoly on public phone booths between AT&T and the regional Bell systems were discriminatory. This resulted in a competitive battle among AT&T, MCI, and Sprint, which continues today.

In March 1990, AT&T launched its new Universal credit card, which is good for long distance calls and consumer purchases. The card is linked with Visa and MasterCard with a variable rate starting at 18.9 percent. In its introductory offer, AT&T offered to waive permanently the traditional annual fee for customers who sign up in 1990 and use the card for a purchase at least once a year. Other selling points included a 10 percent discount on long distance calls made with the card and 90-day insurance coverage for retail purchases.[18]

AT&T's Universal card credit terms are shown in Figure 3–2.

Charge Cards

As was pointed out earlier, the Fair Credit and Charge Card Disclosure Act of 1988 defined a charge card as "a card, plate, or other single credit device that may be used from time to time to obtain credit which is not subject to a finance charge."

American Express, Diners Club, and Carte Blanche are the leaders in the charge card field.[19] Diners Club (see Figure 3–3 for a Diners Club

---

[16]"Benefits of Private Label Credit," *The Credit World,* September–October 1988, p. 22.

[17]David Thompson, "MCI Takes on AT&T in the Phone Card War," *Credit Card Management,* March–April 1989, p. 84.

[18]See "AT&T Crashes the Credit-Card Party," *Business Week,* April 9, 1990, p. 23; Paul G. Kahn, "Not 'Just Another Credit Card,' " *The Credit World,* May–June 1990, p. 38.

[19]Diners Club and Carte Blanche are now owned by Citicorp Diners Club, Inc. Also see the Suggested Readings at the end of the chapter.

FIGURE 3–2

AT&T *Universal Card* Credit Terms

I understand that Universal Bank or its affiliate may obtain a consumer report about me now and from time to time in the future and, if I ask, that Universal Bank or its affiliate will tell me if it has obtained a consumer report and the name and address of the agency that supplied the report. I understand that I must be 18 years of age or older to get an *AT&T Universal Card*. By using the card, authorizing its use, or not cancelling my account within 30 days after I receive the card, I agree to the terms of the *AT&T Universal Card* Agreement which will be sent with the card. This offer is non-transferable and is not applicable to a corporate account.

Annual Percentage Rate	18.9%*.	**Notice to Ohio Residents:** The Ohio laws against discrimination require that all creditors make credit equally available to all creditworthy customers, and that credit reporting agencies maintain separate credit histories on each individual upon request. The Ohio Civil Rights Commission administers compliance with this law.
Variable Rate Information	The annual percentage rate (APR) may vary. It will be based on the prime rate published in *The Wall Street Journal* plus **8.9%**.	
Minimum Finance Charge	**$.50** whenever a finance charge is imposed.	**Notice to California Residents:** If you are a married applicant you may apply for credit in your own name.
Grace Period for Purchases	If you pay your new balance in full within 25 days of your statement closing date each month, you will avoid finance charges on purchases.	**Notice to Illinois Residents:** You may contact the Illinois Commissioner of Banks and Trust Companies for comparative information on interest rates, charges, fees and grace periods at State of Illinois-CIP, P.O. Box 10181, Springfield, Illinois 62791, 1 800 834-5452.
Balance Calculation Method for Purchases	Average daily balance (including new purchases).	
Annual Membership Fee	None.	**Married Wisconsin Residents Only:** No provision of any marital property agreement, unilateral statement, or court order applying to marital property will adversely affect a creditor's interests unless, prior to the time credit is granted, the creditor is furnished a copy of the agreement, statement or court order, or has actual knowledge of the provision. In addition, I must send you the name and address of my spouse within 15 days to *AT&T Universal Card*, P.O. Box 45173, Jacksonville, FL 32232-5173 so that you can provide my spouse with a disclosure required under Wisconsin law.
Cash Advance Transaction Fees	At ATMs, **2%** of the cash advance or **$1**, whichever is greater. At branches, **2%** of the cash advance or **$5**, whichever is greater.	
Late Payment Fee	**$10** if you do not make a payment within 20 days of the payment due date.	
Fee for Exceeding Your Credit Limit	**$10** in each billing cycle in which you exceed your credit limit.	The *AT&T Universal Card* is issued by Universal Bank or its affiliate.

*This corresponds to the calculated variable rate using the prime rate in effect as of the printing date, 10%.

Source: American Telephone and Telegraph Co.

application form) is the granddaddy, dating back to 1950; American Express entered the field in 1958. These plans were formerly known as T & E (travel and entertainment) plans. Under these plans, the customer pays an annual fee to the issuing organization, can charge goods and services at member establishments, and then receives one itemized monthly statement of the charges. The monthly statement gives the customer an itemized record of expenditures and travels and proof of legitimate business expenses for tax purposes. Firms that agree to honor the cards pay a stipulated percentage discount in order to be reimbursed for the customer's charges.

The three major charge card companies vary in the number of outlets serviced; the annual fee charged customers; the plan followed for extended payments, if any; the cash-advance feature allowed; and the minimum income of applicants.

American Express issued its green card in 1958, its gold card in 1966, and its platinum card in 1984. Each card carries a different annual fee and a different array of financial services. Table 3–2 compares the three American Express cards.

The decade of the 1990s is bound to be the battleground for the infighting among the charge card companies and the outfighting with the array of other credit card plans.

FINANCING RETAIL INSTALLMENT TRANSACTIONS

Consumer installment accounts may originate when consumers purchase goods from a retail outlet. Retailers, whether they carry their own paper or not, take the customer's credit information, execute the security agreement, and complete other tests necessary to establish the installment account. Retailers also inform the customer of the terms of the contract and

FIGURE 3–3

Apply Today for the Diners Club Card

> Place your silver
> sticker here.

Don't pass up this opportunity to apply for Diners Club
Card membership. Apply for the Card that gives you Club
Rewards[sm], $350,000 Automatic Air Travel Accident Insurance,
and thousands of dollars in future purchasing privileges.

■ Diners Club Membership Form ■

Fill in this Form completely and mail in enclosed envelope.

Please print your full name as you wish it to appear on the Card. (25 spaces maximum)	Employer Name Your Position
Please print your business title or company name if you wish it to appear on the Card.	Employer Address Street
ADDITIONAL CARD: Please issue an additional Diners Club Card, $30 each annually, with separate monthly itemized listing for the above family or household member. **Married Applicants may each apply for separate accounts.**	City State Zip
Please indicate whether or not you wish Additional Cardmember to also have access to the Club Cash[sm] Account. ☐ YES ☐ NO	( ) Self-employed: Yes ☐ No ☐ Business Telephone (include area code)
Number of dependents (include yourself) _____	
Social Security Number Birth Date	Annual Wages or Salary (must be provided): _____
Highest Level of Education Completed: ☐ Graduate School ☐ College ☐ High School	If your annual salary is less than $25,000—indicate source and amount of other income, and individual (Banker, Broker, Employer, etc.) we may contact for confirmation. Please understand that your total annual income from all sources **must** be at least $25,000 to be considered for Cardmembership.
Home Address Street	Disclosure of income from alimony, child support or separate maintenance required only if you wish it to be considered for purposes of this application.
City State Zip	
( ) _____ Years at current address: _____ own ☐ rent ☐ other ☐ Home Telephone (include area code)	Other income $_____ Source _____
	( ) _____ Name of individual for additional income verification. Phone
Previous Home Address (if less than 1 year at present address)	
City State Zip	Address City State Zip
Indicate your banking relationships:	Please provide all requested information so your Membership Form may be promptly processed. Send no money now. Upon our approval, we will bill you for the non-refundable $55 annual MEMBERSHIP FEE (subject to change).
☐ Checking ☐ Money Market ☐ Savings ☐ NOW ☐ Other _____ Bank Name	**I have read both sides of this application and agree to its terms.**
☐ Checking ☐ Money Market ☐ Savings ☐ NOW ☐ Other _____ Bank Name	X _____ Signature of Primary Applicant Date
Check which charge cards you have: American Express ☐ Visa ☐ MasterCard ☐ Oil Company Cards ☐ Sears ☐ Ward's ☐ J.C. Penney ☐ Other Store Cards ☐	X _____ Signature of Additional Applicant, if any Date

SEE REVERSE SIDE FOR IMPORTANT INFORMATION

answer the customer's questions. Some retailers carry their own installment paper; others let a financial institution assume this burden. Retailers who carry their own paper need more capital to compensate for a
decline in their working capital turnover. They also need more capital if

FIGURE 3–3 *(concluded)*

Annual fees	Transaction fee for cash advances and fees for paying late	
Annual fee for Primary Cardmembers: $55 per year.	Transaction fee for Club Cash Advances:	4% of each Club Cash Advance.
Annual fee for each Additional Cardmember: $30 per year.	Late payment fee for Diners Club Charges:	2½% per month on the entire past due balance if any amount is shown as past due on two consecutive billing statements (approximately 60 days past due) and a one-time $10 charge.
	Late payment fee for Club Cash Advances:	2½% per month on the entire past due balance if any amount is shown as past due on two consecutive billing statements (approximately 60 days past due).

All charges made on this charge card are due and payable when you receive your periodic statement.

By signing this Application, Applicant(s) authorizes Citibank (South Dakota), N.A., and its affiliates, to investigate, verify and exchange information regarding their creditworthiness. Consumer reports may be requested in connection with the processing of this Application and subsequently in connection with any update, renewal or extension of credit. Upon request, each Applicant will be informed of the names and addresses of any consumer reporting agencies which have provided such reports. Primary and Additional Cardmembers agree that the account information will be reported to credit bureaus in their names. Additional Cardmembers will be responsible for payment of their own charges if the Primary Cardmember fails to pay these charges. Additional Cardmember's credit record may be affected by non-payment of the account.

Applicant(s) agrees that use of any Card(s) issued as a result of this Application will be governed by the Agreement provided at the time the Card(s) is(are) issued.

MARRIED WISCONSIN RESIDENTS ONLY: No provision of any marital property agreement, unilateral statement, or court decree, applying to marital property will adversely affect a creditor's interests unless prior to the time credit is granted the creditor is furnished with a copy of the agreement, statement, or decree, or has actual knowledge of the provision. In addition, you must send the name and address of your spouse within 15 days to: Diners Club, P.O. Box 5824, Denver, CO 80217-5824, so that we can provide your spouse with a disclosure required under Wisconsin law.

© 1989 Citicorp Diners Club Inc.

Source: Diners Club.

they increase sales volume by offering installment credit services. Retailers who want a faster turnover of their own capital and desire to shift much of the credit risk burden may sell their paper to a sales finance company, commercial bank, or other type of consumer finance institution. Those who do so transfer the credit function to specialists in installment credit and free their own organization to concentrate on merchandising.

Today retailers carry only a small portion of the debt they are influential in creating. Commercial banks and finance companies hold most installment paper.

TABLE 3–2 **How American Express Charge Cards Compare**

Green Card	Gold Card (includes all Green Card Features)	Platinum Card (includes all Green and Gold Card Features)
Introduced 1958 Annual Fee: $55	Introduced 1966 Annual Fee: $75	Introduced 1984 Annual Fee: $300
No preset spending limit Signed receipt with bills 24-hour customer service AmEx Travel Service Office Network Emergency card replacement Buyer's Assurance Protection Plan Purchase Protection Plan Global Assist Hotline Car rental loss and damage insurance $100,000 travel accident insurance Baggage insurance plan Express cash $1,000 emergency fund Assured reservations	$2,000 line of credit Nonresident membership in 90 private U.S. clubs Envoy personalized travel service	Travel emergency assistance Personalized travel service Minimum $10,000 line of credit Nonresident membership in 26 exclusive clubs worldwide Preferred Welcome Worldwide Personal Assistance to locate goods and services

Financing by Commercial Banks

Today's high standard of living would not be possible without bank credit, particularly bank installment credit.

Many bankers think that the Federal Housing Administration (FHA) was the major factor in influencing banks to enter the field of installment credit. Under the blanket insurance arrangement provided by the FHA in the early 1930s, commercial banks were able to handle direct property improvement loans and acquire paper from contractors and dealers who supplied materials and labor. Banks' satisfactory experience in this area provided the impetus to explore other fields of installment credit.

Basically, a commercial bank has different methods available for acquiring installment business—the direct approach and the indirect approach. Banks may also use a combination of both methods.

DIRECT METHOD. Direct loans generally involve only two parties, the bank and the borrower. In this approach, the bank solicits the customer directly and makes loan commitments to creditworthy borrowers. The bank in turn can control its credit policies, as well as the ratio and volume of business it accepts.

Direct lending has many advantages over indirect installment lending:

1. The bank can apply its credit policies consistently.
2. The bank has greater flexibility in its operations.
3. Only two parties are involved.
4. The bank can better determine and evaluate the borrower's financial and personal characteristics.
5. The bank can influence the size of the loan.
6. Direct lending broadens a bank's base of operation within its trading area.

The principal disadvantage of direct lending is smaller volume generated at a slower pace. In addition, the bank's trading area may be too small to generate a large volume of walk-in direct installment loans, and the bank may have more difficulty with repossessions because it lacks a relationship with a dealer.

INDIRECT OR DEALER METHOD. This method involves three parties: the dealer, the borrower, and the bank. The dealer takes the credit application and prepares the necessary contracts and other forms. The dealer presents the paper to the bank for discount and, if approved, receives from the bank the amount financed by the borrower. In most cases the bank sends the borrower a payment coupon book.

Banks need to recognize the following fundamental differences between direct and indirect (or dealer) methods when considering a dealer arrangement:

1. The bank doesn't see the installment purchasers and thus doesn't have an opportunity to appraise them.
2. The attitude of many installment purchasers toward their obligations is different from the attitude of direct borrowers. When borrowers receive money from a bank in a direct loan transaction, they realize they must repay the obligation in money. When installment purchasers buy goods through a dealer, however, they sometimes think they can cancel their obligation by returning the goods, or they feel justified in refusing to make their installment payments if the goods are unsatisfactory.
3. Fraud, forgery, and misrepresentation are possible in any credit transaction where the bank doesn't see the obligor personally.

All experienced installment credit department managers in commercial banks know that the risks involved in indirect financing are substantially greater than they are in direct installment credit. Dealers have to be carefully policed in indirect financing, and often, the bank doesn't know as much as it would like about prospective borrowers. Yet indirect business can produce a high volume fairly quickly. As a result, indirect business offers the bank an opportunity to generate substantial loan volume with little effort.

In formulating policy on indirect installment sales, an installment loan department first considers the quality of the retail paper. In most cases this paper is only as good as the dealer that initiates it. As a result, the dealer's moral and financial qualifications are extremely important and must be reviewed carefully. Most banks spend considerable time reviewing the dealers' "track records," including details about their financial and business history. When deciding whether to finance a dealer's paper, the bank generally investigates the following areas of the dealer's background:

1. Current and past financial operating statements.
2. Deposit relations with the bank.
3. Trade references.
4. Distributor or manufacturer relations.
5. Credit reporting agencies.
6. Experiences with other financial institutions.
7. Standing with local office of the Better Business Bureau.

Once a bank accepts a dealer relationship, it must consider a wide range of other policies, including the following:

1. The ability to give speedy and prompt decisions on loans the dealer submits to the bank.
2. The development of experienced bank personnel who thoroughly understand the dealer's selling and credit problems.
3. Effective and economically feasible collection practices.
4. The adoption of competitive rates and terms.
5. Provisions for an adequate inventory financing program for the dealer.
6. The maintenance of adequate bank records to be able to review the condition of each dealer's accounts.
7. The ability to extend additional bank services to the dealer.

A variety of financing plans are available. Those selected depend on the competitive conditions prevailing and on the bank's credit policy. Some commercial banks offer their dealers a choice of several plans; others make only one program available and handle all paper purchased under that plan. The purchase of installment paper by commercial banks comes under three major classifications: the full recourse plan, the nonrecourse plan, and the repurchase plan. In each of these three plans, consumer default "triggers" the plan's provisions.

1. Full Recourse. Under the full recourse plan, dealers sell or sign over to the bank the installment sale paper that they originate. They do so with an unconditional guarantee: they accept full responsibility for the paper should the purchaser become delinquent. In the event of default, the dealer must repurchase the obligation from the bank for the balance due. The dealer is also responsible for reconditioning and reselling the product. Dealers like full recourse arrangements because of the lower bank discount rate—particularly if the consumer is a good credit risk.

2. Nonrecourse.   Under the nonrecourse plan, dealers have no responsibility if the customer defaults. They only have to warrant the genuineness of the paper, terms of sale, title, and so forth. The commercial bank buys the paper solely on the credit quality of the installment purchaser. In the event of repossession, the commercial bank assumes the full responsibility of retaking, reconditioning, and reselling the product.

3. Repurchase.   Under this plan, if the consumer defaults, the dealer has to buy back the property for the unpaid balance after it has been repossessed by the bank. The property must be delivered to the dealer's place of business within a specified number of days after maturity of the oldest unpaid installment. Generally, the bank has 90 days to locate the property and return it to the dealer.

Bank installment credit department managers and others involved in these decisions should judge dealer paper based on its individual merits. Banks should maintain a flexible credit policy at all times and make allowance for the financial strength of the dealer, the plan in effect, the quality of the paper purchased, the reserves available, and the borrower's equity. Some retailers request the privilege of a nonnotification plan. Under this plan, the dealer's customers have no knowledge that their sales contracts have been discounted at a commercial bank. Banks usually restrict nonnotification plans to highly reputable dealers with strong financial responsibility. The dealer's full recourse endorsement is generally required.

DEALER RESERVE.   In consideration of the dealer's part in originating the business and also to offset whatever liability the dealer assumes, banks frequently establish a reserve from a portion of the finance charge. Under a dealer participation arrangement, the finance charge to the customer must be higher than the bank rate to the dealer. The difference between the two is frequently set aside in a reserve account, giving the bank some protection on the dealer's contingent liability. Funds generally accumulate in the reserve account until the balance in the account achieves a certain percentage of the total outstanding paper that the dealer maintains with the bank. From time to time the bank will pay the dealer any excess.

Dealer reserve accounts are a policy decision, and they frequently differ from one type of dealer to another and often with the same dealer class. Although some states regulate dealer reserves, banks retain some flexibility. They often base their percentage of outstandings for a certain dealer on their judgment of the dealer's creditworthiness.

INVENTORY FINANCING. Also known as flooring, floor planning, and wholesale floor plan, inventory financing is a form of credit extended by a lender to a retail dealer to enable the dealer to carry an adequate supply of goods for display and sale.

Most commercial banks don't consider inventory financing as a separate activity but rather an integral part of the installment sale financing relationship with the dealer.[20] The low yield the bank obtains from this type of financing is a trade-off to the higher yield derived from the dealer's installment paper. Floor planning thus is an accommodation granted to retail dealers for two basic reasons: (1) in consideration for their agreement to discount with the bank the majority of their retail installment contracts and (2) to gain other cross-selling business activities.

Inventory financing first developed for car dealers, and they utilize it to a great extent. Car dealers have to pay cash for cars delivered to the dealership. The manufacturer draws a sight draft on the dealer, and this draft is payable on receipt of the cars. If dealers used their own capital to pay for the cars, many would have all of their working capital tied up in inventory, thus seriously limiting the quantity of cars they could purchase. Commercial banks thus floor plan the shipments from manufacturers by paying the manufacturer for the dealer. In exchange for this financing, the dealer delivers to the bank a security interest in the cars the dealer acquires. As a result, the commercial bank has title to the cars but the dealer retains possession. Dealers store the cars or use them for display or demonstration. When the dealer sells a car, the dealer must immediately or within a stipulated period satisfy the bank's lien. Of course, the commercial bank involved would also like to handle the buyer's car loan.

In extending flooring credit, the soundness of the dealer is vitally important. Although there are exceptions, experienced dealers with proven managerial ability offer the best risk.

Financing by Sales Finance Companies

The sales finance company is not to be confused with cash lending institutions such as small loan companies, consumer finance companies, and personal loan companies, which lend money directly to consumers and operate under special state legislation.[21] A sales finance company is a specialized type of institution that engages primarily in buying consumer installment contracts from retail dealers and in providing wholesale

---

[20]Technically, inventory financing is a form of commercial credit rather than consumer credit, in that the cash loan is made directly to a business. However, it is generally considered an integral part of the installment sale financing relationship with the dealer, so it is explained at this point.

[21]As will be pointed out in a subsequent section, some sales finance companies "wear two hats." In addition to their regular sales finance operation of buying retail installment paper, they also carry on a small loan operation under state regulation. In addition, refer to the discussion on consumer finance companies in Chapter 4.

financing for these dealers and that charges rates competitive with those of commercial banks and other lenders for equivalent services.

Writing on *The Role of the Sales Finance Companies in the American Economy*, Professor Clyde W. Phelps made these excellent observations:

1. The rise of the sales finance companies is an excellent illustration of two important principles: that institutions arise in response to social needs, and that when established institutions fail to meet the changing needs of society, new institutions come into being.

2. For many years after automobile production began, cars were sold only for cash. The limited financial resources of early car manufacturers made it impossible for them to sell vehicles on credit to automobile dealers, and they demanded cash on delivery from the latter. The dealers' financial resources were small and, therefore, they had to require cash for cars from the public.

3. As a result of this situation, the well-to-do and rich got automobiles and the masses did without. Furthermore, mass production and mass distribution of automobiles—which would make possible better cars, lower prices, increased opportunities for employment, and the advancement of the standard of living of the American people—appeared impossible.

4. The solution to this problem called for a new type of financing service which would do two things: provide wholesale financing to dealers, involving extremely large advances in proportion to their own invested capital; provide retail financing for consumers, involving installment payments.

5. In the early years of this century, before the rise of our specialized financial institutions, the commercial banks were the established institutions upon which society depended for financing the movement of goods from producer to consumer. The commercial banks were unwilling or unable to provide the new financing service required, and the institutions now known as finance companies came into being to meet the emerging social needs.

6. The sales finance companies pioneered in the creation and development of new financing services, and have made great contributions in the way of social benefits which are of interest to students of economics, history, sociology, and to the public generally. The automobile revolutionized American life, and its rapid growth to the position of our No. 1 industry was dependent for its wholesale and retail financing upon the sales finance companies—banks and other institutions did not offer such financing until long after the automobile business had become our leading industry. Also, the early growth of other industries producing consumers' durables, such as radios and household appliances, was dependent upon the sales finance companies for its wholesale and retail financing.[22]

---

[22]Clyde W. Phelps, *The Role of the Sales Finance Companies in the American Economy* (Baltimore, Md.: Commercial Credit Co., 1952), pp. 9–10. While this publication is out of date, it still presents an excellent picture of the current operations of sales finance companies.

Sales finance companies originated in the early 1900s. The *Saturday Evening Post,* in its March 31, 1900, issue, carried its first "horseless carriage" advertisement, but not until 1909 did the production of motor vehicles (both passenger cars and trucks) exceed 100,000. The first sales finance companies supplied working capital to manufacturers and wholesalers by buying open accounts and purchasing drafts and notes receivable. It was not until the increased acceptance of the automobile that sales finance companies, as we know them today, were organized.

These companies grew rapidly. In 1916 the Commercial Credit Company began to purchase automobile paper, and by 1919 the General Motors Corporation formed the General Motors Acceptance Corporation to facilitate the sale of its products by its dealers throughout the nation. In 1929 Ford Motor Company formed the Universal Credit Corporation, which was purchased during the late 1930s by Commercial Investment Trust. More recently the Ford Motor Company formed the Ford Motor Credit Company on a basis similar to GM and GMAC. These giants, with complete national coverage, compete with thousands of smaller regional and local concerns. Many independent sales finance companies are members of a national association, the American Financial Services Association.[23]

In addition, during the 1950s and early 1960s, many of the nation's largest nonfinancial corporations established subsidiary companies to hold notes receivable produced from the parent company's sales. These so-called captive finance companies were primarily designed to raise needed debt capital.

When buying a car or some other high-priced durable good with installment credit, customers usually have to fill out application forms that request fairly detailed information on employment, income, and other pertinent factors. These application forms vary, however, from retail dealer to retail dealer. After the buyer signs the application, it is usually witnessed and signed by a salesperson or the dealer. The usual installment sale contract is then prepared.

If the retail dealer decides not to carry the paper to maturity, the contract may be offered to a sales finance company based on a prearranged agreement between the dealer and the sales finance company. The sales finance company usually performs the credit investigation (although the dealer may do it at certain times) to make sure all the documents are in order and, if everything is acceptable, to make the purchase. The customer's account is then opened, and the customer usually is notified that the sales finance company purchased the contract. The customer makes payments directly to the sales finance company.

---

[23]This association was formerly known as the American Industrial Bankers Association. In May 1971, consumer finance companies, sales finance companies, and industrial banks, through their respective trade associations, joined forces into one organization known as the National Consumer Finance Association. It is now called American Financial Services Association.

As with commercial banks, the purchase of installment paper by sales finance companies comes under three major classifications: the full recourse plan, the nonrecourse plan, and the repurchase plan. In case of customer default, the provisions of these plans come into effect in the same manner as described under commercial bank financing.

In the recourse plan, the *dealer reserve* protects the dealer to some extent against losses. This fund, set aside by the sales finance company out of the finance charges, is refunded to the dealer under specified conditions. The dealer reserve covers expenses of repossession and other encumbrances against the vehicle. The dealer reserve account, which is set up in the accounting records of the sales finance company, ordinarily totals about 1½ percent on the amounts advanced on new cars and approximately 2 to 3 percent on used cars. Thus the retail dealer can be reimbursed on repossession from two sources, the car resale and the accumulated dealer reserve.

When buying installment contracts, sales finance companies' methods, contract forms, and procedures are similar to commercial banks. The interest rates of both are highly competitive in most communities.

In addition to buying installment paper from retailers, particularly car dealers, sales finance companies provide wholesale financing to durable-goods dealers. Such financing arrangements are similar to those provided by commercial banks.

Sales finance companies have changed and expanded over the years and have diversified in at least four ways:

1. In addition to cars, they now deal in installment paper on manufactured homes, boats, aircraft, and farm machinery.
2. They are moving into other types of financing, such as small loans and commercial lending.
3. They are moving into new fields that may or may not be related to the finance industry. An example of this would be the acquisition of a bank by a sales finance company.
4. Some independent sales finance companies are establishing insurance subsidiaries.

THE HOLDER IN DUE COURSE DOCTRINE

The holder in due course doctrine has been closely associated with the financing in retail installment transactions. In an explanation of this doctrine, Philip G. Schrag, professor of law at Columbia University, made the following comments:

> Sellers of goods and services would require consumers to sign negotiable promissory notes, which they would then endorse to banks or finance companies with whom they did business on a regular basis. The third-party purchaser of the paper would then claim the rights of holder in due

course of commercial paper; specifically, freedom from any claims or defenses that the buyer might have asserted against the seller with whom he dealt.

For example, if a man purchased a food freezer or vacuum cleaner from a door-to-door salesman, and signed such a note, he would soon learn that the note had been sold to a bank, and he would be told to make his monthly payments to that institution. However, the man might stop making his payments when he discovered that he'd been cheated by the salesman's fraudulent statements about the nature of the merchandise. In a suit by the bank on the note, the buyer would not be permitted to assert defenses (other than "real" defenses), provided that the bank took the note in good faith, for value, and without notice of the buyer's defenses. If the seller deliberately lied to the buyer about the goods, if the merchandise was unmerchantable, or even if the goods were never delivered (failure of consideration), the buyer would have to pay. Of course, he would still have a right of action against the seller, but asserting it would require finding the seller solvent and initiating a new proceeding against him, rather than merely interposing a defense.[24]

For years consumer advocates have tried to abolish this doctrine. Successful judicial attacks on the doctrine, once a rarity, became more common in the late 1960s. Nevertheless, as late as 1971 the doctrine was still applied in approximately 40 states.

However, in November 1975 the Federal Trade Commission adopted a trade regulation rule designed to protect consumers' rights against sellers when consumers purchase on credit and become obligated to a financial institution.[25] The rule, which took effect May 14, 1976, substantially limited the effect of the holder in due course doctrine. It assured consumers of a continuing right to raise claims and defenses based on misconduct by sellers, including breach of contract, breach of warranty, misrepresentation, and fraud. The FTC justified this rule on the basis that many sellers used credit contracts that cut off consumers' rights by requiring consumers to continue payments to a financial institution regardless of whether the seller lived up to the terms of the bargain.

DISCUSSION QUESTIONS

1. What are the characteristics of bank credit card plans?
2. Trace the development of bank credit cards.
3. What are the advantages of bank credit card plans? The limitations?
4. If you were a retailer, would you join such a plan? Why or why not?

---

[24]Philip G. Schrag, *Consumer Protection* (St. Paul, Minn.: West Publishing Co., 1973), p. 1084.

[25]It should be remembered, however, that bank credit card issuers are no longer protected by the holder in due course doctrine because of the passage of the Fair Credit Billing Act (see Chapter 6).

5. Discuss the recent developments in retail electronic banking.

6. Explain why prestige cards are gaining in popularity.

7. Discuss the advantages and disadvantages of Sears' Discover card.

8. Explain the various ways retailers can finance their installment accounts.

9. What factors should retailers consider in choosing a method of financing installment accounts?

10. What are the two methods available to a commercial bank for acquiring installment business? Explain each method.

11. Distinguish clearly between the full recourse, the nonrecourse, and the repurchase plans of buying paper. Which plan is best for the consumer? For the retailer? For the commercial bank or the sales finance company?

12. What is the primary purpose of a dealer reserve?

13. What is floor plan financing? Why is it especially important in the automobile industry?

14. What is the primary reason for the existence of sales finance companies?

15. Trace the development of the sales finance company in the United States.

16. Discuss the main activities of captive finance companies.

17. Explain how the activities of sales finance companies have been changing in recent years.

18. What is the holder in due course doctrine? Explain how this doctrine affects you as a consumer.

19. Explain how the American Express Company, Diners Club, and Carte Blanche plans operate.

20. Discuss the growing importance of credit card fraud.

21. Explain the difference between a credit card plan and a charge card plan. Give an example of each.

22. Should a bank employ an independent sales organization to expand its credit card program? Why or why not?

23. What is an affinity credit card? Do you have one in your community?

24. Explain the characteristics of a secured-card program.

25. Why did American Express launch its Optima credit card?

26. Would you apply for a Universal credit card? Why or why not?

SUGGESTED READINGS

Independent Sales Organizations (ISOs)

"A Leaner ISO Business Bounces Back." *Credit Card Management,* December 1989, p. 5.

BOOMSTEIN, ANITA. "How Not to Get Stung by an ISO." *Credit Card Management,* March–April 1989, p. 16.

JARVIS, KATHLEEN. "Branchless Banking." *Credit,* March–April 1987, p. 23.

NEUMANN, WILLIAM D. "Protecting Banks from Themselves." *Credit Card Management,* September 1989, p. 101.

STEWART, JOHN. "Here Come the Tin Men." *Credit Card Management,* March–April 1989, p. 66.

Affinity Credit Cards

CANTRELL, WANDA. "Labor's Love Affair with Plastic." *Credit Card Management,* July–August 1988, p. 54.

"The 'Grandaddy' of Affinity Card Marketing." *ABA Banking Journal,* October 1987, p. 134.

HICKS, JOHN. "Credit Unions Can Compete in Consumer Credit Card Marketplace." *The Credit World,* November–December 1987, p. 36.

MANN, DAVID C. "Is Your Affinity Real or Imagined?" *ABA Banking Journal,* June 1989, p. 56.

PUNCH, LINDA. "Can Banks Derail the Credit Unions' Plastic Express?" *Credit Card Management,* March 1990, p. 69.

SLAWSKY, JEFF H. "Ethnic Marketing: The Ultimate Affinity." *Credit Card Management,* April 1990, p. 57.

"Two More Affinity Cards." *Consumer Trends,* October 5, 1989, p. 3.

Interest Rates on Bank Credit Cards

BLINDER, ALAN S. "Plastic Puzzle: Why Rates for Credit Cards Don't Go Down." *Business Week,* August 7, 1989, p. 14.

CANNER, GLENN B., and JAMES T. FERGUS. "The Economic Effects of Proposed Ceilings on Credit Card Interest Rates." *Federal Reserve Bulletin,* January 1987, p. 1.

"Credit Card Come-Ons." *Consumer Reports,* November 1988, p. 720.

Future of Bank Credit Cards

COCHEO, STEVE. "Bank Cards at the Crossroads." *ABA Banking Journal,* September 1987, p. 66.

FRANCINI, J. PINO. "Using Television Technology to Crack New and Lucrative Markets." *Credit Card Management,* January–February 1989, p. 30.

HALL, DANIEL. "Going for the (Plastic) Gold." *ABA Banking Journal,* September 1989, p. 102.

"The Hidden Power of Plastic." *Consumer Reports,* February 1987, p. 119.

"It's Nail-Biting Time." *Credit Card Management,* May 1989, p. 66.

PETERS, KURT T. "A New Frontier for Credit Cards." *Credit Card Management,* September 1989, p. 36.

RAHMER, PETER. "Canada's Credit Card Ward: New Tactics North of the Border." *Credit Card Management,* September–October 1988, p. 98.

SCHULTHEIS, F. ALAN. "Silver Lining: Banks' Future in T&E Cards." *Credit Card Management,* September–October 1988, p. 52.

STEWART, JOHN. "Card Marketers Start Sharp Shooting." *Credit Card Management,* July–August 1988, p. 30.

WEBER, AUSTIN. "Invasion of the Alien T&E Cards." *Credit Card Management,* December 1989, p. 33.

Debit Cards

"Debit Cards and Supermarkets." *The Credit World,* January–February 1987, p. 38.

"Debit Cards: Who Needs Them?" *Changing Times,* September 1987, p. 51.

"Entree Is Dead . . . Long Live Debit Cards!" *ABA Banking Journal,* September 1990, p. 109.

"POS a Hit at Lucky Stores." *ABA Banking Journal,* September 1989, p. 112.

PUNCH, LINDA. "The Credit-Debit War." *Credit Card Management,* April 1990, p. 36.

SMITH, ALEX. "POS: Where Have We Been? Where Are We Going?" *ABA Banking Journal,* September 1988, p. 104.

WOODWORTH, JEAN. "1988: The Year of the Debit Card?" *The Bankers Magazine,* July–August 1988, p. 34.

Sears' Discover Credit Card

ABERTH, JOHN. "Squeezing More from Cards." *ABA Banking Journal,* June 1988, p. 34.

"Discover: Why the Fresh-Faced Kid Is Smiling." *Credit Card Management,* May 1989, p. 76.

GORDON, ANDREA. "Fee for All? Why Some Say Discover Must Charge a Fee." *Credit Card Management,* January–February 1989, p. 42.

"Premium Discover." *Consumer Trends,* July 5, 1989, p. 6.

PUNCH, LINDA. "Are Gold Cards Losing Their Shine?" *Credit Card Management,* September 1989, p. 36.

Charge Card Plans

"Can AmEx Win the Masses—and Keep Its Class?" *Business Week,* October 9, 1989, p. 134.

"The Failed Vision." *Business Week,* March 19, 1990, p. 108.

LOVE, JOHN. "AmEx: Selling Snob Appeal to the Masses." *Credit Card Management,* November–December 1988, p. 20.

PUNCH, LINDA. "AmEx's Platinum-Plated Profit Machine." *Credit Card Management,* August 1989, p. 52.

―――――. "The Escalating Battle for the Corporate Card Market." *Credit Card Management,* March–April 1989, p. 56.

Retail Private-Label Credit Cards

CANTRELL, WANDA. "The Search for Store Card Users Heats Up." *Credit Card Management,* June 1990, p. 58.

EKEDAHL, DAVID D., and DAVID R. NISSEN. "Retailing's Private-Label Shake-out Thrusts GE into the Spotlight." *Credit Card Management,* November–December 1988, p. 50.

"Private-Label Cards in the U.S." *Consumer Trends,* February 5, 1989, p. 3.

STEWART, JOHN. "Store Cards Fight Back." *Credit Card Management,* June 1990, p. 52.

Types of Consumer Credit—Cash Loan Credit

The Objectives or Goals of Chapter 4 Are:

1. To explain why consumers need cash loans.
2. To describe the characteristics of cash loan plans in commercial banks.
3. To illustrate the changing character of commercial banks and their customers.
4. To trace the origin, development, and growth of credit unions.
5. To explain the operations of consumer finance companies.
6. To compare the relative costs of consumer lending institutions.

The financial services industry experienced rapid deregulation during the 1980s. On March 31, 1980, the president signed the Depository Institutions Deregulation and Monetary Control Act (DIDMCA), which changed some of the most important rules under which U.S. financial institutions had operated for nearly half of a century. (See Chapter 6 for details of the law.)

Two years later the Garn-St Germain Depository Institutions Act was signed into law. That widened the sources of depository institution funds, removed interest rate ceilings, and granted regulators temporary emergency powers to deal with current depository institution crises. (See Chapter 6 for details of the law.) These changes complicate the discussion of cash loan credit, as new roles have rapidly replaced the traditional roles of financial institutions and as an increasing number of firms compete in more diverse financial areas.

Over the years, a vast system of financial institutions has provided consumers with cash in exchange for credit. In analyzing consumer credit, it should be recognized that cash loan credit is credit in the form of money, as opposed to credit in the form of goods and services.

Consumers have borrowed money throughout history. Before 1900 all types of consumer credit were of only nominal importance in the United States, but since that time the expansion of cash loan credit has been almost as rapid and dramatic as that of retail installment credit. American consumers need to borrow money more today because they depend heavily on credit to fulfill their varied wants and desires. Just as the several forms of consumer credit developed in response to American consumers' diverse credit needs, so did cash loan credit become an important segment in the consumer credit field.

The system of financial institutions that has evolved supplies most people with various types of cash loans, much as various types of credit are available to facilitate the acquisition of goods and services. Commercial banks, consumer finance companies, credit unions, industrial banks, savings and loan institutions, and a number of other institutions (including philanthropic organizations and illegal lenders) supply cash loans to consumers. Most personal loans are made by commercial banks, credit unions, and consumer finance companies. Home mortgage loans will be covered in Chapter 5, along with the importance of savings and loan associations, life insurance companies, commercial banks, mutual savings banks, mortgage companies, and individual investors.

USE OF CASH LOANS BY CONSUMERS

The consumer who borrows money from a consumer financial institution does so mainly to consolidate existing debts into one lump sum, pay for emergency services, or purchase merchandise and services. Loans made to cover these broad purposes, for example, may be used for medical and dental expenses, home repair and modernization, tax bills, and educational expenses, as well as for furniture, appliances, and cars. Individual consumers, with their varied needs and desires, differ greatly in their ability to satisfy their wants. Some borrowers need nominal sums of money; others require larger sums. Some are able to repay their loan in a matter of 60 to 90 days; others need longer terms. Some prudently compare interest and service charges; others regard immediate cash as more important than cost. A number of borrowers need the security of a comaker, while others are able to borrow on their signature alone. In addition, consumer borrowers differ in their ability to handle funds wisely. Consequently, the U.S. cash-lending industry confronts a different set of circumstances with each loan. The numerous and varied uses of cash loan credit combined with different consumer characteristics explain to a great extent the need for a wide variety of types of loans.

Why do consumers borrow money to purchase goods and services when they can use other types of credit? Many consumers calculate the cost of other types of credit, compare this cost with that of a personal loan, and use the cheapest money available. Prestige or association with a particular financial institution may provide an additional explanation. Typically, professional and managerial groups have had long and pleasant associations with commercial banks, while skilled and semiskilled workers have fully utilized the services of commercial banks only in recent years. Consequently, individual preferences for dealing with a particular financial institution and the cost of money from each source explain some of the apparent duplication of credit services. Most consumers face a number of opportunities and situations that cannot be met except by cash loans.

CONSUMER CASH-LENDING INSTITUTIONS

Commercial banks, credit unions, consumer finance companies, and industrial banks are the principal sources of cash loans made to consumers. Each of these institutions was originated either to serve a particular consumer segment or to meet specific consumer needs not being met by existing credit facilities. The types of loans offered by lending institutions are so varied and numerous that relatively few American consumers have no ready source of cash credit. The variety of cash-lending institutions exemplify an effort to meet diverse consumer needs.

Cash-lending institutions can be thought of as "sellers of money." This concept clearly establishes them as *merchandisers* of credit. The supply and cost of money for cash-lending institutions have a parallel in the supply and cost of goods for retail firms. Cash-lending institutions build a customer group that seeks cash loans and will return when the need again exists; retailers of other commodities strive for goodwill, promotion, and repeat sales to satisfied customers. The interest rates and service charges of the cash-lending institutions represent the cost of money to the borrower, as prices of goods and carrying charges represent costs to the buyer of goods and services. Furthermore, the profit motive attracts capital, institutions, and personnel to the lending industry just as it lends impetus to most economic activity. Consequently, sellers of money are confronted with many of the same problems facing other types of merchandising establishments, and the degree of their success frequently hinges on methods that are the same as or similar to those used by successful merchandisers of goods and services.

Commercial Banks

Commercial banks were slow to adopt the practice of lending cash to consumers. Before 1930, commercial banks were active in the real estate loan field but made only a few customer loans to individuals, and these were single-payment loans made to individuals with high incomes.

In the late 1920s, banks began consumer cash lending. By this time they were fairly sure that consumer credit was a mature economic force, and more importantly, they could see the profitable experience of the pioneering sales finance and consumer loan institutions. The National City Bank of New York opened the first consumer loan department in 1928. Gradually the early stigma of consumer credit diminished, and cash lending to consumers became as accepted and commonplace as loans to businesses.

Cash credit, as offered by commercial banks, has changed considerably in recent years, and many credit plans have been developed. These present-day plans, while varied and ingenious, can best be classified into three forms of cash loan plans: conventional installment loans, other types of installment loans, and single-payment loans.

CONVENTIONAL INSTALLMENT LOANS. In addition to the personal installment loans made to consumers, commercial banks have aided consumers in their installment purchases in other ways. Consumer installment credit held by commercial banks covers purchases of cars and mobile homes, as well as home improvements. Commercial banks are also involved in transactions covered by bank credit cards. The Federal Reserve System considers bank credit card transactions as installment transactions. In this book, however, bank credit cards are considered primarily as a means of financing retail option-terms revolving credit transactions and service credit transactions.[1]

OTHER TYPES OF INSTALLMENT LOANS. As previously mentioned, the banking scene contains a wide variety of installment loan plans. These include cash advances on bank credit card plans, overdraft plans, home equity lines of credit, and student loan plans.

1. Cash Advances on Bank Credit Card Plans. A common addition to bank credit cards is the cash-advance feature. In some instances, banks have used this feature to consolidate processing of all their small personal loans through their bank credit card operations. The total dollar amount that can be loaned by this method to an individual consumer depends on the bank's policy and the customer's creditworthiness. Finance charges on cash advances usually are imposed from the date of the cash advance—that is, the consumer is not given the "free" period generally given in retail and service transactions. In addition, some banks have installed 24-hour teller services, enabling customers to use machines to obtain cash advances by using their bank credit card with a magnetic strip on the back.

2. Overdraft Plans. Overdraft plans, which are basically a form of installment credit, developed independently of bank credit cards. These plans have appeared in a variety of forms and names.

Some plans give customers a choice of two methods of drawing on the reserve: (1) customers simply write a check, or checks, for any amount up to the agreed maximum, regardless of their checking account balance; or (2) customers give prior notification to the bank to transfer funds from the

---

[1]See Chapter 3.

loan reserve to their checking account, when they anticipate using the reserve. In some plans, the bank provides a loan that is exactly the amount of the overdraft; in others, the bank credits the account with loans in increments of $50 or $100. The individual then repays the loan on a revolving basis, sometimes liquidating it by making ordinary deposits to a checking account or by making more formal, separate loan repayments to the bank.

In the so-called Redicheck® Overdraft Credit Line of one commercial bank, some of the more important provisions of the plan are as follows:

> A credit reserve that's available when you need it most—that's Redicheck. You use it exclusively through your First Florida Regular or NOW checking account, just by writing a check. Once you're approved, you'll have a line of credit for $300, $400, or more.
>
> Whenever you find that "special something" you need, but it costs more than your checkbook balance, the extra funds will be automatically credited to your Regular or NOW checking account in increments of $50. Then you simply repay the amount you've borrowed in easy monthly payments.[2]

In evaluating these plans, it is important to look at the potential benefits accruing to the customers as well as to the bank. Customers need to apply for credit only once. If their application is approved and if this credit is handled in the designated manner, they may continue to revolve within the line as long as they want. In addition, these plans are easy and convenient for customers to use; customers are not limited to "certain" merchants, as with bank credit card plans. Such a credit arrangement is often viewed as a prestige type of borrowing in that only customers who measure up to certain credit criteria can secure it. This service appeals to many customers as a way to meet recurring need for short-term financing of small purchases and vacation needs and as a contingency reserve.

There are some disadvantages, however. Customers not only face the temptation to stay in debt for longer periods, but they also must pay an interest charge for this privilege.

Some banks have combined their overdraft plans with their bank credit card plans.

3. Home Equity Lines of Credit. The home equity line of credit is among the leading innovations in consumer cash lending. Consumer interest in home equity credit line plans dates to 1986, when the Tax Reform Act mandated the gradual removal of federal income tax deductions for interest paid on nonmortgage consumer credit. As a result, consumers began using mortgage instruments to fund expenditures that typically have been

---

[2]Overdraft credit line agreement of the First Florida Bank, Clearwater, Florida, as of April 1990.

financed by consumer loans. In addition, borrowing against home equity carried a favorable interest rate compared with rates on many types of consumer credit, particularly credit cards and charge cards.

A home equity line is a form of revolving credit in which a consumer's home serves as collateral. The home usually is a consumer's largest asset, and most homeowners use their credit lines only for major expenditures, such as payment of other debts, home improvements, automobile purchases, education, and medical care. Home equity accounts are ongoing arrangements, often without a fixed maturity date, that allow the borrower flexibility in the size and timing of borrowing and subsequent repayments. Home equity accounts refer exclusively to these new lines of credit and not to the conventional types of first and second mortgages.[3]

Commercial banks, savings and loan institutions, savings banks, and credit unions are the primary sources of home equity lines of credit. These lenders usually set a credit limit on a home equity loan by taking a percentage (say, 75 percent) of the appraised home value and subtracting any balance owed on an existing mortgage or mortgages. For example:

Appraisal of home	$100,000
Percentage	× 75%
Percentage of appraised value	$75,000
Less mortgage debt	− $40,000
Potential credit line	$35,000

When determining a consumer's actual credit line, lenders also will consider the borrower's ability to repay by looking at the borrower's income, debts, other financial obligations, and credit history.

In its booklet, *When Your Home Is on the Line: What You Should Know about Home Equity Lines of Credit,* the Federal Reserve Board points out:

> Home equity plans often set a fixed time during which you can borrow money, such as 10 years. When this period is up, the plan may allow you to renew the credit line. But in a plan that does not allow renewals, you will not be able to borrow additional money once the time has expired. Some plans may call for payment in full of any outstanding balance. Others may permit you to repay over a fixed time, for example, 10 years.
>
> Once approved for the home equity plan, usually you will be able to borrow up to your limit whenever you want. Typically, you will be able to draw on your line by using special checks. Under some plans, borrowers can use a credit card or other means to borrow money and make purchases using the line. However, there may be limitations on how you use the line. Some plans may require you to borrow a minimum amount each time you draw on the line (for example, $300) and to keep a minimum

---

[3]See Chapter 5 for the details of home mortgage lending. Also see the Suggested Readings at the end of the chapter.

amount outstanding. Some lenders also may require that you take an initial advance when you first set up the line.

* * * * *

Home equity plans typically involve variable interest rates rather than fixed rates. A variable rate must be based on a publicly available index (such as the prime rate published in some daily newspapers or a U.S. Treasury bill rate); the interest rate will change, mirroring fluctuations in the index. To figure the interest rate you will pay, most lenders add a margin, such as 2 percentage points, to the index value. . . .

* * * * *

Variable rate plans secured by a dwelling must have a ceiling (or cap) on how high your interest rate may climb over the life of the plan. Some variable-rate plans limit how much your payment may increase, and also how low your interest rate may fall if interest rates drop.[4]

Two statutes, the Competitive Equality Banking Act of 1987 (CEBA) and the Home Equity Loan Consumer Protection Act of 1988 (HELCPA), added truth-in-lending requirements regarding credit linked to home equity (see Chapter 6 for details of these laws).

4. Student Loan Plans. The idea of student loan plans was commendable; the results were not. In 1957 the federal government began to channel billions of dollars into universities for college student tuition loans. It was deemed that the loans would be both an investment in the future of America and a good bet to be paid back by the well-educated graduates. Unfortunately, this has not occurred, partly because of the shift in cultural attitudes among students and partly because of economic conditions.

An interesting observation on student loans was made recently:

Postsecondary education is expensive, and experts tell us that the cost of a college education is not going to get any cheaper. Tuition has risen at almost twice the rate of inflation for the past 10 years, making a heavy burden of student loan debt a reality for most college graduates. Plus, jobs with high salaries upon graduation do not always materialize. Still, these graduating students (often before they graduate) are offered easy to get credit that invites them to acquire more debt than they can pay. Many students cannot say no, and are unable to afford their payments in the years ahead.[5]

Table 4–1 provides repayment estimates for various loan limits at an 8 percent interest rate.

---

[4]*When Your Home Is on the Line: What You Should Know about Home Equity Lines of Credit* (Washington, D.C.: Board of Governors of the Federal Reserve System, August 1989), pp. 3–4.

[5]Art Bilski, "Student Loans—What Do They Mean?" *The Credit World,* May–June 1990, p. 22. Used with permission.

TABLE 4–1 **Repayment Term Estimates—8% Interest Rate**

Amount Borrowed	Months in Payment	Monthly Payment	Amount Borrowed	Months in Payment	Monthly Payment
$1,000	22	$50.00	$10,500	120	$127.39
1,500	34	50.00	11,000	120	133.46
2,000	47	50.00	11,500	120	139.53
2,500	62	50.00	12,000	120	145.59
3,000	77	50.00	12,500	120	151.56
3,500	95	50.00	13,000	120	157.73
4,000	115	50.00	13,500	120	163.79
4,500	120	54.60	14,000	120	169.86
5,000	120	60.66	14,500	120	175.93
5,500	120	66.73	15,000	120	181.99
6,000	120	72.80	17,250	120	209.29
6,500	120	78.66	20,000	120	242.66
7,000	120	84.93	25,000	120	303.32
7,500	120	91.00	30,000	120	363.98
8,000	120	97.06	35,000	120	424.65
8,500	120	103.13	40,000	120	485.31
9,000	120	109.19	45,000	120	545.97
9,500	120	115.26	50,000	120	606.64
10,000	120	121.33	54,750	120	664.27

SINGLE-PAYMENT LOANS. Single payment loans are frequently made for 30, 60, or 90 days and for longer periods such as six months, nine months, or even a year. These loans may be made on either an unsecured or a secured basis, depending on the overall quality of credit risk relative to the amount of the loan. The collateral, if requested, for these loans is usually government bonds and other securities, cash value of life insurance policies, savings accounts, cars, and other personal property that can readily be converted to cash in the event of default.

INTEREST RATES. An interest rate quoted by commercial banks on single-payment loans approaches the actual rate. Whether or not the quoted percentage actually is the true rate depends on the method and time of collecting the interest. If the interest is discounted at the time the loan is made, the borrower has use of the principal *less* the interest; hence, the actual rate will be somewhat higher than it would be if interest and principal had been paid on the loan's maturity date. The so-called prime rate, which is the rate banks charge their commercial customers with the best credit rating, in actual operation is the base price from which negotiations start, but each loan is a separate negotiation.

The simple interest method is challenging the add-on (or discount) method for figuring interest on installment loans. The simple interest method is different from the add-on method in that it is figured on a daily interest rate—usually 1/365th of the annual finance charge—which is added to the daily outstanding balance of the cash loan. Under the add-on method of figuring interest, the amount of the finance charge is computed before the loan is made and is added to the loan amount. The customer then pays the loan proceeds, plus the interest, in a series of installment payments. The annual percentage rate (APR) for the add-on method is nearly twice the indicated rate because the customer only has average use of about half the loan proceeds. Small loan companies and credit unions have used the simple interest approach for years.

To explain even more clearly the daily simple interest method, the Federal Reserve Bank of Philadelphia provides the following:

> The advent of the computer age has enabled lenders to accrue interest on loans on a daily basis by the application of a daily periodic rate to the outstanding balance. This means that a borrower's paying habits will determine the amount of a final payment, whenever it is made. If a borrower habitually makes the periodic payments before the due date, the last payment will be lower. This occurs because the loan balance will reduce more rapidly and less interest will accrue on a daily basis.
>
> On the other hand, a borrower who makes scheduled payments habitually late will end up paying more. Depending upon state law, daily simple interest loans may or may not be subject to late charges for payments after a grace period in addition to the interest that may have continued to accrue.[6]

On January 30, 1981, an opinion letter issued by the Federal Deposit Insurance Corporation held that state-chartered, federally insured banks have "most favored lender" status and may charge interest rates up to the highest authorized by the states in which they are located for any type of lender. As an alternative, such banks may charge interest at 1 percent over the discount rate. If rates allowed under these alternatives would be lower than the rates specifically authorized by state law for state-chartered banks, they may charge the state-authorized rates. This letter followed the action taken by the Federal Home Loan Bank Board on January 1, 1981, allowing federally insured savings and loan associations to charge for consumer loans any interest rate allowed to any other lender located in the same state.

THE CHANGING CHARACTER OF COMMERCIAL BANKS AND THEIR CUSTOMERS.[7]

From the customer's viewpoint, today's commercial bank is a very different institution than it was two or three decades ago. Historically, commercial banks were established to serve the financial needs of businesses. Dealings with business usually involve fairly large sums of

---

[6]*Paying a Loan Off Early—Things You Should Know* (Philadelphia, Pa.: Federal Reserve Bank of Philadelphia, May 1989), p. 3.

[7]See the Suggested Readings at the end of the chapter.

money, and the risk element can be rather accurately appraised. Banks' services to the needs of commerce are still their main function; change and adjustment to current needs of business contributed to their growth and overall importance to our economy. Traditionally, banks have been conservative financial institutions and were so regarded by most consumers. The conservative nature of their management, the early stigma associated with consumer installment financing, the legal requirements, and, in general, their preoccupation with commercial needs all tended to slow the banks' entrance into the financing of consumer needs.

Most present-day banks set out to overcome such negative attitudes and now accept all kinds of consumer credit. In adopting the policy that consumer financing was sound and in aggressively seeking consumer credit customers, they have gradually become one of the dominant sources for consumer loans.

In expanding their present-day customer group, banks had to compete against other aggressive consumer loan institutions. They accomplished much of this expansion through sales promotion. Banks adjusted their hours to customers' convenience; provided friendly, convenient, comfortable, and attractive loan quarters; and used the most effective advertising media and techniques. Using the "full-service" banking concept, some banks adopted the so-called personal banker plan in which each customer is assigned a single bank officer who is responsible for the bulk of the customer's relationships with the bank. The specific objective of such a plan is to eliminate inconvenience, runaround, and loss of customer identity. In addition, some banks for a small monthly fee provide customers with an array of banking services that may include a free checking account, overdraft privileges on their checking account, free traveler's checks, a safe-deposit box, and reduced rates on installment loans. In addition, banks recognized the value of providing services for older customers who were in a financial position to want these services and to furnish a growing source of profit for the participating banks.

Banks became more competitive in the interest rates paid to their depositors. On November 1, 1978, the Federal Deposit Insurance Corporation and the Federal Reserve System authorized member commercial banks to automatically transfer funds from savings accounts to checking accounts, with the customer's approval. For banks, this is the equivalent of interest-paying checking accounts.

Banks and savings and loan institutions heavily advertise their NOW (negotiable order of withdrawal) accounts. At times, they encourage customers to switch from their conventional bank checking accounts to NOW accounts to avoid service charges and to earn an interest return on their deposits. The decision hinges on the cost of the customer's present plan, the number of checks he or she writes, and the amount of cash the customer can move into a NOW account. A number of the larger credit unions offering share draft programs (similar to interest-earning checking accounts) use a low minimum balance requirement and pay interest on the money invested.[8]

Bankers also face an increasing array of competition. People can hide their money in a mattress, where they earn no interest, or deposit it in a savings account where they can withdraw it at any time and it is insured by the federal government for up to $100,000. Thrift institutions, such as savings and loans, may pay a higher interest rate on these accounts than commercial banks can. Other savings choices include saving certificates, which are time deposits paying more interest than a savings account. The saver loses a substantial part of his or her interest, however, if the deposit is withdrawn early. Likewise, savers may choose money market certificates, which are government-insured time deposits carrying a large minimum deposit and a penalty for early withdrawal. Treasury bills, notes, and bonds are also available; maturities, yields, and minimum denominations vary. Another competitor is money market funds—portfolios of securities sold to investors as a mutual fund. Customers can usually write checks against their accounts, deposits are not insured, and interest rates fluctuate daily.

Commercial banks are in a competitive market (see Table 4–2) for the consumer dollar invested in individual retirement accounts (IRAs). These plans were authorized in 1974, were modified in 1982, and were greatly changed by the Tax Reform Act of 1986. Increased attention to self-directed (individuals determine where the funds are to be invested) IRAs has added to the competitive woes of commercial banks. Currently, a consumer may contribute each year up to $2,000 or 100 percent of earned income, whichever is less. If both spouses work, a total of $4,000 per couple may be contributed. IRA contributions are federal income tax deductible if:

- Neither spouse is an active participant in an employer's retirement plan.
- The investor's adjusted gross income (AGI) for the year does not exceed specific dollar limits set by the federal government.

To determine how much of an IRA contribution is deductible if either spouse is covered by an employer retirement plan, refer to Table 4–3.

Beginning December 14, 1982, banks and other financial institutions began offering newly authorized high-interest, federally insured (hifi) money market deposit accounts in an aggressive attempt to raid the billions of dollars Americans hold in money market mutual funds. Effective January 5, 1983, financial institutions were able to offer more competition through so-called Super NOW accounts, which combine deregulated interest with unlimited checking and other transactions.

---

[8]See a subsequent section of this chapter for a discussion of credit unions and share draft programs.

TABLE 4–2 **Individual Retirement Account Assets** ($ billions)

	Year-end 1987		Year-end 1988	
Financial Intermediary	Amount	Percentage	Amount	Percentage
Thrift institutions	$ 77.1	23.1%	$ 90.0	22.9%
Commercial banks	77.0	23.1	88.0	22.4
Mutual funds	72.2	21.6	86.0	21.9
Brokerage industry (self-directed)	58.9	17.6	68.0	17.3
Life insurance companies	26.0	7.8	36.0	9.2
Credit unions	22.6	6.8	25.0	6.4
Total IRA assets	$333.8	100.0%	$393.0	100.0%

Note: Components may not add to totals due to rounding.

Source: *1989 Savings Institutions Sourcebook* (Chicago: United States League of Savings Institutions, 1989), p. 22.

TABLE 4–3 **Tax Filing Status**

		Adjusted gross income is	
		Single	Married/ Joint Return
Get tax-deferred benefits and full deductions	if	less than $25,000	less than $40,000
Get tax-deferred benefits and a partial deduction	if	$25,000 to $35,000	$40,000 to $50,000
Get tax-deferred benefits only	if	over $35,000	over $50,000

Today's consumers are more aware of what commercial banks can and will do for worthy cash loan customers. Bankers have found that this type of credit can be extended safely to large numbers of consumers and offers advantages and growth possibilities to commercial banks.

FDIC PROTECTION. One of the strongest promotional features of commercial banks is the Federal Deposit Insurance Corporation (FDIC)[9] deposit protection. Deposit guarantee legislation, beginning with the 1933 establishment of the FDIC, was enacted to prevent bank system failures like those of the Great Depression of the 1930s. This remained virtually unchanged until enactment of the Depository Institutions Deregulation and Monetary Control Act in 1980. This act covers a variety of credit activities, one of the most important being increased coverage for all federal deposit insurance from $40,000 to $100,000.

---

[9]See Suggested Readings at the end of the chapter.

BANK HOLDING COMPANIES. A number of observers in many circles are questioning the future course of commercial banking. Closely connected to the future of commercial banking operations is the bank holding company movement, which is of increasing interest to both economic and political sectors. Bank holding companies have made substantial inroads into a number of bank-related activities. Formation of a bank holding company is used to overcome many restrictions on banking activities and expand services to the public. The Bank Holding Company Amendments of 1970 ended the exemption of one-bank holding companies from federal control and also liberalized the activities in which bank holding companies were permitted to participate.

The bank holding company form of organization has a number of advantages for banking firms. It also is being recommended for enforcing corporate separation of traditional banking from expanded banking activities.[10]

AUTOMATED TELLER MACHINES (ATMs).[11] In the early 1970s automated teller machines began to grow in popularity. These machines enable consumers to perform various banking transactions such as deposits, cash withdrawals, inquiries as to account balances, and interaccount transfers without the aid of a human teller. Certain states have mandatory sharing laws that require institutions that own ATMs to share their off-premises machines for a "reasonable fee" with any other financial institution in the state. The use of these machines has not lived up to expectations, however, as many customers—even active ATM users—still prefer the human teller.

AVAILABILITY OF FUNDS. A 1988 law limits how long financial institutions may delay a customer's ability to use deposited funds. The Expedited Funds Availability Act specifies that commercial banks must let a consumer use funds deposited in checking and NOW accounts within a stated number of days. Banks also must tell the consumer in writing how soon deposits may be used (see Chapter 6 for details of the law).

Credit Unions

The credit union industry has changed dramatically. Many credit unions have obtained community charters, adopted practically every service and loan type offered by commercial banks, and built outstanding full-service facilities. The community charters generally specify geographical bonds among members, so anyone living or working in a certain area may join

---

[10]Randall Johnston Pozdena, "Banks Affiliated with Bank Holding Companies: A New Look at Their Performance," Federal Reserve Bank of San Francisco *Economic Review,* Fall 1988, p. 29. Also see J. Nellie Liang and Donald T. Savage, "The Nonbank Activities of Bank Holding Companies," *Federal Reserve Bulletin,* May 1990, p. 280.

[11]See Suggested Readings at the end of the chapter.

the credit union. This approach has broadened the potential membership group and resulted in credit unions being strong competition for other lenders.

A credit union is an association of people who decide to save their money together and make loans to each other at relatively low interest rates.[12] In other words, it is a cooperative financial institution. A credit union is organized by people who share a common bond—for example, employees working for the same employer, members of a fraternal order or labor union, or residents of the same community. Some credit unions serve multiple groups, but each group has its own common bond. In addition, participating in the ownership and control of the credit unions creates another common bond among members. As of year-end 1989, 15,086 credit unions operated in the United States and its territories, with approximately 60.4 million members, more than $134.9 billion in loans outstanding in the United States, and over $203 billion in assets.

ORIGIN OF CREDIT UNIONS.   Credit unions began in Germany in 1849. A mayor of a small town reasoned that the town citizens could save money together and make loans to each other at low interest rates. The idea spread rapidly, and by 1888 more than 425 credit unions had been formed. In 1900 Alphonse Desjardins founded the first credit union in North America in Lévis, Quebec.

Credit unions came to the United States in 1909, due largely to the efforts of Edward A. Filene, a well-known Boston merchant. In 1921 Fllene hired Roy F. Bergengren to direct the Credit Union National Extension Bureau and oversee the rapidly growing credit union movement. In 1934 the Credit Union National Association was formed to serve the needs of the thousands of established credit unions.

STRUCTURE AND ORGANIZATION OF THE U.S. CREDIT UNION MOVEMENT.   More than 90 percent of U.S. credit unions are affiliated through an extensive system of state and national credit union service organizations. This means that credit unions, too, work together for the benefit of credit union members. Members of affiliated credit unions govern this service organization structure through their democratically elected representatives. Credit unions in a community or specific geographic area may join or form a chapter. Chapters sponsor educational programs and undertake joint promotion and public relations projects.

Leagues are voluntary associations of credit unions within a given state or geographic area. Leagues are governed by their member credit unions and offer management advice and bookkeeping assistance, legal

---

[12]See Suggested Readings at the end of the chapter.

counsel, legislative and regulatory support, training programs, public relations, insurance counseling, and other essential services.

The Credit Union National Association, Inc. (CUNA), is the national credit union confederation of U.S. leagues. It provides legislative, public relations, research, educational, and development support for the national credit union movement. By joining a league, credit unions become affiliated with CUNA and have access to the services provided by its affiliates, including data processing and investment, interlending, and liquidity management programs, as well as marketing assistance and printing and supply materials.

The CUNA Mutual Insurance Society, the credit union insurance company, serves credit unions and their members with an insurance program wholly oriented to the purposes and objectives of the credit union movement. As a mutual company, it returns all income, after operating expenses and reserves, to policyholders in the form of dividends.

The CUMIS Insurance Society, Inc., a stock insurance company, is the property, casualty, and fidelity insurance arm of the credit union movement. Ownership of the company is vested in credit union members, credit unions, chapters, credit union leagues, and CUNA Mutual. In addition to providing the nonlife insurance needs of credit unions and their organizations, CUMIS offers them homeowner and tenant insurance plans and life, health, and car insurance.

CHARACTERISTICS OF CREDIT UNIONS. Credit unions may be chartered under either state laws or the Federal Credit Union Act of 1934 and its subsequent amendments. The organizing group should consist of at least 300 persons. The common bond of membership may be employment, church affiliation, residence, labor union membership, and the like.

Credit unions adhere to the basic principles commonly associated with other cooperative ventures. The savings and loan facilities are their main function, and they operate only for the benefit and use of their members. Credit unions acquire capital from membership savings, which are invested in credit union shares. Besides shares, credit union capital consists of reserves and undivided earnings. The movement recognized capital's growing importance to credit unions, and in December 1980 a National Credit Union System Capitalization Commission was established. Among its recommendations for increasing the capital position of credit unions, the commission suggested that credit unions create a membership share account that would have all the equity features of the present share account but none of the liability features. The commission also suggested use of annual or one-time membership fees, as well as raising the par value of shares as ways to raise the capital level of credit unions. Additional capital may be borrowed from commercial sources, but such borrowing is subject to legal limitations usually related to the credit union's unimpaired assets. Shares usually accumulate in $5 units, and amounts deposited that are less than this are applied to the purchase of a share. The credit union's capital is available for loans to shareholding members. Each member, irrespective of the amount of holdings in the credit union, is entitled to one vote in the election of its board of directors and its committee members who manage the organization. Additional dividends may be declared on members' shares after expenses are paid and legal reserves set aside.

State laws regulating the operation of credit unions vary substantially, but the more common requirements and general provisions of the federal law indicate their characteristics. Both federal and state laws emphasize protection of the members against imprudent management, while still providing the members with a ready source of cash credit at relatively low interest rates. The credit union's accounting records are examined regularly by government authorities. Surety bond requirements give the members further protection. The treasurer and each officer who handles money must be bonded. The National Credit Union Administration supervises credit unions operating under federal charter, and in most states the state banking commission supervises those under state charter. The Federal Share Insurance Act, enacted in the fall of 1970, requires federal credit unions and permits state-chartered credit unions to provide share insurance on members' savings comparable to the FDIC program offered by banks and savings and loan associations. A number of share and deposit insurance plans also provide coverage to savers in state-chartered credit unions. As of year-end 1989, more than 99 percent of all member savings in credit unions were insured.

CHARACTER OF LOANS.   A credit union member is one who owns one or more credit union shares, which earn dividends; a shareholder is eligible for the credit union's lending services. The credit committee, which is elected by the members, meets as often as necessary to approve or reject loan applications. Authority to approve loans within specified limits may also be delegated to staff loan officers. Installment loans are normally granted and repaid in equal installments according to a schedule established by the organization. Small amounts may be repaid in 6 months, in 12 months, or over longer periods, depending on the amount borrowed and requirements of the borrower. Car loans typically are made for a maximum of 48 months. The borrower may repay the entire remaining balance of a loan at any time without penalty and thus save interest. Most credit unions offer loan protection insurance, primarily through CUNA Mutual Insurance Society. The credit union generally pays the premium for this insurance out of earnings, at no additional charge to the borrower. If the insured borrower dies or is disabled before the loan obligation is fully met, the insurance pays off the loan balance.

Individuals borrow money from credit unions for essentially the same reasons they borrow money from other sources: for cars, home repairs, debt consolidation, taxes, medical expenses, vacations, and education, and to take advantage of various financial opportunities.

GROWTH AND INCREASING IMPORTANCE OF CREDIT UNIONS. Since 1921 credit unions in the United States and Canada have grown rapidly. Except during the war years of 1943–45, credit unions have increased in members and assets practically every year. At the same time, services have increased gradually.

Much of the growth and present-day success of credit unions is due to their relatively low rate of interest, which is made possible by the low cost of operation. Credit unions, at times, enjoy the privilege of free office space provided by the sponsor; they are exempt from some taxes because of their cooperative nature; and frequently they receive the services of management (except for the treasurer) free because elected officers serve voluntarily without pay. The larger credit unions, which are growing in number, maintain scheduled and longer hours of operation and are staffed with paid employees. Members regard the saving feature of credit unions as advantageous, because dividends paid to shareholders have at times been higher than interest on similar savings in commercial banks and savings and loan associations. Share drafts have become popular among credit union members; 15 million members of 6,000 credit unions wrote more than 3.5 billion share drafts in 1989. A share draft is a unique type of financial instrument (see Figure 4–1). Some of its characteristics are as follows:

1. The share draft is payable by the credit union out of the member's share draft account.
2. The share draft is payable through a bank or some other clearing facility. This is the same type of payable-through system used for drafts on nonbank institutions such as insurance companies. Recently, some large credit unions have begun clearing their own share drafts.
3. The request for payment of the draft is transferred electronically from the payable-through bank to the credit union—the draft itself is not transferred.
4. Members are given statements that list share drafts in numerical order by share draft number.
5. The member has a carbon copy of each share draft for recordkeeping.
6. A microfilm copy of each original draft is available on request to the member who wrote the draft, but no copy is returned to the member by the credit union.
7. Dividends on share draft accounts are typically paid monthly on the low balance for the month, but some credit unions pay interest on the average daily balance. Seventy-five percent of credit

FIGURE 4–1 **Example of a Share Draft**

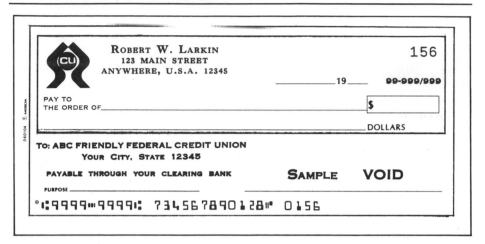

unions offering share drafts levy no routine charges on these accounts.

Despite the apparent advantages enjoyed by credit unions, there are some limitations on most ventures of a cooperative nature. At times, it is difficult to recruit spokespersons and workers for organizations of this type because they are not paid for their time and effort. Another limitation on credit union growth is the number of people with a common bond needed before a credit union can be organized. Groups of this size are not easy to organize in many professional, trade, and clerical fields. In 1982, however, the National Credit Union Administration amended its chartering policies to allow existing federal credit unions to take in small employee and associational groups as members. This has significantly extended credit union service to groups previously too small to have their own credit union.

An increasing number of credit unions offer a variety of consumer credit and savings plans. They also participate in the new electronic payments systems and give their customers the convenience of automated teller facilities and bill-paying plans at their credit union locations.

Consumer Finance Companies

Consumer finance companies (often referred to as small loan companies, personal finance companies, and licensed lenders) make loans to consumers under state-enacted regulations. The characteristics of their loans, their customers, their methods of operation, and the state statutes under which they do business are the principal distinguishing features of these institutions. Consumer finance companies are almost exclusively installment loan institutions, and the average amount of their loans is considerably less than commercial bank loans.

A consumer finance business conducted under the Uniform Small Loan laws may be an individual proprietorship, a partnership, or a corporation. The incorporated company was at first rare, but with the enactment of the Uniform Small Loan Law in most states, the corporate enterprise has become the dominant form of organization.[13] Typically, large corporations operate on a national scale, with licensed offices in hundreds of cities of all sizes. Smaller companies usually operate regionally, while the smallest firms with one or a few offices operate locally.

Consumer finance companies' rapid growth and present-day position in the lending industry are a direct result of the small loan laws enacted by most states. Before the enactment of such laws, this business was characterized by deceptive interest charges and abusive collection practices. In 1907 and 1908 the Russell Sage Foundation, a philanthrophic organization, financed studies that dealt with existing small loan conditions and the demand for loans of this type. These studies disclosed a large demand for small loans by wage earners and other consumers of small means, the need for legitimate lending agencies to supply the demand, and the necessity of subjecting the business to state supervision. In 1916 the foundation, in cooperation with a group of moneylenders, drafted a model small loan law known as the Uniform Small Loan Law. Improved drafts of the model law have been made from time to time by the foundation and by the National Consumer Finance Association.

The first Uniform Small Loan laws tended to reduce the number of lenders subjected to regulation, because some lenders found it unprofitable to operate at the interest rates permitted by law. Before long, however, lenders who formerly shunned this business were attracted to the small loan field, and large numbers of new companies were organized to transact small loans under regulation. The small loan industry encourages state regulation as the basis for attracting ethical personnel and sufficient capital to meet the demand for small loans. The industry's support of the model Uniform Small Loan Law testifies to its opposition to illegal lenders who prey on wage earners and charge usurious interest rates in states without effective legislation. Today the National Consumer Finance Association promotes effective state legislation.

PROVISIONS OF AN EFFECTIVE SMALL LOAN LAW. An effective small loan law must provide for an interest charge that is sufficient to attract capital to the business and at the same time protect borrowers from abusive practices. Most states have enacted laws that meet this

---

[13]In 1911 Massachusetts enacted small loan regulatory laws based on the early recommendations of the Russell Sage Foundation. New Jersey followed with legislation in 1914; New York, Ohio, and Pennsylvania, in 1915.

requisite. Many states have modified the model Uniform Small Loan Law to suit local conditions or particular interests.

Interest charges for cash loans generally vary from 36 percent annually on the smallest to 18 percent on larger, well-secured loans. The Russell Sage Foundation originally recommended a maximum loan size of $300. The need for larger loans readily became apparent, and in some states today the loan ceiling is $25,000.

The lender must be licensed, and each office operated by a chain company must be licensed by the state in which the business is conducted. Each office is subject to annual and special examinations, must be bonded, and usually must submit to a test of ethical and financial fitness.

Under the provisions of the Truth in Lending Act (see Chapter 6), the lender has to disclose the amount financed, the finance charge, the annual percentage rate, the prepayment procedure and total of payments, delinquency or early payment charges, the rebate calculation procedure, and whether a security interest is taken in connection with the extension of credit. The lender may collect no fees other than recording fees. The licensee must accept payment from the customer in advance of the due date, and interest charged can be only for the time the borrower has had use of the money. Civil and criminal penalties are provided for violation of the provisions of the act.

While the above are the principal provisions of the Uniform Small Loan Law (in association with the Truth in Lending Act), there are many other important specific requirements. States that have enacted small loan legislation have varied from these provisions, but essentially with the same fundamental objectives. Some states prohibit any other business to be operated in conjunction with a small loan office; others permit insurance writing to minimize the degree of risk; and still others stipulate somewhat different methods of interest computation.

THE CONSUMER FINANCE CUSTOMER.   Borrowers from consumer finance companies generally come from different occupational groups than do borrowers from commercial banks. Most finance company loans are made to two occupational groups: craftsmen, foremen, and kindred workers; and operatives, laborers, and kindred workers. They borrow funds for the same reasons that other occupational groups borrow, such as consolidation of overdue bills; refinancing existing obligations; payment of medical, dental, and hospital bills; and other financial emergencies.

The services of consumer finance companies frequently differ from those of commercial banks. Finance companies are usually located for the customer's convenience. Their offices accept loan applications, investigate applicants, accept payments by mail and on the premises, and handle delinquencies and other necessary matters.

Individual customers of these companies borrow, on the average, smaller sums than bank customers do. Historically, customers of the small loan business are wage earners and others of limited means, and it is this group that the business has so successfully attracted and served. Generally, the customers' income and occupation are less stable than those of the commercial banks' customers. Although customer groups of consumer finance companies and commercial banks borrow for similar reasons, the amount borrowed generally is in line with the borrower's income and other factors.

CHANGING CONSUMER ATTITUDES.   General acceptance of the small loan business accompanied the widespread change of consumer attitudes and the acceptance of consumer credit of all types during the first half of the 20th century. Most consumers, at some time, experience a temporary need for a small loan when obligations exceed income and savings. This need would exist whether or not the Uniform Small Loan laws existed.

An individual who borrows $100 from a consumer finance company at a monthly rate of 3 percent and repays the loan in 12 equal monthly installments will pay a total interest cost of $20.60, or 36 percent true rate of interest. This amount appears high unless the cost of lending small amounts is clearly understood. The cost of capital for these businesses is higher than it is for commercial banks. The alternative to the Uniform Small Loan Law, which has attracted capital and ethical businesses to this field, is the loan shark and illegal lender. From the standpoint of social necessity, it is better for consumers to have convenient and fair access to small loans rather than be subjected to the lending and collection methods of illegal lenders. Also, the small loan company is the only available cash credit source for many families, whereas typical commercial bank customers can easily qualify for and borrow funds from several sources. Consequently, if a state wishes to make small consumer loans available to its wage earners and lower-income borrowers, it must sanction interest charges that will cover the high expenses this kind of business incurs. If it wants this business to be conducted ethically, it must provide for effective regulation and supervision.

The phenomenal growth in both the number of lenders and the number of consumer borrowers is some indication of the American consumer's widespread acceptance of the small loan business. Today consumer finance companies range from a single-office company to vast chains that operate hundreds of offices throughout the country. However, finance companies now face increased competition among themselves and with commercial banks and credit unions.

Industrial Banks and Loan Companies

Industrial banks are one of the most complex types of consumer lending institutions because of the varied nature of their services. They are governed by nonuniform state laws. In some states, they are similar to commercial banks in many respects. In others, their services are restricted by law, and they operate like small loan companies or the consumer loan departments of commercial banks. The operation of industrial banks is permitted by law in some states. In these states the firm may use the word *bank* in its advertising, contracts, and general literature. The laws of these states authorize such banks to accept deposits and make loans, and the banks may become members of the Federal Deposit Insurance Corporation. Some states do not authorize industrial banks as such, but do permit the operation of industrial *loan* companies. In these states such firms are commonly known as industrial loan companies or industrial credit corporations, and the use of the term *bank* is prohibited. The remaining states have no specific legislation covering these institutions. If they want to conduct business in one of these states, they must be awarded a charter under the laws applicable to commercial banks or secure a license and comply with the state small loan law and operate accordingly.

Except in states that authorize industrial banks to accept deposits, "investment certificates" or "shares of stock" are used to circumvent usury laws. These institutions devised this method because state banking laws, as originally conceived, did not cover interest paid on loans that were repaid in installments. A borrower from an industrial bank must subscribe to an equal amount of noninterest-bearing investment certificates to be "purchased" through a schedule of deposits. When the amount of the deposits equals the value of the investment certificates, the certificates revert to the industrial bank and the loan is thereby paid off. Today industrial banks operate under one of the several methods suggested, depending on the legislative restrictions of the particular state. Some accept deposits from borrowers and nonborrowers and make loans for both consumer and commercial purposes. Others use the investment certificate device to avoid being accused of usurious interest rates. In some states industrial loan companies neither accept deposits nor use investment certificates, but they lend money to consumers or businesses in a manner similar to other consumer lending institutions. Whatever the particular method of operation, all industrial banks and industrial loan companies originated with Arthur J. Morris during the early 1900s. His company has evolved into the largest group of industrial banks, now known as the Morris Plan Banks or Companies.

Savings and Loan Associations

The issue of savings and loan associations as competitors of commercial banks resurfaced in the 1980s when Congress granted all thrifts, including savings and loans, the power to make consumer and commercial loans and to issue transaction accounts. Congress passed the Depository Institutions Deregulation and Monetary Control Act (DIDMCA) in 1980 (see Chapter 6) to help the thrift industry retain its deposit base and to improve its profitability. This 1980 law allowed thrifts to make consumer loans up to 20 percent of their assets, issue credit cards, accept negotiable order of withdrawal (NOW) accounts from individuals and nonprofit

TABLE 4-4 **New Powers Granted to Federally Chartered Thrifts**

New Powers	DIDMCA (effective March 31, 1980)	Garn-St Germain (effective October 15, 1982)
Consumer loans	Consumer loans up to 20 percent of total assets Educational loans up to 5 percent of total assets Issue credit cards	Consumer loans up to 30 percent of total assets
Commercial loans	Commercial real estate up to 20 percent of total assets Unsecured construction loans up to 5 percent of total assets	Commercial real estate loans up to 40 percent of total assets Other commercial loans up to 5 percent of total assets before January 1, 1984 (7.5 percent of total assets for savings banks), and up to 10 percent of total assets thereafter Equipment leasing up to 10 percent of total assets
Transaction accounts	NOW accounts from individuals and nonprofit organizations	NOW accounts from government units Demand deposits from persons or organizations that have established "a business, corporate, commercial or agricultural loan relationship" with the institution

organizations, and invest up to 20 percent of their assets in commercial real estate loans.

Further deregulation took place in 1982 with passage of the Garn-St Germain Depository Institutions Act (see Chapter 6). As shown in Table 4-4, this law increased the proportion of assets that thrifts could hold in consumer and commercial real estate loans and allowed thrifts to invest 5 percent of their assets in commercial loans (7.5 percent for savings banks) until January 1, 1984, when this percentage increased to 10 percent.

This deregulation has created tremendous problems for the savings and loan industry. Chapters 5 and 6 look at the causes of savings and loan failures in the 1980s and at the resultant federal government actions.

Other Types of Lenders

No estimate has been made of the volume of loans made by friends and relatives, philanthropic organizations, church societies, and fraternal orders, but the amount is believed to be sizable. Some people have the distinct advantage of borrowing from friends and relatives, thereby enjoying less formal contractual arrangements and, on most occasions, strict secrecy. The interest charge and enforcement of payment depend almost entirely on the relationship and mutual trust between the individuals.

Philanthropic organizations, church societies, educational institutions, and fraternal orders make loans to individuals under special circumstances. These institutions function to provide temporary financial assistance to deserving people. Some loans may take the form of an outright gift, while others are made with the understanding that complete repayment will be made at some future date. Variations exist from institution to institution.

The pawnbroker[14] is another source of cash loans to individuals. Interest rates may run as high as 36 percent, but no inquiry is made into an individual's credit standing. Insurance companies are still another source; individuals can often borrow on their life insurance polices, paying an interest rate of approximately 5 to 8 percent. Some investment houses lend up to 70 percent of the market value on some blue-chip stocks.

In defiance of state laws, some illegal lenders charge interest rates as high as 700 percent. Typically, illegal lenders are more interested in earning exorbitant charges than in actually collecting the principal. They prefer victims who will obligate themselves deeply and be submissive to the lenders' collection methods. Collections are enforced by threat of wage assignments, loss of employment, and even physical violence. The debtor is frequently of limited means and "buys off" the threats, at least temporarily, by paying interest charges, but the debtor seldom has enough to meet the full principal and exorbitant interest charges.

RELATIVE COSTS OF CONSUMER LENDING INSTITUTIONS

To fully appreciate the interest rates charged by various consumer lending institutions, we must examine their costs of operation. Interest rates, or the "price of money," are usually relative to the costs of doing business and the degree of risk the lender assumes. The costs of conducting consumer loan activity may be quite high or relatively low, depending largely on the number and extent of the functions performed. Furthermore, relative costs of capital have an important influence on the interest rate. The factors that influence the costs of conducting a cash loan business are discussed in the following paragraphs. These brief discussions cover only legal lenders

Types of Risk Accepted

The average loan made to wage and salary earners by consumer finance companies is small. When the amount of the loan is modest, the dollar cost

---

[14]John P. Caskey and Brian J. Zikmund, "Pawnshops: The Consumer's Lender of Last Resort," Federal Reserve Bank of Kansas City *Economic Review,* March/April 1990, p. 5.

per loan of acquiring and servicing customers is relatively high. Because consumer finance companies usually deal with borrowers of limited means, the greater risk they incur influences their ability to attract capital, bad-debt ratios, and costs of investigation. Commercial banks, in particular, and credit unions accept credit from more stable customer groups and therefore incur less risk. Some occupations have greater income stability than others. The occupational groups attracted by banks and credit unions are qualitatively more acceptable from the credit risk standpoint. This factor alone contributes heavily to the higher cost of credit from consumer finance companies.

Investigation

The cost of investigation incurred by commercial banks and credit unions is generally less than the cost incurred by consumer finance companies. The types of risk accepted by the latter mean that those who are dishonest and those who can't or won't pay must be screened out by investigation. The borrower's identity, stability, and general reputation must be verified. Also, income, expenses, and outstanding obligations must be established. On the other hand, commercial banks and credit unions frequently appraise former applicants. Each of these institutions accepts deposits, and in many instances someone in the organization knows the loan applicant. Furthermore, each institution realizes that the apparent risk governs the extent and intensity of investigation. Consequently, consumer finance companies conduct rather extensive and costly investigations because of the higher risk element associated with their customers.

Capital

The cost of capital for commercial banks, credit unions, and some industrial banks is less than that for consumer finance companies. The three former institutions accept deposits, and their deposits are several times as large as their own capital. They have been able to attract capital more successfully because of the lower risk of their lending operations. Consumer finance companies, on the other hand, cannot accept deposits and must borrow from commercial banking facilities or other financial institutions or supply their own funds. They thus pay higher rates for their capital irrespective of the source. For these same reasons, consumer finance companies need somewhat higher net profit to attract investors.

Bad-Debt Losses

The greater degree of risk incurred by consumer finance companies is reflected in higher bad-debt losses. Another factor that contributes to a high bad-debt loss ratio is the low average loan size. Even though a consumer finance company has a well-managed collection system, the cost of collecting nominal sums that are about to become bad-debt losses is usually prohibitive. Furthermore, numerous legal actions against wage earners and others of small means might threaten the social acceptance and goodwill the small loan industry has built. The threat of legal action by a commercial bank or credit union to collect larger average sums usually results in a settlement because the customers they deal with prefer to avoid embarrassment. Interest rates to be charged must take into account the relative amount and frequency of bad-debt losses.

Collection Costs

The collection costs on an installment account are much higher than those of a single-payment loan. Commercial banks have a large volume of single-payment loans, while consumer finance companies primarily make installment loans. In addition, other installment lenders are not subject to the same expenses as consumer finance companies. In an effort to protect borrowers from abuse, the Uniform Small Loan laws of the various states impose costly procedures on this type of business. Consumer finance companies must account for each installment loan in detail, make many individual calculations, and give the borrower detailed informative receipts. The consumer finance company also has accounts that require special handling. Again, the modest amount of its loans makes for higher collection costs. Delinquencies must be remedied by constant reminders, personal letters, and even personal contact with the debtor.

Sources of Income

Commercial banks have many sources of income. They receive income from operation of their lending and trust departments, from their bank credit card operations, from the purchase and sale of federal government and municipal securities, from safe-deposit boxes, from the sale of traveler's checks, and from the operations of the companies that are part of bank holding arrangements. On the other hand, consumer finance companies' income is derived almost exclusively from interest on consumer loans.

Services

Consumer finance companies, by the nature of their business, establish offices for their customers' convenience. These offices are not generally housed within another institution, as are consumer credit departments of commercial banks and credit unions. The services rendered frequently involve more time and relatively more personnel. Most consumer finance companies have gone to considerable expense to establish debt amortization programs for their customers. Each borrower who needs this service presents different problems.

Many, if not most, commercial banks have expanded their customer services. They now advise and counsel their customers on money matters and arrange for debt amortization on a level competitive with that of other types of cash-lending institutions. Commercial banks' introduction of the many new installment loan plans illustrates that they see the necessity of being more customer conscious.

This chapter attempted to clarify much of the widespread misunderstanding associated with particular types of lending institutions. Interest charges are simply a pricing matter, similar to the pricing problem confronted by merchandisers of goods and services. Interest rates, like prices, must be sufficient to cover the total costs of operation and provide a net profit high enough to attract sufficient capital. As the cash-lending industry continues to grow and aggressive competition continues to exist among legal lenders, greater efficiency, and hence lower-cost methods of operation, will contribute to the future health of the industry.

DISCUSSION QUESTIONS

1. How does cash loan credit differ from retail credit? From service credit?
2. Discuss the statement "Consumers have borrowed money throughout history."
3. Why do some consumers borrow money to purchase goods and services when they could use other types of credit to make these purchases?
4. Why do some consumers borrow money to purchase goods and services when they have enough savings to make the purchases?
5. Distinguish carefully between the different sources of cash loans to consumers.
6. Why did commercial banks enter the consumer cash loan field so late?
7. Explain the differences among single-payment loans, conventional installment loans, and the newer types of installment loans commercial banks are making.
8. Survey the commercial banks in your community to discover which types of consumer loan plans are in operation.
9. Check the laws in your state to discover the interest rates allowed on cash loans to consumers.
10. How do you account for the fact that the commercial bank of today is a very different institution than it was one or two decades ago?
11. What are the potential benefits of overdraft plans to the individual customer? To the bank?
12. Explain the cash-advance feature on bank credit card plans.
13. Explain why a cash-advance feature on a bank credit card plan might be beneficial to you.
14. Trace the development of the credit union movement in the United States.

15. Explain the structure and organization of the U.S. credit union movement.

16. How do you account for the growth and increasing importance of credit unions?

17. Explain why a share draft is a unique type of financial instrument.

18. Visit a credit union in your community and discuss the share draft plan with its officials.

19. What provisions should a small loan law have in order to be effective?

20. How do you account for consumers' changing attitude toward consumer finance companies?

21. How does an industrial bank differ from a commercial bank? From a credit union? From a small loan company?

22. Discuss the reasons advanced to justify the varying interest rates charged by various consumer lending institutions.

23. Discuss the growing importance of home equity loans.

24. What are the advantages of a home equity loan? The disadvantages?

25. What is the daily simple interest method?

26. Are you eligible to join an IRA plan? Why or why not?

27. If a bank is not covered by FDIC insurance, would you make a deposit there? Why or why not?

28. What is meant by a bank holding company?

29. Do you use an ATM? Why or why not?

30. If you deposit a check in your commercial bank, how soon can you draw on it?

SUGGESTED READINGS

Home Equity Line of Credit

"A Mortgage That Pays You." *Changing Times,* July 1987, p. 67.

"An Important Study: Who Are Home Equity Borrowers?" *Credit,* March–April 1989, p. 10.

BAREFOOT, JO ANN S. "It's Time for Home (Equity Loan) Improvements." *ABA Banking Journal,* July 1989, p. 25.

CAMPBELL, GEOFFREY A. "Home Equity—the Darling of Lenders and Consumers." *Credit,* May–June 1987, p. 12.

CANNER, GLENN B., and CHARLES A. LUCKETT. "Home Equity Lending." *Federal Reserve Bulletin,* May 1989, p. 333.

CANNER, GLENN B.; JAMES T. FERGUS; and CHARLES A. LUCKETT. "Home Equity Lines of Credit." *Federal Reserve Bulletin,* June 1988, p. 363.

FRITZ, MICHAEL. "Fine-Tuning the Reverse Mortgage." *Forbes,* May 2, 1988, p. 116.

MCKEW, ROBERT. "Consumer Protection and Home Equity Lines of Credit: How an Idea Becomes a Law." *Credit Magazine,* November–December 1989, p. 16.

SMITH, FRANCES B. "Home Equity Lines of Credit." *Credit,* May–June 1987, p. 16.

FDIC Insurance

KAREKEN, JOHN H. "Deposit Insurance Reform; or, Deregulation Is the Cart, Not the Horse." Federal Reserve Bank of Minneapolis *Quarterly Review,* Winter 1990, p. 3.

KUPRIANOV, ANATOLI, and DAVID L. MENGLE. "The Future of Deposit Insurance: An Analysis of the Alternatives." Federal Reserve Bank of Richmond *Economic Review,* May–June 1989, p. 3.

TALLMAN, ELLIS. "Some Unanswered Questions about Bank Panics." Federal Reserve Bank of Atlanta *Economic Review,* November–December 1988, p. 2.

WALL, LARRY D. "A Plan for Reducing Future Deposit Insurance Losses: Puttable Subordinated Debt." Federal Reserve Bank of Atlanta *Economic Review,* July–August 1989, p. 2.

Automated Teller Machines

LADERMAN, ELIZABETH S. "The Public Policy Implications of State Laws Pertaining to Automated Teller Machines." Federal Reserve Bank of San Francisco *Economic Review,* Winter 1990, p. 43.

"What Role for ATMs?" *ABA Banking Journal,* November 1988, p. 45.

Credit Unions

"Credit Unions Fail, Too, Report NCUA Economists." *Savings Institutions,* November 1987, p. 27.

"Credit Unions May Be Tempting Fate." *Business Week,* December 18, 1989, p. 112.

FLOEN, KEITH. "Credit Unions Find Growing Strength in Numbers." *Credit Card Management,* November–December 1988, p. 70.

KOBLINER, BETH. "Why Credit Unions Now Look Spooky." *Money,* December 1988, p. 66.

SHERIDAN, JOHN A. "Unions Prepare to Move on Banks." *The Bankers Magazine,* May–June 1989, p. 67.

Real Estate Credit

The Objectives or Goals of Chapter 5 Are:

1. To explain how a home may be financed.
2. To clarify the differences between conventional mortgage, VA-guaranteed, and FHA loans.
3. To discuss the activities of the so-called second-layer lenders.
4. To compare savings and loan associations, commercial banks, and various other sources as places for the consumer to go for home financing.
5. To describe the characteristics of adjustable-rate mortgages [ARMs] as well as the point system in mortgage lending.
6. To discuss the provisions of the Depository Institutions Deregulation and Monetary Control Act and the Garn-St Germain Depository Institutions Act.
7. To explain the problems caused by deregulation for savings and loan organizations.
8. To discuss the provisions of the Financial Institutions Reform, Recovery and Enforcement Act of 1989 (FIRREA).

The high rate of home ownership in the United States represents a response to many social, historical, demographic, and economic forces. Home ownership is one of the outstanding characteristics of our society; at the close of 1988 nearly 64 percent of the nation's homes were owner-occupied. Table 5–1 gives the trend of home ownership since 1890.

The United States League of Savings Institutions made the following observation on home ownership in its *1989 Savings Institutions Sourcebook:*

> Widespread ownership is one of the distinctive characteristics of American society. Nearly 64% of all residential units in the United States are owner-occupied.
>
> Building, buying, and maintaining the housing units in the U.S. account for hundreds of billions of dollars annually. Housing is a major force in the economy, by any measure. Private residential construction in recent years has accounted for 3.9% to 4.4% of GNP.

TABLE 5–1 **Home Ownership, Selected Years, 1890–1989**

Year	Percentage Owned	Percentage Rented
1890	47.8%	52.2%
1900	46.7	53.3
1910	45.9	54.1
1920	45.6	54.4
1930	47.8	52.2
1940	43.6	56.4
1950	55.0	45.0
1960	61.9	38.1
1970	62.9	37.1
1980	65.6	34.4
1981	65.4	34.6
1982	64.8	35.2
1983	64.7	35.3
1984	64.5	35.5
1985	63.9	36.1
1986	63.8	36.2
1987	64.0	36.0
1988	63.8	36.2

Source: Bureau of the Census.

At year-end 1988, savings institutions accounted for more than 50% of the residential loans outstanding in the private sector—more than all other lenders combined. Even with government and federal agencies factored in, savings institutions held more than 31% of all outstanding residential loans.

Savings institutions hold more than $763 billion in residential mortgage loans. As a major type of credit, residential mortgage loans are exceeded only by the national debt, and savings institutions are the largest single source of home mortgage credit.[1]

In recent years manufactured homes have become important in the housing market. The fact that as early as 1970 more than one out of three families moving into a single-family unit was moving into a mobile home points out that these pre-engineered, factory-built units have rapidly become a widely accepted substitute for the traditionally constructed one-family dwelling. Mobile home data shown in Table 5–2 covers shipments, not sales.

The American consumer usually goes through three steps when buying a home:

---

[1] *1989 Savings Institutions Sourcebook* (Chicago: United States League of Savings Institutions, 1989), p. 8.

TABLE 5–2 **Mobile Home Shipments, Selected Years, 1960–1984**

Year	Number of Units	Percent of Private Starts	
		Total	Single Family†
1960	103,700	8.3%	9.4%
1965	216,470	14.7	18.3
1970	401,190	28.0	33.0
1971	496,570	24.2	30.1
1972	575,940	24.4	30.6
1973	566,920	27.7	33.4
1974	329,300	24.6	27.0
1975	212,690	18.3	19.2
1976	246,120	16.0	17.5
1977	277,000	13.9	16.0
1978	275,900	13.7	16.1
1979	277,400	15.9	18.9
1980	221,600	17.1	20.6
1981	240,900	22.2	25.5
1982	239,600	22.6	26.6
1983	295,800	17.4	21.7
1984	295,700	16.9	21.4
1985	283,900	16.3	20.9
1986	244,300	13.5	17.2
1987	232,800	14.4	16.9
1988*	218,300	14.7	16.8

*Preliminary.
†Single-family conventional homes and mobile homes.
Sources: Department of Commerce; Manufactured Housing Institute; National Conference of States on Building Codes and Standards.

1. Locating a desirable home and negotiating for the purchase. This step includes the preparation of and agreement to the contract in which the price and terms of sale are included.
2. Arranging for a loan, usually from a savings and loan association, a commercial bank, a mortgage company, an insurance company, relatives, or friends. An application is completed, the home is appraised, the buyer's credit is checked, and the loan is approved or denied.
3. Closing the sale, usually with the help of the real estate agent involved and of the lawyers representing the seller and the buyer. The "happy day" of taking possession is now at hand.

The purchase of a home is probably the largest monetary transaction in the life of the American consumer. This chapter is primarily concerned with Step 2 in this important process.

RESIDENTIAL FINANCING

Closely associated with home ownership is home mortgage loan credit.[2] This topic is usually discussed in books covering personal finance but not in books on credits and collections. Your author has changed this.

The housing market is one of the largest users of borrowed funds in the American economy. In fact, the need for residential mortgage credit has grown more rapidly over the past quarter-century than has any other single type of capital or credit requirement. The supply of residential credit has been marked by high volatility, which in turn reflects the volatility of deposit growth at thrift institutions. Savings associations have been, and continue to be, the major source of residential credit. However, the so-called second-layer lenders (organizations such as Federal National Mortgage Association and the Federal Home Loan Mortgage Corporation) have become a significant source of credit in recent years.

Loans outstanding on one- to four-family homes, which represented the largest segment of mortgage loans as of the close of 1988, totaled $2,127 billion. Table 5–3 shows mortgage debt outstanding, by type of property, for the year-end from 1960 through 1988.

Before looking at the various sources of financial aid to borrowers, it is important to understand *FHA insurance, GI loans,* Private Mortgage Insurance, and the federal credit agencies that conduct secondary market actions in buying and selling loans or provide credit to primary lenders in the form of borrowed money

Federal Housing Administration Programs

The National Housing Act of 1934 created the Federal Housing Administration (FHA), which was established primarily to increase home construction, reduce unemployment, and operate various loan insurance programs.

The FHA makes no loans, nor does it plan or build houses. As in the GI-loan program, the applicant for the loan must make arrangements with a lending institution. This financial organization then may ask if the borrower wants FHA insurance on the loan or may insist that the borrower apply for it. The federal government, through the Federal Housing Administration, investigates the applicant and, having decided that the risk is

---

[2]Entire books have been written about home mortgage lending. This book devotes only one chapter to the subject. The author believes that students need exposure to some of the most important aspects of home mortgage financing.

When the first edition of this book appeared in 1960, some reviewers criticized the author for including home mortgage loan credit in the book. Today, some reviewers are suggesting that two chapters should be devoted to this area.

Prospective home buyers, after acquiring some fundamental knowledge of this subject, should rely strongly on the expert advice of their experienced real estate agent, banker, savings and loan executive, insurance agent, and other executives in this field. Much grief can be avoided by following the advice of experts.

TABLE 5–3   **Mortgage Debt Outstanding, by Type of Property, for Selected Years, 1960–1988** ($ billions)

Year-end	Residential Properties			Commercial Properties	Farm Properties	All Properties
	One- to Four-Family	Multi-Family	Total			
1960	$ 141.9	$ 20.3	$ 162.2	$ 32.4	$ 12.8	$ 207.5
1965	220.5	37.2	257.7	54.5	21.2	333.3
1970	297.4	60.1	357.5	85.6	30.5	473.7
1971	325.9	70.1	396.0	95.9	32.4	524.2
1972	366.5	82.8	449.3	112.7	35.4	597.4
1973	407.9	93.1	501.0	131.7	39.8	672.6
1974	440.7	100.0	540.7	146.9	44.9	732.5
1975	482.1	100.6	582.7	159.3	49.9	791.9
1976	546.3	105.7	652.0	171.2	55.4	878.6
1977	642.7	114.0	756.7	189.7	63.9	1,010.3
1978	753.5	124.9	878.4	211.8	72.8	1,163.0
1979	870.5	134.9	1,005.4	236.3	86.8	1,328.4
1980	965.1	142.3	1,107.4	255.5	97.5	1,460.4
1981	1,039.8	142.1	1,181.9	277.5	107.2	1,566.7
1982	1,080.0	145.7	1,225.7	300.9	111.3	1,637.9
1983	1,198.5	160.7	1,359.2	352.4	113.7	1,825.4
1984	1,334.3	185.4	1,519.7	419.3	112.4	2,051.4
1985	1,488.0	214.5	1,702.5	481.5	105.9	2,289.8
1986	1,698.5	247.8	1,946.3	555.0	95.8	2,597.2
1987	1,925.2	273.8	2,199.0	655.2	88.9	2,943.1
1988*	2,127.8	293.2	2,421.0	713.5	86.8	3,221.3

Note: Components may not add to totals due to rounding.
*Preliminary.
Source: Federal Reserve Board.

favorable, insures the lending institution against loss of principal in case the borrower fails to meet the terms and conditions of the mortgage. The borrower, who pays an insurance premium of one half of 1 percent on declining balances for the lender's protection, receives two benefits: a careful appraisal by an FHA inspector and a lower interest rate on the mortgage than the lender might have offered without the protection.

Until the latter half of the 1960s, the Federal Housing Administration served mainly as an insuring agency for loans made by private lenders. However, in recent years this role has been expanded as the agency became the administrator of interest rate subsidy and rent supplement programs. Important subsidy programs were established by the Housing and Urban Development Act of 1968.

In 1974 the Housing and Community Development Act was passed. Its provisions significantly altered federal involvement in a wide range of housing and community development activities. The new law made a variety of changes in FHA activities, although it did not involve (as had been proposed) a complete rewriting and consolidation of the National Housing Act. It did, however, include provisions relating to the lending and investment powers of federal savings and loan associations, the real estate lending authority of national banks, and the lending and depositary authority of federal credit unions.

Further changes occurred in the 1977 Housing and Community Development Act, which raised ceilings on single-family loan amounts for savings and loan association lending, federal agency purchases, FHA insurance, and security for Federal Home Loan Bank advances. In 1980 the Housing and Community Development Act was passed; it permitted negotiated interest rates on certain FHA loans and created a new FHA rental subsidy program for middle-income families.

GI Loans (VA-Guaranteed)

The original Servicemen's Readjustment Act, passed by Congress in 1944, extended a wide variety of benefits to eligible veterans. The loan guarantee program of the Veterans Administration has been especially important to veterans. Under the law, as amended, the Veterans Administration is authorized to guarantee or insure home, farm, and business loans made to veterans by lending institutions. The VA can make direct loans in certain areas for the purpose of purchasing or constructing a home or farm residence, or for repair, alteration, or improvement of the dwelling. The terms and requirements of VA farm and business loans have not induced private lenders to make such loans in volume during recent years.

The Veterans Housing Act of 1970 removed all termination dates for applying for VA-guaranteed housing loans. This 1970 amendment also provided for VA-guaranteed loans on mobile homes. More recently, the Veterans Housing Benefits Improvement Act of 1978 expanded and increased the benefits for millions of American veterans.

Despite a great deal of confusion and misunderstanding, the federal government generally doesn't make direct loans under the act.[3] The government simply guarantees loans made by ordinary mortgage lenders (descriptions of which appear in subsequent sections) after veterans make their own arrangements for the loans through normal financial circles. The Veterans Administration then appraises the property in question and, if satisfied with the risk involved, guarantees the lender against loss of principal if the buyer defaults.

---

[3]The basic intention of the VA direct home loan program is to supply home financing to eligible veterans in areas where private financing is not generally available. Eligible areas are designated by the VA as housing credit shortage areas and are generally rural areas and small cities and towns not near metropolitan or commuting areas of large cities.

Private Mortgage Insurance

Private mortgage insurance (PMI) guarantees home mortgage loans that are *conventional,* that is, nongovernment loans. This private business loan program is equivalent to the FHA and the VA loan programs.

The PMI company insures a percentage of the consumer's loan to reduce the lender's risk; this percentage is paid to the lender if the consumer does not pay and the lender forecloses the loan.

Lenders decide if they need and want private mortgage insurance. If they so decide, it becomes a requirement of the loan. PMI companies charge a fee to insure a mortgage loan; the VA insures a loan at no cost to a veteran buyer; the FHA charges a fee to guarantee the loan.

Second-Layer Lenders

A group called *second-layer lenders* became an important force in the residential mortgage market in the latter half of the 1960s. These federal credit agencies, which include the Federal Home Loan Mortgage Corp., the Federal National Mortgage Association, and the Government National Mortgage Association, conduct secondary market activities in the buying and selling of loans and provide credit to primary lenders in the form of borrowed money.[4] They do not have direct contact with the individual consumer.

FEDERAL HOME LOAN MORTGAGE CORPORATION. In 1970 the Federal Home Loan Mortgage Corporation, sometimes known as Freddie Mac, was established. This corporation is designed to promote the flow of capital into the housing market by establishing an active secondary market in mortgages. It may by law deal only with government-supervised lenders such as savings and loan associations, savings banks, and commercial banks; its programs cover conventional whole mortgage loans, participations in conventional loans, and FHA and VA loans.

FEDERAL NATIONAL MORTGAGE ASSOCIATION. Known in financial circles as Fannie Mae, this association was chartered as a government corporation in 1938, rechartered as a federal agency in 1954, and became a government-sponsored, stockholder-owned corporation in 1968. Fannie Mae, which has been described as "a private corporation with a public purpose," basically provides a secondary market for residential loans. It fulfills this function by buying, servicing, and selling loans that, since 1970, have included FHA-insured, VA-guaranteed, and conventional loans. However, purchases outrun sales by such a wide margin that some

---

[4]For articles on second layer lenders, see the Suggested Readings at the end of the chapter.

observers view this association as a lender with a permanent loan portfolio rather than a powerful secondary market corporation.

GOVERNMENT NATIONAL MORTGAGE ASSOCIATION. This association, which is often referred to as Ginnie Mae, operates within the Department of Housing and Urban Development. In addition to performing the special assistance, management, and liquidation functions that once belonged to Fannie Mae, Ginnie Mae has an important additional function—that of issuing guarantees of securities backed by government-insured or guaranteed mortgages. Such mortgage-backed securities are fully guaranteed by the U.S. government as to timely payment of both principal and interest.

HOW CONSUMERS MAY FINANCE A HOME

One way to buy a home is to pay cash. But the typical American family is not in a position to do this, and thus must arrange to finance its home purchase. Most families can afford only a modest down payment and are forced to secure the remainder of the purchase price by mortgage from some lending institution. The larger the down payment, the smaller the total interest payment over the term of the mortgage. Buyers, however, should not use all of their savings for the down payment, thus depriving themselves of any reserve to fall back on if extraordinary expenses arise or income falls in the future.

Sources of These Finances

The family seeking assistance in buying or constructing a home generally has several possible loan sources available. The amount of the loan sought, however, is usually less important than the ratio of the loan to the value of the property. At certain financial institutions, this ratio is a direct determining factor as to the applicant's eligibility.

A home buyer or builder can obtain financial aid from savings and loan associations, commercial banks, savings banks, mortgage bankers and brokers, life insurance companies, credit unions, federal agencies, individual investors, and builders. See Table 5–4 for data on the various types of lenders that hold mortgage loans on one- to four-family residences for selected years from 1960 to 1988. In deciding on the most advantageous source, applicants should consider a number of factors, such as the size of the loan needed, maturity of the loan, interest rate, method of paying off the loan, and other characteristics.

Savings and loan associations lead by a wide margin in the total amount of credit provided to owners and buyers of homes. Their loans exceed the combined holdings of commercial banks, savings banks, and life insurance companies.

TABLE 5–4 **One- to Four-Family Mortgage Loans Outstanding, by Lender, Selected Years, 1960–1988** ($ billions)

Year-end	Savings Associations	Savings Banks	Commercial Banks	Life Insurance Companies	Federally Supported Agencies†	All Others	Total
1960	$ 55.4	$ 20.6	$ 19.2	$24.9	$ 7.1	$ 14.7	$ 141.9
1965	92.0	33.8	30.4	29.6	6.6	28.1	220.5
1970	121.9	42.1	42.3	26.7	24.7	39.7	297.4
1971	136.6	43.4	48.0	24.6	30.5	42.8	325.9
1972	160.2	46.2	57.0	22.3	36.1	44.7	366.5
1973	182.4	48.8	68.0	20.4	41.9	46.4	407.9
1974	197.7	49.2	74.8	19.0	52.0	48.0	440.7
1975	218.8	50.0	77.0	17.6	65.9	52.8	482.1
1976	254.0	53.1	86.2	16.1	77.6	59.3	546.3
1977	300.8	58.1	105.1	14.7	96.3	67.7	642.7
1978	345.4	63.3	129.2	14.4	119.6	81.6	753.5
1979	384.8	66.1	149.5	16.1	154.1	99.9	870.5
1980	411.0	67.5	160.4	17.9	183.2	125.1	965.1
1981	426.8	68.2	170.3	17.2	209.7	147.6	1,039.8
1982	392.2	64.2	173.8	16.8	270.7	162.3	1,080.0
1983	414.3	69.1	182.5	15.3	346.1	171.2	1,198.5
1984	459.7	71.5	196.2	14.1	401.4	191.4	1,334.3
1985	485.8	75.9	213.4	12.4	492.5	208.0	1,488.0
1986	485.6	82.0	235.8	12.8	646.9	235.4	1,698.5
1987	502.0	94.1	275.8	13.2	777.9	262.2	1,925.2
1988*	552.1	104.9	311.8	15.3	871.8	271.9	2,127.8

*Preliminary.
†Includes mortgage pools.
Source: Federal Reserve Board.

SAVINGS AND LOAN ASSOCIATIONS. The most important purpose of these institutions is to make mortgage loans on residential property. These organizations, which also are known as savings associations, building and loan associations, cooperative banks (in New England), and homestead associations (in Louisiana), are the primary source of financial assistance to a large segment of American homeowners. As home-financing institutions, they give primary attention to single-family residences and are equipped to make loans in this area.

Some of the most important characteristics of a savings and loan association are:

1. It is generally a locally owned and privately managed home-financing institution.
2. It receives individuals' savings and uses these funds to make long-term amortized loans to home purchasers.

3. It makes loans for the construction, purchase, repair, or refinancing of houses.

4. It is state or federally chartered.

For most of its history, the savings and loan institution was a remarkable success. Started in 1930, it grew from a small, mutually owned organization into the prime supplier of mortgage money for the American home buyer.

But the 1980s were a different story! As mentioned in Chapter 4, Congress in 1980 granted all thrifts, including savings and loan associations, the power to make consumer and commercial loans and to issue transaction accounts. Designed to help the thrift industry retain its deposit base and to improve its profitability, the Depository Institutions Deregulation and Monetary Control Act (DIDMCA) of 1980 allowed thrifts to make consumer loans up to 20 percent of their assets, issue credit cards, accept negotiable order of withdrawal (NOW) accounts from individuals and nonprofit organizations, and invest up to 20 percent of their assets in commercial real estate loans. In 1982, the Garn-St Germain Depository Institutions Act was passed and increased the proportion of assets that thrifts could hold in consumer and commercial real estate loans and allowed thrifts to invest 5 percent of their assets in commercial loans until January 1, 1984, when this percentage increased to 10 percent. (See Table 4–3 for the new powers granted to federally chartered thrifts.)

The following is a detailed summary of the major causes for losses that hurt the savings and loan business in the 1980s:

1. Lack of net worth for many institutions as they entered the 1980s, and a wholly inadequate net worth regulation.

2. Decline in the effectiveness of Regulation Q in preserving the spread between the cost of money and the rate of return on assets, basically stemming from inflation and the accompanying increase in market interest rates.

3. Absence of an ability to vary the return on assets with increases in the rate of interest required to be paid for deposits.

4. Increased competition on the deposit gathering and mortgage origination sides of the business, with a sudden burst of new technology making possible a whole new way of conducting financial institutions generally and the mortgage business specifically.

5. A rapid increase in investment powers of associations with passage of the Depository Institutions Deregulation and Monetary Control Act (the Garn-St Germain Act), and, more important, through state legislative enactments in a number of important and rapidly growing states. These introduced new risks and speculative opportunities which were difficult to administer. In many instances management lacked the ability or experience to evaluate them, or to administer large volumes of nonresidential construction loans.

6. Elimination of regulations initially designed to prevent lending excesses and minimize failures. Regulatory relaxation permitted lending, directly and through participations, in distant loan markets on the promise of high returns. Lenders, however, were not familiar with these distant markets. It also permitted associations to participate extensively in speculative construction activities with builders and developers who had little or no financial stake in the projects.

7. Fraud and insider transaction abuses were the principal cause for some 20% of savings and loan failures the past three years and a greater percentage of the dollar losses borne by the FSLIC.

8. A new type and generation of opportunistic savings and loan executives and owners—some of whom operated in a fraudulent manner—whose takeover of many institutions was facilitated by a change in FSLIC rules reducing the minimum number of stockholders of an insured association from 400 to one.

9. Dereliction of duty on the part of the board of directors of some savings associations. This permitted management to make uncontrolled use of some new operating authority, while directors failed to control expenses and prohibit obvious conflict of interest situations.

10. A virtual end of inflation in the American economy, together with overbuilding in multifamily, condominium type residences and in commercial real estate in many cities. In addition, real estate values collapsed in the energy states—Texas, Louisiana, Oklahoma particularly—and weakness occurred in the mining and agricultural sectors of the economy.

11. Pressures felt by the management of many associations to restore net worth ratios. Anxious to improve earnings, they departed from their traditional lending practices into credits and markets involving higher risks, but with which they had little experience.

12. The lack of appropriate, accurate, and effective evaluations of the savings and loan business by public accounting firms, security analysts, and the financial community.

13. Organizational structure and supervisory laws, adequate for policing and controlling the business in the protected environment of the 1960s and 1970s, resulted in fatal delays and indecision in the examination/supervision process in the 1980s.

14. Federal and state examination and supervisory staffs insufficient in number, experience, or ability to deal with the new world of savings and loan operations.

15. The inability or unwillingness of the Bank Board and its legal and supervisory staff to deal with problem institutions in a timely manner. Many institutions, which ultimately closed with big losses, were known problem cases for a year or more. Often, it appeared, political considerations delayed necessary supervisory action.[5]

---

[5]Norman Strunk and Fred Case, *Where Deregulation Went Wrong* (Chicago: United States League of Savings Institutions, 1988), pp. 15–16. Reprinted with permission.

As a result, the Financial Institutions Reform, Recovery and Enforcement Act of 1989 (FIRREA) dramatically changed the savings and loan industry and its federal regulation. Here are the highlights of this legislation, signed into law August 9, 1989:[b]

1. The Federal Home Loan Bank Board (FHLBB) and the Federal Savings and Loan Insurance Corporation (FSLIC) were abolished.

2. The Office of Thrift Supervision (OTS), a bureau of the Treasury Department, was created to charter, regulate, examine, and supervise savings institutions.

3. The Federal Housing Finance Board (FHFB) was created as an independent agency to oversee the 12 federal home loan banks (also called district banks).

4. The Savings Association Insurance Fund (SAIF) replaced the FSLIC[7] as an ongoing insurance fund for thrift institutions. SAIF is administered by the Federal Deposit Insurance Corp.

5. The Resolution Trust Corporation (RTC) was established to dispose of failed thrift institutions taken over by regulators after January 1, 1989. The RTC will make insured deposits at those institutions available to their customers.

6. FIRREA gives both Freddie Mac and Fannie Mae additional responsibility to support mortgages for low- and moderate-income families.

The savings and loan industry is in an unprecedented situation; its importance in consumer residential real estate is uncertain; the impact of FIRREA is not clear. What the future holds for the savings and loan industry is not known. Only time will tell!

COMMERCIAL BANKS. In the past, commercial banks have not been greatly interested in real estate loans and have placed only a relatively small percentage of their assets in mortgages. As their name implies, such financial institutions secured their earning primarily from commercial and consumer loans and left the major task of home financing to others. However, due to changes in banking laws and policies, commercial banks are increasingly active in home financing.

Changes in banking laws now allow commercial banks to make home mortgage loans on a more liberal basis than ever before. In acquiring mortgages on real estate, these institutions follow two main practices. First, some of the banks maintain active and well-organized departments whose primary function is to compete actively for real estate loans. In

---

[b]"FIRREA—It's Not a New Sports Car," *The Credit World,* September–October 1989, p. 20. Also see the Suggested Readings at the end of the chapter.

[7]Like the FDIC, the FSLIC was a permanent corporation that insured savings and loan accounts up to $100,000.

areas lacking specialized real estate financial institutions, these banks become *the* source for residential and farm mortgage loans. Second, the banks acquire mortgages by simply purchasing them from mortgage bankers or dealers.

In addition, dealer service companies, which were originally used to obtain car loans for permanent lenders such as commercial banks, wanted to broaden their activity beyond their local area. In recent years, however, such companies have concentrated on acquiring mobile home loans in volume for both commercial banks and savings and loan associations. Service companies obtain these loans from retail dealers, usually on a nonrecourse basis. Almost all bank/service company agreements contain a credit insurance policy that protects the lender if the consumer defaults. The service company usually receives 1.5 percent per year of the scheduled terms of the original amount financed. In addition, most service companies perform other functions, including collection efforts after the loan becomes more than 30 days past due, repossession if necessary, sale of repossessed collateral, and collection of monthly payments.

SAVINGS BANKS.   These depository financial institutions are federally chartered, primarily accept consumer deposits, and make home mortgage loans. Historically, these institutions were of the mutual (depositor-owned) form and were chartered in only 16 states, the majority being in New England.

MORTGAGE BANKERS AND BROKERS.   Mortgage bankers are companies or individuals who originate mortgage loans, sell them to other investors, service the monthly payments, and may act as agents to dispense funds for taxes and insurance.

Mortgage brokers basically present the consumer home buyer with their attempts to find the best loan from a variety of loan sources. Their income comes from the lender making the loan plus an extra fee, usually 1 percent of the mortgage.

LIFE INSURANCE COMPANIES.   Life insurance companies are another source of financial assistance. These companies lend on real estate as one form of investment and adjust their portfolios from time to time to reflect changing economic conditions. Formerly, farm loans were looked on with favor by life insurance companies. In recent years, however, these institutions have reduced their activity in residential mortgages. Individuals seeking a loan from an insurance company can deal directly with a local branch office or with a local real estate broker who acts as loan correspondent for one or more insurance companies.

CREDIT UNIONS.   These cooperative financial institutions are organized by people who share a common bond—for example, employees of a company, a labor union, or a religious group. (See Chapter 4 for a detailed description of the activities of a credit union.) Some credit unions offer home loans in addition to other financial services.

FEDERALLY SUPPORTED AGENCIES. As previously discussed, under certain conditions and fund limitations the Veterans Administration makes direct loans to creditworthy veterans in housing credit shortage areas designated by the VA's administrator. Such areas are generally rural areas and small cities and towns not near the metropolitan or commuting areas of large cities—areas where GI loans from private institutions are not available.

The federally supported agencies referred to here do not include the so-called second-layer lenders who enter the scene after the mortgage is arranged between the lending institution and the individual home buyer.

OTHER SOURCES. Individual investors constitute a fairly large but somewhat declining source of money for home mortgage loans. Experienced observers claim that these lenders prefer shorter term obligations and usually restrict their loans to less than two-thirds of the value of the residential property. Likewise, building contractors sometimes accept second mortgages in part payment of the construction price of a home if the purchaser is unable to raise the total amount of down payment above the first mortgage money offered.

Finally, real estate investment trusts (REITs), which began when the Real Estate Investment Trust Act became effective January 1, 1961, are available. REITs, like savings and loan associations, are committed to real estate lending and can and do serve the national real estate market, although some specialization has occurred in their activities.[8]

COMPETITION AMONG LENDERS FOR LOANABLE FUNDS

To be able to provide home buyers and builders with the funds needed, financial institutions must compete for deposits—and in the last decade this competition has become intense.

Consumer lending institutions compete for loanable funds not only among themselves but also with the federal government and private corporations. Called *disintermediation,* this process involves the movement of dollars from savings accounts into direct market instruments: U.S. Treasury obligations, agency securities, and corporate debt. One of the greatest factors in recent years in the movement of deposits was the tremendous growth of money market funds whose higher interest rates attracted consumer deposits.

---

[8]See the Suggested Readings at the end of the chapter.

To compete for deposits, savings institutions offer many different types of plans:

- *Passbook or ordinary accounts*—permit any amount to be added to or withdrawn from the account at any time.
- *NOW and Super NOW accounts*—function like checking accounts but earn interest. A minimum balance may be required on Super NOW accounts.
- *Money market accounts*—carry a monthly limit of preauthorized transfers to other accounts or persons and may require a minimum or average balance.
- *Certificate accounts*—subject to loss of some or all interest on withdrawals before maturity.
- *Notice accounts*—the equivalent of certificate accounts with an indefinite term. Savers agree to notify the institution a specified time before withdrawal.
- *Individual retirement accounts (IRAs) and Keogh accounts*—a form of retirement savings in which the funds deposited and interest earned are exempt from income tax until after withdrawal.
- *Checking accounts*—offered by some institutions under definite restrictions.
- *Club accounts and other savings accounts*—designed to help people save regularly to meet certain goals.

PROVISIONS OF HOME MORTGAGES

Lenders offer a wide array of home mortgage loans. The two most popular mortgage instruments today are the fixed-rate mortgage and the adjustable-rate mortgage (ARM). Under both of these instruments, the amortized form of mortgage lending is followed.

Amortization

Amortization may be defined as the systematic and continuous payment of the principal balance on an obligation through installments until the debt has been paid in full. All government mortgage financing institutions, such as the FHA, insist on the amortized form of mortgage lending. This direct-reduction mortgage provides for a fixed monthly payment that not only covers interest—and perhaps taxes and insurance—but also reduces the principal of the mortgage debt. Table 5–5 shows an amortization schedule.

Using the material in Table 5–5, it is easy—and amazing—to figure how much a buyer actually pays for the home over the years. In examples A and B, comparative figures are shown for an 11½ percent mortgage over 15 years and over 30 years:

TABLE 5–5 **Amortization Schedule**

| | Monthly Payment to Amortize $1,000 Loan, Including Interest at Rate of— | | | | | |
	8½%	9½%	10½%	11½%	12½%	15%
In 15 years	$9.85	$10.45	$11.06	$11.69	$12.33	$14.00
In 20 years	8.86	9.33	9.99	10.67	11.37	13.17
In 25 years	8.06	8.74	9.45	10.17	10.91	12.81
In 30 years	7.69	8.41	9.15	9.91	10.68	12.65

Example A: $60,000 home with $10,000 down payment for 15 years at 11½%

Monthly payment	$ 11.69 per $1,000
	× 50
	$ 584.50 for $50,000 mortgage
For 15 years or 180 months	× 180
	$105,210 total dollar payments
Down payment	+$ 10,000
	$115,210 total cost of home*

*Does not include taxes and insurance.

Example B: $60,000 home with $10,000 down payment for 30 years at 11½%

Monthly payment	$ 9.91 per $1,000
	× 50
	$ 495.50 for $50,000 mortgage
For 30 years or 360 months	× 360
	$178,380 total dollar payments
Down payment	+$ 10,000
	$188,380 total cost of home*

*Does not include taxes and insurance.

The difference between Example A and Example B (same home, same down payment, same interest rate, but longer pay-off period) is $188,380 − $115,210 = $73,170.

TABLE 5–6 **Actual Interest Rate on a 20-Year Mortgage if Paid Off in 10 or 20 Years**

Number of Points Paid	10 Percent Paid Off	
	10 Years	20 Years
1	10.175	10.146
2	10.353	10.296
3	10.534	10.447
4	10.717	10.601
5	10.903	10.758
6	11.092	10.918
7	11.283	11.080
8	11.477	11.245
9	11.675	11.413
10	11.875	11.584

The "Point" System in Mortgage Lending

Over the years mortgage lenders have frequently charged "points." This practice, while generally misunderstood and often ignored, is vitally important to understanding mortgage lending operations. A point is 1 percent of the face value of the mortgage; thus, if a homeowner is charged four points on a $20,000 loan, the lender deducts $800 and the home buyer receives only $19,200. However, the home buyer has to repay the entire $20,000. This, of course, means that the true annual rate of interest is more than the stated rate.

The figures in Table 5–6 show the actual interest rate, depending on the number of points charged, that the buyer will pay on a 20-year, 10 percent mortgage, paid off in 10 or 20 years.

Points may also be charged to the seller. These points, however, do not affect the interest rate; they simply reduce the amount the seller receives. Points may be charged as prepaid interest in some loans, often in order to get a more attractive rate for the term of the loan. Some lenders also express their loan origination (or processing) fees as points. In this case, some points are included in the amount financed, whereas other points represent out-of-pocket costs that the buyer pays when the loan is closed.

Home buyers should seek expert advice as to the terms of their mortgage and the points charged before making any final decision.

Fixed-Rate Mortgages

For many years the most common mortgage instrument was the fixed-rate mortgage loan. This loan is easy to understand; the biggest difference between the two most popular forms, the 15-year and the 30-year fixed rate, is the length of maturity (see examples A and B). People who want to know exactly how much their monthly payments will be for the length of the loan, no matter what happens to interest rates, tend to choose this type of loan.

This type of loan was considered the standard of home mortgage loans until high interest rates made it unaffordable for the average home buyer. Today, however, most of these loans are sold to investors, thus limiting the number of fixed-rate mortgage loans available. Even so, the Federal Home Loan Mortgage Corporation reported that in 1988 nearly 20 percent of the new mortgages made were 15-year fixed-rate loans. Reasons cited for this were (1) major savings in interest expense, (2) rapid increase in owner's equity, and (3) loan paid off in a relatively short period.

Balloon Mortgages

This loan has the same interest rate with the same monthly payment with one big exception. Computed on a 30-year payback, for example, the entire loan is due and payable in full at the end of the 15th year. The buyer's payments are those of a 30-year loan, thus keeping payments down, but the buyer has only 15 years to pay. This type of loan can be computed on a fixed-rate loan for any number of years payback with a balloon payment placed at any given year. The loan may or may not have a provision to refinance at the time of the balloon. Otherwise, it is the buyer's responsibility to locate new refinancing.

Adjustable-Rate Mortgages (ARMs)

The *adjustable-rate mortgage (ARM)* has become prominent in home mortgage lending. Shopping for a mortgage used to be a fairly simple process. In the past, most home mortgages had interest rates that did not change over the life of the loan. Today, however, many loans have interest rates (and monthly payments) that can change from time to time. Thus to compare one ARM with another or with a fixed-rate mortgage, buyers need to know about indexes, margins, discounts, caps, negative amortization, and convertibility. Buyers need to know the maximum amount their monthly payment could increase and to compare the possible increase with their future ability to pay. Adjustable-rate mortgages thus transfer some of the risk of changes in market interest rates from lenders to borrowers.

The most important basic features of ARMs are:

1. *Initial interest rate.* This is the beginning interest rate on an ARM.
2. *The adjustment period.* This is the length of time that the interest rate or loan period on an ARM is scheduled to remain

unchanged. The rate is reset at the end of this period, and the monthly loan payment is recalculated.

3. *The index rate.* Most lenders tie ARM interest rates changes to changes in an index rate. Lenders base ARM rates on a variety of indexes, the most common being rates on one-, three-, or five-year Treasury securities. Another common index is the national or regional average cost of funds to savings and loan associations.

4. *The margin.* This is the percentage points that lenders add to the index rate to determine the ARM's interest rate.

5. *Interest rate caps.* These are the limits on how much the interest rate or the monthly payment can be changed at the end of each adjustment period or over the life of the loan.

6. *Initial discounts.* These are interest rate concessions, often used as promotional aids, offered the first year or more of a loan. They reduce the interest rate below the prevailing rate (the index plus the margin).

7. *Negative amortization.* This means the mortgage balance is increasing. This occurs whenever the monthly mortgage payments are not large enough to pay all the interest due on the mortgage. This may be caused by the payment cap contained in the ARM.

8. *Conversion.* The agreement with the lender may have a clause that allows the buyer to convert the ARM to a fixed-rate mortgage at designated times.

9. *Prepayment.* Some agreements may require the buyer to pay special fees or penalties if the ARM is paid off early. Prepayment terms are sometimes negotiable.

It should be obvious that the choice of a home mortgage loan is complicated and time consuming.

As a help to the buyer, the Federal Reserve Board and the Federal Home Loan Bank Board prepared a mortgage checklist (see Figure 5–1).

HOME EQUITY LOANS

A relatively new concept, home equity loans enable people to convert their homes into cash without selling them. Simply, home equity conversion allows homeowners to draw on the equity they have accumulated. Some plans provide income over a specified period, and others guarantee a lifetime income.

Features of home equity loans vary by state and by lender. However, the concept is basically the same. The homeowner applies for a revolving line of credit secured by the value of the home. The owner may be able to borrow up to 70 percent or 80 percent of the current value of the home, less the remaining balance on any mortgage on the home. See Chapters 4 and 6 for details of this type of consumer borrowing.

FIGURE 5–1   **Mortgage Checklist**

	Mortgage A	Mortgage B
Mortgage amount	$	$
Basic Features for comparison		
Fixed rate annual percentage rate		
(the cost of your credit as a yearly rate which		
includes both interest and other charges)	_____	_____
ARM annual percentage rate:		
Adjustment period	_____	_____
Index used and current rate	_____	_____
Margin	_____	_____
Initial payment without discount	_____	_____
Initial payment with discount (if any)	_____	_____
How long will discount last?	_____	_____
Interest rate caps: Periodic	_____	_____
Overall	_____	_____
Payment caps	_____	_____
Negative amortization	_____	_____
Convertibility or prepayment privilege	_____	_____
Initial fees and charges	_____	_____
Monthly payment amounts		
What will my monthly payment be		
after 12 months if the index rate:		
Stays the same	_____	_____
Cooc up 2%	_____	_____
Goes down 2%	_____	_____
What will my monthly payments be after		
three years if the index rate:		
Stays the same	_____	_____
Goes up 2% per year	_____	_____
Goes down 2% per year	_____	_____
Take into account any caps on your mortgage		
and remember it may run 30 years.		

DISCRIMINATION IN MORTGAGE LENDING

As pointed out in Chapter 6, the Equal Credit Opportunity Act prohibits credit discrimination on the basis of race, color, religion, national origin, sex, marital status, and age (provided that a person has the capacity to enter into a binding contract); because all or part of a person's income derives from any public assistance program; or because a person in good faith has exercised any right under the Consumer Credit Protection Act. The provisions of this act apply in any decision-making activity in regard to home mortgage lending.

Likewise, some mortgage lenders have been the target of criticism because of certain "redlining" practices—that is, setting aside certain areas in a community as undesirable credit risk zones.

DISCUSSION QUESTIONS

1. Why might home mortgage loan credit be considered as a type of consumer credit? Why might it not be so considered?
2. Why would you want to buy a home? To rent instead?
3. How do you account for the acceptance of mobile homes as a form of residential housing?
4. Distinguish between an FHA-insured, a VA-guaranteed, and a conventional loan.
5. What is meant by the term *second-layer lenders?*
6. Distinguish carefully between Freddie Mac, Fannie Mae, and Ginnie Mae.
7. What sources are available to the American family to finance the purchase of a home?
8. Check with a savings and loan association, a life insurance company, a commercial bank, and a savings bank (if there is one in your area) as to their requirements for home financing.
9. Check the interest rates being paid to individual depositors in the various types of financial institutions in your area. In which institution would you prefer to place your own deposits? Why?
10. What are the advantages and disadvantages of the adjustable-rate mortgage to the home buyer? To the lending institution?
11. What is meant by the "point" system in home mortgage lending? Why might you as a home buyer be in favor of the point system? Why might you object to it?
12. What is private mortgage insurance (PMI)?
13. Explain the effects of deregulation on the savings and loan industry.
14. Discuss the provisions of FIRREA.
15. What is meant by amortization?
16. Distinguish between a fixed-rate mortgage and an adjustable-rate mortgage.
17. What are the disadvantages of a balloon mortgage? The advantages?
18. Explain the most important basic features of ARMs.
19. Would you want to take out a home equity loan? Why or why not?

SUGGESTED READINGS

Home Mortgage Loans

A Consumer's Guide to Mortgage Closings. Washington, D.C.: Federal Reserve Board and Federal Home Loan Bank Board, undated.

A Consumer's Guide to Mortgage Lock-Ins. Washington, D.C.: Federal Reserve Board and Federal Home Loan Bank Board, undated.

A Consumer's Guide to Mortgage Refinancing. Washington, D.C.: Federal Reserve Board and Federal Home Loan Bank Board, undated.

ARM White Paper. Beverly Hills, Calif.: Great Western Financial Corporation, 1989.

BRIDGES, JAMES E., and DEBORAH J. BRIDGES. *Mortgage Loans: What's Right for You?* 2nd ed. White Hall, Va.: Betterway Publications, Inc., 1989.

Consumer Handbook on Adjustable Rate Mortgages. Washington, D.C.: Federal Reserve Board and Federal Home Loan Bank Board, undated.

How to Shop for a Loan. Beverly Hills, Calif.: Great Western Financial Corporation, 1989.

MALMGREN, JEANNE. "Navigating the Mortgage Maze." *St. Petersburg Times,* November 12, 1989, p. 1H.

PEEK, JOE. "A Call to ARMS: Adjustable Rate Mortgages in the 1980s." Federal Reserve Bank of Boston *New England Economic Review,* March–April 1990, p. 47.

REITs

CHAMBLISS, LAUREN. "A Buyer's Guide to REITs." *Financial World,* June 13, 1989, p. 81.

GUSTKE, CONSTANCE. "Gold Among the REITs." *Financial World,* June 16, 1987, p. 118.

Savings and Loan Reform

"A Closer Look Reveals New Realities." *Savings Institutions,* October 1989, p. 28.

"At the 'El Dorado of Impaired Assets,' Everything Must Go." *Business Week,* November 6, 1989, p. 176.

CACY, J. A. "Thrifts in the Troubled 1980s: In the Nation and the District." Federal Reserve Bank of Kansas City *Economic Review,* December 1989, p. 3.

CHESSEN, JAMES. "Strong Medicine." *ABA Banking Journal,* October 1989, p. 63.

"Compared to CEBA, FIRREA Falls Short on the QTL Test." *Savings Institutions,* April 1990, p. 22.

"Faced with a Fiscal Curfew, the RTC Plays Beat-the-Clock." *Savings Institutions,* November 1989, p. 64.

"FIRREA Amendment Reappraises Appraisers." *ABA Banking Journal,* November 1989, p. 20.

"FSLIC's Fate Sparks Debates Over Viable Solutions." *Savings Institutions,* November 1988, p. 6.

"Making the Most of the New Law." *ABA Banking Journal,* December 1989, p. 10.

"Man of Many Hats." *ABA Banking Journal,* October 1989, p. 74.

ROBERTS, STEVEN M. "FIRREA: The $166 Billion Solution." *The Bankers Magazine,* January–February 1990, p. 5.

"The Response—FIRREA Rewrites Management's Agenda." *Savings Institutions,* October 1989, p. 54.

"The S&L Mess—and How To Fix It." *Business Week,* October 31, 1988, p. 130.

"Solving the FSLIC Puzzle." *ABA Banking Journal,* November 1988, p. 31.

"Thrift Rescue: Now the Hard Work Begins." *ABA Banking Journal,* September 1989, p. 12.

"To Work, the RTC Must Be Given Independence." *Savings Institutions,* April 1990, p. 25.

Second-Layer Lenders

"Freddie and Fannie Clean up after the S&L Mess." *Business Week,* June 5, 1989, p. 112.

"Freddie's New Board." *Savings Institutions,* March 1990, p. 17.

"Ginnie's and Freddie's More Predictable Cousins." *Business Week,* February 13, 1989, p. 104.

"Sallie Mae Still Plays a Vital Role as a Lender." *Savings Institutions,* October 1990, p. 80.

"Should You Do the 'Two-Step' With Fannie Mae?" *Business Week,* April 9, 1990, p. 88.

TAUB, STEPHEN. "Fannie Mae's Private Parts." *Financial World,* August 25, 1987, p. 52.

Regulation of Consumer Credit

The Objectives or Goals of Chapter 6 Are:

1. To trace the historical development of consumer credit regulation.
2. To point out the provisions of:
   a. The Truth in Lending Act.
   b. The Credit Card Issuance Act.
   c. The Fair Credit Reporting Act.
   d. The Fair Credit Billing Act.
   e. The Equal Credit Opportunity Act.
   f. The Fair Debt Collection Practices Act.
   g. The Electronic Fund Transfer Act.
   h. The Depository Institutions Deregulation and Monetary Control Act.
   i. The Garn-St Germain Depository Institutions Act.
   j. The Competitive Equality Banking Act.
   k. The Expedited Funds Availability Act.
   l. The Fair Credit and Charge Card Disclosure Act.
   m. The Home Equity Loan Consumer Protection Act.
   n. The Financial Institutions Reform, Recovery and Enforcement Act.
3. To trace the passage of state regulations of consumer credit.

Credit is an easy way for people to purchase items they want now but can't afford to pay for immediately. Almost all credit carries a cost, in the form of either interest or carrying charges. Consumers must weigh the enjoyment they will derive from the things they wish to purchase today against the necessity of having to pay for those items—at a cost—in the future. Because not all consumers use good judgment in their use of credit, federal and state action has established controls over the use of consumer credit. This chapter traces the history of federal and state credit regulation in the United States.

FEDERAL REGULATION OF CONSUMER CREDIT

Federal regulation of consumer credit began during World War II. Much new federal credit legislation was passed during the 1960s, 1970s, and

1980s. Each law attempted to reduce the problems and confusion surrounding consumer credit, whose complexity increased with its wider use. These laws are designed to set a standard treatment for individual consumers in their financial dealings.

Early Consumer Credit Legislation

Passage of Regulation W during World War II was the first attempt at consumer credit regulation. The regulation (1) dealt with the amount of down payments and the length of the repayment periods in installment selling and (2) prohibited continued activity on 30-day charge accounts that were past due for a specified period. The actual results of Regulation W are questionable. During World War II, few consumer durable goods were available and consumer income was unusually high. Consequently, sales declined for goods targeted by Regulation W for reasons other than the regulation.

The effect of regulation during the postwar period and the Korean conflict was mild. Perhaps only lower-income groups and those with heavy obligations on their incomes had to delay purchases of durable goods. The incomes of the major portion of consumers were high enough and their savings sufficient to meet the regulatory standards. Further, a scarcity of goods prevailed for several years after World War II, and by the time the United States was involved in the Korean conflict, the ineffective results of the previous regulations were well understood. Regulation during the Korean conflict was mild and applied only to the down payment and length of the repayment periods on installment sales contracts. In this instance the goods under regulation were very limited, while all other goods were free of controls.

Credit Control Act

The Credit Control Act was one of the many credit-related federal enactments that appeared during the 1960s and 1970s. Signed into law December 24, 1969, this legislation empowered the president "at any time at his discretion to authorize complete and total control of all forms and types of credit by the Federal Reserve Board—even over rates and licensing." To enforce the provisions of this act, the Federal Reserve Board was empowered, with permission from appropriate courts, to issue permanent or temporary injunctions or restraining orders against violators or suspected violators and to assess civil penalties or bring criminal charges against willful violators.

In conjunction with President Jimmy Carter's program to control inflation and with his invocation of the Credit Control Act on March 14, 1980, the Federal Reserve Board announced it was imposing restraints on the growth of certain types of consumer credit extended by banks, retailers, finance companies, and others. Credit-tightening steps taken under the act included:

- The establishment of a 15 percent "special deposit" requirement for banks, finance companies, retailers, gas and travel companies, and others on new credit extended. However, this measure was not designed to affect lending for mortgages, home improvements, cars, or other durables.
- The setting of a 10 percent "special deposit" rule for nonmember banks of the Federal Reserve System on so-called managed liabilities, which were large certificates of deposit and dollars borrowed from abroad.
- A requirement that money market mutual funds hold 15 percent of the increase of their assets in reserve.
- These controls did not apply to creditors with outstandings from covered types of credit totaling less than $2 million.

These credit-tightening steps were removed July 3, 1980. As of June 30, 1982, the law expired, and it has not been reinstated.

Truth in Lending Act—Title I of the Consumer Credit Protection Act

In 1960 the federal government made a serious but unsuccessful attempt to regulate consumer credit activities in the form of a "consumer credit labeling bill" (S. 2755). This bill, among other things, would have required that a statement of the total finance charges in dollars and cents and of the "simple" annual rate accompany every consumer credit transaction. According to its sponsors, the bill would "assist in the promotion of economic stabilization by requiring the disclosure of finance charges in connection with extension of credit." This bill was reintroduced in 1961 under the interesting title, "truth in lending bill" (S. 1740), and its leading spokesman was Paul H. Douglas (then U.S. senator from Illinois). Congress held extensive hearings on this and similar bills introduced during the early 1960s. In January 1967, William Proxmire (U.S. senator from Wisconsin) introduced his version (S. 5) of the so-called truth in lending bill, which was subsequently passed and signed into law. It became effective July 1, 1969.

As originally passed, the Truth in Lending Act is Title I of the Consumer Credit Protection Act; Title II deals with extortionate credit transactions; Title III is concerned with wage garnishment, and Title IV provides for the creation of a National Commission on Consumer Finance. For most consumer-business transactions, compliance with the law is under the general supervision of the Federal Trade Commission, which has been given part of the responsibility for enforcing Regulation Z. This regulation, which implements the Truth in Lending Act, was issued by the Board of Governors of the Federal Reserve System and is designed to tell business executives how to comply with the act. It also adds substantive requirements necessary to carry out the disclosures required by the act. One interesting provision of the regulation is that the board may exempt from federal disclosure requirements certain transactions within a state if it determines that the state law imposes substantially similar requirements and that adequate enforcement is provided. Regulation Z, however, spells out the detailed procedures creditors must follow if they decide to comply with any provisions of a state law that are inconsistent with the federal disclosure requirements.

The main purpose of the truth in lending portion of the act is to assure a meaningful disclosure of credit terms so that consumers will be able to readily compare the various credit terms available to them and to avoid the uninformed use of credit. The Truth in Lending Act is simply a disclosure law; it does not set maximum interest rates.[1] It does specify, however, that the most important credit terms—the dollar amount of the finance charge and the annual percentage rate—be disclosed to the customer.

One important amendment to this act became effective June 7, 1974, at which time the Federal Trade Commission's regulation gave buyers a three-business-day right of cancellation in home sales of consumer goods or services with a purchase price of $25 or more.

On October 28, 1974, the Depository Institutions Act was signed into law. This included a variety of amendments to the Truth in Lending Act. Among the provisions adopted were these requirements:

- Any advertisement relating to extensions of credit repayable in more than four installments without an identified finance charge must state that the cost of the credit is included in the price of the goods or services.
- A maximum limit on class action liability is set at $100,000 or 1 percent of the creditor's net worth, whichever is less.[2]
- An exemption from truth in lending disclosures for agricultural credit is allowed for transactions that exceed $25,000.

---

[1]Unfortunately, some business firms used this law as a basis to start charging interest on their credit accounts. Following is a paragraph of a letter sent by a retailer grocer to his customers: "We also must reluctantly announce that at the same time we are forced to start charging a service charge under the provisions of the Federal Truth in Lending Legislation which became effective July 1, 1969. This charge will be 9% per annum, or ¾ of 1% per month for any account not paid in full within a 30 day period." This is, of course, false and misleading, and such action should be condemned whenever it occurs.

[2]Class action is an old legal device that permits a few people with a claim against a company or an individual to join together in a single suit, representing not only themselves but also all others who have similar claims.

- Fraudulent use of a credit card to obtain money, goods, or services having a value aggregating $1,000 is made a federal crime, enforceable by the Justice Department.

Effective October 1, 1982, the Federal Reserve Board decided the most important provisions of a totally revised Regulation Z would require or allow:

1. Easier consumer waiver of rescission rights.
2. Disclosure of the effect of required deposit balances on APR (annual percentage rate) accuracy.
3. Tolerances for accuracy in the disclosure of finance charges as well as APRs.
4. Disclosure of a representative example, with respect to variable-rate loans.
5. "Bona fide" error defense to include good faith calculation, clerical errors, and printing errors.
6. Sixty days, instead of 15, for voluntary correction of unintentional disclosure errors.
7. Encouragement of early disclosure by exempting any need for additional disclosures unless the APR is increased by more than one-eighth of 1 percent.
8. Limitation of disclosures in "refinancing" to only those transactions in which an old debt is satisfied and replaced by a new obligation.

If any creditor fails to disclose information required under truth in lending or gives inaccurate information, it may be sued for actual damages (any money loss suffered). In addition, the individual can sue for twice the finance charge in the case of a credit transaction. In any successful lawsuit, the individual is entitled to court costs and attorney fees.

The Truth in Lending Act makes it fairly easy for the consumer to understand the terms creditors are offering, but it is difficult at times to estimate the dollar difference from various terms. Assume a consumer is buying a $7,500 car, puts down $1,500, and needs to borrow $6,000. Compare the three credit arrangements shown in Table 6–1.

TABLE 6–1 **Three Possible Credit Arrangements**

	APR	Length of Loan	Monthly Payment	Total Finance Charge	Total of Payments
Creditor A	14%	3 years	$205.07	$1,382.52	$7,382.52
Creditor B	14%	4 years	$163.96	$1,870.08	$7,870.08
Creditor C	15%	4 years	$166.98	$2,015.04	$8,015.04

How do these choices compare? The answer depends on what the buyer actually needs:

1. The lowest cost loan is available from Creditor **A**.
2. If the buyer is looking for lower monthly payments, he or she could get them by paying off the loan over a longer period. However, the buyer would have to pay more in total costs. A loan from Creditor B will add about $488 to the finance charge.
3. If that four-year loan were available from Creditor C, the APR of 15 percent would add another $145 to the finance charges as compared with Creditor B.

The buyer should look at all the terms before making the credit choice.

Credit Card Issuance Act—Title V of the Consumer Credit Protection Act

In October 1970 a federal law on credit card issuance became effective. Under this law, no credit card may be issued except in response to a request or application. This requirement, however, does not apply to renewals or substitutions for previously accepted cards.

On May 18, 1970, the Federal Trade Commission issued a Trade Regulation Rule on unsolicited mailing of credit cards, but it was determined that the FTC rule did not apply to banking institutions. The new law, however, applies to all card users, including banks, oil companies, and entertainment firms.

In addition to stopping the mailing of unsolicited cards, the law limits the consumer's liability on lost or stolen credit cards. After the consumer has notified the credit card company of the loss or theft of any credit card, he or she does not have to pay any unauthorized charge. Regardless of how much is charged before the missing card is reported, the most the consumer will have to pay for any unauthorized charges is $50 on each card. A card company may not collect any loss from the consumer—even the first $50—unless it can prove the following four things:

1. The card was issued at the consumer's request, the card was issued as a renewal or substitute for an accepted card, or the consumer used it at least once before it was lost or stolen.
2. The consumer was provided something on the card, such as a signature line, to identify the consumer as the authorized party to use it.
3. The consumer was notified of the potential $50 liability.
4. The consumer was notified he or she may give oral or written notification that the card was lost or stolen. The consumer must be given a means of notification, such as a telephone number, an address, or both.

Fair Credit Reporting Act—Title VI of the Consumer Credit Protection Act

This amendment to the Consumer Credit Protection Act became law in April 1971. The provisions of this act affect all grantors of consumer credit and all local retail credit bureaus. One of the major requirements on credit grantors is the provision making it mandatory for the business to inform consumers whenever credit is refused on the basis of a credit report and, further, to inform them of the name and address of the bureau making the report. If credit is denied on the basis of information received from a source other than a credit bureau, the business must inform consumers of their right to request in writing the nature of the information on which the denial was based.

The act places new restrictions on credit bureaus as to the inclusion of obsolete information in any consumer report they release; spells out the conditions under which bureaus must disclose in-file information to consumers; prescribes the procedure to follow in case of dispute about the accuracy of information contained in a report; places certain restrictions on investigative consumer reports; and sets forth the bureaus' liability in connection with their operations.

More details of the act as amended and as interpreted by the Federal Trade Commission, which has the responsibility for enforcement of the act, will be covered in Chapter 9 on consumer credit reporting agencies.

Fair Credit Billing Act

The Fair Credit Billing Act became effective October 28, 1975, as a result of an amendment to the Truth in Lending Act. The act is designed to protect consumers against inaccurate and unfair credit billing practices by credit card issuers and other "open-end" creditors. Revolving, flexible, option, 30-day, 90-day, and other types of credit accounts are included under the definition of open-end accounts if a credit card is used or a finance charge imposed. The act provides procedures for prompt resolution of billing disputes.

The major provisions of the act are as follows:

1. If a customer thinks a bill is wrong or wants more information about it, he or she should notify the creditor in writing within 60 days of the bill's mailing date. The letter should include the customer's name and account number, a statement indicating the bill contains an error, an explanation of why it is believed there is an error, and the suspected amount of the error.

2. While waiting for an answer, the customer does not have to pay the disputed amount or any minimum payments or finance charges that apply to it. The customer, however, is still obligated to pay all parts of the bill that are not in dispute.

3. The creditor must acknowledge the customer's letter within 30 days, unless the bill is corrected before that. Within two billing periods—but in no case more than 90 days—either the account must be corrected or the customer must be told why the creditor believes the bill is correct.

4. If the creditor made a mistake, the customer does not have to pay any finance changes on the disputed amount. The account must be corrected either for the full amount in dispute or for a part of that amount along with an explanation of what is still owed. If no error is found, the creditor must promptly send the customer a statement of what is owed. In this case the creditor may include any finance charges accumulated and any minimum payments missed while the bill was being questioned.

5. If the customer still is not satisfied, the creditor should be so notified within the time specified to pay the bill.

6. Once the customer has written about a possible error, the creditor may not give out information about the customer to other creditors or credit bureaus or threaten to damage the customer's credit rating. Until the letter is answered, the creditor also may not take any collection action on the disputed amount or restrict the account because of the dispute.

7. The customer may withhold payment of any balance due on defective merchandise or services purchased with a credit card, provided a good faith effort has been made to return the goods or resolve the problem with the merchant from whom the purchase was made. If the store that honored the credit card was not also the issuer of the card, two limitations apply to this right: the original amount of the purchase must have exceeded $50, and the sale must have taken place in the customer's state or within 100 miles of the customer's current address.

Creditors must provide customers with a complete statement (see Figure 6–1) of their fair credit billing rights when the customers first open an account and at least twice annually (or send a shorter version with each billing).

A creditor who fails to comply with rules applying to the correction of billing errors automatically forfeits the amount owed on the item in question and any finance charges on it, up to a combined total of $50—even if the bill was correct. The customer also may sue for actual damages plus twice the amount of any finance charges, but in any case not less than $100 or more than $1,000. Court costs and attorney fees are allowed in a successful lawsuit. Class action suits also are permitted.

Private enforcement of the act is supplemented by administrative enforcement by several federal agencies. Compliance by banks, for example, is enforced by the appropriate bank regulatory agency. The Federal Trade Commission has enforcement responsibility for all creditors not specifically assigned to other federal agencies (for example, department stores and other retailers, consumer finance companies, and all nonbank credit card issuers).

FIGURE 6–1 **Statement of Fair Credit Billing Rights**

IN CASE OF ERRORS OR INQUIRIES ABOUT YOUR BILL

The Federal Truth in Lending Act requires prompt correction
of billing mistakes.

1. If you want to preserve your rights under the act, here's what to do if you think your bill is wrong or if you need more information about an item on your bill:
   a. Do not write on the bill. On a separate sheet of paper write the following (you may telephone your inquiry, but *doing so will not preserve your rights under this law*).
      i. Your name and account number.
      ii. A description of the error and an explanation (to the extent you can explain) why you believe it is an error. If you only need more information, explain the item you are not sure about and, if you wish, ask for evidence of the charge such as a copy of the charge slip. Do not send in your copy of a sales slip or other document unless you have a duplicate copy for your records.
      iii. The dollar amount of the suspected error.
      iv. Any other information (such as your address) which you think will help the creditor to identify you or the reason for your complaint or inquiry.
   b. Send your billing error notice to the creditor. Mail it as soon as you can, but in any case, early enough to reach the creditor within 60 days after the bill was mailed to you. If you have authorized your bank to automatically pay from your checking or savings account any credit card bills from that bank, you can stop or reverse payment on any amount you think is wrong by mailing your notice so the creditor receives it within 16 days after the bill was sent to you. However, you do not have to meet this 16-day deadline to get the creditor to investigate your billing error claim.
2. The creditor must acknowledge all letters pointing out possible errors within 30 days of receipt, unless the creditor is able to correct your bill during that 30 days. Within 90 days after receiving your letter, the creditor must either correct the error or explain why the creditor believes the bill was correct. Once the creditor has explained the bill, the creditor has no further obligation to you even though you still believe that there is an error, except as provided in paragraph 5 below.
3. After the creditor has been notified, neither the creditor nor an attorney nor a collection agency may send you collection letters or take other collection action with respect to the amount in dispute; but periodic statements may be sent to you, and the disputed amount can be applied against your credit limit. You cannot be threatened with damage to your credit rating or sued for the amount in question, nor can the disputed amount be reported to a credit bureau or to other creditors as delinquent until the creditor has answered your inquiry. *However, you remain obligated to pay the parts of your bill not in dispute.*
4. If it is determined that the creditor has made a mistake on your bill, you will not have to pay any finance charges on any disputed amount. If it turns out that the creditor has not made an error, you may have to pay finance charges on the amount in dispute, and you will have to make up any missed minimum or required payments on the disputed amount. Unless you have agreed that your bill was correct, the creditor must send you a written notification of what you owe; and if it is determined that the creditor did make a mistake in billing the disputed amount, you must be given the time to pay which you normally are given to pay undisputed amounts before any more finance charges or late payment charges on the disputed amount can be charged to you.
5. If the creditor's explanation does not satisfy you and you notify the creditor *in writing* within 10 days after you receive the explanation that you still refuse to pay the disputed amount, the creditor may report you to credit bureaus and other creditors and may pursue regular collection procedures. But the creditor must also report that you think you do not owe the money, and the creditor must let you know to whom such reports were made. Once the matter has been settled between you and the creditor, the creditor must notify those to whom the creditor reported you as delinquent of the subsequent resolution.
6. If the creditor does not follow these rules, the creditor is not allowed to collect the first $50 of the disputed amount and finance charges, even if the bill turns out to be correct.
7. If you have a problem with property or services purchased with a credit card, you may have the right not to pay the remaining amount due on them, if you first try in good faith to return them or give the merchant a chance to correct the problem. There are two limitations on this right:
   a. You must have bought them in your home state or if not within your home state within 100 miles of your current mailing address.
   b. The purchase price must have been more than $50.
   However, these limitations do not apply if the merchant is owned or operated by the creditor, or if the creditor mailed you the advertisement for the property or services.

Equal Credit Opportunity Act (ECOA)—Title VII of the Consumer Credit Protection Act

The Equal Credit Opportunity Act (ECOA), effective October 28, 1975, became Title VII of the Consumer Credit Protection Act. Implementing regulations—Regulation B—have been issued by the Federal Reserve Board. The act and regulations apply to all who regularly extend or offer to extend consumer credit or who arrange consumer credit for any purpose or in any amount.

As originally passed, the Equal Credit Opportunity Act prohibits discrimination by creditors on the basis of sex or marital status. As originally written, Regulation B, implementing the act, contains partial exemptions from procedural provisions for business, securities, and public utilities creditors. These partial exemptions, however, do not exempt such creditors from the basic prohibitions against discrimination on the basis of sex or marital status. Regulation B also exempts from numerous specific procedural provisions credit issued as an incident to doing business (such as credit given by dentists, doctors, or small retailers) not obtained by use of a credit card; credit where no finance or late charge is made; and where there is no agreement making the credit payable in more than four installments.

The principal provisions of Regulation B, as originally issued, are as follows:

1. Creditors may not make statements discouraging applicants on the basis of sex or marital status.
2. Creditors may not refuse, on the basis of sex or marital status, to grant a separate account to a creditworthy applicant.
3. Creditors may not ask the marital status of an applicant applying for an unsecured separate account, except in a community property state or as required to comply with state law governing permissible finance charges or loan ceilings (effective June 30, 1976).
4. Neither sex nor marital status may be used in credit scoring systems.
5. Creditors may not inquire into childbearing intentions or capability or birth control practices or assume from an applicant's age that an applicant or an applicant's spouse may drop out of the labor force due to childbearing and thus have an interruption of income.
6. With certain exceptions, creditors may not require or use unfavorable information about a spouse or former spouse where an applicant applies for credit independently of that spouse and can demonstrate that the unfavorable credit history should not be applied.

7. A creditor may not discount part-time income but may examine the probable continuity of an applicant's job.

8. A creditor may inquire about and consider whether obligations to make alimony, child support, or maintenance payments affect an applicant's income.

9. A creditor may ask to what extent an applicant is relying on alimony or child support or maintenance payments to repay the debt. The applicant must first be informed that such disclosure is unnecessary if the applicant does not rely on such income to obtain the credit.

10. Creditors must provide the reasons for terminating or denying credit to applicants who so request.

11. No later than February 1, 1977, creditors must inform holders of existing accounts of their rights to have credit history reported in both names.

12. Creditors must, with certain exceptions, give applicants the following written notice: "The Federal Equal Credit Opportunity Act prohibits creditors from discriminating against credit applicants on the basis of sex or marital status. The federal agency which administers compliance with this law concerning [insert appropriate description—bank, store, etc.] is [name and address of the appropriate agency]" (effective June 10, 1976).

13. With certain exceptions, creditors may not terminate credit on an existing account because of a change in an applicant's marital status without evidence that the applicant is unwilling or unable to pay.

The adoption of extensive amendments to the Equal Credit Opportunity Act in March 1976 necessitated a revision of Regulation B. The statutory amendments expanded the act's prohibition of discrimination to include discrimination based on race, color, religion, national origin, age, receipt of income from public assistance programs, and the good faith exercise of rights under the Consumer Credit Protection Act. Some of the following amendments went into effect immediately, but the more important provisions took effect March 23, 1977:

1. Creditors are required to notify applicants of action taken on their applications and to provide reasons for adverse action either automatically or on request.

2. Creditors are authorized to ask about and consider an applicant's age in order to favor the applicant.

3. The statute of limitations for instituting actions under the act is lengthened from one year to two years, and the maximum award for punitive damages in a class action is increased from

$100,000 to the lesser of $500,000 or 1 percent of the creditor's net worth.

4. Creditors are authorized to differentiate among applicants on a prohibited basis such as race in connection with special-purpose credit programs.

5. Creditors are forbidden to use age in a credit scoring system unless the system is demonstrably and statistically sound and the age of an elderly applicant is not assigned a negative factor or value.

On December 29, 1976, the Federal Reserve Board issued another series of revised regulations, of which the following are the most important:

1. Creditors that rely on judgmental rather than credit scoring systems for evaluating creditworthiness are permitted to consider age to evaluate the amount and probable continuance of income levels, credit history, length of employment, and other "pertinent elements of creditworthiness."

2. A creditor that uses an empirically derived credit scoring system is permitted to consider age only if the system is "demonstrably and statistically sound." The regulation establishes standards such systems must meet in order to qualify as "demonstrably and statistically sound."

3. Even in such a sound credit system, creditors may not assign a negative factor or value to the age of an elderly applicant.

4. Creditors are barred from terminating an account or denying credit because the applicant's age makes credit insurance unavailable.

5. When adverse action (primarily denial of credit) is taken, creditors are required to meet more extensive notification requirements.

If an applicant thinks he or she has adequate proof of discrimination by a creditor for any reason prohibited by the act, the individual may sue for actual damages plus punitive damages of up to $10,000 if the violation is proved to have been intentional. Court costs, attorney fees, and class action suits also are possible.

In total, the Equal Credit Opportunity Act requires that all credit applicants be considered on the basis of their actual qualifications for credit and not be turned away because of certain personal characteristics.

Regulation Q

Federal Reserve Regulation Q established interest rate ceilings on deposits at commercial banks that are members of the Federal Reserve System. Ceilings at insured nonmember banks were set by a regulation of the Federal Deposit Insurance Corporation (FDIC) and were the same as for member banks. The Banking Acts of 1933 and 1935 were the basis of these regulations. Until 1966, there were no explicit nationwide regulations on interest and dividend rates at savings and loan associations and savings banks. In that year, legislation brought rates paid by federally insured mutual savings banks under the control of the FDIC, and rates paid at savings and loan associations that are members of the Federal Home Loan Bank Board were placed under the control of the board.

Under the provisions of the Depository Institutions Deregulation and Monetary Control Act of 1980, Regulation Q's interest rate controls ended March 31, 1986.[3]

Fair Debt Collection Practices Act—Title VIII of the Consumer Credit Protection Act

The Fair Debt Collection Practices Act, which became effective March 20, 1978, covers the collection practices of third-party debt collectors—those who collect debts for others. This law applies only to collectors dealing with individuals, not to agencies seeking payment from businesses.

The major provisions of the law are as follows:

1. Collectors may not phone debtors at inconvenient times or places. This provision forbids calls between 9 P.M. and 8 A.M.
2. If a debtor engages an attorney, the collector must deal only with the attorney.
3. The collector may not call a debtor at the debtor's place of work if it is known or suspected that the debtor's employer prohibits such communication.
4. If the collector is notified in writing that the debtor refuses to pay the debt, the collector must stop communicating with the debtor, except to describe the additional measures that are being taken.
5. The collector is obliged to give a debtor the following information in writing: the amount owed; the creditor's name; a statement that the debt amount is assumed to be correct, unless the debtor informs the collector otherwise within 30 days; a promise that if the debt is disputed, the debtor will be sent verification of the debt or a copy of the judgment entered against the debtor.

Electronic Fund Transfer Act

Electronic fund transfer (EFT) is the application of electronic technology to financial payments now made by cash and checks. While EFT is designed to displace some cash payments, it is primarily an alternative to checks.

---

[3]R. Alton Gilbert, "Requiem for Regulation Q: What It Did and Why It Passed Away," Federal Reserve Bank of St. Louis *Review,* February 1986, p. 26.

The Electronic Fund Transfer Act was passed October 15, 1978, and took effect 120 days later. The EFT Act was passed as an amendment to the Financial Institutions Regulatory and Interest Rate Control Act and provides for required disclosures, receipts, notices, and periodic statements as consumer safeguards, including penalty provisions. It prohibits both financial institutions and others from requiring a consumer to establish an EFT account, particularly the making of an extension of credit conditional on repayment by EFT or employers forcing employees to use EFT in direct deposit of paychecks. It also gives the Federal Reserve Board rule-making authority to implement its requirements and prohibitions.

Some of the key provisions of the Electronic Fund Transfer Act are listed here.

1. Permits exemptions for check verification or guarantee systems, wire transfers, purchase or sale of securities, automatic transfers from savings to checking accounts, and nonrecurring telephone transfers that are not part of a prearranged plan.

2. Allows limited consumer right to stop payment in preauthorized transfer plans.

3. Sets a $50 consumer liability limit for unauthorized transfers, except in cases of fraud, improper use by a person entrusted with an EFT card, or failure to report unauthorized use within two business days of discovering the unauthorized use. Sets a $500 liability limit for a person's failure to report a lost or stolen card within 60 days of receiving a statement.

4. Requires investigation of a reported EFT error within 10 days, along with 1 day for correction of an error, if found.

5. Permits distribution of unsolicited debit cards if a personal identification number (PIN) or access code will be provided only on written request.

6. Requires the Federal Reserve to use cost-benefit analysis, especially in relationship to paperwork for compliance, in exercising its rule-making authority. Also authorizes the Federal Reserve to modify compliance requirements for small institutions to ease their burden.

The Electronic Fund Transfer Act applies to all types of financial institutions that offer EFT services to consumers, including banks, savings and loan associations, credit unions, savings banks, finance companies, and firms that install EFT point-of-sale terminals or other similar devices.

If a financial institution fails to comply with any provisions of the EFT Act, the individual concerned may sue for actual damages (or, in the case of failure to correct an error or recredit an account, three times actual damages) plus punitive damages of not less than $100 nor more than

$1,000. If an institution fails to make an electronic fund transfer, or to stop payment of a preauthorized transfer when properly instructed to do so, the individual concerned may sue for all damages following from the failure. The individual also is entitled to court costs and attorney fees in a successful lawsuit; class action suits also are permitted.

Depository Institutions Deregulation and Monetary Control Act (DIDMCA)

On March 31, 1980, the president signed into law the Depository Institutions Deregulation and Monetary Control Act. This legislation marked the culmination of many years of effort to change some of the rules under which U.S. financial institutions operated for nearly half a century.

The provisions of this act cover a wide variety of credit activities, the most important of which are:

1. Increased the maximum coverage for all federal deposit insurance from $40,000 to $100,000.
2. Gave statutory authority for banks' automatic services for transfers from savings to checking accounts, saving and loan remote service units, and credit union share drafts.
3. Imposed federal override of state usury ceilings on residential mortgages, including mobile homes.
4. Gave authority for NOW accounts to be offered nationwide; required full reserve requirements on NOW accounts.
5. Increased the interest rate credit unions could charge for consumer loans from 12 to 15 percent.
6. Gave authority for state and national banks to charge interest on business and agricultural loans of more than $25,000 at up to 5 percentage points more than the Federal Reserve district bank's discount rate plus surcharge.
7. Gave authority to repeal Regulation Q on March 31, 1986.

Table 4–3 detailed the new powers granted to federally chartered thrifts under DIDMCA.

The Garn-St Germain Depository Institutions Act

This complex and detailed act, effective October 15, 1982, dealt with different areas of financial reform. It became a rapid step toward a deregulated financial system. At the time of passage, many observers viewed the Garn-St Germain Act as primarily a rescue operation for the savings and loan institutions and the savings banks. The act also increased the options of other depository institutions, however, and gave regulators greater flexibility in handling crisis situations in which banks and thrifts ceased to be viable.

The provisions of the act were directed toward widening the sources of depository institution funds, contributing to the removal of interest rate ceilings, permanently expanding the uses of funds and other powers, and temporarily granting regulators emergency powers to deal with current depository institution crises. Table 4–3 contains information pertinent to the most important provisions of this legislation.

This deregulation created tremendous problems for the savings and loan industry. Chapter 5 looked at the causes behind the savings and loan failures in the 1980s and at the resultant federal government actions, in the form of the Financial Institutions Reform, Recovery and Enforcement Act, which will be more fully explained later in this chapter.

Debt Collection Act

On October 25, 1982, the president signed the Debt Collection Act of 1982, allowing government agencies to report delinquent debtor information to credit bureaus and to contract with third-party collection agencies in an effort to recoup approximately $33 billion in delinquencies.

Beginning November 30, 1983, the Office of Management and Budget began requiring government agencies to comply with the Debt Collection Act of 1983 by reporting delinquent debts to credit reporting agencies. Government agencies also have to purchase credit reports on prospective borrowers.

Competitive Equality Banking Act

Federal regulatory agencies' rulings in 1987 granted commercial banks certain additional securities underwriting powers. The first of these was by the Federal Reserve, which ruled in April 1987 that banks could underwrite commercial paper, municipal revenue bonds, and mortgage-backed securities. These activities were to be conducted through nonbank subsidiaries. In July 1987, the Federal Reserve Board also approved the underwriting of securities backed by consumer receivables. However, Congress imposed a moratorium beginning in March 1987 prohibiting all federal bank agencies from granting any new nonbanking powers for one year.

This moratorium, contained in the Competitive Equality Banking Act of 1987 (CEBA), prohibited regulatory approval of any new securities, real estate, or insurance activities. The congressional moratorium ended without any legislative action on this issue, so the ban on further regulatory approvals was lifted. However, clarification of this issue is pending.

FIGURE 6–2

Type of Deposit	When the Funds Must Be Available
• Cash	The next business day after the day of deposit (certain conditions may apply—check with the institution)
• The first $100 of any deposit of checks	
• Government, cashier's, certified, or teller's checks	
• Checks written on another account at the same institution	
• Direct deposit and other electronic credits	
• Checks written on local institutions	The third business day after the day of deposit
• Checks written on nonlocal institutions	The seventh business day after the day of deposit
• Deposits made at an automated teller machine not belonging to the institution	

Expedited Funds Availability Act

The Expedited Funds Availability Act (EFA)[4] regarding holds placed on funds deposited in checking, share draft, or NOW accounts in commercial banks, savings and loan associations, savings banks, and credit unions, took effect September 1, 1988. The new law does not require a financial institution to delay a consumer's ability to use deposited funds; it only limits how long the delay may last. How quickly the funds must be available depends on the type of deposit made and on the likelihood it will be paid.

Figure 6–2 shows the longest times institutions can delay a consumer's use of deposited funds under this law.

In certain circumstances, EFA allows an institution to delay a customer's use of deposited funds longer than the usual limits. This gives

---

[4]For details of the law, see *Making Deposits—When Will Your Money Be Available?* (Washington, D.C.: Board of Governors of the Federal Reserve System, undated). Also see the Suggested Readings at the end of the chapter.

extra time to make sure a deposit is backed by sufficient funds. This longer limit may be used in the following instances:

- The customer has redeposited a check previously returned unpaid.
- The customer has overdrawn his or her account repeatedly in the previous six months.
- The customer has deposited checks totaling more than $5,000 on any one day.
- The institution has good reason to believe the check being deposited will not be paid.

If the institution uses the longer limit, it must inform the customer why it has done so and when the deposited funds will be available.

Regulation CC, a 300-page document issued in mid-May 1988, is the Federal Reserve's implementation of EFA. The regulation affects check processing, teller procedures, accounting, and data processing.

Fair Credit and Charge Card Disclosure Act

The distinction between credit card plans and charge card plans appeared in the Fair Credit and Charge Card Disclosure Act of 1988. Under this act, which was signed into law November 4, 1988, a charge card is defined as "a card, plate, or other single credit device which is not subject to a finance charge." On the other hand, a credit card is subject to a finance charge.

This new law requires that disclosures be made on applications and brochures, in mailed solicitations for credit cards and charge cards, in published advertisements for these cards, and in telephone solicitations. These regulations apply only to applications for consumer credit. Figure 6–3 shows a guide to the disclosure provisions of the law.

FIGURE 6–3 **A Guide to Disclosure Provisions**

Credit Card Issuers Must Reveal . . .	Charge Card Issuers Must Reveal . . .
• APR and how determined	• All items at left, except APR
• Balance-calculation method	• That all charges are payable on receipt of statement
• Grace period	
• Annual, transaction, and account-maintenance fees	
• Minimum finance charge	
• Cash-advance fee*	
• Late fee*	
• Fee for exceeding credit limit*	

*Does not apply to telephone solicitations.

Telephone solicitations for new accounts can be handled differently. All of the disclosures shown in Figure 6–3 (except for the late fee, cash-advance fee, and the overlimit fee) are required for telephone solicitations. Disclosures can be mailed within 30 days after a request for the card but not later than the card itself.

This new federal law is tougher than most of the state application disclosure laws in effect.

Home Equity Loan Consumer Protection Act

As was pointed out in Chapter 4, a home equity line is a form of revolving credit in which a consumer's home serves as collateral for a loan. The Home Equity Loan Consumer Protection Act (HELCPA) was enacted November 23, 1988. This law and the implementing regulations adopted by the Federal Reserve Board require extensive new disclosures to the consumer at an early stage in the loan application process.

In its explanation of home equity lines of credit, the Federal Reserve Board recommended the consumer be familiar with the following terms:

Annual membership or participation fee. An amount that is charged annually for having the line of credit available. It is charged regardless of whether or not you use the line.

Annual percentage rate (APR). The cost of credit on a yearly basis expressed as a percentage.

Application fee. Fees that are paid upon application. An application fee may include charges for property appraisal and a credit report.

Balloon payment. A lump-sum payment that you may be required to make under a plan when the plan ends.

Cap. A limit on how much the variable-interest rate can increase during the life of the plan.

Closing costs. Fees paid at closing, including attorneys' fees, fees for preparing and filing a mortgage, for taxes, title search, and insurance.

Credit limit. The maximum amount that you can borrow under the home equity plan.

Equity. The difference between the fair market value (appraised value) of your home and your outstanding mortgage balance.

Index. The base for rate changes that the lender uses to decide how much the annual percentage rate will change over time.

Interest rate. The periodic charge, expressed as a percentage, for use of credit.

Margin. The number of percentage points the lender adds to the index rate to determine the annual percentage rate to be charged.

Minimum payment. The minimum amount that you must pay (usually monthly) on your account. In some plans, the minimum payment may be "interest only." In other plans, the minimum payment may include principal and interest.

Points. A point is equal to one percent of the amount of your credit line. Points usually are collected at closing, and are in addition to monthly interest.

Security interest. An interest that a lender takes in the borrower's property to assure repayment of a debt.

Transaction fee. A fee charged each time you draw on your credit line.

Variable rate. An interest rate that changes periodically in relation to an index. Payments may increase or decrease accordingly.[5]

The Federal Reserve Board also prepared a checklist (see Figure 6–4) and recommended the consumer ask the lender for help in filing it out.

Financial Institutions Reform, Recovery and Enforcement Act

Deregulation and passage of the Financial Institutions Reform, Recovery and Enforcement Act (FIRREA) dramatically altered the savings and loan industry. Chapter 5 presented highlights of this legislation, passed on August 9, 1989. Pertinent articles relating to this law are listed in the Suggested Readings at the end of Chapter 5.

STATE REGULATION OF CONSUMER CREDIT

Until recent years, most U.S. businesses believed they could sell goods and services at one price for cash and at a higher price on time without violating the interest and usury laws.[6] This view arose from the generally accepted idea that a sale of goods and services was involved and that a loan of money was not connected with the transaction—an idea based on a judicially created doctrine that originated in England in 1774. The English court at that time ruled that the words *loan* and *forbearance* were used to designate transactions to which the usury law applied and that a sale of merchandise on time by a merchant was neither a loan of money nor a forbearance of a debt.

Legislative and court actions in various parts of the United States, however, raised pertinent but confusing questions as to the applicability of interest and usury laws to the sale of goods on a time basis. The first deviation from the time-price doctrine occurred in 1957 in the Arkansas *Sloan* v. *Sears, Roebuck & Co.* case (308 S.W. 2d 802). Here the court decided the usury law in Arkansas was not limited to finance charges on

---

[5]*When Your Home Is on the Line: What You Should Know about Home Equity Lines of Credit* (Washington, D.C.: Board of Governors of the Federal Reserve System, undated). Also see the Suggested Readings at the end of Chapter 4.

[6]At times, usury is defined as a premium paid by a consumer for the loan of money. In a stricter legal framework, usury is defined as interest in excess of a legal rate charged to a borrower for the use of money.

FIGURE 6–4 **Checklist for Home Equity Loans**

	Plan A	Plan B
Basic features		
Fixed annual percentage rate		
Variable annual percentage rate		
Index used and current value		
Amount of margin		
Current rate		
Frequency of rate adjustments		
Amount/length of discount (if any)		
Interest rate caps		
Length of plan:		
Draw period		
Repayment period		
Initial fees:		
Appraisal fee		
Closing costs		
Application fee		
Repayment terms		
During the draw period:		
Interest and principal payments		
Interest only payments		
Fully amortizing payments		
When the draw period ends:		
Balloon payment		
Renewal available		
Refinancing of balance by lender		

loans or forbearances but covered credit sales as well. In 1963 the second deviation occurred in Nebraska in the case of *Lloyd* v. *Gutgsell* (124 N.W. 2d 198), in which the court held that usury laws applied to credit sales where financing was arranged through and by a third-party finance company.

By the end of the 1960s, most states had statutes, special or regular, spelling out in detail the cash price-time price concept. In other states, the fundamental issue still involved was simply whether a finance charge or service charge should be considered an interest charge. And the confusion as to whether a revolving credit account came under the time-price doctrine further clouded the legal issue. To help reduce this confusion almost all of the states have passed specific legislation on revolving credit accounts and have specified the maximum rate that can be assessed on these accounts.

Uniform Consumer Credit Code (UCCC)

The Uniform Consumer Credit Code has been defined as:

> An Act relating to certain consumer and other credit transactions and constituting the uniform consumer credit code; consolidating and revising certain aspects of the law relating to consumer and other loans, consumer and other sales of goods, services and interests in land, and consumer leases; revising the law regulating to usury; regulating certain practices relating to insurance in consumer credit transactions; providing for administrative regulation of certain consumer and other credit transactions; imposing fees making uniform the law with respect thereto; and repealing inconsistent legislation.[7]

The new Uniform Consumer Credit Code was drafted by the National Conference of Commissioners on Uniform State Laws to replace the former code set forth in 1968. At its annual meeting in August 1974, the conference approved the code for enactment in all states. Currently 11 states (Colorado, Idaho, Indiana, Iowa, Kansas, Maine, Oklahoma, South Carolina, Utah, Wisconsin, and Wyoming) and Guam have enacted the code. The main purposes of the code are:

1. To simplify, clarify, and modernize the law governing consumer credit and usury.
2. To provide rate ceilings to assure an adequate supply of credit to consumers.
3. To further consumer understanding of the terms of credit transactions and to foster competition among suppliers of consumer credit so that consumers may obtain credit at reasonable cost.
4. To protect consumers against unfair practices by some suppliers of consumer credit, having due regard for the interests of legitimate and scrupulous creditors.

---

[7]*Uniform Laws Annotated,* Business and Financial Laws, Master Edition 7A (St. Paul, Minn.: West Publishing Co., 1985), p. 17.

5. To permit and encourage the development of fair and economically sound consumer credit practices.

6. To conform the regulation of disclosure in consumer credit transactions to the Federal Truth in Lending Act.

7. To make uniform the law, including administrative rules, among the various jurisdictions.

In the areas of consumer sales, leases, and loans, the major protective provisions of the UCCC are found in six categories: rate ceilings, disclosure of finance charges, limitations on multiple agreements between the buyer and the seller, limitation on various practices (such as default payments and balloon payments), rules governing home solicitation sales, and limitations on the creditors' remedies.

In its prefatory note describing the 1974 code, West Publishing Co. made the following observations:

> Enactment of the Code would abolish the crazy-quilt, patch-work welter of prior laws on consumer credit and replace them by a single new comprehensive law providing a modern, theoretically and pragmatically consistent structure of legal regulation designed to provide an adequate volume of credit at reasonable cost under conditions fair to both consumers and creditors. Upon its enactment, no longer would credit regulation within a State consist of a number of separate uncoordinated statutes governing the activities of different types of creditors in disparate ways.
>
> All creditors dealing with consumers would be covered by the same statute. Under this Act, the total consumer credit process—from advertising through collection—would be within the scope of regulation, with variations in the law based on functional differences in the kinds of transactions rather than on the kinds of creditors involved. Whether a consumer is financing an automobile with a sales finance company or borrowing money from a consumer finance or small loan comany, certain basic protections would apply across-the-board to safeguard the consumer.
>
> Thus the Conference has chosen to approach consumer credit in much the same way it did so successfully with respect to secured transactions under Article 9 of the Uniform Commercial Code: Function should prevail over form.

* * * * *

Events occurring after promulgation of the 1968 Text have made it desirable to revise it. Experience in the States which enacted the Code has proved that the Code works and that both consumers and creditors are pleased with it, but this experience has also turned up a few unforeseen problems of the kind that come to light only after a law has been in effect. The revision has dealt with these matters as well as with some of the variations from the 1968 Text that were enacted in several of the States.

The late 1960s and early 1970s have seen a number of important legislative and judicial developments in consumer credit. Information gained from legal services attorneys has thrown new light on the needs of poverty-level consumers, but has also revealed that those needs cannot be met solely by consumer credit legislation of general application. The National Consumer Law Center has produced a number of legislative proposals. The United States Supreme Court revolutionized debtor-creditor law in its *Sniadach* decision in 1969. Developments at both the federal level (Consumer Credit Protection Act, Regulation Z, Fair Credit Reporting Act) and the state level (Wisconsin Consumer Act) have invited a review of the U3C. Then, too, new ways of granting consumer credit appeared on the scene during this period. The concept of a nationwide credit card was in its infancy when the 1968 Text was being prepared in the 1960s; today it is a reality.

A major factor calling for a review of the U3C is the Report of the National Commission on Consumer Finance (NCCF). This landmark study, the product of three years of work by a federally sponsored Commission, is the first comprehensive examination in the United States of the whole field of consumer finance. The recommendations of the Commission reflect both objectivity and understanding of the complex consumer credit process.[8]

Uniform Commercial Code

The Uniform Commercial Code is a uniform body of rules designed to deal with all situations ordinarily arising in the handling of a commercial transaction. It was designed by the National Conference of Commissioners on Uniform State Laws and the American Law Institute. Passed at the state level, this law affects all commercial transactions.

The Uniform Commercial Code, 1962 Official Text with variations, is the law in all states (except Louisiana), the District of Columbia, and the Virgin Islands. The code is divided into 10 articles as follows: General Provisions; Sales; Commercial Paper; Bank Deposits and Collections; Letters of Credit; Bulk Transfers; Warehouse Receipts, Bills of Lading, and Other Documents of Title; Investment Securities; Secured Transactions, Sales of Accounts, Contract Rights, and Chattel Paper; and Effective Date and Repealer.

DISCUSSION QUESTIONS

1. Explain why there were no consumer credit controls before World War II
2. Discuss the arguments for and against the control of consumer credit.
3. Explain why a president of the United States might have been reluctant to invoke the Credit Control Act.

---

[8]Ibid., pp. 1–3.

4. What do you believe are the most important provisions of the Truth in Lending Act? Why did you choose the ones you did?

5. What is the main purpose of the Credit Card Issuance Act?

6. What are the main provisions of the Fair Credit Reporting Act?

7. Explain what you believe the Fair Credit Billing Act has attempted to accomplish. How successful do you believe the act has been?

8. What effect has the Equal Credit Opportunity Act had on you as a consumer?

9. What changes do you anticipate will be made in the Equal Credit Opportunity Act in the next few years?

10. What did the Fair Debt Collection Practices Act and the Debt Collection Act attempt to accomplish?

11. Explain the main provisions of the Electronic Fund Transfer Act.

12. How did the DIDMCA and the Garn-St Germain Act affect the country's financial system?

13. What did the Competitive Equality Banking Act attempt to accomplish?

14. How has the Expedited Funds Availability Act affected you?

15. Explain the main provisions of the Fair Credit and Charge Card Disclosure Act.

16. Check with three financial institutions in your community and see what effect the Home Equity Loan Consumer Protection Act has had on their operations.

17. What effect has FIRREA had on the operations of savings and loan institutions in your community?

18. Discuss what is meant by the cash price-time price doctrine.

19. What is the status of the Uniform Consumer Credit Code in your state?

20. What is the Uniform Commercial Code?

SUGGESTED READINGS

Expedited Funds Availability Act

"Alert: Expedited Funds Availability Act Now in Effect." *The Credit World,* September–October 1988, p. 32.

BROWN, ROYCE D., and ROGER J. SNELL. "Roll Up Your Sleeves, Reg CC is Coming." *ABA Banking Journal,* July 1988, p. 48.

————. "Unclear Terms." *ABA Banking Journal,* August 1988, p. 36.

BROWN, ROYCE D.; ROGER J. SNELL; and RANDLE P. HAGA. "The Exit Poll on Reg CC." *The Bankers Magazine,* March–April 1989, p. 27.

FEDDIS, NESSA. "Analyzing the Revised Reg CC." *ABA Banking Journal,* July 1988, p. 59.

HALL, DANIEL. "Life with Reg CC." *ABA Banking Journal,* October 1989, p. 118.

Fair Credit and Charge Card Disclosure Act

BOOMSTEIN, ANITA. "The Credit Card Game Just Got Tougher to Play." *Credit Card Management,* January–February 1989, p. 16.

"Credit Card Disclosure Bill Becomes Law." *Communicator,* November–December 1988, p. 1.

"Disclosure Bill Approved." *Consumer Trends,* November 5, 1988, p. 8.

FEDDIS, NESSA EILEEN. "New Credit Card Regs: 18 Questions Answered." *ABA Banking Journal,* June 1989, p. 14.

"Get Ready for New Card Disclosure Rules." *ABA Banking Journal,* December 1988, p. 20.

Also see the Suggested Readings at the end of Chapter 3.

Home Equity Loan Consumer Protection Act

See the Suggested Readings at the end of Chapter 5.

FIRREA

See the Suggested Readings at the end of Chapter 5.

Management and Analysis of Consumer Credit

Management of Consumer Credit

The Objectives or Goals of Chapter 7 Are:

1. To explain how consumer credit management is a profession.
2. To outline the basic functions of the retail credit manager, the service credit manager, and the financial credit manager.
3. To discuss the various organizations of credit executives.
4. To discuss the use of promotion in retail and service credit operations.
5. To illustrate the use of promotion in financial institutions.
6. To explain the diffusion of innovations theory and its relation to the adoption process.

Chapter 7 and the next four chapters deal with the fact that consumer credit management involves all the activities and responsibilities connected with the following: how credit operations fit into company objectives; what sources of information may be used in making the actual decision to accept or reject the credit; how to handle the decision-making process, the setting of credit limits (or lines), and the details of the credit transactions themselves; and what procedures to follow in setting collection procedures and practices involving satisfied customers.

Consumer credit management in today's credit-based economy cannot be considered as a specialized tool or as an isolated function. Instead, consumer credit management must continuously and increasingly familiarize itself with the problems, procedures, and possibilities of its credit function as an integral part of a company's total operations and as a path to potential future profits.

Experience, ability, and education are essential in consumer credit management.[1] Opportunities in this field are increasing with the expanding economy, and demands and standards of performance are rising simultaneously.

The management of consumer credit activities involves the fundamental principles of management found in all other types of operations.

---

[1]See the Suggested Readings at the end of the chapter.

Essentially, managing is the art of doing and management is the body of organized knowledge that underlies the art. For successful credit management, planning, organizing, directing, and controlling credit activities must take place in an efficient and coordinated manner. The task of credit management varies depending on such factors as the type of business, the size of the operation, the organizational framework, the ownership plan, the authority delegated to the credit executive, and the firm's overall goals and policies. These vary, of course, depending on whether the organization is a retail firm, a service organization, or a financial institution.

Consumer credit management has come a long way over the years. It has had to face the fact that to some people credit occupies a negative role in business operations. This position in which credit has found itself on various occasions often was the fault of credit people themselves. For a number of years, such negative thinking contributed to a lack of fresh and creative ideas, constructive imagination, and positive leadership. When such conditions prevail, rigor mortis tends to set in, and aspiring young people look elsewhere for positions that offer more opportunities.

Fortunately, in recent years consumer credit management has come to be recognized as the positive and constructive force that it is, and a new brand of leadership has raised credit management to the status of a profession. More than ever before, credit people as a group are demonstrating technical competence in all the important phases of credit administration.

RETAIL CREDIT MANAGEMENT

Once a retail store decides to include credit among its selling tools, it faces the tasks of establishing a credit policy to serve as the cornerstone of sound credit administration, setting up a credit department, securing the services of competent and well-trained individuals to carry out credit activities, and directing and controlling credit operations to attain sound credit management.[2]

Policy Determination

A well-managed organization operates on the basis of sound policies to guide its action. Since a policy is a course of action that will be followed over a considerable period, it is imperative that clear thinking prevail and that the problems involved and the results desired be carefully appraised before a firm decides on a consumer credit policy.

A variety of credit plans are now being used, so firms can't simply say, "We sell on credit." What type of credit plan or plans to adopt immediately becomes a vital segment of policy determination. The preceding chapters

---

[2]Assuming the retail firm decides to handle its own credit operations and does not turn over all of its credit operations to some outside credit plan, such as Visa or MasterCard.

described these various arrangements. Out of this assortment, the firm must select the one type or combination of types that best fits its business and that it believes will produce the results desired. It has been pointed out that many factors—effect on sales and profits, costs of operation, desires of customers, capital available, competition, type of goods, availability of credit information, availability of credit card plans, and legal restrictions—are involved in the firm's choice. These factors vary widely and must be analyzed separately for each type of credit under consideration.

A credit manager is entitled to a written statement of policy—a policy that should be accepted and clearly understood by the other executives of the firm. Such a spelled-out policy statement should include, at minimum, an accurate description of the types of credit plans in effect, the terms of each, the basis for accepting a customer's credit, the willingness with which it is accepted, and the relationship of credit to the store's other major policies. Some policy statements on credit are more detailed and more descriptive than the minimum. At the same time, a surprisingly large number of retail firms attempt to carry on credit activities without any specifically defined policy or with an inadequate policy.

A successful credit policy should strike a definite note for positive thinking, positive creativeness, and positive action. Often the words used in carrying out a credit policy can be of great importance in arriving at the desired objectives. Such expressions as "dunning," "delinquency," "rejected," "turned down," "problems," and so on have been contributing factors to negative thinking on the part of credit management. Positive wording can be an influential factor in positive thinking and positive action.

Basic Functions of the Retail Credit Manager

Regardless of the type of retail store involved and the type of organization under which the retail credit department operates, retail credit managers must perform certain basic functions for their department to accomplish its duties. These basic functions usually include the following:

1. Maximizing sales and profits.
2. Minimizing bad-debt losses.
3. Utilizing invested funds efficiently.
4. Cooperating with other internal and external departments.
5. Emphasizing public relations and the retention of customer goodwill.

MAXIMIZING SALES AND PROFITS. Credit should be introduced and continued in use in a retail store only as long as it increases the volume of sales and, in turn, profits. Credit is a means to an end; a store does not (or should not) accept credit in its operations unless such a policy is to the store's advantage. Of course, if asked, some retailers would reply that they are using credit simply because competition is forcing them to do so. However, this is the same as saying that unless credit were used, sales and profits in their stores would decline.

MINIMIZING BAD-DEBT LOSSES. Credit managers not only are faced with the task of using credit as a tool to sell more goods and to make more profit, but they also have to watch the trend of bad-debt losses that occur. In no way does this imply that an exceedingly low bad-debt loss automatically signifies high sales and profits and efficient credit management. In fact, an exceedingly low bad-debt loss may signify that the store is accepting only the best credit risks and in a sense is simply operating on a "deferred" cash basis. Thus retail credit managers constantly walk a tightrope. They must determine how much risk they will accept in order to expand sales and profits to a maximum and at the same time hold a tight rein over bad-debt losses. This determination will (or should) vary depending on the type of credit being accepted.

Some credit managers feel that this is only part of the story—that the real attempt is to minimize all credit expenses, which include bad-debt losses. Such an approach is realistic, but it raises the question of what are strictly credit expenses and what are general office operating expenses.

UTILIZING INVESTED FUNDS EFFICIENTLY. Once a retail store accepts credit, the transaction becomes an account receivable on the books of the retailer until the customer pays the account. In case of nonpayment, the account may be changed to a note receivable or charged off as a bad-debt loss. Also, some accounts may be sold to financial and other types of institutions.

The retail store, having invested its funds in its inventory (assuming that the store pays its own bills quickly in order to take advantage of any cash discount), thus finds that these funds are tied up in the accounts receivable representing the goods that have been bought on credit and still are owed for by customers. Thus the retail credit manager has the responsibility of handling and accounting for these invested funds—a responsibility that is just as vital and important as that of a retail buyer in deciding what inventory to invest in or that of a financial executive of the firm in deciding what kind of investment to make in order to secure a return on surplus funds.

COOPERATING WITH OTHER INTERNAL AND EXTERNAL DEPARTMENTS. The day is long past when credit managers "sat on their credit information" and refused to share data with other departments. Credit information can be used to improve the operations of the entire store because credit policy is tied in closely with all the other store policies. Thus there is an ever-present need for close cooperation between credit operations and those relating to sales promotion, merchandise returns, financing, accounting, delivery, and so on.

Likewise, retail credit managers have learned that sharing their information with credit managers of other retail firms through credit bureaus or through direct interchange helps them make better and more reliable credit decisions. Thus, directly or indirectly, credit managers are increasingly cooperating with fellow credit people in the mutual exchange of credit data.

EMPHASIZING PUBLIC RELATIONS AND THE RETENTION OF CUSTOMER GOODWILL. There are two sides to the marketing concept: profit and customer satisfaction. Thus credit management must recognize that the customer is "king" or "queen" and that credit activities must be designed to attain this goal.

Organization of Retail Credit Departments

The particular organization in any store is a product of many factors. What is suitable for a large store is impractical for a small store. Ownership and personality may also affect the type of organizational arrangement.

In small single-proprietorship stores, owners or managers are jacks-of-all-trades. In addition to other duties, they may have to supervise credit and collect slow accounts.

In a small department store, credit activities may become a staff function under the authority of a treasurer-controller.

As the department store becomes larger and more departmentalized, credit activities tend to become the responsibility of the controller, who is the head of one of the four or five major divisions. The controller, in cooperation with the credit manager, often has the responsibility for coordinating the objectives of the credit operations with the overall objectives of the firm. If a firm wants to adopt a more lenient credit policy in an effort to stimulate sales, the controller, in cooperation with the credit manager, has to translate this policy change into a new program of decision making in the credit department. Of course, the actual operating head of the credit section is the credit manager. The activities of this section may be divided into promoting, interviewing, authorizing, and collecting. Interviewing personnel gather data about credit applicants and help determine whether to accept the credit. The authorization people have the responsibility for certain phases of identification and authorization. Credit promotion may be assigned to one or more people. Those involved in collection keep slow accounts on a paying basis or stop granting credit to bad risks.

In the typical chain store organization, the controller has responsibilities similar to those of the department store controller. A major responsibility of the controller is credit. However, handling credit has become such an important function that today the top credit manager of a chain organization frequently has a staff of workers (not counting the credit staff in each store) as large as the entire controller's division of a few years ago.

Credit-Related Associations

In 1912 retail credit managers recognized the need for closer cooperation among themselves and with the organizations that furnished consumer credit data. As a result, the Retail Credit Men's National Association was formed. In 1927 the name of this trade association for retail credit granters was changed to the National Retail Credit Association. Today this association is known as the International Credit Association (ICA) and is located in St. Louis, Missouri. Through its local and district associations, it conducts a continuing program of education and service for the personnel of credit-related companies.

In an effort to raise professional standards and improve the practices of credit executives and their personnel, the International Credit Association organized a professional advancement program, and in 1958 it authorized the formation of the Society of Certified Consumer Credit Executives, now known as the Society of Certified Credit Executives (SCCE). The purpose of the society was stated as follows:

> The society was established to create a professional organization for management-level credit executives who have a common interest in improving industry operations and to advance the knowledge of its fellows through academic training, research, technical publications, seminars, and forums for the exchange of education information.
>
> To achieve this purpose, the society, as a division of the International Credit Association, will:

A. Encourage high standards of ethics and professional conduct among its fellows.

B. Develop, expand, and improve the professional skills of its fellows through the exchange of information and experience gained in practice.

C. Maintain an active clearinghouse for the collection and distribution of credit education information.

D. Broaden the knowledge and understanding of credit among its fellows and others.

E. Make its fellows available as consultants to government agencies, elected officials and others to assist in the development of credit programs and projects that are fair and equitable to the business community and to the consumer.

F. Conduct research directly related to policies and procedures in the field of credit independent of, in cooperation with, or for other associations, foundations, or business organizations.

G. Conduct such other activities as are consistent with the advancement of the purpose and objectives of the society.

The professional certification program of the Society of Certified Credit Executives has three levels: a credit associate (CA) level; an associate credit executive (ACE) level; and the highest level, certified consumer credit executive (CCCE), certified credit bureau executive (CCBE), certified collection agency executive (CCAE), and certified financial counseling executive (CFCE).

The first (CA) level in the program is open to an employee with one year of on-the-job experience in an operation granting credit, a credit bureau, a collection agency, or a credit counseling service. The second (ACE) level is the intermediate or supervisory level of recognition. The prerequisites are a minimum of three years of credit management experience at the supervisory level or above and a background of professional association membership and community activity. For the highest level of recognition—certified consumer credit executive (CCCE), certified credit bureau executive (CCBE), certified collection agency executive (CCAE), or certified financial counseling executive (CFCE)—the candidate must have a minimum of five years of supervisory and/or managerial experience in a particular aspect of credit. The candidate must also have a background of professional association membership and community leadership activity. By late 1991 the Society of Certified Credit Executives plans to incorporate into the certification process an examination on basic credit concepts and procedures in addition to the existing requirements.

The Society of Certified Credit Executives has an active awards program. The Outstanding Fellow Award is presented to the individual who has performed outstanding service on behalf of the credit industry and the SCCE. Nominees must have:

1. Active membership in the society.
2. Certification at the top level in the society.
3. A record of service as an officer, director, or committee member at the local, state, district, or international level in a professional association.
4. Evidence of continuing service to SCCE.

The SCCE Membership Award is presented to the ICA district with the highest percentage of increase in persons certified for the year.

Another organization made up of retail credit personnel is Credit Women–International. Started in 1934, this active group now has a membership of approximately 12,200 women engaged in credit activity in the United States and Canada. Edith Shaw, the founder of this association, believed its clubs would be forums for mutually helpful discussions, classrooms for a study and review of changing retail credit techniques, and sororities for social contacts and acquaintances. The clubs have been successful in developing close contact among credit women, in establishing better relations between credit managers and local credit bureaus, and in stimulating interest in the continuing education of credit personnel.

A third organization of retail credit personnel is the National Retail Merchants Association's Credit Management Division. This association includes department, specialty, dry goods, and apparel stores among its members. Since 1934, when it was established, the Credit Management Division of the association has furnished a special research service to the credit managers of member stores. Through meetings, surveys, and publications, this division constantly works to keep its members up to date on new developments and changing techniques in the retail credit field.

SERVICE CREDIT MANAGEMENT

Service credit has become an important segment of the consumer credit field in regard to hospital credit, medical and dental credit, and legal credit arrangements. The increasing age of the American consumer has brought greater need for service credit in these areas. Medicare and Medicaid have met some of the financial problems of the aging population, but many American consumers have recognized the need for private, supplemental insurance to help meet these increasing expenses. Those who decide not to obtain this supplemental coverage must make their own financial arrangements or simply do not pay debts incurred for such services.

There is little basic difference between retail stores and service concerns—such as accountants, lawn service people, plumbers, roofers, carpenters, automobile repair people, contractors, home maintenance individuals, financial consultants, and so on—in the management of credit activities. Usually, the size of the service establishment is small, the type of ownership is the independent proprietorship, and the owner serves as the credit executive, the credit analyzer, and the collector. Generally, credit accepted in the service operation is for a relatively short period. However, more and more service firms are using installment and revolving credit plans.

MANAGEMENT OF CONSUMER CREDIT ACTIVITIES IN COMMERCIAL BANKS

Consumer Installment Credit

Effective management of installment credit in a commercial bank involves a wide variety of complex skills and tasks. In addition to the fundamental management tasks, the installment credit manager should:

- Analyze the department's basic structure and organization to identify areas for improvement.
- Develop appropriate policies and techniques for operating efficiently.
- Establish and maintain good relationships with other departments.

- Understand and explore various marketing strategies so the department can satisfy consumer needs effectively.
- Carefully recruit and train personnel.

Installment credit departments in most commercial banks, regardless of size or services offered, generally perform four major functional activities: business development, credit determination, operating functions, and collections. Figure 7–1 is a simplified chart that reflects the typical functions of an installment credit department.

The business development section identifies the community's needs for bank services and develops and implements installment credit programs to meet these needs. The credit determination section reviews and evaluates applicants and makes the final decision. The operating functions group does credit investigation, maintains records and retrieves information required for credit decisions, and determines loan discount schedules. Finally, the collection section works to make sure the department maintains the lowest delinquency and loss rates consistent with bank policy. Variations in operations occur depending on whether the bank emphasizes direct lending, indirect lending through the buying of dealer paper, or some combination of the two.

Professor Lon L. Mishler made the following comments about installment loan activity in commercial banks:

> The basic flow process begins with solicitation of existing customers or inquiry about a possible loan. . . . As the deregulation of this industry has progressed, many credit grantors find themselves offering the same basic set of products. Increasing emphasis is being placed on marketing and sales efforts by employees who come into contact with customers.
>
> The next step involves the actual application. It is at this point that legal compliance becomes so very important. Many banks, for example, are currently trying to decentralize the application-taking process by having more personal bankers and other platform workers take applications instead of loan officers. . . .

FIGURE 7–1 **Organization of Installment Credit Department**

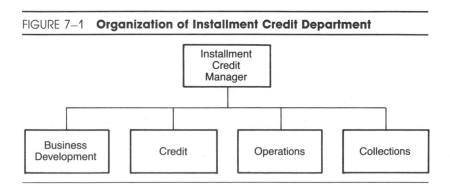

The next step in the granting flow process involves various screen techniques and/or calculations. . . .

* * * * *

The screening activities are often undertaken to determine if further investigation is warranted. Beyond this point, the expenditures for an actual investigation begin to tally up. It is better to turn down a client early in the process than to complete an expensive investigation and eventually end at the same point of turn-down. One expenditure arises, for example, when the credit bureau report is obtained in the next step. Mention should be made that most lenders are currently on-line with the credit bureaus at this point, and the reports are printed out at terminals in the bank buildings.

Next, direct inquiries are made to verify residence, verify employment, and get current ratings from listed credit references. Other calls, of course, may be made to check out inquiries, derogatory reports, and other information found in the credit bureau report.

After the investigation and decision is complete, the loan closing occurs. . . . APR and other disclosure forms must be provided for. The various security agreements (CC forms) must be signed and perfected. And the opportunity exists to do valuable credit counseling by instructing the borrower to call the lender if any problems develop in making prompt payments.

The loan has been made, but various control measures are now used to "watch" the loan. In the more sophisticated retail computer systems, programs actually monitor payments to automatically adjust credit lines up or down. Other programs attempt to predict bankruptcies and other collection problems before they occur. Within the financial institutions, delinquency and other watch lists are generated for employees to monitor the repayment process.

Finally, collection activities must be implemented, in varying degrees, to ensure that funds will be repaid. . . .[3]

Installment credit departments have altered their organization structure considerably in recent years. The past years have seen changes in credit products and services, more advanced computer capabilities, and influential demands from employees for more satisfying work.

Bank Credit Cards

If a commercial bank operates a bank credit card plan, another officer is usually in charge of this operation and is responsible for its management, including soliciting retail and service concerns to become members of the plan, encouraging consumers to use their bank credit cards at participating firms, and all the internal operations of approving customers'

---

[3]Personal correspondence with Professor Lon L. Mishler, Northeast Wisconsin Technical College, January 1990.

purchases, billing, collecting, ensuring legal conformity, and improving customer satisfaction and goodwill.

Decisions must continually be made as to how bank funds may be used to meet the needs of consumers and businesses and make the best return for the bank. Thus division of funds between commercial loans, regular consumer installment loans, bank credit card operations, home equity loans, and long-term home mortgage loans requires constant consideration by executive management. Changes in the banking industry have been widespread in the past decade, and more changes are inevitable.

ORGANIZATIONS OF MANAGERS OF FINANCIAL INSTITUTIONS

Most of the associations described in this section devote a considerable portion of their efforts to raising the educational background of credit management personnel so they will continue to improve, recognize, and adopt new developments and techniques.

The American Bankers Association (organized in 1875) is a national organization representing more than 93 percent of U.S. banks and more than 99 percent of the nation's banking resources. This association has carried out a diverse program designed to meet the many different needs for education as a basis for career development in the banking field. As part of the association's educational program, the Installment Lending Division of the ABA has prepared a variety of manuals on the important aspects of installment credit policies and procedures. Many banks also found that they needed further assistance. As a result, a correspondent bank program on installment credit was inaugurated. This program encouraged larger city banks to make their specialized knowledge and experience in this field available to their correspondents.

The American Bankers Association also has been active in establishing, developing, and promoting an off-duty banking educational program offered by the American Institute of Banking (AIB). The institute sponsored its first classes in 1902 and was the first formal educational program of its type directed toward the education of a large adult group. One of the most important areas covered in this program is that of installment credit.

Hundreds of additional educational programs for bankers are available each year, covering many areas and carrying a variety of titles. A number of these programs are called "banking schools," and the American Bankers Association maintains an up-to-date listing of resident banking schools, classified by broad category. Some state banking associations sponsor banking schools primarily designed for local bankers, while other associations concentrate on conferences, clinics, and other shorter programs.

Other financial associations include the American Financial Services Association and the Consumer Bankers Association (CBA). In May 1971, consumer finance companies, sales finance companies, and industrial banks, through their respective trade associations, joined forces into one organization. This organization has established a school for the personnel of its member firms; the school is held at Marquette University and is known as the Consumer Credit Institute. Likewise, the Consumer Bankers Association has established its School of Consumer Banking to raise the standards of credit management among its members.

The Credit Union National Association, Inc. (CUNA), is the national confederation of U.S. credit union leagues. It provides legislative, public relations, research, educational, and developmental support for the national credit union movement. By joining a league, credit unions become affiliated with CUNA.

The United States League of Savings Institutions serves the savings and loan business and the public interest by furthering thrift and home ownership.

ORGANIZATION OF MANAGERS OF RETAIL CREDIT BUREAUS

The Associated Credit Bureaus, Inc. (ACB), is the national association of retail credit bureaus.[4] It offers its members such widespread benefits as interbureau reporting rosters, standardized reporting forms, trade publications, national public relations, educational services, credit bureau research, special information reporting services, and annual meetings and conventions.

ORGANIZATION OF MANAGERS OF COLLECTION SERVICES

The American Collectors Association (ACA) was organized in 1939 and is an international organization of professional collection services. It is the world's largest organization of debt collection services. Its international voluntary membership serves more than 11,000 communities throughout the United States, Canada, and over 100 other nations.

Membership in ACA signals clients that their collection agency subscribes to high operating standards. ACA members serve credit grantors by contacting consumers with past-due accounts and counseling them on ways to repay their debts. ACA is made up of 44 state or multistate units.

ACA publishes *Collector* magazine, which updates members monthly on developments in the collection industry. ACA is organized into three departments: public affairs, insurance, and public relations.

The ACA Education Program consists of separate schools. Each school is designed to be presented as a one-day seminar so that students can improve their knowledge without a great time commitment. Some schools also are available as half-day seminars in conjunction with unit meetings.

The schools are divided into three groups:

---

[4]These are discussed in detail in Chapter 9.

1. Collector track schools:
   Fair Debt Collection Practices Act School
   Professional Telephone Collectors Techniques School
   Communications and Collections School
   Employee Motivation School
   Skip-tracing School
2. Sales track schools:
   Sales and Marketing School
   Creditors' Seminar School
   Public Relations School
   Public Speaking School
   RFPs, Proposals, and Contracts School
3. Management track schools:
   Professional Liability School
   Top Managers' Seminar
   Human Resources Management School
   Legislative Action School
   Managing for Profit School
   Managing the Computerized Collection Office
   Supervisory Practices for Collection Agencies

The education department also offers a number of self-paced training programs designed for use in the collection office.

THE CREDIT RESEARCH CENTER

The Credit Research Center (CRC) was established at Purdue University in 1974. Headed by Dr. Robert W. Johnson, the center was launched with the stated purpose of compiling, analyzing, summarizing, and disseminating information affecting all aspects of the consumer credit industry. The major direction of the center's activities are fourfold:

1. To look into the future issues of "consumerism."
2. To identify strategic problems common to various segments of the industry.
3. To provide hard, impartial research data and analysis for responsible decision making by credit grantors, legislators, and the courts.
4. To broadly communicate research findings relevant to important credit problems.

MANAGING PROMOTION IN CREDIT OPERATIONS

No magic formula exists for the successful use of promotion in credit operations. Necessary ingredients include timing, place, message, and form as well as an ample budget.

The continued success of retail firms, service concerns, and financial institutions reflects their ability to respond rapidly to changing conditions and to provide the broadest range of profitable products and services to the greatest number of people. However, consumers not only must be made aware of these products and services, but they also must be convinced they will personally benefit.

Diffusion of Innovations

For years behavioral scientists in many areas have been studying how consumers react to new products and services. In their studies, they have used the term *diffusion of innovations* to describe the process by which a new product or service spreads from its source to ultimate users or adopters. The diffusion process is directly related to the adoption process—the process whereby an individual moves from unawareness of a product or service through five distinct steps: (1) awareness, (2) interest, (3) evaluation, (4) trial, and (5) adoption or rejection.

1. Awareness. At this stage, sometimes called exposure, individuals are exposed to the new product or service but lack complete and full information about it. Here individuals are not yet motivated to seek further information, even though they are aware of the innovation. Some studies, however, point out that information about new ideas often does not create awareness, even though individuals may be exposed to this information, unless the individual has a need that the new product or service promises to solve.

2. Interest. Here individuals become interested in the new product or service and decide to seek additional information about it. They are beginning to look favorably on the innovation in a general way but have not yet considered it in terms of their own situations. The function of this stage is primarily to increase the individual's information about the new product or service. Here information is actively sought, whereas at the former stage the individual merely listened or read about it.

3. Evaluation. Here individuals go through a form of mental trial in that they compare the advantages of the innovation with the disadvantages. If the advantages are greater, they then will decide to try the new product or service. The trial itself (the next stage) is distinct from the decision to try the innovation. Since the innovation carries a risk to individuals, they are in need of some reinforcement at this stage to convince them that they are thinking correctly. Such reinforcement will probably come from the advice and suggestions of friends rather than from mass communication messages.

4. Trial. At this stage, individuals actually use the innovation on a small scale in order to determine its applicability. The main function of this stage is to demonstrate the innovation in the individual's own situation and to determine its usefulness for possible complete adoption. At this trial stage, individuals may seek specific information about the method of using the innovation.

5. Adoption or Rejection. At this stage, individuals may decide to continue the full use of the innovation, or they may decide to reject it (actually rejection may occur at any stage in the adoption process). Many products or services never become successful because customers are not made aware of them or because consumer interest is not sufficiently stimulated.

The diffusion process is a social process by which an innovation moves from those individuals who use it first to all possible adopters within a community. Behavioral scientists tell us that customers do not adopt a new product or service as one homogeneous group. Instead, they form heterogeneous groups segmented by the degree of their receptivity to the innovation.

In his book *Diffusion of Innovations,* Everett M. Rogers provided a five-way classification of potential users: (1) innovators, (2) early adopters, (3) early majority, (4) late majority, and (5) laggards.[5]

INNOVATORS. Innovators are venturesome, willing to accept the risks of trying new products or services, and therefore likely to try almost any innovation. They are of the highest social status, wealthy, and young. They have relatively little effect on other groups, however, because of their almost indiscriminate adoption of innovations.

EARLY ADOPTERS. This group consists of people who are respected in their communities, have a reputation for intelligent use of new products or services, and are very important in new product or service marketing because of their influence on later adopters. If early adopters accept an innovation, the early majority will follow along. If they do not, the innovation is destined for failure.

EARLY MAJORITY. This category will adopt new products or services but first must deliberate about them. The people in this category will consider adoption only after their peers have adopted the innovation.

LATE MAJORITY. Skeptical of new ideas, this group needs the overwhelming pressure of public opinion before it will adopt the product or service.

---

[5]Everett M. Rogers, *Diffusion of Innovations* (New York: Free Press, 1962).

LAGGARDS. This group has been called traditional in that it will adopt the new product or service only after the innovation has been around long enough to be thought of as tradition.

The adoption process and the diffusion process have many implications for credit operations. For example, credit managers must decide whether they want to focus their future marketing efforts on getting current users to use certain services more often or to pitch their marketing strategy to obtaining new users. If they decide on the latter, they must realize that the lifestyles of today's nonusers differ considerably from those of current users. A change in strategy will undoubtedly be required, and new forms of advertising and other types of promotion will probably have to be used in order to entice persons with these new lifestyles to use certain services.

Promotion in Retail Credit Operations

Retail credit sales come from three sources: new account solicitation, which may include new customers or cash customers that are converted; reactivation of accounts that have become inactive; and sales of more merchandise to present credit customers.

Stimulating profitable credit sales is an important but often neglected function of credit management. Credit transactions are becoming so common that firms often ignore solicitation. Credit managers need to apply the principles of salesmanship to this key function of the credit department. Building the number of active accounts takes on significance when we evaluate the reasons for losing credit customers.

SHOULD CREDIT CUSTOMERS BE SOUGHT? The proportion of sales volume directly attributable to credit customers varies considerably from store to store. Although many retail stores do not sell on credit, one-third to one-half of all retail sales are made on credit. Many merchants, particularly those selling very high-quality or prestige merchandise, report that credit sales represent 80 percent or more of their total sales volume. Department stores typically have a heavy volume of credit sales; many do more than half of their volume on credit.

Why are credit customers important to a retail store? Properly used, credit can increase a store's sales volume. But, to increase profits, the costs of opening, controlling, and collecting the accounts must be kept low relative to the store's gross margin. Merchants need to analyze the pitfalls of consumer credit and adopt wise credit policies to overcome them. Credit customers increase sales volume because as a group they (1) retain close ties to stores where they have an active account, (2) have less resistance to price, and (3) tend to buy higher-quality merchandise.

Credit customers appear to form a habit of buying at stores where they have credit privileges. Cash customers are restricted in the amount of their purchases and hence can be more easily attracted by other merchants' offers. Conversely, credit customers become well acquainted with the offerings of the stores in which they buy on credit. They become better acquainted with the personnel, are susceptible to the quality of merchandise offered, and are generally regarded as preferred customers. These factors create goodwill and a high degree of loyalty in the customer's mind. The ease and convenience of a credit account and the attitude displayed by the store toward credit customers help develop a credit-customer group that habitually trades with the same merchants. The average sale to the credit customer is likely to be larger because credit customers are less price conscious. They don't have to be as cautious as cash buyers, who fear the embarrassment of being short of funds. The credit customer can make purchases anytime and, not having to wait for payday, is susceptible to the dictation of desires. The credit customer is a *selected* customer. During the selection process, less able customers are excluded.

Even though credit customers are a distinct advantage to a store, problems naturally arise. Within a profitable credit-customer group, some accounts will become inactive for a variety of reasons. Customers die, trade elsewhere, move, meet with misfortune, have fluctuations of income, and change from credit to cash customers of their own volition. Slightly more than 10 percent of accounts become inactive each year. This ratio agrees with department store experiences, but may be high or low depending on the type of vendor. So sales promotion must be applied continuously in order to build a profitable credit-customer group.

HOW TO GET NEW RETAIL CREDIT CUSTOMERS. New credit customers may come from any of three sources—present cash customers, potential customers residing in the store's trade area, and new residents in the community.

Present cash customers are a frequent source for new credit accounts. A cash customer may have already gained a favorable impression of the store, its personnel, and its quality of merchandise and services. Aggressive credit managements have been alert to the possibility of converting cash customers to credit customers. In doing this, they adopt methods of account solicitation that make it more convenient, pleasant, and complimentary for the customer. Much of the effort in converting these customers is applied in the retail store. Salespeople can be of valuable assistance here and perhaps are the principal force in motivating a good cash customer to open a credit account. At times, they are financially reimbursed for opening new credit accounts. Salespeople need to be trained in the art of account solicitation. They must have a thorough understanding of the store's policy with regard to the various credit plans as well as an appreciation of how a credit account can better serve their customers. Trained salespeople can then answer customers' questions more intelligently and approach them more effectively.

Newspapers, direct mail, and credit account promotion within the store play important roles in sales promotion plans. Advertising for new credit accounts is most effective when patterned after the store's overall

merchandising policies. High-quality stores use refined and carefully selected copy to reflect the quality, luxury appeal, and prestige expected.
Merchandisers who appeal to a large cross section of the population solicit
credit customers with more aggressive and showmanlike techniques. Ven
dors who make no class appeal and promote price to a greater extent than
quality usually sell credit terms in the same manner.

Altering credit terms and installments can help sell some merchandise. Durable good sales are frequently stimulated during periods of low
business activity by giving customers more convenient terms. "No down
payment," "no payments until next year," and extending installments over
more months are typical ways to build installment sales. Promotions of
this type are timed to attract credit accounts when the incentive to buy on
credit might otherwise be low.

Employee campaigns and contests can produce new credit customers.
Credit departments can develop their own employee contests or turn to a
sales promotion consulting firm. The advantage of professional assistance
lies in its ability to overcome contest inequities, set reasonable and profitable goals, and assume responsibility for successful execution of the contest. Despite the cost of professional help, management may gain a more
successful campaign and avoid most of the problems associated with promotions of this type.

New families in the community are one of the most productive sources
of new credit customers. A new family usually has immediate and long-
run needs in establishing a comfortable and convenient place to live.
Home furnishings, floor coverings, housewares, and small and large appliance departments should be particularly alert for such new customers.
Most communities have organized methods to find new families and determine whether they own or rent their homes. In soliciting a new family,
retailers should quickly extend an invitation to visit the store and use its
services. Otherwise, this valuable source of credit business may be lost to
other stores that made their approach sooner. Whatever the method used,
it should help the new family associate with the store before competitors
have the same opportunity.

The consumer credit industry is increasingly aware of the expanding
teenage market. Long before they acquire full-fledged credit status, teenagers have woven the use of credit (their own or their parents') into their
social and economic lives. Teenagers today have an active influence in determining tomorrow's kind of credit climate.

HOW TO GET MORE SALES FROM RETAIL CREDIT CUSTOMERS. A
well-organized and successful campaign for promoting credit sales must
also solicit present credit customers. Present credit customers need almost
continuous solicitation to keep their accounts active and sufficient in dollar
volume.

Inactive credit accounts come about for a number of reasons. The
customer may have had an unfortunate experience with the store's

merchandise or sales personnel; may be buying in some departments but not others; may be shopping elsewhere; may have been the subject of an aggressive collection method or have an overdue account; or may become indifferent for no apparent reason. Of the various methods for increasing credit sales, direct mail and personal solicitation can be effectively employed in some of the above situations.

When the reason for inactivity rests with the collection department, the problem is with the store and not with the customer. If the collection effort is too strict or too lenient, the store will lose sales. A high percentage of customers are concerned about their indebtedness, particularly if they are delinquent. If the sole objective of a firm's policy is a high collection ratio, customer goodwill may be destroyed. To achieve a high collection ratio without evaluating its effect on sales volume is shortsighted. On the other hand, a collection policy that is too lenient is likely to result in many overdue accounts. In either case, sales are lost. Customers who harbor resentment and ill will are of no greater sales potential than customers who are overburdened with debt.

An analysis of credit customer accounts reveals many interesting facts to management. Some accounts have a large amount of activity, and their average monthly credit purchases contribute importantly to the store's total sales volume. Some reveal trading on a storewide basis. Customers who concentrate their purchases with a particular store and in many of its departments are regarded as "ideal" credit customers. Many accounts, however, won't measure up to this ideal. Some customers use their accounts on rare occasions, make few purchases, and charge small amounts. Other accounts remain inactive for months and even years for no apparent reason. Building credit sales volume through occasional customers or those with inactive accounts is a difficult promotional problem. Direct mail, personal solicitation at the home, and solicitation by salespeople in the store are the most effective methods in these cases.

Too frequently, the sales force fails to appreciate the significance of credit as a selling tool. If salespeople understand management's attitudes on credit and the reasons for having various credit plans, they may be more willing to emphasize credit to their customers. They must, however, be told that (1) consumer credit is a selling tool without which the business would suffer; (2) no customer should ever be embarrassed in the use of credit, but encouraged and complimented on this wise choice; (3) there are reasons for all the various credit plans, and a plan is available for almost every customer; (4) free and easy credit is not the policy of management, but sound beneficial credit plans are offered to good customers; and (5) they should learn more about the wise use of credit and how different credit plans are coordinated with the store's merchandising policies.

SELLING CREDIT TO THE RETAIL ORGANIZATION. To achieve the greatest total benefit from a credit department, its purpose, objectives, and policies must be coordinated with and understood by all segments of the firm. Top management must know what contribution the credit department makes to the total firm effort. The credit department can increase sales volume, the volume from present customers, and the number of credit customers. In accomplishing these objectives, the firm expects a profit. Profit is one of the aims of a credit department, too, as it functions to increase sales volume at low operating costs. As another store service, credit stimulates goodwill and sales volume. The objectives of the firm and the aims of the credit executive are the same.

For greatest effectiveness, the credit department function must be coordinated with all other departments and personnel—merchandising, store operations, sales promotion, control, and personnel divisions. Total effectiveness can be nullified by malfunctioning of any segment. The credit department is particularly susceptible to malfunctioning because of the false impressions, prejudices, and traditions associated with consumer credit. These problems cannot be overlooked when credit management strives for complete cooperation with other departments.

Promotion in Service Operations

This area is often overlooked. For years it was against tradition to promote medical, dental, and legal services. In fact, if these professionals

FIGURE 7–2

Source: *St. Petersburg Times,* May 27, 1990, p. 40. Reprinted with permission.

attempted to promote, primarily by advertising, their activities, the American public reacted negatively. This is no longer true, however, and such promotion has become common. See Figure 7–2 for an example of an advertised legal service, Figure 7–3 for a medical health and nutrition clinic, and Figure 7–4 for a medical knee center.

Consumers using these services may pay their bills by cash or personal check, various insurance plans, different credit card plans, or different types of credit plans between the service institutions and themselves. No accurate statistical data of this increasing drain on consumers' income exists, but such outlay is growing each year.

Promotion in Financial Institutions

The continued success of financial institutions reflects their ability to respond rapidly to changing conditions and to provide the broadest range of profitable financial services to the greatest number of people. For example, in recent years commercial banks have developed the concepts of one-stop banking and full-service banking to meet the needs and wants of the American public, while at the same time recognizing their responsibility to their depositors and to their stockholders.

FIGURE 7–3

Source: *St. Petersburg Times*, June 4, 1990, p. 3. Reprinted with permission.

FIGURE 7–4

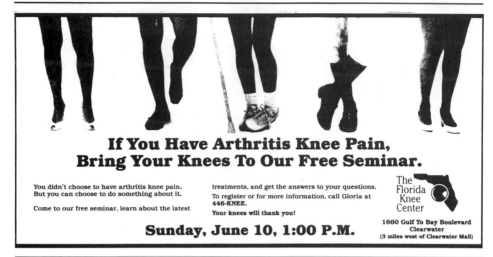

If You Have Arthritis Knee Pain, Bring Your Knees To Our Free Seminar.

You didn't choose to have arthritis knee pain. But you can choose to do something about it.

Come to our free seminar, learn about the latest treatments, and get the answers to your questions. To register or for more information, call Gloria at 446-KNEE.

Your knees will thank you!

The Florida Knee Center

1660 Gulf To Bay Boulevard
Clearwater
(3 miles west of Clearwater Mall)

Sunday, June 10, 1:00 P.M.

Source: *St. Petersburg Times,* June 4, 1990, p. 2. Reprinted with permission.

Today's consumer, while better educated and more knowledgeable than predecessors, finds himself or herself in the midst of an ever-increasing array of confusing plans and terms. And these plans are not only from commercial banks, but also from retail concerns, service establishments, credit unions, savings and loan associations, small loan companies, credit card companies, and many more. In the past, the American consumer thought of a particular retail store when he or she planned to buy a desired product. And the consumer's mind immediately turned to a particular financial institution when he or she wanted to deposit or borrow money. Decisions were relatively easy. But times have changed.

More recognition is being given to the trends that have forced commercial banks—and other financial institutions—to acknowledge the growing importance of marketing (including promotion and advertising) and its application to internal operations and outside activities. These trends include the following:

1. Changes in federal and state laws.
2. Changes in public attitudes.
3. Increased education and changing attitude of financial executives and other personnel.
4. Addition of popular consumer credit services.
5. Improved promotion, including advertising and publicity.
6. Recognition of increasing social responsibility to the consuming public.

FIGURE 7–5

JUMBO CD's $100,000 AND OVER

Premium Rates
Safety Plus Security

44 Offices
Call **539-9770** for
current rates

 **Barnett Bank
of Pinellas County**

All Barnett Banks are members of FDIC

Source: *St. Petersburg Times,* June 4, 1990, p. 23. Reprinted with permission.

7. Improved operations (standards, practices, and systems).
8. More inviting atmosphere in the financial structures.

Financial management today uses advertising as one of the basic tools in its total marketing program. Figures 7–5 and 7–6 are illustrations of advertising being used by financial institutions. Financial advertising brings to the public's attention news and information of a financial service and the reasons for its use. Advertising is most effective when it points out a need or creates a desire, at the same time explaining how the financial service will satisfy that need or desire.

FIGURE 7–6

MAKE UP TO $25,000 IN LESS THAN AN HOUR.

Introducing one of the fastest, easiest home equity loans known to man. The Homemade Loan.

All you have to do is pick up the phone. Answer a few simple questions. And in 59 minutes or less,* we'll have an answer for you on an equity loan of up to $25,000.

From start to finish, the whole application process is easier.

And a lot less time-consuming.

What's more, it's even less expensive. There are no points to worry about. And the interest payment, in many cases, is fully tax deductible.

For more information, simply give us a call at 407-283-8950 and ask about our Homemade Loan.

Or come by the Glendale Federal Bank office in Stuart and apply in person if you like.

We'll make it worth your time.

GLENDALE FEDERAL BANK F.S.B.

The way a bank should work™

*May be subject to title search, income verification and appraisal. Applies to owner-occupied, single-family residences. ©1990 Glendale Federal Bank, F.S.B.

Source: *St. Petersburg Times*, May 29, 1990, p. 11A. Reprinted with permission.

Advertising produces the best results if it is (1) informative, (2) persuasive, (3) persistent, and (4) timely. Regardless of the medium used, each advertising message should meet the following objectives: (1) gain attention, (2) inform or explain clearly, (3) present the benefits of the service to the prospective consumer, (4) urge action on the part of the consumer, and (5) achieve identification.

Managing consumer credit activities in retail firms, service concerns, and financial institutions is a difficult, time-consuming operation if the desired results are to be attained.

DISCUSSION QUESTIONS

1. What is meant by the term *credit management?*
2. Distinguish between retail credit management, service credit management, and credit management in money-lending institutions.
3. What are the basic functions of the retail credit manager? Describe each function clearly.
4. Explain the function of "utilizing invested funds efficiently."
5. How can the retail credit manager cooperate with other internal and external departments?
6. Describe the organization of the credit department in a typical large independent department store.
7. What is the International Credit Association? Trace its history and its activities.
8. If you were working in the field of consumer credit, why should you be interested in knowing about the Society of Certified Credit Executives?
9. What are the purposes of the Credit Women–International?
10. Explain the activities of the Credit Management Division of the National Retail Merchants Association (NRMA).
11. Check with your local bankers and discover the courses being offered by the AIB in your community.
12. Check with a collection agency in your community and discover why it is, or is not, a member of the American Collectors Association, Inc.
13. From what sources do retail credit sales come?
14. Do you believe that credit customers should be sought by the retail credit department of a firm? Why or why not?
15. Why do some stores prefer credit customers to cash customers?
16. Explain why credit accounts may become inactive.
17. What is meant by the expression "The alteration of terms and installments"?
18. Why are newcomers in a community often one of the most productive sources of new retail credit customers?
19. How do you suggest getting more sales from retail credit customers? How are stores in your community doing this?

20. What procedures are the leading department stores in your community following to reactivate "dead" retail credit accounts? Do you believe these procedures have been successful?

21. What can be done to encourage salespeople to appreciate the significance of retail credit as a selling tool?

22. What is meant by the term *diffusion of innovations?*

23. What are the five steps normally found in the adoption process?

SUGGESTED READINGS

CLARK, WILLIAM M. "Controlled Architecture—Building Your Own Credit House." *Business Credit,* May 1988, p. 23.

Consumers and Credit—Bankruptcy . . . A Ten-Year Mistake. St. Louis, Mo.: International Credit Association, undated, pp. 1–4.

KRAMER, DONALD B. "Most Common Errors of Credit Executives." *The Credit World,* May–June 1988, p. 28.

LAWRENCE, DAVID B. "Here Come the Credit Risk Managers." *Credit Card Management,* January–February 1989, p. 52.

Solving Credit Problems. Washington, D.C.: Federal Trade Commission, 1985, pp. 1–8.

8

Basis of the Credit Decision

The Objectives or Goals of Chapter 8 Are:

1. To set forth the credit qualities that should be investigated.
2. To outline the information the credit applicant supplies to the credit analyst.
3. To summarize the advantages and disadvantages of direct inquiry.
4. To discuss the information supplied from in-file facts.
5. To explain the differences between facts and opinions.
6. To point out the importance of economic conditions in decision making.
7. To explain the differences between investigation and verification.

A credit investigation is undertaken to aid in making a sound credit decision. It is not an activity to satisfy curiosity; it has a much more immediate and practical purpose. The investigation does not seek information for the sake of information; it seeks information pertinent to the specific credit decision and sufficient to assure that the decision will fall within the probability range for payment set by the operating policies. Credit analysts must thus ask themselves what they need to know in order to make a proper credit decision. The information pertinent to that decision then becomes the guide to the type of information sought. The extent of the investigation should similarly be governed by the degree of certainty necessary for a proper decision.

At all times credit executives also must weigh the value of additional information about a credit prospect against the cost of obtaining such information. They thus are faced on the one hand with needing sufficient information from which to make valid decisions and on the other hand with paying the cost of acquiring that information. Credit managers must carefully decide when they have enough information from the viewpoint of completeness, accuracy, and cost. They then have the continuing problem of determining when the information obtained is really enough.

FACTS OR OPINIONS

Credit investigators must keep in mind that references, informants, and credit reporting agencies do not create credit information. Credit information is created only by consumers, who are constantly creating information about themselves through their conduct and activities. Such information becomes credit information when it can be used to predict a credit applicant's future behavior; it is important credit information when, if known, it would influence a credit decision.

Some information may be of that objective and verifiable type known as fact; much is likely to be of that somewhat subjective type known as opinion. Opinions may rest on facts or prejudice or imagination. An opinion may be soundly based on objective facts and be the result of careful and logical analysis of the situation; it may be as sound as or sounder than the opinion the analyst would form after making an analysis, but it is still the opinion of someone else.

Operating credit managers who substitute the opinions of others for their own judgment have permitted these outsiders to become credit managers for their departments and have themselves become merely credit clerks. Opinion should be given consideration in one respect only, that is, when the opinion of others is itself treated as fact and is so used in the analysis. Such opinions, soundly based or not, do affect the quality of the credit performance expected and so have a place in the analysis. But these opinions should be regarded as simply a category of facts and in the analysis should be weighed in the same way as any other factual category.

When making a credit investigation, the credit executive should do so in a manner designed to collect facts rather than opinions. Questions should be phrased to induce informants to reply factually rather than with loosely stated opinions or judgments. Informants should be asked questions they are likely to know the answer for. Asking informants questions about things they are not likely to know is an invitation to reply with opinion rather than fact and is also a temptation not to reply at all.

WHAT TO INVESTIGATE

When the question of what to investigate is raised, it has been the custom to repeat the "four horsemen" of credit: character, capacity, capital, and conditions.[1] These so-called four Cs of credit have been cited by thousands of credit managers and have been discussed over and over again in textbooks, articles, and speeches.

Figure 8–1 gives an example of the questions asked on a credit application form of a retail department store chain.

---

[1] Some credit managers, especially in the finance field, consider collateral as a fifth C. Others, however, consider collateral as simply part of capital.

FIGURE 8–1

JBYRONS **Application for Credit**

To find out about changes in the information in this application for credit you may call us at 1 (800) 821-1111.

☐ **Individual Account**—Is based on your own creditworthiness. Complete sections A, B, C, E. You may designate one authorized user, for whose payments you will be responsible, by writing only his/her name and relationship in section D.

☐ **Joint Account**—Is based on the creditworthiness of both parties, and both will be responsible for payment. Complete sections A through E.

FOR OFFICE USE ONLY

STORE | ASSOCIATE NO. | DATE

Section A—Tell us about yourself

LAST NAME | FIRST NAME | MIDDLE | SOCIAL SECURITY NO. | AGE

HOME ADDRESS | APT. | NO. OF DEPENDENTS (EXCLUDING SELF)

CITY | STATE | ZIP CODE | HOME PHONE ( )

☐ OWN ☐ RENT FURNISHED ☐ ROOM & BOARD ☐ RENT UNFURNISHED ☐ LIVE WITH PARENTS ☐ MOBILE HOME ☐ OTHER | TIME AT THIS ADDRESS YRS. MOS. | MONTHLY RENT OR MORTGAGE PAYMENT $

PREVIOUS HOME ADDRESS (IF LESS THAN 3 YEARS AT PRESENT ADDRESS) | TIME AT PREVIOUS ADDRESS YRS. MOS.

NAME AND ADDRESS OF NEAREST RELATIVE NOT LIVING WITH APPLICANT | RELATIVE HOME PHONE ( )

Section B—Tell us about your employment

BUSINESS OR EMPLOYER | TYPE OF BUSINESS | BUSINESS PHONE ( ) EXT.

BUSINESS ADDRESS | CITY | STATE | ZIP CODE | EDUCATION ☐ ELEMENTARY ☐ HIGH SCHOOL ☐ COLLEGE ☐ POST COLLEGE

POSITION OR TITLE | HOW LONG WITH THIS EMPLOYER YRS. MOS. | ANNUAL SALARY $

IF SELF EMPLOYED, PLEASE GIVE YOUR BUSINESS BANK REFERENCE AND ACCOUNT NUMBER

PREVIOUS BUSINESS/EMPLOYER (IF LESS THAN 3 YEARS AT THIS JOB) | HOW LONG YRS. MOS. | POSITION OR TITLE

OTHER INCOME: ALIMONY, CHILD SUPPORT, OR SEPARATE MAINTENANCE INCOME NEED NOT BE REVEALED IF YOU DO NOT WISH TO HAVE IT CONSIDERED AS A BASIS FOR REPAYING THIS OBLIGATION. | ANNUAL AMOUNT $ | SOURCE

Section C—Tell us about your credit and banking relationships

BANK REFERENCES—NAMES OF BANKS AND BRANCH LOCATIONS | ACCOUNT NUMBERS

1. | | ☐ CHECKING ☐ SAVINGS ☐ NOW/MONEY MKT. (CHKG. & SAVINGS)

2. | | ☐ CHECKING ☐ SAVINGS ☐ NOW/MONEY MKT. (CHKG. & SAVINGS)

CREDIT REFERENCES—ACCOUNTS WITH DEPT. STORES, BANK CARDS, OIL COMPANIES | ACCOUNT NUMBERS | BALANCE

1. | | $

2. | | $

3. | | $

OUTSTANDING LOANS (NAME OF CREDITOR/CREDIT UNION/FINANCE COMPANY)

OTHER CREDIT REFERENCES | HAVE YOU EVER HAD ANOTHER JBYRONS ACCOUNT | YES | NO | ACCOUNT NUMBER (IF KNOWN)

Section D—Information regarding joint applicant or authorized user

LAST NAME | FIRST NAME | MIDDLE | SOCIAL SECURITY NO. | AGE

BUSINESS OR EMPLOYER | TYPE OF BUSINESS | BUSINESS PHONE ( ) EXT.

BUSINESS ADDRESS | CITY | STATE | ZIP CODE | EDUCATION ☐ ELEMENTARY ☐ HIGH SCHOOL ☐ COLLEGE ☐ POST COLLEGE

POSITION OR TITLE | HOW LONG WITH THIS EMPLOYER YRS. MOS. | ANNUAL SALARY $

RELATIONSHIP TO APPLICANT | OTHER INCOME: ALIMONY, CHILD SUPPORT, OR SEPARATE MAINTENANCE INCOME NEED NOT BE REVEALED IF YOU DO NOT WISH TO HAVE IT CONSIDERED AS A BASIS FOR REPAYING THIS OBLIGATION. | ANNUAL AMOUNT $ | SOURCE

Section E—Please sign below and on reverse side

I (We) understand that you may investigate my (our) credit record and may report information concerning the credit experience of the Account for individual and joint accountholders and authorized users to consumer reporting agencies and others.

If Applicant signs on behalf of Joint Applicant, Applicant represents that he or she is authorized to make this application and enter into this Agreement on behalf of Joint Applicant.

I (We) agree to terms of the **RETAIL INSTALMENT CREDIT AGREEMENT** on reverse side.

X APPLICANT'S SIGNATURE | DATE

X JOINT APPLICANT'S SIGNATURE | DATE

Courtesy of JByrons

What is character? It may be defined as an intangible sum of personal attributes, and these attributes are revealed indirectly rather than directly. The elements entering into character may be personal, and thus be concerned with family situation or personal habits and attitudes such as drinking, gambling, and so forth. They may include virtues such as honesty and courage, or the reverse. Character also may be inferred or revealed by business or professional conduct, such as payment of obligations, tendency to make unwarranted claims or to return goods without cause, attitude toward obligations, speculative tendencies, and respect for the rights of others. Being an inward thing—in effect an intangible personal quality—character can be correctly inferred only to the extent that it is revealed. In some respects good character may be the result of never having faced adversity.

"How has this individual paid a bill with you?" is a better question than "What is the individual's credit reputation?" It becomes an even better question by asking the year the account was opened, the balance now owing, the highest recent credit, and whether payment is in 30, 60, or 90 days or longer. Attitude toward obligations is better revealed by a question asking whether the person makes unjustified claims or acts in accordance with the contract than by general questions about attitude toward obligations.

Character is an inward thing that probably cannot be measured or appraised exactly by even those most intimately associated with an individual, certainly not by the measures available during a credit investigation. Nevertheless, the credit investigation can come closer to interpreting this quality correctly when it asks for specifics that can be ascertained and gives each of these specifics its proper weight in the analysis. Although they can be summarized under the heading of character, they are investigated by inquiries about specific and tangible elements. Evidence that is largely factual can be gathered about the specifics. Seeking evidence about the general obtains only opinions.

Likewise, capacity is a credit quality that rests on a widely diverse group of specific conditions. In a narrow sense, it may mean simply the ability to pay a specific dollar obligation when it is due. But in a much wider sense, it measures the sources of the ability to pay. Such information is often summarized under the headings of income and employment. While capacity is essentially a question of an individual's earning power, income by itself should not be the sole determinant of an individual's ability to secure credit. The average consumer makes expenditures and meets contractual payments out of current income rather than from accumulated savings. As a result, unless the credit investigator can get a fairly complete picture of previous commitments, the firm may find that it is dealing with an individual whose income is earmarked by debts previously incurred—regardless of the volume of income involved. Thus the adequacy of income should be tested by comparing it with the individual's current contractual obligations and present expenditure pattern.

In the field of consumer credit, the credit analyst gives more weight to specific qualities that reveal an individual's character and capacity than to those that reflect an applicant's capital. To the credit manager, capital means the financial strength of the risk in case the applicant is unable (because of decreased capacity) or merely unwilling (because of certain traits of character) to pay obligations when due. While the quantity of the capital is important, the credit manager is also interested in the nature of the assets in which the capital is invested and the proportion invested in each. While many consumers have relatively little capital to be used as a backstop, information about the capital they do possess (home ownership, household furnishings and personal effects, bank accounts, stocks and bonds, real estate holdings, and so forth) may help add to the information already available and give the credit manager better insight into the individual's true character and capacity.

CREDIT QUALITIES TO INVESTIGATE

The preceding discussion illustrated the basic issue raised earlier. Character, capacity, and capital may not be clearly defined classifications of the credit investigation, and specific bits of information must be sought to have the raw material for proper analysis of each of these. Thus it seems desirable to list the personal credit qualities that appear to be the most essential to investigate. It is not claimed that the credit qualities listed here include all of the qualities it might be desirable to investigate. It is not even claimed that they are all of the most important credit qualities, but it is believed that these are the credit qualities that in the great majority of cases are most pertinent to the credit decision. If the investigation reveals information about these qualities, there should be sufficient information at hand to enable the analyst to reach a sound credit decision. And as will be seen later, a suggested method of analysis of the individual's credit rests on these very same credit qualities.

Obviously, some information will be more important in certain cases than in others. Credit judgments are individual judgments. A credit prospect—the subject of each investigation—is an individual. The weight given to various credit qualities must necessarily conform to the circumstances of the individual case, so the importance of certain qualities rises and falls in the particular case. The need for and importance of these credit qualities also vary with the circumstances surrounding the credit offered by the consumer—whether it is to initiate the establishment of credit for the first time or to secure added credit on an existing account.

Most large firms process a tremendous volume of credit requests. To do so, they often try to categorize credit applicants. They may use scoring guides as a preliminary screening device and turn down applicants who do not attain some minimum score. Credit (or sometimes called *numerical*) scoring plans are gaining acceptance in evaluating credit risk. Credit scores typically assign points to characteristics on the application and on the credit bureau report. These points are then totaled to determine the score for the credit applicant. Each firm using such a system will have its own schedule of assigning points and setting the number required for credit acceptance. Credit scoring does have limitations, however. Although preferred by many credit executives, it still is not a perfect predictor of creditworthiness.

This topic will be discussed in more detail in connection with decision making in Chapter 10.

Payment Record

The most important point to consider here is not whether the consumer can pay but whether *he or she will pay.* Some individuals have the money available to meet credit payments, but they simply do not want to or will not let go of that dollar. Character thus plays a vital role.

Payment record usually is considered the most important factor revealed in an investigation. It shows not only the manner of the consumer's payments and thus is important as a predictor of behavior, but it shows past payment habits as well. The credit investigation should seek facts as to the type or types of account involved, the amount currently owed, the amount past due, the highest recent credit, and the manner of payment. The manner of payment should be stated specifically—pays in 30 to 60 days, pays in 90 days, and so forth. The adjectives *prompt, good,* and *slow* can have a variety of meanings; 60 to 90 days may be considered prompt by one firm and slow by another, depending on the type of account involved.

The date of the experience also should be established. This is especially important when an applicant has a varied record containing some derogatory data. It is important to know whether the profit and loss charge-off, or the collection through judgment, or the paid only after call by collector, or the repossession occurred in the past or is the most recent experience. Investigators draw a different conclusion if the bad record occurred some time ago and the applicant has a good current record than from the opposite sequence.

Income

Since most customer debts are to be paid from income, investigation of income is essential. The amount of income and its regularity should be ascertained, and the probability of its continuance estimated. Income must be evaluated relative to the demands placed on it by individual or family needs and obligations. Such demands may include prior commitments, such as retail installment purchases, installment cash loans, home mortgage loans, contingent obligations that result from agreeing to be a comaker on another person's loan, and alimony payments.

There are differences of opinion as to how income should be defined. For instance, should investigators count overtime pay, unemployment compensation, bonuses, and profit-sharing plans?

Under the Equal Credit Opportunity Act of 1975, creditors cannot discount part-time income but can examine the probable continuity of an applicant's job. In addition, creditors can inquire about and consider whether obligations for alimony, child support, or maintenance payments affect an applicant's income. Likewise, creditors can ask to what extent an applicant is relying on alimony, child support, or maintenance payments to repay a debt, but applicants must first be informed that such disclosure is unnecessary if they do not rely on such income to obtain the credit.

Employment

Employment is probably the principal source of income, so it should be investigated along with income. Employment information should include, at minimum, the name of the employer, the type of business, and the applicant's position. In addition, investigators should try to determine how long the individual has been employed by the current employer. When employment has been for a comparatively short time (three to five years is considered short), it may be advisable to investigate previous employment. Investigation of credit prospects who are self-employed should be especially extensive, since applicants themselves supply their own employment and income information.

Residence

Check of residence is first of all a routine verification of identity. In addition, residence information should show the length of time at the present location and any previous residences in the last three to five years. If necessary, these facts can be used as the basis for more intensive investigation in the local area. They also may reveal certain information about the other credit qualities of the applicant. In addition, the investigation should determine whether the applicant owns or rents the property. If the applicant owns the property, the investigator should determine the amount of the mortgage and the mortgage payment. The amount of the rent and the manner of payment should be determined if the property is rented.

Marital Status

This area has been the subject of a great deal of controversy in recent years. Marital status used to be considered a significant quality in most consumer credit transactions, so credit investigators sought this information. Now, under the Equal Credit Opportunity Act of 1975, a firm cannot refuse to grant a person credit on the basis of sex or marital status. However, the firm can inquire about a person's marital status to determine the rights and remedies available under applicable state law. Likewise, a firm can ask for joint signatures from a married couple on a credit application in order to comply with state legal requirements involving liens, garnishments, or wage-assignment situations. In addition, a husband and wife can ask for separate credit accounts voluntarily, in which case the accounts cannot be combined for billing purposes.

Under the provisions of the Housing and Community Development Act of 1974, lenders are required to consider the combined incomes of husband and wife in extending mortgage credit.

It should be noted that the three types of acceptable terms are *unmarried, married,* or *separated.* Previous terms such as *divorced* or *widowed* are no longer acceptable.

Age

With the young, the investigation should establish that the applicant is of legal age to sign a contract. With most investigations, age is not an important credit quality. However, extremes of youth or age can be crucially important, and in these instances this quality is considered. Under the 1976 amendments to the Equal Credit Opportunity Act, creditors can ask about and consider an applicant's age in order to *favor* the applicant; they can't use age in a credit scoring system unless the system is demonstrably and statistically sound and the age of an elderly applicant is not assigned a negative factor or value. Some studies show that credit risk generally decreases with increasing age, especially above 50.

Reserve Assets

In only a few instances should a creditor rely on reserve assets for payment of a consumer credit obligation. In most cases reserve assets are additional surety that both debtor and creditor hope will not be needed. In some cases, especially with older customers who are living on a pension or on income from investments, the investigation of reserve assets may be essential in order to establish capacity to handle the credit obligation. However, when considering property ownership, analysts must avoid attributing a positive effect to something that, when carefully analyzed, should be given negative weight. Homeowners may have such heavy mortgage payments that, instead of the home being an addition to reserve assets, they are earmarking too much current income to assume any additional commitments. Analysts need sufficient detail about such situations to assure they don't overlook a recurring heavy payment.

Equity in Purchase

An additional credit quality, equity in the purchase, is a major concern, especially in consumer installment purchasing. Strictly speaking, equity in purchase concerns the market value of the property. The presence of this market value, as it is available to the creditor through the terms of the lien contract, may raise an otherwise unacceptable credit risk well above the level of acceptability. When the equity is large and is maintained by the amount and frequency of payment, the major question may not be, "Will the individual pay?" but instead, "Can the property always be found and retaken?" To the extent that the equity is smaller and is not maintained by the amount and frequency of payments, personal credit qualities should be analyzed more carefully and should be correspondingly stronger to attain equal safety. In addition, the proportion of the initial equity may reflect the attitude of the buyer toward the obligation. When the initial equity or ownership is large, through a significant down payment, it will appear that the buyer fully intends to complete the contract as agreed, and by inference this is indicative of character. Conversely, when the initial equity is small, it may reflect an attitude of possession through rental rather than a sense of ownership—by inference, a potential adverse indication of character.

Collateral

While collateral, an element of capital, is lacking in most retail and service credit transactions, it is often involved in cash loans made to consumers. Collateral—some tangible asset owned by the individual and offered as additional security to the lending institution—is another credit quality to consider. The value of the collateral varies, however. Commercial banks prefer savings, bonds, stocks, and insurance policies, followed by real estate, automobiles, mobile homes, boats, aircraft, and further down the list various types of unsecured collateral.

INFLUENCE OF ECONOMIC CONDITIONS

While credit analysts today can obtain a fairly reliable picture of an individual through a series of specific questions, they always face the problem of interpreting this information in terms of the current economic environment.

Knowledge of the economic environment must be part of the analyst's general knowledge. Some of this knowledge is secured by keeping abreast of local business and community affairs. Are strikes affecting certain industrial plants, or are such labor curtailments imminent? Is the weather too dry or too wet, and is the farmer going to be hurt as a consequence? Are some area businesses expanding rapidly and thus drawing new residents to the community? In other words, credit analysts must know "How's business?" in their own line, other lines, their own town, and surrounding towns.

Perhaps a knowledge of this short-term economic climate is easier to acquire than the ability to predict the long-run economic picture. The background, experience, and training of credit managers will be vital factors in how they look at the future. Their political beliefs, their international views, their financial position, and their experiences in attaining their present position also color their views.

Consistent with their short-run and long-run views of economic conditions, credit managers must interpret the information they obtain about a credit applicant and make the decision to accept or to reject the credit.

INVESTIGATION AND VERIFICATION

The investigation is a way to develop information not at hand. It is also a way to verify the information supplied. Most credit verifications start when an individual asks for credit and supplies some personal credit information. If an investigation is necessary, good credit managers use it to verify some of the information supplied by the applicant. The credit executive may confirm some of the most vital and important facts that the credit applicant has supplied by seeking information concerning them from several separate and independent sources. The credit executive has to judge how much verification is needed based on the overall quality of the credit applicant and the manner in which the information supplied coincides with that already known or easily secured.

HOW MUCH TO INVESTIGATE

A credit investigation is undertaken to aid in making a sound credit decision. Now the credit analyst must face the problem of how much investigation is needed because every bit of information secured through investigation costs money. Credit executives always walk a tightrope in deciding when they have enough information in terms of completeness, accuracy, and cost.

Insufficient information can cause errors in judgment. Inadequate information means that some pertinent fact was not known that, if known, would have caused a different decision. An even more probable cause of error is that the analyst either did not give sufficient weight to certain information or, even worse, interpreted the information incorrectly.

Extensive investigations cost money and take time; meanwhile, a decision is delayed, with consequent loss of customer goodwill and friction with salespeople. The accumulation of additional bits of information is costly, whether the information is purchased from sellers of credit information or developed by direct inquiry. Unless the information is used and useful, it is not worth what it costs in either time or money. A mass of factual data may actually interfere with the analysis and decision. The sheer extent of the evidence may result in its being incorrectly weighed or misinterpreted. More pertinent evidence may be buried under a mound of nonpertinent detail.

The proper time to seek information from the applicant and to decide on the extent of the investigation is when credit is first requested. Should the information supplied by the applicant be unusually complete and the case appear sound, the investigation may be limited to payment experience only or to payment experience and verification of employment and residence. Should the information obtained from the applicant be limited, as it sometimes is with retail charge accounts, the investigation should be much more extensive. It is possible for an account to be accepted without investigation—that is, without verification of the information supplied by the applicant. In some cases the "no-investigation" policy is advisable. In fact, creditors often waste money verifying the obvious. It is far better to save investigation budgets for cases where there is a probability of trouble.

It is not desirable to gather all possible evidence before reaching a credit decision. The desirable amount is just the amount needed to reach a decision based on the judgment and experience of the credit executive.

WHERE TO INVESTIGATE

What, then, should the investigation do? It should seek specific information from sources that possess the information or can get it accurately, completely, quickly, and at minimum cost. (Note: Since information is the raw material of credit decisions, the credit managers must *give* as well as *get* credit information. The best basis for a full flow of clear credit information is an exchange of information.)

Information sources that are accurate, complete, speedy, and reasonably priced include credit applicants themselves, direct investigation, in-file ledgers, and consumer credit reporting agencies, banks, and other miscellaneous sources.

INFORMATION SUPPLIED BY APPLICANTS

Most consumer credit investigations start with information supplied by the applicant. Such information, which should be regarded as a part of the credit investigation, is treated as statements of fact that have not been verified. Certain facts may be accepted without verification; others may be verified through further investigation. The first credit decision is whether any facts need to be verified. If so, a second and third determination becomes necessary: which facts to verify through investigation and what sources to use.

The Credit Application

Most credit departments use a formal procedure for opening a credit account—usually involving an application for credit signed by the applicant. The signature is a vital factor in credit transactions (particularly installment and revolving credit) that result in a finance charge. Figure 8–2 shows a warning to the buyer before signing a credit agreement. The

FIGURE 8–2

NOTICE TO THE BUYER: 1. DO NOT SIGN THIS CREDIT AGREEMENT BEFORE YOU READ IT OR IF IT CONTAINS ANY BLANK SPACE. 2. YOU ARE ENTITLED TO A COMPLETELY FILLED IN COPY OF THIS CREDIT AGREEMENT. 3. KEEP IT TO PROTECT YOUR LEGAL RIGHTS.

A copy of this Retail Installment Credit Agreement, along with information regarding your rights to dispute billing errors, will be delivered with your credit card if this application is approved.

_____

Vice President
Chief Financial Officer

X_____

Buyer Signs   Date

X_____

Co-Buyer Signs   Date

---

extent of the information sought varies considerably, depending on the firm's policies, the type of account requested, and the customs of the trade and region.

THE CASE FOR A FORMAL APPLICATION.   Those who argue for a formal application procedure have a number of reasons for their view.

Complete information can best be obtained by asking the applicant to fill out a comprehensive application. Certain facts are likely to be known only to the applicant and, unless asked for at the time the account is opened, such facts may not be developed through the investigation; in fact, they may not even be sought. It is more economical to obtain such leads from the applicant and simply verify them through further investigation if verification is considered desirable.

An applicant may have a more serious attitude toward credit obligations if the application is rather formal and complete. When the opening of the account seems a rather minor or routine procedure, the applicant may not be properly impressed with the value of credit or with the necessity of conforming to the terms established. When an account is opened, the creditor has an unusual opportunity to educate the customer in proper credit behavior. First, people tend to esteem anything that is difficult to get. If they are impressed with the fact that not everyone can receive credit, they are more likely to regard the account as a privilege and not as a right. Second, the best time to establish sound habits or behavior patterns is with the first transaction. Payment according to terms is a habit that should be established early. By making the opening of the account a formal process, applicants take the first step toward establishing good credit habits. Third, the customer is more likely to respect a credit department that operates in a careful and businesslike manner. A casual attitude toward the acceptance of credit is likely to impress the customer as being typical of all operations of the business. The best way to achieve this serious attitude is to combine a personal interview between the credit prospect and the credit manager with the completion of the credit application blank.

THE CASE FOR AN INFORMAL APPLICATION.   Some firms strongly believe that informality in credit investigation is more desirable. They point out that credit is just as much a sales promotional tool as advertising. Advertising is easily viewed and read by customers; thus credit should be made easily obtainable. A brief application form for credit may be made readily accessible to the credit prospect at various convenient points. The prospect simply fills out the short form, mails it to the credit department, and usually has no direct contact with anyone in the credit department.

Such stores count on the idea that the vast majority of people pay their accounts. Thus, they reason, why bother to spend money on interviews. To these stores it appears better to conserve funds to secure payment from those who don't live up to the provisions of the credit arrangement. Of course, such a view presupposes that the credit department will know exactly when and how to go after reluctant payers and that these collection efforts (which cost money) will be successful.

WHAT INFORMATION SHOULD BE REQUESTED?   The bare minimum is simply identifying information—the name and address of the credit prospect. For the sake of accurate posting to the account, it is desirable to secure the complete given name and at least the middle initial. Some retail stores handle thousands of accounts and may have a number of Carl Johnsons, Edward Smiths, or Mary A. Smiths. A minimum addition to the identifying information is place of employment and occupation, as well as the length of time at each (and previous address or employment if less than one year). A rule-of-thumb often used in retail credit departments is that residence and employment should be known for five previous years. Such information enables investigators to develop facts or verify information over a sufficient period of time to satisfy doubts as to current behavior. Investigation at earlier places of residence or employment may then be undertaken whenever there is reason to question the consistency of credit behavior. With the widespread movement of population, such caution seems indicated.

Sales finance companies and cash lenders commonly use more detailed application blanks than retailers.[2] They may need the additional

---

[2] See Figure 8–3 for a detailed application form from a commercial bank. Figure 8–4 is a less detailed form used by a retail firm.

FIGURE 8–3 **Detailed Form Used by a Commercial Bank**

FIRST FLORIDA BANK

Select the accounts for which you are applying by checking the appropriate boxes. Flex-Line Home Equity Line of Credit and Mortgages require special applications. See your Personal Banker for details.

☐ Flex-Line Executive ☐ Redichek ☐ Gold MasterCard ☐ Visa Gold ☐ Regular MasterCard ☐ Classic Visa ☐ Installment Loan

Credit Amount Request $_____ Purpose _____

☐ NEW ACCOUNT ☐ REISSUE REQUEST ☐ REQUEST LIMIT INCREASE

ACCOUNT NUMBER ☐☐☐☐☐☐☐☐☐☐☐☐☐☐☐☐☐

IMPORTANT:
Read these Directions before
completing this Application
and Check Appropriate Box

☐ If you are applying for an individual account in your own name and are relying on your own income or assets and not the income or assets of another person as the basis for repayment of the credit request, complete only Sections A, C, D.
☐ If you are applying for a joint account or an account that you and another person will use, complete all Sections, providing information in B about the joint applicant or user.
☐ If you are applying for an individual account, but are relying on income from alimony, child support, or separate maintenance or on the income or assets of another person as the basis for repayment of the credit requested, complete all Sections to the extent possible, providing information in B about the person on whose alimony, support, or maintenance payments or income or assets you are relying.

SECTION A — APPLICANT

FIRST NAME	MIDDLE NAME	LAST NAME	SOCIAL SECURITY NUMBER	BIRTHDATE MO/DAY/YR

STREET ADDRESS | APT. NO. | CITY | STATE | ZIP | HOW LONG? | HOME PHONE NO. ( )

☐ OWN ☐ RENT ☐ BUYING ☐ LIVE W/RELATIVES | PREVIOUS STREET ADDRESS | CITY | STATE | ZIP | HOW LONG? | NO. DEPENDENTS: Ages:

EMPLOYED BY | HOW LONG? | ADDRESS | MONTHLY SALARY $ (GROSS)

BUSINESS PHONE ( ) | POSITION | PREVIOUS EMPLOYER | ADDRESS | CITY | STATE | HOW LONG

NAME OF NEAREST RELATIVE NOT LIVING WITH YOU | STREET ADDRESS | CITY | STATE | PHONE NO. ( ) | RELATION

BANK WITH | BRANCH | ☐ CHECKING ACCOUNT NO. | ☐ LOAN
| | ☐ SAVINGS ACCOUNT NO. | ☐ CREDIT CARD

ALIMONY, CHILD SUPPORT, OR SEPARATE MAINTENANCE INCOME NEED NOT BE REVEALED IF YOU DO NOT WISH TO HAVE IT CONSIDERED AS A BASIS FOR REPAYING THIS OBLIGATION.

OTHER INCOME Source(s) of other income: | ALIMONY, CHILD SUPPORT, SEPARATE MAINTENANCE, RECEIVED UNDER:
$ | ☐ COURT ORDER ☐ WRITTEN AGREEMENT ☐ ORAL UNDERSTANDING

SECTION B — JOINT APPLICANT

FIRST NAME	MIDDLE NAME	LAST NAME	SOCIAL SECURITY NUMBER	BIRTHDATE MO/DAY/YR	HOME PHONE NO. ( )

STREET ADDRESS | APT. NO. | CITY | STATE | ZIP | HOW LONG? | NO. DEPENDENTS: AGES:

☐ OWN ☐ RENT ☐ BUYING ☐ LIVE W/RELATIVES | PREVIOUS STREET ADDRESS | CITY | STATE | HOW LONG? | RELATIONSHIP TO APPLICANT IF ANY

EMPLOYED BY | HOW LONG? | ADDRESS | MONTHLY SALARY $ (GROSS)

BUSINESS PHONE ( ) | POSITION | PREVIOUS EMPLOYER | ADDRESS | HOW LONG

NAME OF NEAREST RELATIVE NOT LIVING WITH YOU | STREET ADDRESS | CITY | STATE | PHONE NO. ( ) | RELATION

BANK WITH | BRANCH | ☐ CHECKING ACCOUNT NO. | ☐ LOAN
| | ☐ SAVINGS ACCOUNT NO. | ☐ CREDIT CARD

ALIMONY, CHILD SUPPORT, OR SEPARATE MAINTENANCE INCOME NEED NOT BE REVEALED IF YOU DO NOT WISH TO HAVE IT CONSIDERED AS A BASIS FOR REPAYING THIS OBLIGATION.

OTHER INCOME Source(s) of other income: | ALIMONY, CHILD SUPPORT, SEPARATE MAINTENANCE, RECEIVED UNDER:
$ | ☐ COURT ORDER ☐ WRITTEN AGREEMENT ☐ ORAL UNDERSTANDING

SECTION C — OBLIGATIONS AND REFERENCES

PLEASE LIST BELOW ALL DEBTS, INCLUDING ANY ALIMONY OR CHILD SUPPORT. YOU MAY ALSO LIST ANY ACCOUNTS (PAID OUT OR OPEN) WHICH YOU WISH THE BANK TO CONSIDER AS A CREDIT REFERENCE. USE SEPARATE SHEET IF NECESSARY.

NAME OF COMPANY OR BANK	ACCOUNT NUMBER	PRESENT BALANCE	MONTHLY PAYMENT	ACCOUNT IN NAME OF
RENT OR MORTGAGE PAYABLE TO				☐ APPLICANT ☐ JOINT APPLICANT ☐ OTHER
AUTOMOBILE FINANCED BY YEAR: MAKE:				☐ APPLICANT ☐ JOINT APPLICANT ☐ OTHER
YEAR: MAKE:				☐ APPLICANT ☐ JOINT APPLICANT ☐ OTHER
				☐ APPLICANT ☐ JOINT APPLICANT ☐ OTHER

Are you co-maker, endorser, or guarantor on any loan or contract? Yes ☐ No ☐ If "yes"

For whom? _____ To whom? _____

Are there any unsatisfied judgments against you? Yes ☐ No ☐ If "yes" to whom owed? _____

Have you been declared bankrupt in the last 10 years? Yes ☐ No ☐ If "yes" where? _____ Year _____

The applicant and joint applicant, if any, hereby request a Revolving Line of Credit, affirm that everything stated in this application is true and correct, understanding that the Bank will retain this application whether or not it is approved, authorize the Bank to check the above credit and employment history and to answer questions about the credit experience with the account, and agree to be obligated by the terms and conditions of the Agreement and Disclosure required by Federal Law as amended from time to time delivered to them. Should a Line of Credit be issued and without limiting the generality of said agreement they specifically agree, jointly and severally to pay for credit extended through the use of the card or any other credit device and all costs incurred in collecting that indebtedness, including a reasonable attorney's fee.

(Seal) (Seal)
_____ _____ _____ _____
Applicant's Signature | Date | Other Signature (where Applicable) | Date

FIGURE 8–3 *(concluded)*

FILL OUT SECTION D ONLY FOR UNSECURED CREDIT REQUESTS IN EXCESS OF $5,000

(When you are relying solely on your present income and credit record as the basis for approval, without including any form of collateral, i.e., property and/or assets, it is considered an Unsecured Credit Request.)

SECTION D — PERSONAL FINANCIAL STATEMENT

ASSETS		LIABILITIES AND NET WORTH	
1. CASH On hand, and unrestricted in banks		18. Notes Payable to Banks, Unsecured Direct borrowings only	$
2. U. S. Government Securities (Guaranteed)		19. Notes Payable to Banks, Secured Direct borrowings only.	
3. Government Agencies Securities		20. Notes Receivable, Discounted With banks, finance companies, etc.	
4. Accounts and Loans Receivable (See Sched. No 1)		21. Notes Payable to Others, Unsecured	
5. Notes Receivable, Not Discounted (See sched. No 1)		22. Notes Payable to Other, Secured	
6. Notes Receivable, Discounted With banks, finance co., etc. (See Sched. No 1)		23. Loans Against Life Insurance (See Sched. No 2)	
7. Life Insurance, Cash Surrender Value (Do not deduct loans) (See Sched. No 2)		24. Accounts Payable	
8. Stock and Securities Other Than Guaranteed U. S. Gov't and Gov't Agencies (See Sched. No 3)		25. Interest Payable	
9. Real Estate Registered in own name (See Sched. No 4)		26. Taxes and Assessments Payable (See Sched. No 4)	
10. Automobiles Registered in own name		27. Mortgage Payable on Real Estate (See Sched. No 4)	
11. Other Assets (Itemize)		28. Brokers Margin Accounts	
12.		29. Other Liabilities (Itemize)	
13. Sub Total $		30.	
14. Less Line No. 31 $		31. Total Liabilities	
15. Net Worth (To be shown on line No. 33) $		32.	
16.		33. Net Worth	$
17. TOTAL ASSETS	$	34. TOTAL LIABILITIES and NET WORTH (Line 31 plus line 33)	$

No. 1 Accounts Loans and Notes Receivable *(A list of the largest amounts owing to me.)*

Name and Address of Debtor	Amount Owing	Age of Debt	Description of Nature of Debt	Description of Security Held	Date Payment Expected

No. 2 Life Insurance

Name of Person Insured	Name of Beneficiary	Name of Insurance Co.	Type of Policy	Face Amount of Policy	Total Cash Surrender Value	Total Loans Against Policy	Amount of Yearly Premium	Is Policy Assigned

No. 3 Stocks and Securities Other Than Guaranteed U.S. Government Securities and Government Agencies

Face Value (Bonds) No. of Shares (Stocks)	Description of Security	Registered in Name of	Cost	Present Market Value	Income Received Last Year	To Whom Pledged?

No. 4 Real Estate *The legal and equitable title of all the real estate listed in this statement is solely in the name of the undersigned, except as follows:*

Description or Street No.	Dimensions or Acres	Improvements Consist of	Mortgages or Liens	Due Dates and Amounts of Payments	Assessed Value	Present Market Value	Unpaid Taxes Year	Unpaid Taxes Amount

No. 5 I have credit accounts with *(List most frequently used accounts)*

Name	Address	Name	Address

The undersigned certifies that each side hereof and the information inserted herein have been carefully read and is true and correct.

Date _____ Signed _____

Courtesy of First Florida Bank

FIGURE 8–4 **Less Detailed Form Used by a Retail Firm**

JCPenney *instant credit* Application

For Office Use Only

To apply for Instant Credit, fill out the application below.
If you have applied for a JCPenney account within the past 60 days, please do not complete this application.

Store Number	Account Number	Type Of Account You Want
		☐ Individual ☐ Joint

Credit Insurance Enrollment

☐ **YES** I wish to protect my JCPenney Account with Credit Insurance for the cost as described above. I understand the insurance is not required.

☐ **NO** I waive my right to enroll for Credit Insurance at this time.

APPLICANT (SIGN TO ENROLL)	Date Of Birth
SPOUSE'S NAME	Date Of Birth

In signing this enrollment form, I authorize J.C. Penney Company, Inc. to advance to J.C. Penney Life Insurance Company and J.C. Penney Casualty Insurance Company amounts equal to the premiums becoming due under the policy applied for and bill such amounts with my JCPenney Credit Account. I agree to pay such amounts when billed.

General Information (Please Print All Information)

Name Of Applicant To Whom Our Billing Statements Should Be Sent (First, Middle Initial, Last)   Applicant's Social Security Number

Name And Relationship(s) To Applicant(s) Of   ☐ Co-Applicant   ☐ Authorized Buyer(s)

Present Address — Street/Apt. ☐ Own ☐ Rent ☐ With Parents ☐ Other | City, State | Zip

Former Address (If At Current Address Less Than One Year) — Street/Apt. | City, State | Zip

Home Phone	Business Phone	Date Of Birth	Co-Applicant's Date Of Birth
( )	( )		

Bank Account
☐ Checking & Savings   ☐ Checking   ☐ Savings   ☐ Loan

Picture I.D. (Driver's License, Student I.D., Etc.)	Number	Major Credit Card	Account Number

Sign here to complete your JCPenney Instant Credit Application.
Your signature(s) mean(s) that you have read, understood, and agree to the terms of the above Retail Installment Credit Agreement.

Applicant's Signature	Date	Co-Applicant's Signature	Date

Courtesy of J.C. Penney Company, Inc.

information because their credit transactions involve larger amounts and longer time periods. Or they may simply be taking advantage of the fact that applicants for such credit will supply more information without resisting. (This practice may be opportunistic or simply represent more careful credit operation.) Additional questions may cover an applicant's income and assets. These lenders are likely to ask about real estate owned, bank balances and other savings, and insurance carried. They seek information as to past credit dealings by asking for other installment contracts currently open and recently paid and other cash loans currently open and recently paid. They usually ask for a list of business references (best asked by the heading "firms with which you have had recent credit transactions") and for a list of personal references. Some also ask the customer's bank and type of account carried.

Some questions may be precautionary in the event the lender has to trace a "skip"—a debtor who deliberately disappears and leaves no forwarding address. When a lender has a lien on property purchased on an installment contract or used as collateral for a loan, both the debtor and the property may be sought. If the property under lien is a car, it may facilitate the debtor's disappearance. Since such a disappearance is deliberate, tracing the debtor involves some detective work. Certain classes of information supplied when the account is opened can be the leads needed to initiate a search. Such requests as "name and address of nearest relative" are used for this purpose.

SIGNATURE AND CONTRACT.   It is good credit practice to have the applicant sign the application. Some credit departments add words above the signature to make the application a formal written contract. This clause may be an affidavit that the information is given for the purpose of obtaining credit and that the facts are complete and correct. The clause may also recite the credit terms and be drawn as a contract between creditor and debtor.

The Credit Interview

Obviously, the nature of the credit interview should be consistent with the character of the application and the philosophy of the credit department. Opinions differ markedly as to the best procedures for conducting a credit interview, especially the procedures for completing an application. Some prefer to develop the answers to questions through the interview and to record the information on the application form themselves. The ability of the credit personnel available for interviewing and the firm's physical facilities are important in deciding these questions.

If applicants fill out the form, a firm needs fewer skilled credit personnel and can accommodate more customers in the same space. A skilled credit interviewer can secure much more information and can also stress the rights and wrongs of credit behavior. If a credit interviewer fills in the application, the form should provide space for recording any extra information (the interviewer should record this additional information *after* the customer leaves). If the customer fills in the application, the interviewer should look over the form to be sure it's complete and probe more deeply into questionable areas.

What appears more important is to develop the right attitude toward the credit interview and to accomplish the objectives sought rather than to prescribe a single procedure for completing the application. The credit interview should be a part of the credit department promotion; in other words, it should be part of the promotion of credit sales. It is an opportunity to convert a credit prospect into a credit customer. Accordingly, the credit interview should not be an inquisition; rather, it should be a business procedure for establishing that the credit offered is suitable to the goods or services sought. The interviewer should proceed with the quiet confidence that the prospect is a valued customer.

Analyzing the Application

The credit application is a source of credit information that has not been verified. The analysis then is directed toward the need for verification and the means of verification to be used. Certain information can be verified by confirmation. For example, an address can be confirmed in a telephone directory or a city directory. In some cases, a directory may also confirm an applicant's occupation. Dates of publication give some indication of length of residence. An address can give the credit analyst who knows the community some additional information. Certain neighborhoods are known to be upper-, middle-, or lower-income areas. Some addresses are warning signals indicating the need for careful investigation, perhaps because they are situated in areas known to have a heavy concentration of residents of poor morals. On the other hand, addresses in neighborhoods known to be beyond applicants' apparent resources and income may indicate that applicants are living beyond their means. Such inferences direct the extent of the investigation.

Brevity of residence or employment may indicate the need for more extensive investigation. Knowledge of employment policies in the community can help direct the extent of the investigation. Certain employers may have a policy of carefully screening employees, and employment with such a firm may permit an inference of reliability.

Sometimes an occupation may indicate the need for more complete investigation. Occupations that are seasonal or that experience considerable fluctuation in income or high turnover call for more complete investigation than do more stable occupations. An interesting yet controversial study attempted to rate various occupations by credit risk.[3] Recently, some

---

[3]The study of occupational credit standings dates from 1931, when Professor P. D. Converse, a pioneer in the field of marketing, first made such an analysis. In 1941 he repeated the survey, increasing the size of the sample and the number of occupations studied ("The Occupational Credit Pattern," *Opinion and Comment*, August 12, 1941, pp. 1–9). A repeat of the earlier studies was undertaken in 1951 by Professor Robert S. Hancock and was published in the August 1952 issue of *Current Economic Comment*.

The author made arrangements with the Research Department of the Associated Credit Bureaus, Inc., to study 1,769 copies of actual reports issued by credit bureaus during the months of January, February, March, and June 1966. The reports were coded on the basis of occupations according to the job classifications of the U.S. Bureau of the Census. The reports were further coded on the basis of the geographic location of the individual applicant. Four hundred towns were represented in a broad geographic coverage. Then the reports were analyzed according to the numerical ratings given on the reports. The

companies have shown interest in this area in an attempt to mechanize some of their decision-making operations.

Certain characteristics do seem to prevail among those in higher-rated occupations (largely professional and highly skilled workers). Stability of income and better utilization of income are two. These are important factors in accepting credit from these groups. Although there are exceptions among all occupations, the sense of responsibility an occupational group may have substantially affects its paying habits. This fact may be attributed to the kind and amount of education or training necessary to perform these better-rated jobs—sometimes years of formal education and personal discipline.

Some occupational groups are made up of transient workers. Such workers have always been regarded as doubtful credit risks because they have less sense of credit responsibility. This is true of workers who move frequently from one town to another—e.g., unskilled factory workers, section hands, and common laborers. Until recently, it was a relatively simple matter for a worker to skip out on debts and assume another name in a new community. The network of credit bureaus throughout the nation, strong union affiliations, social security registration, and income tax laws have significantly hampered this practice.

Stability of income is as important as the amount of income in credit risk appraisal, so it plays an important role in credit study. Credit selling is most effective when directed toward those who have the financial ability to pay installment or revolving credit purchases or the recurring amounts due on open account purchases. Selling techniques should attract the largest number of people with a reasonably regular income to move the product from the retailers' shelves.

INDICATING THE INVESTIGATION TO MAKE. The decision whether to make a further credit investigation and, if so, to what extent is based on an analysis of the application, in the case of an initial request for credit. Of course, a distinction must be made between an initial application for credit[4] and a request from an established credit customer for a larger amount of credit. The application and interview are the primary sources for determining further action with the initial credit applicants. On the other hand, payment record data from in-file information plays a dominant role in deciding whether to expand a customer's credit.

---

results of this study appeared in the June 1967 issue of *ACBofA Management*. The author's final conclusion was that this limited study suggested extreme caution in the use of occupation as an indicator of credit risk.

[4]Today, many larger credit firms have computerized this process. Clerical workers simply type in the data from the application; the computer calculates the score, decides who gets a card, establishes the credit line, and sends the card to the applicant. For further discussion of this procedure, see the material on credit scoring systems in Chapter 10.

What to investigate and what sources of credit information to use should be carefully considered by the credit analyst. Selection must be made between the various sources, and each source must be selected on the basis of type of information desired; speed, accuracy, and completeness of the response; and relative cost of obtaining the information.

INFORMATION SUPPLIED BY DIRECT INQUIRY

Direct inquiry is a common method of obtaining information to verify facts presented on an application or during an interview. Likewise, direct inquiry is also used to obtain additional facts needed to decide whether to accept the credit of an initial applicant or to enlarge the amount of credit accepted from an established customer. This section covers credit information obtained by direct inquiry from sources other than the applicant. A careful distinction is made between obtaining credit information directly from sources with such facts and buying somewhat similar credit data in the form of prepared reports from consumer credit reporting agencies.

Although investigation may be done by direct inquiry or by purchase of reports from professional sources of credit information, direct inquiry is not *free*. Direct inquiry incurs costs in time and personnel, and purchase fees in some instances may be lower. But direct inquiry may be faster, and it gives the investigator the ability to ask specific questions, develop additional information as needed, and confine the response to pertinent information. For instance, on the basis of preliminary analysis of the application, a credit analyst may decide to verify only the applicant's employment and its duration. A telephone call or a letter to the employer may suffice, and the case is closed in a matter of minutes. If an inquiry doesn't confirm the information supplied by the application or raises some additional questions, the investigation can be extended.

Direct inquiry can result in duplication, and the information supplied may be incomplete and not uniform for all accounts. When a number of people possess the same information, a middleman is usually the most efficient way to exchange such information. For each creditor to know the experience of six other creditors, for example, each must send out six inquiries and reply to six inquiries. If they all submit information to a central clearing agency, each creditor only has to make one inquiry and submit one reply—a total of only seven inquiries and seven replies. Figure 8–5 illustrates the economy of centralized clearance, of which the local credit bureau is a leading example. The local credit bureau and other consumer credit reporting agencies are described in detail in Chapter 9.

Inquiry by Mail

Direct inquiry by mail may be directed to the employer, firms that have had credit dealings with the applicant, the applicant's bank, attorneys who

FIGURE 8–5 **The Economy of Centralized Clearance**

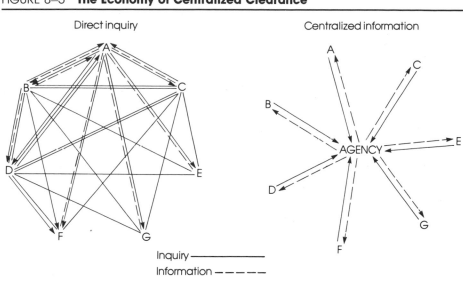

Direct inquiry

Centralized information

Inquiry ————————
Information — — — — —

might have had contact with the applicant, and other references. In each case the reference letter should be carefully framed to solicit information that the informant is expected to have and reveal and that is pertinent to the credit decision. The questions should be phrased as specifically as possible and the form designed so it is easy for the respondent to reply. In all cases an offer to reciprocate should be made and a self-addressed, stamped envelope supplied for reply. While communication by letter is more common, some firms use double-return postcards with the name of the applicant coded on the reply card to avoid possible legal complications. It is usual to indicate that the information is needed because of a request for credit, and in some cases the nature of the transaction is indicated. Since such information should be and usually is on a give-and-get basis, some firms submit their own experience when asking for the experience of others. It also is usual to state if the inquiry is directed to a person whose name was supplied as a reference.

Questions should be phrased to permit specific and unequivocal answers. So far as possible the questions should require factual response rather than opinion or judgment. The questions should not indicate or invite bias in either inquiry or reply. The whole tone should be tactful and considerate of the respondent.

Appropriate questions to be directed to the employer include:

Employed since? _____ or How long employed? _____
Position?_____ or Occupation? _____
Confirmation of salary given by applicant: Yes _____ No _____

And if a former employer, it is appropriate to ask:

Employed? From _____ to _____
Position _____ or Occupation? _____
Reason for separation? _____

Appropriate questions to trade creditors include:

Type of account? _____
What account was opened? _____
Present balance? $_____
Highest recent credit? $_____
Payment experience: Pays when due _____
                                Within 30 days _____
                                In 30 to 60 days _____
                                In 60 to 90 days _____
                                Other _____
(If experience has been unsatisfactory, please state the nature of the difficulty, the manner of collection, and if there was a charge to profit and loss.) $_____
Date?_____

Appropriate questions to banks include:

Is applicant a depositor? Yes? _____ No? _____ Checking? _____
Saving? _____
Approximate amount of the usual balance? $_____
Have you had lending experience with applicant? Yes _____ No _____
Was the lending experience satisfactory? Yes _____ No _____
Would you recommend? _____

This last question, which violates the precept not to ask for opinion, is included because some bankers won't answer specific questions but will make a recommendation.

Developing Additional Informants

Specific questions can glean usable information even from biased sources, since few reputable business executives actually falsify credit information. They are more likely to bias their reply by not mentioning any unfavorable points or by being vague, even generous, in response to requests for opinion or judgment. It is sometimes surprising to the credit analyst—and would be even more surprising to the prospect—how frank some answers can be.

Despite these mitigating factors, such predictable bias impels skillful investigators to develop evidence from informants not supplied by the prospect. Ingenuity and knowledge of the market often help the investigator to add sources. For example, utilities usually have experience records. Public record information can also be used. Ownership of property can be checked against tax records. The presence of liens can be determined by examining public records. Police records are sometimes revealing. While every case doesn't warrant such a costly and time-consuming investigation, when circumstances indicate it, the investigation can be extended in unusual directions.

Inquiry by Telephone

Inquiry by telephone can be used in place of a mail inquiry and the same or similar questions asked. The interviewer records replies on a form similar to that used in mail inquiries. Standard questions result in uniform responses, but trained telephone investigators should be skilled enough to probe further if indicated.

Telephone inquiry has an advantage over mail: replies are received immediately. The cost per completed inquiry compares favorably with the cost of a mail inquiry. But a telephone inquiry may disrupt the respondent's normal work procedures and take more time than replying to a letter.

Inquiry by Outside Representative

Some firms, particularly cash lenders and sales finance companies, use their own employees as credit investigators. The employees, or outside representatives, may be assigned the dual task of outside or personal collector and credit investigator. They usually are supplied with the names of employer, landlord, and business firms and are expected to call these people and ask questions similar to those asked in a mail investigation. Here too there is an advantage in using standardized questions and a standard form for recording answers.

Outside representatives should be aggressive in developing additional informants and in extending the depth of the inquiry. Although a mail investigation cannot readily be extended, good outside representatives analyze the information supplied as it accumulates. They thus extend their inquiries to the point where they decide that they have sufficient information to accept or to reject. By discreet inquiries, they may develop information that no other means of direct investigation can match. Inquiries can be made of neighbors and local tradespeople, even the mail carrier or a police officer.

Some cash loan companies, lending on the collateral of household effects, believe that personal examination of the home can supply useful credit information. Such information as the type and quality of the furnishings, quality of housekeeping, and pride or lack of pride in the home can indicate the credit quality of the applicant.

Inquiry through Credit Group Meetings

The technique of group meetings is more common in commercial credit transactions, but in some communities creditors selling consumer goods use it to exchange ledger facts and other valuable information. While such meetings are often held under the auspices of the local retail credit bureau, the technique is a result of direct inquiry.

The purpose of such group meetings, which often are held in conjunction with a social luncheon or dinner, is to provide a quick and easy means of exchanging information about initial applicants for credit, slow-pay customers, and other accounts exhibiting unusual behavior. Usually, each participating store is limited in the number of names it can bring up in discussion.

INFORMATION SUPPLIED FROM IN-FILE LEDGER FACTS

In-file ledger facts are one of the most important sources of information in deciding whether to accept or reject a larger amount of credit from an established credit customer. Applicants for a larger credit base have already been interviewed and investigated and had their applications analyzed and verified.

In-file records indicate the firm's experience with the customer. Credit analysts know the customer's payment habits, any complaints registered, and any collection efforts needed. In many cases such information is sufficient; in others the credit executive will seek more information, called "purchased information," from professional sources. Such sources will be covered in the next chapter.

DISCUSSION QUESTIONS

1. What is meant by the statement "Credit information is created only by the subject of the credit inquiry"?
2. What is the basic purpose of a credit investigation?
3. Distinguish between subjective information and objective information.
4. Explain the statement "The credit investigation brings together historical information which, through analysis, is used as a basis for a prediction of future behavior."
5. What are the "four horsemen" of credit?
6. Explain the term *character*.
7. When the term *conditions* is used, does it apply to conditions surrounding the applicant's status or to general local, national, and international economic conditions? Explain your answer.
8. What credit qualities should credit executives normally evaluate in their credit determination? Why these qualities?

9. What additional qualities would you recommend be applied to the list appearing in the text?

10. Check with several firms (retail, service, and financial) in your community as to the importance they place on each of the credit qualities suggested.

11. Distinguish between collateral and equity in purchase.

12. Why are economic conditions an important factor in determining credit risk?

13. Why is the question "How much to investigate?" difficult to answer?

14. What information sources are available to credit managers?

15. Distinguish between direct investigation and internal company data.

16. Explain the statement "The extent to which consumer-supplied information is verified or expanded through additional investigation depends on the judgment of the credit analyst."

17. Should credit applications be signed? Why or why not?

18. Why is a signature on an application form particularly important in installment and revolving credit transactions?

19. Check with the leading retail stores in your community to determine what type of credit application they use.

20. How would you conduct a credit interview? Why did you include the steps that you did?

21. How is the direct inquiry method accomplished? What are its advantages and disadvantages?

22. Explain the differences between purchased information and free information.

23. Attend a luncheon of retail credit executives in which an interchange of credit information on certain slow-pay customers takes place.

24. When is it desirable to use information supplied from in-file ledger facts?

25. Why do sales finance companies and cash lenders use more detailed application forms?

CHAPTER

9

Basis of the Credit Decision (continued)

The Objectives or Goals of Chapter 9 Are:
1. To distinguish between the various types of consumer credit reporting agencies.
2. To trace the history, development, organization, and operation of local credit bureaus.
3. To discuss the activities of Associated Credit Bureaus, Inc. (ACB).
4. To explain the activities of CBR Information Group, Inc.
5. To point out the legal restrictions on credit bureau operations under the Fair Credit Reporting Act, including recent interpretations by the Federal Trade Commission.
6. To discuss automated credit bureau reporting.
7. To explain the activities of TRW Information Systems and Services, of Trans Union, and of Equifax Inc.

Information about the credit history or paying habits of individuals and families may be secured from many sources. Each source has its own special merits as well as some disadvantages.

The direct method of investigation is "free" only in the sense that the creditor pays no fee to an outside organization. A direct technique may be more costly than a fee service, and the product supplied may be inferior. Yet, in any credit investigation, quality of information is a prime consideration. Because credit investigations have become so specialized, it is usually best to rely on specialists. In addition, special agencies avoid unnecessary duplication of effort. Credit information in the files of credit reporting agencies can be used more than once; in fact, multiple use of the same information is the principle on which this type of organization is founded. Credit information gathered by direct methods is available only to the firm doing the investigation.

There are several types of consumer credit reporting agencies:

1. Reporting firms that have their own computer database and have national files. The primary source of their data is accounts

receivable tapes of credit grantors. They also obtain public record data from court records. There are three major firms in the United States today: TRW Information Systems and Services, Trans Union, and Equifax Inc. The files of CSC Credit Services are stored in the computer of this latter firm.

These three competing firms operate their own branch offices, and each one has branches in over 30 locations. In addition, all other computerized credit bureaus have arranged for immediate access to the database of one of these firms. Counting both the branch offices and the affiliated bureaus, there are about 700 computerized credit bureaus in the United States.

2. Noncomputerized credit bureaus in towns far removed from metropolitan areas have access to Consumer Credit Associates, a privately owned firm that provides them with the same infor- mation available to the computerized bureau. The number of manual bureaus is decreasing steadily as they are unable to com- pete in marketing their services over a wide area, as the larger bureaus can.

3. Bureaus that, by contract agreement, have access to the data in the three databases, but are not owned by them. They pay monthly fees for access to the file data.

Any credit bureau, whether computerized or not, has immediate access to the records of all other credit bureaus, through a long- standing arrangement. The credit file of a family that moves is available to credit grantors in the new location through interbureau reporting arrangements.

Another kind of reporting organization, termed an *investigative re- porting* company, produces consumer reports primarily for insurance firms to use in evaluating applicants for insurance. Equifax Inc., a leader in this field, offers detailed investigations by its staff of field representatives. Equifax does not draw from a pool of information as do other credit bureaus.

HISTORY AND ORGANIZATION OF CREDIT BUREAUS

Credit bureaus are one of the most important sources of information about consumers' paying habits. Credit grantors need such information to extend credit privileges promptly and knowledgeably.

Beginning and Development of Local Credit Bureaus

Local credit bureaus are primarily a 20th-century development. The first so-called credit bureau was organized as early as 1860 in Brooklyn, but credit bureaus grew and developed slowly before World War II. Until then few retailers sold on credit, and those that did confined their credit business to well-known customers. Movement of people was limited because of the lack of rapid transportation and communication facilities.

Many of the old-time credit exchanges used lists of known poor credit risks. In effect, such lists closed the barn door after the horse had been stolen.

From this humble beginning, credit bureaus grew to the position of importance they now occupy.[1] Credit bureaus have become the principal clearinghouses for information furnished by their subscribers, members, and other outside sources and are one of the best examples of close cooperation among business firms serving the American public.

Origin and Growth of the Trade Association for Credit Bureaus

The organized exchange of consumer credit information between local areas started about the turn of the century. In 1906 William H. Burr, owner of a "credit company" in Rochester, New York, asked the managers of several other consumer credit reporting agencies to meet with him to discuss the possibility of forming a national association of credit bureaus. Before that time there were no rosters of credit bureaus, no system for interchanging reports between bureaus, and no standardized forms. This 1906 meeting resulted in the formation of the only national organization of credit bureaus, then called the National Association of Retail Credit Agencies but now known as Associated Credit Bureaus, Inc. (ACB). The need for closer cooperation between credit bureaus and credit grantors soon became evident, and in 1912 the Retail Credit Men's National Association (now known as the International Credit Association) was formed as a trade association of retail credit managers.

From its 1906 beginning, when six small credit reporting agencies incorporated and agreed to exchange credit information, ACB has grown rapidly. Today it is the only trade association in the consumer credit industry, offering its members traditional trade association benefits such as lobbying, group purchasing, national public relations, and training aids for employees through seminars, forums, and institutes.

ACB also operates a comprehensive certification program so that credit reporters and consumer interviewers receive thorough training in the laws that govern their activity. The certification, which is usually renewed every two years, is often used to prove the operational procedures and the employees are carefully monitored.

---

[1]See John Aberth, "Larger Role for Credit Bureaus," *ABA Banking Journal,* August 1988, p. 21. Also, Ralph E. Spurgin, "Standard Credit Bureau Reporting," *The Credit World,* May–June 1988, p. 29.

CBR Information Group, Inc.

CBR Information Group, Inc. (formerly Credit Bureau Reports, Inc.), is a national marketing company that functions as a sales organization for local credit bureaus. During the 1970s, as the individual credit bureaus throughout the United States began to automate, the long-term future for CBR's "network" of manual credit bureaus was not as positive as it had been. Thus the network has been expanded to include the newly automated credit bureaus as well. Through this manual/automated network, CBR provides regional and national users of credit information with access to credit information on individuals throughout the United States.

Over the past 15 years, CBR has embarked on a corporate diversification program designed to allow greater growth by offering additional products and services to the financial services community. During this period, CBR has purchased and operated credit bureaus on the TRW, CBI, and Trans Union systems. CBR has also purchased collection agencies in major metropolitan areas. Through its National Credit Marketing Services (NCMS) division, CBR now offers direct-mail production, list acquisition, data processing, and prescreening of consumer names to determine creditworthiness.

As a result, CBR has moved from an integral part of the credit bureau industry to an integral part of the financial services industry.

Organization and Ownership of Local Credit Bureaus

In the past most credit bureaus were community cooperative or nonprofit associations operated for the benefit of users. Others were owned by local chambers of commerce, which operated them for the benefit of their members. Today most credit bureaus are owned by individuals and corporations and operated for profit.

As with any private business, credit bureaus may change owners. Most bureaus are incorporated. The three major databases mentioned earlier acquire new branch offices occasionally when they purchase bureaus formerly affiliated by contract arrangements. The number of offices owned by Trans Union, TRW, and Equifax increases steadily.

Regardless of ownership, the principle of credit bureau operation is constant. All credit bureaus rely on the cooperation of credit grantors to contribute their accounts receivable tapes and to purchase credit reports. All bureaus interview consumers, explain their function to all who are interested, attempt to reconcile differences between consumers and credit grantors, and correct errors as they are detected. The Fair Credit Reporting Act crystallized the methods and formats, so that today treatment of consumers is uniform. However, bureaus are receiving an increasing number of challenges to the file information. As a result, ACB is publicizing its Consumer Relations Code of Ethics (see Figure 9–1).

FIGURE 9–1 **ACB Consumer Relations Code of Ethics**

Members of Associated Credit Bureaus pledge to:

1. Educate consumers on the role credit reporting agencies play in our economic system and how credit reporting agencies can better serve their needs.
2. Maintain reasonable procedures to assure maximum accuracy of credit information provided to credit grantors.
3. Train consumer interviewers to qualify for certification.
4. Provide fair and equitable procedures for disclosing information to consumers as expeditiously as possible.
5. Maintain effective procedures to expedite prompt reverification of information.
6. Advise consumers of their rights under the Fair Credit Reporting Act, including reinvestigation and notification.
7. Provide appropriate procedures for handling consumer disputes.

At one time reporting firms needed a physical location. Today computers have made that unnecessary. All a credit grantor—or even another credit bureau—needs is access to a computer terminal.

Credit bureaus are conscious of the need for security measures to protect the integrity of their data. Each credit bureau develops a security program tailored to its own needs. Depending on the bureau's experience, the security systems range from complex automated systems to simple precautions to prevent unauthorized access to credit records.

Security programs need constant updating to provide better protection and to become as standardized throughout the industry as different operating environments permit.

Security touches almost all aspects of credit bureau operations. ACB requires certain basic security measures of its members and recommends others depending on the size and location of the credit bureau. Computerized bureaus especially adopt stringent methods to prevent unauthorized access to stored data.

The residents who live in a wide area around any city where a credit bureau is located will find that their credit files are readily available because the data from the national credit grantors are accessible from the three major firms through the affiliated bureaus.

OPERATION OF CREDIT BUREAUS

Credit bureaus must maintain control of the data they collect. To comply with the Fair Credit Reporting Act, credit bureaus must carefully verify the identity of all who request credit information, whether it be a credit grantor, an employer, or even the subject of the report itself.

Principal Sources of Credit Information

Since the primary activity of a credit bureau is to furnish credit reports on consumers applying for credit, it is important to explore the principal sources of data for such reports.

Credit files may be drawn up on computer screens or on printers located in the credit grantors' offices. Each of the three major database firms has customized the once-standard credit report format so it provides all of the information needed. Although the information in each database is theoretically identical, the display of the information and its treatment will be different, depending on the database source.

The ACB format, called Crediscope, is designated Form 2000 (see Figure 9–2).[2] Credit information is gathered from a variety of sources located in one or more trading areas that are willing to exchange information. The credit bureaus arrange to secure the necessary data from as many creditors and other sources as possible. In addition to the data from Trans Union, TRW, and Equifax, affiliate bureaus arrange for computerized banks, finance companies, retailers, and so on to add their tapes to the files and enrich the credit histories in the bureau. Bureaus also add new and current employment information to each person's file as that information becomes available, usually from a credit application.

Ledger information on Form 2000 shows, in outline form, the manner in which individuals meet their credit obligations. The present status of the consumer is of paramount importance, but the reader of a credit report is vitally interested in the historical status—how often the consumer was significantly late in paying bills. The period covered by each trade line is expressed in months under the column heading "No. of months history reviewed."

The credit history section of Form 2000 tells the reader many other facts:

1. Who is responsible for paying the account. This information is necessary to comply with the Equal Credit Opportunity Act and is discussed at length later.

2. The kind of business reporting the information. Actual names of credit grantors are shown on automated bureau reports.

3. The date the credit bureau received the information. Bureaus with access to major creditors' automated accounts receivable tapes receive updated data every 30 days.

4. The method of reporting. (This is of value to the reader only because manual data remain static, whereas automated tapes are updated monthly.)

---

[2]Although Form 2000 is shown in Figure 9–2, the actual forms prepared by the "big three" firms show considerable variation because of computerization. It is not possible to show a generic computerized report form. Form 2000 is merely shown as an illustration.

FIGURE 9–2 **Form 2000**

NAME AND ADDRESS OF CREDIT BUREAU MAKING REPORT

☐ SINGLE REFERENCE ☐ IN FILE REPORT ☐ TRADE REPORT

☐ FULL REPORT ☐ EMPLOY & TRADE REPORT ☐ PREVIOUS RESIDENCE REPORT

☐ OTHER_____

	Date Received	**CONFIDENTIAL**
FOR	Date Mailed	crediscope® REPORT
	In File Since	Member Associated Credit Bureaus, Inc.
	Inquired As:	

| REPORT ON: LAST NAME | FIRST NAME | INITIAL | SOCIAL SECURITY NUMBER | SPOUSE'S NAME |
| ADDRESS: CITY | STATE: | ZIP CODE | SINCE: | SPOUSE'S SOCIAL SECURITY NO. |

| PRESENT EMPLOYER: | POSITION HELD: | SINCE: | DATE EMPLOY VERIFIED | EST. MONTHLY INCOME $ |

DATE OF BIRTH	NUMBER OF DEPENDENTS INCLUDING SELF:	☐ OWNS OR BUYING HOME	☐ RENTS HOME	OTHER: (EXPLAIN) ☐
FORMER ADDRESS:	CITY:	STATE: FROM:	TO:
FORMER EMPLOYER:	POSITION HELD:	FROM:	TO:	EST. MONTHLY INCOME $
SPOUSE'S EMPLOYER:	POSITION HELD:	SINCE:	DATE EMPLOY VERIFIED	EST. MONTHLY INCOME $

WHOSE	KIND OF BUSINESS AND ID CODE	DATE REPORTED AND METHOD OF REPORTING	DATE OPENED	DATE OF LAST PAYMENT	HIGHEST CREDIT OR LAST CONTRACT	PRESENT STATUS				HISTORICAL STATUS				TYPE & TERMS (MANNER OF PAYMENT)	REMARKS
						BALANCE OWING	PAST DUE		NO. OF PAYMENTS	NO. MONTHS HISTORY REVIEWED	TIMES PAST DUE				
							AMOUNT				30-59 DAYS ONLY	60-89 DAYS ONLY	90 DAYS AND OVER		

This information is furnished in response to an inquiry for the purpose of evaluating credit risks. It has been obtained from sources deemed reliable, the accuracy of which this organization does not guarantee. The inquirer has agreed to indemnify the reporting bureau for any damage arising from misuse of this information, and this report is furnished in reliance upon that indemnity. It must be held in strict confidence, and must not be revealed to the subject reported on, except as required by law.

FORM 2000-5/80

5. The date the account was opened.
6. The date of the last payment.
7. The highest amount of credit extended or the amount of credit represented by the last contract with the customer.
8. Whether the account is open charge, revolving, or installment. If known, the amount of monthly payments agreed to is shown.
9. Explanatory remarks to help the reader obtain a clearer picture of the consumer's paying habits. The explanatory remarks are three-letter abbreviations that amplify and explain the reference on that line.

When a credit bureau receives a request for an updated report, it routinely checks with the employer of record to verify employment. If the report ordered is an "in-file" report, the bureau furnishes the name of the last known employer along with other employment information stored in the file.

Credit bureaus check public records regularly to gather credit-related data. A bankruptcy petition, judgment for money due, or a tax lien may affect a consumer's paying ability, regardless of his or her previous record.

As the population becomes more mobile, consumers make many purchases outside their local trading areas. And increasing numbers of families move from one city to another. In both circumstances, one credit bureau must request a credit report from another bureau. Through an interbureau reporting system, the record of an individual in other markets is readily available.

NEED FOR FACTS—NOT OPINIONS. Credit bureaus have long distinguished between facts and statements of opinion. In the distant past, credit reports included opinions of credit grantors and even comments about the subject's parents. To ensure compliance with the Fair Credit Reporting Act, bureaus refuse to place in their files anything other than verifiable data.

The Equal Credit Opportunity Act changed how credit reports are prepared. Before passage of the ECOA, almost all files, both credit grantor and credit bureau, were in the name of the husband. The ECOA requires creditors, when reporting credit history, to make clear what responsibility the subject has toward the accounts listed. Form 2000 provides several options coded in the extreme left-hand column headed "Whose." The most widely used designations are:

1. Individual account for individual use.
2. Joint account with contractual liability.
3. Authorized user (usually a spouse).
4. Comaker of a promissory note.

Scope of Bureau Operation

The primary purpose of the credit bureau is to supply information. How this information is furnished to credit grantors is explained in the following sections.

In all major cities, computers assemble data swiftly and efficiently; in isolated communities, noncomputerized bureaus maintain files manually.

PREPARATION AND MAINTENANCE OF THE BUREAU FILE. The bureau files are the source of credit information from which data can be obtained quickly and easily and in turn, transmitted to inquirers.

The basic stock-in-trade of a bureau is its "in-file" information obtained from two major sources: local creditors and national or regional creditors' accounts receivable tapes.

Local firms that have credit experience with the subject of an inquiry are asked for current information covering their recent experience with that subject. Subjects usually name credit references when filling out a credit application. The contract credit grantors sign to become bureau subscribers specifies that they will provide their ledger experience promptly and accurately.

When the process works properly, the basic file accumulates automatically and reflects the credit experience of creditors with information about the subject's paying habits. Obsolete data, as defined in the Fair Credit Reporting act, is deleted.

A bureau file reveals such data as details of each creditor's last transaction with the customer, the current status of the account, and a historical status that may cover varying lengths of time. Both automated and noncomputerized bureaus have access to the accounts receivable tapes of major credit grantors.

A private firm, Consumer Credit Associates, arranges with many national creditors to receive their accounts receivable data, convert them into microfiche, and sell the fiche to the smaller credit bureaus according to ZIP codes.

In addition to ledger experience, the credit bureau files contain information about each credit user, such as current and past addresses and current and former employment data. Public records of civil judgments for money, bankruptcy filings, and tax liens are added as they are obtained from court records.

TYPES OF CREDIT REPORTS. Credit bureaus offer several kinds of credit reports either in printed form or orally.

When an oral report is requested by a member credit grantor, he or she identifies his or her company by a prearranged code to ensure confidentiality of the information. Then the credit grantor provides complete identification of the subject to include name, address, social security number, spouse's name, employment, and previous address. The credit bureau operator then reads the file to the credit grantor.

The reporter will then advise the caller of the date of the last data revision in the manual file. Computer tape data furnished at 30-day intervals may be adequate, or the caller may request that the in-file data be updated also. This is especially true if references indicate slow paying habits or other adverse data. In the automated credit bureau, oral reports can be more expensive than computer terminal displays. Today the vast majority of credit reports are either received in machine-readable format (CPU to CPU) between a credit grantor and a credit bureau or by one of the thousands of dial-up remote terminals found in large and small credit grantors' offices.

Credit bureaus are prepared to provide many specialized reports. For example:

Residential Mortgage Credit Report. This comprehensive report contains more information than a regular consumer credit report, including verification of almost everything in the file.

Employment Report. This report is used by a prospective employer to evaluate the ability of the applicant to live within his or her means and to verify the data the applicant wrote on the application.

Some credit bureaus provide two other kinds of reports, but they require different source data:

1. Business reports. Usually prepared in response to a specific request, the business report contains all the information the bureau is able to collect on smaller commercial firms. The business report may be supplemented by credit reports on the owners, although great care is exercised to separate consumer credit histories from business credit transactions.

2. Personnel reports. Usually prepared in response to specific requests from prospective employers, the personnel report is compiled by checking the sources listed by the firm requesting the report. Many personnel reports contain academic records, extensive employment history, public records, and a consumer credit history. Where items of public record become part of a personnel report, up-to-date revision of this data is required by the Fair Credit Reporting Act to ensure that an employment or promotion opportunity is not jeopardized by incorrect or outdated public information.

STANDARDIZATION OF TERMINOLOGY. Standardization of terminology within the credit industry was once a problem. Credit language was ambiguous, confusing, and sometimes misleading. A department store with a lenient credit policy might state that the consumer was "slow but satisfactory," yet a bank with a strict policy would describe the same paying habit as "very unsatisfactory."

With computerization, standardized language was vital between credit grantors and credit bureaus. For this reason, ACB and a cross section of the country's credit grantors devised "Crediscope," and by mutual cooperation, the present terminology emerged. Crediscope simplifies credit reporting and guarantees consumers that all creditors use the same criteria to judge the same kinds of paying habits. It provides one of the most thorough means available for including only objective information in a credit report.

Figure 9–3 shows a completed sample credit report Form 2000. An explanation of the credit history shown on sample Form 2000 is given in Figure 9–4. Figure 9–5 explains the terms that might appear on any Form 2000.

Supplementary Credit Bureau Services

Services discussed so far are tailored for the inquiring subscriber. But bureaus also provide other services that are not individually tailored in response to an order.

LISTS OF PROSPECTIVE RETAIL CUSTOMERS.   By carefully following antidiscrimination laws, credit bureaus can offer retailers lists of potential new credit customers. The credit grantor must first provide the bureau with a list of its standards and requirements, such as income, length of time on present job, and other permissible specifications.

The bureau selects names and addresses from its files that meet the designated requirements and furnishes the list to the credit grantor for a predetermined fee. The credit grantor then mails those listed an invitation to open a credit account; it does not send them credit cards because this is illegal.

COLLECTION SERVICE.   Most bureaus, either through a collection department or an affiliate, offer retail debt collection service to creditors in their trade areas.

EDUCATIONAL ACTIVITIES.   ACB offers its bureau members a wide variety of educational activities to upgrade and enhance the skills of both management and reporters. Seminars, institutes, audiovisual training aids, and publications are constantly improved, so people working in a credit bureau are familiar with the law and time-tested techniques in efficient reporting service.

Associated Credit Bureaus, Inc., has produced several brochures about credit and credit bureaus and suggests its members use them to advise consumers of their rights under the various federal consumer credit laws.

FIGURE 9–3 **Sample Form 2000**

NAME AND ADDRESS OF CREDIT BUREAU MAKING REPORT

- [ ] SINGLE REFERENCE
- [ ] IN FILE REPORT
- [ ] TRADE REPORT
- [X] FULL REPORT
- [ ] EMPLOY & TRADE REPORT
- [ ] PREVIOUS RESIDENCE REPORT
- [ ] OTHER _____

Credit Bureau of Anytown
1311 Main St.
Anytown, Anystate 12345

Date Received 10/11/91	**CONFIDENTIAL** crediscope® REPORT
Date Mailed 10/12/91	
In File Since 1973	■ Member Associated Credit Bureaus, Inc.
Inquired As: 2	

FOR   First National Bank
      Anytown, Anystate 12345

REPORT ON:	LAST NAME Consumer	FIRST NAME Robert	INITIAL B	SOCIAL SECURITY NUMBER 123-45-6789	SPOUSE'S NAME Betty

ADDRESS:	CITY	STATE:	ZIP CODE	SINCE:	SPOUSE'S SOCIAL SECURITY NO.
812 Elm St.	Anytown Anystate	12346	1975	987-65-4321

PRESENT EMPLOYER:	POSITION HELD:	SINCE:	DATE EMPLOY VERIFIED	EST. MONTHLY INCOME
Research Engineer Inc.	Sr. Vice Pres.	5/81	3/21/89	$ 3600

DATE OF BIRTH 4/48	NUMBER OF DEPENDENTS INCLUDING SELF: 2	[X] OWNS OR BUYING HOME	[ ] RENTS HOME	OTHER: (EXPLAIN) [ ]

FORMER ADDRESS: 123 Oak St. Thattown	CITY: Anystate	STATE:	FROM: 1973	TO: 1975
FORMER EMPLOYER: Sun Research	POSITION HELD: Engineer	FROM: 1978	TO: 1981	EST. MONTHLY INCOME $ –
SPOUSE'S EMPLOYER: Gift World	POSITION HELD: Owner	SINCE: 1984	DATE EMPLOY VERIFIED 3/21/89	EST. MONTHLY INCOME $ 1800

WHOSE	KIND OF BUSINESS AND ID CODE	DATE REPORTED AND METHOD OF	DATE OPENED	DATE OF LAST PAYMENT	HIGHEST CREDIT OR LAST CONTRACT	PRESENT STATUS				HISTORICAL STATUS				TYPE & TERMS (MANNER OF PAYMENT)	REMARKS
						BALANCE OWING	PAST DUE AMOUNT	NO. OF PAYMENTS	NO. MONTHS HISTORY REVIEWED	TIMES PAST DUE 30-59 DAYS ONLY	60-89 DAYS ONLY	90 DAYS AND OVER			
3	D-608	Jones Department Store 9/91A	2/83	6/91	$172	$85	$34	2	12	1	1		R-$17	
1	B-319	Bank of Anytown 9/91M	8/85	8/91	2400	00	00		24				I-$100	
2	C-526	Styles of Today, Inc. 9/91A	1980	7/91	$1264	100	50	1	12	2	1		R-$50	
3	N-772	Ready-Credit 9/91A	2/81	7/91	$350	160	–	–	12	1			0	DRP
0	D-490	Everybody's Dept. Store 5/89M	1979	6/90	$700	00	0	–					R-$150	

Public Record
County Small Claims Court Case SC-1001, 5/31/91.
Plaintiff Ace Stereo Sales $825 Paid 8/91.

FIGURE 9–4 **Explanation of Credit History on Sample Form 2000**

Trade line 1. This is a shared account that Mr. Consumer's wife is permitted to use. Department store (D608) last reported the account on computer tape September 1991 with a high credit of $172; the account owes $85, of which $34, amounting to two payments, is currently past due. The creditor reviewed the last 12 months' history of the account. Under historical status, note that in addition to the two payments currently past due, the account has also been past due on the other occasions. This is a revolving account with a $17 monthly payment. Bureaus assign internal code numbers to help them keep each firm separate. One department store might be D608, while another might be D853.

Trade line 2. Individual account with a bank (B319) in the husband's name. Trade reported manually 9/91. The creditor reviewed 24 months' history with installments of $100 monthly. The account was never as much as 30 days past due and is now paid in full.

Trade line 3. Clothing firm (C526) revolving account, high $1,264, for which both spouses are contractually liable. The account currently owes $100, of which one $50 payment is past due. In addition, note that on two other occasions in the past 12 months, the account balance became 30 to 59 days past due and that once it became 60 to 89 days past due.

Trade line 4. A national credit card account on which the spouse is an authorized user. All or part of the present balance of $160 is disputed and was reported by the creditor as DRP (disputed—resolution pending). Under the Fair Credit Billing Act, the creditor suppresses any information as to the amount past due and the number of payments past due. The "1" in the 30–59 days past-due column under historical status does not refer to the current condition of the account. Rather, it indicates that at one other time within the 12 months reviewed, the account was in this condition and that it was not disputed at that time.

Trade line 5. Legally, favorable information can be reported indefinitely, but users of credit reports prefer that it not be retained so long that it distorts the consumer's present paying trends. In this instance the data is over one year old, and the account is inactive.

Charges for Credit Bureau Services

Whether operated as a merchant-owned service or a profit-oriented corporation, credit bureaus must charge for their services.

Most bureaus charge a monthly fee or "dues" billed to all members according to the membership contract. Usually the fee is a base charge only; the bureau depends on the sale of a volume of reports for its income.

Each report furnished a subscriber is counted and listed on a monthly statement showing the quantity and price. Each bureau establishes its own prices.

CREDIT BUREAU OPERATIONS AND THE LAW

The Fair Credit Reporting Act (Title VI amendment of the Consumer Credit Protection Act) regulates the credit reporting industry. It became effective in 1971.

FIGURE 9–5 **Explanation of Abbreviations Used in Sample Form 2000 (Figure 9–3)**

Terms of Sale

Open account (30 days or 90 days)	O
Revolving or option (open-end a/c)	R
Installment (fixed number of payments)	I

Kind of Business Classification

Code	Kind of Business	Code	Kind of Business
A	Automobile	O	Oil companies
B	Banks	P	Personal services other
C	Clothing		than medical
D	Department and variety	Q	Mail-order houses
F	Finance	R	Real estate and public
G	Groceries		accommodations
H	Home furnishings	S	Sporting goods
I	Insurance	T	Farm and garden supplies
J	Jewelry and cameras	U	Utilities and fuel
K	Contractors	V	Government
L	Lumber, building materials, hardware	W	Wholesale
M	Medical and related health	X	Advertising
N	National credit card companies	Y	Collection services
	and air lines	Z	Miscellaneous

A. Column 1, whose account, provides a means of showing how a credit grantor maintains the account for ECOA purposes. Examples: 0–Undesignated, 1—Individual account for individual use, 2—Joint account contractual liability, 3—Authorized user spouse, 4—Joint, 5—Comaker, 6—On behalf of account, 7—Maker, 8—Individual account of spouse, 9—Subject no longer associated with account.

B. Column 3, method of reporting, indicates how a trade item was placed in file: A—Computer tape or TVS, M—Manual.

C. When inserting dates, use month and year only (example: 12–90).

D. Remarks codes (examples):

ACC—Account closed by consumer.	RLD—Repossession. Paid by dealer.
AJP—Adjustment pending.	RLP—Repossession. Proceeds applied
BKL—Account included in bankruptcy.	to debt.
CCA—Consumer counseling account.	RPO—Repossession.
Consumer has retained the	RRE—Repossession, redeemed.
services of an organization that	RVD—Returned voluntarily. Paid by
is directing payment of his	dealer.
accounts.	RVN—Returned voluntarily.
CLA—Placed for collection.	RVP—Returned voluntarily, proceeds
DIS—Dispute following resolution.	applied to debt.
DRP—Dispute resolution pending.	RVR—Returned voluntarily, redeemed.
JUD—Judgment obtained for balance	STL—Plate stolen or lost.
shown.	WEP—Wage earner plan account
MOV—Moved. Left no forwarding	(Chapter 13 of the
address	Bankruptcy Act).
PRL—Profit and loss write-off.	

E. Account numbers, if shown, should appear on second line just below each trade item.

F. Disputes and comments associated with specific trade lines should be printed on second or third line in cases where account numbers are printed.

According to the authors of the bill, Congress explained the need for such a law in these words:

1. The banking system is dependent upon fair and accurate credit reporting. Inaccurate credit reports directly impair the efficiency of the banking system, and unfair credit reporting methods undermine the public confidence which is essential to the continued functioning of the banking system.
2. An elaborate mechanism has been developed for investigating and evaluating the creditworthiness, credit standing, credit capacity, character, and general reputation of consumers.
3. Consumer reporting agencies have assumed a vital role in assembling and evaluating consumer credit and other information on consumers.
4. There is a need to ensure that consumer reporting agencies exercise their grave responsibilities with fairness, impartiality, and a respect for the consumer's right to privacy.[3]

The Fair Credit Reporting Act established, among other things, the length of time that adverse information may remain in a consumer's credit file:

1. Bankruptcies which, from date of adjudication of the most recent bankruptcy, antedate the report by more than 10 years.[4]
2. Suits and judgments which, from date of entry, antedate the report by more than seven years or until the governing statute of limitations has expired, whichever is the longer period.
3. Paid tax liens which, from date of payment, antedate the report by more than seven years.
4. Accounts placed for collection or charged to profit and loss which antedate the report by more than seven years.
5. Any other adverse item of information which antedates the report by more than seven years.[5]

The Fair Credit Reporting Act distinguishes between "consumer report" and "investigative consumer report" because these are radically different in context. This chapter deals almost exclusively with the former. Investigative consumer reports contain information on a consumer's character, general reputation, personal characteristics, or mode of living

---

[3]Sec. 602 of the Fair Credit Reporting Act (Title VI of the Consumer Credit Protection Act), effective April 1971. Also see Walter R. Kurth, "Fair Credit Reporting Act (FCRA)," *The Credit World,* May–June 1990, p. 16.

[4]The Bankruptcy Code of 1978 reduced the time that bankruptcies can be kept in a consumer's credit file from 14 to 10 years, effective October 1, 1979.

[5]Sec. 605 of the Fair Credit Reporting Act.

obtained through personal interviews with the consumer's neighbors, friends, or associates, whereas consumer credit reports are composed of factual ledger experience only. Investigative consumer reports are used mostly by insurance companies to evaluate applicants for their insurance policies. The Fair Credit Reporting Act provides that underwriting purposes is the specific permissible purpose for this kind of report, so they may not be used when claims are filed.

The Federal Trade Commission, which is responsible for enforcing the act, has announced interpretations that have affected credit bureaus' mode of operation. Two of the more interesting are:

1. Prohibition of books containing credit ratings of individual consumers (called credit guides), unless the ratings are coded to ensure that consumers can't be identified by name.
2. Permission to credit bureaus to offer promotional lists (described earlier in this chapter) so long as the user of such a list certifies that every person on the list will receive the solicitation.

If a credit grantor declines credit privileges to an applicant based on information in a consumer credit report, the credit grantor must advise the applicant and provide the name and address of the credit bureau. This applies even if the credit report was only partly responsible for the decision. Notification is customarily provided in writing.

The business is not required to give any information to the consumer as to what the report contains. In fact, the contractual agreement between the credit bureau and the business concern prohibits such disclosure. One reason is that the firm that compiles the report (the bureau) is in a much better position to explain it and to be helpful to the declined applicant.

Further, if the credit grantor denies credit based on data from sources other than a credit bureau, the consumer must be informed at the time of denial of the right to request in writing, within 60 days, the nature of the information on which the rejection was based. For example, a jewelry store might have asked the credit department of a hardware store how regularly the applicant pays. The intent of the law is that the consumer be given enough facts to be able to refute or challenge the accuracy of the information. The law does not require the credit grantor to tell the consumer the names of the sources checked.

Since the FCRA became law, credit grantors have been acutely conscious of the definition of a credit reporting agency. Legally, if a credit grantor relays third-party data as distinguished from its own ledger information, it becomes a credit reporting agency itself. For example, suppose a jewelry store calls a hardware store about a consumer's paying habits and the hardware store passes along secondhand information learned from a clothing store. The hardware store is then considered to be a consumer reporting agency and is liable for all the record-keeping and interview procedures in the FCRA.

One of the most important provisions of the act is the right of consumers to know what is on file about them in credit bureaus. The law provides that every consumer reporting agency reveal the following on request and proper identification of the consumer:

1. The nature and substance of all information (except medical information) in its files on the consumer at the time of the request.
2. The sources of the information; except that the sources of information acquired solely for use in preparing an investigative consumer report and actually used for no other purpose need not be disclosed: Provided, that in the event an action is brought under this title, such sources shall be available to the plaintiff under appropriate discovery procedures in the court in which the action is brought.
3. The recipients of any consumer report on the consumer which it has furnished—
   a. for employment purposes within the two-year period preceding the request, and
   b. for any other purpose within the six-month period preceding the request.[6]

The law states that consumers cannot be charged for an interview if, within the past 30 days, they have been denied credit because of a credit report from a credit bureau or have received a notice from a collection department affiliated with a credit bureau. Bureaus usually charge for interviews if the consumer just wants to find out what the file contains and has not been refused credit.

Individuals can sue any creditor or credit reporting agency for violating the law about who can have access to its credit records and about correcting errors in its files. The individual is entitled to actual damages plus punitive damages as allowed if the violation is proved to be intentional. In any successful lawsuit, court costs and attorney fees are awarded. An unauthorized person who secures a credit report—or a credit reporting agency employee who supplies a credit report to unauthorized persons—may be fined up to $5,000 or imprisoned for a year, or both.

AUTOMATED CREDIT BUREAU REPORTING

Operating a noncomputerized credit bureau in a major city in the United States now is impossible. Developments and refinements have even made computerization available to credit bureaus in smaller towns.

Four major organizations—TRW, Trans Union, Equifax, and CSC Credit Services—either own credit bureaus or provide bureaus with

---

[6]Sec. 609 of the Fair Credit Reporting Act.

computer service. CSC Credit Services in Houston, Texas, has its file data in Equifax's computer system, leaving only three database systems.

Consumer Credit Association (CCA), formerly ACB Services, Inc., delivers account information from national and regional credit grantors to smaller, manually operated bureaus. Using a method called *Trade Verification Service* (TVS), CCA obtains computer receivable tapes monthly from major retailers, bank credit card companies, and charge card plan companies. At a processing center, these accounts receivable tapes are put into a standardized format, sorted by ZIP code, and merged into alphabetical consumer name sequence. CCA then sells this information to bureaus that request it to supplement their files. The data may be in one of three forms—paper printout, microfiche, or disk tapes—depending on which form the receiving bureau requests.

Computerized bureaus also provide prescreened mailing lists of people whose files indicate good credit histories, according to the criteria supplied by the credit grantors. Lenders and retailers purchase these for mass-mail solicitations for loans and credit and charge cards.

TRW INFORMATION SYSTEMS AND SERVICES

One of TRW Inc.'s best known businesses, TRW Credit Data, is part of the company's Information Systems and Services group. TRW Information Systems and Services is made up of seven other businesses ranging from a commercial credit reporting division to a division that develops and manufactures image processors for financial institutions.

TRW Credit Data, one of the nation's largest consumer credit bureaus, provides computerized credit reporting services to qualified subscribers as permitted by law and company policy. The subscribers include credit grantors, employers, and insurers. TRW's consumer credit database contains factual credit history information on nearly 170 million consumers nationally.

In order to access the database, subscribers must transmit a subscriber code and password in addition to the required identifying information about the consumer. Identifying information includes the following: full name (including generation, such as junior or senior), current and previous addresses for the past five years, social security number, and year of birth. The information is transmitted from the subscriber's computer terminal to TRW's data center in Anaheim, California, over a private data communications network. Within 3 to 10 seconds, the credit information is retrieved from TRW's database and transmitted back to the subscriber in the form of a credit report.

TRW's consumer credit report, called the TRW Credit Profile Report (see Figure 9–6), contains identifying and credit-related information about consumers. Information that identifies a consumer is used to locate and display a complete credit history about the consumer. Name, addresses, social security number, year of birth, and employer's name are all part of the identifying information. The main portion of the report contains factual credit history information about open and closed credit accounts as well as selected public record information, limited to bankruptcies, judgments, and tax liens. All of this information is reported to TRW monthly.

FIGURE 9–6

The TRW Credit Profile Report

With input from our subscribers, the TRW Credit Profile report was designed in an easy-to-read format. Information has been included which will enhance your decision-making capabilities. Similar data elements are grouped together so you can analyze data faster.

Files on nearly 170 million credit active consumers nationwide are maintained in the TRW data base. Your inquiry initiates a search of this data base which produces an applicant's credit history—the TRW Credit Profile report. An illustration and description of a sample Profile report are shown in this brochure.

1 A code which identifies the **TRW or Credit Bureau office** nearest to the consumer's current address. Use for consumer referrals.

2 Consumer's **name and address** as recorded on automated subscriber tapes, including date of most recent update.

3 Consumer's **Social Security number.**

4 Consumer's **year of birth.**

5 **Spouse's first name initial.**

6 **Employer's name and address** as reported via a subscriber inquiry as of the date shown.

7 **FACS+ Summary:** contains messages related to the FACS+ fraud prevention services.

8 Message which displays if a consumer's Social Security number has not been issued or if the number is not valid, based on a check of Social Security Administration records.

9 The number of previous inquiries using this consumer's Social Security number within the last four months. **Optional.**

10 The number of previous inquiries using this consumer's current address within the last four months. **Optional.**

11 The **nonresidential** type of **establishment,** address and telephone number displays if a consumer's address matches an address listed in TRW's file of nonresidential addresses.

12 **The Profile Summary:** contains 16 significant calculations from the Profile report. **Optional.**

13 The total number of public record items.

14 Total installment loan account balance owed by the consumer.

15 Total real estate loan account balance owed by the consumer.

16 Total revolving charge account balance owed by the consumer.

17 Total dollar amount of past due payments owed by the consumer.

18 The combined total of scheduled and estimated monthly payments owed by the consumer.

19 Total dollar amount of real estate payments owed by the consumer.

20 Total percentage of revolving credit still available to the consumer.

Note: An **asterisk** following any Profile Summary total indicates not all trade lines had an amount which could be included in the total.

21 Total number of inquiries.

22 Total of inquiries made within six months preceding the date of the Profile report.

23 Total number of trade lines on the Profile report.

24 Total of accounts which have been paid satisfactory or paid after having been previously delinquent.

25 Total of accounts which are current or paid satisfactory.

26 Total of accounts which are now delinquent or derogatory.

27 Total of accounts which were delinquent or derogatory, and either have been paid in full, or brought current.

28 The date the oldest trade line on the report was opened.

29 **Risk model score:** generated if you use one of TRW's credit risk models. **Optional.**

30 **Score factors:** codes which contributed to the risk model score generated if you use one of TRW's credit risk models. **Optional.**

31 **Public record:** court name, case number, filing date, plaintiff, court code, amount and type of public record. Public record information consists of bankruptcies, liens, and judgments against a consumer.

32 An **asterisk** preceding public record information or a trade line indicates that information may need further review.

FIGURE 9–6 (continued)

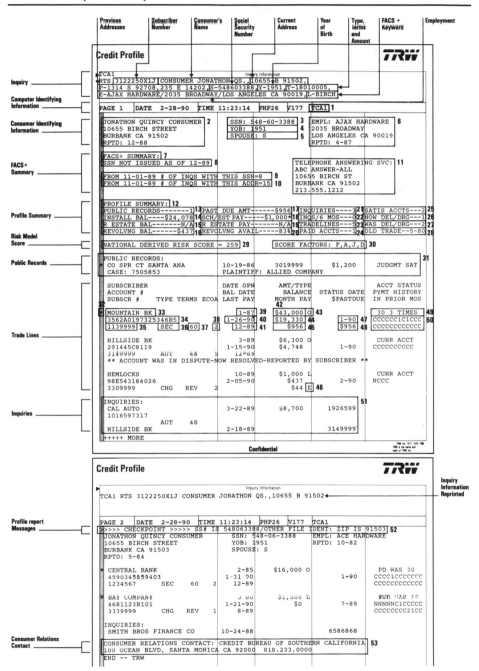

FIGURE 9–6 (continued)

33 Reporting **subscriber's name.**

34 Consumer's **account number.**

35 Reporting **subscriber's identification number.**

36 Type of account.

37 Terms of account.

38 Code describing **consumer's association** to the account per the Equal Credit Opportunity Act.

39 Date the account was **opened.**

40 Balance date: the date balance information was extracted from the subscriber's accounts receivable file.

41 Date of consumer's **last payment** on the account.

42 The **amount** of the loan or credit established.

43 Indicates if the amount is an original loan **(O)**, credit limit **(L)**, high balance **(H)**, or charge-off **(C)**.

44 Current balance of the account.

45 Monthly payment amount the consumer is scheduled to pay each month on the account. **Note:** a scheduled monthly payment is indicated if there is no qualifying character directly after the amount.

46 Estimated monthly payment amount: indicated by the qualifying character "E" directly after the monthly payment amount.

47 Status date: the date the account status was reported to TRW.

48 The **amount past due** for the account.

49 Account status comments indicate the payment condition of the account as of the status date.

50 The **consumer's payment history** during the past 24 months. The codes reflect the status of the account for each month and are displayed for balance reporting subscribers only.

C	Current
N	Current account/zero balance reported
1	30 days past the due date
2	60 days past the due date
3	90 days past the due date
4	120 days past the due date
5	150 days past the due date
6	180 days past the due date
—(Dash)	No history reported for that month
Blank	No history maintained; see account status comment.

51 Inquiries: indicate a Profile report was received by the subscriber listed. Inquiring subscriber, account number, date of inquiry and subscriber identification number are shown. Type, terms and amount may display and are from the subscriber's inquiry input for that particular report.

52 Profile report messages: display certain differences between consumer identifying information supplied in the inquiry and information in the data base.

53 Name, address and telephone number of **TRW office or Credit Bureau** nearest to the consumer's current address. Use for consumer referrals. **Optional.**

TRW Credit Data does not collect information about checking account deposits, savings accounts, race, religion, sex, salary, income, personal lifestyle, medical history, or criminal records.

Open, current accounts remain on the report indefinitely while closed or paid accounts are removed within 10 years. As set by federal law, adverse credit information remains on file for a maximum of seven years, with the exception of bankruptcies, which remain for a maximum of 10 years. Inquiries to a consumer's file are retained up to two years.

Federal law allows consumers to question report information that they believe to be inaccurate. The bureau, in turn, is required to reverify the information with its source and report the results of the investigation to the consumer. There is no charge for this type of investigation.

FIGURE 9–6 (concluded)

The TRW Credit Profile Report Messages

〉〉〉〉〉 **CHECKPOINT** 〉〉〉 **SSN NOT ISSUED AS OF 08/87**
This Checkpoint message appears on the Profile report if the applicant's Social Security number has not been issued as of the date displayed in the message. In general, Checkpoint messages alert you to pertinent information about specific applicant identifiers. When you see a Checkpoint message, you may want to further investigate the information supplied by the applicant.

〉〉〉〉〉 **CHECKPOINT** 〉〉〉〉〉 **SS# IS 524479971**
A Checkpoint Variation message will appear when the information in TRW's file relating to the applicant's Social Security number, generation or year of birth does not correspond to the information entered in the subscriber's inquiry. **It is possible that the information may not pertain to the individual inquired upon.**

〉〉〉〉〉 **CHECKPOINT** 〉〉〉〉〉 *****AKA SEARCH *** LASTNAME IS SMITH**
The AKA Search enhancement is designed to automatically retrieve and display additional consumer data associated with alternative surnames— such as aliases, misspelled names and maiden or previous surnames. **It is possible that the information may not pertain to the individual inquired upon.**

〉〉〉〉〉 **CHECKPOINT** 〉〉〉〉〉 ***** NICKNAME SEARCH *** 1ST NAME IS BOB**
The Nickname Search enhancement includes a Nickname Table containing alternative first names which may be used by an individual. This Nickname Table is automatically referenced for each inquiry and searches with both the given name and the nickname to retrieve additional credit information on an individual. **It is possible that the information may not pertain to the individual inquired upon.**

------***ATTN* FILE VARIATION: MID INIT IS J**
A File Variation message will appear when there are variations in minor identifiers in TRW's file relating to the applicant's middle initial, spouse initial, street initial, last three digits of the zip code or the second and third characters of the first name. **It is possible that the information may not pertain to the individual inquired upon.**

------ **FILE IDENT: MID INIT IS Q**
A File Ident message will appear when information is not given on input, but exists on file.

CAUTION THE ABOVE REPORT MAY CONTAIN ITEMS FOR OTHER MEMBERS OF THE SAME FAMILY
This message may appear when names and addresses are similar. It means that closer checking of the application or with the applicant may be necessary. **It is possible that the information may not pertain to the individual inquired upon.**

****AUTO-FILE—CONTAINS AUTOMATED SUBSCRIBER INFORMATION ONLY****
This message indicates geographic areas which, in general, contain data received from national companies. Local credit grantor and public record information is not yet available.

CONSUMER STATEMENT
TRW Credit Data will accommodate statements on the Profile report in accordance with the Fair Credit Reporting Act and state reporting laws.

Courtesy of TRW Information Systems and Services

In addition to its base product credit report, TRW Credit Data offers a variety of services[7] that assist subscribers with account management through account monitoring and statistical modeling. TRW has in-house statisticians who develop models that assess a consumer's future credit risk. One of the company's newest products values loan portfolios and

---

[7]See "A Credit Report That's Easy on Your Eyes," *Business Week*, February 21, 1990, p. 88E; Wanda Cantrell, "Richard Whilden: Guiding the Growth of TRW's Information Systems Group," *Credit Card Management*, November–December 1988, p. 6; John Stewart, "The Battle of the Bureaus," *Credit Card Management*, August 1989, p. 47.

identifies the amount of cross-sell opportunities. This automated evaluation results in written reports.

TRW was the first credit reporting agency to use artificial intelligence in combination with an expert system to monitor access to its database. In 1989 TRW purchased one of its primary competitors, Dallas-based Chilton Corp., and strengthened its file in the Midwest and South. Chilton's consumer credit database was merged with TRW's that same year. TRW kept Chilton's collection business, renaming it TRW Receivables Management Services. It is based in Dallas.

Both the Credit Data and the Business Credit[8] divisions are headquartered in Orange, California.

TRANS UNION

Trans Union is one of the nation's leading consumer credit information companies. It maintains more than 220 million names from all 50 states in its computerized database at corporate headquarters in Chicago. The database is comprised of accounts receivable data from national, regional, and local credit grantors.

Trans Union has provided national credit reporting services since 1988 and has followed a strategy of acquiring regional credit bureaus, signing contracts with other private or merchant-owned bureaus to bring them into the network, and opening owned bureaus in key locations. In 1980 Trans Union was comprised of seven large, owned bureaus and a scattering of contract service bureaus. In 1990 Trans Union had 45 owned bureaus and more than 220 contract service bureaus. Credit grantors now can locate people who have moved to any part of the country.

The existence of national consumer credit files also has allowed credit grantors, such as bank card issuers and major retailers, to centralize their operations into large credit centers serving multiple geographic areas. Trans Union gathers and continuously updates accounts receivable information from credit grantors at all levels, even those that do not maintain large mainframe computer systems. It also collects full public record information in every county and state nationwide.

Trans Union introduced the Credit Reporting On-Line Network Utility System (CRONUS) in 1971. It was the first on-line information storage and retrieval data processing system to compliment the automated techniques used by credit grantors. CRONUS provides credit grantors across the country with fast and accurate one-source credit information on consumers. Each bureau within CRONUS electronically maintains and enriches consumers' credit reports continuously, both on-line and off-line.

With oral inquiries, an operator keys in the subject's identifying information: name, current address, previous address, social security number,

---

[8]The Business Credit Division of TRW is discussed in Chapter 16.

and name of spouse. Within seconds, the consumer's credit file is displayed on the screen. The operator then reads the information to the prospective credit grantor. There are two other methods of obtaining credit reports: via teletype and with CPU-to-CPU hookups.

Because operators can access any of the credit bureau's databases, they can get information on consumers residing in any city served by Trans Union. By adding or reconciling file information, the operators can update a consumer's file on line.

In-house clerical handling of credit inquiries can be reduced by mailing credit applications to the credit bureau. An operator then keys in the application information, receives a Trans Union credit report, attaches it to the application, and forwards both to the credit grantor all in the same day.

A Trans Union credit report combines demographics with trade and financial data. It is kept valid with information supplied by national, regional, and local credit grantors who ship accounts receivable tapes to Trans Union for updating. To help credit grantors spot potential problem areas at a glance, tradelines are categorized from worst to best on the basis of current ratings. The report also provides a 24-month history of payments, giving the lender a clear picture of an account's status with specific credit grantors and how it has performed over the past two years.

Trans Union and other credit reporting companies have branched into providing broad lines of consumer credit products, enhancements, and services, spanning many applications. Among the innovative products now offered are:

- Point scoring systems to predict account delinquencies and bankruptcies.
- Alert messages to pinpoint file discrepancies or unusual credit activities that call for further investigation.
- Fraud databases to protect against illegal activities.
- Search features to locate customers who have moved, changed their names, or "skipped."
- Reports that provide credit grantors, financial institutions, and marketing organizations with information on how, where, and by whom credit is being used in their markets.

Because of the depth of its database, Trans Union provides direct marketing and mailing list services. Trans Union's subsidiary, TransMark, goes several steps beyond basic list compilation. List offerings based on Trans Union's national database include names of people who have moved to new residences in the past 90 days and people who have applied for a mortgage and may be moving soon. Prescreening identifies creditworthy consumers before a mailing is made, and "cluster groups" of people of similar affluence and lifestyles can be targeted. In the future, credit bureaus may become a one-stop shopping place for all of a credit grantor's solicitation and promotion marketing needs—from targeting of customers, to preparation and distribution of mailings, to processing of responses.

Other expanded capabilities within the credit bureau industry include automated credit application processing and score card monitoring products. These recently have become available through Trans Union's newest subsidiary, TransAction, under a long-term exclusive agreement with CCN Systems Ltd., Europe's largest credit reporting company. TransAction can compile, analyze, score, and evaluate all the application information necessary to make an informed credit decision and pass it on to the credit grantors with a recommendation for approval, rejection, or further review, based on the credit grantor's criteria. The application can be entered on-site by the client or at a processing center.

Like many corporations, Trans Union is expanding beyond the United States. The company is already well established in Puerto Rico and the Virgin Islands, and last year it entered the Canadian marketplace with offices in Montreal, Toronto, and Vancouver.

EQUIFAX INC.

Equifax Inc., founded by Guy and Cator Woolford in 1899, was formed to provide local Atlanta businesses with individuals' credit histories. Today the company serves more than 60,000 customers in business and industry. Equifax Credit Information Service's consumer reporting companies are Equifax Inc. and Acrofax in the United States, and Equifax Services Inc. in Canada. In 1987 CSC Credit Services and Equifax Credit Information Services merged their databases. With some 16,000 employees in 1,100 locations throughout the United States, Canada, and Europe, this organization provides informational services and automated systems to help its customers evaluate risk and market products and services.

Through five broad service areas, Equifax provides:

1. Consumer Credit and Collection Services. This national credit bureau network provides information for the completion of consumer credit transactions, services for the management and collection of accounts receivable, and the detection and prevention of fraud.

Customers include retailers, financial institutions, charge card companies, consumer finance businesses, and automobile finance and leasing firms.

2. Insurance and Special Services. These are systems and services for insurance underwriting, claim investigations, premium auditing, rate and policy management, and agency communications. Also included are employment selection services, mortgage loan origination services, floor plan auditing, and residential and commercial energy audits.

Customers served include property and casualty insurers; life and health insurers; mortgage lenders; financial services companies;

employers of all types of manufacturers and distributors of consumer goods and capital equipment; government agencies; and public utilities.

3. Marketing Information Services. These activities include marketing-related products and services pertaining to marketing analysis, targeted demographic information, automated application processing, credit prescreening, statistical modeling, project management, data processing, account acquisition services, and marketing research.

Customers include insurance companies, retailers, banks, consumer credit companies, manufacturers and marketers of consumer goods and services, public utilities, direct-mail marketers, and government agencies.

4. Technology Information Services. Activities included here are systems, analysis, research, operations, and support for the company's various technological resources. It functions to increase technological responsiveness to improve data processing and systems operations.

5. Equifax Canada. This area provides consumer credit reports, automated business credit reports, accounts collection, and insurance underwriting services and systems.

Customers served include retailers, banks and other financial institutions, most major insurance companies in Canada, manufacturers and distributors of consumer goods, and government agencies.

SPECIALIZED CREDIT BUREAUS AND OTHER SOURCES

There are many specialized credit reporting agencies throughout the United States. Some of these serve particular professional groups, while others handle specialized types of reporting. The medical and dental professions can use the Medical Credit Bureau, which has a collection service as well as a credit reporting service. Physicians and dentists have had a history of poor financial management, but the educational programs of the American Medical Association, the American Dental Association, and credit groups have done much to overcome past business practices. Services and reports to medical and dental users do not differ fundamentally from those provided to businesses.

Small loan companies and a few other financial institutions have established lenders' exchanges. These exchanges operate in some metropolitan markets for the express purpose of servicing particular types of lending and financing institutions. They keep master records of all loans or contracts financed by their members so they can rapidly check outstanding loans against a prospective loan customer. Subscribers can make telephone inquiries and receive immediate reports consisting of lists of outstanding loans against a potential debtor and the names of the lenders. Then lenders can be questioned about their experience with the subject. Subscribers or members of the exchange must disclose their borrowers by name, so that a complete record of the subject's similar dealings is available. Exchanges frequently service the small loan industry in a particular metropolitan area. In some cities, banks and sales finance companies also use similar facilities.

DISCUSSION QUESTIONS

1. What effect has the Fair Credit Reporting Act had on credit bureaus? On credit grantors? On consumers?
2. Discuss the several types of consumer reporting agencies.
3. Trace the beginning and development of the local credit bureau.
4. What are the principal activities of Associated Credit Bureaus, Inc.?
5. Explain why credit bureau work must be highly confidential.
6. Discuss the principal sources of credit bureau information.
7. What data is reported on Form 2000?
8. Discuss the variety of services available from local credit bureaus.
9. Which of these services is the local credit bureau in your community providing its subscribers?
10. Describe the methods that credit bureaus use to charge for their services.
11. How valuable is the local credit bureau serving your community?
12. Tour your local credit bureau, and discuss with bureau executives their views of the future of automated credit reporting.
13. Explain the operations of TRW Information Systems and Services.
14. Does TRW's credit report contain sufficient information? If not, what information should be added?
15. Explain how Trans Union carries out its operations.
16. If you were the owner of a credit bureau, would you want to be serviced by Trans Union? Why or why not?
17. Explain the organization of Equifax Inc.
18. Discuss the five service areas of Equifax.
19. Check to see if there is a lenders' exchange in your community.
20. What does TRW Credit Data provide?
21. What identifying information does the TRW Credit Profile report contain?
22. What consumer credit information does TRW Credit Data *not* collect?
23. Why did TRW purchase Chilton Corp.? What did it gain by doing so?
24. What comprises the database of Trans Union?
25. Explain the operations of Trans Union's CRONUS and TransMark.
26. How has Trans Union become a global corporation?

10

Decision Making, Limit Setting, and Transaction Handling

The Objectives or Goals of Chapter 10 Are:

1. To explain why decisions are the heart of all credit work.
2. To discuss grading as an analytical device.
3. To explain the use of the credit grading form.
4. To illustrate the use of the credit grade in actual operations.
5. To discuss the advantages and disadvantages of credit scoring plans.
6. To comment on discrimination in decision making.
7. To distinguish between identification and authorization.
8. To discuss automated approaches to credit control.

Decisions are the heart of all credit work. Customers offer credit for goods, services, and money, and credit managers must decide whether to accept or refuse the credit transaction. Judgment should be based on the information that is readily and economically available and most pertinent to the problem and on an analysis that is sufficiently penetrating to make the available data yield the greatest help possible in arriving at a correct decision. Generally, information available without excessive cost or undue delay is incomplete. The facts obtained through the credit investigation must be used to the utmost to offset the common deficiency.

Good judgment is one of the most difficult skills to develop but one of the most necessary to the credit manager. Because it is so difficult to develop good credit judgment, too many credit managers emphasize the negative aspects of credit decisions. Errors of judgment as revealed by bad-debt losses are obvious, but errors of judgment resulting in lost sales are well hidden. Thus the easy route is to err through excessive refusals of doubtful credit transactions. Sales lost for this reason are difficult to total.

Errors of judgment may arise from insufficient information, misleading or false information, or improper interpretation of the data on hand. The investigation should supply sufficient information on which to base a decision and should reveal false information as well as give a basis for properly interpreting data that otherwise would be misleading. Unfortunately, the pressures of time and costs and the desire for sales often cause inadequate investigations and faulty decisions. Faulty investigations tend to increase collection costs and bad-debt losses; excessive investigations tend to increase investigation costs, lost time, and customer irritation. The credit manager walks a narrow path between extremes, hoping to compensate for the lack of data by more careful analysis.

The credit investigation brings together the raw materials that are processed through the credit analysis in order to get the final product—*the credit decision*. This end product is the objective of all the efforts directed toward gathering information and all the skill exercised in analyzing the information.

DECISIONS—THE ESSENCE OF CREDIT WORK

The credit offered must be examined before a decision is made to accept or reject it. Making such decisions is the single most important credit activity. The success of the credit operation rests squarely on the appraisal and acceptance of the credit offered; the activities of the credit department in administering its work and collecting accounts may make the operation more successful or less successful, but they cannot replace decisions.

The credit executive must appraise or evaluate an individual's credit against the standards set by a firm's established policy. In order to appraise, the credit executive must have information supplied by a credit investigation. Analysis and decision are aided by proper operating procedures, which assure needed and accurate information made meaningful by proper analytical processes. After policy is established and standards are set, the subsequent stages are gathering information through investigation, evaluating and analyzing the information, reaching the decision to accept or reject, and carrying out the credit department operations to reach the ultimate goal—payment by a satisfied customer.

Analysis and decision are necessary in every consumer credit transaction. At the time of acceptance, the firm expects that the individual will pay the amount at some predetermined future date. When a predictable loss account is accepted, it should be called by its proper name—charity, not credit.[1] Of course, some accounts that appear safe when they are opened or when additional charges are added eventually fail to pay. Such defaults are inevitable, especially when a forecast is made on the basis of incomplete information. In the face of sometimes inaccurate and incomplete information, greater analytical skill must be employed. The goal is

---

[1]Failure to recognize the distinction between charity and credit causes many doctors to complain of large bad-debt losses. Doctors often feel that they cannot refuse to give a patient the benefit of their skill even though there is no prospect of payment. If such contributions were correctly labeled as charity rather than entered on the books as credit, doctors would not confuse their charity cases with bad-debt losses.

not perfection in the sense of no losses. Rather, it is losses within the limits set by the credit policy.

Credit information is necessarily somewhat incomplete, and it is needlessly costly and time-consuming to try to make it complete. In addition, not all information is verified; some information must be accepted as the basis for decision without verification, and some can be verified only by reasonable inference. Despite these limitations, the first step of the analysis should be to evaluate the credit information at hand. This step should be based on a complete review of the credit file and an examination of all the information in it. During this examination, the two questions "How complete is the information?" and "Is the information verified?" should always be in the forefront of the analyst's thinking. The source of the information lends greater or lesser credibility to certain statements. Other statements may be considered reliable because they are consistent with other facts. By way of illustration, credit analysts may not verify an applicant's income through the applicant's employer or other sources if they know it is consistent with the community level for similar occupations or with the amounts paid by that employer. They may not verify the applicant's length of employment either, if it coincides with information at hand on the applicant's age and period of residence in the community. Information from known informants may be considered more reliable than that from unknown informants, or information from a professional credit reporting source may be evaluated higher than information from personal sources.

Evaluation of credit information should not be made a separate part of the credit analysis; however, before analysis the entire file should be reviewed for credibility and completeness. If sufficient information is not available, the investigation should be extended. In this case, the specific information needed is known, and the investigation can focus on obtaining it. When the information is not reliable or believable, the investigation can focus on clearing up such doubts. In addition to this review before the analysis, the evaluation should be continued during the analysis. As each element of the credit case is examined, it should be evaluated for completeness and credibility. Thus, when the final credit decision is reached, its reliability or unreliability can be based on the completeness and credibility of the source information.

CREDIT IS RELATIVE

A particular credit transaction must be measured against the certainty of payment and found acceptable or unacceptable on the basis of the firm's credit policies. In effect, the credit department must decide whether or not the particular case falls within the limits established by these credit policies. Judgment is necessarily relative. If the credit department approves only accounts that will undoubtedly pay under all circumstances, the firm will gain very little extra business from its credit service. To put it another way, a soundly operating credit department should have some losses—if it doesn't, it is selecting its accounts too strictly and thus rejecting some profitable business.

Standards aren't always exact. From time to time, the need for volume, general economic conditions, the nature of the clientele sought, the territorial conditions, or various other environmental situations may cause a firm to change its previous standards.

Credit standards are intimately related to other marketing policies. If a firm is selling a high-quality product to preferred customers, its credit standards can be quite high. Conversely, when a firm is selling an economy product to a mass market, somewhat lower credit standards may be indicated.

Stricter terms are usually associated with lower credit standards. For installment sales of durable goods, the lower the credit standard, the more necessary it is to obtain down payments that establish a feeling of ownership and monthly payments high enough and frequent enough to steadily increase this equity. When a firm accepts credits of lower standard, it is more important that the time and the amount of the payments be adjusted to the time income is received and to the amounts received. Unhappily, easier terms attract lower-rated credit risk, and the task of rejecting risks that are truly substandard becomes more difficult.

Difficult as it may be to set exact standards, credit departments must compare specific cases against the standard established. The easy cases are those that are clearly acceptable and those that are definitely substandard. The credit department must then concentrate its efforts on selecting acceptable accounts from the rest. The clearly good cases will not need a credit department; the clearly bad can be detected easily. The talent must all be exercised on those that fall into the probably-good-enough class.

GRADING AS AN ANALYTICAL DEVICE

The quality of the whole is the sum of the quality of a number of credit elements or pieces. When credit analysts consider each factor separately, they can judge each independently without the halo effect that certain elements are likely to cast over the whole. When a credit decision is made on an overall basis—the credit is acceptable, or the credit is not acceptable—one or two elements usually exercise an undue influence. The decision-making process is better when each pertinent element is considered separately and properly appraised. This tends to avoid overlooking pertinent items or giving relatively unimportant items excessive weight, and it gives more assurance that all available evidence is brought to bear on the problem.

Two major points should be recognized: (1) credit quality is a relative evaluation, not an absolute measurement; and (2) measurement of a number of specific factors is likely to be more accurate than a single overall judgment. In the decision-making process these two generalizations may be attained through the device of grading the credit. *Grading the credit is the orderly examination of evidence and recording of the quality judgment drawn from specific evidence bearing on specific factors.* It involves assigning a quality grade or rating to each pertinent element of the credit appraisal and a summary grade to the combined judgments of the whole credit.

Separate grading of all the factors pertinent to the decision permits specific factors to be appraised independently on the basis of evidence relevant to each. When a quality grade is assigned, the relative evaluation is recorded for that factor. Skilled and experienced credit personnel do this automatically, perhaps unconsciously. A formal grading device assures that less experienced people will follow the same procedure. By working through a formal method of grading, beginners gain sound analytical skills and good habits of analysis. A grading system results in improved and more standardized credit decisions.

If the grading process is formal and systematic, beginners can be assured that they have considered all pertinent elements and used all available evidence. They can also see the extent to which the information has been verified; if they are unable to reach a decision because of insufficient verification or inadequate information, they can verify more evidence or gather additional information.

Elements to Be Graded

Certain classifications of evidence are standard subjects for analysis in any consumer credit appraisal. Evidence relative to income, employment, and payment habits is essential; such additional qualities as residence, age, and reserve assets are more debatable.[2] Obviously, no one list of qualities is accepted by all credit analysts, and no one list meets the needs of all credit situations. For example, analysis of an installment purchase becomes more meaningful when equity in the purchase is added. When the dealer has some contingent responsibility, as often occurs when such paper is discounted with a sales finance company, the dealer's credit standing attains added importance. Similarly, when analyzing a cash loan, the grade assigned to collateral usually has considerable meaning, and the purpose of the loan also may be graded.

Credit Grading Form

The grading forms shown in Figures 10–1 and 10–2 illustrate classifications of information important to a credit decision and include those qualities sufficient to assure an appraisal of the credit applicant. For practical

---

[2]The Equal Credit Opportunity Act restricts the use of age as a quality in making a credit decision.

FIGURE 10-1 **Option-Terms Revolving Credit Account Grading Form**

| Credit Qualities | Grade | | | Verified |
	Good 1	Fair 2	Poor 3	
Income				
Employment				
Residence				
Age				
Reserve assets				
Payment record				
Summary—overall appraisal				
Limit:	Accept _____		Refuse _____	
Special conditions:				

reasons, the credit qualities to be graded should be limited in number. Too long a list makes the operations unduly time-consuming and also causes difficulty in appraising the evidence. Too brief a list may not bring all the evidence into focus, since it causes judgments to be formed on the basis of an unrepresentative list of qualities. The items suggested fall between an extended list and an abbreviated list and are what experience shows to be practical.

The evidence obtained during the course of the investigation does not fall into neat and mutually inclusive classifications consistent with the qualities being graded. The same items of evidence, or the same factual information, may be used in determining the grade on several qualities.

For example, John Doe receives an income of $375 a week. With these limited facts, it is difficult to grade his income; we know nothing of the certainty of its continuance or the demands on it. We can't judge if it's adequate without knowing, Adequate for what? or if it's certain without knowing, Relative to what? If we call Doe's employer and find out that Doe is a cutter in a local shoe factory, has been employed there for 7 years, and is 31 years old, we can judge that his income is likely to continue based on age and length of employment. We can make a better judgment if we know something about the shoe business and the market position of the local shoe factory. Knowledge is further improved when we know something about the employment policies of the local company. These comments

FIGURE 10–2 **Cash Loan Grading Form**

Credit Qualities	Grade			Verified
	Good 1	Fair 2	Poor 3	
Income				
Employment				
Residence				
Age				
Reserve assets				
Payment record				
Collateral				
Purpose of loan				
Summary—overall appraisal				
Accept _____ Refuse _____				

illustrate how valuable general knowledge of local and national business conditions is to credit analysts.

With the facts now before us, we might be warranted in assigning a grade of 1 to Doe's income, although we still wouldn't be able to grade exactly on income adequacy. (The information about income is verified and may be so noted on the grading form.) Other facts may help us grade this factor. Suppose we add the information that Mrs. Doe works part-time in a dress shop, approximately 20 hours a week, for an hourly wage of $4.75. On the basis of the information now before us, we might assign a grade of 1 to income and to consider the grade verified.

Some facts might be uncovered that would make the income appear inadequate—the existence of other obligations, for example. Suppose the credit bureau reports that the Does have purchased a home and will be making payments of $360 a month; they also bought a car five months ago, on which they have to make 24 payments of $135 a month; a department store reports a balance due of $175 with payments slow; a clothing store reports a balance of $75, payments 60 days slow; and a men's store reports no balance now but slow previous payments. The Does have two children, ages eight and two. Because their income may not be adequate relative to their obligations, a grade of 2 may be assigned to the income in the light of these new facts. A grade of 3 would be warranted if the information indicated the continuance of the income to be doubtful—for example, information that the shoe factory was about to shut down for 60 days because of lack of orders.

PROCEDURE IN USING GRADING FORMS. When using the grading forms previously illustrated, or similar forms, credit analysts record their appraisal of each credit quality in the appropriate column. These columns may be labeled good, fair, or poor, or they may be given numerical grades: 1, 2, or 3. Three divisions are best, since finer gradations may confuse the process. General grading standards are as follows:

Good, 1:   Credit qualities that indicate the credit will be redeemed with no more than normal difficulty or effort.

Fair, 2:   Credit qualities that indicate the credit will be redeemed but only after abnormal difficulties or delays and in response to active collection effort.

Poor, 3:   Credit qualities that indicate the credit will not be redeemed.

Grading should predict credit experience. This prediction, or forecast, should reflect the best possible overall judgment considering all the evidence. Earlier, grading was recommended as a device that would assure all pertinent factors were considered and would avoid undue influence by a single especially favorable or unfavorable piece of evidence. Now caution is suggested against *not* considering a single unfavorable or favorable credit quality. In some circumstances, a single highly unfavorable quality (for example, inadequate or uncertain income or a very adverse payment record) should dictate the grade. Any one of the above might justify a grade of 3 even though all other elements of the credit appraisal are favorable. After all, the end result is a credit decision that, after considering all the evidence and properly analyzing it, forecasts the credit experience it is reasonable to expect. Although the forecast cannot be 100 percent correct, orderly and systematic analysis should improve the accuracy of decision making.

Summary grades can be defined as follows:

Good, 1:   Predicts excellent to satisfactory experience. Clearly, the credit is acceptable.

Fair, 2:   Predicts possible unsatisfactory experience but not so clearly predictable as to warrant rejection. Although credit losses and excessive costs will arise from handling such accounts, it is not possible to label the applicant as a certain loss. The maximum investigation and the most penetrating analysis should be lavished on such credits in order to screen out and reject those that should more correctly be labeled 3.

Poor, 3:   Predicts unsatisfactory experience with sufficient certainty that it warrants rejection. In other words, rejection does not deprive the creditor of a potential profit or prevent a worthy customer from having credit accepted. Instead, it saves the creditor from a predictable loss, and it prevents debtors from adding to their unredeemable obligations.

Use of Credit Grade in Operations

The usefulness of credit grades may extend beyond the aid they supply in making credit decisions.

The summary grade is a prediction of future experience. This prediction may be used to determine the type of collection effort needed and the time to apply it. When a credit that was highly questionable at the time of acceptance is up for collection, gentler collection reminders should be abandoned quickly and more severe collection devices applied. Routine and reminder types of collections are not appropriate, and early personal handling is indicated. Thus grading guides the intensity of collection effort and assists in obtaining satisfactory results from lower quality credits.

The quality of business also can be analyzed by means of the credit grades assigned. New accounts can be compared with older accounts, and a larger or smaller proportion of 2 credits can be taken to indicate that better or poorer quality credits are being accepted. Or when business comes from different areas in a city, the firm can compare the quality generated by various areas based on the proportion of 1 and 2 accounts. Various means of promoting credit sales—direct mail, newspaper advertisements, or solicitation on the floor—can be compared on the same basis. The comparisons that grading makes possible enable the credit department to operate more intelligently and purposefully.

When several people are employed in a credit department, analysis of the grades assigned by each can be helpful in comparing their operations. For educational purposes, actual experience with accounts can be compared with the grade initially assigned.

The development of the grading technique and learning how to apply it is in itself a useful educational device. Credit analysis can become better because of the emphasis on improving grading skill, and comparison of actual experience with predicted experience helps with self-criticism and self-improvement. Also, newer employees learn the art of making sound credit decisions more quickly when their decision making is directed by a grading system.

Grading accomplishes the "easy" part of separating cases that are clearly acceptable from those that are definitely substandard. Credit decision making faces its greatest challenge in the number 2 category. Some credit analysts believe that credit scoring, as described in the subsequent section, may hold a key to solving this problem.

CREDIT SCORING PLANS

Henry Wells, a statistician who worked for Aldens Inc. and Spiegel Inc. in the late 1930s and early 1940s, was the first to use statistical methods to evaluate a credit applicant's repayment potential. He devised a point scoring system for new mail-order time payment applications.

Applying mathematical and statistical models to the credit-granting decision gained recognition when David Durand of the National Bureau of Economic Research in New York published his 1941 study entitled *Risk Elements in Consumer Installment Financing*. He was the first to use discriminant analysis to measure credit risk. Subsequently, various attempts were made to investigate statistical credit systems, but the credit industry did not seriously consider credit scoring models until the mid-1960s.

The following statistical procedures are necessary to develop a point scoring system:

   a. Application samples are taken to include those that would be approved with and without a credit report and those rejected with and without a credit report.

   b. Factors on the application are correlated with the performance of these accounts over a period of time—6 months, 12 months, 18 months, and so on.

   c. Weights are derived from statistical techniques and the position of the particular group of applicants characterized by these factors.

   d. Statistical methodologies will attempt to measure the discriminating power of any single application factor, or any combination of factors, to the degree that the success or failure of the factor by itself indicates possession of the ability being measured. In credit point scoring, the ability being measured or predicted is payment ability.

   e. Certain predictions are inferred from payment performance measured over time for each group of applicants characterized by certain factors.

   f. Numerical weights are assigned to factors and the total of these weighted factors are plotted on a curve.[3]

The following definition of credit scoring has been given:

> A typical credit scoring system assigns points to certain characteristics deemed an indication of creditworthiness. The points are added together to determine an applicant's score. If the score is above a designated level, the applicant will receive credit. If the score is below another level, credit is refused. If an applicant scores within a range which makes him or her a possible good risk, then the company will run a credit check to further

---

[3]Stanley L. Mularz, "Statistical Origins and Concepts of Point Scoring," *The Credit World,* March–April 1987, p. 50.

FIGURE 10–3 **Credit Scoring System—Example**

Monthly Income	Points Awarded
Less than $400	0
$400 to $650	3
$651 to $800	7
$801 to $1,200	12
$1,200+	15
Age*	
21–27	11
28–35	5
36–48	2
48–61	12
61+	15
Years at Address	
Below .5	2
.5 to 2.49	8
2.5 to 5.49	19
5.5 to 12.49	25
12.49–over	30

*Some credit scoring systems award fewer points to people in their 30s and 40s because these individuals often have a relatively high amount of debt at that stage of their lives. The law permits using properly designed credit scoring systems to award points based on age. People who are 62 or older must receive the maximum number of points for this factor.

If, for example, you needed a score of 25 to get credit, you would need to make sure you had enough income at a certain age (and perhaps enough years at your present residence) to qualify for credit.

Remember, this example shows very generally how a credit scoring system works. Most systems consider more factors than this example—sometimes as many as 15 or 20. Usually these factors are obviously related to your creditworthiness. Sometimes, however, additional factors are included that may seem unusual. For example, some systems score the age of your car. While this may seem unrelated to creditworthiness, it is legal to use factors like these as long as they do not illegally discriminate on race, sex, marital status, national origin, religion, or age.

Source: "Just What Is a Credit Score?" *The Credit World,* January–February 1988, p. 59. Used with permission.

determine creditworthiness. Scoring systems may incorporate information on as few as 5 or as many as 350 characteristics.

Credit scoring systems are developed by evaluating a pool of recent applicants, both accepted and rejected, to determine what common characteristics the good credit risks had and what characteristics were common to applicants who subsequently defaulted or were slow to pay.[4]

To illustrate how credit scoring works, Figure 10–3 shows an example that uses only three factors to determine whether someone is creditworthy. (Most systems have 6 to 15 factors.)

---

[4]Reprinted by permission of *Credit* magazine, September 1, 1977, copyrighted 1977 by the National Consumer Finance Association. Also see the Suggested Readings at the end of the chapter.

Computers in Credit Scoring[5]

Computers are being used in credit scoring more frequently and efficiently than ever before. Some of the reasons for this increase include the following:

1. Software availability. Credit scoring programs have been written to run on mainframes down to the single-station personal computer. This allows organizations of any size to benefit from an automated approach to credit scoring. While programs that run on mainframe computers are more powerful and are able to store more data, some traits are common to all programs. The most important of these traits allows companies to set acceptance criteria based on management's weighting of risk factors.

2. Cost. From a cost standpoint, the purchaser of computers and software has benefited over the past few years. The power and speed of today's computers has gone up, while the price has declined.

3. Competitive pressures. With the increasingly automated approach to credit control, an office that does not computerize may soon find itself unable to compete effectively.

Once an organization computerizes its scoring system, it can expect to realize several benefits:

1. Ability to use more complex mathematical scoring models.
2. Immediate updating of scoring criteria.
3. Access to on-line credit bureau information.
4. Faster turnaround time for customers to be notified whether their application has been accepted.
5. Better tracing of customer data to prevent duplicate applications, fraud, or inaccurate customer information. This information also will provide a databank of information that can be tapped for possible sale of other products or services.
6. More time to spend on the percent of applications that fall into the questionable acceptance range.
7. Employees' lack of knowledge about the weight being given to specific scoring criteria. This eliminates employees doctoring applications based on their personal feelings versus the actual situation.

While the benefits of computerizing the credit scoring process are many and profound, there are some disadvantages. These include training costs and lost productivity during the training period. Also, customers

---

[5]The author thanks Richard L. Cole, vice president of Cole Enterprises, Inc., Clearwater Beach, Florida, for his help in preparing this section.

may feel alienated by having a computer decide their acceptance. Although not as true today as in the past, management might resist trying credit scoring systems. Because developing a truly accurate system is costly, some firms take shortcuts and never gain full benefit.

As the volume of new credit applications continues to increase and more firms develop some automated system of credit control, an increasing number of firms will begin to experiment with and adopt some type of numerical scoring plan.

DISCRIMINATION IN DECISION MAKING

The 1975 Equal Credit Opportunity Act prohibits discrimination by creditors on the basis of sex or marital status. Extensive amendments in March 1976 expanded the act's prohibition of discrimination to include color, race, religion, national origin, age, receipt of income from public assistance programs, and the good faith exercise of rights under the Consumer Credit Protection Act. As a result of this amended federal act and various state laws, certain credit qualities have diminished in importance or disappeared as factors in credit decisions.

However, the Equal Credit Opportunity Act did specify that credit grantors can employ credit scoring techniques that are "demonstrably statistically sound" and "empirically derived" if they do not include factors prohibited by law. The board of governors of the Federal Reserve System is responsible for developing the criteria for a "statistically sound and empirically derived" credit scoring system.

On April 1, 1983, the Federal Reserve Board adopted an interpretation dealing with the treatment of income on credit scoring systems. This interpretation "prohibits creditors from discounting or excluding the income of an applicant (or the spouse of an applicant) from consideration because of a prohibited basis or because the income is derived from alimony, child support, separate maintenance, part-time employment, retirement benefits, or public assistance. A creditor may consider, however, the probability of any income continuing in evaluating an applicant's creditworthiness and may consider the extent to which alimony, child support, or separate maintenance is likely to be consistently made." The board also made another interpretation, this time regarding the selection and disclosure of reasons for adverse action. The board stated "the reasons for adverse action must relate to factors actually scored or considered by the creditor" in both credit scoring systems and judgmental systems. Thus, if a creditor takes adverse action because of bankruptcy, the specific factor must be disclosed.

SETTING THE CREDIT LIMITS AFTER THE DECISION

Credit personnel use the term *retail credit limits* to refer to the maximum amount of credit the customer is permitted to charge. A better term might be *guide* or *line,* since the limits are not absolutes but merely guides in the handling of an account. They can be changed freely should circumstances warrant it. Regardless of what they are to be called, limits are useful in the operation of the credit system.

At the time an account is opened, it is subjected to the most complete review and examination it is likely to have for some time. At that moment, credit managers or credit analysts may be able to set a more definite limit than they will be in a position to do later. They have just completely analyzed the information available and have thought carefully about the account's payment possibilities. The effort to set a specific amount makes them subject the account to a more careful and penetrating analysis.

In addition, by using credit guides, credit managers free themselves of the responsibility of making day-to-day decisions. They exercise their judgment at the opening of the account, and if their judgment is sound, it will continue to govern. During the life of the account, responsibility for additional charges can safely be delegated to other personnel. This relieves credit managers of much of the routine work of handling daily transactions, so they can concentrate on other difficult tasks. If they were responsible for routine tasks as well as the major decisions on policy and other difficult problems, they might perform the routine tasks carelessly, attempting to approve day-to-day purchases from memory or after only a cursory examination of the credit file. With set limits, the judgment is carefully reached, and future transactions are maintained in accordance with this original judgment by a routine, matter-of-form check. In fact, even if credit managers handled all authorization personally, they would probably find it a convenience and an economy in handling routine tasks to set limits and follow them.

Further, credit limits permit finer control of the account during day-to-day operations. Suppose a person with weak credit wants to open an account. While the credit is not strong enough to be carried on an unrestricted basis, the credit manager may believe that it is not bad enough to reject and that the customer deserves a trial period. Without limits it is hard to enforce this period of trial, but with limits such accounts can be easily handled. They may be opened with a very small limit, or with no limit on a straight refer basis. This way the account has every credit purchase scrutinized from a credit standpoint and, during the trial period, is very closely supervised. After the trial period, the account may be put on a larger credit limit or on an unrestricted basis. Limits also help the credit department handle slow-pay accounts.

Possible Techniques to Be Used

Although the advantages of using limits are well recognized, no one method is best for setting the limit. Methods are necessarily inexact and, in many instances, arbitrary. Variations occur between the types of credit plans involved—for example, between the option-terms revolving credit plan, the installment plan, and the open charge account plan. Variations also occur between retail transactions, service transactions, and cash loans from financial institutions.

Some credit departments attempt to limit the account to a certain period of time—a month's purchases, a week's purchases, and so on. In some lines of trade this makes a normal limit. Utilities, such as the water, light, and phone companies, are almost compelled by the nature of the business to follow such a procedure. They may reduce the risk exposure somewhat by requiring a meter deposit or advance payment, but some utility companies are abandoning such practices.

Some credit managers, in the course of the credit interview for opening a regular 30-day account, persuade customers to set their own limit. This is sometimes accomplished by asking, "What do you want as a limit on your purchases?" or "Do you have any amount you want to place as a limit on your purchases?" Others approach the matter a little more tactfully by asking, "About how much do you think you will buy in the course of the month?" After the customer gives an amount, the next question may be, "Shall we then consider this as the limit you place on your purchases?"

Completely uniform standards are not necessary for the creditor firm to determine the quantity of credit acceptable from any one debtor. These matters are determined by individual firms and enforced through the operations of their credit departments. The policy on the quality of credit to be accepted should be adjusted to the firm's general sales policies, clientele, location, line of goods carried, and local and general business conditions. The policy on the quantity of credit to be accepted from any one debtor should be adjusted to the financial resources of the creditor, the credit standing of the debtor, and the type of credit plan involved.

HANDLING THE TRANSACTION

After a retail account has been established, some systems must be set up so credit management can control the purchases of individual customers. Two phases—identification and authorization—are involved in controlling approval of day-to-day purchases. The next step in most credit transactions is billing the customer for purchases made during the previous month. This step may involve cycle billing and descriptive billing.

Identification

The identification phase makes sure that the person purchasing is the person who has an account and not an impostor—namely, someone attempting to buy on someone else's account or against a nonexistent account. Identification is especially necessary with charge-take purchases—that is, purchases that customers want to take with them. With charge-send purchases the task of identification is much simpler because the store sends the merchandise to the address of the party with the account.

The speed element further complicates identification. After making a selection, customers don't want any delays receiving the merchandise. They may ask to see every article in stock and spend hours making a selection, but once they make a decision, they want the article instantly. Therefore, an identification system must be speedy to avoid customer ill will. Further, identification must be handled with the least embarrassment to the customer. Certain positive means of identification are not readily available because they seem to accuse the customer of lying. The customer knows perfectly well that she is Sally Jones and does not see why anyone else should doubt this fact. Therefore, the best identification systems are those that are not obvious to the customer.

IDENTIFICATION BY CREDIT CARD. Identification may be handled by issuing credit cards or some similar device. This method is commonly used by credit card and charge card plans and certain retail stores. When presented to the salesperson, the card serves to identify the customer. Bank credit card plans furnish listings of lost or stolen credit cards to credit grantors. Credit grantors can then compare the number on an offered card with those reported lost or stolen. The bank sponsoring the plan sometimes gives salespeople a financial reward for recovering a card that a customer is attempting to use fraudulently.

IDENTIFICATION BY SIGNATURE. Another identification technique is having the customer sign the sales ticket. Should the customer claim that the purchase was not made, the signature on the sales ticket proves otherwise or is good evidence in case the creditor has to institute legal action.

IDENTIFICATION BY PERSONAL RECOGNITION. In some smaller stores, the clerk or store manager recognizes customers personally, and there is no need for more elaborate identification systems.

Authorization

Authorization is the second phase in handling the day-to-day charges to customers' accounts. Authorization involves controlling the quantity of credit customers' use. An account is open, but not for an indefinite amount of credit. The store must set a credit limit for each customer and establish some way to control day-to-day purchases to keep the total within or near this maximum. A limit may be fixed by the credit line established at the time the account was opened or by the store's own credit guides. To enforce a credit limit, there must be some checks on the freedom to use the credit account.

The credit card, in addition to serving as a means of identification, also may be used as a device for authorization. In a telephone system, each sales section is connected directly with the authorization section of the credit department. After the sale is made, the salesclerk calls the credit department and repeats to the authorizer the name and address of the customer as shown on the sales slip and the dollar amount of the purchase. If the authorizer finds the account in the files and the purchase is within the limit the authorizer is permitted to approve, he or she furnishes an authorization number to the salesperson, who then records the number on the sales slip.

When a bank credit card is used, the retailer or service concern operator must receive authorization from the bank for a consumer purchase above an agreed-on amount ($50, for example). If such authorization is not received and the consumer defaults, the business firm and not the bank suffers the loss. However, if authorization is received and the customer defaults, the bank and not the business firm suffers the loss.

If the credit is not authorized, the customer usually is asked to go to the credit department. It is unwise to allow salespeople to handle credit questions with customers, since noncredit personnel are usually less able to do so tactfully than is possible in the privacy of the credit department.

Computerization and Credit Control[6]

Computers are being used by more retail businesses and to a greater degree than ever. And this increase is expected to continue.

Computer programs help credit managers achieve more effective control over operations and better decision making. In addition, a purely objective, carefully customized system enables credit managers to express their credit policies in concrete numerical terms.

Retailers can use computer programs to analyze sales from store level down to individual items, reduce labor costs, gather useful information for soliciting credit accounts and for collections follow-up, review inactive accounts, and improve record-keeping accuracy.

Thus the increasing use of on-line management systems affects every aspect of credit management, integrating initial decision making, identification, authorization of credit purchases, and control functions.

The decreasing cost of computers and the availability of prepackaged software eliminates the need for in-house programmers, so smaller retailers can now realize the benefits of computerizing their credit operations. Figure 10–4 is an example of the way computer vendors are tailoring computer programs to aid various retail operations.

Figure 10–5 shows an actual checkout system produced by the National Cash Register Corporation. NCR says the NCR 2126 Retail System provides the retailer with total system versatility. The NCR 2126 terminal enables a retailer to automate transaction processing and back-office applications on an as-needed basis. System features and options include

---

[6]The author wishes to acknowledge the help of Richard L. Cole in the preparation of this section.

FIGURE 10–4 **Tailored Computer Programs**

Free IBM Seminars

It's great to have a growing business or profession. But your costs may be growing faster. At a free IBM Seminar, you'll find out how the latest computer solutions can help you control costs – and improve your company's productivity and profitability.

Seminars are presented with IBM Business Partners who know *your* industry and can answer questions about your specific needs.

For a fresh point of view on the challenges you face every day, join us at a seminar where your business is the subject.

Seating is limited. Call to reserve your place now.*

IBM SOLUTION SEMINARS FOR YOUR KIND OF BUSINESS

DISTRIBUTION
Barcoding for Order Processing — Aug. 23, 9:30-Noon
Industrial Tool & Supply — Aug. 7, 1:30-4pm
Plumbing & Irrigation Supplies — Aug. 16, 9:30-Noon

MANUFACTURING
Computer Integrated Manufacturing - CIM — Jul. 31, 9-11am;
Aug. 28, 9-11:30am

MEDICAL/HEALTH
Dental Office Management — Aug. 29, 2-4pm;
Aug. 29, 6-8pm

OTHER
AIX® RISC System/6000™ - Product Overview —
Aug. 14, 1-3pm
Cemetery Control & Management — Aug. 1, 9:30-Noon
MIS for Printing & Graphic Art Companies —
Aug. 28, 1:30-4pm
Retail Furniture Management — Aug. 8, 1:30-4pm
RISC System/6000-Based MRP in the '90s —
Sep. 11, 9:30-Noon

At the IBM Customer Center
LakePointe One, 4th Flr.
3109 W. Buffalo Ave., Tampa
For reservations call:
872-2800, 24 hours/7 days (from Tampa)
461-1404, ext. 2800 (from Pinellas County)
683-7851, ext. 2800 (from Polk County)

*All seminars require confirmed reservations 24 hours in advance.

IBM®

Courtesy of International Business Machines Corporation

FIGURE 10–5 **NCR Retail Checkout System**

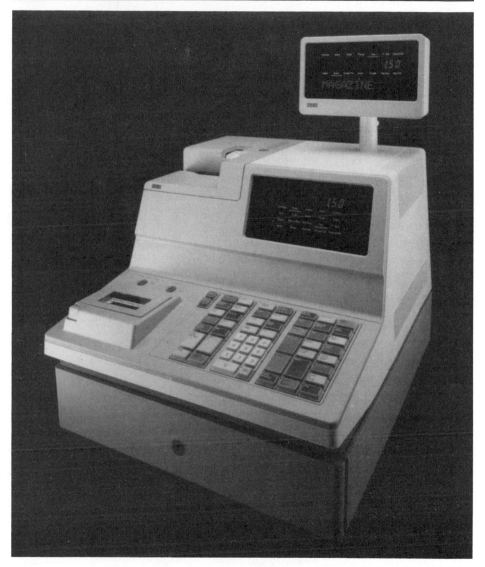

Courtesy of NCR Corporation

number/price lookup, scanning, item level data collection with cassette or flexible disk, negative check, and credit authorization. In-store and high-order communication system options provide consolidated terminal management reports, broadcasting, and transmission of data between stores and central headquarters or warehouses.

Consumers also benefit from computerized retail operations in the form of expanded customer services. One of these expanded customer services is electronic funds transfer (EFT) or point-of-sale (POS) technology. The retail industry has made considerable progress in developing and implementing point-of-sale transaction processing systems. Across the entire spectrum of retailing—food, drug, specialty store, and mass merchandising—these innovative retail information systems have provided many benefits to management, store personnel, and customers.

POS is the electronic transfer of funds—initiated from the point of sale at a retailer (hence the name)—from a consumer's account to a retailer's account to pay for purchases or services.

It works like this: A customer walks up to the counter with a basket of food. The cashier rings up the items as usual. The customer then puts his order bank card (a debit card, probably an ATM card) through a slot on a card reading device and enters his or her personal identification number on a keypad. If there are sufficient funds, the account is debited for the amount of the purchase, and the store's account is credited for the same.

This on-line transaction is completed at the time of the sale or at least by the end of the day. POS transactions can also be made using an off-line system.[7]

Figure 10–6 illustrates a POS transaction. The POS technology yields the following advantages:

- Eliminates delay at checkout caused by writing and cashing of customer checks.
- Provides customer with an additional payment option.
- Deducts payment automatically from customer's bank account in a debit card transaction.
- Requires minimum checker/cashier intervention.
- Provides easy-to-follow, lead-through instructions in POS terminal display.
- Creates potential increase in sales.
- Improves cash flow.
- Creates potential source of revenue from financial institutions.
- Eliminates check cashing charges.
- Reduces amount of cash and checks subject to theft at store level.

One drawback to electronic funds transfer is that it requires three primary participants: the bank, the retailer, and the consumer. If any one is missing, it will not operate. All of these must realize benefits over current

---

[7]Alec Smith, "POS: Where Have We Been? Where Are We Going?" *ABA Banking Journal,* September 1988, p. 104.

FIGURE 10–6 **Visual Presentation of a POS Transaction**

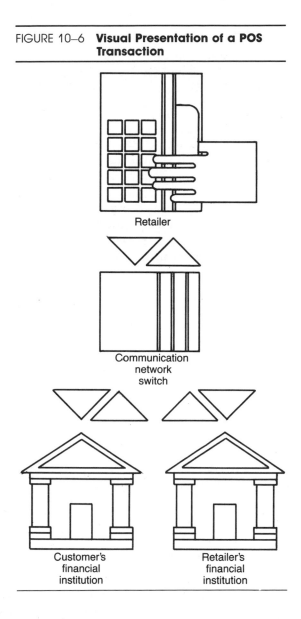

Retailer

Communication
network
switch

Customer's
financial
institution

Retailer's
financial
institution

methods of payment to make the change profitable. POS and EFT technology have been discussed in the literature for the past 20 years and has yet to realize the complete success many predicted. But the limited use it enjoys today merits the discussion in this edition.

The main disadvantages to computerizing credit operations for retailers include training costs, the possibility of acquiring so much information that it becomes difficult to identify pertinent data, and the possibility that some consumers may view additional automation as another step away from the more personalized service they once enjoyed and expected.

Billing the Customer

The next step in most credit transactions is billing the customer for purchases made during the previous month. On a certain date each month, all information about an individual's charges, credits, and payments is used to make up a bill.

CYCLE BILLING. The date on which a bill is expected to be paid changed in the early 1940s with the introduction of cycle billing. Instead of sending all bills on or around the first of the month, the names in the credit files are divided systematically and statements are prepared for a different group of customers each working day of the month. The cycle-billing technique has proved extremely valuable to large retail establishments, which otherwise would face a tremendous work load on the first few days of each month and inefficient utilization of personnel during the slack period.

DESCRIPTIVE BILLING VERSUS COUNTRY CLUB BILLING. Most firms with automated credit control use descriptive billing. The customer gets a machine-produced monthly statement that may show: (1) previous balance, (2) a dollar figure for each purchase together with a code number indicating the department in which each item was bought, (3) total purchases, (4) total payments or credits, (5) finance charges, (6) new balance, (7) minimum payment due, and (8) statement date. The use of descriptive billing in connection with a bank credit plan is shown in Figure 10–7.

On the other hand, country club billing, which once was very popular, has practically disappeared. Under this plan, sales slips are sent to the customer at billing time, along with a statement showing the total amount owed. The store, of course, keeps a photocopy of the sales slips and the statement.

Time and Expense Problems

In identification, authorization, and billing, emphasis generally is placed on speed and cost of operation and on maintaining customer goodwill. At times this necessarily means a relaxation in credit safeguards. Most stores believe this is justified, since the savings of time and money may more than compensate for the small number of customers who take advantage of a lax system. The systems described here are primarily large-store systems. In many smaller stores, the same results can be accomplished with less formal procedures because the store manager (or owner) is usually personally acquainted with most of the store's customers. In any event, whether the system is formal and routinized or whether it is informal and nonroutinized, the essential features of the task remain the same.

FIGURE 10–7 **Example of Descriptive Billing**

BANK CARD SERVICE CENTER
PO BOX 80999
LINCOLN NE 68501-0999   1W   7 15 2

VISA	MINIMUM PAYMENT DUE	PAST DUE AMOUNT	PAYMENT DUE DATE	NEW BALANCE	ACCOUNT NUMBER	PLEASE WRITE IN AMOUNT OF PAYMENT ENCLOSED
	83.00	0.00	05/17/90	1667.81		$.

Payments received at the mailing address below before 2:00 p.m. will be credited to your account as of the date of receipt. Payments received at any other location may be subject to a delay in crediting of up to 5 days after the date of receipt. Use enclosed envelope and make payment to:

PLEASE DETACH AND ENCLOSE
TOP PORTION WITH PAYMENT.

BANK CARD SERVICE CENTER
PO BOX 80999
LINCOLN NE 68501-0999

|||.|.|.||.|...||.||||...   4413 0000   3008

V00044130012500920008300601667815000441300125009 2

ACCOUNT NUMBER	CREDIT LIMIT	AVAILABLE CREDIT	DAYS IN BILLING CYCLE	BILLING CYCLE CLOSING DATE	PAYMENT DUE DATE	MINIMUM PAYMENT DUE
4413 001 250 092	3750	2070	32	04/22/90	05/17/90	83.00

DATE OF TRANS.	POST.	REFERENCE NUMBER	CHARGES, PAYMENTS AND CREDITS SINCE LAST STATEMENT	AMOUNT
0415	0422	A7H2600FZMEU00332	HOWARD JOHNSONS NO 157 COLUMBIA MO	8.70
0420	0422	B041300G008QFRGVN	MILLER & PAINE GATEWAY LINCOLN NE	26.25
		FINANCE CHARGE *PURCHASES $11.00 *CASH ADVANCE $0.00		11.00

PREVIOUS BALANCE	PAYMENTS	CREDITS	PURCHASES AND CASH ADVANCES	DEBIT ADJUSTMENTS	FINANCE CHARGE	NEW BALANCE
551.59	27.00	0.00	1132.22	0.00	11.00	1667.81

AN AMOUNT FOLLOWED BY A MINUS SIGN (–) IS A CREDIT OR A CREDIT BALANCE UNLESS OTHERWISE INDICATED.
TOLL FREE CUSTOMER SERVICE NUMBER.
(NEBRASKA) 1-800-742-0107 (OUTSIDE NEBRASKA) 1-800-228-9145
TO REPORT LOST OR STOLEN VISA OR MASTERCARDS CALL:
(LINCOLN RESIDENTS) 475-0577 (OMAHA RESIDENTS) 399-3600
(NEBRASKA RESIDENTS) 1-800-642-9370
(OUTSIDE NEBRASKA RESIDENTS) 1-800-228-1122

Send Notice of Billing Errors to: BANK CARD SERVICE CENTER   P.O. BOX 81068   LINCOLN, NE 68501

	UNDER RATE CHANGE POINT		DOLLAR POINT AT WHICH RATES CHANGE	OVER RATE CHANGE POINT		1. Total Current Billing Cycle Purchases	2. Average Daily Balance of Previous Billing Cycle Purchases
	CASH ADVANCES	PURCHASES		CASH ADVANCES	PURCHASES	1132.22	192.63
ANNUAL PERCENTAGE RATES	18.00%	18.00%	N/A	N/A %	N/A %	3. Average Daily Balance of Old Purchases	4. Average Daily Balance of Cash Advances
MONTHLY PERIODIC RATES	1.500%	1.500%		%	%	541.46	0.00

A **FINANCE CHARGE** on Old Purchases and Cash Advance ... ... the date payment is credited to your account and will be billed on your next statement. If the New Balance is paid in full by the Payment Due Date, no **FINANCE CHARGE** ... ... in this statement. Current Billing Cycle Purchases.

NOTICE: See reverse side for important information.

DISCUSSION QUESTIONS

1. Explain the statement "Decisions are the heart of all credit work."
2. Is there really any difference between bad-debt losses and charity cases? Explain your point of view.
3. Why is it not suggested that evaluation of credit information be made a separate part of the credit analysis?
4. Why is credit a relative matter? Explain your answer clearly in view of the discussion of this point in this chapter.
5. Discuss why credit standards are intimately related to other marketing policies established by a firm.
6. Define the expression "grading the credit." Is your definition different from that in the text? Why or why not?
7. What qualities are usually graded in the option-terms revolving credit account grading form? In the cash loan grading form?
8. Can you think of any other qualities that should be graded? Any qualities that should be eliminated?
9. What does the grade of 1 or good stand for in the grading forms? In the final summary overall appraisal?
10. Explain the procedure to follow in using the grading forms.
11. Discuss how the use of credit grades can be extended beyond the aid they supply to the making of credit decisions.
12. Discuss the advantages and the disadvantages of setting credit lines or limits.
13. What methods may be used in setting credit limits in a retail store? Can you think of any other techniques? Explain.
14. What is meant by the term *credit scoring?*
15. Discuss the advantages and disadvantages of credit scoring plans.
16. Distinguish between identification and authorization.
17. What possible techniques might be used for identification and for authorization?
18. Visit the leading stores in your community to discuss what use they are making of automated systems of credit control.
19. Distinguish between cycle billing and descriptive billing.

CREDIT REPORT PROBLEMS

Figures 10–8, 10–9, and 10–10 show fictitious Form 2000 credit reports. Based only on the data given in the reports, would you accept or reject the applicant for:

a. A new 30-day account, with a limit of $150, in a small clothing store?
b. A $150 sportcoat purchase in a men's clothing store on an option-terms revolving credit account? The account has never been used before.

FIGURE 10–8

NAME AND ADDRESS OF CREDIT BUREAU MAKING REPORT

Credit Bureau of Anytown
1234 Main St.
Anytown, Anystate 12345

☐ SINGLE REFERENCE ☐ IN FILE REPORT ☐ TRADE REPORT
☒ FULL REPORT ☐ EMPLOY & TRADE REPORT ☐ PREVIOUS RESIDENCE REPORT
☐ OTHER _____

FOR ┌ Jones Department Store 5th and A Streets Anytown, Anystate 12345 ┐	**Date Received** 7/10/90 **Date Mailed** 7/12/90 **In File Since** 1980 **Inquired As:** 2

CONFIDENTIAL
crediscope® REPORT
🔲 Member
Associated Credit Bureaus, Inc.

REPORT ON:	LAST NAME	FIRST NAME	INITIAL	SOCIAL SECURITY NUMBER	SPOUSE'S NAME
	Adams	James	C	563-25-2817	Mary

ADDRESS:	CITY		STATE:	ZIP CODE	SINCE:	SPOUSE'S SOCIAL SECURITY NO.
	110 Raven	Anytown	Anystate	1234	1979	991-82-7773

PRESENT EMPLOYER:	POSITION HELD:	SINCE:	DATE EMPLOY VERIFIED	EST. MONTHLY INCOME
Self - Ace Janitor Service	Owner	1981	1/16/89	$ 1800

DATE OF BIRTH	NUMBER OF DEPENDENTS INCLUDING SELF:			OTHER: (EXPLAIN)
1935	2	☐ OWNS OR BUYING HOME	☐ RENTS HOME	☒ Owns mobile home

FORMER ADDRESS:	CITY:	STATE:	FROM:	TO:
663 Cloverdale	Cincinnati	Ohio	1975	1979

FORMER EMPLOYER:	POSITION HELD:	FROM:	TO:	EST. MONTHLY INCOME
D-Plus Broom Co.	Salesman	1977	1981	$ 1100

SPOUSE'S EMPLOYER:	POSITION HELD:	SINCE:	DATE EMPLOY VERIFIED	EST. MONTHLY INCOME
not employed				$

WHOSE	KIND OF BUSINESS AND ID CODE	DATE REPORTED AND METHOD OF REPORTING	DATE OPENED	DATE OF LAST PAYMENT	HIGHEST CREDIT OR LAST CONTRACT	PRESENT STATUS BALANCE OWING	PAST DUE AMOUNT	NO. OF PAYMENTS	NO. MONTHS HISTORY REVIEWED	TIMES PAST DUE 30-59 DAYS ONLY	60-89 DAYS ONLY	90 DAYS AND OVER	TYPE & TERMS (MANNER OF PAYMENT)	REMARKS
2	F-30	Acme Finance 7/90m	3/88	4/90	400	325	70	2	12					I-$35
2	C-61	Clothing Fair 6/90A	1/89	5/90	550	210	25	1	12	1				R-$25
2	H-92	General Hardware 12/89	1985	5/90	290	50	–	–	8		1			R-$30

Public Record

Small claims court SC - 81754
Medical clinic for $280
Judgment for plaintiff
not paid

FIGURE 10-9

NAME AND ADDRESS OF CREDIT BUREAU MAKING REPORT

☐ SINGLE REFERENCE ☐ IN FILE REPORT ☐ TRADE REPORT

☒ FULL REPORT ☐ EMPLOY & TRADE REPORT ☐ PREVIOUS RESIDENCE REPORT

Credit Bureau of Anytown
1234 Main St.
Anytown, Anystate 12345

☐ OTHER _____

FOR Jones Department Store Fifth and A Streets Anytown, Anystate 12345	**Date Received** 8/17/90
	Date Mailed 8/19/90
	In File Since 1982
	Inquired As: 2

CONFIDENTIAL crediscope® REPORT

■ Member Associated Credit Bureaus, Inc.

REPORT ON:	LAST NAME	FIRST NAME	INITIAL	SOCIAL SECURITY NUMBER	SPOUSE'S NAME
	Alvarado	Jose	S	155-25-2515	Kay

ADDRESS:	CITY	STATE:	ZIP CODE	SINCE:	SPOUSE'S SOCIAL SECURITY NO.
6321 Sweetbriar	Anytown	Anystate	12346	1984	315-15-6189

PRESENT EMPLOYER:	POSITION HELD:	SINCE:	DATE EMPLOY VERIFIED	EST. MONTHLY INCOME
Pilgrim House Furniture	Warehouseman	7/89	10/89	$1400

DATE OF BIRTH	NUMBER OF DEPENDENTS INCLUDING SELF:		OTHER: (EXPLAIN)
1949	4	☒ OWNS OR BUYING HOME ☐ RENTS HOME	☐

FORMER ADDRESS:	CITY:	STATE:	FROM:	TO:
1021 Grand St.	Portland	Oregon	prior	1982

FORMER EMPLOYER:	POSITION HELD:	FROM:	TO:	EST. MONTHLY INCOME
National Chemical Co.	Inspector	1982	1985	$ not known

SPOUSE'S EMPLOYER:	POSITION HELD:	SINCE:	DATE EMPLOY VERIFIED	EST. MONTHLY INCOME
Crater Oil Co.	Research Assistant	1984	7/7/89	$1200

WHOSE	KIND OF BUSINESS AND ID CODE	DATE REPORTED AND METHOD OF REPORTING	DATE OPENED	DATE OF LAST PAYMENT	HIGHEST CREDIT OR LAST CONTRACT	PRESENT STATUS BALANCE OWING	PAST DUE AMOUNT	NO. OF PAYMENTS	NO. MONTHS HISTORY REVIEWED	HISTORICAL STATUS 30-59 DAYS ONLY	60-89 DAYS ONLY	90 DAYS AND OVER	TYPE & TERMS (MANNER OF PAYMENT)	REMARKS
1	D-81	Standard Stores 6/90A	5/89	7/90	$890	$310	150		12					R-$20
2	B-63	Bank of Anytown 7/90A	1988	7/90	$2500	$2000			18					I-$200
2	C-10	Ed's Clothiers 5/90	6/88	6/90	$750	$100			12					0
2	N-99	Century Charge 7/90A	1986	7/90	$1950	0			12					R
2	B-51	First Savings Bank 12/89	1984	5/90	$650	0			6					I

This information is furnished in response to an inquiry for the purpose of evaluating credit risks. It has been obtained from sources deemed reliable, the accuracy of which this organization does not guarantee. The inquirer has agreed to indemnify the reporting bureau for any damage arising from misuse of this information, and this report is furnished in reliance upon that indemnity. It must be held in strict confidence, and must not be revealed to the subject reported on, except as required by law.

FORM 2000-5/80

FIGURE 10–10

NAME AND ADDRESS OF CREDIT BUREAU MAKING REPORT		

Credit Bureau of Anytown
1234 Main St..
Anytown, Anystate 12345

☐ SINGLE REFERENCE ☐ IN FILE REPORT ☐ TRADE REPORT
☒ FULL REPORT ☐ EMPLOY & TRADE REPORT ☐ PREVIOUS RESIDENCE REPORT
☐ OTHER_____

FOR
Jones Department Store
Fifth and A Streets
Anytown, Anystate 12345

Date Received: 10/1/86
Date Mailed: 10/2/86
In File Since: 1980
Inquired As: 1

CONFIDENTIAL
crediscope® REPORT
◆ Member
Associated Credit Bureaus, Inc.

REPORT ON:	LAST NAME	FIRST NAME	INITIAL	SOCIAL SECURITY NUMBER	SPOUSE'S NAME
	Cook	Ella	Y	516-39-6166	Wid Sam F.

ADDRESS:	CITY	STATE:	ZIP CODE	SINCE:	SPOUSE'S SOCIAL SECURITY NO.
333 East First St.	Anytown	Anystate	12345	1981	

PRESENT EMPLOYER:	POSITION HELD:	SINCE:	DATE EMPLOY VERIFIED	EST. MONTHLY INCOME
Needles 'N' Threads	Seamstress	6/83	7/20/90	$ 1050

DATE OF BIRTH	NUMBER OF DEPENDENTS INCLUDING SELF:				OTHER: (EXPLAIN)
est 1934	1	☐ OWNS OR BUYING HOME	☒ RENTS HOME		☐

FORMER ADDRESS:	CITY:	STATE:	FROM:	TO:
not known				

FORMER EMPLOYER:	POSITION HELD:	FROM:	TO:	EST. MONTHLY INCOME
not known				$

SPOUSE'S EMPLOYER:	POSITION HELD:	SINCE:	DATE EMPLOY VERIFIED	EST. MONTHLY INCOME
				$

WHOSE	KIND OF BUSINESS AND ID CODE	DATE REPORTED AND METHOD OF REPORTING	DATE OPENED	DATE OF LAST PAYMENT	HIGHEST CREDIT OR LAST CONTRACT	PRESENT STATUS BALANCE OWING	PAST DUE AMOUNT	NO. OF PAYMENTS	NO. MONTHS HISTORY REVIEWED	HISTORICAL STATUS TIMES PAST DUE 30-59 DAYS ONLY	60-89 DAYS ONLY	90 DAYS AND OVER	TYPE & TERMS (MANNER OF PAYMENT)	REMARKS
1	B-88	Bank of Anytown - Auto Loan 9/90	1989	9/90	$3100	$1400			12					I-$100
1	D-22	Fields Stores, Inc. 9/90	1989	8/90	$520	$50		1	12					R-$25

This information is furnished in response to an inquiry for the purpose of evaluating credit risks. It has been obtained from sources deemed reliable, the accuracy of which this organization does not guarantee. The inquirer has agreed to indemnify the reporting bureau for any damage arising from misuse of this information, and this report is furnished in reliance upon that indemnity. It must be held in strict confidence, and must not be revealed to the subject reported on, except as required by law.
FORM 2000-5/80

c. A purchase of a $500 color television set on a 12-month installment plan from an appliance store?

d. An installment loan (to be repaid in 12 months) from a commercial bank to install air conditioning in a car?

e. A loan of $500 (single repayment in 90 days) from a commercial bank, signature loan?

Do you need any additional information? If so, state what you need.

SUGGESTED READINGS

Credit Scoring

ALEXANDER, WALTER. "What's the Score?" *ABA Banking Journal,* August 1989, p. 58.

CONNORS, MIKE. "Credit Scoring." *Business Credit,* April 1988, p. 51.

"Credit Application System Supports Scoring Model." *Credit Card Management,* January–February 1988, p. 100.

DAWSON, GREGORY, and NORM EAGER. "The Paperless Credit Office." *Business Credit,* January 1988, p. 18.

FRAZIER, ARLENE. "How to Get the Most out of Scoring." *Credit Card Management,* February 1990, p. 59.

GOTHE, PER. "Credit Bureau Point Scoring Sheds Light on Shades of Gray." *The Credit World,* May–June 1990, p. 26.

LYNCH, DEBORA, and JAMES DIRLAM. "Creating a Modern Credit Approval Environment." *The Credit World,* September–October 1988, p. 24.

MCALLISTER, PETER. " 'Early Warning' on Delinquencies." *The Credit World,* September–October 1987, p. 36.

PELLEGRINO, MARY K. "The Evolution of Scoring in the 1980s." *The Credit World,* November–December 1988, p. 26.

SMITH, MURRAY. " 'Neurocomputing' May Make Credit Scorecards Obsolete." *Credit Card Management,* November–December 1988, p. 77.

"Software Selection." *Business Credit,* May 1988, p. 32.

STEWART, JOHN. "Credit Scoring's New Era." *Credit Card Management,* September 1990, p. 60.

Consumer Collection Policies and Practices

The Objectives or Goals of Chapter 11 Are:

1. To explain why collections are an inherent part of any credit business.
2. To explain the purpose and objectives of consumer credit counseling services.
3. To discuss the factors affecting a collection policy.
4. To discuss the area of consumer credit insurance.
5. To set forth the four stages of a general collection system.
6. To discuss the various types of actions that might take place during the drastic or legal action stage.
7. To outline the problems connected with consumer bankruptcy.

Collections are an inherent part of any credit business. Credit has limited acceptance because of the risk and time elements involved. Accompanying these two elements is the factor of nonpayment.

Any collection system must get the money. Yet this objective becomes difficult to attain when the company also has to retain customer goodwill, rehabilitate the debtor, encourage prompt payment, and operate economically. If promptness is the firm's major objective, it may handle all collections immediately. However, the methods it uses may be very costly in dollars and goodwill. On the other hand, if a firm's major objective is to retain goodwill, its appeals and techniques will be very gentle, even delicate, and collections will be slow. The best approach for rehabilitating a debtor largely depends on the type of individual involved.

The word *collections* does not mean the same thing to all people, not even to all credit personnel. Does the collection effort start the moment the customer is reminded of an indebtedness, regardless of whether the credit period agreed on has expired? Advocates of this view consider the billing statement part of the firm's collection efforts. However, in this book the word *collections* refers to efforts made *after* the credit period agreed on by the debtor and creditor has expired. Thus collections start only in case of nonpayment of indebtedness in the time established prior to or at the time of sale.

The fundamentals of establishing and maintaining effective controls over the problem of bad-debt losses are relatively simple, regardless of the procedure followed in accepting the credit of the consumer. To have a successful collection policy, the three most important requirements when extending credit are:

1. A clear understanding of the terms when a credit transaction is initiated.
2. A systematic and careful follow-up of every account.
3. A periodic age analysis of every outstanding account.

The longer an account is kept on the books, the less chance there is of successful collection. Surveys taken by the American Collectors Association, Inc., show that the potential bad-debt personality falls into one or more of the following groups:[1]

1. Habitually slow pay.
2. Financially immature.
3. Irresponsible as to employment and usually irresponsible as to family obligations.
4. Unavoidably involved in debt.
5. Incapable of handling his or her own problems.
6. "Skip," runs away from debt.
7. Deliberate "credit criminal," at the time he or she buys, has little or no intention of paying.
8. Tries to reduce debts through unfair complaints.

CONSUMER CREDIT INSURANCE

Before discussing regular collection policies and practices, it is important to recognize a collection device followed in certain consumer credit transactions: consumer credit insurance.

During recent years, the use of life and disability insurance in connection with consumer credit transactions has risen rapidly. Many different types of credit-granting institutions now offer debtors this special kind of insurance, called consumer credit insurance. The insurance names the creditor as the first beneficiary. If the insured dies, the insurance company pays the debt in full. If the insured becomes disabled, the insurance company pays his or her periodic installments. Consumer credit insurance is divided, then, into two major categories: credit life insurance and credit

---

[1]*A Collection Guide for Creditors* (Minneapolis, Minn.: American Collectors Association, Inc., undated), p. 9.

accident and health insurance. Some lenders also now offer unemployment coverage in the event the borrower faces an involuntary unemployment situation.

Credit grantors can make the insurance available to their customers by offering individual policies, for which the debtor usually pays the premium, or by offering certificates of insurance under a group policy. The cost of group coverage may be paid by the creditor, or it may be shifted to the debtor through an identifiable charge. Unfortunately, some customers believe credit insurance is automatically included with their loan, while others have the misconception that it is required to obtain a loan. Misunderstandings about product features of the credit insurance are an even greater problem.[2]

Nature of the Insurance

Credit insurance is written for the duration of a consumer loan or installment sale contract in an amount equal to the indebtedness. It is issued to debtors without benefit of a medical examination, with no restrictions for physical impairments or occupational hazards, and with a uniform charge regardless of the insured person's age.

Individual credit life insurance policies may be written either on a decreasing-term or a level-term basis. Decreasing-term coverage provides a benefit that decreases as the installment debt reduces, so that the protection is always equal (or approximately equal) to the debt. If the coverage is level term, the amount of insurance in force remains the same for the duration of the debt. Decreasing-term coverage is the more popular of the two.

There are two basic kinds of credit accident and health insurance policies: those with an elimination period and those with a retroactive period. Under either plan, the insurance company assumes installment payments only after a stated period of disability—usually 14 days. If the policy has an elimination period, the disabled debtor is not reimbursed by the insurance company for any payments made during the waiting period. If coverage is retroactive, the insurance company reimburses the debtor for payments made during the waiting period.

Consumer credit insurance benefits both debtors and creditors. Debtors benefit because the insurance gives them protection and peace of mind, permits them to make greater use of their credit, enables them to get cosigners when needed, and is available without exclusions. Creditors benefit because the insurance serves as an added security device and relieves them of onerous collection duties. In addition, goodwill accrues to the

---

[2]Bud Elsea, "Making the Most of Credit Insurance," *ABA Banking Journal,* September 1988, p. 52.

creditor when benefits are paid as the result of death or disability and because large numbers of consumer-debtors want such coverage.

The growth of consumer credit insurance in recent decades has been the result of several factors: (1) the public's desire for security, (2) the benefits provided by the insurance, (3) the increased use of consumer credit, (4) the passage of favorable state laws, (5) the great variety of creditors offering the protection, (6) the competitive selling efforts of the insurance companies, (7) the favorable publicity it has received, and (8) the "fee income" revenue to the creditor institution from the sale of the credit insurance to the debtor.

However, states regulate consumer credit insurance because: (1) the consumer is in an inferior bargaining position and is generally not versed in matters relating to insurance; (2) the insurance companies, as a selling device to creditors, tend to grant higher commissions than necessary; and (3) unscrupulous creditors, in the absence of effective laws, might use the insurance as a means of extracting extra charges from their customers.

The following rules help prevent abuses:

1. Charges for individual and group insurance and the compensation received by creditors must be limited.
2. Coverage must never exceed the amount of the debt or the term of indebtedness.
3. Debtors must be free to acquire the insurance from sources other than the creditor.
4. Creditors must give insured persons a statement or copy of the policy that describes the coverage.
5. Insurance must be canceled and unearned charges refunded when debts are prepaid or refinanced.
6. Claims must be paid by the insurance company rather than by the credit grantor.
7. Insurance companies writing the policies must be authorized to do business in the state.
8. Creditors selling individual or group coverage must be licensed or authorized by the state insurance department.
9. All policies must be reviewed and approved by the insurance department.

CONSUMER CREDIT COUNSELING SERVICE

Credit counseling service is discussed before collection policies and practices because this service results in fewer collection problems in the future; it is not a service called on after other collection efforts fail.

The consumer can get credit counseling from a number of sources: nonprofit counseling centers, for-profit counseling centers, credit unions, lawyers, and many more. However, the consumer should choose his or her advisor carefully.[3]

Nonprofit credit counseling centers are helpful to people having trouble paying their debts because the centers contact the creditors and try to arrange a repayment plan. The Consumer Credit Counseling Service (CCCS) has more than 350 nonprofit offices in 47 states. CCCS counselors help the consumer set up a realistic budget and, on the basis of that budget, try to arrange a repayment plan. Counselors also aid consumers in developing a spending plan to cover living expenses, debt payments, and other financial obligations. The meeting between counselor and client is an opportunity for the consumer to discuss any financial-related concerns and to plan for future expenses.

If the consumer's debt is beyond a monthly budget, CCCS may suggest a debt management plan, in which creditors are asked to accept smaller payments over a longer period. CCCS disburses funds monthly until all accounts are paid in full. Some creditors stop finance charges for clients on the CCCS debt management plan. Clients agree to incur no further credit obligations while in the program.

Figure 11–1 shows a form that one nonprofit credit counseling center uses in the conference between the client and the counselor.

The National Foundation for Consumer Credit is engaged primarily in efforts to inform and educate people who use consumer credit. This program of education is conducted not only for young people who will become the consumers of tomorrow but also for adult consumers who have allowed themselves to become overburdened with debt and who need immediate professional advice. The National Foundation for Consumer Credit has been dealing with the problem of consumer credit for more than 25 years through the sponsorship of locally organized and managed Consumer Credit Counseling Service offices nationwide.

DEVELOPING A COLLECTION POLICY

Businesses need to establish a collection policy, but this does not mean that once a policy is established it cannot be changed. On the contrary, changes are vital to keep any policy up to date. But the basic plan should change slowly, so that customers, firm personnel, and other interested individuals are familiar with the general procedure being followed.

There are four general policies from which to choose:

1. Liberal credit—strict collection.
2. Strict credit—liberal collection.

---

[3]See C. Philip Johnston, "Credit Counseling: Chipping Away at Chargeoffs," *Credit Card Management,* January–February 1989, p. 84, and Harold Kane, "These 'Doctors' Are Giving the Credit Card Business Headaches," *Credit Card Management,* June 1989, p. 65.

FIGURE 11–1 **Form Used By Nonprofit Credit Counseling Center**

CONSUMER CREDIT COUNSELING SERVICE
OF PINELLAS COUNTY, INC.
801 West Bay Drive, Suite 313
(Southeast Bank Building)
Largo, Florida 34640
(813) 585-0099

Date _____

Name _____ Age _____

Name _____ Age _____

Home Address _____ Apt. # _____

City _____ Zip _____ How long? _____

Telephone _____ Number children _____ Ages _____

- -

Referred to CCCS by _____

Recently denied credit? _____ Type _____ Company _____
                  (yes/no)   (loan/credit card)   (by whom?)

Previous bankruptcy? _____ Date _____ Where _____
               (yes/no)

- -

Employed by _____ How long? _____

Occupation _____ Gross Salary _____

Income Received: _____ Take-Home Amount _____
   (monthly, weekly, biweekly, bimonthly?)

Telephone _____ Extension _____

Employed by _____ How long? _____

Occupation _____ Gross Salary _____

Income Received: _____ Take-Home Amount _____
   (monthly, weekly, biweekly, bimonthly?)

Telephone _____ Extension _____

Other income source _____ Amount _____

FIGURE 11–1 (continued)

INSTRUCTIONS: Please list the amounts you owe for mortgages, car payments, loans, installment payments, credit cards, medical bills, and any other personal debts.
IMPORTANT: DO NOT LIST YOUR ACCOUNT NUMBERS. NO Account Numbers, please!

TO WHOM DEBT OWED	BALANCE	MONTHLY PAYMENT	DATE LAST PAID
MORTAGES:			
CAR PAYMENTS:			
Make _____ Model _____ Year _____ Date Purchased _____			
Make _____ Model _____ Year _____ Date Purchased _____			
CREDIT UNION LOANS:			
Payroll deduction? (yes/no) _____			
INSTALLMENT LOANS:			
Date originated? _____ Purpose _____			
Date originated? _____ Purpose _____			
Date originated? _____ Purpose _____			
CREDIT CARDS:			
MEDICAL BILLS			
Patient's name _____			
Patient's name _____			
Patient's name _____			

FIGURE 11–1 (concluded)

Other debts:

Do not include normal household bills, even if unpaid this month. DO list personal loans, unpaid bills for discontinued service, legal expenses, vet bills, and all other debts not previously listed.

TO WHOM DEBT OWED	BALANCE	MONTHLY PAYMENT	DATE LAST PAID

- -

Authorization for Financial Counseling

The undersigned (hereinafter called the "client") hereby applies to the Consumer Credit Counseling Service of Pinellas County, Inc. (hereinafter called the "agency") for Financial Counseling and requests the agency to develop a budget based on the information provided by the client.

The client agrees that all information furnished to the agency is accurate and complete. The agency agrees that all information shall be kept confidential and used only to provide the requested service.

The client hereby agrees to hold the agency, its employees, officers, and agents harmless from any claim, suit, action, or demand of themselves, their creditors, or any person which might arise out of this application, or any action taken by the agency.

_____   _____
(Client signature)   (Date)

_____   _____
(Client signature)   (Date)

3. Liberal credit—liberal collection.
4. Strict credit—strict collection.

The first two are the most common, especially in retail stores and service establishments. Professional people often find themselves involved with the third policy, much to their dismay.

As long as customers regard credit solely as a service rather than a mutual privilege, creditors' collection problems may be troublesome. When customers begin to think of credit primarily as a business transaction, collection problems tend to become simpler, sentimentality lessens, and creditors are not as afraid to insist on payment for fear of incurring their customers' ill will. Closely connected with this view is creditors' growing realization that no credit transaction is complete until the debtor pays in full; payment is made more readily if the indebtedness is incurred recently; terms established between debtor and creditor must be respected; and slow-paying customers not only cost additional money for collection efforts but also are often reluctant to patronize the same business until they pay off their indebtedness.

Recognizing that unwillingness is usually a more important reason for nonpayment than inability, many creditors start out new credit customers with the understanding that prompt payment is expected and that everything possible will be done to collect any indebtedness incurred. "Accounts well opened are half collected." It is vitally important at the time the account is opened to impress on the customer the importance of paying promptly.

Factors Affecting Collection Policy

In deciding which type of collection policy to adopt, a firm must recognize that many factors influence policy determination. Capital, competition, type of goods, and class of customers are among the most important and influential factors, although they by no means constitute a complete list.

CAPITAL. One of the most important factors affecting collection policy is the amount of capital the firm owns or has available. Regardless of how liberal a collection policy creditors may wish to follow, if they are operating with a limited capital structure, they are usually forced to adopt a "strict" collection policy in order to meet the demands of their own creditors. Most business firms are not blessed with an overabundance of working capital; they depend on the turnover of their goods to provide needed funds. But a mere turnover of goods is not enough, if these goods are sold on credit. One step is added to the process—completion of the credit transaction by receipt of cash payment. How quickly this step must be completed depends on how badly the firm needs capital. Thus capital availability and need play a vital role in determining what type of collection policy a firm must adopt, despite the fact that a different policy might be more desirable in view of some of the other factors involved.

COMPETITION. Another influence in the formation and development of a collection policy is, "What is the competition doing?" Community size plays a role; there is generally more room for different policies among large-city competitors than among small-town competitors. Regardless of community size, however, customers become aware of widely varying credit and collection policies, and a firm must know what its direct and indirect competitors are offering these mutual customers.

TYPE OF GOODS. The type of goods handled by the retail firm also influences the determination of collection policy. The greater the perishability of the good, the greater is the need for prompt payment of the account and thus the stricter is the collection policy. On the other hand, if the goods involved are hard goods and repossession (although undesired) is possible, the need for a strict collection policy is lessened. This is not to say, however, that a strict collection policy is never followed by a firm handling hard goods, but it does point up that such a policy is dictated by some factor other than the type of goods involved.

CLASS OF CUSTOMERS. Collection work would be easier and the results better if there were some magic way to classify each account as to the reason for nonpayment and the collection method that would be most effective. Sorting devices to perform such miracles unfortunately are not yet available, and until such devices become economically and mechanically feasible, the responsibility for any classification rests with credit personnel.

Some customers pay regularly and automatically. Those in this desirable classification solve one part of the classification problem and remove themselves as possible collection cases.

Thus, in deciding on what collection policies and practices to adopt, many firms attempt to decide whether their customers will pay promptly and need only slight reminders, if any. In these cases, if pressure is ever needed, it will be applied gradually and slowly. Included in this classification are debtors who, although they may be having difficulty in making payment, respond fully to any inquiry by explaining the reason for nonpayment and indicating when full payment may be expected.

With customers at the other extreme, if the company realizes it made a mistake in accepting their credit in the first place, little is gained by using gradual and weak devices. Experience shows that such individuals respect only strong efforts. An immediate threat of legal action may be the only way to get results.

Between prompt payers and known deadbeats is the group of debtors with whom judgment and experience play a vital role in determining how strict to be, how severe a collection method to use, and when to apply pressure. With these debtors the problem of classification is most acute.

A GENERAL COLLECTION SYSTEM[4]

The ideal collection system solves the problem of volume of work by being routine in operation and solves the problem of classification by letting debtors classify themselves by their own actions. When properly adapted to the needs of the creditor firm and when correctly fitted to the characteristics of the customers, such a system should get the money and should do so promptly, economically, and without loss of customer goodwill. By understanding the principles of such a system, an actual operating system can be developed by any competent credit manager.

Promptness and regularity of payment must be built into any system for the following reasons:

1. A lax collection policy often indicates incompetent management. This can affect the purchaser's attitude toward the products the firm sells.

2. Experience shows that there is a definite correlation between the length of time debts are unpaid and the volume of resulting bad-debt losses.

3. Slow collections tend to result in the loss of future sales because slow-paying customers are reluctant to buy from firms they already owe money to. Of course, creditors may show an even stronger reluctance to sell to such customers.

4. Failure to enforce collection encourages imprudent purchasers. Thus foolhardy buyers may plunge headlong into unwise buying, knowing that a firm will permit an excessively long time to pass before it takes drastic legal action, if it ever does so.

A well-designed collection system can be compared to a series of screens. Earlier screens are low in cost and handle the customer gently to preserve goodwill. Later screens are less routine, cost more to apply, may be somewhat sharper in action and thus not preserve goodwill with such certainty, and tend to classify reluctant debtors into much smaller and more exact assortments.

A general collection system can be divided into four stages based on the collection effort involved:

1. The impersonal routine stage.
2. The impersonal appeals stage.
3. The personalized appeals stage.
4. The drastic or legal action stage.

The collection devices appropriate to each stage and the classes of debtors expected to respond at that stage are indicated in Figure 11–2.

---

[4]See the Suggested Readings at the end of the chapter.

FIGURE 11–2 **A General Collection System**

Stage of System	Collection Devices Available for Use	Debtors Involved
Impersonal routine	Statement—1st, 2nd, 3rd, etc. Statement inserts and stickers Notes on statements Form letters of reminder type (Note: These refer only to devices used after expiration of credit period.)	Those awaiting notice Honestly overlooked Temporarily financially embarrassed Careless or procrastinating
Impersonal appeals	Form letters appealing to: "Anything wrong" tone "Tell us your story" tone Pride in credit responsibilities Sense of fair play Seeking reply from debtor: Telephone Special letters: Registered Special delivery Trick reply	Honestly overlooked Careless or procrastinating Temporarily embarrassed Overbought Accident or misfortune Disputed account
Personalized appeals	Personal collector: Telephone Personal interview Personal letters to: Debtor Employer Credit bureau	Overbought Eventual insolvents Accident or misfortune Frauds—no intent to pay Disputed account
Drastic or legal action	Extension agreement Composition arrangement Collection agency Garnishment or wage assignment Repossession Attorney Suit Other actions	Same as debtors shown in the *personalized appeals* stage (all should have assets)

Self-classification on the part of debtors is accomplished at each stage. The devices suggested for each stage are too numerous to incorporate into one operating system. When developing a system to use in a particular situation, credit managers select the devices most appropriate to their collection task and determine the frequency of use and the time that should elapse between uses. They tailor the devices used to their own situation, considering the needs of their firm and the character of their customers. They should also conform to the customs of their lines of business and territory and should deviate from custom only on the basis of well-informed judgment.

This general system conforms to the principles of effective collection. It assures that lower-cost and routine methods are used for the majority of accounts and that customers with more desire and means to pay meet their obligation during the early stages of the system. After the bulk of the accounts has been reduced by various low-cost methods that also preserve goodwill, the higher-cost methods are applied selectively to the remaining small number of accounts. These stronger and more emphatic methods have lower percentage returns because the potential of the group to which they are applied is lower. At this point, creditors aren't as concerned about retaining goodwill because the self-classification process has already eliminated accounts whose goodwill is important. Thus, through the four stages, the collection department gradually increases pressure up to the point that the debtor should (but unfortunately not always does) feel that there is no more desirable alternative than paying and that there is no escape from this conclusion.

The general system will give a sound, effective, and logical organization to the collection efforts. Skill in selecting the devices, the quality of the devices individually prepared, and appropriate timing should assure that the system is properly adapted to the firm's situation and the nature of its customers.

The Impersonal Routine Stage

This stage is where the self-classification of debtors begins. Many debtors pay within the credit period established and thus are never considered in any of the four collection stages. The impersonal routine stage does not begin until the established credit period expires.

Some common collection devices used in this stage are impersonal statements (or bills) sent to customers, statement inserts and stickers, stamped or written notes on the statements, and various form letters of the reminder type (see Figures 11–3 and 11–4). Debtors that respond to the collection devices of this stage are generally those who are simply awaiting some notice that the account is overdue, those who have honestly overlooked making payment, careless or procrastinating debtors, and those who are temporarily financially embarrassed.

Mail is one of the most important means of contacting debtors. Whether using statements, inserts, or form letters, creditors should remember that their collection device is attempting to sell the debtor on the idea that the account must be paid at once. Frequent change in the wording of notes on statements and form letters is advisable. In fact, some firms keep a record of the pulling power of each form letter they use. Some firms also experiment with colored paper or colored printing to see whether it increases the effectiveness of the collection device used.

In this impersonal routine stage, the firm uses a gentle nudging without giving the idea that it is seriously concerned over nonpayment. Just how soon this gentle nudging starts after expiration of the credit period varies depending on company policy as well as the type of credit account involved. Thus with weekly or semimonthly payments, a three-day grace

FIGURE 11–3 **Examples of Impersonal Routine Stage (stickers for statements)**

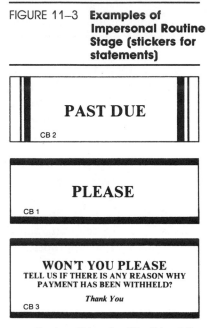

Courtesy of International Credit Association

period is common. Since installment accounts generally are paid from current income, a missed payment usually means the debtor must wait until the next pay period for future payments. Such considerations are often overlooked in planning a collection system.

The Impersonal Appeals Stage

If the mild notices in the first stage fail to produce payment or to gain some response from the debtor, a more forceful means is used to bring the indebtedness to a speedy conclusion. That is the purpose of this second stage. In this stage collection efforts are still "impersonal" but change from a routine procedure to a nonroutine or an appeals basis. The form letters used are no longer the routine impersonal type; they take the "anything wrong?" or "tell us your story" tone or appeal to the customers' pride in meeting their credit responsibilities or to their sense of fair play.

The use of the telephone as a collection device has increased tremendously over the past several years. In addition to its direct appeal, the telephone has a cost advantage over the use of the mails. Many firms, recognizing the value of the telephone as a collection device, consider when deciding to accept credit whether an individual has a telephone listing.

FIGURE 11-4 **Example of Impersonal
Routine Stage (form letter)**

We've searched HIGH . . .

. . . and LOW for
Your payment.

We haven't found it yet.

Will you please send it?

Nancy J. Friedman suggests 10 tips to maximize the telephone's potential:[5]

1. When making a telephone call, be prepared for the called person to be absent.
2. Don't let your negative emotions move from one call to the next.
3. Use your name over the phone.
4. Try to be nice over the phone.
5. Be sure to return all phone calls.
6. Tell certain vendors that you do not want to hear from them again.

---

[5]Nancy J. Friedman, "Ten Terrific Telephone Tips," *The Credit World,* May–June 1990, p. 34.

7. Treat internal calls as politely as external calls.

8. If the party called is not available, try stating the reason for the call to someone else.

9. If you are out of the office, be sure to check whether any messages were left for you.

10. The secret of good phoning is to be friendly—smile over the phone.

Unusual letters (such as special delivery, registered, or trick reply, in which debtors are given the choice of filling a lengthy questionnaire or paying their bill) are also used to secure some indication of whether the debtor received the inquiry. After writing to a person who does not respond but who gives every indication of residing at the address used, the creditor has several alternatives that may be more effective but involve increased costs. These include the use of certified mail, restricted delivery to addressee only, returned postage receipt showing the name of the person who signed for it, and return receipt showing address where delivered.

The debtors involved in this stage generally include those who: have honestly overlooked the amount in arrears, are in a temporarily embarrassing financial position, are careless in making payments or are procrastinators, have suffered a misfortune since incurring the debt and cannot meet their obligation, have overbought, believe the amount owed is incorrect, or raise questions involving some phase of the transaction and thus dispute the amount.

The Personalized Appeals Stage

This third stage incorporates both the personal aspect and the appeals approach. All efforts are directed toward the debtor on a highly personalized basis—efforts that are the last ones before the creditor takes some type of drastic or legal action (see Figure 11–5). Debtors who force the creditor to this stage include those who: overbought, will eventually become insolvents (and may even resort to bankruptcy), met with some accident or misfortune, are habitual frauds with no intent of paying, or believe the amount owing is incorrect and dispute the bill.

The collection devices commonly used in this stage include personal letters (usually a series, spaced at different intervals) pointing out the drawn-out procedure the creditor has been forced to go through up to this stage. This stage may also include personal letters to the debtor's employer, as well as notification to the local credit bureau of the impairment of the debtor's credit standing. Personal collectors and personal contacts by phone are also commonly used at this stage.

The costs of the actions in this stage are greater than those involved in the first two stages. Personally dictated letters are one of the main weapons employed. Although personally dictated letters are initially

FIGURE 11–5 **Example of Personalized Appeals Stage**

Date

Mr. John C. Slow
000 Main Street
Your City, Your State

Dear Mr. Slow:

You expect fairness from us, don't you?

Our entire collection procedure has been based on courtesy
and consideration. We have been willing to cooperate with
you in every way.

All, alas, to no avail.

Now, our last message to you . . . sent in all fairness.

Your account will be placed with a professional collection
agency unless you pay it in full, or make satisfactory
arrangements, within the next five days.

Be fair to yourself . . . your immediate action will prevent
serious trouble.

Cordially yours,

(Signature)
Name typed
Title

Courtesy of International Credit Association

expensive, they permit more varied and persuasive appeals than do stock form letters, debtor reaction is generally more favorable, and the result is greater pulling power.

Drastic or Legal Action Stage

In the previous three stages, creditors consider customer goodwill before taking any action, but in this last stage the gloves are off and the honeymoon is over. The debtors involved at this stage are of much the same type as the debtors of the third stage, but the creditor now should consider what assets the debtor owns before undertaking a legal action, such as suit. Many firms don't use the techniques discussed in this section, however, because of the possible ill feelings they can create.

EXTENSION AGREEMENT.   Under this agreement, honest and sincere people who are temporarily unable to meet their obligations may be given a longer time to pay their debts. Creditors should allow this only when they are convinced that both parties will benefit from such an arrangement.

COMPOSITION ARRANGEMENT.   Under this arrangement, a group of creditors agree to accept a reduced amount as settlement of their indebtedness in full. This scaling down is done only if the debtor is honest and sincere and free from any taint of fraud. Such an arrangement enables the debtor to recover a debt-free position, while creditors receive x cents on the dollar of their indebtedness without any more drastic action.

COLLECTION AGENCY.   Another drastic action that a creditor can take is referring an account to a collection agency. Although there are thousands of collection agencies in the country, one of the better known groups is the Collection Service Division of Associated Credit Bureaus, Inc. Members are located in all parts of the United States and Canada and form what might be termed a network collection service. Each local collection service office may (and does) call on any one of the other offices for help in locating the debtor of a local creditor. The account is usually forwarded to any of the other offices involved, and personal collection effort is expended on the local level to collect the account. These local collection service offices generally have their own established collection systems, which may closely resemble the four stages just outlined.

The costs of collecting through such an agency vary considerably, although the average runs between one-third and one-half of the amount collected. The 50 percent figure is used primarily with accounts $25 or under, accounts 12 months past due, accounts that require skip tracing or litigation, and when necessary to receive payments of $5 or less.

Once an account is turned over to a collection agency, the creditor should insist that all dealings be made through the agency, that the agency furnish periodic progress reports, and that arrangements be made as to how and when collections should be remitted.

The American Collectors Association, Inc. (ACA),[6] is a trade association representing collection agencies located in the United States, Canada, and more than 100 countries overseas. To become a member of ACA, a collection service makes an application to an affiliated state or multistate association. Once accepted at that level, it becomes an ACA member. All association members are bonded as required by their state or through ACA. ACA provides educational programs not only for collectors but for creditors and consumers as well. Since more than two-thirds of the states license or regulate collection services in some way, one of ACA's functions is to keep members informed of changing state (and federal) regulations.

GARNISHMENT OR WAGE ASSIGNMENT.   These two actions are combined to illustrate techniques available for collecting amounts due by securing part of the debtor's income. The two actions vary considerably, however, in how they are carried out.

The right of garnishment exists in some form or other in practically every state, although it is called by varying names. It requires a court order, in which a creditor may acquire a right to hold a third party (in whose possession goods, money, or credits of the debtor are found) liable for the debt of the defendant.

On July 1, 1970, Title III, the restrictions on garnishment section of the federal Consumer Credit Protection Act, went into effect. The main features of these restrictions on garnishment have been described as follows:

> For the first time in the history of this country, Congress has passed a law that imposes a federal limitation on the garnishment of an employee's wages. To put it simply, the new law limits weekly garnishments to either (1) 25 percent of after-tax pay or, (2) after-tax pay minus 30 times the federal minimum wage, whichever is less.
>
> While it is true that technically the law covers only those engaged in "interstate commerce" the courts over the past few years have established such broad standards for this term that almost every business today can be considered to be involved in interstate commerce in one way or another, and therefore would very likely be subject to this restriction in the new law.
>
> It should also be remembered that this new federal garnishment law prohibits employers from firing an employee simply because his wages have been subject to garnishment for one indebtedness.[7]

---

[6]Also see the material on the ACA in Chapter 7.

[7]Max A. Denney, "Restrictions on Garnishment," *Industrial Banker,* March 1970, p. 11. For provisions of the federal Fair Debt Collection Practices Act, see Chapter 6.

The minimum amount of disposable earnings immune from garnishment increases with each increase in the minimum wage rate set forth in the Fair Labor Standards Act.

Under a wage assignment, the debtor signs an agreement (usually at the time the credit transaction is made) to the effect that in case of nonpayment, the creditor may seek a certain portion of the debtor's wages without a court order. Such an arrangement is pertinent only to the employer named in the wage assignment. Generally speaking, when a wage assignment is presented to an employer, the employer is bound to recognize the terms agreed on by debtor and creditor.

However, there are exceptions to these provisions. In some states, state employees cannot be bound by garnishment proceedings and wage assignments. Federal government employees and members of the armed forces are not generally subject to these collection devices.[8] However, effective April 22, 1978, the U.S. Postal Service was required to honor valid court-ordered wage garnishments. This decision was based on the fact that five federal appellate courts had held that the U.S. Postal Service was not entitled to the defense of sovereign immunity in wage garnishments.

REPOSSESSION.   Although generally the creditor's last desire is to retake merchandise that is not paid for, this may be the only action left. The right of repossession is generally found under the right of replevin. This right specifies that if the creditor can show a title or a possessory right superior to that of the debtor, then the merchandise can be retaken in case of nonfulfillment of the terms of the contract. However, the varying state laws set forth widely different provisions as to the circumstances under which replevin is applicable.

Repossession can take place only when the creditor has a secured interest in the merchandise (typical of the installment-type contract) or when a writ of replevin has been obtained after suit has been filed and judgment rendered.

ATTORNEYS.   Another technique is to turn the account over to an attorney who will act like a collection agency in attempting to secure payment. Two different approaches are found under this arrangement: (1) use of the company's own attorney, who usually contacts the debtor as a private lawyer and not as an employee of the company; and (2) use of a separate and independent attorney who attempts to collect the indebtedness on a fee or commission basis.

---

[8]Effective May 7, 1979, the Office of the Secretary of Defense instituted a rule that revised DOD policies regarding the processing of claims of delinquent indebtedness against members of the armed forces. Generally, the rule stated that armed forces personnel were expected to pay just financial obligations in a proper and timely manner and that the DOD had no legal authority to require members of the armed forces to pay private debts or to divert any part of their pay for the satisfaction of such debts, even debts reduced to judgment, except for the payment of alimony or child support.

SUIT. Collection by suit is generally considered when all other collection methods fail and when the debtor has sufficient assets against which to execute a judgment. Suit action, which is generally looked on with disfavor by the creditors of consumer debt because of possible bad publicity, accomplishes two things: (1) it establishes the legal fact that the debt exists and that it is of such an amount; and (2) it provides the creditor with a legal remedy and aid in collecting the debt. However, just obtaining a judgment does not guarantee payment. Creditors should make sure the debtor has sufficient assets against which the judgment can be entered before instituting suit.

The effectiveness of collection by suit is reduced by two modifications. First, a debt cannot be held forever. Every state has statutes of limitations that spell out in detail the length of time during which a debt may be collected and the provisions for renewing the limitation period. Second, various state laws stipulate what property and what percentage of earnings are not subject to seizure by suit. These exemptions are allowed because of the traditional belief it is an injustice to society and to the debtor to strip the debtor of all personal assets and income.

OTHER ACTIONS. Small amounts can be collected in various small claims courts or, as they are known in some states, justice of the peace (JP) courts. Again, state laws governing the actions of these courts vary. No attempt has been made to list all possible drastic or legal means.

PROBLEMS WITH CONSUMER BANKRUPTCY

Another method, this time usually initiated by the debtor, that modifies the individual's indebtedness is the action that can be taken under the federal Bankruptcy Act, as amended. The first Bankruptcy Act was passed in 1800, and a thorough revision was made in 1938. On November 6, 1978, the president signed the Bankruptcy Reform Act of 1978, which became effective October 1, 1979, and applied to all bankruptcy cases filed after that date.

The Bankruptcy Reform Act of 1978 had an unintended impact on consumer bankruptcies. Personal bankruptcies jumped 75 percent during the first 12 months the new law was in force—far in excess of what was expected on the basis of historical experience. The number of individual bankruptcies being filed under the Bankruptcy Reform Act posed a problem that could not be ignored by anyone engaged in the consumer credit field. Bankruptcies rapidly became one of the nation's chief domestic problems; the amount of money involved was tremendous. Contrary to common belief, business failures accounted for only a small percentage of the total bankruptcies; the bulk occurred among the wage earner and salaried worker class.

In July 1984 the president signed the Bankruptcy Amendments and Federal Judgeship Act, ending months of congressional dispute and repeated deadline extensions. The new law included consumer credit reforms directed toward reducing the alleged abuses by both debtors and creditors under the 1978 Bankruptcy Reform Act.

Highlights of the 1984 act include:

There are a number of specific parts, or chapters, of the federal bankruptcy law, and these offer alternatives to debtors. Chapter 11 of the federal bankruptcy act is generally not intended for consumer borrowers because of the expense and complexity of the proceedings. Consumer borrowers typically utilize Chapter 7 or 13. Proceedings under Chapter 7 (straight bankruptcy) involve taking a portion of the borrower's property (non-exempt assets, as explained later) and distributing it among his or her lenders. Bankruptcy plans under Chapter 13 typically extend the time for repayment, but involve repaying a portion of the debt in installments from the borrower's income. Under any chapter, once the bankruptcy proceeding is concluded (lenders have been paid the debts due them) you are no longer liable. In legal parlance, you are "discharged" from the debts and start financially with a clean slate.

* * * * *

Chapter 13 is the most commonly used alternative within the bankruptcy code. It allows a person who has a steady income to pay all or a portion of his or her debts. Under Chapter 13, you file a bankruptcy petition and a proposed payment plan with the U.S. Bankruptcy Court. Under the rules for a Chapter 13 filing, your payments must represent all of your disposable income (whatever is not needed for shelter, food, and other necessities). Chapter 13 is available only to borrowers with less than $100,000 in unsecured debts (such as credit cards) and less than $350,000 in secured debts (such as mortgages and car loans). Anyone with greater debts generally must declare bankruptcy under Chapters 7 or 11 of the bankruptcy act. (Chapter 11 covers businesses which are restructuring while continuing operations, but a Chapter 11 filing by an individual is possible.)

* * * * *

A repayment plan under Chapter 13 typically extends your time for paying debts (usually up to three years or, with special permission of the court, up to five years) and may allow you to repay less than you owe. With this kind of plan you usually turn over a fixed sum of money every month to the trustee, who then pays the lenders.[9]

One of the more important changes under the 1984 law was that judges are now permitted to dismiss a case if they believe that granting relief would be a "substantial abuse" of Chapter 7 of the bankruptcy code (Chapter 7 provides for straight discharge of debts). The court may consider future income in assessing the need for relief, whereas formerly it considered only assets and liabilities. In addition, the debtor and debtor's

---

[9]*Your Legal Guide to Consumer Credit* (Chicago: American Bar Association, Public Education Division, 1988), p. 37. Also see the Suggested Readings at the end of the chapter. Reprinted by permission of the American Bar Association.

attorney must show that the debtor was made aware of alternative relief under different chapters of the bankruptcy code.

Under the new law, the debtor is prevented from "loading up" before filing for bankruptcy. Debts of more than $500 for luxury goods and services incurred within 40 days before the order of relief are nondischargeable, as are cash advances of more than $1,000 that are extensions of consumer credit under an open-end credit plan and that are obtained within 20 days before the order. There is an exemption for household goods of $4,000 per household. Consumers have 45 days from the date of filing for bankruptcy to tell the court which items they wish protected from creditors. In the past, consumers could exempt an unlimited amount of household goods valued up to $200 per item.

Filings of individual bankruptcy petitions were expected to drop as a result of the changes in the law. However, this has not happened, as shown in Table 11–1, which gives the number of nonbusiness petitions by state for 1984 to 1989, and in Table 11–2, which gives bankruptcy petitions from 1981 through 1988.

AUTOMATED COLLECTIONS

Automation is becoming an important ingredient in the collections process of some firms, since effective and timely handling of delinquent accounts is a key to successful operation and profitability. The following comments are pertinent to the trend toward automation.

> Several computer systems firms now offer software packages that can identify delinquent accounts and can even make telephone calls to past-due customers. The software packages interface with existing computer operations and are designed to increase collector productivity and management control while reducing delinquencies and losses.
>
> Even though the software is available, relatively few offices currently have automated collections capability. AFSA members Credithrift and General Electric Credit Corporation (GECC) are two examples of companies where such systems are in place. Credithrift has eight dedicated outgoing WATS lines that are used to deliver electronic past-due notices for first delinquencies. (Seriously overdue accounts are switched to the mainframe computer or are handled by live collectors.) The software package for Credithrift supports a computerized calling procedure that can make up to 400 calls per hour with only one operator needed to monitor the system. The system is in place only for the company's new card division, and is in the testing stage for the branch office system.
>
> GECC combines software and hardware in a system that uses 4–8 lines at once and can make up to 200–300 calls in an hour. One operator is needed to front the calls. In the case of a busy signal, the system is programmed to redial according to parameters set by GECC. Also, the GECC automated collection system services three different departments.
>
> With most automated collections systems, the collections process begins the moment the account has been past due for a predetermined

TABLE 11-1 **Number of Nonbusiness Bankruptcy Petitions**

	December			Average Change	
	1984	1988	1989	1984–88	1988–89
District of Columbia	533	1,008	996	22.28%	−1.19%
Maine	421	771	955	20.78	23.87
Massachusetts	1,766	2,832	4,244	15.09	49.86
New Hampshire	382	646	1,004	17.28	55.42
Rhode Island	583	822	1,119	10.25	36.13
Connecticut	1,513	2,331	3,218	13.52	38.05
New York	11,291	17,753	22,600	14.31	27.30
Vermont	114	262	154	32.46	−41.22
Delaware	390	641	711	16.09	10.92
New Jersey	5,490	7,617	9,373	9.69	23.05
Pennsylvania	7,655	11,798	13,003	13.53	10.21
Maryland	3,345	7,282	7,966	29.42	9.39
North Carolina	4,038	7,477	8,605	21.29	15.09
South Carolina	1,804	3,885	4,358	28.84	12.18
Virginia	7,202	13,164	15,033	20.70	14.20
West Virginia	1,429	2,800	3,041	23.99	8.61
Louisiana	5,637	11,136	11,556	24.39	3.77
Mississippi	4,293	8,960	9,973	27.18	11.31
Texas	9,676	34,220	35,013	63.41	2.32
Kentucky	5,729	9,940	11,626	18.38	16.96
Michigan	7,458	14,108	15,949	22.29	13.05
Ohio	17,322	28,588	32,145	16.26	12.44
Tennessee	12,548	26,349	30,095	7.50	14.22
Illinois	21,342	29,474	31,512	.53	6.91
Indiana	10,661	17,674	20,046	16.45	13.42
Wisconsin	5,701	8,011	8,637	10.13	7.81
Arkansas	2,974	5,406	6,034	21.20	7.97
Iowa	2,279	3,827	4,065	16.98	6.22
Minnesota	3,708	9,240	11,379	37.30	23.15
Missouri	5,314	9,883	11,404	21.50	15.39
Nebraska	1,952	2,703	3,027	9.62	11.99
North Dakota	337	917	828	43.03	−9.71
South Dakota	913	829	928	−2.30	11.94
Alaska	213	1,013	1,132	93.90	11.75
Arizona	3,447	12,098	13,912	62.74	14.99
California	51,860	90,282	94,022	18.52	4.14
Hawaii	389	735	757	22.24	2.99
Idaho	1,566	3,464	3,589	30.30	3.61
Montana	732	1,454	1,396	24.66	−3.99
Nevada	2,255	5,369	5,372	34.52	0.06
Oregon	4,618	8,825	9,731	22.78	10.27
Washington	8,609	15,580	15,407	20.24	−1.11
Colorado	4,480	13,736	13,773	51.65	0.27
Kansas	3,473	6,389	7,067	20.99	10.61
New Mexico	1,310	2,643	3,464	5.44	31.06
Oklahoma	5,510	12,267	12,595	3.66	2.67
Utah	2,541	6,437	7,252	38.33	12.66
Wyoming	532	1,269	1,281	34.63	0.95
Alabama	8,982	18,309	21,657	25.96	18.29
Florida	6,136	20,132	26,026	57.02	29.28
Georgia	11,500	24,698	32,588	28.69	31.95
Total	284,534	549,831	616,753	23.31%	12.17%

Source: A. Charlene Sullivan, "Charting the Course of Personal Bankruptcies," *Credit Card Management,* August 1990, p. 58.

TABLE 11–2 **Bankruptcy Petitions Filed and Pending, by Type and Chapter— 1981 to 1988**

[*For years ending June 30.* Covers only bankruptcy cases filed under the Bankruptcy Reform Act of 1978. **Bankruptcy:** *legal recognition that a company or individual is insolvent and must restructure or liquidate. Petitions "filed" means the commencement of a proceeding through the presentation of a petition to the clerk of the court; "pending" is a proceeding in which the administration has not been completed*]

Item	1981	1982	1983	1984	1985	1986	1987	1988
Total, filed	360,329	367,866	374,734	344,275	364,536	477,856	561,278	594,567
Business[1]	· 47,415	56,423	69,818	62,170	66,651	76,281	88,278	68,501
Non-business[2]	312,914	311,443	304,916	282,105	297,885	401,575	473,000	526,066
Voluntary	358,997	366,331	373,064	342,828	362,939	476,214	559,658	593,158
Involuntary	1,332	1,535	1,670	1,447	1,597	1,642	1,620	1,409
Chapter 7[3]	265,721	255,098	251,322	232,994	244,650	332,679	397,551	423,796
Chapter 9[4]	1	4	3	4	3	7	10	3
Chapter 11[5]	7,828	14,059	21,207	19,913	21,425	24,443	25,566	18,891
Chapter 12[6]	(X)	(X)	(X)	(X)	(X)	(X)	4,824	3,099
Chapter 13[7]	86,778	98,705	102,201	91,358	98,452	120,726	136,300	148,771
Section 304[8]	1	–	1	6	6	1	27	7
Total, pending	361,664	461,287	537,306	577,567	608,945	728,577	808,504	815,497

– Represents zero.
X Not applicable.
[1]Business bankruptcies include those filed under chapters 7, 9, 11, or 12.
[2]Bankruptcies include those filed under chapters 7, 11, or 13.
[3]Chapter 7, liquidation of nonexempt assets of businesses or individuals.
[4]Chapter 9, adjustment of debts of a municipality.
[5]Chapter 11, individual or business reorganization.
[6]Chapter 12, adjustment of debts of a family farmer with regular annual income, effective November 26, 1986.
[7]Chapter 13, adjustment of debts of an individual with regular income.
[8]11 U.S.C., Section 304, cases ancillary to foreign proceedings.
Source: Administrative Office of the U.S. Courts, *Annual Report of the Director.*

number of days. At that time, the computer dials the customer's telephone number and when contact is made, a brief written outline of that customer's account record shows up on the computer terminal. The collections operator then comes on the line to make positive identification of the cardholder before asking the person to hold for a prerecorded message. Where the call goes after that time is determined by the software package.[10]

IMPACT OF A SOUND COLLECTION POLICY

Collection work is trying, and collection managers and their staffs need patience, persistence, and resourcefulness. How well collection managers perform their jobs determines the impact that collection activities have on

---

[10]Lourie Shaker, "Automated Collections," *Credit*, March–April 1985, p. 16. Also see John Y. Coffman and J. Stephen Darsie, "Collection Scoring," *The Credit World*, September–October 1986, p. 26.

their firms. They always walk a tightrope, trying to decide just how much effort to make and how much expense to incur in attempting to bring an indebtedness to a satisfactory conclusion.

Collection managers, working at times under the direction of credit managers, have the following responsibilities.

1. To aid the working capital position of the firm by securing collections of receivables as quickly, cheaply, and completely as possible.

2. To reduce bad-debt losses. This involves deciding when an account should be considered a loss. It generally is recommended that any amount six months past the credit period should be considered bad and charged off. This does not mean collection efforts should stop at this time—accounts charged off as bad-debt losses can still be recovered.

3. To aid the sales effort. An individual free of overdue debt is much more likely to make purchases at the firm than a customer with a guilty conscience over an overdue bill. Such customers make future purchases at competing firms.

4. To ease pressure between customer and firm by straightening out any misunderstanding that stands in the way of payment. In fact, here the collection manager doubles as a public relations person.

5. To help make policy decisions concerning credit and collections. For example, what policy should be established concerning paid-up slow accounts seeking new credit?

DISCUSSION QUESTIONS

1. How do you account for the fact that collections are an inherent part of any credit business?

2. Why doesn't the word *collections* mean the same thing to all people involved in the credit and collections business?

3. What is the purpose of consumer credit insurance?

4. Survey the leading stores in your community and see if they are using consumer credit insurance.

5. Explain the two main categories of consumer credit insurance.

6. Why should states regulate this type of insurance?

7. Explain the purposes of consumer credit counseling services.

8. What four general policies can be followed in collection activities? Which would you recommend?

9. Discuss the factors that are involved in setting up a collection policy.

10. A general collection system is usually divided into four stages. What are these stages?

11. How do you account for the types of debtors that are usually involved in each of the four stages?

12. When would you recommend that an extension agreement be used? A composition settlement?

13. Visit a collection agency in your community and compare the charges of this agency with those shown in the chapter.

14. Discuss the new restrictions on garnishment as set forth in the Consumer Credit Protection Act.

15. What is the primary purpose of bankruptcy? How does consumer bankruptcy procedure vary from that of a business firm?

16. Outline the main provisions of the 1984 Bankruptcy Amendments and Federal Judgeship Act.

SUGGESTED READINGS

A General Collection System

FANNING, DEIRDRE. "Playing by the Rules." *Forbes,* March 9, 1987, p. 76.

GILLESPIE, TOM. "What's New in the Collection Department of the 90s?" *The Credit World,* May–June 1990, p. 36.

HORN, RICHARD L. "Working with Collection Agencies." *The Credit World,* January–February 1987, p. 34.

JEWEL, GARY L. "Collect with Care." *ABA Banking Journal,* December 1988, p. 57.

JOHNSON, JOHN W. "The Rapid Evolution of the Debt Collection Business." *The Credit World,* July–August 1987, p. 38.

LUCAS, PETER. "Are You Ready for Kinder, Gentler Collectors?" *Credit Card Management,* June 1989, p. 32.

YOUNG, ORVILLE D. "Keys to a Long-Term Productive Collector." *The Credit World,* March–April 1987, p. 38.

Bankruptcy

BUCKHOLTZ, TINA. "Consumer Bankruptcy: Don't Let It Hit Your Blind Side." *The Credit World,* January–February 1988, p. 39.

LUCKETT, CHARLES A. "Personal Bankruptcies." *Federal Reserve Bulletin,* September 1988, p. 591. Reproduced with permission in *The Credit World,* March–April 1989, p. 22, and *The Credit World,* May–June 1989, p. 36.

MAPOTHER, WILLIAM R. "Magical Bankruptcy Strategies." *The Credit World,* January–February 1989, p. 18.

Busir **al Credit**

dit.

ommercial credit.

le in commercial credit.

f sale.

e.

ent rates of interest

t, and these next 9 chap-
fication of credit as out-
ed into two categories:
ial) credit. This chapter

as mercantile or trade
nd services in exchange
ly in connection with a
esale. Commercial credit
ause the value received
ated to consumer credit
businesses. Commercial
such as manufacturers,
s. The services included
d in connection with the
nduct of the enterprise.
f short-term credit used
ber of transactions, the
ounting procedures nec-

oods through successive
important function is

frequently supplemented by other forms of credit, businesses rely on commercial credit far more than other sources.

Financing the Movement of Goods

A simple example illustrates the use of commercial credit in production and distribution. When producers of raw materials sell to processors and manufacturers, the goods may be financed in several ways. If these original producers are financially capable, they may accept their customers' credit, thus creating commercial credit. If raw materials suppliers are financially weak, the burden of financing the goods falls on the purchasers, who may use their own capital or borrow from a bank or some other lending institution.

As the raw materials are processed or converted into semiprocessed goods, they are sold to manufacturers of finished goods who may offer their credit in exchange. This is known as commercial credit because the manufacturers are acquiring goods for further fabrication or for the operation of their businesses. (Other forms of credit, in whole or in part, help the manufacturer pay workers, meet overhead, and cover other manufacturing costs.) As the goods are manufactured into finished products, they are sold to wholesalers or industrial supply houses. This transfer is again accomplished by commercial credit—wholesalers offer their credit to the manufacturer in exchange for the goods. And, finally, retailers offer their credit to obtain an inventory of finished goods. Commercial credit transactions take place each time goods change ownership until they are purchased by the final consumer.

Commercial credit, then, is used by all kinds of business enterprises to finance the acquisition of goods or services. The transaction may be very informal: one business orders goods or services and another delivers. Evidence of the transaction is an account receivable or a note receivable claim in the seller's accounting records. The buyer's evidence of the transaction is an account payable or note payable obligation in its accounting records. Few businesses are free from frequent credits and debits to these asset and liability accounts. Furthermore, although there is no precise data to support the point, the vast majority of all goods and services flowing through the production and marketing processes are financed this way.

At times (in a "credit crunch" period) some of the largest and best-rated companies slow down their payments to smaller and weaker creditors, thus forcing the smaller companies to "carry" them.

The United States is far more advanced than other countries in its use of commercial credit. U.S. businesses offer and accept much more credit than businesses in any other nation. Not only is our system simple and informal, but it is also much more extensive. This is principally due to our unique and well-developed network of interchanging credit information.

Essential to a Mass-Distribution Economy

Some method of relieving the financial problem in the various stages of production and distribution is essential to the effectiveness of a mass-distribution economy. If businesses depended exclusively on bank loans and their own capital, they couldn't marshal the financial capacity they do with commercial credit.

The widespread use of commercial credit and much of its importance as a form of business finance stem from the nation's economic developments. As the nation grew, so did the distances between manufacturers and their customers. With the development of transportation and communication systems, population and businesses scattered over vast geographic areas. Paralleling these developments, mass-production and mass-distribution methods assumed their place in the economy. Retailers also increased in number, and large-scale retailing became necessary to meet the wants of a growing population. As a result, trade was transacted on a more impersonal basis and over greater distances. Speed of commercial transactions became essential as competitive forces intensified. To achieve effective production and distribution systems in this changed economy, businesses needed some method of financing goods as they moved through production and marketing phases.

Changing Attitudes toward Commercial Credit

Commercial credit is not a recent invention. In colonial America, commercial credit was the backbone of trade with England and other European countries. However, the attitudes associated with credit and the credit instruments themselves differed greatly.

Early laws and attitudes concerning delinquent debtors were rigid and harsh. Punishments ranged from imprisonment or enslavement to death in some instances. This state of affairs placed the risk squarely on the debtor, not on the creditor. Furthermore, considering the consequences for default, prospective debtors had to give serious thought to any credit transaction, thus inhibiting the role credit could play in an expanding economy. Only recently have such rigorous laws been abolished and more lenient attitudes toward delinquent debtors emerged. Today only debtors who commit fraudulent credit transactions can be imprisoned. Creditors who deal with businesses today regard themselves more as business partners than as people in a position to ruthlessly enforce a claim. Credit between business enterprises is recognized as mutually profitable. Risk is now assumed by debtors *and* creditors. In a sense, then, because both have risk capital invested in the business, an attitude of partnership is easily fostered.

The changing economic environment has also contributed to the changed attitude toward credit. Before the Civil War, retailers had to estimate their inventory requirements for six months or longer. They took annual or semiannual trips to the market, where they purchased large quantities of merchandise. Because of the large amount of credit needed and the lack of an adequate communication system, the credit was secured with a trade acceptance, promissory note, or draft. As transportation and communication improved, businesses didn't need to estimate their inventory requirements so accurately. Suppliers' salespeople could travel to distant locations, and retailers could visit the market more often. The open-book account, as evidence of a commercial credit transaction, supplanted the trade acceptance, promissory note, and draft. Because retailers no longer had to estimate requirements over an unrealistic time period, they didn't have to obligate themselves so heavily, and shorter credit terms prevailed. Shorter terms meant that retailers could liquidate their obligations faster, thereby increasing the turnover rate of suppliers' receivables. Today computerized commercial credit transactions are commonplace and customary.

TERMS OF SALE

In each commercial credit transaction, the seller and buyer must understand the conditions for payment, generally known as the *terms of sale, credit terms,* or *payment terms.*[1] It is sound business practice to quote terms of sale on all invoices covering the shipment and all instruments associated with the sale contract. See Figures 12–1 and 12–2 for examples of invoices with terms of sale quoted on the invoices. If specific terms of sale are not quoted, the buyer can legally presume that any terms customary in that line of trade are applicable. The buyer's obligation to meet the terms of sale arises when the seller delivers the goods or services or meets other specified conditions of the sale. The terms of sale applicable in commercial credit transactions are peculiar to this type of credit.

Establishing Terms of Sale

Credit terms offered to customers should be determined by executives responsible for policy decisions. Credit policies deserve just as careful consideration as other elements of the sales program. While credit policies and terms may vary in particular situations, certain general principles are common.

---

[1]For a discussion of credit terms, see Calvin M. Boardman and Kathy J. Ricci, "Defining Selling Terms," *Credit & Financial Management,* April 1985, p. 31. Also see Charles M. Tatelbaum, "Don't Get Caught Outdated," *Business Credit,* July–August 1990, p. 42.

FIGURE 12–1 **Sample Invoice with Terms of Sale**

```
                THE FLORIDA SPECIFIER


                          I N V O I C E


TECHNICAL COMMUNICATIONS GROUP INC          Invoice No 24451
385 WEST FAIRBANKS AVENUE
POST OFFICE DRAWER 2027                    Customer No 63681
WINTER PARK, FL 32790-2027
Telephone 407/740-7950                   Invoice Date 07/02/90




Bill To:                          Ship To:
CLIPPING SERVICE OF FLORIDA       CLIPPING SERVICE OF FLORIDA
636 MANDALAY AVE                  636 MANDALAY AVE
CLEARWATER, FL 34630              CLEARWATER, FL 34630


ROBB COLE PRESIDENT




        THE FLORIDA SPECIFIER                    265.00

        AD PRODUCTION                             20.00

        1/6 STANDARD PAGE AD - JULY 1990 ISSUE

        THANK YOU!




TERMS:  NET DUE 30 DAYS, 1 1/2% SERVICE CHARGE ON OPEN BALANCES OVER 30 DAYS.




                        NonTaxable Subtotal    285.00
                        Taxable Subtotal         0.00
                        Tax                      0.00
                        Total                  285.00

TO ASSURE PROPER CREDIT TO YOUR ACCOUNT,
PLEASE RETURN COPY WITH YOUR CHECK.
```

FIGURE 12–2 **Sample Invoice with Terms of Sale**

CLIPPING BUREAU OF FLORIDA
PRESS CLIPPING SERVICE
P.O. Box 3159 • Clearwater, Florida 34630-8159

JULY 19, 1990

ROB MIDDLEMAS
SENIOR VICE PRESIDENT
DEAN WITTER REYNOLDS, INC.
P.O. BOX 30789
PALM BEACH GARDENS, FL 33420

THE PULSE OF FLORIDA
WE CHECK IT DAILY!

```
                       INVOICE # 1360-04
                       -----------------

MONTHLY READING FEE:     06/20   TO    07/19/90        $    39.00

CLIPPING CHARGE:        26  @  45¢                          11.70

CLIPPING CREDIT:         5  @  45¢                          -2.25

SPECIAL MAILING:    $15.00--DAILY, $7.50--TWICE WEEKLY       0.00

FAXING CHARGE:           0  @  $1.50                         0.00
                                                          ------

CURRENT AMOUNT DUE:                                        48.45

PREVIOUS BALANCE:   INVOICE #1360-03,  6/19/90            53.40


                                                          ------

TOTAL AMOUNT DUE:                                     $   101.85
                                                          ======

TERMS: NET 15 DAYS      ---     08/03/90
```

THANK YOU FOR YOUR BUSINESS! IF YOUR RECORDS EVER VARY FROM OURS
AS TO TOTAL CLIPS, PLEASE CONTACT US FOR A DAILY ITEMIZATION.

OVER 1,000 FLORIDA PUBLICATIONS MONITORED
STATE 800-442-0332 / CLEARWATER 813-442-0332

Two major variables are involved in all terms of sale. The first is the *credit period,* also called the net credit period, which is the length of time allowed the buyer before payment is considered past due.

> The use of the postmark date in determining when a bill is paid is another current trade practice of corporate management that seems to be an anomaly in the age of instant satellite communications. That is, a large percentage of companies still maintain that if an envelope containing a payment is postmarked by the quoted discount or due date, it qualifies for the discount or will be deemed to be paid when due. The reaction one might get when questioning a credit manager about the origin of this practice is that the Uniform Commercial Code requires it.
>
> In researching this question through legal texts, however, one finds that the practice really comes out of contract law rather than statute. Lawyers generally call it "the mailbox rule." Two early landmark cases established its use. The first case established the time of acceptance of an offer as being the moment the mailed acceptance was turned over to the postal system. (*Adams* v. *Lindsel,* 1818). The second case established the mail as a satisfactory method for communicating that acceptance (*Henthorn* v. *Fraser,* 1892).
>
> In spite of its clouded origin, the postmark date is still a very important benchmark in both corporate cash and credit management. With respect to collection systems, once a check is in the mail, the collector attempts to intercept it as soon as possible by locating lockboxes in close proximity to the mailing point. Conversely, in disbursing funds, a bill is considered to be paid once it is in the mail and the payer then hopes for as much disbursement float time as possible.[2]

The second major variable is the *cash discount.* This is a reduction allowed the buyer if payment is made before the end of the net credit period. The period of time the cash discount is allowed is known as the *cash discount period.* Not all firms allow cash discounts, but they are common in many trades. The cash discount should not be confused with the trade discount, which is a pricing device and bears no relationship to the time of payment.

In addition to the importance of quoting terms of sale, sellers and buyers need a clear understanding as to the credit instrument employed. The most frequent evidence of a commercial credit transaction is the seller's accounts receivable ledger. However, in some instances the seller may use a promissory note, trade acceptance, or time draft, all of which require the buyer's signature. Use of one of these instruments should be specified. To avoid disputes and eventual loss of customers, sellers must be sure that

---

[2]Theodore O. Johnson, "Credit Terms," *Credit & Financial Management,* January 1984, pp. 23–24. Reprinted with permission from *Credit & Financial Management,* Copyright 1984, published by the National Association of Credit Management, 520 Eighth Avenue, New York, NY 10018–6571.

buyers understand the terms of sale, the credit instrument, delivery dates, and all other details of the credit transaction.

Another detail of the credit transaction is known as "anticipation." By contract or custom, most sellers allow customers an anticipation rate, equivalent to the "normal going interest" rate. The anticipation rate is an added inducement to get the buyer to pay early. There is no agreement as to whether this anticipation rate should be given to encourage prompt payment within the cash discount period or whether it should be offered to customers who let the cash discount period expire and need an inducement to pay before the end of the net period. Customs of the trade determine which view prevails in any transaction.

Factors Influencing Terms of Sale

Even though American industries use various terms of sale, many trades tend toward standardized selling terms, referred to as *customary* or *regular* terms of sale. When conditioning factors influence the members of a trade to adopt similar selling policies over time, such policies become customary or standardized for a trade.

Despite this trend, most companies have several terms of sale that serve as credit department guideposts. Once a company establishes its selling terms, they are likely to correspond to the selling terms of the rest of the trade. Established terms, however, often have to be adjusted for a particular customer or circumstance. The following factors are the most important influences on the adoption of particular selling terms and their occasional adjustment.

EFFECT ON SALES AND PROFITS. The decision on what terms of sale to adopt depends primarily on the effect on sales and profit that the business firm expects these terms to have.

RATE OF STOCK TURNOVER. Sellers commonly finance buyers through at least a portion of their turnover periods. Accordingly, there is a relationship between the time it takes to convert merchandise into cash and the time allowed for payment of the indebtedness. Lines of trade with rapid turnover of merchandise generally have a short credit period, and those with relatively slow rates of stock turnover generally have a longer credit period. For example, most food products have a short credit period and clothing items have a relatively longer credit period.

LOCATION OF CUSTOMER AND TRANSPORTATION FACILITIES. Sellers dealing in distant markets are often at a disadvantage compared to local producers. If the time for payment starts from the date of the invoice, distant customers do not have as much time to pay after they receive the shipment. To overcome this handicap, sellers may attempt to equalize the distance and transportation factors by allowing a longer credit period

FIGURE 12–3 **Collection Float**

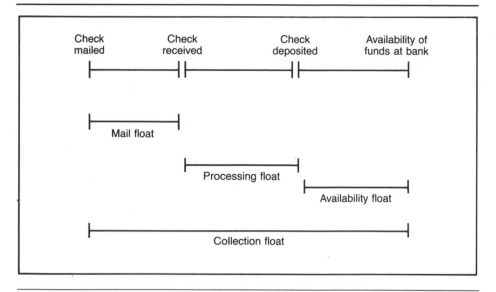

Source: Cathy L. Rollins, "Would a Bank Lockbox Make Sense for You?" *Business Credit,* December 1987, p. 34.

or by allowing terms starting with receipt of goods or receipt of invoice. In this way, the seller's terms of trade compensate for time lost in transportation and the expense of carrying a larger stock.

Because the distance between a seller and buyer becomes a time factor in the seller receiving payment, the use of bank lockboxes close to the mailing point has become increasingly popular since they were introduced in 1945.[3] The use of lockboxes thus can influence the terms of sale offered by a seller. Mail directed to a lockbox not only minimizes delivery time, but also improves the availability of funds because the bank having the lockbox processes mail throughout the night. Because many banks send checks directly to the drawee banks by courier, the seller usually obtains quicker availability on its checks. See Figure 12–3 for a graphic picture of a collection float.

REGIONAL DIFFERENCES. When selling in certain sections of the country, sellers may have to adjust terms to local conditions. While not as important today as it was in the past, this influence is still real in many areas. Crop farming, for example, is more seasonal than dairy farming. To as reasonable an extent as possible, commercial credit selling terms should be adjusted to this condition. Sellers may have to make a similar adjustment in major industries where customers' income is very irregular.

---

[3]Also see the comments on the use of bank lockboxes in Chapter 20.

CHARACTER OF THE GOODS. Adoption and adjustment of terms may be based on the character of the goods. If a firm sells a wide variety of products, a single selling term may not apply equally well to all of them. Different products on the same invoice may or may not carry a cash discount. Likewise, the credit period may vary from one line of goods to another even though the goods are all sold by the same supplier. Variations in terms of sale may thus be the result of such factors as profit margin, perishability, the novelty of the product, and even seasonal characteristics. For example, goods that are very perishable and those that afford a narrow profit margin usually have a short credit period and little or no cash discount. Conversely, sellers usually grant a longer credit period and a larger cash discount when goods are seasonal, new, and yield a wide margin of profit.

NATURE OF CREDIT RISK. The terms of a particular trade may not be uniformly applied to all customers. Terms may vary according to the nature of the credit risk. Thus buyers who are poor credit risks may be sold on a cash basis or on COD (cash on delivery) or CBD (cash before delivery) terms, whereas better credit risks get more liberal terms of sale. When most buyers in a particular trade are weak credit risks, the above terms may become standard practice, and sellers may continue to use them even after this reason ceases to exist.

CLASS OF CUSTOMER. Variations in selling terms may also exist because of customer differences. Customers can be classified in numerous ways—e.g., by size of order, by type of buyer (wholesaler or retailer), and even by type of wholesaler or type of retailer. Customers who make small purchases are frequently allowed shorter terms than the standard terms for the trade. On the other hand, large buyers who represent an important portion of the supplier's total volume may be given terms that are more lenient than is customary. A related factor is the customer's ability to perform important marketing functions for the supplier. Large buyers, for example, are frequently in a position to assume the storage function, provided the selling terms are adjusted to their requirements and other discounts are made available. Usually, as a matter of industry trade practices, wholesalers get different terms than retailers.

COMPETITION. Competition often has the strongest influence on selling terms. Sellers frequently modify customary terms of sale to meet the actions of their competitors. Because of this, they grant extra datings or seasonal datings (datings designed to delay the buyer's payment date) to various customers. Certain customers, because of the competitive pressures they are able to exert, may also be granted terms of MOM (middle of month) or EOM (end of month). Too frequently, competition causes a departure from an originally sound policy. At first, some of these modifications are made to favored customers and considered exceptions. Competitors, however, come to adopt the same terms, so the more lenient terms generally become standard trade practice. When this happens, terms of sale are no longer effective in stimulating sales, and the entire trade may find itself following unsound practices without any firm deriving special benefit.

FINANCIAL RESOURCES OF THE SELLER. The seller's ability to carry accounts receivable may force some modification of terms. A new business venture that is short of working capital has to sell on shorter terms than a well-established business with adequate resources to carry large accounts receivable. If many firms in a particular industry are financially weak, this policy may be adopted by the entire industry. For example, the shortage of working capital of the early car manufacturers led the industry to adopt cash terms. The same policy persisted long after car manufacturers had adequate working capital.

ECONOMIC CONDITIONS. Business activity is influenced by economic conditions, and hence some business practices are modified according to the business cycle. Firms tend to adjust selling terms in periods of prosperity or depression. Probably the ideal adjustment to cyclical changes is to tighten terms during prosperity and to liberalize them during depression.

In practice, customers demand longer terms during depression or recession, and sellers often accommodate them. During prosperity, however, sellers seldom tighten their terms. By tightening terms during prosperity, overstimulation of business activity would ease somewhat; and by liberalizing terms during depression, a stimulus to business would be in operation when it is most needed. Credit could thus be used to aid or abate business stimulation rather than to make it less stable. And credit would also be working with the coming trend rather than against it. Unfortunately, not all business policies are made for logical reasons, nor do all competitors operate rationally. Accordingly, and all too frequently, sellers don't adjust terms to changing economic conditions.

ATTITUDE OF CREDIT MANAGERS. Credit managers can influence selling terms. Their degree of influence, however, depends on their position in a company relative to other policy-making positions and the relationship they have with other selling departments. If credit managers consider it their sole responsibility to eliminate bad-debt losses and if they impose this attitude throughout a company, the seller may unduly shorten the credit terms. This extreme, and even the opposite extreme, will abort the function of the credit department, to the detriment of the seller and customers. Such narrow and one-sided attitudes on the part of credit managers conflict with the role of credit management in our economy.

TERMS OF SALE CLASSIFIED

Terms of sale can be classified into the following groups:

- Prepayment
- Cash
- Ordinary
- Single-payment or lumped-order
- Special-datings
- Consignment

Prepayment Terms

This class of terms includes CBD (cash before delivery), COD (cash on delivery), CWO (cash with order), CIA (cash in advance), and SD-BL (sight draft with bill of lading attached). Technically, prepayment terms are not common in commercial credit transactions. When prepayment terms are used, the element of risk inherent in credit transactions is absent or slight.

Aside from a few instances where they are customary in certain lines of trade, the above terms indicate the seller's unwillingness to accept the credit risk. The buyer may have always been a poor credit risk, or the buyer's creditworthiness may have deteriorated to the point of unacceptability. Not only is the seller unwilling to accept the buyer's credit, but the buyer also is often required to submit payment by certified check or cashier's draft; thus the seller does not even assume the risk of check clearance.

Unlike the other prepayment terms, COD terms and SD-BL terms are not entirely free of risk. The risk involved centers on the possibility that the buyer may reject the shipment after it arrives at its destination. In such instances the seller can accept the round-trip transportation costs, enter into a questionable credit arrangement with the original buyer, or, as a last resort, seek out another customer nearby. Sellers should insist on cash or a certified or cashier's check in payment of COD shipments.

SD-BL terms, which are a modification of COD terms, involve an order bill of lading, properly endorsed, attached to a sight draft. The seller sends these instruments to a bank in or near the buyer's city. When the merchandise arrives, the buyer may check the condition of the shipment and then pay the sight draft at the bank. In return for paying the sight draft, the buyer receives the bill of lading, which grants title and possession of the shipment. Once a shipment is made on SD-BL terms, the seller should be wary of buyers who plead lack of funds when the goods arrive. Coupled with this claim, such buyers usually encourage the seller to permit the bank to release the shipping papers, promising payment in 10 days. Since the alternatives are so unattractive, the seller may be strongly tempted to accept this arrangement. However, to do so means accepting credit from a customer whose credit was unsatisfactory a few days earlier.

Cash Terms

Cash terms do not indicate an immediate cash payment but the acceptance of credit for approximately 10 days from the date of invoice. Cash terms are a step removed from prepayment terms, as the credit period is very short. The time interval allows the buyer time to inspect and accept the shipment, and the seller's risk is lessened compared to more common, longer terms. With cash terms the buyer usually gets no discount privilege. Since the seller has no special recourse if the buyer fails to pay, the seller incurs the usual degree of credit risk. In "net plus 30 days" terms, no discounts are allowed, and the total amount is due in 30 days. Sometimes the net 30 days terms are combined with a service charge on open balances over 30 days, as shown in Figure 12–1.

Ordinary Terms

In many lines of trade, the terms of sale (referred to as ordinary terms) are the net credit period, the cash discount, and cash discount period. One of the frequently used ordinary terms is "2/10, net 30" (2 percent discount if paid within 10 days, full amount due in 30 days). If a customer receives an invoice for $300 dated March 15, terms 2/10, net 30, the customer has the choice of paying $294 on or before March 25 or $300 by April 14. By electing to pay the $300, the buyer pays $6 for the use of $294 for 20 days—a figure equivalent to 36 percent annual interest. Buyers should take advantage of all cash discounts.

Single-Payment or Lumped-Order Terms

In a number of industries, sellers permit customers to accumulate their obligations over a short period of time. These arrangements are used when individual buyers purchase and repurchase frequently. Rather than bill the customer for each order, the seller accumulates orders, usually for a month, and bills the customer as of one date.

Single-payment terms are really a special form of dating. The terms used may be based on EOM (end of month), MOM (middle of month), and proximo (a specified date in the following month). If EOM terms are used, all sales made during a given month are dated as of the first day of the following month. The cash discount period and net credit period commence with this date.[4] Under terms of 8/10 EOM, common in the apparel trades, all deliveries in the month of October are included in the statement rendered as of the last business day of October, and payment must be made by November 10 to take advantage of the 8 percent discount.

---

[4]Under EOM terms, the 25th day of the month in which the invoice is dated is commonly considered the end of the month. Thus, on a purchase made on May 26 with terms of 2/10 EOM, the cash discount could be taken through July 10. This is subject to negotiation between buyer and seller.

MOM terms, a variation of EOM terms, allow for a shorter total credit period. Under MOM terms, all purchases made between the 1st and the 15th of any month are consolidated and a statement rendered as of the 15th. Purchases made between the 16th and the end of the month are similarly consolidated as of the last day of the month (or the first of the next month). Hence, all purchases invoiced during the first half of a month are to be paid less discount as of the 25th, and purchases accumulated during the last half of the month are due the 10th of the following month to earn a cash discount.

Proximo terms specify a date in the month following shipment by which the cash discount must be taken. In many instances, there is no distinction between proximo terms and EOM terms; one or the other just becomes customary in a particular trade. Proximo terms, however, often provide for a shorter discount period than the net credit period. Hence, terms of 2/10 prox., net 30 set the discount date as of the 10th of the month following shipment and a due date the last day of that month.

Special-Datings Terms

Special datings, which extend the credit period, are used to adjust terms to conditions peculiar to a trade or its customers. "Season" dating and "extra" dating are two common credit terms denoting special dating.

If the demand for a product is seasonal, sellers use season dating to induce buyers to purchase and accept delivery well ahead of their selling season. Sellers benefit because they can plan their production more in accord with their sales curve, and they can shift some of the storage burden to the buyer. Buyers have the goods on hand without an immediate investment of their own funds. This type of dating compensates the buyer for the storage burden and brings the payment date closer to the buyer's selling season. Summer wearing apparel, for example, may be purchased in October and delivered in January on terms of 2/10, net 60, but the invoice may be dated May 1. These terms permit the discount on or before May 10 and establish the net due date as no later than July 1. This same arrangement can be accomplished by extending the regular selling terms an additional 30, 60, or 90 days during the preselling season months.

Extra dating is another method of giving customers long discount and credit periods. Extra dating terms treat the discount period and credit periods as identical, but rather than state the terms as 2/70/70, they are customarily stated as 2/10-60 ex. Under these terms, the purchaser is expected to pay the stated amount of the invoice, less 2 percent, 70 days after the date of invoice.

ROG (receipt of goods) and AOG (arrival of goods) terms and a few similar arrangements are used to compensate for disadvantages imposed on distant buyers. Such terms, in effect, adjust the beginning date of the discount period and often of the net credit period. Since terms may start with the date of the invoice, ROG and AOG terms adjust the entire discount period so that the first day of the discount period corresponds to the receipt or arrival of goods, whichever is applicable. Terms of this type are often competitively necessary for sellers dealing with distant customers.

Consignment Terms

Consignment terms are most often used for other than credit reasons. Agricultural products are customarily sold on consignment terms with commission agents. New products, and for that matter *any* merchandise for which a distributing organization refuses to accept the purchase risk, may be handled on consignment terms. And some goods of very high unit value move through marketing channels under these terms. Sellers also use consignment terms when the buyer's creditworthiness doesn't justify ordinary terms of sale and when the buyer lacks the resources for prepayment arrangements such as COD or SD-BL. Title to consigned goods remains with the seller, while the recipient acts as an agent for the seller. Because of the legal implications, credit managers must use consignment terms cautiously. Consigned goods must be physically segregated from other goods; proceeds from the sale of such goods must be separately accounted for; the shipper must carry insurance on the merchandise in the name of the consignor; and periodic sales and inventory reports and remittances by the consignee must be provided for. Credit managers should seek legal help to draw up consignment contracts and prepare the necessary directions to the consignee.

CASH DISCOUNTS AND EQUIVALENT RATES OF INTEREST

Cash discounts are very attractive to buyers as indicated by Table 12–1. If the equivalent interest rate is higher than current interest rates, businesses should borrow money to take advantage of discounts rather than forgo this attractive return. In some businesses, particularly retail enterprises, the discounts taken can make the difference between a profit and a loss. Several offices of the National Association of Credit Management distribute complete tables, similar to this, to inform their members of the advantage of taking all cash discounts.

THE PROBLEM OF UNEARNED DISCOUNTS

Some retailers take unearned discounts—that is, they send the manufacturer a check for the amount due less the cash discount even though the cash discount period has expired. The seller than has to decide whether to accept the payment as a completed transaction, bill the buyer for the cash discount erroneously taken, or return the uncashed check and demand

TABLE 12–1	**Rates of Interest Equivalent to Selected Cash Discounts***

Terms	Annual Rate
½/10, net 30	9%
1/10, net 30	18
2/10, net 60	14.4
2/30, net 60	24
2/10, net 30	36
3/10, net 30	54
3/30, net 60	36
4/10, net 60	26.8

*To compute such equivalents, find the number of days' difference between the cash discount period and the net credit period. This represents the number of days the seller gains in the use of funds when the buyer remits within the discount period. The potential number of times this is apt to occur is 360 days × the rate of discount = the equivalent rate of interest per year. For example, for terms 2/10, net 30, 360 ÷ 20 = 18 × 2% = 36%.

the net amount due. There is no one correct procedure; sellers have to consider customer goodwill, competitive conditions, and their own capital position.

TERMS OF SALE AND FEDERAL LEGISLATION

Sellers can use terms of sale to practice price discrimination. Price discrimination exists when sellers vary discounts to buyers in the same class. Credit terms came under the scrutiny of the federal government during the 1930s, when the Robinson-Patman Act became law. The Robinson-Patman Act prohibits price discrimination that results from discriminatory credit terms. Sellers are allowed to grant uniform discounts to all customers of the same class (i.e., all the manufacturer customers, all wholesaler accounts, and all retailer customers). They cannot give larger cash discounts to one buyer than to another of the same class, accept terms insisted on by "terms chiselers," and allow late discounts when not appli cable uniformly to all customers of the same class.

In this connection, the following material on a decision by the U.S. Supreme Court is pertinent:

A recent U.S. Supreme Court decision, reversing the decisions of two lower federal courts, held that credit terms fall within the legal definition of "price" under the Sherman Antitrust Act. Thus, an agreement of competing wholesalers to fix credit terms violates federal laws against price-fixing under the *per se* rule.

The case was *Catalano, et al v. Target Sales, Inc., et al.* . . .

* * * * *

Thus, the Catalano decision would appear to continue the Supreme Court's support for the legality of exchanging terms and other credit information—*so long as there are no agreements or common actions based upon that information.*

This decision also makes abundantly clear that courts will view credit terms as an element of price, and if agreements to fix, standardize or otherwise interfere with terms should occur, such agreements will be judged harshly under the antitrust *per se* standard.[5]

CASH DISCOUNTS OR TRADE DISCOUNTS?

The cash discount is a *reward* to prompt-paying customers for (1) saving the seller additional costs associated with a slower turnover of receivables and (2) avoiding the collection difficulties involved in handling slow-paying accounts. It is also a *penalty* assessed against slow-paying customers to compensate for the higher costs and inconveniences of handling their business. In the former case, the quoted price is considered the list price, and the cash discount allowed roughly equals the expenses saved by doing business with prompt-pay customers. In the latter case, the net price is the true realized price; the penalty collected from slow-paying customers approximately equals the expense of doing business with them.

Sellers would have difficulty collecting this penalty if it were so labeled, and efforts to enforce "fines" for delinquency would be strongly resisted and cause much ill will. Psychologically, it is better to collect the penalty as a benefit withdrawn. Loss of the discount then appears to buyers as the withdrawal of a gain that, through their own fault, they did not obtain. As a penalty assessed against slow-paying customers, the cash discount, to be equitable, must be no larger than necessary to recover the additional costs involved.

The costs to be recovered by the penalty are for: (1) use of the seller's capital during the extra time allowed for payment, (2) the assumed risk of potential bad-debt losses, and (3) increased billing and collection costs. Most trades allow a cash discount of 1, 2, or even 3 percent, an amount that seems to correspond to the cost savings incurred. Yet, under the guise of a cash discount, many sellers offer discounts as high as 6, 7, or 8 percent, and higher. And some accept these discounts even though payment is late. Such liberal discounts are *trade discounts*—not cash discounts—

---

[5]William J. Parsons, "Supreme Court Rules on Trade Credit Case," *Credit & Financial Management*, September 1980, pp. 32–33. Reprinted with permission from *Credit & Financial Management*, Copyright 1980, published by the National Association of Credit Management, 520 Eighth Avenue, New York, NY 10018–6571.

and so are special-dating terms if the discount is not disallowed because of late payment. Similarly, when the discount period and the net credit period are synonymous, some credit managers view the cash discount as a trade discount.

DISCUSSION QUESTIONS

1. Explain the function of commercial credit.
2. Discuss the statement "The reliance of businesses on commercial credit outweighs alternative sources of credit."
3. Why do receivables difficulties rank first as a fundamental cause of business failure?
4. How can large companies force small companies to "carry" them during periods of a "credit crunch"?
5. Comment on the changing attitudes toward commercial credit.
6. What are the major variables involved in terms of sale?
7. How do buyers' rates of stock turnover influence terms of sale? How do other factors exert an influence?
8. Define and distinguish between:
   a. Prepayment terms.
   b. Cash terms.
   c. Ordinary terms.
   d. Single-payment or lumped-order terms.
   e. Special-dating terms.
   f. Consignment terms.
   g. Cash discount and cash discount period.
   h. Trade discount.
   i. Net period.
   j. Anticipation.
9. Why does the rate of anticipation tend to vary directly with the prevailing interest rate at commercial banks?
10. Why are terms of sale often negotiable?
11. Why would a manufacturer use consignment terms rather than establish price under resale price maintenance arrangements?
12. How do you compute rates of interest equivalent to selected cash discounts?
13. Is there a logical basis to believe that some cash discounts are really trade discounts?
14. Explain the relationship between the Robinson-Patman Act and a manufacturer's terms of sale.
15. Explain the function of bank lockboxes.

Business Use of Cash (Financial) Credit

The Objectives or Goals of Chapter 13 Are:

1. To distinguish between financial credit and commercial credit.
2. To explain the differences between various types of business loans made by commercial banks.
3. To point out what compensating balances do to the actual rate of interest paid for a loan.
4. To distinguish between ordinary accounts receivable financing and factoring of accounts receivable.
5. To explain how commercial paper acts as a source of funds.
6. To discuss the need for long-term borrowing.
7. To explain the activities of the Small Business Administration (SBA).

While commercial credit is used to finance some of a firm's current assets (its acquisition of merchandise and services), most businesses require additional financial assistance. Borrowing may be short-term, intermediate-term, or long-term. Businesses use short-term borrowing to acquire current assets not covered by commercial credit or by the owners' investment. They use intermediate-term and long-term borrowing, on the other hand, to finance both current and fixed assets. Commercial banks and business finance companies (primarily factors and commercial finance companies) are the principal sources for short-term and intermediate-term loans. Another source of funds for short-term needs is the issuance and sale of commercial paper. Long-term loans are available from such sources as insurance companies, investment houses, trust companies, and, to some extent, the Small Business Administration, wealthy individuals, and commercial banks.

COMMERCIAL CREDIT MANAGEMENT VERSUS CASH CREDIT MANAGEMENT

Commercial credit management concerns a highly specialized type of business credit—facilitating the sale of merchandise and services in exchange for credit. With such specialization, individual managers tend to think of their activities apart from the entire credit structure. Yet, if they are to play the important role of guiding, suggesting, and recommending in regard to their companies and customers, they must have a clear and concise knowledge of all classes of business credit.

Whether credit executives are directly involved with their companies' financial needs frequently depends on their position in the organizational structure. Organizational structures vary according to the number and types of functions to be performed. A small or medium-sized enterprise may employ a single executive to deal with both commercial credit administration and the company's working capital requirements. This person may be designated as the treasurer, with a subtitle, credit manager. To work both sides of the fence—that is, customers' credit and the company's credit—the executive must be intellectually equipped to cope with the several types of business credit. Large businesses, on the other hand, often divide financial responsibilities among several executives. Commercial credit management may be established in a separate department headed by a credit manager. The short-term, intermediate-term, and long-term capital requirements of the company may be administered by an executive designated as the treasurer or by the treasurer and a select group of company officers. Whatever policy the company follows, these executives need specialized knowledge to perform their tasks effectively. Because of the close relationship between credit management and debt management, such executives need knowledge of all phases of business credit.

Irrespective of titles, organizational structure, and company size, executives responsible for commercial credit management frequently advise credit customers on their financial problems. The increased tendency for credit managers to counsel their business customers is fostered by the present-day partnership concept of creditor and debtor. Many commercial credit managers report that the customer-counseling aspect of their credit departments is one of the most valuable services they render. Their clear understanding of other sources of working capital and their ability to recommend these sources often give new life to a marginal or deteriorating customer. Similarly, cash loan managers must recognize the financial role played by commercial credit in financing a portion of their customers' current assets. Hence, both commercial credit managements and cash loan managements need more than a casual grasp of all types of business credit to better serve their employers and their debtor customers.

The parts of this book devoted to business credit can be a valuable source of information for cash-lending executives. Selling merchandise and services on credit and handling business loans have a marked degree of similarity. They use similar credit information, a similar decision-making process, and similar collection policies. Differences between the two involve dependence on various sources of credit information, differences in credit standards, methods of controlling customers' accounts, and various governmental regulations.

COMMERCIAL BANK LOANS

As a source for short-term and intermediate-term loans, no other institution is as dominant as the commercial bank.[1] The tremendous financial resources of our commercial banking system make it the largest and most frequently used source for borrowed capital.

Need for Loans

Most business enterprises need cash credit to finance a portion of their assets. Cash loans help balance a firm's financial requirements with its production and marketing operations. Businesses' cash needs, though, are seldom constant or regular. Sometimes they need large amounts of working capital and other times only small sums.[2]

Retailers, for example, may borrow from their banks shortly after a heavy buying season to take advantage of cash discounts. Wholesalers may borrow to acquire inventory and take advantage of suppliers' special offerings. Manufacturers may borrow to acquire working capital for current manufacturing operations. These examples illustrate how businesses use commercial bank loans to supplement commercial credit. This is only one possible use of bank loans. Realistically, when a business borrows from a commercial bank, it may use the deposit money created to fulfill a number of business needs. The need for commercial bank loans stems from the very nature of business; that is, disbursements don't coincide with the receipt of income.

Credit Policy of Commercial Banks

A business firm can enjoy a long and continuous financial relationship with its commercial bank. Other than acting as a depository for business funds, the bank stands ready to serve its customers by providing an important segment of their financial needs. A commercial bank, however, usually has higher credit standards than those involved in commercial credit transactions. Businesses that can't meet the standards must acquire cash by borrowing from other, frequently less attractive, sources.

Banks have high credit requirements because they are entrusted with the public's money. A bank must guard this trust above all else to maintain its reputation and its customers' confidence. A Federal Reserve member bank cannot ask for extensions of its obligations without impairing its position in the system. And the liquidity of banks depends largely on the

---

[1]See the Suggested Readings at the end of the chapter.

[2]At times it is hard to tell the lenders from the borrowers. Manufacturers of countless products are offering customers an increasing number of lease deals, installment credit plans, and trade financing arrangements, and are then turning to lenders to fill their own cash gap.

liquidity of their customers. The requirement that banks always be in a position to meet their obligations limits the extensions they can grant their customers. Banks do grant extensions, but the number can't exceed a safe limit without impairing the bank's liquidity.

Another factor that contributes to banks' credit standards is that their stock-in-trade is money and not merchandise. Merchandise creditors have a wider margin of profit from the sale of merchandise than banks have from the lending of money. Because of this, merchandise creditors may be more willing to accept marginal risks and grant extensions not considered prudent by a bank. Furthermore, the amount of credit involved in a commercial credit transaction may represent only a small portion of the debtor's total obligations; bank loans frequently represent a major portion of the firm's total debt. An extension granted by a merchandise creditor has very different implications from an extension granted by a bank.

Finally, banks are subject to supervision of state and federal banking authorities. They are restricted on the size of loan made to any one borrower; they are not permitted to lend on the security of their own stock; and they are limited in the amount they may lend to an officer of the bank. There are exceptions to the above restrictions; but, more importantly, bank loans are periodically examined. Bank examiners and their supervisors are responsible for enforcing the numerous administrative regulations that affect bank loan activities. To be regarded highly by the Federal Reserve System and its examining bodies, a bank must not have a record of lending money to a high proportion of weak credit risks. Thus legal regulations are another factor affecting the standards imposed on business borrowers.

Kinds of Loans

Traditionally, businesses obtained loans to finance their short-term needs, and loan maturities corresponded to the normal terms of sale (30, 60, or 90 days). During the 1930s, commercial banks changed their policies with respect to loan maturities and adjusted their lending terms to conform to the needs of borrowers. Short-term loans left many business firms with inadequate funds for continuous working capital and capital to refinance their bond issues. Since that time banks have been making intermediate-term loans, with maturities from one to five years, and long-term loans, with maturities in excess of five years.

BUSINESS INSTALLMENT LOANS. Traditional loans to businesses were single-payment loans, but today business installment loans have become more and more important in the banking industry. In analyzing the various forms of installment (or term) loans, the following comment is valuable:

> There are no steadfast rules for structuring the repayment schedule for term loans. Because each such loan is the result of a particular need, it

makes sense to design a payment schedule which is tailored to conform to the anticipated cash flow of the borrower. The most simple form is the serial term loan, in which the proceeds are advanced at once and are repaid over a stated number of years. Payments may be called for monthly, quarterly, or even annually, though quarterly payments are most frequently used. It is not entirely uncommon for the repayment schedule to call for less than proportionate payments in the early years of credit, with stepped-up payments in the final years.[3]

SECURED OR UNSECURED LOANS. Bank loans are also classified according to security—either secured or unsecured. A secured loan relies not only on the borrower's promise to pay but also on the pledge of some specified property. The bank can exercise its lien on the collateral in the event the borrower doesn't pay. Banks prefer security that can be readily converted into cash. Government bonds, for example, which are easily converted into cash, are the highest quality of collateral. Businesses may, and often do, pledge inventories, stocks, bonds, mortgages, equipment, real estate, accounts receivable, and other property of value.[4]

An unsecured loan is based solely on the creditworthiness of the borrower. Evidence of this type of loan is usually the borrower's promissory note. An unsecured loan made on the basis of a single business or a person's signature is known as *single-name paper.*

Another type of unsecured loan is paper (trade acceptances and promissory notes used between buyers and sellers in some lines of business) that is discounted at the commercial bank by the borrower. Sellers who hold this paper may endorse it and discount it at their banks, thus giving rise to the terms *two-name, double-name,* or *endorsed paper.* Some banks also refer to this as a personal guaranty or a continuing guaranty. The borrower (seller) by endorsing the instrument assumes a contingent liability, and hence the bank has the specific promise of the buyer of the goods to pay the indebtedness as well as the contingent promise of the seller (borrower). Most U.S. businesses use the open-book account method of selling their merchandise; therefore this type of paper is relatively scarce.[5]

---

[3]Claude H. Booker, Jr., and W. C. Henry, "Longer Term Lending to Business," in *The Bankers' Handbook,* ed. William H. Baughn and Charles E. Walker (Homewood, Ill.: Dow Jones-Irwin, 1978), p. 668.

[4]Financing goods (usually commodities) held by third parties in warehouses is not a new or untried method of lending. Many banks are quite successful at such loans in terms of volume, profitable return, and loss history.

[5]Under certain circumstances, drafts or bills of exchange are drawn against the buyer's bank, and, on acceptance, the instrument becomes a *banker's acceptance.* Sellers may hold these until maturity or discount them at their banks. In effect, when a bank places its signature on the draft or bill of exchange, it guarantees the buyer's credit. If the bank that accepts the instrument is well known, the instrument is regarded as "prime" paper and, as such, is sought by other banks for use as a secondary reserve. Acceptances of this type can be converted into cash at a low rate of interest. In banking circles, this and the discounting of notes and trade acceptances are sometimes referred to as *open-market loans.*

Double-name paper may be distinguished from an *accommodation endorsement*. Because of weak credit or other circumstance, some businesses and people are required to bolster the quality of their credit by supplying a comaker or endorser to their promissory note. The comaker lends personal creditworthiness as an accommodation. Such loans are classified as secured, whereas loans resulting from an endorsed trade acceptance or note are classed as unsecured. The endorser of a promissory note as an accommodation guarantees payment and is legally liable for payment in the event the maker defaults.

Bank Interest Rates—Discount Rates

Interest rates on bank loans are determined by a number of factors. An established rate of interest does not apply to all customers. Rather, the rate charged a business customer is determined by the amount and term of the loan, the borrower's credit standing, the tightness or abundance of bank funds, the compensating balance maintained on deposit with the lending bank, the bank's geographic location, and the demand for loans. In general, small businesses pay higher rates than large ones, and rates vary inversely with the size of loan.

Commercial banks employ two methods of collecting interest charges. In the case of short-term loans of 30, 60, or 120 days, banks deduct the interest charge at the time the loan (advance) is made. Technically, this charge is referred to as the *discount, bank discount,* or *discount rate.* The discount rate a customer pays is not the same as the rate of interest paid on other loans. For example, if a $10,000 note that is to mature in six months is discounted at 14 percent, the discount would be 0.07 of $10,000, or $700. The business borrower receives $9,300 as the proceeds of the loan, and on maturity of the note a payment of $10,000 is due the bank. The borrower has use of $9,300 and not $10,000, and hence the discount rate is higher than the interest rate. Interest on other loans is usually calculated on the daily balance of the loan and charged to the borrower monthly.

Line of Credit and Compensating Balances

Once a business establishes a relationship with a bank, the bank may set a line of credit. A line of credit is the maximum amount the bank is willing to lend. Lines of credit are established after the bank has thoroughly analyzed the customer's needs, credit standing, and frequency of cash needs. Once established, a line of credit is much more convenient for the bank and for the customer; the customer can borrow needed amounts within the line without the formalities of a new credit investigation, analysis, and credit decision. A line of credit in no way obligates the bank to lend that amount, nor does it obligate the business customer to use the entire amount. Banks, however, normally maintain lines of credit for firms that preserve their credit standing.

When establishing a line of credit, a bank may set two requirements. One is that the customer maintain a *compensating balance* on the deposit at all times—i.e., a fraction of the line of credit that the borrower is expected not to withdraw. Generally, compensating balance requirements range from 10 to 20 percent. This rule, though not uniformly applied, is customary in many banks. Some banks institute variations of the principle by requiring borrowers to maintain on deposit a fraction of the total loans made. The other requirement is that the borrower clean up loans periodically. This assures the bank that the loan is fulfilling its proper purpose and is not being used for investment purposes. Businesses' seasonal needs are the basis for a line of credit, and loans used to meet such needs should be self-liquidating. Firms unable to meet this requirement from their own funds must borrow from other banks to clean up their loans and at the same time have their financial affairs scrutinized by other banks.

ACTIVITIES OF THE SMALL BUSINESS ADMINISTRATION (SBA)

In 1953 Congress created the Small Business Administration[6] as a permanent, independent government agency to help small businesses grow and prosper. Small manufacturers, wholesalers, retailers, service concerns, and other businesses can borrow from the agency to construct, expand, or convert facilities; purchase buildings, equipment, or materials; or obtain working capital. One important restriction applies to all SBA loans. By law, the agency cannot make a loan if a business can obtain funds from a bank or some other private source. Businesses, therefore, must first seek private financing before applying to the SBA—i.e., they must apply to a local bank or other lending institution for a loan.

To be eligible for SBA loan assistance, the business must be operated for profit and qualify as small under SBA criteria (except for sheltered workshops under the handicapped assistance loan program). Loans cannot be made to businesses involved in the creation or distribution of ideas or opinions such as newspapers, magazines, and academic institutions. Other types of ineligible borrowers include businesses engaged in speculation or investment in (rental) real estate.

For business loans, size standard eligibility is based on the average number of employees for the preceding 12 months or on sales volume averaged over a three-year period. Some industry standards are shown here.

---

[6]*Business Loans from the SBA* (Washington, D.C.: Office of Business Development and the Office of Finance and Investment, May 1989). Also see the Suggested Readings at the end of the chapter.

Manufacturing: Maximum number of employees may range from 500 to 1,500, depending on the type of product manufactured.

Wholesaling: Maximum number of employees may not exceed 100.

Services: Annual receipts may not exceed $3.5 to $14.5 million, depending on the industry.

Retailing: Annual receipts may not exceed $3.5 to $13.5 million, depending on the industry.

Construction: General construction annual receipts may not exceed $9.5 to $17 million, depending on the industry.

Special trade construction: Annual receipts may not exceed $7 million.

Agriculture: Annual receipts may not exceed $0.5 to $3.5 million, depending on the industry.

Basic Types of Business Loans

SBA offers two basic types of business loans:

1. *Guaranty loans.*   These are made by private lenders, usually banks, and guaranteed up to 90 percent by the SBA. Most SBA loans are made under this program. The maximum guaranty of loans exceeding $155,000 is 85 percent. The SBA can guarantee up to $750,000 of a private-sector loan. The lender plays the central role in the loan delivery system. The small business submits the loan application to the lender, which makes the initial review and if approved forwards the application and analysis to the local SBA office. If approved by the SBA, the lender closes the loan and disburses the funds.

2. *SBA direct loans.*   These loans have an administrative maximum of $150,000 and are available only to applicants unable to secure an SBA-guaranteed loan. The applicant must have first sought financing from his or her bank and been refused. In cities of over 200,000 population, one other lender must have refused the loan. Direct loan funds are very limited and at times are available only to certain types of borrowers (e.g., borrowers located in high-employment areas, or owned by low-income individuals, handicapped persons, Vietnam-era veterans, or disabled veterans).

Terms of Loans

Working capital loans generally have maturities of five to seven years, with a maximum maturity of 25 years. The longer maturities are used to finance fixed assets such as purchase or major renovation of business premises. Interest rates in the guaranty program are negotiated between the borrower and lender and are subject to SBA maximums. Interest rates on direct loans are based on the cost of money to the federal government and are calculated quarterly.

Collateral Needed

The SBA requires that sufficient assets be pledged to adequately secure the loan to the extent required. Personal guaranties are required from all the principal owners and from the chief executive officer of the business. Liens on the personal assets of the principals also may be required when business assets are considered insufficient to secure the loan.

Statistics on Small Business Administration loans to all small businesses from 1978 through 1988 are shown in Table 13–1.

ACCOUNTS RECEIVABLE FINANCING

The credit executive needs to have knowledge of accounts receivable financing because such financing may be used by the credit manager's own company or by its suppliers. Equally important, a firm's customers may finance certain phases of their operations this way, and familiarity with this type of financing is then necessary for proper analysis and decision making.

In accounts receivable financing, a financing agency either makes loans or advances to a borrower secured by an assignment of its accounts receivables or purchases the accounts receivables outright. As a firm's sales volume expands, it needs more capital to provide increased plant and

---

TABLE 13–1 **Small Business Administration Loans to All Small Businesses: 1978 to 1988** (for fiscal year ending in year shown)

A small business must be independently owned and operated, must not be dominant in its particular industry, and must meet standards set by the Small Business Administration as to its annual receipts or number of employees. Loans include both direct and guaranteed loans to small business establishments. Does not include Disaster Assistance Loans.

Loans Approved	Unit	1978	1979	1980	1981	1982	1983	1984	1985	1986	1987	1988
Loans, all businesses	1,000	31.7	30.2	31.7	28.7	15.4	19.2	21.3	19.3	16.8	17.1	17.1
Loans, minority-owned businesses	1,000	6.1	5.5	6.0	5.2	2.5	2.7	3.1	2.8	2.0	2.1	2.2
Percent of all business loans	Percent	19	18	19	18	16	14	15	15	12	12	13
Value of total loans*	Mil. dol.	3,314	3,407	3,858	3,668	2,038	3,007	3,450	3,217	3,013	3,232	3,434
Value of loans to minority-operated businesses†	Mil. dol.	402	428	470	454	238	295	383	324	265	299	343

*Includes both SBA and bank portions of loans.
†SBA direct loans and guaranteed portion of bank loans only.
Source: U.S. Small Business Administration, unpublished data.

equipment, to carry larger inventories, to support growth in accounts receivable, to meet larger payrolls, and so on. One of the ways now widely used to obtain more operating cash is receivables financing.

The two basic types of accounts receivable financing—ordinary accounts receivable financing and factoring—are subject to much misunderstanding. Ordinary financing of accounts receivable differs from factoring in the following major respects:

1. Commercial banks and commercial financing companies[7] are the principal sources of accounts receivable financing, whereas specialized companies generally known as factors are the source for factoring.

2. Businesses finance their accounts receivable for fundamentally different reasons than they engage in factoring.

3. The methods of operation, procedures, costs, and service charges are basically different in each type of financial arrangement.

4. Finally, there is a marked difference in the relationship between the parties involved in accounts receivable financing as contrasted with factoring.

The following definitions point out the differences and similarities of these methods.

1. Ordinary accounts receivable financing involves an agreement under which a financing institution (a) purchases the open accounts receivable of its customers or advances them loans secured by the pledge of such receivables (b) with recourse to them for any losses and (c) without notice to their trade debtors.

2. Factoring involves a continuing agreement under which a financing institution (a) assumes the credit and collection function for its client and (b) purchases their open accounts receivable as they arise (c) without recourse to them for credit losses and (d) with notice to their trade debtors.

The above definitions imply the reasons a business may enter into one or the other type of financing arrangement. Businesses use ordinary accounts receivable financing for one major reason—to acquire needed capital. Specific reasons are numerous and varied, but all such needs for capital can usually be met by short-term or intermediate-term borrowing. Factoring, on the other hand, is entered into for two reasons—first, to acquire operating capital by selling the receivables outright, and second, to shift the entire credit and collection burden to the financing institution.

---

[7] These companies serve the business community by making secured loans to manufacturers, wholesalers, and jobbers, just as sales finance and consumer finance companies serve the financial needs of the consumer.

Ordinary Accounts Receivable Financing

Commercial banks and commercial finance companies are the sources that normally finance accounts receivable. Commercial banks may follow the procedure of making a *loan* with the accounts receivable as security. Finance companies *purchase* the receivables for some stated amount of cash or accept assigned receivables as security for a loan much as a bank does.

Both types of lenders normally make their advances with *recourse* to the borrowing firm, but without notice to the borrower's trade debtors.[8] Recourse gives the lending institution protection against slow-paying accounts and losses that occur due to uncollectible accounts. Because of the recourse provision of the transaction, the lender assumes little or no risk; in essence, the assigner guarantees payment of all assigned accounts. The lending institution, whether bank or finance company, examines the quality of the accounts receivable offered. To be acceptable, the major proportion (about 75 to 80 percent) of the assigned receivables must have the high or the second-high rating granted by Dun & Bradstreet or some other commercial credit reporting agency. The contract between the parties under the nonnotification plan: (1) sets forth the lender's advances and charges; (2) provides that the assigner act as the assignee's agent in collecting accounts; (3) establishes the method and time by which the assigner transmits collections to the lending firm; (4) provides for the assigner to guarantee all assigned accounts; and (5) provides that the assignee may inspect the accounting records of the assigner at any time. These and other provisions of the contract, as well as other technicalities of the transaction, dictate that the borrower give a precise accounting of all funds received that are to be credited to the assigned accounts receivable.

The American Bankers Association recommends that the loans based on accounts receivables should be no more than 80 percent of the face value of the receivables, less trade and other discounts allowed to customers and consideration for merchandise returns. Commercial finance companies may advance 70 to 95 percent of the face value of the receivables. Each of the quoted percentages depends on the quality of the receivables and the lender's standards of acceptability. The difference between the percentage and the net value of the receivables is a margin of safety against deductions, shrinkages, and bad-debt losses.

---

[8]Assignment of accounts receivable may be done either by the *notification* plan or by the more common *nonnotification* plan. Under the former plan, trade debtors are notified of the assignment or purchase of their receivables and informed that they are to make payment, when due, to the financing institution. Frequently, such notification is made on the face of the debtor's invoice. Under the latter plan, no notice to trade creditors is given; the assigned or purchased accounts are borrowed on without the debtor's knowledge. The borrower (assigner) then acts as an agent, accepts collections of the accounts, and in turn pays the assignee.

Bank rates on this type of lending vary widely and are determined by a group of complex factors. The rate may be set on the basis of the risk involved, the credit standing of the trade debtor's accounts that are assigned, the assigner's terms of sale, the borrower's credit and collection practices, and other factors previously discussed.

Rates charged by commercial finance companies also vary widely, although larger companies generally have lower rates. While the method of computing these rates is quite different from the bank method, the two institutions' rates are generally competitive.

A business executive may turn to a commercial finance company for the following reasons: to increase volume by extending longer or more generous credit terms for desirable business; to manufacture and launch a new seasonal product at the right moment; to phase production in advance of peak seasonal demands, thus eliminating overtime and reducing costs; to pay bills promptly or in advance and gain cash discount or price, delivery, and service concessions; to increase production and cut costs by purchasing new, more efficient machinery and equipment; to expand production and sales by increasing the number of employees; to help finance the purchase of another company; to buy out a partner; to save on transportation costs by buying car-load-lots; and to take advantage of favorable raw materials prices. In addition to financing accounts receivable, commercial finance companies offer a number of supplementary loan services, including loans on inventory; installment financing of machinery and equipment, and other durables; loans on fixed assets and other collateral; and note loans to businesses. Many businesses find that finance companies are more flexible to deal with and more closely meet their needs. Because finance companies provide such a wide variety of financial services, they enjoy a close working relationship with their customers. Because these companies operate on a branch-office basis and are not hampered by the restrictions imposed on banks, they can acquire a more diversified group of risks and hence accept greater risk.

However, some executives and lenders view accounts receivable financing as undesirable. Their principal objection seems to be that assigning receivables deprives trade creditors of protection against losses. Yet this objection is not as valid as it was before the 1930s. Many creditors now recognize the need for this type of financing as a desired alternative method of acquiring capital, and a large number of banks presently make such loans. Furthermore, the American Bankers Association has recognized that (1) accounts receivable financing is becoming increasingly important, (2) the security is often the most liquid a borrower has to offer, (3) the necessity to borrow arises not from failure but from growth problems, and (4) as a business grows, it faces financial stress from its large volume of receivables, and it is logical to resort to this asset for necessary relief.

Borrowing on the basis of accounts receivable is also an alternative to other financing possibilities. Most businesses face short-term financial problems. Rather than gain relief by increasing its long-term debt, a business can increase its line of credit at the bank. If this isn't possible, it can secure an additional loan from the bank by pledging its accounts receivable. Some businesses don't qualify for an additional bank loan or prefer to seek financial aid from a commercial finance company. Whatever the source of the funds, businesses are usually better off with a self-liquidating loan than a long-term debt burden.

Factoring Accounts Receivable

The financing aspect of factoring is often secondary to the desire and need to shift the entire credit and collection management phase to the factor.[9]

The factor purchases accounts receivable from clients without recourse for credit losses and assumes all credit risks involved. It is the only known arrangement that completely assumes the entire commercial credit and collection function for clients. Trade debtors, accordingly, are notified that payments are to be made directly to the factoring company. In addition to these services, factors advance cash for receivables whenever clients so desire. In other words, they can advance cash immediately for receivables purchased or hold cash in the client's account until it is needed. This service lets clients reduce interest charges paid to the factor, because they pay interest only for cash actually advanced. Factors, in addition to their primary activity, make loans to businesses on their inventory, fixed assets, open accounts, and other security. Most factors maintain an advisory service to counsel customers on production, marketing, and financial matters.

METHOD OF OPERATION. A factor may deal differently with different clients. The specific relationship and the responsibilities of the parties are set forth in the factoring contract. The following steps indicate the factoring procedure after the assignment of existing accounts on the books:

1. Before clients ship any merchandise to a customer as a result of sales, they must submit the list of customers, amounts of the orders, terms of sale, and any other essential information to the factor for approval.

2. The factor investigates each account and makes the credit decision to accept or reject the order. The order copies with the proper notations "accepted" or "rejected" are returned to the clients. If, at this point, the clients want to ship to rejected accounts, they do so at their own risk.

3. After shipments are made on the approved orders, clients sell the accounts to the factor by signing and transmitting to the factor an assignment schedule supported by a copy of each invoice and shipping order. The

---

[9]For articles relating to factoring, see the Suggested Readings at the end of the chapter.

assignment schedule provides space for a complete description of the sale and shipment (e.g., customer name, address, terms of sale, due dates, and amounts of invoices). The invoices in turn are stamped before mailing, giving notification to the account that payment must be made directly to the factor. Sufficient copies of each instrument are made so that the factor and the client have complete records.

4. The factor credits the client's account for all accounts receivable purchased and remits the proceeds as mutually agreed on by the factor and the client. If a client doesn't want to withdraw the funds immediately, withdrawal can be made at regular intervals. The method of paying the client is normally geared to the client's working capital needs. The factor pays the client interest on all money that accrues on matured accounts and isn't withdrawn.

5. Clients receive a monthly statement (called an *account current*) showing their financial standing with the factor. This record lists accounts receivable purchased, charges for returns and allowances, the factor's commission and interest charges, and other items that may affect the account.

EXTENT OF FACTORING. Once heavily concentrated and traditional in the textile industry, factoring operations are spreading into many other lines of business.

FACTOR TERMS AND CHARGES. Factoring charges include (1) a commission or service charge and (2) an interest charge. Factors determine the exact amount of commission by taking into consideration the kind of industry the client represents, the client's annual sales volume, the credit standing of the client's customers, and so on. Commission is based on the actual value of the accounts receivable, less cash discounts, merchandise returns, and other normal allowances. The interest charge is computed on the average daily net debit balance.

In comparing factoring costs with the costs of borrowing funds from other sources, business must consider factors' other services including complete credit and collection management.

USE OF FACTORING OPERATIONS BY BUSINESSES. Contrary to common opinion, factoring doesn't imply a financially weak business. Although a factoring service may be used by a business whose credit isn't acceptable elsewhere, many financially strong companies use factoring to good advantage. Factoring helps firms avoid the costs of maintaining a commercial credit department, including overhead, investigation costs, accounting costs, collection expenses, and the ever-present expense of bad debts. A firm that factors all of its accounts receivables, as many textile companies do, can eliminate this important but often costly business function. Another advantage is that factoring frees management from credit and collection problems so it can concentrate on production and other marketing problems. In a sense factoring provides a form of complete credit insurance and at the same time frees the business from its investment in accounts receivable. Finally, factoring increases the client's net working capital, provided the cash received is put to work to pay current obligations.

The principal objection to factoring accounts receivable is cost. However, only the interest rate should be considered when comparing this method of financing with alternatives. The factoring commission is not entirely a charge for advancing funds but, more accurately, a charge for credit and collection management.

COMMERCIAL PAPER AS A SOURCE OF FUNDS

Businesses' issuance and sale of commercial paper is a relatively simple way for them to enter the marketplace and secure funds for short-term needs. Unlike loans, however, such paper is not renewable. Usually, in times of tight money, cash is still available in the money market—the large pool of funds that financial institutions and individuals lend temporarily. Another reason businesses sell commercial paper is that it may cost less to borrow in the commercial paper market than at a bank even without the cost of keeping cash idle in "compensating balances."

The favorable aspects of the commercial paper market were greatly questioned in 1970 when Penn Central Transportation Company announced it could not meet its commitments in connection with the issuance of commercial paper. For decades size was regarded as almost foolproof insurance against bankruptcy; the Penn Central's financial floundering proved just the opposite.

LONG-TERM LOANS

Up to this point, we have discussed businesses' short- and intermediate-term financing needs. Yet long-term borrowing is often one of the first forms of financing a business uses. When a business acquires funds through long-term borrowing arrangements, it is using its *investment credit*.

The Need for Long-Term Financing

Almost all firms need and use long-term financing. Firms often use long-term financing at startup to provide costly production or marketing facilities. Such fixed assets include land, buildings, equipment, and machinery. (Owners may avoid using investment credit if they furnish their own capital—equity capital.)

As they grow and prosper over the years, many businesses need to expand or replace their facilities. They use long-term financing both to expand their fixed assets and to increase current assets. Often a portion of the needed current-asset expansion is financed by long-term methods rather than the previously discussed short-term methods. During periods of rapid expansion, firms may find it more desirable to rely on long-term financing rather than short-term financing to keep a reasonable balance between current assets and current liabilities. In addition, such financing can be used to renew existing indebtedness, to retire some debts, and to acquire the assets of another company under merger arrangements.

Forms and Sources of Long-Term Borrowing

Long-term financing may take one or a combination of the following three forms: (1) long-term loans, (2) real estate mortgage loans, and (3) the issuance of secured or unsecured bonds. In each instance the business uses its investment credit as a power to obtain funds in exchange for its promise to pay an equivalent value at some date in the relatively distant future.

Long-term loans are those with maturities longer than five years. Although not a major lending function of commercial banks, some do deal in this type of loan. Evidence of the transaction is the promissory note, either secured or unsecured. Loans made over long periods are often renewed again and again, thus resulting in a more or less "permanent" obligation on the part of the business borrower. Usually, such loans are repaid at specified intervals mutually agreed on by the lender and borrower. The borrower then gives the lender a series of notes maturing, say, at six-month intervals over the years until the entire loan is repaid. Some borrowers arrange to have the payments gradually increase with each succeeding interval.

Real estate mortgage loans for business concerns may be a single-payment type, also known as the *straight-payment loan,* whereby the borrower makes no payment on the principal until the entire amount is due. Usually, borrowers pay interest on such loans at stated intervals and have prepayment privileges if they want to make partial or full payment on the mortgage before maturity. The direct-reduction mortgage loan, also known as the *amortized loan,* is the other common type of mortgage contract. This instrument specifies monthly, quarterly, semiannual, or annual repayments of principal plus interest.

Corporations that issue bonds to acquire investment capital guarantee to pay a specified sum at some future date, with interest at a fixed rate. Maturity dates usually exceed 10 years (dates of 15, 20, 25, or 30 years are common). When borrowing by this method, the business sells the entire issue to investment bankers, who in turn sell the bonds to the general public or to a single holder, such as a life insurance company.

Some firms sell stock for long-term financing. It is important to understand the differences between stocks and bonds from both sides of the transaction—the firm's position in trying to raise funds, and the investor's involvement in trying to obtain a good return.

DISCUSSION QUESTIONS

1. Why should commercial credit managers be well informed on business needs, uses, and sources of cash credit?
2. In what ways can bank loans be classified? Distinguish each type.
3. Explain double-name paper and accommodation paper.
4. Distinguish between bank interest rates and bank discount rates.
5. What are the principal reasons commercial banks have high credit standards and requirements?
6. Discuss the activities of the Small Business Administration.
7. What are the principal differences between ordinary accounts receivable financing and accounts receivable factoring?
8. Is ordinary accounts receivable financing a desirable or undesirable business practice? Explain.
9. Under what circumstances can a business use factoring to a good advantage?
10. Explain the use of commercial paper as a source of funds for business concerns.
11. What is investment credit?
12. How have life insurance companies helped business concerns in their long-term financing needs?

SUGGESTED READINGS

Managing Financial Credit

BAREFOOT, JO ANN S. "Are Commercial Lenders Killing Compliance?" *ABA Banking Journal,* April 1990, p. 34.

BERGEN, MONA. "What's Really Happening in Bank Automation." *Bankers Monthly Magazine,* April 15, 1986, p. 16.

BRYAN, LOWELL L. "The Future of the Credit System." *The Bankers Magazine,* January–February 1986, p. 67.

"Could You Collect This Loan?" *ABA Banking Journal,* June 1990, p. 33.

McNEIL, JANE H. "Guiding Credit/Loan Approval." *Credit & Financial Management,* June 1986, p. 13.

TAYNE, LAWRENCE H. "Finding Funds." *Credit & Financial Management,* December 1985, p. 25.

WITKINS, JAMES P. "Cash Management Has to Be Sold." *Bankers Monthly Magazine,* May 15, 1986, p. 14.

Factoring Accounts Receivable

KUNDEY, GARY E. "Target Industries: Can Factoring Expand into New Markets?" *Business Credit,* June 1988, p. 41.

GRIMALDI, JOSEPH A. "Factoring Programs." *Credit & Financial Management,* December 1985, p. 17.

RUBIN, DAVID. "The Future of Factoring." *Business Credit,* June 1988, p. 39.

Small Business Administration

"Can James Abdnor Revive SBA?" *ABA Banking Journal,* June 1987, p. 52.

"The Iran-Contra Scandal of the Small Business World." *Business Week,* June 4, 1990, p. 63.

"A Mother Lode of Loans for Small Business." *Business Week,* June 19, 1989, p. 104.

Management and Analysis of Commercial Credit

Responsibilities of the Commercial Credit Manager

The Objectives or Goals of Chapter 14 Are:

1. To understand the status, place, and functions of the commercial credit executive.
2. To explain the changing status and qualifications of credit management.
3. To discuss where the credit department fits into a company's organizational framework.
4. To spell out the basic functions of commercial credit management.
5. To explain the classification of the sources of commercial credit information.
6. To point out the factors that should be considered in selecting sources of commercial credit information.
7. To compare internal information and direct investigation.
8. To explain the problems leveraged buyouts (LBOs) create for the commercial credit manager.

The position of the present-day commercial credit manager continues to grow in importance. The reasons for this are: (1) practically all production and marketing institutions rely on commercial credit for short-term financing; (2) commercial credit is a customary means of selling goods and services and the most frequently used type of business credit; (3) the volume of commercial credit is far larger than other types of business credit; and (4) credit executives are assuming the duties of business advisors, one of the most dramatic changes in credit management in recent years.

Some indication of the importance of the commercial credit executive can be gained from estimating the volume of commercial credit. Ninety to 95 percent of all commercial and industrial transactions between business executives are made on the basis of commercial credit. Because the receivables item is one of the largest and most liquid assets on most manufacturers' and wholesalers' balance sheets, commercial credit management is concerned with a financial aspect of business as demanding, important, and significant as many other financial tasks. Commercial credit management must safeguard the receivables asset with sound, intelligent, and effective credit and collection policies.

COMMERCIAL CREDIT EXECUTIVE—STATUS, PLACE, AND FUNCTIONS

Commercial credit managers occupy a respected and responsible position in their companies' organizational structures.[1] They manage the acceptance of customers' credit and the collection of their debts. Simple as this appears, effective credit management involves several major tasks, all of which depend on numerous routine operations.

Credit managers have the same aim as their companies—to earn a profit. And their policies have a significant impact throughout a company. If credit managers' attitudes and policies are too conservative, customers whose credit is less than prime must buy elsewhere. On the other hand, if their attitudes and policies are too lenient, a company may be stuck with low-quality receivables. In the former instance the company's sales and financial gains suffer; in the latter sales may increase, but the company suffers financial losses on low-quality credit customers. *Managing commercial credit sales is the efficient employment of all the devices at one's command to create the most profitable balance between company sales and company revenue.*

What kind of person measures up to the demands, responsibilities, and opportunities of commercial credit work? Some of the character traits, work habits, temperament, mental capabilities, and social virtues that favor success in this field include:

1. Imagination.
2. Resourcefulness in new and changing conditions.
3. Ability to get along with others.
4. Perseverance.
5. Ingenuity in eliciting pertinent information.
6. Communication through speech and writing.

Responsibilities of the commercial credit executive include:

1. Classifying receivable risks.
   a. Prime—no apparent risk.
   b. Moderate risk—temporarily unbalanced financial position.
   c. High risk—lack of management talent; undercapitalized.
   d. Cash only.

---

[1]For articles relating to this topic, see the Suggested Readings at the end of the chapter.

2. Managing receivables.
3. Troubleshooting.
   a. Collecting delinquent accounts—a substantial volume of credit activity comes from marginal accounts.
   b. Customer counseling—help customers overcome financial difficulties; try to restore an acceptable credit standing; retain customers as a profitable partner in future transactions.
   c. Cooperating with other departments within the company.

Changing Status and Qualifications of Credit Management

A major factor contributing to the changing status and qualifications of commercial credit management has been the rapid and tremendous growth of American industry and commerce. When most businesses were small sole proprietorships, credit approval was a simple, personal matter. Fifty to 75 years ago, buyers visited markets once or twice a year. Proprietors had an opportunity to "size up" buyers and either approve or disapprove their credit. As commerce developed, the personal relationship was lost, and business needed some other basis to manage commercial credit.

This task logically fell on someone within the company, usually the "bookkeeper." But as commerce and industry grew, one person couldn't handle both bookkeeping and credit duties.

NATIONAL ASSOCIATION OF CREDIT MANAGEMENT.[2] With the organization of the National Association of Credit Management (NACM) in 1896, the significance of professional credit management was realized. Improved sources of credit information developed; better accounting methods became universal, and the techniques of financial statement analysis were refined. Managements recognized the professional character of credit work and its significant relationship to their marketing and financial operations. An increased number of highly qualified people sought credit work as a career and profession. The complexities of modern-day business and the need for specialization fostered the status held by today's credit managers. Credit management is now an established business profession, with prerogatives, responsibilities, standards, and ethics.

Qualifications for success in credit management had to change too. Bookkeeping knowledge is not sufficient, as it was many years ago. Nor does credit management rely solely on knowledge of accounting principles and financial statement analysis, as some businesspeople and educators still believe. Modern business techniques and the operation of an effective credit department demand that credit management be intimately knowledgeable of credit's relationships to the financial, production, marketing,

---

[2]For a complete discussion of the National Association of Credit Management, see Chapter 16. Also see the Suggested Readings at the end of this chapter.

and other aspects of the business. As a result, credit managers need broader qualifications, with greater emphasis on formal training in both specialized and general areas of credit management.

The NACM has continually recognized the importance of education for its members. In 1918 it added the National Institute of Credit to its list of major services provided to members. In 1949 the Credit Research Foundation, Inc., which maintains a close affiliation with the NACM, was established to carry on research and education in credit and financial management.

The National Institute of Credit (NIC), administered by the Credit Research Foundation, is the oldest and broadest-based educational activity of the NACM, benefiting people with different educational and business backgrounds. NIC chapters cooperate with educational institutions through a college affiliation program. Students also may undertake a coordinated program leading to a credit management certificate or degree. Approved courses also prepare people for the credit business associate (CBA), credit business fellow (CBF), and certified credit executive (CCE) designations, which are recognized nationally. The CCE designation is based on a satisfactory review of personal data and successful completion of a comprehensive written examination.

Figure 14–1 lists the current requirements for the CBA and CBF designations. Both the CBA and CBF requirements refer to a "Career Roadmap," shown in Figure 14–2, that shows the process followed to receive a designation and assigns points to each segment.

The NACM Graduate School of Credit and Financial Management, conducted by the Credit Research Foundation, offers a program of executive professional development for experienced credit executives. Registrants attend a two-week resident session for each of three years. The programs are offered at Dartmouth College and Santa Clara University. Other graduate programs include the advanced credit executive studies (ACES), held at Northwestern University, designed for those who have completed the Graduate School of Credit and Financial Management or its equivalent and other lower division programs for middle management and supervisory level people—i.e., the Mid-Career School, Pine Mountain, Georgia, and the Credit Management Leadership Institute, Baylor University.

Short-term, on-campus residential programs and conferences of one to four days on topics of interest to credit administrators are held nationwide. The Credit Research Foundation conducts basic and applied research in business credit and receivables management and publishes studies on significant trends.

In addition to the above specialized and general educational programs, many colleges and universities offer day and evening programs designed to help equip the credit manager. Schools of business administration usually offer the best programs including specialized training in marketing, management, finance, economics, and accounting. In addition, many firms

---

FIGURE 14–1

Current Requirements Under Credential Reform
(CBA) Credit Business Associate

1. Complete a registration form which is available from NIC or your NACM Affiliate.

2. Attach the following documentation to the registration form:
   Transcripts or grade reports showing satisfactory completion
   (grade average must be C or better)
   of the following seven courses:
   2 accting courses
   2 economics courses
   1 financial analysis course
   1 credit & collections principles course
   1 business communications course.

3. Complete a "Career Roadmap" and return for certification by your local NACM affiliate.

4. Pass the CBA exam.

Note: See Plan B below under CBF. Under study is a Plan B for the CBA with the same equivalency provision.

(CBF) Credit Business Fellow

1. Notify your local NACM affiliate that you are ready to apply for the CBF designation. (You must have already earned the CBA.)

2. Complete a "Career Roadmap" and attach the following documentation (100 points are required):

   Plan A:
   Transcripts or grade reports showing satisfactory completion (grade average must be C or better)
   of the following 9 courses:
   2 business law courses:
   1 public speaking course
   1 marketing course
   1 cases in credit management course
   1 psychology course
   1 management course
   2 elective business courses.

   Plan B:
   Under revision during 1990 by the National Education Committee. The revised Plan B will include a provision for members to petition for equivalency, supported and certified by the local NACM affiliate and approved by the NIC director.

3. Pass the CBF exam.

Source: Maurice Margotta, Jr., "Advance Your Career," *Business Credit,* April 1990, p. 27. Permission granted by the National Association of Credit Management, *Business Credit.*

conduct their own training programs. There is no cut-and-dried formula for a successful training program; each firm must determine the type and extent of training that best suits its needs.

Thus most people, regardless of educational background, can develop the *personal, experience,* and *educational* qualifications necessary for the credit management profession.

FIGURE 14–2

NATIONAL INSTITUTE OF CREDIT
CAREER ROADMAP CRITERIA

EDUCATION

	POSSIBLE POINTS	MAXIMUM	TOTAL POINTS
College Education (Other than CCA & ACCA) (Transcripts Required)	5 per 25 credit hours	(max. 25)	_____
Graduate School (GSCFM) yr. ____	10	(max. 30)	_____
Advanced Credit Executive Studies yr. ____	10	(max. 10)	_____
Electronic Data Interchange yr. ____	5	(max. 5)	_____
Credit Management Leadership Institute yr. ____	10	(max. 10)	_____
Mid-Career School yr. ____	10	(max. 10)	_____
Credit Admin. (CAP)	5 per course	(max 20 if certif. achieved)	_____
or Advanced Credit Admin. (ACAP)	5 per course	(max. 10)	_____
Prequalified Seminars yr. ____	2 per seminar	(max. 20)	_____
Other (Home Study, e.g., AMA, RMA Courses to be determined by COO on a case-by-case basis) yr. ____	2-5	(max. 15)	_____
CRF Round Table Workshop	3 per seminar	(max. 12)	_____
		EDUCATION SUBTOTAL	_____

PARTICIPATION

(Local NACM)	POSSIBLE POINTS	MAXIMUM	
Committee Member	3 ea. year	(max. 21)	_____
Committee Chairman	5 ea. comm.	(max. 20)	_____
Industry Group Chairman	10	(max. 10)	_____
Board Member yr(s)	3 ea. year	(max. 12)	_____
Chief Elected Officer yr____	10	(max. 10)	_____
Attended Local Seminars (past 3 years)	2 ea.	(max. 10)	_____
Regional Conference General Chairman	10	(max. 10)	_____
Attended Regional NACM Conference (past 5 yrs)	5 ea. year	(max. 10)	_____

(CFDD and/or NIC Activities)			
Committee Member	3 ea. year	(max. 9)	_____
Committee Chairman	5 ea. comm.	(max. 10)	_____
Board Member yr(s)____	3 ea. year	(max 9)	_____
Chief Elected Officer yr____	10	(max. 10)	_____
Attended Regional Conf. (past 5 yrs)	5 ea. year	(max 10)	_____
Regional Conference General Chairman	10	(max. 10)	_____

(National NACM)			
Attended National Credit Congress (past 5 years)	5 ea. year	(max. 15)	_____
National Committee Member	3 ea. year	(max. 15)	_____
National Task Force Groups	2 ea. year	(max. 10)	_____
National Board Member yr(s)____	5 ea. year	(max. 20)	_____
National Officer yr____	10	(max. 10)	_____
Attended Legislative Conf. (past 5 yrs)	5 ea. year	(max. 15)	_____
Nat'l Industry Day Chairman	10	(max. 10)	_____

(Special Interest)			
Mentor	5 ea. mentee	(max. 10)	_____
Mentee Achieves Assoc. or above	5 ea. Award	(no max.)	
College Instructor (credit courses)	5 ea. qtr.	(max. 20)	
* NACM Panelist/Instructor	3 ea.	(max. 15)	
Published Article(s) (copies required)	5 ea.	(max. 20)	
* Instructor of seminar, workshop, industry day/CFDD Speaker			
		PARTICIPATION SUBTOTAL	_____

WORK EXPERIENCE

	POSSIBLE POINTS	MAXIMUM	
Work Experience (credit)	2 ea. yr. 1st 5 yrs.	(max. 10)	
	1 ea. yr. 6-15 yrs.	(max. 10)	
Special Consideration	Equivalency recommended by C.O.O.	(max. 5)	_____
		WORK EXPERIENCE SUBTOTAL	_____
		ROADMAP TOTAL	_____

CREDIT SUPERVISORY CANDIDATE	50 pts. - Qualifies participant for admission to CBA
CREDIT MANAGER CANDIDATE	100 pts. - Qualifies participant for admission to CBF
CREDIT EXECUTIVE CANDIDATE	125 pts. - Qualifies participant for admission to CCE

NAME: _____ SSN _____

COMPANY _____ NACM Officer _____

ADDRESS _____ NAME OF LOCAL NACM _____

CITY _____ STATE _____ ZIP _____ BY (NAME) _____ TITLE _____

DATE _____ PHONE _____ SIGNATURE _____

CERTIFIED BY NACM OFFICER _____

The Roadmap leads to the three nationally recognized designations: Credit Business Associate (CBA), Credit Business Fellow (CBF), and Certified Credit Executive (CCE).

CR 89

Source: Donald R. Mosher, "Success: A Process or a Miracle?" *Business Credit*, January 1990, p. 25. Permission granted by the National Association of Credit Management, *Business Credit*.

The Credit Department in the Organization Framework of the Company

Well-run organizations clearly define lines of authority and responsibility to ensure effective performance of the credit function. The credit department must be organized to conduct numerous routine activities, decision-making processes, collection phases of the operation, and supplemental services to customers and the company.

When a business organizes a commercial credit department, the question of its place in the company's organizational framework arises. This question can't be easily resolved due to variations in company size, department size, and the firm's principal business activity. Service companies generally have fewer credit problems and less opportunity to fulfill all the basic credit functions. Manufacturers and wholesalers, especially large ones, need a full-fledged, effective department. Small firms frequently delegate credit and collection functions among the owners, salespeople, or accounting personnel.

In large companies where the credit function plays an integral role in accomplishing major objectives, the credit department may be part of the sales, financial, or accounting areas, or it may be separate and independent.

CREDIT DEPARTMENT IN THE SALES AREA. It is common to have the credit department as part of the sales area if the company is in a highly competitive industry, if company policies are almost entirely sales-oriented, and if the company emphasizes credit service to customers. The principal arguments advanced for and against this type of organizational plan are:

For	*Against*
1. Both sales and credit have the same objective—that of maximizing sales.	1. The sales philosophy is too liberal with respect to credit risk.
2. Salespeople can help gather credit information.	2. An overly liberal credit policy can as easily create ill will among customers as an overly strict one.
3. Closer cooperation results between sales and credit personnel.	3. The decision-making process is not free from subjective influences.
4. Credit manager has a better opportunity to build goodwill by keeping alert to weak customers and new customers, as reported by sales personnel.	
5. The processing of sales orders is facilitated.	

CREDIT DEPARTMENT IN THE FINANCIAL AREA. Many credit managers are under the supervision of company treasurers. Such companies place great emphasis on utilizing invested capital efficiently. The arguments for and against this type of organizational plan are:

For	*Against*
1. The control of funds invested in accounts receivable is improved.	1. The maximizing of the sales function is likely to suffer under the financial-oriented and not sales-oriented department.
2. A better working relationship between the treasurer and credit manager is fostered.	2. The treasurer is more importantly charged with managing company debt, not customers' credit.
3. The current financing of the company is closely related to the performance of the credit department.	3. Credit and collection policies tend to be conservative and harsh, hence creating poor customer relations.
4. The total financial plan of the company includes accounts receivables, and the treasurer needs control to forecast the company's financial requirements.	

CREDIT DEPARTMENT IN THE ACCOUNTING AREA. While most credit departments are placed under the sales department or the treasurer's office, there are some advantages to placing them in the accounting area. The main advantage of this type of organizational setup involves recordkeeping. Both accounting and credit personnel need access to the accounts receivable ledger, which is usually maintained by accounting personnel to satisfy both accounting and credit activities. All pertinent data on current and inactive accounts is then centralized, mutually available, and readily accessible. In this arrangement, credit management and accounting management should have positions of coordinate rank. The principal objection to this arrangement is that credit managers may fail to realize their greatest potential by being *inward* rather than *outward* in their policies and decisions, to the detriment of other company departments and the company's customers.

THE INDEPENDENT CREDIT DEPARTMENT. If the credit department doesn't have some independence, it may be best to change the company's organizational structure. Whether or not this is necessary depends on the management personalities involved. If the credit manager is incapable in certain activities, the credit department should remain under the control of another executive. Conversely, it may be best to establish a separate credit operation if a dominant but shortsighted sales executive, financial officer, or accounting head lacks appreciation of credit's role.

If an independent credit department is organized, it is the responsibility of the senior executives and the credit manager to see that close cooperation between function and operation exists among the various departments in the company. Furthermore, the credit manager should occupy a place in the structure coordinate with that of other executives. Independent credit departments should be able to function more effectively because they are free of the supervision of other department managers. Without the one-sided dominance of another department, the credit department can enhance its cooperation with all other departments.

Basic Functions of Commercial Credit Management

The functions of modern-day credit management, first conceived by Dr. Theodore N. Beckman of The Ohio State University, are as follows:

1. To maximize sales and profits.
2. To minimize bad-debt losses.
3. To utilize invested funds efficiently.
4. To cooperate with other internal and external departments.

(See Chapter 7, where these functions were explained in connection with consumer credit activities.)

NEED FOR CREDIT INFORMATION

Commercial credit management confronts the inherent uncertainties and risks caused by the time element in the credit transaction. Because of this, decision making is the core of commercial credit management, just as it is for other types of credit. The decision maker attempts to improve the quality of the credit accepted and to assure a more profitable relationship by minimizing risk on the one hand and establishing a basis for confidence on the other. But confidence, based on past and present facts soundly obtained and appraised, can remove some uncertainty.

The questions of whether an account *can* and *will* pay can be answered only after a series of more specific questions about the risk have been answered. Even though no two customers are alike, the same specific questions usually arise and the types of information needed to answer them are usually quite similar. To answer the "can" and "will" question, credit managers must get answers to the following questions:

1. Can we establish this account's *identity and legal responsibility* so we know the order comes from a bona fide business?
2. What is the *history and business background* of this account?

3. What is the general *character and responsibility of the account's management?* Can we anticipate a continuous and healthy business relationship?
4. What is the *financial ability and capability* of this account?
5. What is the *financial strength and outlook* of this account?
6. Does the account's *past and present payment record* inspire confidence? What can we expect in the future?

Credit investigations give credit analysts answers to these questions. There are numerous sources and types of credit information. Credit management may use several sources or vary their use depending on the firm's particular needs. Experienced and resourceful credit managers can select the most suitable combination of sources to supply useful data quickly, economically, and accurately.

Classification of Sources of Commercial Credit Information

The sources of credit information available to commercial and other business-type creditors can be classified as internal or external as follows:

I. Internal information.
   A. Credit manager's personal knowledge.
   B. In-file information on previously established accounts.
II. External information.
   A. Mercantile agencies.
      1. General.
      2. Special.
      3. Interchange bureaus.
   B. Trade association bureaus.
   C. Interviews.
      1. By sales representatives.
      2. By credit manager and other authorized representatives of the creditor.
   D. Financial statements furnished by the account or new customer directly to the creditor.
   E. Banks.
   F. Attorneys.
   G. Public records.
   H. Correspondence with subject, creditors, or references.
   I. Inventors' manuals and services.
   J. Newspapers, magazines, trade journals, and other publications.

Sources of credit information are not only internal or external but are also commercialized or noncommercialized. Commercialized sources are mercantile agencies, trade association bureaus, and investors' manuals and services. A commercialized source is an organization whose main function is supplying credit information for compensation.

On the other hand, no internal sources of information are commercial ventures, so these sources are called noncommercialized. The credit manager's personal knowledge and in-file information on previously established accounts are available to most credit analysts. Several external sources of credit information are also noncommercialized—e.g., banks, attorneys, references, interviews, and other creditors. These external sources are often willing to supply information because of reciprocity, custom, courtesy, or informal compensation. Most noncommercialized sources are available to all credit personnel on an equal basis. The amount and usefulness of information from these sources depend on the type of business activity, the creditor's contacts, and the efficiency of the credit department.

Credit managers must be thoroughly familiar with the various sources of credit information and the types of credit information each supplies. They must know how the available types of information will best serve the needs of their firms and what each source can contribute toward sound credit decisions. By having an intimate knowledge of the sources, credit managers can get information at the proper time, of adequate amount and quality, and within the cost limits imposed by their budgets and the characteristics of each account.

Selecting Sources of Credit Information

The particular sources of credit information chosen depend on the characteristics of each source. The most important factors that should be considered are: accuracy of information, content of reports, speed of reporting, cost of the service, trade coverage, geographic coverage, variety and number of reports, and supplemental services that fulfill particular or occasional creditor needs.

ACCURACY OF INFORMATION. Accuracy of information supplied to a creditor is paramount. While most sources report all facts accurately, human frailties cause some errors. Today, automatic processing and duplicating equipment help safeguard against such errors. Foremost to take advantage of these technological improvements were the mercantile agencies. Much information, particularly financial data supplied to the agencies by firms being reported on, is now duplicated mechanically. These more reliable methods of recording facts contrast starkly to the once-prevalent manual operations.

CONTENT OF CREDIT REPORTS. Credit report content varies depending on the source and the characteristics of the business. Businesses need comprehensive and detailed reports to answer questions on new accounts; they can periodically revise existing accounts with limited information of a specific nature. In appraising the creditworthiness of most accounts, commercial credit management may need a complete financial picture. If adequate financial information is not available from mercantile agencies, credit managers should request such information from the customer or other sources. This type of information is essential to the appraisal and decision-making functions. Each credit instance dictates the kind and amount of additional information needed to reach a decision. The situation may warrant obtaining information on the aging of accounts payable, the aging of accounts receivable, or even the current status of inventories. Payment record (ledger) information is required for most new accounts because it reveals the likely payment pattern a creditor can expect. There are sources available for all information needs, but cost and time often restrict the choices.

SPEED OF THE REPORTING SERVICE. Speed is important to assure credit decisions are made within a reasonable time. Modern communications systems and duplicating devices greatly speed the compilation of credit information. Despite these improvements, some types of information can be gathered only with time and effort. Furthermore, credit departments can't delay a sale or shipment until they tap *all* sources of information. Competitive conditions in the market establish the speed required to prevent lost sales. While many credit losses occur when decisions are based on inadequate information, credit managers have to decide when to sacrifice adequacy for speed, or vice versa.

COST OF CREDIT INFORMATION. Credit costs must be evaluated and justified in the same way as other marketing costs. Creditors dealing with a nominal number of accounts may spend a few hundred dollars a year to acquire credit information. But large businesses with thousands of accounts may spend tens of thousands of dollars with a single source. Mercantile agencies usually scale their fees so unit costs decrease as quantity of reports and services increase.

The cost of acquiring and maintaining up-to-date information on each account is nominal with a sizable unit sale. On the other hand, the cost of investigating small orders is frequently disproportionate to their value. To compensate for this relatively high cost, the credit department may conduct a less thorough investigation. Some businesses don't investigate exceptionally small orders. Whether or not a credit investigation is warranted depends on the profit involved, whether the order is from a one-time customer, and whether the overall losses justify the costs.

Another aspect of costs involves risk. Obviously, exposure to more risk dictates more effort, greater costs, and more complete information. Alert credit managers keep costs in line with risk and profit.

TRADE AND GEOGRAPHIC COVERAGE. Information sources should cover the same geographic area as the creditor. Businesses that sell in a number of markets and to different types of customers need sources capable of supplying broad information. Not all agencies have national and international coverage, nor do they report on customers in all lines of trade. Credit managers must know these factors to select the most effective source. The variations in these factors become apparent in the next few chapters.

VARIETY AND NUMBER OF REPORTS. Sources differ considerably in the variety and number of reports they supply. Some accounts can be appraised most accurately with particular types of reports supplied by credit department request. Other accounts, particularly those where the degree of risk is high and continuous, require a series of reports supplied at specified intervals. Again, the characteristics of individual accounts must correspond to the services rendered.

SUPPLEMENTAL SERVICES. Supplemental services fulfill particular or occasional credit needs. Credit information sources may maintain credit reference books, make recommendations or decisions, render opinions, and supply foreign credit reports and standardized financial statements. Credit reference books are particularly valuable for preliminary credit checks and in appraising small orders that don't warrant a complete credit investigation. Some sources make recommendations with regard to the acceptability of an account—a valuable service if the credit department is staffed by a part-time credit manager or other circumstances make it desirable to shift the decision-making process. Most creditors' needs are not completely satisfied by the *basic* credit information services. Supplemental services help refine the decision-making process and overcome peculiar circumstances inherent in trading with a diverse group of customers.

INTERNAL INFORMATION AND DIRECT INVESTIGATION

In some respects there is no better source of information than the internal information on the debtor business itself, or the information gathered by direct investigation. However, in today's economy, large-scale production, more complex organizational structures, and the increasing distance between customers and suppliers all restrict a creditor's ability to gather sufficient credit information directly. Yet, even though it is seldom possible for a credit manager to interview a customer personally, other company representatives may have a chance to do so. Typically, a creditor's sales force has direct contact with the account, and it may be mutually beneficial for both the credit and sales departments to cooperate in the gathering of credit information. Many business credit managers require application forms from prospective customers. Traditionally, the direct gathering of credit information has been thwarted (limited) by sales staff involvement and concerns regarding customer harassment. Without detailed information from the prospective customer, the credit manager is more dependent on other sources.

Internal Information

The credit office is a storehouse of credit facts. Each time a credit department accepts a new account, a file on the customer is established. The information contained in these files is known as "in-file information." This source of information and the credit manager's own knowledge are the principal sources of internal information.

Perhaps the most arbitrary factor affecting the credit risk, and yet a valuable source of information, is the credit manager. The information credit managers acquire through experience and what they already know about their customers sharpen their decisions and methods of operation. Much of what they know they acquire through their attention to in-file information in making decisions and through the help they give their office associates in making routine decisions.

The customer's ledger record is also a valuable source of information. Each time an active or inactive account reorders, credit analysts can review the recorded data, basing a decision on the assumption that past experience will be repeated. They may note the size of the new order and compare it with previous orders. If they see radical differences and the time between orders is lengthy, they may initiate a new investigation.

Direct Investigation

The term *direct investigation* applies when a creditor is *directly* involved in gathering basic facts from any noncommercialized sources of information. Such an investigation involves either (1) direct contact with the customer to acquire credit information or (2) direct contact with individuals and institutions that may have useful credit information bearing on the account. It does not involve information supplied by any commercialized source.

CUSTOMER-SUPPLIED INFORMATION. Credit managers often get the most accurate information about a firm's operation and financial condition from its owners or principals. But, though customers can supply financial data, trade and bank references, and other pertinent information, limitations affect the use of this source. Direct contact with the customer depends on the customer's degree of cooperation, the distance from the creditor, the time available to conduct the investigation, and the amount of the credit requested.

Direct contact (by mail, phone, or personal interview) gives the creditor an opportunity to establish goodwill and an enduring business relationship. Creditors can also use direct contact to clarify credit and collection policies and to answer customers' questions. The first contact with a customer is perhaps the most important. If creditors state their information requirements firmly but courteously during the first contact, customers should remain cooperative in subsequent dealings.

Salespeople are frequently in an excellent position to furnish the credit department with valuable information on their customers. Few salespersons, however, are suited to be good credit reporters because their interests, experiences, and temperaments usually are not conditioned toward this goal. On the other hand, it is in their interest to supply information to the credit department when possible, so the account can be adequately appraised and credit approved quickly.

A salesperson usually has the first contact with a customer; if all goes well, the salesperson may be the only company representative who calls on the account. During these calls, the salesperson can become acquainted with the customer's operation and local reputation. Salespeople should be able to furnish information on business identity and legal responsibility, management ability, habits, local reputation, desirability of location, local conditions, bank and creditor references, and the financial status of the business.

DIRECT INTERCHANGE.   Another source of credit information is other creditors who have experience with the customer. It is common practice for creditors to exchange their experience as evidenced by accounting records. Some credit managers believe this source is one of the most valuable at their disposal.

Creditors may exchange ledger information by correspondence or personal contact or through trade group meetings sponsored by the National Association of Credit Management. Personal contact is the most costly method—because it consumes the valuable time of credit managers or their representatives. This method should be limited to cases involving substantial credit exposure in which other methods are not feasible. On the other hand, correspondence with other interested creditors is low cost and takes little of the credit manager's time. However, respondents don't always reply promptly.

Trade group meetings sponsored by the National Association of Credit Management take place each month throughout the country. Credit executives in the same or allied lines of business, or who sell to the same customers, meet to discuss their joint problems and their experiences with individual accounts.

Although the quantity of information supplied by direct interchange may vary with the approach used and the type of creditors contacted, this source can supply the age of the account, the highest recent credit approved, the manner in which the account has been paid, the terms of sale, the current status of the account, and any trade abuses. The advantages of soliciting information from other creditors are:

- Because the information is the result of the other creditors' experiences, the inquirer can reasonably expect any future experience to be similar.
- The information comes from people qualified to recognize the problems confronting a fellow creditor.
- The inquirer tries to solicit data from credit managers who have demonstrated their cooperativeness, reliability, and good judgment.
- The information, under most circumstances, can be obtained quickly.
- The information is up-to-date and therefore of current value.
- The financial conditions of a mutual customer change from time to time. Contacts with others who are selling the same account prevent debtors from becoming seriously past due without other business knowing about it.

Banks and commercial creditors can be mutually helpful in gathering credit information because typical businesses have many credit dealings with banks. Similarly, most businesses depend on commercial credit to meet their inventory, equipment, and miscellaneous requirements. Hence, both banks and commercial creditors have similar credit information needs. They complement each other in that they both maintain extensive credit files.

Despite the help each could be to the other, both banks and commercial creditors fall short in cooperation. Some banks refuse to reveal some or all of the data requested, and commercial creditors are more inclined to inquire of banks than banks are to inquire of them. To improve their relationships with banking institutions, businesses should examine their methods of approach and the content of their requests. One of the best ways to get complete information from a bank is by personal contact. Credit managers should become well acquainted with the members of their bank's credit department. Furthermore, credit managers may be able to influence the placing of their companies' deposits. Once this relationship is cultivated and mutual confidence develops, credit managers should be able to acquire more complete information.

Evaluation of Internal Information and Direct Investigation

Noncommercial sources of credit information can be used by most credit managers. The types of information supplied by these sources can be helpful in determining the creditworthiness of new accounts and in revising the credit lines of existing accounts. The credit analyst needs various types of credit information when deciding whether to accept a customer's credit. Before commercial creditors can adequately appraise an account, they have to answer questions involving an account's identity and legal responsibility, history and business background, managerial character and responsibility, financial ability and capacity, financial strength and outlook, and payment record.

By tapping the noncommercial sources, credit managers may be able to acquire the information needed to make a logical and sound credit decision. All information, whether acquired directly or indirectly, originates with the account under investigation. Practically, however, a single source of information seldom supplies *all* the data needed. Credit managers should check other noncommercial sources. They can check the subject's record by examining their own files; they can ask other creditors about their experiences; they can develop financial information and verify financial statements by contacting the customer's bank; or they can tap any other "free" source.

Despite all these possibilities, credit managers should not rely entirely on the limited number of noncommercial sources. Weak accounts can keep their records clean with a limited number of suppliers. They may even be highly regarded by their banks, close business associates, and the creditor's salespeople. In other circles, their financial deterioration is recognized.

More important to all credit managers is the fact that they are too concerned with other financial problems of the business to become expert credit investigators. Therefore, noncommercial sources are best utilized as a supplemental source of credit information; purchased information comes from a much greater storehouse of credit facts.

Of all the sources of credit information available to the credit analyst, the most extensive are the reports of commercialized organizations, which are discussed in subsequent chapters. The major purpose of these organizations is to gather and report all types of information that affect the quality of a firm's credit.

COMMERCIAL CREDIT MANAGERS' PROBLEMS WITH LEVERAGED BUYOUTS

In recent years, one of the biggest headaches for the commercial credit manager has been the growing impact of leveraged buyouts (LBOs).

> An LBO is any situation in which an individual, group of individuals, or a corporation buys a company using borrowed money to finance the purchase. A large amount of money is often needed to finance an LBO. Typical sources of financing for LBOs are asset-based lenders, mortgage bankers, who set up the so-called junk bond offerings, and banks.
>
> Often, the buyer pledges the assets of the company that is being purchased as collateral for the loans taken out to purchase it. In other words, the buyer may not personally borrow the money but will structure the deal so that the corporation to be purchased actually owes the money.

As a result, the first and most obvious principle that must be kept in mind is that following any LBO, the company in question is riskier from a credit perspective than it was before the buyout. Equity is replaced with debt, often creating significantly greater interest payments.

The profit margin is often squeezed because of astronomical interest payments due to the increased debt load. In extreme situations, the company is forced to sell portions of its own assets to enable it to make the interest payments on its debt.[3]

A credit manager needs to be able to spot an LBO that may cause trouble. Determining the specific background of all new owners is vital. The credit manager should attempt to discover any silent partners and their complete background. The following quotation describes the sources of information that should be explored:

To determine the background of the new owners of a company purchased in an LBO, the credit manager often must be aggressive. All available sources of information should be tapped, including: credit reporting agencies that normally include antecedent information on their reports; the company itself; industry group meetings; the financier of the LBO (its lender); or the NACM Loss Prevention Department.[4]

Experts predict that if leveraged buyouts have run their course, then the new era of less-leveraged buyouts (LLBOs) is about to begin.

DISCUSSION QUESTIONS

1. Explain why the position of the commercial credit manager continues to grow in importance.
2. What is the Credit Research Foundation, Inc.?
3. Comment on the changing status and qualifications of commercial credit management.
4. Discuss the main objectives of the National Institute of Credit.
5. What are the arguments for organizing the credit department within the sales area? Within the financial area?
6. Where should the commercial credit department be placed in the organizational framework of a manufacturing firm? Why?
7. What basic functions are usually attributed to commercial credit management? Evaluate the probable effects of placing too much emphasis on any one of these functions.
8. Discuss the general questions that should be answered before the credit of a commercial credit customer can be appraised objectively.

---

[3]Robert Lawson, "LBO Bustout," *Business Credit,* July–August 1989, p. 4. Permission granted by the National Association of Credit Management, *Business Credit.*

[4]Ibid., p. 6. Also see the Suggested Readings at the end of the chapter.

9. Explain the classification of sources of commercial credit information.

10. How do these sources vary from those used in consumer credit transactions?

11. What should a credit manager consider in selecting sources of credit information?

12. Which one of these considerations do you believe to be the most important?

13. What is meant by the statement "The credit office is a storehouse of credit facts"?

14. Should salespersons be required to gather credit information? Explain your position on this point.

15. What is meant by the term *direct investigation?*

16. What is the purpose of the trade group meetings of the NACM?

17. How do you believe the relationship between commercial credit managers and bank personnel dealing in credit work could be improved?

18. What types of credit information can usually be supplied by commercial banks?

19. Assume you are a commercial credit manager of a manufacturing firm. Would you use direct investigation to acquire credit information? Explain your answer.

20. Explain why leveraged buyouts (LBOs) have created problems for the commercial credit manager.

SUGGESTED READINGS

The Commercial Credit Executive

BUTTERBAUGH, ALAN. "Communicating with Top Management." *C&FM*, March 1987, p. 34.

EICHORN, ROBERT W. "A Myriad of Functions." *Credit & Financial Management,* July–August 1986, p. 27.

GRASSEL, PETER J. "Advancing Credit Management." *Credit & Financial Management,* July–August 1986, p. 16.

MERCHANT, JOHN E. "The Interrelated Roles of Sales and Credit: Viewpoint of a Sales Exec." *C&FM,* May 1987, p. 33.

REIMER, HAROLD I. "Explaining Yourself." *Business Credit,* January 1989, p. 30.

RUTHERFORD, R. D. "Meeting Company Targets." *C&FM,* May 1987, p. 29.

SCHNEIDER, ALAN J. "Beyond Managing Cash, to Managing Cash Flow." *Financial Executive,* November–December 1988, p. 54.

WATSON, W. ALVIN. "Credit Management Principles." *Credit & Financial Management,* March 1986, p. 9.

Leveraged Buyouts

HENZE, WILLIAM F. "Reality Confronts LBOs." *Business Credit,* February–March 1990, p. 14.

"Leveraged Buyouts Fall to Earth." *Business Week,* February 12, 1990, p. 62.

LOOMIS, CAROL J. "LBOs Are Taking Their Lumps." *Fortune,* December 7, 1987, p. 63.

MORRIS, DANIEL M. "Making a LBO Work, by Learning the Signals." *Financial Executive,* May–June 1989, p. 14.

TAUB, STEPHEN. "LBOs: The Next Lap." *Financial World,* October 31, 1989, p. 24.

TIMM, DANIEL. "LBOs: Concerns for Tomorrow." *Business Credit,* October 1989, p. 18.

TURSMAN, CINDY. "LBOs: Lax Standards or Good Management?" *Business Credit,* October 1989, p. 14.

National Association of Credit Management

GLAUS, O. D., JR. "What CCE Means to the Credit Profession." *Business Credit,* September 1989, p. 16.

MARGOTTA, MAURICE, JR. "Advance Your Career." *Business Credit,* April 1990, p. 26.

————. "Career Path Reforms Progress on Schedule." *Business Credit,* November 1989, p. 5.

————. "The Graduate School of Credit and Financial Management." *Business Credit,* December 1987, p. 57.

MOSHER, DONALD R. "Success: A Process or a Miracle?" *Business Credit,* January 1990, p. 24.

Basis of the Commercial Credit Decision—Dun & Bradstreet Business Credit Services

The Objectives or Goals of Chapter 15 Are:

1. To discuss the origin and development of Dun & Bradstreet.
2. To explain the present-day activities of Dun & Bradstreet Business Credit Services.
3. To explain the principal types of credit reports prepared by D&B.
4. To clarify the use of the *Reference Book.*
5. To evaluate the services of Dun & Bradstreet Business Credit Services.

Credit management has at its disposal a variety of commercialized sources of credit information, in addition to the noncommercialized sources discussed in the previous chapter. A commercialized source of credit information supplies credit information for compensation. This chapter and the next cover the commercialized sources of information for commercial creditors and commercial bank creditors. There are three types of commercialized sources of credit information:

1. The general mercantile agency, Dun & Bradstreet Business Credit Services, reports on any business enterprise in response to subscribers' credit inquiries (discussed in this chapter).
2. The Business Credit Reporting Service of the National Association of Credit Management operates for the systematic exchange of ledger information among members (see Chapter 16).
3. The specialized mercantile agencies report on business enterprises in particular lines of trade on a subscriber's request (see Chapter 16).

The services of the commercialized sources of credit information are quite varied and somewhat complex, so credit management must be thoroughly familiar with these sources. To arrive at a sound judgment of a credit risk, credit managers must have a wealth of credit information at their disposal. One of the most important of the commercialized sources is the general mercantile agency.

THE GENERAL MERCANTILE AGENCY

The activities of Dun & Bradstreet Business Credit Services are more extensive than those of any other credit reporting organization. In fact, D&B Business Credit Services is frequently referred to and classified as the only "general agency." The general agency's primary function is to supply credit reports on business concerns of *all sizes,* in *all lines* of trade, *located anywhere* in the United States and many foreign countries. However, even with its widespread operations and numerous services, Dun & Bradstreet does not have a monopoly in the field of credit reporting. It must compete with various specialized agencies that often serve the creditor's interests more completely, economically, and effectively. Despite the competitive atmosphere in credit investigation, Dun & Bradstreet has grown and prospered. Its scope of operations is so vast that it is the most frequently used source of credit information. D&B has offices in the principal cities of the United States and leading centers of world trade.

Origin and Development of Dun & Bradstreet

A century ago or even less, the possibility of securing organized and factual data was remote. Credit decisions were often hit-or-miss affairs. Terms were long, the relationship between debtor and creditor was often personal, and some credit transactions were based solely on references furnished by customers. As a result, business experienced large credit losses that had to be offset by greater margins of profit.

During the panic of 1837, Arthur Tappan and Company failed. Lewis Tappan, who was associated with the firm, had gained a wide reputation as an excellent judge of a credit risk. His personal interest in credit investigation, his reputation in appraising a credit risk, and the steady growth of the nation's economy suggested the idea of organizing a central credit reporting bureau. In 1841 he organized The Mercantile Agency to collect and disseminate information for the benefit of creditors.[1]

The impetus for developing organized sources of credit information grew out of the uncertainties and losses experienced during the panic of 1837, the rapid changes in the country's economic structure, and the expansion of trading areas. Manufacturers and suppliers needed credit to trade over wider geographic areas. This meant that credit judgment could no longer be based on personal relationships, nor could adequate

---

[1]For an authoritative and detailed account of the origin and development of Dun & Bradstreet, see Roy A. Foulke, *The Sinews of American Commerce* (New York: Dun & Bradstreet, Inc., 1941).

information be gathered in the immediate vicinity of the creditor. Consequently, a system of organized credit reporting evolved to eliminate some of the major uncertainties of trade.

Soon after Lewis Tappan founded The Mercantile Agency in New York, he developed a branch-office system to penetrate major trade centers. Reporters visited each community to interview new and established business executives. R. G. Dun, an employee of The Mercantile Agency in 1851, became the sole proprietor of the company in 1859 and changed the name to R. G. Dun & Co. In 1849 John M. Bradstreet, an attorney in Cincinnati, founded The Bradstreet Company. This company operated in a manner similar to The Mercantile Agency and served the same fields of trade for many years. In 1933 the two firms merged into Dun & Bradstreet, Inc.

In 1973, following more than a decade of expansion and diversification, Dun & Bradstreet Companies, Inc., was formed as the parent corporation of D&B and a number of subsidiaries, including the Reuben H. Donnelley Corporation and Moody's Investors Service, Inc. In 1979 The Dun & Bradstreet Corporation succeeded the so-called Companies as the parent company.

THE ORGANIZATION, SERVICES, AND ACTIVITIES OF DUN & BRADSTREET BUSINESS CREDIT SERVICES TODAY

To facilitate the tremendous task of collecting, assembling, analyzing, and disseminating credit information, Dun & Bradstreet employs 1,300 to 1,400 full-time reporters. These people gather credit information from business firms in the United States, Puerto Rico, and the U.S. Virgin Islands. In addition, D&B has reporters and correspondents in over 100 offices in many other parts of the free world. The entire operation of D&B Business Credit Services is administered and controlled from the general offices located in Murray Hill, New Jersey.

By early 1974 Dun & Bradstreet had equipped its U.S. offices with computer installations, and in 1975 the computers were linked to the D&B National Business Information Center at Berkeley Heights, New Jersey. This network forms one of the largest private computer operations in the world. The center functions as the central processing, mailing, and storage point for the entire company, replacing most of the manual files and mailing operations previously maintained at offices across the country. Through their own terminals, the offices are able to transmit data electronically to the center and retrieve any of the report information maintained on more than 9 million U.S. businesses. (Dun & Bradstreet does not prepare consumer reports.) The National Business Information Center responds to almost 16 million requests for information each year. Over 80 percent of all inquiries are answered directly from computer files the same day they are received; the balance are sent to field offices for investigation.

Principal Activities of Dun & Bradstreet

Dun & Bradstreet's principal activity is supplying business information, and over the years it has developed a number of services for the business community. Its diverse activities include the following:

1. *Report services*—D&B investigates, analyzes, and edits Business Information Reports on commercial and industrial enterprises. All reports have the same basic characteristics, but each is prepared to reflect the complexities of varied financial structures. International Reports cover the rapidly expanding overseas markets. In recent years, report formats have been expanded to include Payment Analysis Reports and Dun's Financial Profiles.[2] These include spreadsheet analyses of payments and finances, respectively (see Figures 15–1 and 15–2).

2. *Automated services*—rapidly developing technology has permitted D&B to develop a wide range of refined services. Automated systems offered by D&B now include Change Notification Service (CNS), Exception Credit Update Service (ECUS), and Key Alert. Under these systems, a subscriber's own account list can be entered into D&B computers for regular monitoring and subsequent notification of significant changes occurring in the D&B information file. The primary difference between the two systems is that CNS and Key Alert output can be printed, while ECUS is intended for computer-to-computer interchange.

In recent years, delivery systems (previously the mail) have been expanded to include DunsDial, DunsPrint, and DunsLink.[3] These systems allow subscribers direct access to D&B's computerized business information center.

3. *Reference Book service*—D&B compiles and publishes the Dun & Bradstreet *Reference Book* six times a year. This book contains businesses' names, their SIC (standard industrial classification) number, and in most instances a key showing their estimated financial strength and composite credit appraisal rating. The January, March, July, and September revisions also are published in state editions. The *Reference Book* is useful to executives and salespersons active in the field. International reference books also are available.

4. *Apparel trades service*—this service meets the special needs of business firms in the apparel field. It is rendered through the Credit Clearing House, a D&B unit that gives credit reports and recommendations especially designed to fit the needs of the apparel trades. The *Apparel Trades Book,* containing listings on approximately 200,000 retailers and wholesalers in the apparel industry, is revised four times a year. Many CCH customers use DunsPrint, whereby credit and marketing information is electronically transmitted to terminals in the offices of customers.

---

[2]These terms will be explained in a subsequent section of this chapter.

[3]These terms will be explained in a subsequent section of this chapter.

5. *Commercial collections*—this service offers accounts receivable control and collection of past-due accounts when necessary.

6. *Publications*—D&B publishes a wide variety of business statistics and operating ratios useful to business management.

7. *Directories*—D&B publishes various directories and other reference books used for credit, sales, publishing, and executive reference, including *Reference Book of Manufacturers* (through Dun's Marketing Services, Inc.), *Reference Book of Corporate Managements,* and *Directory of Principal International Businesses.*

8. A recent addition to the D&B services is Duns Reference Plus, which uses the latest CD-ROM technology to give customers faster access to more information with great flexibility. Customers now have instant access to the exact level of D&B information needed to make a wide variety of business decisions.

Duns Reference Plus is a high-speed workstation (see Figure 15–3) that combines:

- A compact disk that gives electronic access to reference data on more than 4 million companies and trade styles.
- Advanced communication software that automatically links the customer to the D&B database and lets full reports be retrieved on more than 9 million U.S. firms.
- Report management capabilities that store D&B reports on the customer's hard disk, giving the flexibility to view, store, print, update, or delete at the customer's convenience.

Yet the most important activity of Dun & Bradstreet is the collecting, assembling, and analyzing of credit information. Many of D&B's other activities are dependent on this one.

Methods of Collecting Credit Information

To accomplish the tremendous task of collecting credit information, Dun & Bradstreet uses personal investigations (both direct and telephone) and mail inquiries. Personal investigations are made by reporters, who are usually assigned a specific territory so they become more intimately acquainted with the sources of credit information and with local business managements. Reporters revise and update reports at stated intervals, so Dun & Bradstreet files contain the latest available information.

Most credit investigations of businesses follow a similar pattern. Reporters first interview the principals of a business, confirm ownership, note details of its operations and methods, obtain a financial statement, and discuss future plans and sales trends. They may also check court and other public records or investigate outside the business (i.e., interview bankers, accountants, and other informed sources) to gather additional facts or verify existing information.

FIGURE 15–1 **Payment Analysis Report**

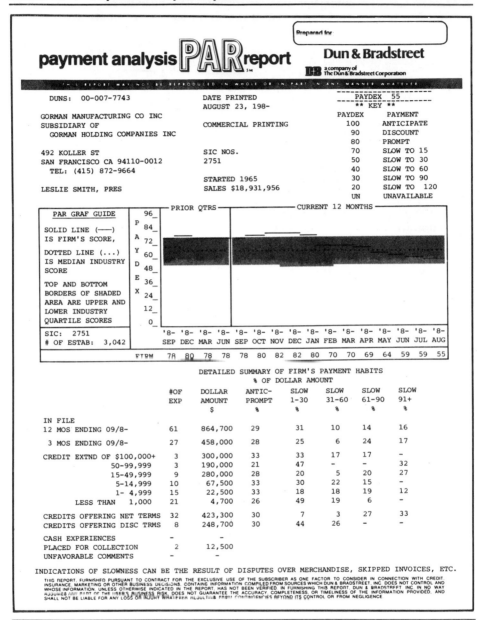

First page of a sample Payment Analysis Report on Gorman Manufacturing Company, a fictitious firm.

FIGURE 15–1 *(concluded)*

payment analysis **PAR** report SM

Prepared for:

Dun & Bradstreet
DB a company of
The Dun & Bradstreet Corporation

THIS REPORT MAY NOT BE REPRODUCED IN WHOLE OR IN PART IN ANY MANNER WHATEVER.

GORMAN MANUFACTURING CO
SAN FRANCISCO CA 94110-0012   * PAYMENT HABITS BY INDUSTRY *   PAGE 2

LINE OF BUSINESS	# EXP	DOLLAR AMOUNT	HIGHEST CREDIT	AVERAGE HGH CR	ANT PPT	SLO 1-30	SLO 31-60	SLO 61-90	SLO 91+
		$	$	$	%	%	%	%	%
AIR TRANS	5	10,250	5,000	2,050	51	–	–	49	–
CHEMICALS WH	1	500	500	500	50	50	–	–	–
COMMUNICATIONS	2	5,750	5,000	2,875	50	7	43	–	–
COMPUTER/DP SVCS	2	3,500	2,500	1,750	–	29	–	35	36
ELEC EQUIP WH	3	261,000	100,000	87,000	21	58	21	–	–
ELEC MACHY MF	5	170,500	100,000	34,100	50	2	47	1	–
EQUIP RENTAL	1	2,500	2,500	2,500	100	–	–	–	–
FUR & FIX MF	1	80,000	80,000	80,000	50	50	–	–	–
FURNITURE RET	1	250	250	250	–	–	100	–	–
INDUSL MACHY WH	6	10,150	10,000	1,692	99	1	–	–	–
LAB INSTRMTS MF	1	50	50	50	–	100	–	–	–
LODGING	2	45,000	40,000	22,500	–	11	–	–	89
MEASURING DEV MF	2	32,000	30,000	16,000	39	23	–	38	–
MEDICAL INSTRU MF	1	50	50	50	–	–	50	50	–
NON CLASSIFIED	2	1,500	1,000	750	–	100	–	–	–
NON ELEC MACHY MF	6	92,600	40,000	15,433	24	3	3	48	22
PAPER PDTS WH	8	103,000	60,000	12,875	100	–	–	–	–
PERSONNEL SVCS	1	1,050	1,050	1,050	1	20	5	–	74
PRIMARY METAL MF	1	7,500	7,500	7,500	–	100	–	–	–
PRINT & PUBLISH	6	33,000	30,000	5,500	90	2	–	8	–
REPAIR SVCS	1	2,500	2,500	2,500	–	–	100	–	–
RUBBER & PLASTIC MF	1	1,000	1,000	1,000	–	100	–	–	–
SOCIAL SVCS	1	1,000	1,000	1,000	–	–	–	–	100
TRANS SVCS	1	50	50	50	100	–	–	–	–

* PAYMENT SUMMARY *

COMPOSITE PAYDEX
CURRENT 12 MONTHS = 71   AVG. HIGH CREDIT = $ 14,175

         HIGHEST CREDIT = $ 100,000

COMPOSITE PAYDEX
PRIOR 12 MONTHS = 79

Second page of a sample Payment Analysis Report on Gorman Manufacturing Company, a fictitious firm.

FIGURE 15-2 Dun's Financial Profiles

Dun & Bradstreet
A company of the Dun & Bradstreet Corporation

0		
GORMAN MANUFACTURING CO INC	PREPARED FOR	DUNS ANALYTICAL SERVICES
492 KOLLER STREET		SUB 230-152050
SAN FRANCISCO CA 94110		DEMO;PB
D&B OFFICE 052		

LAST INDUSTRY UPDATE: 06/29/90   DATE PRINTED: 08/02/90

DUNS 00-007-7743	SALES 13,007,229
SICS 2752	WORTH 5,627,497
STARTED 1965	INDUSTRY ASSET RANGE:
EMPLOYS 500	OVER $5 MILLION WEST
	0003

	FISCAL DEC. 31,1989 (30 FIRMS)				FISCAL DEC. 31,1988 (22 FIRMS)				FISCAL DEC. 31,1987 (27 FIRMS)		
		% CHANGE	SUBJECT %	INDUSTRY %		% CHANGE	SUBJECT %	INDUSTRY %		SUBJECT %	INDUSTRY %
CASH............	1,323,364	132.5	17.4	7.3	569,144	33.0	9.0	7.4	428,032	6.1	6.7
ACCOUNTS RECEIVABLE...	1,725,814	3.4	22.7	31.2	1,668,942	(19.8)	26.4	28.7	2,082,249	29.7	25.3
NOTES RECEIVABLE......	-	-	-	0.6	-	-	-	0.5	-	-	0.8
INVENTORY.............	1,711,769	1.4	22.5	11.8	1,688,738	(14.6)	26.8	13.1	1,977,928	28.2	12.9
OTHER CURRENT.........	537,075	297.5	7.1	2.7	135,100	8.6	2.1	4.7	124,355	1.8	3.7
TOTAL CURRENT.........	5,298,022	30.4	69.6	53.6	4,061,924	(11.9)	64.4	54.4	4,612,564	65.7	49.4
FIXED ASSETS..........	1,795,021	(7.1)	23.6	35.4	1,932,321	(7.0)	30.6	34.4	2,078,000	29.6	38.1
OTHER NON CURRENT.....	523,772	65.3	6.9	11.0	316,806	(4.4)	5.0	11.2	331,411	4.7	12.5
TOTAL ASSETS..........	7,616,815	20.7	100.0	100.0	6,311,051	(10.1)	100.0	100.0	7,021,975	100.0	100.0
ACCOUNTS PAYABLE......	745,204	64.0	9.8	11.8	454,377	(44.6)	7.2	10.7	820,175	11.7	9.3
BANK LOANS............	-	-	-	0.1	-	-	-	0.3	-	-	0.3
NOTES PAYABLE.........	-	-	-	5.0	-	-	-	3.9	-	-	5.7
OTHER CURRENT.........	880,514	119.0	11.6	13.5	401,993	(49.4)	6.4	17.0	794,374	11.3	15.4
TOTAL CURRENT.........	1,625,718	89.8	21.3	30.4	856,370	(47.0)	13.6	31.9	1,614,549	23.0	30.7
OTHER LONG TERM.......	185,000	(14.4)	2.4	26.9	216,000	28.6	3.4	26.0	168,000	2.4	25.4
DEFERRED CREDITS......	178,600	3.1	2.3	0.6	173,247	(22.5)	2.7	0.8	223,586	3.2	1.7
NET WORTH.............	5,627,497	11.1	73.9	42.1	5,065,434	1.0	80.3	41.3	5,015,840	71.4	42.2
TOTAL LIABILITY/WORTH.	7,616,815	20.7	100.0	100.0	6,311,051	(10.1)	100.0	100.0	7,021,975	100.0	100.0
NET SALES.............	13,007,229	26.0	100.0	100.0	10,325,582	(6.8)	100.0	100.0	11,082,639	100.0	100.0
GROSS PROFIT..........	4,777,675	47.8	36.7	27.9	3,232,728	(11.4)	31.3	28.2	3,649,732	32.9	29.3
NET PROFIT AFTER TAX..	633,883	754.0	4.9	5.8	74,224	(67.5)	0.7	5.2	228,180	2.1	5.3
DIVIDENDS/WITHDRAWALS.	24,360	-	0.2	5.6	-	-	-	6.6	24,915	0.2	2.7
WORKING CAPITAL.......	3,672,304	14.6	-	-	3,205,554	6.9	-	-	2,998,015	-	-

FIGURE 15–2 (concluded)

DUNS ANALYTICAL SERVICES

Dun & Bradstreet — a company of The Dun & Bradstreet Corporation

GORMAN MANUFACTURING CO INC
492 KOLLER STREET
SAN FRANCISCO CA 94110
DUNS NO. 00-007-7743

PREPARED FOR
SUB 230-152050
DEMO;PB

LAST INDUSTRY UPDATE: 06/29/90   DATE PRINTED: 08/02/90
0004

RATIOS	1989 (30 FIRMS) SUBJECT	% CHANGE	-INDUSTRY QUARTILES- UPPER	MEDIAN	LOWER	1988 (22 FIRMS) SUBJECT	% CHANGE	-INDUSTRY QUARTILES- UPPER	MEDIAN	LOWER	1987 (27 FIRMS) SUBJECT	-INDUSTRY QUARTILES- UPPER	MEDIAN	LOWER
(SOLVENCY)														
QUICK RATIO..(TIMES).	1.9	(26.9)	2.2	1.0	0.9	2.6	62.5	1.4	1.0	0.8	1.6	1.8	1.0	0.7
CURRENT RATIO.(TIMES).	3.3	(29.8)	3.0	1.5	1.3	4.7	62.1	2.5	1.5	1.1	2.9	2.4	1.4	1.2
CURR LIAB TO NW..(%)..	28.9	71.0	33.4	67.2	156.6	16.9	(47.5)	40.4	92.1	170.8	32.2	23.5	49.8	213.0
CURR LIAB TO INVT.(%)..	95.0	87.4	161.6	289.9	388.7	50.7	(37.9)	155.7	284.8	355.0	81.6	147.2	235.9	338.2
TOTAL LIAB TO NW.(%)..	35.3	43.5	70.9	179.2	290.4	24.6	(38.5)	74.8	258.0	339.8	40.0	54.1	99.4	272.9
FIXED ASSETS TO NW.(%)	31.9	(16.3)	58.4	116.3	183.4	38.1	(8.0)	64.9	174.1	204.7	41.4	55.9	94.6	168.0
(EFFICIENCY)														
COLL PERIOD..(DAYS)...	48.4	(18.0)	40.7	50.2	68.6	59.0	(14.0)	43.4	48.5	56.9	68.6	45.9	58.8	65.7
SALES TO INVT.(TIMES).	7.6	24.6	24.3	16.9	10.0	6.1	8.9	21.0	16.6	10.7	5.6	21.9	15.8	8.3
ASSETS TO SALES.(%)..	58.6	(4.1)	48.8	59.8	73.4	61.1	(3.6)	38.9	51.2	69.0	63.4	54.0	67.7	78.2
SALES TO NWC.(TIMES)..	3.5	9.4	16.4	8.7	4.8	3.2	(13.5)	24.2	8.1	4.9	3.7	17.4	7.0	5.1
ACCT PAY TO SALES.(%).	5.7	29.5	3.7	6.1	8.1	4.4	(40.5)	3.6	5.0	5.8	7.4	4.8	6.0	7.8
(PROFITABILITY)														
RETURN ON SALES..(%)..	4.9	600.0	6.5	2.7	0.3	0.7	(66.7)	6.4	3.7	1.3	2.1	5.9	4.5	1.4
RETURN ON ASSETS.(%)..	8.3	591.7	9.1	4.6	1.5	1.2	(62.5)	9.6	8.3	2.6	3.2	10.4	6.4	2.3
RETURN ON NW....(%)..	11.3	653.3	23.3	12.7	4.2	1.5	(66.7)	21.5	15.0	9.1	4.5	23.5	14.3	7.1

TO HAVE A FINANCIAL SPECIALIST PREPARE A WRITTEN ANALYSIS OF THIS BUSINESS, ORDER A PRO REPORT THROUGH DUNS DIAL OR YOUR LOCAL DUN & BRADSTREET OFFICE

THIS REPORT MAY NOT BE REPRODUCED IN WHOLE OR PART IN ANY MANNER WHATEVER

FIGURE 15–3 **The Duns Reference Plus System**

SEPT 1988 EDITION

What you see...
Pictured here are the physical hardware components of the Duns Reference Plus system: The Duns Reference Plus CD-ROM disc (actual size), an IBM or 100% compatible personal computer (640K RAM), a compact disc reader with Microsoft Extension support and interface card, and a color or monochrome monitor.

What you don't see...
You can't see the behind-the-scenes activities that are part of the Duns Reference Plus system. For instance, you can't see the system automatically connecting to the D&B data base and downloading complete D&B reports for you. You can't see those reports being stored and managed electronically for you. Or the detailed information on millions of companies that the system puts at your fingertips. And you can't see here, how fast and efficient the system is, or how much it can increase your productivity...but when you try it, you will!

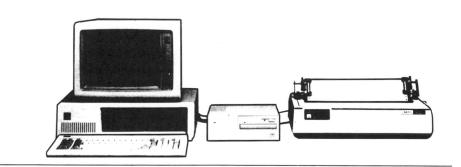

D&B also collects payment data in many forms. It uses the traditional methods of collecting payment data from suppliers by mail and phone. On a daily basis, the National Business Information Center machine generates payment experience request forms and mails them to 700,000 suppliers nationwide. Reporters also ask for payment experiences when they update the Business Information Report.

The primary method of collecting payment data is Dun-Trade and, for banking information, Dun-Bank. These two methods eliminate all paperwork and phone calls by regularly collecting the same data as the traditional methods (e.g., manner of payment, high credit, amount owing, past dues, terms of sale, and date of last sale) on computer tapes, diskettes, and disks. D&B is also developing a method to accept payment data directly from customers' computers via communication lines. The payment information collected by mail, phone, and computer is added to the business data gathered by reporters and other third-party sources to make up the Business Information Report.

As a further means of ensuring that its reports are accurate and fair, Dun & Bradstreet's policy has always been to make copies available to businesses being reported on. For some years, D&B mailed a copy of pertinent report data to millions of companies covered by D&B reports. More recently, D&B sends a copy of the entire report (either an initial report or a full revision) to the chief executive of the firm being reported on with a request for review and, if appropriate, suggested revisions. The costs of writing a report are assumed by D&B subscribers, never by the subjects themselves.

PRINCIPAL TYPES OF REPORTS

All D&B reports contain the same basic elements, but some reports use specialized forms to fit the credit and sales requirements of various subscribers. VIP Reports cover short-term credit and management problems and contain highly detailed information along with a specific credit recommendation. International Reports are written on overseas concerns in principal free-world markets.

Senior business analysts handle the more complex and active cases, and, generally, the largest companies are handled by a group of highly trained national business analysts.

Business Information Reports

D&B sends the Business Information Report (see Figure 15–4) in response to all subscriber inquiries from its National Business Information Center. A computer-merged Business Information Report is divided into 10 basic elements—6 of which appear in all cases: summary, payments, finance, banking, history, and operation. Four other elements appear as necessary: special events, changes, update, and public filings.

Most report information is developed through direct contact with principals of the company on which the report is being written, but many details also come from public records, suppliers, and other sources.

Since a Business Information Report reflects investigations conducted at different times, no single date is applicable to all of the information in the report. The lead date at the top is merely the date on which the report was printed out by computer in response to an inquiry.

FIGURE 15–4 **Business Information Report**

Summary: For quick appraisal and an overview of the company—the D&B Rating, company history and operation performance.

Special Events: Your decisions about a firm may be affected by the late-breaking events that could appear: criminal proceedings, bankruptcies, burglaries, fires, changes in ownership or acquisition.

Payments: A brief review of the company's payments including high credit extended, amounts owed and past due, and time period since last sale so you can evaluate how you will be paid.

Changes: Alerts you to shifts in management, business expansion or changes to legal structure, such as the incorporation of a proprietorship. Or changes in location or business name, so you can keep your records current.

Update: Provides you with recent changes in operation since the report was last revised.

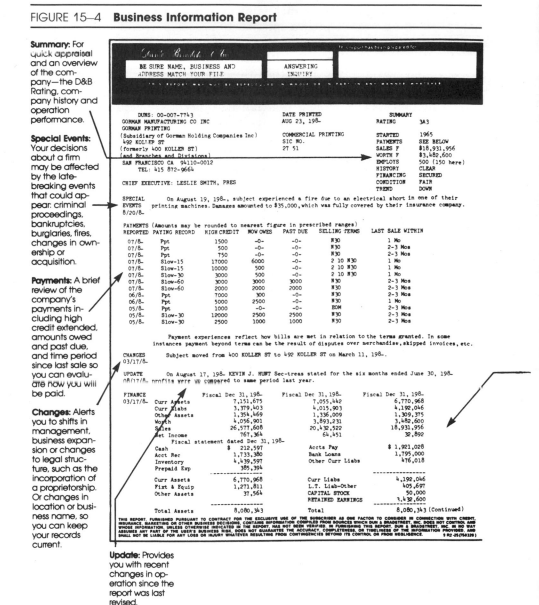

Heading and Summary of the Business Information Report

The Heading and Summary of a Business Information Report provide a concise, at-a-glance picture of a business. Reading across the top, an analyst can quickly obtain the basic identification information about a company: the name and address, telephone number, principal owner or executive, four-digit U.S. Standard Industrial Classification code

FIGURE 15–4 (concluded)

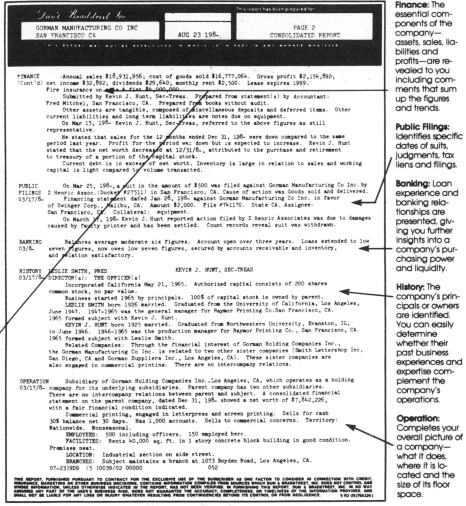

All information may not be available on every company.

Finance: The essential components of the company—assets, sales, liabilities and profits—are revealed to you including comments that sum up the figures and trends.

Public Filings: Identifies specific dates of suits, judgments, tax liens and filings.

Banking: Loan experience and banking relationships are presented, giving you further insights into a company's purchasing power and liquidity.

History: The company's principals or owners are identified. You can easily determine whether their past business experiences and expertise complement the company's operations.

Operation: Completes your overall picture of a company—what it does, where it is located and the size of its floor space.

(designating the company's product line and function), and a written description of the company's line of business.

In the upper left-hand corner is the *DUNS* number, a unique nine-digit identification code assigned to every company in the D&B computerized files. (Each location of a company has its own separate number.)

In the upper right-hand corner is the *Dun & Bradstreet Capital-and-Credit Rating,* designating the estimated financial strength and the composite credit appraisal (see the key to ratings in Figure 15–5). In addition, for quick review, the *Summary* at the upper right gives important points

FIGURE 15–5 **Key to Ratings**

Estimated Financial Strength			Composite Credit Appraisal			
			High	Good	Fair	Limited
5A	$50,000,000	and over	1	2	3	4
4A	$10,000,000 to	$49,999,999	1	2	3	4
3A	1,000,000 to	9,999,999	1	2	3	4
2A	750,000 to	999,999	1	2	3	4
1A	500,000 to	749,999	1	2	3	4
BA	300,000 to	499,999	1	2	3	4
BB	200,000 to	299,999	1	2	3	4
CB	125,000 to	199,999	1	2	3	4
CC	75,000 to	124,999	1	2	3	4
DC	50,000 to	74,999	1	2	3	4
DD	35,000 to	49,999	1	2	3	4
EE	20,000 to	34,999	1	2	3	4
FF	10,000 to	19,999	1	2	3	4
GG	5,000 to	9,999	1	2	3	4
HH	Up to	4,999	1	2	3	4

General Classification based on Estimated Strength and Composite Credit Appraisal

Estimated Financial Strength	Composite Credit Appraisal		
	Good	Fair	Limited
1R $125,000 and over 2		3	4
2R $50,000 to $124,999 2		3	4

Explanation
When the designation "1R" or "2R" appears, followed by a 2, 3 or 4, it is an indication that the Estimated Financial Strength, while not definitely classified, is presumed to be in the range of the ($) figures in the corresponding bracket, and while the Composite Credit Appraisal cannot be judged precisely, it is believed to fall in the general category indicated.

"INV" shown in place of a rating indicates that Dun & Bradstreet is currently conducting an investigation to gather information for a new report. It has no other significance.

"FB" (Foreign Branch). Indicates that the headquarters of this company is located in a foreign country (including Canada). The written report contains the location of the headquarters.

Absence of a Rating - - The Blank Symbol
A blank symbol (--) should not be interpreted as indicating that credit should be denied. It simply means that the information available to Dun & Bradstreet does not permit us to classify the company within our rating key and that further inquiry should be made before reaching a credit decision.

Absence of a Listing
The absence of a listing in the Dun & Bradstreet Business Information File or in the Reference Book is not to be construed as meaning a concern is non-existent or has discontinued business. Nor does it have any other meaning. The letters "NQ" on any written report mean "not listed in the Reference Book." The letters "FBN" on any written report also mean that the business is not listed in the Reference Book and that the headquarters is located in a foreign country.

Employee Range Designation (ER)

Certain businesses do not lend themselves to a Dun & Bradstreet rating. Instead, reports on these businesses carry an Employee Range Designation (ER) which is indicative of size based on number of employees. No other significance should be attached to this classification. The ER listings in the Reference Book represent those businesses on which there has been subscriber interest in the past year. Additional ER listings are stored and updated in the D&B Business Information File.

Key to Employee Range Designation

ER 1	1000 or more	Employees
ER 2	500-999	Employees
ER 3	100-499	Employees
ER 4	50- 99	Employees
ER 5	20- 49	Employees
ER 6	10- 19	Employees
ER 7	5- 9	Employees
ER 8	1- 4	Employees
ER N		Not Available

derived from more detailed report information. Besides the D&B rating, these points usually include the year started, payments, sales, worth, number of employees, history, financing, condition, and trend.

STARTED. Ordinarily, this figure is the year the present ownership came into financial control of the business. In older, family-owned businesses and publicly owned companies, however, it may be the year the business originally commenced operations.

PAYMENTS. This section always says SEE BELOW because the trade data is updated daily and any abbreviated description may be inconsistent due to recently received data.

SALES. This figure is the company's annual sales or revenue. It may be shown as a range of annual sales.

WORTH. This figure—sometimes referred to as the estimated financial strength—attempts to show the tangible net worth of a business after all intangible assets have been deducted. Some specific intangible assets are not deducted in computing net worth. When an *F* precedes the figure, sales or worth is based on figures taken from the books of account. (Such figures have not necessarily been prepared by a public accountant and an opinion expressed. That can be determined from the Finance section in the body of the report.) When the sales or worth figure is based on signed estimates from the owner or management, the amount is preceded by an **E.** If there is neither an *F* nor an **E,** the figure has been estimated by the management or by others.

EMPLOYS. The figure for number of employees includes all those who are paid wages for their services, including full-time and part-time employees, as well as the owner, partners, or officers. In some instances the figure is the latest one available; in others it represents an average number employed over a year's time. If the company's employment is seasonal, a range is usually shown.

HISTORY. One of four descriptive words are used in this category: *clear, business, management,* or *incomplete.*
   Clear indicates that *nothing* in the background of a business or its management is likely to be of special interest to the report reader, including such items as significant suits, judgments, liens, or business failures.
   Business indicates that *something* in the background of a business or its management is likely to be of interest to the reader. *Management* indicates that the report contains similar items pertaining to one or more of those who manage or own the business. *Incomplete* indicates that the identity of one or more of the owners or managers is incomplete or significant background information is unavailable or could not be satisfactorily confirmed.

FINANCING. The caption "Financing" appears when a business is borrowing and the loan is secured by receivables and/or inventory. If the caption is followed by the word *secured,* either there are such loans outstanding or a financing statement has been filed that makes such loans available to the business. If the caption is followed by *secured-unsecured,* both types of loans are outstanding.

CONDITION. One of four descriptive words follow this caption: *strong, good, fair,* or *unbalanced.* This word describes the financial strength of the business but generally also ties in closely with the composite credit appraisal, as reflected in the second part (the letter) of the D&B rating (i.e., *strong* = high, *good* = good, *fair* = fair, and *unbalanced* = limited). However, there are exceptions. If business throughout the trade is slow, the rating could be "good" or "fair" while the firm's condition is "strong." Or the rating may be "blank" ("—") by reason of a criminal conviction even though the firm's condition is "strong" or "good."

TREND. Trends in earnings, worth, and sales are all important, but the "Trend" caption usually reflects *earnings.* In some cases large withdrawals of earnings may make the *worth* trend more significant. If earnings and worth information is unavailable, the trend will reflect *sales.* In instances of conflicting factors, the D&B analyst must judge which is most significant.

Other Sections of the Business Information Report

PAYMENTS. This section shows a company's payment position with its vendors, as reported by suppliers. Each listing in the section will include one or more of the following: the paying record, high credit, amount owing, amount past due (if any), selling terms, and period of time since the last sale. A separate line shows a supplier's comments (for example, "Account in dispute" or "Special agreement"). The dates to the left of the paying record indicate when that particular information was reported.

Some "slowness" generally appears in every representative trade section, and small percentages are not usually considered significant by credit executives. A fair way to calculate the percentage of prompt payments is to count the number of 1s (prompt or better), 2s (mixed, such as "prompt-slow" or "disc-slow"), and 3s (slow). Each user should establish guidelines for an acceptable amount of slowness. Even in the strongest companies, 20 percent of payments may show some slowness. Where the risk is greater, some analysts prefer a deeper analysis, such as dollar weighting.

From the Payments section, a supplier intending to open a new account receives a good indication of what to expect when dealing with the customer—based on the previous payment experiences of others.

FINANCE. This section includes essential facts for determining the financial condition and trend of a business. Many reports contain financial information in the form of audited figures prepared by a certified public accountant (with or without qualification in the accountant's opinion), unaudited figures from the books of account (not prepared by an outside accountant), or management's own estimate of assets, liabilities, sales, expenses, and profit. In any event, no audit is conducted by Dun & Bradstreet.

Principals of some concerns decline to furnish detailed figures, and financial figures may therefore be based on bank and supplier comment, investigation of public records, or the D&B business reporter's own estimates of certain estimated tangible balance sheet items.

Financial information is also frequently supplemented with information regarding leases, insurance coverage, and other pertinent details. Comment in the Finance section is devoted to further necessary explanation of the figures and to a description of sales and profit trends. D&B bases its rating to a large extent on the degree of financial stability and the trend reflected in this section.

BANKING. Information on banking relations may include average balances, previous and current loan experience, whether loans are secured or unsecured, the length of time the bank has had the account, and whether the bank considers the account satisfactory. A date to the left indicates when this information was reported to D&B.

Sometimes the report provides the names of some or all of the account's banks, though not necessarily in order of importance.

HISTORY. This section contains the names and past business experience of the firm's principals or owners. Such information is usually obtained from the firm's management. Past business experience and outside affiliations of principals are important considerations in evaluating a company's management. D&B uses its own files where feasible to verify and augment the information provided by management. Other background information is usually not verified.

D&B reports any criminal proceedings it learns of for as long as they are pending. If a conviction results, it is reported for 25 years. In general, historical information is not repeated after 25 years, except for such items as corporate charter or trade-style registration dates and principals' educational background and date of birth.

The History section can be used to verify ownership; identify owners, partners, or officers; and reveal the outside interests of the principals.

OPERATION. This section describes what a company does and the nature of the premises, the neighborhood, and the size of floor space. Also described—wherever applicable—are the lines of merchandise it sells or the kinds of services it supplies, as well as the price range, classification of customers, selling terms, percentage of cash and credit sales, number of accounts, seasonal aspects, and number of employees.

By describing the machinery of production and distribution, the Operation section gives the reader a better understanding of the company's balance sheet and profit and loss figures. The report user is also better able to judge whether capital is adequate or debt is excessive. Sales departments use this section to determine whether the company could be a profitable outlet for their lines of merchandise. Purchasing departments use the information to determine the vendor's capacity to deliver an order or support guarantees.

SPECIAL EVENTS. This section highlights significant events that might vitally affect a present credit relationship or pending credit decision, including recent changes of chief executive, legal structure, partners, control, business location, or business name, bankruptcy updates, business discontinuances, criminal proceedings, burglaries or embezzlements, and fires and other disasters.

The Special Events section appears after the Heading and Summary so it can be noticed immediately.

PUBLIC FILINGS. This section identifies public civil filings, such as bankruptcies, suits, judgments, Uniform Commercial Code filings, liens, and record item updates and releases. While it is impossible to provide coverage of all public record information, D&B provides many significant items. The Public Filings section appears between the Finance and Banking sections of the report.

Payment Analysis Reports (PAR)

These reports (see Figure 15–1) provide an in-depth but concise report card on a firm's payment habits. Subscribers use PAR as a complement to the D&B Business Information Report on new or important accounts or by itself to periodically check smaller or more established customers. The key to PAR is the PAYDEX, a single numerical value that serves as an at-a-glance indicator of a company's current payment posture. The PAYDEX is used to compare the payments of an individual company with other companies in the same line of business and same size range. PAR provides a valuable monthly summary of a firm's payment habits for the previous 12 months and summarizes both the amounts of "credit extended" and the firm's "manner of payment" in an easy-to-read format.

Dun's Financial Profiles

These profiles (see Figure 15–2) provide extensive financial spreadsheets on over 1 million U.S. firms, publicly held and private, large and small, in a format that makes it possible for readers to quickly and easily evaluate financial trends and analyze how these firms compare with their own line-of-business groups (by Standard Industrial Classification number and by asset size range). The profiles also provide a screening service to identify qualified prospects for marketing acquisition or investment purposes using a wide variety of selection criteria provided by the subscriber.

Continuous Service

This service provides automatic notification of recent developments affecting accounts on which the subscriber has ordered a D&B report. It is a "watchdog" service for monitoring key or marginal accounts that a subscriber has registered with D&B. Continuous PAR, another monitoring service, notifies subscribers when any of the accounts that they have registered with D&B undergoes a change in payment score of more than 10 points up or down.

VIP Reports/Special Purpose Reports

Subscribers who need information beyond that found in the Business Information Report or supplied by Continuous Service can use D&B's VIP Reports. Each of these reports furnishes comprehensive and detailed information in answer to specific questions raised by individual subscribers. VIP Reports provide facts on important customers in answer to subscribers' questions.

Subscribers indicate the nature of their question or problem on a special-request form. After a comprehensive investigation and analysis, D&B prepares a report to meet the particular need. Because of their comprehensive nature, the detailed and lengthy investigation, and the time necessary to complete them, these reports cost more than the Business Information Reports.

Use of Credit Reports by Subscribers

Subscribers use detailed credit reports for a variety of business purposes. While credit reports usually serve credit purposes, much of the same information is valuable for other business activities. Subscribers normally request reports for the following credit purposes:

1. To appraise the creditworthiness of a new account for which the subscribers have no data on file and for which the D&B *Reference Book* rating is not a sufficient basis for a credit decision.
2. To review active credit files to keep informed of the progress and current condition of accounts. Periodic review of accounts is the basis on which customers' lines of credit and terms of sale are adjusted to their financial standing.
3. To determine the underlying causes of slow and doubtful accounts. Current information often helps subscribers convert such accounts into profitable customers.

4. To provide a sound basis for decision making when customers want to expand their line of credit or when marked changes in paying habits occur.

In addition to the uses cited above, credit reports should be requested whenever the credit manager's confidence in the debtor has been shaken. A number of circumstances can create this condition, such as radical fluctuations in a firm's buying policies and financial dealings, suspected fraud or misrepresentation, legal proceedings, and "acts of God."

Sales departments can use credit reports on new businesses and prospective customers not only to provide a basis for extending credit but also to determine the prospect's sales potential. Salespeople are better equipped to sell when they have advance knowledge of a prospect's operations, scope of activities, and financial capacity. Similarly, such reports help sales departments determine if a firm warrants a higher line of credit or has not reached its full sales potential.

The coordinated use of detailed credit reports as suggested above results in the greatest possible advantages to the subscriber. When credit reports serve more than one purpose, it is easy to justify their costs.

THE DUN & BRADSTREET *REFERENCE BOOK*

The Dun & Bradstreet *Reference Book* contains the names and credit ratings of almost 3 million commercial, industrial, and service enterprises located throughout the United States, Puerto Rico, and the U.S. Virgin Islands. Although D&B is well known for this activity, the preparation of credit reports is the backbone of the organization. Information gathered for credit reports contributes to the financial ratings and changes that occur in the *Reference Book*. Despite the fact that this function is of secondary importance at D&B, *Reference Book* ratings are frequently referred to by credit managers. In fact, checking a firm's capital-and-credit rating is frequently the first step in credit risk appraisal. In many instances this rating alone is sufficient to reveal a high degree of creditworthiness.

Contents of the *Reference Books*

The *Reference Book,* which is prepared in four separate sections, is published every two months and leased to subscribers. It contains a complete listing of most businesses in every city, town, and village in the United States, Puerto Rico, and the U.S. Virgin Islands. Other editions of the *Reference Book* are also available; one covers only the United States, a *State Sales Guide* covers each state, and a number of sectional editions include listings of several states. These smaller editions are exact copies of the state or metropolitan information contained in the larger volumes and are published in a convenient 9-by-11-inch briefcase size. Company representatives, especially salespeople, use the state editions to appraise customers conveniently, build prospect lists, and gain helpful information about their territories.

The books contain ratings on manufacturers, wholesalers, retailers, and other businesses on which Dun & Bradstreet has written a Business Information Report. Listings are alphabetical by state, then by town within the state. Following the town name is the population and the county in which the community is located. This information is followed by an alphabetical listing of businesses.

Each business name is preceded by a U.S. Standard Industrial Classification code number, which indicates the nature of the business. For example, 52 51 is the SIC code designating retail hardware, and all hardware stores have this code number preceding the business name. The number immediately after some of the business names indicates the business was started within the last 10 years. The number is the last digit of the year within the 10-year period. To the extreme right, and following this information, is the firm's rating. If the business is new to the current edition of the *Reference Book,* the letter *A* is posted to the left of the business classification code; the letter *C* in the same place means a rating change occurred with the current edition. An illustration of a *Reference Book* page is shown in Figure 15–6.

Explanation of Ratings

A Dun & Bradstreet rating consists of two elements: (1) a firm's established financial strength and (2) its composite credit appraisal. The estimated financial strength is expressed in the letter portion of the rating. (See Figure 15–5 for the Dun & Bradstreet key to ratings.) These 15 codes (5A to HH) designate the company's range of net worth or financial strength. The composite credit appraisal is a general credit grade of high, good, fair, or limited, expressed by number.

Estimated financial strength is a conservative estimate of the firm's tangible net worth. This is arrived at by analyzing the firm's financial statements or other financial data, after allowances for intangible items such as goodwill or patents.

The composite credit appraisal, an evaluation of the firm's ability and willingness to pay and of its past history in meeting its obligations, is based on the length of time in business, the abilities of management, general financial condition, the trend of the business, payment record data, and the like. If these factors are judged to be strong, D&B may assign the firm a high credit rating; if they are judged to be weak, it may assign a lower rating. The exact credit rating used depends on the strength or weakness of all the above factors in relation to one another.

The assignment of the rating is made by the reporter at the time of report revision. An automated rating assistance algorithm (RATE)

FIGURE 15–6 **Specimen Page from the Dun & Bradstreet *Reference Book***

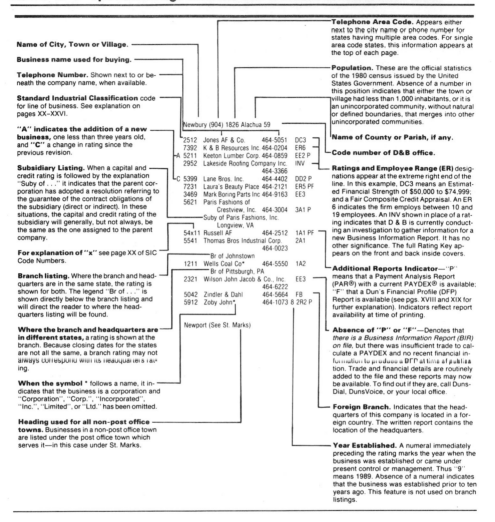

suggests a rating to the reporter based on the company's position relative to industry norms and D&B guidelines.

As new data such as late financial information, changes in manner of payment, or courthouse information is added, the RATE algorithm compares the existing rating to the proposed rating. Each case or revision is reviewed by a D&B specialist, and a new rating, based on the latest data, may be applied.

In some instances, D&B isn't able to assign a capital or credit rating, or both. The symbols used to denote these uncommon circumstances are explained in Figure 15–5 in the key to ratings.

Use of the D&B *Reference Book* by Credit Managers

The D&B *Reference Book* contains a large amount of useful information for credit managers. In general, the books are highly regarded throughout the credit profession because they frequently offer a basis for quick approval of orders. Experienced credit managers, however, use them with caution; although a new *Reference Book* is published every two months, the information is not always current. In any event, *Reference Books* are not normally used as a basis to refuse credit but rather may indicate the need for additional information. Any publication as vast in scope and detail as the *Reference Book* cannot be produced without some errors. However, D&B now uses computers and advanced printing technology, and timeliness has been improved.

Serious shortcomings may be due not to the publication task but to the nature of the investigating task. It is impossible to investigate each name immediately before a revised edition. Furthermore, ratings are the result of human judgment based on the information available. No rating system is infallible, and the merits of a rating system cannot compensate for the deficiencies in human judgment. Credit reporters may gather insufficient information or rely too heavily on certain sources. Some businesses won't reveal their financial condition and other facts, so the reporter must rely on the best available sources of indirect information. In these cases, *estimates* of financial condition are made, errors in judgment occur, and the actual status of the company may not be fully ascertained. However, since 1974 D&B has assigned no full capital-and-credit rating *without book figures* if tangible net worth exceeds $50,000.

Despite these limitations, subscribers to the *Reference Book* can use it to advantage in the following circumstances:

Credit departments can:
> Set up credit lines by ratings.
> Check small and sample orders.
> Review continuously important changes in customers and
>> prospects.

Purchasing departments can:
> Locate sources of supply.
> Verify credit standings of suppliers.
> Determine responsibility of vendors.

Sales departments can:
> Brief salespersons on accounts.
> Estimate purchasing power.
> Build and revise prospect files.
> Spot new prospects (names prefixed by *A*).

Reclassify prospects (rating changes highlighted by *C*).

Select prospective distributors.

Guide sales research in selected areas.

OTHER ACTIVITIES

DunsDial

Within seconds, this direct, toll-free telephone service gives regular subscribers access to information on any one of the businesses with data stored in the D&B computerized business information files. Since early 1989 computerized delivery of the reports via fax transmission has been available.

DunsPrint

This access system puts hard-copy Business Information Reports and other information formats in D&B subscribers' hands within minutes. DunsPrint is the ultimate in business information communications—the instant relay of information to personal computers and/or print terminals located on the customer's premises. (A two-page Business Information Report ordinarily takes less than one minute to print.) Formats available are:

Business Information Reports (full display).

Credit Advisory Service (CAS).

Bankers Advisory Service (BAS).

Payment Analysis Reports (PAR).

Dun's Financial Profiles.

Rating & Verification Display.

Summary Display.

Family Tree Service.

Credit Clearing House Recommendation.

EVALUATION OF DUN & BRADSTREET

Dun & Bradstreet follows the previously set criteria in selecting information supplying the information credit analysts need. The important selection factors are: accuracy of information, contents of reports, speed of reporting, cost of service, trade coverage, geographic coverage, variety and number of reports, and supplemental services offered. And credit managers need the following information: identity and legal responsibility, history and business background, character and responsibility of management, financial ability and strength, and payment experience.

While D&B is not free of limitations and errors, it meets the above criteria. The agency's interest is to report facts as accurately and completely as possible. As the most comprehensive source of commercial credit information, D&B reports the facts as it knows them. The procedures of reporting are constantly being improved, and Dun & Bradstreet requests that its subscribers report errors.

D&B's trade and geographic coverage are the most complete in the credit reporting industry. With its large number of reporters, the agency can supply a credit report on any business located anywhere in the country. Dun & Bradstreet does not claim to gather information from sources that would be unavailable to creditors; it acquires its information from the same sources available to all credit managers. Creditors can undertake their own direct investigation, but Dun & Bradstreet's facilities are tailored to this purpose.

Dun & Bradstreet reports give creditors much of the information necessary to make an informed credit decision. If certain types of credit information are not available or the firm has failed to supply financial statements, such shortcomings in the data are clearly apparent to the subscriber. Subscribers can then conduct direct investigations to acquire any necessary missing data. The agency's variety of reports, Continuous Service, *Reference Books,* and collection services fulfill the requirements of most commercial creditors. The broad scope of the agency's services alleviates problems associated with making credit decisions, controlling and collecting accounts receivable, and periodically revising information.

The final responsibility for the credit decision, however, rests with the credit executives. They must decide the amount of information they need, the sources they should use, the reliability of the information, and the weight they should give to the various data they have.

DISCUSSION QUESTIONS

1. Why is it necessary for credit managers to have knowledge of a variety of sources of credit information even though they may use only a few?

2. Why is Dun & Bradstreet referred to as the "general agency"?

3. How did economic and business developments in the early 1900s influence credit risk and the need for organized sources of credit information?

4. List the principal activities of Dun & Bradstreet, and explain each one briefly.

5. Of the various activities of Dun & Bradstreet, which one is the "backbone" of the agency's business? Why?

6. Discuss the credit managers' need for and the usefulness of D&B's Key Accounts Reports and its Continuous Service.

7. Under what circumstances would you request the agency's credit reports? Why wouldn't you request them for each credit decision?

8. What is the basis for the ratings used in D&B's *Reference Book?*

9. What credit and other business uses do the *Reference Book* ratings serve?

10. Do the services of Dun & Bradstreet fulfill the credit information needs of credit management? Can you note any deficiencies in the services?

11. What qualifications do you believe a reporter of Dun & Bradstreet should have?

12. What is the Standard Industrial Classification? Why does Dun & Bradstreet use it?

13. Do you believe the rating system used by Dun & Bradstreet is satisfactory? Why or why not?

14. Who has the ultimate responsibility for the credit decision? Why?

CHAPTER

16

Basis of the Commercial Credit Decision—Other Commercial Credit Reporting Agencies

The Objectives or Goals of Chapter 16 Are:

1. To explain the organization and activities of the National Association of Credit Management (NACM).
2. To discuss the operations of the Business Credit Reporting Service of NACM.
3. To point out the contents and interpretation of a National Business Credit Report.
4. To appraise the credit interchange system of the NACM.
5. To cover the activities of the Business Credit Division of TRW.
6. To investigate Dun & Bradstreet's interest in specialized credit reporting.
7. To explain the activities of the Credit Clearing House.
8. To appraise the credit services of specialized agencies.

Other commercial credit reporting agencies include the Business Credit Reporting Service of the National Association of Credit Management, the Business Credit Division of TRW, as well as a number of specialized mercantile agencies.

NATIONAL ASSOCIATION OF CREDIT MANAGEMENT

The National Association of Credit Management is the oldest and largest professional and service association representing commercial and financial credit personnel in the United States. In 1896, when the association was formally organized, credit managers operated in a vastly different climate. Fraud and misrepresentation were common, and creditors lacked adequate commercial laws to prosecute the guilty and protect their business. For example, it was almost impossible to prosecute debtors who, on the verge of insolvency, sold the assets of their business and pocketed the proceeds. Such actions ignored the interests of creditors and violated the present-day theory that an insolvent business belongs to its creditors. This situation was further aggravated by the rapid growth of interstate commerce and the absence of a uniform federal bankruptcy law to deal with financially distressed businesses. The few state laws at the time were contradictory and complex and generally failed to protect creditors.

Financial statements, though used infrequently in analyzing a risk's creditworthiness, could not be relied on, and no laws protected the creditor. Credit managers did not exchange credit information, and many creditors deliberately attempted to deceive by revealing inadequate or incorrect information.

Any individual attempt to improve the ethical standards of the profession or to raise the quality of the credit structure was recognized as futile. All credit managers, however, working together could impose ethical standards on the industry, raise the quality of the credit structure, and develop a scientific approach to the mutual problems of credit management. The National Association of Credit Management realized that cooperation was necessary to cope with such problems, which were intensifying through a growing demand for credit. From a humble beginning of less than 600 members, NACM today numbers more than 40,000 members from leading manufacturing, wholesaling, and financial institutions.

Organization

Today, with headquarters in Columbia, Maryland, the association is organized into affiliated local chapters representing most of the nation's major and minor markets. Each local chapter is governed by elected officers, and most chapters employ a full-time administrator of association activities as well as full-time clerical help. Local units are organized into departments for the various services they render, such as legislation, education, business credit reporting, and collection.

The coordinating unit is NACM, which is governed by elected officers and a board of directors. The activities of the national association are directed by a full-time president and a paid staff. Dues grant membership in both the local chapter and the national association.

Activities

In addition to operating credit interchange bureaus, the association fulfills its objectives and meets the individual needs of its membership by engaging in the following activities:

1. *Loss prevention.* The loss prevention department[1] detects and prosecutes perpetrators of commercial frauds.

---

[1]Jim Choplick, Jr., "Conference Opens Eyes to Far-Reaching Fraud," *Business Credit,* May/June 1990, p. 32.

2. *Education.* The National Institute of Credit offers educational opportunities in the credit, banking, business law, and merchandising fields to members, their associates and assistants, and others who want to train for a career in credit work. Credit institutes and seminars are conducted at major universities throughout the country.

3. *Legislation.* The legislative department has a continuing program for the correction, modification, repeal, or enactment of both federal and state laws that affect credit and finance.

4. *Adjustments.* Adjustment bureaus of NACM[2] are maintained throughout the United States and specialize in the orderly administration of distressed businesses. The bureaus function for the benefit of creditors by acting as assignee, trustee, or receiver and by attending creditors' meetings and making recommendations.

5. *Collections.* NACM operates a nationwide collection service for members.

6. *Publications.* NACM publishes the *Credit Manual of Commercial Laws* annually and *Business Credit,* a monthly magazine.

7. *Research.* The Credit Research Foundation, founded by NACM in 1949, sponsors and encourages credit research concerned with credit conditions and practices of either a general or specific nature. It has prepared and edited the *Credit Management Handbook* and other publications.

8. *Industry and trade group meetings.* NACM sponsors industry and trade group meetings made up of credit and financial management people who meet regularly to discuss credit problems and economic trends. Trade group meetings also give members the opportunity to discuss their experiences with specific accounts.

9. *Foreign credit interchange.* Finance, Credit, and International Business, established in 1919, provides a ready source of payment record data on thousands of foreign buyers located throughout the world. Members of NACM may subscribe to its services on a cost basis.

BUSINESS CREDIT REPORTING SERVICE (NACM)

Originally called credit interchange bureaus, the service was at first operated on a local-market basis. It was soon found that information gathered from one market was insufficient for members' requirements, and a system for interchanging ledger experience among bureaus was developed. In 1919 a central bureau was organized in St. Louis so various bureaus, although independently operated, could exchange their information and reports. Not until 1921 did NACM take over the central bureau, and with 15 participating bureaus it established the National Credit Interchange System.

---

[2]Gary L. Wartik, "NACM Adjustment Bureaus," *Business Credit,* April 1988, p. 8.

Organization

Today the National Business Credit Reporting Service is entirely an operation of the National Association of Credit Management.[3] The system comprises a coordinating unit, the Service Corporation of NACM, and 59 local bureaus (plus bureaus in Hawaii and Canada) covering major and minor markets. Each local bureau operating in the system is member-owned and member-operated under the supervision of the local NACM association. Membership is open to manufacturers, wholesalers, and other middlemen, and bankers, regardless of trade line or geographic location. The underlying principles of each bureau are (1) member direction and control and (2) service charges just adequate to cover the costs of operation. The bureaus serve as mediums for assembling and disseminating the credit information supplied and used by member-creditors.

The entire system is administered by NACM.

Method of Operation

The successful and efficient operation of the Business Credit Reporting Service depends almost entirely on the cooperation of its members. To encourage member cooperation and to perpetuate an efficient system, the mechanics of the operation have been coordinated and standardized.

The system operates on the basis of information accumulated in a national databank; each participating member furnishes aged trial balance information every 30 days.

Knowing how a customer company or a prospective customer company pays its bills is the base of any sound credit decision. NACM credit reports have been providing this information since 1904. In the fast-paced economy of the 1990s, when credit decisions must be made quickly, NACM associations use automation instead of the old mail/telephone system of gathering credit information.

NACM associations today offer their members fast, accurate, current, and objective information within minutes after a request for a credit report has been received. Information in the automated files of NACM is supplied by a broad spectrum of local, regional, and national firms.

National Business Credit Reports answer many key questions about a customer. Does it pyramid its buying? Does it pay one creditor on time but not others? Is it using the creditor's working capital? Are its total purchases within safe limits? What is the trend of its business?

---

[3]*Facts about NACM* (Columbia, Md.: The National Association of Credit Management, 1990).

CONTENTS AND INTERPRETATION OF A NATIONAL BUSINESS CREDIT REPORT

An illustrative National Business Credit Report is shown in Figure 16–1. Unlike many other types of credit reports, this one offers no recommendations or opinions. Personal views that are not based on actual ledger experience are not included. The report merely presents facts based on creditors' actual ledger experiences arranged in an orderly manner for rapid appraisal. Because the report contains a large amount of information, it should be appraised carefully and properly. A quick and superficial appraisal may result in faulty interpretation and failure to uncover the true significance of the data.

FIGURE 16–1 **NACM National Business Credit Report**

The National Business Credit Report of the National Association of Credit Management (NACM) has been created to display information needed for a prompt, informed credit decision. Coverage is national in scope. The form was designed by credit experts working directly with experienced technical personnel. This has ensured a standardized format that is objective and easy to read, concerning how businesses pay their suppliers.

The report displays the following categories of information:

PAYMENT HISTORY—Ledger experience from individual member companies including: Member Number Identification • Business Category • Year Opened • Date Information Reported • Last Activity • High Credit • Total Owing • Account Balances Displayed in Current and Past Due Categories • Payment Terms • Member Remarks

TRADE LINE TOTALS—Summary of the individual reported trade experiences both in dollar totals and percentages of the columns pertaining to "Account Balance" and aging of "Account Status."

MONTHLY PAYMENT TREND—Summary of account balances and aging for the three preceding months—again, by both dollar totals and percentages.

QUARTERLY PAYMENT TREND—Derived from summaries within the previous three calendar quarters, this feature provides a comparison or trend of the paying habits of the subject business.

NATIONAL ASSOCIATION OF CREDIT MANAGEMENT

NATIONAL BUSINESS CREDIT REPORT

REPORT ON: ID# DATE JANUARY 1, 1990

ACME INDUSTRIES
2840 COAST HIGHWAY
PANORAMA CITY, CA 90001

REPORT FOR MEMBER # 95-4102

JOHN DOE COMPANY INC
2300 W OLYMPIC BLVD
LOS ANGELES CA 90006

ON FILE SINCE

BUSINESS CATEGORY	YR OPEN	DATE REPTD	LAST ACTIVITY	HIGH REPTD	ACCOUNT BALANCE					PAYMENT TERMS	RMKS
104738GEMD	82	1289	1289	10000	8800	8800				110N30	
100236ESMF	81	1289	989	50000	42000	2000	18000	10000	12000		COD
950152ESNF	80	1189	1089	45000	25300	5000	20300			VARIOUS	
950512INDS	80	189	1289	38900	38900			38900		N30	
890211MISC	80	189	1289	21600	15600	4000	4000	7600		210N30	UDS
952792NFER	79	1189	1189	2500	1500	1500				210N30	SAT
943441TIMF	80	189	1289	12000	8000	6000	2000			N10	
954295ALWO	81	1289	989	6300	5000				5000	NET	DIP
965201ETRO	80	189	1089	25000	20000	3000	7000	10000			SPT
950013TRUC	82	1289	1289	60000	10000	10000				110N30	
TRADE LINE TOTAL			10 ACCOUNTS		175100	40300	90200	27600	17000		
						23.0%	51.5%	15.8%	9.7%		
MONTHLY PAYMENT TREND											
	1289		8 ACCOUNTS		144400	63800	60600	10000	10000		
						44.1%	42.0%	6.9%	6.9%		
	1189		9 ACCOUNTS		125000	65000	40000	20000			
						52.0%	32.0%	16.0%			
	1089		9 ACCOUNTS		125000	65000	40000	20000			
						52.0%	32.0%	16.0%			
QUARTERLY PAYMENT TREND											
	0989		8 ACCOUNTS		150000	72000	42450	30550	5000		
						48.0%	28.3%	20.4%	3.3%		
	0689		7 ACCOUNTS		92000	29500	30500	24000	8000		
						32.1%	33.1%	26.1%	8.7%		
	0389		7 ACCOUNTS		80000	20000	30000	30000			
						25.0%	37.5%	37.5%			

CONFIDENTIAL

The accuracy of this report is not guaranteed. Its contents have been gathered in good faith from members, but no representations can be made as to the accuracy of the information gathered and contained in the report. This bureau disclaims liability for the negligence of any person or entity resulting in an inaccuracy in the report. This report is prepared and distributed for use in the extension only of commercial and business credit.

FIGURE 16–1   (concluded)

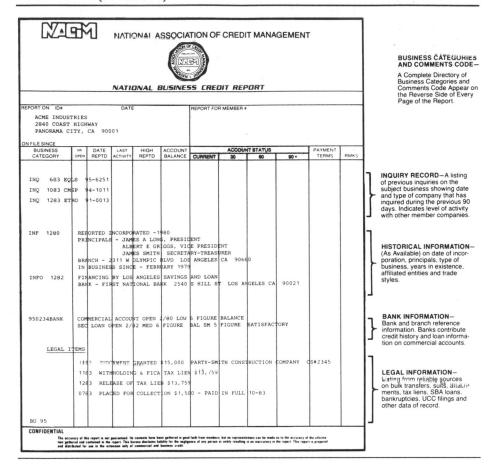

Comments

This part of the report provides space for information that can clarify the ledger facts recorded in preceding columns. The trend of payments experienced by creditors often appears in this column. In general, data that shows no change, improvement, slowness, and the like is valuable in determining the stability of the risk. Any report that shows a large number of unfilled orders in this column should signal further investigation. When comments are particularly unfavorable, such as "collect" or "legal," users should appraise the general character of the report—particularly, the date of the transaction involved so that unfavorable information of long standing is not regarded as current.

NACM recommends that creditors request a National Business Credit Report to investigate a new order, when they receive an unusually large order from a customer, and when they receive a large number of direct inquiries on a customer. Likewise, a report should be requested on all slow-pay accounts and when the creditor is anticipating special collection action against the debtor. Furthermore, the association recommends that creditors keep close watch on important customers and doubtful accounts, by using the automatic revision service. This service gives members a series of new, up-to-date reports at intervals they designated. Such reports permit creditors to keep a close check on the paying habits of their customers and also to determine the share of volume secured from good customers.

APPRAISAL OF THE NACM CREDIT SYSTEM

The NACM credit system is one of the most widely and frequently used sources of credit information. The system's strength accrues from its operation by NACM, which is one of the nation's largest, most respected, and most influential trade associations. Each company represented in the association is either a National Business Credit Report user or a potential member of the system. The varied services of the association and the high esteem with which members regard these services add to the system's strength and overall value.

Perhaps the system's greatest weakness stems from the fact that it is a cooperative venture and hence must depend on its many members reacting in a like manner in supplying ledger information and answering subsequent inquiries. For maximum total effectiveness of the system each member must be prompt, thorough, and truthful. In addition, each credit department member who answers inquiries and analyzes reports affects the quality of the system. Unless these people are trained to understand the reports and the workings of the system, the system itself can't operate with maximum effectiveness. In areas where communication is easy and where members of the NACM credit system are actively interested in using and promoting the system, it seems to work well. In some areas, though, these qualities are lacking.

Despite these weaknesses, a cooperative method of gathering ledger information is the most efficient method known in the industry. To overcome the shortage of trained credit department personnel, the association has developed educational programs and publishes a great deal of literature.

Other than what users can imply from a careful analysis, the National Business Credit Report does not reveal information concerning either the subject's business background or the character and responsibility of management. The credit report is most comprehensive when dealing with a customer's immediate past and present payment record. The report does not estimate the subject's financial condition (but users can do so if they analyze the data properly). For these reasons, some credit executives regard the report as supplemental to other types of reports.

Despite the fact that the National Business Credit Report does not fill all the needs of credit management, ledger information is one of the most important types of information used in the industry, followed by the financial statement, the creditor's past experience, and then history and antecedents. While credit management needs several types of credit information, there is considerable variation in the value attached to each and in the frequency with which some kinds of data are needed. The superiority of the National Business Credit Report stems from the frequency with which ledger data can change; antecedents, method of operation, and financial statements change only over extended periods of time. The rapidity with which ledger data changes contributed to the development of NACM's credit system. Because ledger information changes frequently, each new credit report should assist the creditor in making proper and current revision of a customer's accounts. Finally, the National Business Credit Report is not intended to replace financial and operating statements but to be used in conjunction with these statements. When credit management does this, it marshals the most valuable data used in making a credit decision.

BUSINESS CREDIT DIVISION OF TRW

In addition to its consumer credit reporting services, TRW also provides commercial credit reports through its Business Credit Division. The company entered this market in July 1976, with the nation's first automated system for collecting and reporting objective and up-to date commercial credit information in all major industries. Subscribers obtain the TRW Business Profile reports within seconds by using a computer terminal. The cost of the report depends on volume and whether the subscriber contributes accounts receivables data to TRW.

In general, the TRW Business Profile report gives commercial credit executives a quick and precise view of how a company is currently paying its bills from suppliers. The report also summarizes how a company has paid its bills during the previous five quarters. More specifically, the Business Profile report includes the following:

- Current and previous payment information.
- Days beyond terms calculation.
- Payment trends.
- Industry payment profiles.
- Public record information.
- Financial information from Standard & Poor's Corp.
- Key facts on the company, such as sales figures, number of employees, and names of company principals.
- Information on debts owed to government agencies.

Information is contributed to TRW every 30 to 90 days by commercial credit grantors across the country.

In addition to the Business Profile report, this TRW division also markets a Small Business Profile, which details credit history of a small-business owner. Introduced in 1988, this report was developed to meet the needs of commercial credit grantors who consider a business owner's personal credit history when deciding on extending a commercial loan.

TRW Business Credit also offers a trade verification service, a public record monitor service, and an account monitor service.

For a summarization of TRW's business services, see Figure 16–2.[4] Both the Business Credit and Credit Data Divisions are headquartered in Orange, California.

SPECIALIZED MERCANTILE AGENCIES

The network of mercantile credit reporting comprises an undetermined number of specialized credit reporting agencies. Some of these agencies are corporate enterprises, others are operated by trade associations. Specialized agencies differ from general agencies in the following ways: (1) all of them restrict the credit information they gather and the reports they render to a single line of trade or to a limited number of allied trades; (2) some restrict geographic coverage to a particular territorial region;[5] and (3) some restrict their credit information to a special type of activity or concentrate on services valuable to the trade involved.

Manufacturers, wholesalers, and other suppliers who merchandise their products to businesses in a particular line or in a few allied fields use specialized agencies' services. As will be shown in subsequent sections, much of the value in using these sources of credit information stems from the specialized nature of their activities.

DUN & BRADSTREET'S INTEREST IN SPECIALIZED CREDIT REPORTING

While Dun & Bradstreet is principally concerned with general agency activities, it entered the field of specialized credit reporting when R. G. Dun & Co. acquired the National Credit Office, Inc. (NCO), in 1931, and Dun & Bradstreet acquired the Credit Clearing House, Inc. (CCH), in 1942.

---

[4]Also see, Andrea Gordon Rosen, "TRW Tries to Make a Science Out of an Art," *Credit Card Management*, August 1990, p. 51.

[5]Typically, when this is the case, the territory covered corresponds to the geographic concentration of the trade.

FIGURE 16–2

Credit Clearing House

The apparel trades are highly competitive, permeated by the vagaries of fashion and afflicted with a high mortality rate among retail outlets. Because of these characteristics, businesses that sell to the apparel trades confront a degree of risk not ordinarily found in other industries. In recognition of this special need, Credit Clearing House, established in 1888 in St. Paul, Minnesota, became one of the largest specialized credit reporting agencies. Now a division of Dun & Bradstreet, Credit Clearing House rates and prepares credit recommendations on businesses in the apparel trades. It also covers a few allied industries such as jewelry, notions, and gifts as well as mass merchandisers.

A unique feature of Credit Clearing House's operations is its recommendation service. This service facilitates credit decisions on orders from new and unfamiliar accounts, orders from accounts owing past-due amounts, orders exceeding a previous high credit limit, orders from accounts where a sizable credit exposure already exists, and orders from other types of problem accounts. For each inquiry, CCH makes a specific recommendation taking into account the dollar amount of the order. For example, if a subscriber receives an order for $5,000, the recommendation service will indicate whether it should ship all or part of the order or whether a "guideline is not established for this transaction." In the latter case, CCH sends the inquiring subscriber a full D&B Business Information Report to aid it in making a decision.

Credit Clearing House analysts, who are familiar with purchasing habits, trade customs, and seasonal factors of the industry, base their recommendations on Dun & Bradstreet reports and data accumulated from trade sources and credit interchange groups.

CCH subscribers have direct access to business information by means of DunsDial and DunsPrint. A D&B customer service representative, using a video-display terminal, calls up a recommendation display on a particular account and reads it to the subscriber. Information in the recommendation display includes both the D&B *Reference Book* and the *Apparel Trades Book* ratings, the recommendation (which considers the actual dollar amount of the order), and coded reasons to back up the recommendation. A confirmation of the recommendation is mailed to the subscriber.

A companion service offers consultation with an industry specialist and is called Credit Clearing House Tel Con. It customizes the credit opinion to the subscriber's needs and often is able to offer a more positive opinion.

The Credit Clearing House division also supervises publication of the *Apparel Trades Book,* which is issued every three months—February, May, August, and November—and rates over 200,000 wholesalers and retailers in the apparel industry. The arrangement of the *Apparel Trades Book* is similar to that of the Dun & Bradstreet *Reference Book,* except that the ratings are more complex. The Dun & Bradstreet rating consists of two elements, while the Credit Clearing House rating consists of three. A code letter indicates the estimated financial strength; a number—1, 2, 3, or 4—indicates the payments appraisal; and a letter—*A, B, C,* or *D*—indicates the composite appraisal. Figure 16–3 shows the *Apparel Trades Book* key to ratings, which explains the rating system in detail.

FIGURE 16–3 **Credit Clearing House Key to Ratings**

Apparel Trades Book Key to Ratings

		Estimated Financial Strength	Payments Appraisal	Composite Appraisal
B	A	Over $1,000,000	1 2 3 4	A B C D
		. . . . (See Note[1])	1 2 3 4	A B C D
	C	Over 500,000	1 2 3 4	A B C D
F	D	Over 300,000	1 2 3 4	A B C D
	E	Over 200,000	1 2 3 4	A B C D
		. . . . (See Note[1])	1 2 3 4	A B C D
	G	Over 100,000	1 2 3 4	A B C D
K	H	Over 50,000	1 2 3 4	A B C D
	J	Over 30,000	1 2 3 4	A B C D
		. . . . (See Note[1])	1 2 3 4	A B C D
	L	Over 20,000	1 2 3 4	A B C D
	M	Over 10,000	1 2 3 4	A B C D
S	O	Over 5,000	1 2 3 4	A B C D
	R	Over 0,000	1 ? 3 4	A B C D
		. . . . (See Note[1])	1 2 3 4	A B C D
	T	Up to 3,000	1 2 3 4	A B C D

X. . . . Not Classified . . . . See Note [2]

$ The dollar sign ($) preceding a rating indicates that an important part of the total worth consists of real estate or other assets not usually considered working capital.

Note[1]   The letters B, F, K, and S in the Estimated Financial Strength column, indicate in a general way what is considered relative in size. To illustrate: the letter B indicates size comparable to concerns classified in the range A to C inclusive; the letter F, comparable to those from D to G inclusive; the letter K, comparable to those from H to M inclusive; and the letter S, comparable to those from O to T inclusive.

Note[2]   The letter X is not to be construed as unfavorable but, in the column or columns in which used, signifies circumstances difficult to definitely classify within condensed rating symbols and should suggest to the subscriber the advisability of reading the detailed report.

OTHER SPECIALIZED COMMERCIAL CREDIT REPORTING AGENCIES

Lyon Furniture Mercantile Agency

The Lyon Furniture Mercantile Agency, established in 1876 by Robert P. Lyon, is the oldest and one of the most important special mercantile agencies. Over the years the Lyon agency has expanded its operations, so that today it reports on credit risks in the furniture, interior decoration, major home appliance, contract furnishings, and mobile home trades, as well as on credit risks among department stores and general stores. Within these trades, Lyon covers a large number of allied fields. For example, in the furniture trade it reports on risk in the carpet, floor covering, upholstery, bedding, bedsprings, juvenile furniture, and baby carriage fields; and in the interior decoration trade, it covers risk in the drapery, mirror, picture frame, lamp, lampshade, gift, and home furnishings fields. Also allied to these trades are the veneer, plywood, and hardwood lumber industries. This incomplete listing indicates the extensive scope of the Lyon agency.

Subscribers to the Lyon agency's services are manufacturers and wholesalers selling in the several fields of specialization. According to Lyon management, more than 95 percent of the businesses in the industries it serves subscribe to its services. Lyon will conduct a credit investigation on any business located anywhere in the United States provided it buys from the specified trades.

The Jewelers Board of Trade

The Jewelers Board of Trade is an example of specialized credit reporting by a trade association. This national association, a mutual nonprofit corporation, was organized to promote the interests of the jewelry industry. Throughout the years it has increasingly emphasized assisting members in credit matters. The association's current credit reporting activities are the result of an amalgamation (dating back to 1874) of several credit organizations that operated in the jewelry field. The membership of the Jewelers Board of Trade includes manufacturers, wholesalers, and importers of jewelry and allied trades.

Coverage

Although there is no accurate information about the number of trades covered by specialized mercantile agencies, the following list indicates the extent of coverage: leather and allied trades; fruits, vegetables, and other processed farm products; lumber and woodworking trades; the construction industry; the stationery, typewriter, and office equipment trades; and the textile, apparel, dry goods, and sporting goods trades.

The following list of specialized agencies illustrates the variety of activities covered:

- Chicago Mercantile Exchange.
- Electrical Manufacturers Credit Bureau.
- Liquor Credit Association.
- Lumbermen's Credit Association, Inc.
- Manufacturers Clearing House of Illinois, Inc.
- Printing Trades Credit Association.
- Sporting Goods Industries Clearing House.
- Credit Exchange, Inc.

Appraisal of Specialized Agencies

Most specialized agencies follow the same method of operation as the general agency, except for distinctive features developed to meet the needs of credit management in particular trades. Although major contributors to the field of credit reporting, some agencies limit their scope of trade coverage. Thus they have somewhat fewer members or subscribers and the information exchanged among creditors is less complete. In general, the services performed by more limited agencies are highly flavored with such sources of trade information as trade bulletins, advisory information pertinent to the trade, and trade-specific rating books.

Specialized agencies are an important source of credit information, and their contributions to better credit judgment are significant. Specialized credit reporting agencies, just like the general agency, meet the needs of credit management by supplying data on a subject's identity and legal responsibility, history and business background, managerial character and responsibility, financial ability and strength, and payment record experience. Their credit services should be measured against these criteria. Specialized agencies are also more flexible in adapting their services to the needs of a particular trade.

Many believe that credit investigators and correspondents employed by specialized agencies gain a more thorough knowledge of their particular field. By confining activities, they frequently have more intimate contact with and knowledge of their subjects, a factor that may contribute to more complete and more satisfactory credit reporting. By specializing research in particular trade lines, it may be possible to get more detailed information of broader significance to the credit manager.

Specialized agencies have some disadvantages too. The information they gather has little significance for credit managers whose businesses sell in a wide variety of markets. Because there are no specialized credit reporting agencies in such trade lines as tobacco, coal, eating and drinking places, and many others, the general agency is an indispensable source of credit information for the many marketers who sell in a large number and wide variety of markets. A common criticism of credit managers is that the ledger experiences of the specialized sources are often incomplete. Agency reporters, because of their preoccupation with a particular trade, may fail to investigate markets in which subjects do the greater proportion of their purchasing.

DISCUSSION QUESTIONS

1. Explain the term *ledger experience.*
2. Compare and contrast the activities of NACM with those of Dun & Bradstreet.
3. Compare and contrast the activities of NACM with those of specialized mercantile agencies.
4. Analyze the report reproduced in Figure 16–1. Would you accept or reject this customer's order for $3,500? Why?
5. Why is it important to analyze the entire NACM National Business Credit Report and not base a decision on one or a few columns?
6. What are advantages or strong points of the NACM credit system? Discuss each advantage or strong point you have listed.
7. List the major weaknesses in the system. How should these be corrected?
8. Would you use other types of credit information to augment the NACM National Business Credit Report? If so, what other types? Explain.
9. Discuss the activities of the Business Credit Division of TRW.
10. Explain what TRW's Business Profile report contains.
11. Explain Dun & Bradstreet's interest in specialized credit reporting.
12. How do specialized agencies differ from Dun & Bradstreet?
13. What are the advantages and disadvantages of specialized credit reporting? Discuss.
14. Explain the recommendation service of Credit Clearing House.
15. Why is it said that the Credit Clearing House uses a three-legged rating while Dun & Bradstreet uses a two-legged rating?
16. Discuss the fields of concentration of several specialized commercial credit reporting agencies.
17. Appraise the credit services rendered by specialized commercial credit reporting agencies.

Financial Statements—Analysis and Interpretation

The Objectives or Goals of Chapter 17 Are:

1. To explain the importance of financial statement analysis in credit decision making.
2. To point out the reasons for financial statements.
3. To show the sources from which financial statements can be obtained.
4. To discuss the various types of accounting opinions appearing on financial statements.
5. To explain the importance of cash flow.
6. To set forth the steps involved in the preliminary appraisal of financial statements.
7. To discuss financial statement legislation.

Credit executives need financial statements for the same reason they need other types of credit information—to arrive at proper and sound credit decisions. Thus analysis of financial statements is one essential part of a credit decision. Such an analysis involves an examination of balance sheet and operating statement details, review of trial balance information and schedules supporting financial statements, and consideration of economic conditions, both general and in the particular industry involved.

The balance sheet is a statement of the financial condition of a company as of a moment in time. In other words, it is a photograph of the business showing its assets, liabilities, and net worth as of the instant in time the "picture is taken."[1] The income statement (sometimes called the profit and loss or operating statement), on the other hand, covers a specific period of time and reflects the sales, cost of goods sold, expenses, and net

---

[1]It is assumed that readers have had a course in the principles of accounting or practical experience in the accounting field. If this is not so, the reader should refer to any basic accounting text for definitions of accounting terms used in this and the succeeding chapter.

profit or loss during the interval covered. The statement of changes in financial position (sometimes called the statement of sources and application of funds) is an outgrowth of the recognition that standard methods of statement analysis provide only partial information about a company's earning power. The statement of changes in financial position is not new, but it has become more popular because of a widening gap between net income or loss and the actual flow of funds.

REASONS FOR FINANCIAL STATEMENTS

As previously stated, credit managers need financial statements to arrive at rational and sound credit decisions.[2] Without this type of information, a credit decision would rest on factors that do not reveal the customer's ability to pay the credit obligation. Because financial information most often reveals this capacity, or probability, credit managers rely heavily on financial statements to guide their decision-making processes. Financial statements also reflect the integrity of the management, which handles the decision-making functions of the business. However, statement analysis is not the sole basis of the credit decision; it is only *one* segment of a larger process known as credit analysis. Supplementary information is often required to correctly interpret what the financial statement reveals.

At this point, a word of caution is appropriate. The credit analyst should not overly rely on financial statements involving accounting subtleties the analyst is unaware of. These can be misleading. For example, problems can arise in the analysis of the "pool of funds concept" valuation of goodwill and in the handling of franchise fees as income rather than a footnoted capital payment.

Other problems in the use of financial statements have been pointed out by Rensis Likert:

> By ignoring a large proportion of their assets, many industries often make sizeable errors in their own financial statements.
>
> These assets include the loyalty and effectiveness of their human organization. They also include supplier loyalty, shareholder loyalty, customer loyalty, and the firm's reputation in the community. But none of these assets is represented in the balance sheet—and virtually no firms keep rigorous quantitative surveillance over them in order to learn whether they are increasing in value from year to year, and by how much.[3]

Requests for financial statements have increased tremendously in recent years, not only between the cash lender and the business borrower

---

[2]For articles on this topic, see the Suggested Readings at the end of the chapter.

[3]Rensis Likert, "Human Resources—The Hidden Assets of Your Firm," reprinted from *Credit & Financial Management,* June 1969, p. 20. Copyright 1969 by the National Association of Credit Management, New York, N.Y. Although this article is out of date, it presents a point of view that is seldom recognized.

Total Contingent Liabilities versus Total Assets, December 31, 1984 (in billions)

Banking Company	Total Contingent Liabilities	Total Assets	Contingent Liabilities as Percent of Total Assets
First National, Chicago	$ 75.054	$ 39.765	188.7%
Bankers Trust	84.773	45.298	187.1
Chemical Bank	91.736	52.957	173.2
Marine Midland	32.264	22.984	140.4
Bank of America	162.103	119.579	135.6
Citibank	194.838	147.071	132.5
Morgan Guaranty	83.248	63.9	130.3
Chase Manhattan	106.529	86.838	122.7
Manufacturers Hanover	70.168	74.492	94.2
Security Pacific	34.571	43.183	80.1
Continental Illinois	24.343	30.524	79.8
Wells Fargo	19.97	27.675	72.2
Crocker National	16.091	22.483	71.6
Mellon Bank	18.234	28.999	62.9
First Interstate	12.543	44.746	28.0

but also between the seller and the buyer of goods. One of the reasons for this increased demand is that a growing number of executives at the credit management level have been trained at universities and colleges in this technique of credit determination. This source of credit information should be used even more in the future as these individuals occupy an even greater number of decision-making positions.

As more firms and banks have called for balance sheets and income statements from their prospective customers, credit applicants have come to recognize the need to make a good showing to obtain credit. Business enterprises that trade on their credit have been forced to adopt accepted accounting practices and techniques, to keep organized and accurate books of record, and to employ the services of competent and recognized accountants who can certify the correctness of the information reported.

As bank regulatory authorities increase the pressure on bank holding companies and banks to strengthen their capital positions, a harder look is being taken at off-balance-sheet liabilities of the banking organizations. Off-balance-sheet liabilities are a worldwide problem. In the United States, the 15 largest banks have about twice as many liabilities off their books as on, as explained in the following quotation and table:

> Some regulators fear that a number of the nation's largest banks—and other banks, as well—have been trying to circumvent the tougher capital rules by reducing the proportion of loans and counterbalancing liabilities in favor of off-balance-sheet items. As a result, a growing number of bankers and analysts expect that at some point the regulators will

require banking companies to attribute capital to at least some of the off-balance-sheet items.

* * * * *

According to these figures, at the end of 1984, contingent liabilities of these 15 banks amounted to $1,026 trillion, or 120.6 percent of their balance sheet assets [see table on page 407].

If federal regulatory authorities decided to apply the full 5½ percent primary capital ratio against the total amount of contingent liabilities—highly unlikely—the nation's largest bank holding companies would have to raise tens of billions of new capital.[4]

SOURCES OF STATEMENTS

The credit grantor can obtain financial statements either from the applicant, from the applicant's bank or accountant, or from a credit agency.

Directly from Risk

The grantor may ask the credit seeker to supply financial statements. Some firms have adopted a policy of asking for a financial statement before the initial credit acceptance and for interim and annual statements. Such a practice becomes almost automatic for the credit customer. Often a standarized form, similar to the one illustrated in Figure 17–1, is furnished to the customer for completion.

Commercial banks and accounting firms are also regarded as "direct" sources of financial statements. Banks sometimes supply financial statements rendered to them for credit purposes. Both the bank and the commercial creditor use the statements for essentially the same purpose. Accounting firms that have certified to the correctness of the customer's accounting procedures, as well as prepared the financial statements, may—on request from the debtor firm—supply statements to creditors.[5]

Indirectly from Mercantile Credit Agencies

The reports furnished by Dun & Bradstreet Business Credit Service and by most of the special mercantile agencies generally contain financial statements that have been furnished to these agencies by the prospective credit customer. In order to show financial trends occurring in the business operation, such reports often contain financial information covering three to five years. These agencies have made a concentrated attempt in

---

[4]Robert Bryant, "Contingent Liabilities—What the Balance Sheet Doesn't Say," *Bankers Monthly Magazine,* August 15, 1985, p. 14. Although more up-to-date data is not available, this quotation and accompanying data present a concept that is often overlooked.

[5]For a discussion of different types of certification, see the subsequent section on types of accounting opinions on financial statements.

FIGURE 17–1 **Financial Statement Form Approved by the National Association of Credit Management**

(This form approved and published by The National Association of Credit Management) FORM 8

FINANCIAL STATEMENT OF

DATE_____ 19____

FIRM NAME_____

Address_____ City_____

At close of business on_____ 19____ State_____

ISSUED TO_____ ◄─── { NAME OF FIRM
Requesting Statement

[PLEASE ANSWER ALL QUESTIONS. WHEN NO FIGURES ARE INSERTED, WRITE WORD "NONE"]

ASSETS	Dollars	Cents	LIABILITIES	Dollars	Cents
Cash in Bank	$		Accounts Payable	$	
Cash on Hand			(For Merchandise)		
			Notes and Acceptances Payable		
Accounts Receivable			(For Merchandise)		
(Amounts Pledged $)			For Borrowed Money:		
Notes and Trade Acceptances Receivable			Notes Payable—Unsecured		
(Amounts Pledged $)					
Merchandise Inventory			Notes Payable—Secured		
(Not on Consignment or Conditional Sale)					
			Income Taxes Payable or Owing		
(Amounts Pledged $)					
Other Current Assets: (Describe)			Other Taxes, including Sales Tax, Owing		
			Rental, Payrolls, Etc., Owing		
			Other Current Liabilities: (Describe)		
TOTAL CURRENT ASSETS			TOTAL CURRENT LIABILITIES		
Land and Buildings (Depreciated Value)			Mortgage on Land and Buildings		
Leasehold Improvements (Amortized Value)			Chattel Mortgage on Merchandise or Equipment		
Machinery, Fixtures and Equipment (Depreciated Value)			Other Liabilities, Unsecured		
			Other Liabilities, Secured (Describe)		
Due From Others — Not Customers					
Other Assets: (Describe)			TOTAL LIABILITIES		
			Capital { Capital Stock $ _____ Surplus $ _____ }		
	$			$	
TOTAL ASSETS			TOTAL LIABILITIES AND NET CAPITAL		

BUY PRINCIPALLY FROM THE FOLLOWING FIRMS:

NAMES	ADDRESSES	AMOUNT OWING
		$

FIGURE 17-1 (concluded)

STATEMENT OF PROFIT AND LOSS FOR PERIOD FROM_____TO_____

NET SALES FOR PERIOD	$		DETAILS OF OPERATING EXPENSES:	$	
Cash $			Salaries — Officers (or owner:) _____		
Credit $					
			Salaries — Employees		
Inventory at start of Period $			Rent, Heat, Light		
			(Include Amortization of Leasehold)		
Purchases for Period $_____			Advertising		
TOTAL $					
Less: Inventory at			Delivery		
Close of Period $_____					
			Insurance		
COST OF GOODS SOLD			Taxes, Including Sales Taxes		
GROSS PROFIT			Depreciation (Fixtures, Trucks, etc.)		
Less: Operating Expense					
			Miscellaneous (Other Operating Expenses)		
NET OPERATING PROFIT				$	
			TOTAL OPERATING EXPENSE		
Other Additions and Deductions (net)					
			SUPPLEMENTAL INFORMATION (DETAILED)	$	
NET PROFIT BEFORE FEDERAL INCOME TAXES			If Incorporated, Amount of Dividends Paid		
				$	
Less: Federal Income Taxes			Interest Paid (Expense)		
	$			$	
NET PROFIT AFTER TAXES			Cash Discount Earned (Income)		

Fire Insurance Carried: On Merchandise $_____On Furniture and Fixtures $_____Other Buildings $_____

Liability Insurance Carried On Premises $_____On Auto and Truck $_____Other Insurance (Type and Am't)_____

Name of Bank_____

Title to Business Premises is in the name of_____

If Premises leased state Annual Rental $_____Lease Expires_____

The foregoing statement (both sides) has been carefully read by the undersigned (both the printed and written material) and is, to my knowledge, in all respects complete, accurate, and truthful. It discloses to you the true state of (our) (my) financial condition on the date indicated. Since that time there has been no material unfavorable change in (our) (my) financial condition other than indicated below under "Remarks."
(We) (I) make the foregoing financial statement in writing intending that you should rely upon it for the purpose of our obtaining merchandise from you on credit. You have my (our) permission to disclose this information in confidence to others in order to facilitate the establishment of additional credit lines with them.

Name of Individual or Firm_____

If Partnership, name partners_____

If Corporation, name officers_____

How long established_____Previous business experience_____
_____where_____

Date of signing Statement_____Street_____City_____State_____

Witness_____Signed by_____

Residence Address
of Witness_____Title_____

REMARKS: (Attach separate sheet if necessary)

recent years to gather financial statements on the business firms they investigate, thus improving their coverage of the financial aspects of credit information for their subscribers.

TYPES OF ACCOUNTING OPINIONS ON FINANCIAL STATEMENTS

Analysts who base a great deal of their credit judgment on financial statements prepared by accountants must understand the kinds of opinions expressed by accountants.

Depending on their findings, accountants may express: (1) an unqualified opinion, (2) an unqualified opinion with qualification as to scope, or (3) a qualified opinion. Accountants express only one kind of opinion on any particular set of financial statements. If they cannot give an opinion under the circumstances, they may present an adverse opinion or a disclaimer of opinion.

A description of the opinions used by accountants is given in the following sections. Although the content of the accountant's report is governed by accepted auditing standards, individual accountants can select language they believe suitable for the circumstances. (It should be noted that some accountants are using three other opinions—audited, reviewed, and compiled.)

Unqualified Opinion

Accountants express unqualified opinions when satisfied that the financial statements present a firm's financial position and results of operations fairly and in conformity with generally accepted accounting principles and practices consistently applied. Accountants should not express unqualified opinions unless they are satisfied in all material respects and have adequate grounds for their opinion.

Unqualified Opinion with Qualification as to Scope

At times the section of an accountant's report dealing with the scope of the examination states that the accountant has not, for example, confirmed the accounts receivable and has not actually observed the taking of inventories. If the receivables and inventories are substantial, the accountant should make a qualification as to the scope of these items. In rare circumstances accountants may have been able to use other auditing procedures to satisfy themselves as to these items; in such cases they should say so and express an unqualified opinion. A qualification as to the scope of the examination does not mean the opinion is qualified.

Qualified Opinion

Accountants express qualified opinions when they believe the statements are a generally fair presentation but they are not completely satisfied on some point or they feel that some part of the financial position or operations is not fairly presented. In general, accountants express qualified opinions when they aren't permitted or are otherwise unable to conduct an examination complete enough to warrant an unqualified opinion or when they discover departures from accepted accounting principles that the firm is not willing to correct.

Adverse Opinion

In an adverse opinion, the auditor states that as a whole the financial statements are not presented fairly in conformity with generally accepted accounting principles. The auditor should have definite evidence of lack of fair presentation, and the exceptions should be so material that a qualified opinion cannot be issued.

Disclaimer of Opinion

Sometimes an auditor is unable to form an opinion as to the fairness of the financial statements and thus disclaims an opinion. For example, an unusual uncertainty may be very material, and the auditor may wish to issue a disclaimer. A disclaimer also should be given if an auditor is not independent.

Other Conditions

Occasionally, credit analysts see financial statements prepared without audit but presented on an accountant's report cover or stationery. Rules of professional conduct, subscribed to by most accountants, state that a warning, such as "Prepared from the books without audit," should appear on each page of such financial statements. The mere appearance of an accountant's name on a financial statement or on the cover of a report does not necessarily mean the accountant has approved it.

PURPOSES OF STATEMENT ANALYSIS

Credit managers approach financial statement analysis with a specific goal in mind. The exact nature of that goal depends on the characteristics of the case at hand. For example, they may have what appears to be a one-time order to approve or disapprove; or they expect a customer to become a repeat buyer and the creditor-debtor relationship to continue over many years. In the former situation they spend less time evaluating the financial statements and arriving at a decision. In the latter circumstance, however, they devote much more time to the financial analysis and attempt to determine the customer's probable continuing profitability. Fortunately, the content and structure of financial statements permit flexibility in analysis, and the precise nature of the analysis can be tailored to the nature of the credit risk.

In general, the analysis of financial statements can determine three major factors: a firm's liquidity, solvency, and managerial efficiency. A credit analyst concerned only with determining the credit case's liquidity is most likely to regard the customer in terms of a one-time order. When the credit risk appears to be one that will be continuing, however, the analyst is more concerned with the customer's long-run financial prospects. Hence the analyst may have to determine liquidity, solvency, and managerial efficiency to arrive at a correct credit decision. The *liquidity* of a business is its ability to meet day-to-day, current obligations. The *solvency* of a business is indicated by its dependence on financial support from creditors contrasted with financial investment by owners. *Managerial efficiency* indicates the firm's ability to operate profitably and successfully over a long period. Whether the analyst approaches the credit case to uncover one, two, or all three financial conditions depends on the nature of the risk and what the analyst must know to arrive at an objective decision.

In any line of trade certain proportions of assets and liabilities are more conducive to successful operation than others and indicate an ability to meet maturing obligations. Thus the proportion of assets to liabilities should be such that the assets supplied by creditors are in no larger proportion than necessary for safety, continued operations, and due division of the risks of the venture between creditors' capital and owners' capital. The debts should also be properly proportioned to liquidity requirements. In a line of trade where most of the assets are highly liquid, these assets may support a larger debt structure than would be true in a line of trade where a large proportion of the resources is invested in fixed or nonliquid form. A proper proportioning of the assets and liabilities also assures continuation of the business—what might be called the safety factor. Too heavy a debt structure is not a sound financial policy to face a period of declining sales. On the other hand, a too conservative borrowing policy may not injure creditors but may interfere with the business's profitable operation.

Acquired assets should be distributed so as to result in profit. Many retail firms make the common mistake of having too large a proportion of assets invested in buildings. Likewise, a manufacturer may have too large a proportion of its resources tied up in fixed form. This often interferes with the business's ability to purchase its desired stock of material. It may interfere with merchants' ability either to carry enough accounts receivable to offer credit service or to stock a sufficiently varied and attractive inventory. Too large an investment in fixed assets leads to the situation sometimes referred to as *frozen*. The firm then may be good, but very slow, in meeting payments. Its resources are invested largely in assets that cannot be quickly converted into cash during normal business processes and that, in the event of emergency, are converted only at considerable sacrifice of value. In case of an emergency the firm may fail despite the possession of large resources because its inability to meet currently maturing liabilities may lead impatient creditors to take drastic legal action.

The business's capital should be in proper proportion to its needs; that is, resources supplied by the investors or owners should be relative to the needs of the business. This may be a matter of both size and proportion. In connection with size, sufficient owner capital should be supplied to enable the business to operate on a scale conducive to success. A business started without sufficient capital to operate efficiently is hampered in competition and growth. Relative to the proportion concept, a sufficient proportion of the capital should be supplied by outside creditors to distribute the risks properly between owned capital and borrowed capital. The proportion of capital supplied by owners should not be so small that creditors are asked to take ownership risks in return for only creditor profits.

The trend, or direction-of-change, concept is slightly different. Credit analysts face the questions both of the firm's current financial status and of where the firm has been and where it is going. These matters are as significant as the current financial position. A firm that falls short of the ideal risk but has been improving may be a better credit risk than a firm that is above the ideal but has been deteriorating over a period of years. The trend concept also recognizes that the standard or ideal may change with business conditions. Deterioration may reflect difficult business conditions; in fact a comparatively small deterioration may be more favorable than a slight improvement under more prosperous conditions.

The credit analyst should be alert to the success or failure of managerial efficiency. Managerial efficiency over a period of time affects the firm's ability to pay even current debts. The credit analyst also may test management's efficiency in meeting new or unexpected conditions. In a period of declining business, has management properly adjusted its asset structure? In a period of business improvement, has management expanded too rapidly without preparing to meet the change that will eventually come? In a period of improvement, has management strengthened the financial structure to be prepared for any future change?

Examination of *all* the financial statements, not just the balance sheet, is crucial to a complete, well-balanced analysis of a business's health. The operating statement should be scrutinized. There are a number of specific devices for testing managerial efficiency. For example, credit analysts may examine the gross profit the firm earns. They may compare the percentage of particular expense items to trade norms. They may see whether the applicant's advertising or selling expenses are too high, whether the firm spends too much for rent, or whether its administrative expense is unduly heavy. Finer classifications of expense items permit very exact and detailed examination of operations.

IMPORTANCE OF CASH FLOW

A basic part of every business operation is cash flow. Since the most important and the most frequently used source of funds for loan repayment comes from the business's normal operations, it is vital that primary consideration be given to cash flow in any credit appraisal. For purposes of financial analysis, cash flow is considered to be the net income for a period, after adding back items deducted as expenses but that currently do not involve the use of cash funds. Likewise, items that are not a current source of funds may be deducted from the net income figure.

Cash flow is one of the most difficult and complicated areas to forecast because many intermixed forces can affect the outcome of business operations. A firm's ability to meet its short-term obligations is important to both the credit analyst and the firm's management, so cash flow forecasting benefits both parties.

A cash flow forecast is a planned procedure for estimating cash receipts and disbursements over a specified time period, usually one year. Since cash is usually budgeted on a monthly basis, management has time to arrange for necessary financing; in turn, the credit analyst can be alerted to situations that may create difficulties in repaying obligations. Although the cash forecast is based primarily on historical data, it also must consider many other factors, including projected expenditures for new plant and equipment, expansion in future sales volume, and the effect of economic conditions on collections and selling terms.

The credit analyst's goal is to predict loan repayment, which is directly correlated with future cash flows. The installment loan officer must know the loan-seeking firm's plans and market estimates before earnings and cash flows can be accurately predicted. In making such predictions, he or she evaluates historical information, forming opinions as to the competency and consistency of the firm's management and evaluating the degree of asset protection. As a general rule, a small business term loan is paid out of earnings rather than out of a liquidation of inventory and receivables, as in commercial credit transactions. Therefore, anticipated earnings, along with the other elements of cash flow, should exceed repayment requirements by a reasonable amount.

Credit professionals and other users of financial statements now use a new financial statement called the *statement of cash flows.*

> During November 1987 the Financial Accounting Standards Board (FASB) issued FAS No. 95, "Statement of Cash Flows." This statement establishes standards for cash flow reporting and supersedes the previous reporting of changes in financial position. A statement of cash flows will now be required for fiscal years ending after July 15, 1988, as part of a full set of financial statements for all business enterprises. The board indicated the primary purpose of a statement of cash flows is to provide relevant information about the cash receipts and cash payments of an enterprise during the reporting period.

It is generally believed that the information presented in a statement of cash flows, when used with the information contained in the balance sheet, income statement and the related notes to the financial statements, should help investors, creditors and others to:

- Assess an enterprise's ability to generate positive future net cash flow.
- Assess an enterprise's ability to meet its obligations and to pay dividends, and its needs for external financing.
- Assess the effects of an enterprise's financial position of both its cash and noncash investing and financing during the reporting period.
- Assess the reasons for differences between net income and associated cash receipts and payments.[6]

Figure 17–2 illustrates a statement of cash flows.

PRELIMINARY APPRAISAL OF FINANCIAL STATEMENTS

The first step in appraising financial statements should be to test the validity of the stated values. Financial statements present certain facts that, if good accounting practices are followed, the accountant states as accurately as possible. Credit analysts, on the other hand, approach the analysis as outsiders. Because of this, they are likely to be skeptical about some features of the statements and hence will examine them critically. Often they will try to determine whether the business management has presented a statement that overstates the financial condition. Most businesses, for obvious reasons, want their financial statements to appear as favorable as circumstances permit. At times, even with no intention of dishonesty, management attempts to present facts in a more favorable light than the situation justifies. Window dressing, undue optimism, inability to reflect current facts, and actual falsification are some of the ways financial statements may be adjusted to present a more favorable appearance.

Window Dressing, or "Putting the Best Foot Forward"

Window dressing is not an attempt to falsify anything but merely to present the business's various aspects in as favorable a light as possible. Knowing that credit analysts look for certain relationships in the statement as a test of goodness, the firm may attempt to manipulate its affairs immediately before statement time to make these relationships highly favorable. For example, knowing that a good cash balance and a very liquid current position are considered desirable by creditors, the firm may,

---

[6]Dennis F. Wasniewski, "Statement of Cash Flows," *Business Credit,* September 1988, p. 26. Permission granted by the National Association of Credit Management, *Business Credit.*

FIGURE 17–2 **Illustrative Example of the Statement of Cash Flows** (direct method)

ENTERPRISE, INC.
Statement of Cash Flows
For the Year Ended July 31, 1988

Cash flows from operating activities:		
Cash received from customers	$14,635	
Cash paid to suppliers and employees	(13,220)	
Income taxes paid	(360)	
Interest received	25	
Net cash provided by operating activities		$1,080
Cash flows from investing activities:		
Proceeds from sale of building	205	
Purchase of equipment	(120)	
Net cash provided in investing activities		85
Cash flows from financing activities:		
Proceeds from issuance of stock	45	
Dividends paid	(23)	
Net cash provided by financing activities		22
Net increase in cash and cash equivalents		1,187
Cash and cash equivalents at beginning of year		13
Cash and cash equivalents at end of year		$1,200
Reconciliation of net income to net cash provided by operating activities:		
Net income		$900
Adjustments to reconcile net income to net cash provided by operating activities:		
Depreciation of fixed assets	$125	
Amortization of deferred organization expenses	3	
Provision for losses on trade accounts receivable	15	
Payment of deferred organization expenses	(16)	
Changes in assets and liabilities:		
Increase in trade accounts receivable	(46)	
Decrease in inventories	49	
Increase in accrued liabilities and other payables	32	
Increase in interest and taxes payable	18	
Total adjustments		180
Net cash provided by operating activities		$1,080

Disclosure of accounting policy:
Cash in excess of daily requirements is invested in U.S. Government obligations whose maturities are three months or less. Such marketable investments are deemed to be cash equivalents for purposes of the statement of cash flows.

Source: Dennis F. Wasniewski, "Statement of Cash Flows," Business Credit, September 1988, p. 27. Permission granted by the National Association of Credit Management, Business Credit.

for the month immediately preceding the year-end, work strenuously to collect its accounts receivable and accumulate cash for statement purposes. Thus at the year-end it may have a better-than-normal cash position. It may also defer certain spending to avoid increasing liabilities or draining cash.

Further, the business may continue making normal purchases but not enter the goods received in the asset account Inventory or the corresponding accounts payable in the liability account Accounts Payable. This might be described as poor accounting practice rather than falsification or deliberate dishonesty.

Just before the statements are prepared, the firm may deposit in the bank a number of items that may be returned unpaid. These items may include NSF and other bad checks that have been held as collection items; they may even include some drafts or notes that have been previously presented and refused. With the cooperation of the bank, a firm may be able to deposit these items and have them included for the last day of the fiscal period as cash in bank, knowing that within a few days they will be returned unpaid. At that time the items have to be charged back to the deposit account and again be included on the firm's books as unpaid items. Opinions differ as to whether this step is window dressing or actual falsification. It's hard to prove falsification in such cases.

Undue Optimism, or "Reluctance to Face Unpleasant Realities"

Like window dressing, undue optimism is not usually considered a form of falsification. Instead it simply reflects the firm's natural hope that certain items on the financial statement will in time return to the value at which they are being carried. For example, certain inventory items may be carried at a much higher figure than their present market value, reflecting the firm's reluctance to face the unpleasant reality that it has done a poor job of buying, selling, or both.

Other items of a current nature, while not deliberately falsified, may be treated with undue optimism. It is not uncommon, on investigation, to find that securities not readily converted into cash are contained in a securities account, sometimes at a value considerably higher than their true market value. Because of the difference in the valuations placed on some of these items by the prospective debtor and the credit analyst, some credit managers refuse to consider such miscellaneous items unless a definite statement is given as to their true composition.

Inability to Reflect Current Facts

The beginner in credit work tends to take the figures shown in financial statements as definite and absolutely accurate. While the depreciated value of certain fixed assets, for example, may be quite accurate from an accounting point of view, their actual value on the present-day market is much more useful and realistic from a credit-determination standpoint. Such reasoning not only applies to the fixed-asset item on the balance sheet but also has merit in setting a "true" value on accounts receivable (less reserve for bad debts) and cash on hand (less commitments made but not always shown on the balance sheet).

Actual Falsification

As a matter of routine procedure, credit analysts should begin their examination by determining whether the statement presents any false conditions. The first thing to do when handling a new statement is to make sure the statement is correctly totaled, to see that it is dated and signed, and, if possible, to see that the evidence of mailing is preserved. The statement with round figures that are clearly estimated rather than book figures should be viewed with suspicion. The business should have noted this condition to forestall any claims of falsification. While credit analysts see few false financial statements, they need to test every statement for correctness and honesty in the presentation of statement facts. Nothing can be gained by analyzing a statement that has been falsified or doctored to present a more favorable position.

Even more deliberately dishonest practices may be used to further exaggerate statement items. Some of these practices are discussed next.

CASH. To be properly understood, the Cash account should be divided into Cash on Hand and Cash in Bank. It is possible to exaggerate the Cash on Hand item by including certain items in the cash drawer that are not actually cash. For example, the firm's owner or members may follow the careless, and probably not approved, practice of taking cash out of the cash drawer and substituting their IOUs. For statement purposes, these IOUs exaggerate the cash item if they are included in Cash on Hand. Firm members also may include as cash certain advances made to the firm's officers. They justify this by saying these items are handled just as petty cash would be handled and that when the expenses are presented, the items will be charged to the proper expense account and, of course, taken out of cash. Temporarily, however, this method exaggerates the cash item. Advances to salespersons for traveling expenses may be handled in the same fashion with the same resulting distortion of the statement values. To check this situation, credit analysts should be skeptical of an unusually large Cash on Hand account. They also determine whether window dressing has been practiced in connection with the Cash in Bank account by observing whether the balance at statement time agrees with the normal balance indicated by the bank in the course of the investigation.

ACCOUNTS RECEIVABLE. This is another item that may be adjusted to show a more favorable situation than the true circumstances warrant. Firms can be unduly optimistic about the collectibility of certain receivables. Continuing to include in accounts receivable items that are not likely to be collected, or that are definitely going to become bad-debt losses, exaggerates this asset's value. The firm may further falsify this item by arbitrarily including certain amounts that are not actually trade receivables, such as amounts due from the business officers and employees. While these are receivables, they are not receivables that will be collected in the ordinary course of business. Including them in accounts receivable presents a more favorable situation than the true circumstances warrant, since this leads the analyst to think of them as current assets when they should be regarded as noncurrent assets that do not contribute to the firm's true liquidity status.

Some firms attempt more deliberate falsification by writing up fictitious accounts receivable. They may set up receivables with existing firms for imaginary transactions or with imaginary firms. This increases the accounts receivable asset falsely and also increases sales figures. Often this device is adopted both to deceive creditors and to cover employee thefts. In the process of covering thefts, other assets may be falsified and nonexistent inventories created or other unreal assets placed on the books. By carefully analyzing the statements, an outside credit analyst can often detect these frauds as soon as or sooner than the owner.

INVENTORY. Merchandise is a very difficult item to evaluate properly. There are numerous opportunities for honest differences of opinion as to the actual value of the merchandise inventory, and it is difficult to arrive at an inventory valuation that is agreed to by all the people concerned. Consequently, a firm attempting to place a more favorable valuation on the inventory than might be justified would have little difficulty supporting this valuation on the basis of honest differences of opinion. While taking and valuing the inventory, the firm can be optimistic or pessimistic. Whichever method is followed changes not only the assets shown but also the profits for the period. Because of this effect on profits, the credit analyst may be deceived as to the true condition. The method used may also change the firm's taxes in a particular year. In addition to unduly optimistic valuations, which may deceive the credit analyst, firms can falsify their statements more deliberately by including in the merchandise inventory certain goods whose invoices are not included in the liability item of accounts payable. This has the double effect of increasing the assets and decreasing the liabilities, thus making the statement even more favorable than would be the case if just one of these items changed.

FIXED ASSETS. Fixed assets may be even more difficult to value than the inventory. The credit analyst naturally wants them to be shown on the statement at their book value with the depreciation reserve shown separately, rather than having the depreciation deducted and only the net value given. For purposes of analysis, it is desirable to know what depreciation policy the firm is following and at least to see whether that policy is conservative and in line with good practice. Since this is another item that directly affects the income statement, the credit analyst also is anxious to test the profit shown by determining whether it is computed on the basis of proper depreciation policies. The analyst can sometimes check the valuation placed on the fixed assets by comparing it with the valuation and description given in an agency report or arising from the credit manager's personal knowledge.

ACCOUNTS PAYABLE. As previously discussed, the liability Accounts Payable may be correspondingly reduced by omitting the invoice as a liability while entering the merchandise received as an asset. The accounts payable item may be readily checked by comparing it with the total owing as revealed by a complete trade investigation. A very unsatisfactory trade experience report, compared with a much more favorable current position than is consistent with the payment record, is another indication of possible minimization of the accounts payable. The possession of a large claimed cash account and a rather liquid position is inconsistent with slowness in the trade or with a small accounts payable item. Comparing accounts payable with purchases to get the turnover should indicate the period of payment; thus, 12 turns of accounts payable roughly indicate payment in 30 days. With this turnover rate, there should be a corresponding trade record of discount and pays when due. If the trade reports do not support the turnover rate shown by this calculation, the accounts payable on the statement may have been reduced, or the firm may have carefully avoided purchases just before statement time, resulting in an abnormal lowering of this item.

OTHER PAYABLES. Notes payable can be checked against bank data to see whether the bank report of the notes payable is consistent with the amounts shown on the statement. Mortgages payable can be compared with agency reports showing the mortgages, which are matters of public record. Any omissions from the statement should be revealed by comparison with the public record information.

Bonds can hardly be omitted because they are public knowledge, and they should be very readily checked against this fact.

Up to this point, the credit analyst may uncover a hint of possible exaggeration or falsification at various points during the analysis. Certain comparisons, or inconsistencies of certain facts with others, should warn analysts to look for some exaggeration or incorrectness in the statement. These indications are further studied in the discussion of analysis methods.

The maximum benefit from falsification is minimization of liabilities. In changing a liability item, the falsification must be a deliberate act rather than the result of a little undue optimism or exaggeration. Because it is harder to prove deliberate falsification of assets, firms may be more cautious about changing liabilities than about exaggerating or being unduly optimistic about their assets.

FINANCIAL STATEMENT LEGISLATION

Because the financial statement may be a vital factor in a firm's decision to sell its goods on credit to a credit seeker, safeguards must be provided to prevent the furnishing of false and misleading information to creditors. For this reason, most of the states[7] and the federal government have enacted legislation that holds certain abuses of financial statements to be a misdemeanor subject to civil and criminal prosecution. Table 17–1 compares state and federal requirements for prosecuting credit seekers who have submitted false financial statements. Although there is no express federal legislation for prosecuting makers of false financial statements, Section 215 of the U.S. Criminal Code is the basis for controlling those who use the mails to transmit false statements to obtain credit.

The requirements for prosecution under various state laws are similar to those under the federal enactment pertaining to offenses against the Postal Service. Under each set of laws, the prosecution must prove that the financial statement was submitted in writing and was signed, that the maker of the statement knew that the statement was false (under most state laws it is sufficient to show that the maker "should" have known it was false), that the statement was made for credit purposes with the intent that it be relied on in any credit decision, and that the false part of the statement misrepresented the facts to such a degree that the decision would have been otherwise if the true facts had been known.

At this point the similarities cease and the important differences begin. These differences often are the deciding factors as to which set of laws may be best for successful prosecution. The concept of fraud has been the subject of many court decisions and legal entanglements. Many state laws do not require proof that property was actually obtained on the basis of a false financial statement; they simply require proof that the facts were misrepresented. On the other hand, some courts (including federal courts) identify fraud with the actual passage of goods as a result of a decision based on a false and "fraudulent" financial statement. Involved parties need competent legal advice as to the conditions prevailing in particular situations.

Use of the mails is a prerequisite for prosecution under federal law, whereas this is not a condition for prosecution under the various state

---

[7] These are generally known as *false pretense* statutes.

TABLE 17–1 **Prosecution of Makers of False Statements** (state and federal laws)

Requirements	State Laws	Federal Law
In writing and signed	Must be proved	Must be proved
Made knowingly	Must be proved	Must be proved
For credit purposes	Must be proved	Must be proved
To be relied on	Must be proved	Must be proved
Materially false	Must be proved	Must be proved
Fraudulent	Need not be proved	Must be proved
Use of mails	Need not be proved	Must be proved
Place of prosecution	Country where statement made	Where statement made or received

laws. To help prove that the financial statement was transmitted through the mails, the self-mailing type of statement form was developed. The postmark on the back of the statement proves that the mails were used to deliver the form to the prospective creditor. A last point of difference is the place of prosecution. Under the various state laws, prosecution may be instituted only in the county in which the statement was made. Prosecution under federal law may be started either where the statement was made or where it was received.

What is the true importance of these preventive laws? Because of the large burden of proof necessary under both federal and state laws, many believe these laws act more as a deterrent to the submission of false statements than as a basis to punish violators.

METHODS OF STATEMENT ANALYSIS

This chapter has been concerned with only one phase of financial statement interpretation. More often than not, credit managers have confidence in their credit customers and rely on the authenticity of the financial statement. After a rapid preliminary appraisal, they may, in view of the requirements of the credit problem, determine the firm's liquidity, solvency, and trend. Four methods are commonly used to determine these factors: (1) the simple evaluation method, (2) the percentage comparison method, (3) the statement of changes in financial position method, and (4) the ratio analysis method. In addition to these methods, some credit managers employ a preliminary scaling-down technique. In this procedure the analyst simply reduces all the items on the balance sheet by some predetermined percentage before making any comparisons. Some believe this procedure is necessary to account for the "optimistic nature" of the people who prepare the financial statement. The four commonly used methods of statement analysis will be discussed in the next chapter.

DISCUSSION QUESTIONS

1. Distinguish clearly between a balance sheet and an income statement.
2. From what sources are financial statements usually available? What are the advantages of using one source over another?
3. Assume a prospective customer refuses to furnish a balance sheet and an income statement. How would you acquire the needed information? Would refusal of this request influence your credit decision? Discuss.
4. Should the loyalty and effectiveness of a firm's personnel be included in its assets? Why or why not?
5. Why has there been an increasing demand for financial statement analysis and interpretation in recent years?
6. How do you account for the different types of accounting opinions on financial statements?
7. Explain the cash flow concept.
8. Do all credit problems require the same degree of financial analysis to arrive at a sound credit decision? Why or why not?
9. What is meant by the following expressions?
   a. The liquidity position of a firm.
   b. The solvency condition of a firm.
   c. The managerial efficiency of a firm.
10. Why is it said that certain proportions of assets and liabilities are more conducive to successful operation of a firm than others?
11. Distinguish clearly between window dressing, undue optimism, and actual falsification.
12. Should window dressing be a crime punishable by law? Why or why not?
13. What are the most common techniques used to exaggerate or falsify the following: cash, accounts receivable, fixed assets, and accounts payable?
14. Why is it believed that financial statement legislation is primarily preventive in nature?
15. In what respects do the state laws and the federal law differ in regard to making and issuing false financial statements?
16. What purpose does the self-mailing type of financial statement serve?

SUGGESTED READINGS

"How to Juggle Numbers So the Debt Doesn't Show." *Business Week,* November 7, 1988, p. 152.

KAISER, CHARLES, JR. "Raising Professional Standards." *C&FM,* September 1987, p. 26.

MAPOTHER, WILLIAM R. "False Financial Statements: Debtors' Lie Can Be Your Gain." *Business Credit,* May–June 1990, p. 6.

PAVLOCK, ERNEST J.; FRANK S. SATO; and JAMES A. YARDLEY. "Accountability Standards for Corporate Reporting." *Business Credit,* September 1990, p. 8.

SWIECA, ROBERT W. "The Whole Picture: A Practical Approach to Financial Statement Analysis." *Business Credit,* October 1988, p. 38.

VALENTI, STEPHEN P. "New Legal Viewpoint." *C&FM,* September 1987, p. 22.

WASNIEWSKI, DENNIS F. "Statement of Cash Flows." *Business Credit,* September 1988, p. 26.

18

Financial Statements—Analysis and Interpretation (continued)

The Objectives or Goals of Chapter 18 Are:
1. To explain the methods of statement analysis.
2. To distinguish between the ratios of liquidity, solvency, and managerial efficiency.
3. To illustrate how standards may be used in statement analysis.
4. To illustrate the use of ratio analysis.
5. To discuss the limitations of statement analysis.

Financial analysis is basically used to decide whether or not the customer can pay in the future. Financial statements divulge trends in the business and help credit managers make decisions. The fruits of today's credit decision will mature in the future. Thus preparation made now will affect many in the years to come.

Financial statement analysis is part of the capacity assessment, and it is used in conjunction with character and capital to make the ultimate credit decision. In analyzing a financial statement, the credit analyst seeks certain fundamental things. One is balance or proportion. To be successful, a firm's relationship of assets to liabilities must be healthy and sound. Also its total assets must be invested to form an efficient business machine. Thus inventory must be in proper proportion to sales; receivables must be in proper proportion to sales and to inventory; excessive amounts must not be frozen in plant and equipment, leaving too little to buy raw materials or pay labor; liabilities must be proportional to assets and to owners' investment. This does not mean there is only one proper proportion or balance for all kinds of businesses, or for the same business at all times. Rather, there is an ideal or best balance for each business at a particular time. It also means certain disproportions are dangerous and definitely indicate that trouble is in store for the business.

Another thing sought in the financial statement is the business's trend or direction. Credit managers naturally are interested in the present balance or proportion of the items in the statement, but they are even more interested in knowing what the items are going to be in the future.

METHODS OF STATEMENT ANALYSIS

The four commonly accepted methods of analyzing financial statements to determine a firm's liquidity, solvency, and management efficiency are: the simple evaluation method, the percentage comparison method, the statement of changes in financial position method, and the ratio analysis method. Regardless of the method or methods used, analysts must know and understand the line of trade in which the business operates, the location of the business, and the date of the statement in order to make their analysis within the proper framework.

Simple Evaluation

This method depends heavily on the analyst's experience and judgment. Here the credit manager merely inspects the dollar items shown. Arranging a spreadsheet or work sheet often facilitates this task. After receiving several statements, the analyst has a picture of the last three to five years. Such an arrangement for either the balance sheets or the profit and loss statements permits a quick appraisal of the company and affords the experienced eye an opportunity to spot any obvious changes in business operations. The comparison of dollar items alone, however, is rather dangerous unless the analyst is unusually skilled. This is not a technique for beginners.

Percentage Comparison

To facilitate comparison, irrespective of the dollar items, the balance sheet may be computed so that each item in the statement is expressed as a percentage of total assets, which is the same thing as a percentage of liabilities plus net worth. Likewise, in the profit and loss statements the net sales figure usually is taken as 100 percent and the other items are computed as a percentage of this total.[1] This has been called the 100 percent or common size method. When this technique is used, changes are more readily apparent than if only dollar figures are used. Increases in the dollar items actually may be decreases in the proportion, or vice versa, and this would be readily apparent only to alert and experienced observers.

Statement of Changes in Financial Position

Another method of indicating not only the direction of change but also its exact amount is by making a statement of changes in financial position comparison. This technique depends on the accounting truism that an increase in an asset must be accompanied by a corresponding decrease in

---

[1]The use of the percentage method is illustrated in Table 18–1.

another asset or by an increase in a liability or net worth. Each statement item that has changed is listed as either a plus or minus, and the sum of the pluses is canceled by the sum of the minuses. This method, based on the accounting equation assets equal liabilities plus net worth, not only emphasizes changes but may also reveal the firm's policies by the increase or decrease in particular statement items. It shows whether the company is increasing its liabilities to purchase additional plant, to invest more in inventory, or for other purposes. The analysis may also reveal unsatisfactory dividend policies and unwise handling of surplus. Thus it will be apparent if the business has continued to pay out dividends, although suffering losses.

Ratio Analysis

Perhaps the most publicized method of statement interpretation is the ratio analysis. Is a firm selling a million dollars worth of goods a year a success? Obviously, a credit analyst needs more information to reach a sound answer. A million-dollar sales figure accompanied by a loss of $50,000 gives a much different picture than a $100,000 net profit (after taxes) on the same volume of sales.

Certain fundamental relationships between statement items are emphasized by stating them as ratios. Such ratios make it easier to interpret balance relationships, and the trend of the business can be easily determined by noting the changes in these ratios. The ratios listed and commented on here are for illustration only; they are not the only ones used or even, in all cases, the most significant.

Ratio analysis received its initial impetus from the article "Study of Credit Barometrics," by Alexander Wall. This study, which was prepared at the request of the Federal Reserve Board, appeared in the March 1919 issue of the *Federal Reserve Bulletin*. In addition, Dun & Bradstreet and Robert Morris Associates have taken an interest in this field.

Rather than a list of ratios and a discussion of how they are computed and what they mean, the following three-way classification will be used: ratios showing the firm's liquidity, or its ability to meet debts as they come due; ratios showing the firm's solvency, or the division of risk between owners and debtors; and ratios showing the firm's trend and managerial efficiency. In several instances the same ratios appear under two classifications.

LIQUIDITY RATIOS. At least seven ratios are generally considered significant in analyzing a firm's ability to meet its debts. Many credit analysts do not attempt to compute and interpret all seven; instead, credit executives develop favorites on which they base their decisions. However, credit analysts must understand all seven before they are experienced enough to pick favorites.

$$\text{Current ratio} = \frac{\text{Current assets}}{\text{Current liabilities}}$$

The current ratio for many years was considered the most important. It is computed by dividing total current assets by total current liabilities, and it shows the number of times current assets exceed current liabilities. The current ratio indicates the business's ability to meet its maturing obligations, which must be met from the cash item. An excess of current assets over current liabilities promises sufficient cash on hand to meet the business obligations without difficulty. The standard most commonly accepted is that current assets should be twice current liabilities—a 2-to-1 ratio.[2] This ratio is no longer considered of paramount significance because of the growing feeling that the composition of the current assets is more important than the amount by which they exceed the current liabilities. Also, many businesses, knowing that the analyst will surely figure the current ratio, strive to make it favorable on their statements and thus artificially bring about a better showing than is justified. Although no longer thought of as the most important ratio, the current ratio is still one that must be considered and one that the analyst should be familiar with.

$$\text{Acid-test ratio} = \frac{\text{Current assets} - \text{Inventory}}{\text{Current liabilities}}$$

The acid-test ratio is computed by dividing total current assets less inventory by total current liabilities. Inventory generally is the slowest of the current assets; when it is deducted from the total, the remaining current assets are already converted or very readily converted into cash without shrinkage. The standard minimum for this ratio is 1 to 1, although variations occur between various lines and during different economic conditions.

$$\text{Stock turnover} = \frac{\text{Net sales}}{\text{Inventory}}$$

The stock turnover may be computed in at least two ways, if the information is available:

$$\frac{\text{Stock turnover}}{\text{(for retailers only)}} = \frac{\text{Net sales at retail}}{\text{Average inventory at retail}}$$

$$\text{Stock turnover} = \frac{\text{Cost of goods sold}}{\text{Average inventory at cost}}$$

Some analysts interpret the term *average inventory* to mean the beginning inventory plus the ending inventory divided by two. Others attempt to se-

---

[2]This proportion varies from one line of business to another and with the various phases of the business cycle.

cure figures more often, such as the amount of inventory at the start of each month. Of course, the inventory control system a firm follows determines its ability to supply such detailed information. In any case this ratio is designed to show the number of times a firm is able to convert its stock of goods into cash or receivables.

Comparing the results of this ratio from year to year for the same company or for different companies for the same year shows how the subject company is utilizing its investment in inventory to generate sales. This is a very important indication of managerial efficiency and operating results. Declining efficiency, as shown by a declining ratio, forecasts slowness in converting assets into cash, decrease in sales volume, capital investment in less productive inventory, and declining profits. Slow turnover of inventory may indicate excessive investment in old and slow-moving stock, which casts doubt on the value claimed for inventory in the current assets. The stock turnover ratio is therefore a test of the firm's current position and may lead the analyst to doubt whether that position is actually as good as the statement indicates.

$$\text{Receivables turnover} = \frac{\text{Net sales}}{\text{Receivables}}$$

The receivables turnover, computed by dividing net sales by receivables, shows the number of times during the fiscal period that the receivables are turned. This indicates the efficiency with which the receivables are being collected. Comparing results for the subject company from year to year or for the subject company with similar companies shows how the subject compares in efficiency of converting receivables into cash. A slowing of receivables, shown by a decline in the ratio, shows investment of capital in slow or uncollectible receivables. This hampers the firm's ability to meet obligations and ties up capital unnecessarily. Dividing credit sales by receivables shows the true turnover of sales on credit and the average number of days it takes the firm to collect its sales on account. Thus, if the turnover is 6 times a year, it collects in 60 days; if 12 times a year, it collects in 30 days; and if 10 times a year, in 36 days. From these figures, the analyst can appraise the soundness of the value claimed for accounts receivable in current assets. The receivables turnover ratio is therefore a means of testing the soundness of the current asset position.

$$\frac{\text{Sales to net}}{\text{working capital}} = \frac{\text{Net sales}}{\text{Current assets} - \text{Current liabilities}}$$

This ratio, computed by dividing the net sales figure by the net working capital (current assets less current liabilities), shows how efficiently the firm is utilizing net working capital to produce the desired results—sales.

$$\text{Payables turnover} = \frac{\text{Purchases}}{\text{Accounts payable}}$$

The payables turnover ratio is figured by dividing purchases by accounts payable. Interpreting this ratio over a period of years, the analyst is able to tell whether current liabilities are being paid more or less promptly than in prior periods. For example, a firm reporting purchases of $60,000 for a specified period (generally a year) and payables of $12,000 at the end of the period has a ratio of 5 to 1. Translated into days (360 days divided by 5), the ratio reveals that this company is taking 72 days on the average to pay its accounts payable. Some accounts are paid in less than 72 days, and some in more, but if a seller is contemplating accepting the firm's credit, the average length of time the seller can expect to wait for funds is 72 days.

$$\frac{\text{Net working capital}}{\text{represented by inventory}} = \frac{\text{Inventory}}{\text{Current assets} - \text{Current liabilities}}$$

This ratio, which is not too well known and is not in general use, shows what proportion of net working capital is made up of inventory that may be too hard to sell. In interpreting the ratio, the analyst should recognize that it may be favorably influenced either by an exceptionally low level of current liabilities or by an excessively low level of merchandise relative to other current assets.

$$\frac{\text{Days sales}}{\text{outstanding (DSO)}} = \frac{\text{Average receivables for 3 months ends} \times 90}{\text{Credit sales for last 3 months}}$$

The controversial nature of days sales outstanding (DSO) and whether it is an accurate way to judge the efficiency of a credit department has become evident since the *Business Credit* DSO contest was introduced about six years ago.[3] When *Business Credit* began the contest, it asked entrants to report their DSO figures on a monthly basis. Some firms boycotted the contest because they disagreed with the premise that the DSO of one company could be compared with the DSO of a firm in another industry with different sales and marketing conditions.

SOLVENCY RATIOS. Seven ratios are capable of showing a firm's solvency condition. In interpreting these ratios, the analyst is answering such questions as: "Is the net worth adequate?" "Is the borrowing proper?" and "Are the fixed assets fitted to the needs of the company, to the capital invested by the owners, and to the demands of outside creditors?" As with the liquidity ratios, credit managers have favorites; they do not usually analyze all those listed and described in this section.

$$\text{Debt to net worth} = \frac{\text{Current debt} + \text{Long-term liabilities}}{\text{Net worth}}$$

---

[3]Judy A. Gordon, "DSO Debate," *Business Credit,* February 1989, p. 29.

The ratio of debt to net worth is computed by dividing total debt by net worth. It shows the proportion of investments by outside creditors in relation to capital investment by the owners. In other words, it indicates the proportional relationship between the dollar value of money and goods secured on credit from outsiders and the sum invested by the owners of the business (owners' equity). Obviously the owners should have an adequate equity in the business to protect the investments made by others. A general rule is that owners' capital should be, at minimum, as great as the outside investments—a 1-to-1 ratio. The desirable ratio is not definite but varies with the nature of the business and other conditions. As the proportion of owners' capital increases, the business is working into a safer position and depending less on creditors. Some analysts also show the ratio of current debt alone to net worth. This is especially valuable when a considerable part of the firm's liabilities are long term.

$$\text{Total assets to fixed assets} = \frac{\text{Total assets}}{\text{Fixed assets}}$$

This ratio is computed by dividing total assets by fixed assets. It indicates the proportion of total assets represented by fixed assets. The ratio is significant only in lines of trade where fixed assets constitute an appreciable portion of the total assets. Businesses must try to avoid the danger of allowing too large a proportion of their assets to become frozen (nonliquid) by tying them up in fixed assets that can't be readily disposed of and that may not contribute to earnings. A study of the total assets to fixed assets ratio can reveal this tendency.

$$\frac{\text{Fixed assets to}}{\text{long-term liabilities}} = \frac{\text{Fixed assets}}{\text{Long-term liabilities}}$$

This ratio is computed by dividing fixed assets by long-term liabilities. The theory is that long-term liabilities are created to acquire fixed assets and are frequently secured by fixed assets. If this is the case, the comparison of these two items is of significance. The ratio shows among other things the extent to which borrowings are being used to carry fixed assets. This may indicate the safety margin of the loans, the prospects of renewing maturing debts, and the possibility of acquiring funds by making additional loans. Large long-term liabilities relative to fixed assets may indicate financial strain and a weakened condition. In some lines of business, however, fixed assets are so small in proportion to total assets that this ratio has little significance and may be omitted.

$$\text{Fixed assets to net worth} = \frac{\text{Fixed assets}}{\text{Net worth}}$$

This ratio is computed by dividing fixed assets (such as plant, machinery, equipment, and other fixed properties) by net worth or owners' equity. A high ratio is a danger signal that the firm may have expanded its fixed assets more rapidly than warranted by normal growth. On the other hand, when this ratio materially exceeds the average for a particular type of operation and line of business, a low working capital is indicated. In fact, it may mean an overworking of the firm's working capital.

$$\text{Sales to net worth} = \frac{\text{Net sales}}{\text{Net worth}}$$

This ratio, which is computed by dividing net sales by net worth, shows the number of dollars in sales that are generated by the owners' net worth. More efficient use of the owners' capital naturally results in a larger ratio. However, this ratio may become "too good." Inadequate investment on the part of the owners for the volume of business being attempted makes the ratio abnormally high. This is known as overtrading. Inefficient use of owners' capital causes a low ratio. Both conditions are unsatisfactory, but overtrading is probably more dangerous than undertrading. Inefficient use of owners' capital is likely to result in lower profits or inadequate returns. Attempting to do too much business on the capital invested means the owners are straining the business. They are relying heavily on borrowed funds and are able to maintain this pace because of very rapid turnover rates of inventory and receivables. Should something happen to slow down this rate of conversion of assets into cash, they would quickly find themselves unable to pay debts as they mature. Slowing down in debt payment makes creditors anxious and hesitant to accept credit for additional amounts. Such a situation is doubly disastrous for a firm in this condition, because the owner-supplied capital is insufficient to give the creditors much margin of protection and the business depends on the rate of operations for success. This ratio should be examined with the ratio of sales to inventory, the ratio of sales to receivables, the current ratio, and the net worth to debt ratio. A combined review of all these ratios will suffice to reveal the condition. A comparison of sales to net working capital (current assets minus current liabilities) may also reveal an attempt to do too large a volume of business on insufficient capital.

$$\text{Sales to total assets} = \frac{\text{Net sales}}{\text{Total assets}}$$

This ratio is computed by dividing net sales by total assets. It shows the number of dollars in sales generated by the total assets invested in the business. More efficient use of the assets results in more dollars of sales; less efficient use results in a falling ratio. This ratio may be more significant than the sales to inventory figure for manufacturing firms or other firms that carry only a small inventory but have a heavy investment in fixed assets. For firms of this type, the sales to fixed assets ratio is sometimes used to supplement other ratios.

$$\text{Sales to fixed assets} = \frac{\text{Net sales}}{\text{Fixed assets}}$$

The ratio shows the dollars of net sales produced with each dollar of fixed assets. When the ratio is low, the degree of plant utilization may be relatively low—in other words, the business may be too large for the volume of business transacted.

TREND AND MANAGERIAL EFFICIENCY RATIOS. The ratios included in this section are designed to answer such questions as: How efficient is the firm in the use of its assets? What is management's ability to meet changing conditions? and How adaptable and flexible is the firm? Six of the ratios normally considered as revealing trend and managerial efficiency have been discussed previously: the stock turnover ratio, the receivables turnover ratio, the sales to net working capital ratio, the sales to net worth ratio, the sales to total assets ratio, and the sales to fixed assets ratio. Three other ratios in this category involve net profit and are related to the firm's net worth, total assets, and net sales. Likewise, an operating expense ratio (total expenses to net sales) should be analyzed.

$$\text{Net profit to net worth} = \frac{\text{Net profit}}{\text{Net worth}}$$

This is computed as a percentage of net profit to net worth and shows the earnings made on the owners' capital. This amount, which is very important to owners and managers, is often considered one of the most important results shown by the financial statements. It shows the efficiency of the firm's overall operations and may be compared for the subject firm over a period of years or to other similar firms. For purposes of comparison with other firms, however, it is not always the best figure to use. The profit on net worth by a particular firm is influenced by both its operations and its financial policy. To make the most exact comparison, both percentage of return on net worth and percentage of return on total assets should be computed.

$$\text{Net profit to total assets} = \frac{\text{Net profit}}{\text{Total assets}}$$

This ratio is computed by dividing net profit by total assets. It is designed to show how efficiently total assets are being used in producing dollars of profit. Used jointly with the ratio of net profit to net worth, as just discussed, it often enables the analyst to more accurately interpret the firm's true condition and future outlook.

$$\text{Net profit to net sales} = \frac{\text{Net profit}}{\text{Net sales}}$$

This ratio is computed by dividing net profit by net sales. The policies a firm follows have a great effect on the ratio. Thus firms employing price-cutting techniques tend to seek large total profits and high sales volumes and show a lower ratio than firms that sell at a high markup and attain a lower sales volume.

$$\text{Operating expense} = \frac{\text{Total expenses}}{\text{Net sales}}$$

This ratio enables the analyst to compare expenses to the net sales figure. Comparisons with previous years and with similar types of companies make the ratio even more significant.

USE OF STANDARDS IN STATEMENT ANALYSIS

The statement analysis procedure becomes more important when the computed percentages and ratios are viewed in light of their trends over several years. These trends may be within the company itself or within the industry in which the company is included.

The two companies most active in compiling material for use in making industry comparisons are Dun & Bradstreet Business Credit Services and Robert Morris Associates.

Dun & Bradstreet Business Credit Services

The material published by Dun & Bradstreet Business Credit Services is one of the most comprehensive and current sources for industry comparisons. One of the pioneers in ratio analysis, this company's compilations first appeared in a series of four articles in the *Dun & Bradstreet Monthly Review,* starting in August 1933.

Robert Morris Associates

The *Statement Studies* of Robert Morris Associates have been published continuously since 1923. These studies are a collection of "composite" balance sheets and income statements for different lines of business—manufacturers, wholesalers, retailers, and service concerns. Many widely used financial ratios are also computed. A separate section provides information on selling and delivery expense, officers' salaries, and other general administrative expenses, all expressed as percentages of net sales. The statements of each industry or trade are tabulated into groups according to asset size.

LIMITATIONS OF STATEMENT ANALYSIS

The techniques of financial statement analysis that have been discussed involve one very material limitation. They are static in the sense that, at best, they can estimate the apparent ability of a company to meet its obligations as of some *past* date. While it is impossible to estimate future debt payment ability accurately, it is still desirable to try to do so.

Creditor firms make daily decisions that deviate from the norm but prove profitable. Exceptions to the rule occur, emphasizing the importance of individual human judgment. Most credit decisions are a result of human judgment exercised after a careful examination of the facts presented.

ILLUSTRATIVE USE OF RATIO ANALYSIS

Table 18–1 provides an illustration of statement analysis. The credit manager may interpret these figures as follows.

Both total assets and total liabilities have decreased. The inventory has decreased $15,000, from 36 to 31 percent of total assets. This decline in inventory has, however, been nearly counteracted by the increase in receivables, so that current assets make up almost as large a part of total assets as before. The current assets to current liability ratio shows that current assets are still considerably in excess of current liabilities, indicating the firm is not in a dangerous condition in this respect.

The acid-test ratio indicates that, even with inventory omitted, the current assets are equal to the current liabilities. For this ratio, the minimum for satisfactory conditions is often stated as 1 to 1. The debt to net

TABLE 18–1 **The Fashion Shop** (retailer of ladies' ready-to-wear)

	19—	Percent	19—	Percent
Cash	$ 10,483	6	$ 4,550	3
Receivables	14,977	9	22,657	15
Inventory	60,642	36	45,318	31
Total current assets	86,102	51	72,525	49
Fixed assets	82,349	49	74,026	51
Total assets	$168,541	100	$146,551	100
Current liabilities	$ 26,872	15	$ 23,880	16
Fixed liabilities	38,000	23	30,000	21
Net worth	104,669	62	92,671	63
Total liabilities and net worth	$168,541	100	$146,551	100
Sales	$225,000		$151,688	
Net profit	7,532		5,221	

Ratio Analysis	19—	19—
Current assets to current liabilities	3.33	3.04
Current assets less inventory to current liabilities (acid test)	0.98	1.14
Debt to net worth	0.61	0.58
Sales to inventory	3.71	3.35
Sales to receivables	15.02	6.69
Sales to net worth	2.15	1.64
Percent net profit to sales	3.35	3.44
Percent net profit to total assets	4.47	3.56
Percent net profit to net worth	7.20	5.63

worth ratio has improved. Despite the decline in net worth, there is a still greater decline in liabilities. Credit managers believe that owners should have, as a general rule, a larger stake in the business than creditors.

The sales to inventory ratio indicates the efficiency with which the management turns its investment in merchandise into sales. This firm has shown a decline in efficiency in this respect, and many firms of this type have a sales to inventory ratio of at least 7 or 8 to 1.

The sales to receivables ratio is alarming. It has deteriorated sharply and shows that the management is not efficient in collecting. This ratio not only has decreased greatly but also has reached the point where it is evident that the firm has accepted credit unwisely. (Assume there has been no change in the type of credit offered.)

The deterioration of both these ratios can be partially explained by the decrease in sales. However, the firm did not adjust to this decline by reducing either its inventory or its receivables to bring them in line with the lessened sales volume. This has kept it from turning these assets into cash and reducing current liabilities accordingly. It has meant the sacrifice of cash and the loss of opportunities to take cash discounts.

The ratio of sales to net worth shows how efficiently owners' capital is being used. Too low a ratio here means that owners' capital is not being used efficiently; too high a ratio shows insufficient capital for the volume of business being attempted. In this case the ratio is too low and is getting worse. The large investment in fixed assets that are not fully productive partially explains the low ratio here.

The three profit percentages are important in this situation. The net profit to sales ratio appears better than it really is because adequate reserves against losses on bad debts have not been set up. The ratios of net profit to total assets and to net worth, although not large, are satisfactory.

Credit managers reviewing this situation will find some indication of satisfactory conditions and some of very unsatisfactory conditions. They have only the two statements. If they had one or two more, they could determine the trend. They must decide whether the trend of sales is a result of national and local economic conditions and whether an improvement can be expected in the near future. Or is this drastic drop a reflection of poor management? There are ample assets to protect creditors, and there appears to be no immediate danger of failure. They might expect payments to be somewhat slow but would feel safe in accepting a moderate amount of credit if they are able to resolve the declining sales figure. Any decision made involves a compromise.

The firm's future prospects depend on what steps management takes to correct the unsatisfactory conditions. The firm must stage a vigorous selling drive to clean out its surplus stock and at the same time must wage an effective campaign to collect debts from delinquent customers. The firm may then use the funds realized from these sources to pay off its own current liabilities, bringing them down to manageable proportions and making the firm liquid enough to take advantage of cash discounts. It also would bring about a proportion of assets to liabilities such that when business conditions improved, the firm could increase its inventory and receivables to keep pace with increased sales. These increases could be managed on credit when accompanied by increased sales, but the wisdom of incurring additional current debt is subject to considerable speculation.

CONCLUSIONS ON STATEMENT ANALYSIS

This discussion of the analysis and interpretation of financial statements has obviously not included all of the acceptable methods. The discussion does, however, introduce the subject. The major goal in making such an appraisal and interpretation is a clear understanding of financial statement facts. Credit analysts must choose the best available methods and consider all pertinent factors to arrive at a sound decision.

DISCUSSION QUESTIONS

1. Explain how financial statements divulge trends in a business and help credit managers in their decision-making process.

2. Discuss the four commonly accepted methods of financial statement analysis. Explain the most important features of each method.

3. Which method is the one most closely dependent on an analyst's experience and judgment? Why?

4. Describe the background, development, and reasoning behind the ratio analysis approach to financial statement analysis.

5. What are the most important liquidity ratios? Explain what each ratio reveals.

6. What are the seven ratios most generally accepted as capable of showing the solvency condition of a firm? Explain what each ratio reveals.

7. List the trend and managerial efficiency ratios that are considered in this chapter, and explain what each of these ratios reveals.

8. Do you believe it possible to determine accurately the managerial efficiency of a business firm by using ratio analysis? Explain your answer.

9. How are standards used in financial statement analysis?

10. Where might such standards be obtained?

11. Discuss the limitations of financial statement analysis.

12. Study Table 18–1. Assume you have received an initial order amounting to $1,750 from the Fashion Shop. The order is to be made up of women's coats and dresses.
   a. On the basis of the analysis accompanying Table 18–1, would you accept or reject this order? Why or why not?
   b. Would you want additional information on this case? What type of information would be particularly helpful?
   c. If you have rejected the order, would you accept it on COD terms? Explain your decision.

13. **The Happy Shoe store.** *Situation:* Assume you are the credit manager for the Royal Shoe Company. Your firm manufactures a complete line of shoes—men's, women's, and children's—and distributes them directly to retail outlets. Your merchandising method is to establish the line with one of the better retail stores and to get the major portion of the trade from the selected outlet rather than to sell to all possible outlets. Thus the number of accounts handled is small, but each account is rather substantial.

   The Happy Shoe Store has been an outlet for approximately 50 years, having become a major outlet during the years 1940 to 1945. During these years, you favored it by allotting it something more than its share of your production, and it expanded substantially. During the past few years, its purchases have been close to $30,000 a year, and the account with you has tended to increase. From a running balance of approximately $3,000, the balance has mounted until it is currently $10,348. The payments that had been discounted have deteriorated, so that now the account would be classified as slow, even unsatisfactory.

   You receive a current financial statement direct from the Happy Shoe Store (see Exhibit 1), and the receipt of the statement for the year 1991 prompts you to review the account completely and to order a current credit report.

EXHIBIT 1

	12/31/88	12/31/89	12/31/90	12/31/91
Assets				
Current assets:				
Cash	$ 10,328	$ 8,238	$ 8,884	$ 7,744
Receivables	2,344	2,190	3,172	13,430
Inventory	48,420	47,526	49,946	51,634
Other current assets	4,200	4,338	5,190	5,248
Total current assets	65,490	62,290	66,992	78,056
Furniture and fixtures	14,244	13,948	13,462	12,852
Total assets	$ 79,734	$ 76,238	$ 80,454	$ 90,908
Liabilities and Net Worth				
Accounts payable	$ 14,116	$ 13,966	$ 18,438	$ 25,284
Notes payable (less than one year)	7,724	4,230	3,948	4,086
Accrued taxes and expenses	2,206	1,962	2,234	2,436
Total current liabilities	$ 24,046	$ 20,158	$ 24,620	$ 31,806
Net worth	55,688	56,080	55,834	59,102
Total liabilities and net worth	$ 79,734	$ 76,238	$ 80,454	$ 90,908
Sales	$148,534	$140,236	$131,634	$141,232
Cost of goods sold	93,504	90,688	85,162	93,226
Gross margin	55,030	49,548	46,472	48,006
Total expenses	44,756	42,526	40,238	41,426
Net profit	$ 10,274	$ 7,022	$ 6,234	$ 6,580

Required:

a. Make a complete analysis of the financial data.
b. Make a careful analysis of the credit information on hand.
c. Recommend appropriate action, and state the reasons for your recommendations.
d. What payment experience could the Royal Shoe Company expect?
e. What collection experience is the Happy Shoe Store having with its accounts receivable?
f. What additional information, if any, would you like to have to make a more complete analysis?

Financial information: Copies of standardized financial statements for the last four years are given.

Credit information: Pertinent information from the credit reports arranged under appropriate headings is presented below.

History and method of operation: The Happy Shoe Store was organized in 1933. During the first five years of operation, the store earned nothing above a bare living, but it made more rapid progress following 1939. In 1941 the owners obtained new quarters, the store was expanded, and substantial progress was made. The rate of progress slowed in later years, but the store is considered the leading store in its line.

Operated as a family shoe store, the Happy Shoe Store carries a complete line of men's, women's and children's shoes. Its principal line is Royal, which is featured in its advertising and display. The store's fixtures are modern and attractive; its windows are attractive; and its stock is orderly and well arranged. It is regarded as a promotional store, and it frequently emphasizes special promotions that are advertised heavily. At the end of 1988, the Happy Shoe Store started promoting its own option-terms revolving credit plan. Within the past several months, it decided to accept the Visa credit card.

Walter Green, the owner, is 55 years old, married, and experienced in the line. He employs an assistant manager and two salespeople on a full-time basis, with additional personnel employed on a part-time basis for the weekend and special sales.

The Happy Shoe Store is located in the downtown section of Middleville, a city of 20,000 people. Middleville is an expanding industrial center and also a trading center for the surrounding area. Within the last 18 months an outlying shopping center has been established. A competing shoe store is located in the shopping center.

Ledger clearance: By direct inquiry of sources, the following information is obtained.

HC	Owes Now	Payments
$2,234	$2,234	$600 now due, balance past due
294	264	Now on COD basis
900	400	Pays when due, formerly discounted
634	—	Discounts
2,600	736	30 to 60 days slow
1,000	—	Pays when due

SUGGESTED READINGS

GORDON, JUDY A. "DSO Debate." *Business Credit,* February 1989, p. 29.

KELLEY, ANTHONY F. "Ratios and Decision-Making Models." *Credit & Financial Management,* January 1986, p. 9.

LAWDER, KEITH E. "Ratios 101." *Business Credit,* June 1989, p. 28.

SHIMKO, THOMAS. "Financial Statements: The Lighter Side of Analysis." *C&FM,* February 1987, p. 28.

Commercial Credit—Analysis, Decision Making, and Credit Lines

The Objectives or Goals of Chapter 19 Are:

1. To discuss the basic purposes of commercial credit data.
2. To explain a "house standard."
3. To point out the importance of credit lines.
4. To explain how to set credit lines.
5. To illustrate the importance of automation in the commercial credit department.

The basic purpose of credit data is to help the credit executive make a better analysis of the credit risk and reach a sounder decision. In other words, will accepting the order result in *profitable* and *continuing* sales? This chapter covers the role of analysis and decision making in commercial credit transactions and the setting of credit lines.

CORE OF THE COMMERCIAL CREDIT TASK

Commercial credit departments perform many operations. They receive orders, institute investigations, open credit files, control accounts, maintain credit records, bill customers, handle collections, and make adjustments. However, as with consumer credit, the critical core of the commercial credit task is decision making.[1] When credit decisions are formed on the basis of accurate information, properly evaluated and carefully analyzed, they reflect sounder and more rational judgments. Credit decisions are not always free from error—because predictions are not always correct—but they should be right in enough cases to conform to the credit policies and objectives the firm has established.

---

[1] See the Suggested Readings at the end of the chapter.

Establishment of a "House Standard"

In order for credit managers to accomplish the objectives top management wants, management must furnish a clearly defined and understood statement of what it expects of the credit department. Once this is accomplished, credit managers can establish a "house standard" or a guide to judge the creditworthiness of the firm's customers. In setting such a house standard, credit managers are influenced by such external or uncontrollable factors as competition, general business conditions, and characteristics of the local market. Certain controllable factors also have an influence. Such factors include profit margin of the seller, type of product, seasonal aspects of the product, use of special terms and special arrangements for marginal and submarginal customers, influence of collection policies and procedures, and personality of the credit manager and other managerial influences. As these factors vary periodically, so does the house standard used to judge whether to accept or reject customer orders. At certain times some of the factors have more weight than others, but no one factor or set of factors is always dominant and conclusive.

EXTERNAL FACTORS. In deciding whether to approve an order, credit managers must determine the account's degree of risk and then compare that risk to the level the firm is willing to accept. In establishing this level, credit managers must consider what their competition is doing in the way of lenient or strict credit, terms, and collections. Regardless of a company's desire to dictate its own house standard, it must consider that competitors are eagerly seeking the customer's order too.

Credit managers need to pay attention to general business conditions. When the economy is booming and demand for a company's products exceeds its production capacity, the credit manager will have a different philosophy of credit acceptance than in periods of reduced business activity or recession. Firms selling in local areas are influenced by local business conditions and may face problems disposing of products even while the overall economy is in the so-called prosperity phase of the business cycle. This situation is pointed up by the popular saying: "It's a recession when the other fellow's products aren't selling, but it's a depression when our products aren't selling."

CONTROLLABLE FACTORS. Although a firm has little or no control over external factors, other factors that influence a house standard are largely controllable within the framework of company policies. Thus the type of product sold, its seasonal or nonseasonal characteristics, and the seller's profit margin all influence a company's level of credit acceptance. Generally, the wider a company's profit margin, the poorer the class of credit risks it can afford to sell. However, not all firms with high profit margins sell to poor risks. Such firms can simply *afford* to do so—if they decide that such a policy is feasible and consistent with other aims.

It isn't always necessary to disapprove orders from marginal and sub-marginal customers; credit managers can make certain arrangements for such orders and still adhere to established house standards. One such arrangement is to use a trade acceptance.

Use of a trade acceptance enables both buyer and seller to complete their transactions without delay. The seller makes out the instrument to his or her own order, drawn on the buyer. The seller takes the trade acceptance in payment for the goods. When the buyer accepts the draft drawn on him or her, the obligation to pay becomes firm. The seller may then discount the trade acceptance at the bank for the full amount therein, negotiate it further, or wait until the buyer honors it.

Other terms used for qualified credit risks include cash (this generally means payment within 10 days of the invoice date), COD (cash on delivery), or split-shipment (part of the goods shipped on cash before delivery and part on regular terms).

The type of collection policy a firm decides to follow often determines the level of acceptance the credit manager sets.[2] If a firm has a very strict collection procedure, chances are that its standard of acceptance is low or lenient. The following combinations are found most often:

Strict acceptance—lenient collection.

Lenient acceptance—strict collection.

Another controllable factor is the personality and "sales ability" of the credit manager. Some individuals have the talent to say no to a customer and still maintain the customer's goodwill to such an extent that the transaction is completed either on a cash basis or on credit terms much stricter than normal.

Once all of these factors are carefully weighed and analyzed, credit managers have some guide by which to judge the creditworthiness of the orders they receive.

Automatic and Nonautomatic Initial Orders

Credit managers need to make a distinction between initial orders and follow-up orders. It is essential, whenever possible, that the first order from a new customer be processed as quickly and expeditiously as possible, without lengthy and extensive investigation. A new order is the first contact between buyer and seller; initial impressions often mean the difference between a long-range series of follow-up orders and a one-time, one-order customer. Some firms consider old customers who haven't bought during the preceding year as "new" customers.

---

[2] The type of credit acceptance policy adopted in turn influences the type of collection policy set. This is the more normal cause-and-effect sequence.

AUTOMATIC INITIAL ORDERS. To expedite the processing of initial orders, credit departments may give blanket approval to all first orders below a specified amount. This amount is influenced by the type of product involved, the nature of the company's operation, its overall credit policy, general market conditions, competitive credit terms, and prior experience in collecting small credit accounts approved in this manner. However, a follow-up procedure is vital for successful future operation.

Some firms appraise initial orders on the basis of ratings given by credit agencies such as Dun & Bradstreet and the various specialized agencies. They assign maximum amounts to each Dun & Bradstreet credit rating. For example, if the initial order of a customer with a certain credit rating falls below the maximum, approval is automatic.[3] Of course, each company that uses such a technique establishes its own first-order limits to meet its own needs and conform to its own policies.

NONAUTOMATIC INITIAL ORDERS. If the company has no established procedures such as blanket and agency-rating approvals, it must decide how to handle initial orders. It may base this decision on answers to the following questions:

1. Is the profit margin on the order large enough to cover the cost of investigation?
2. Should the account be cultivated because of the potential future sales volume?
3. What public relations benefits might the company gain because of the sale?

If the company decides to investigate, a further decision must be made as to how extensive the investigation should be. Where present and expected sales potential justifies an intensive and direct investigation, the credit department should seek all available information regarding historical and forecast data, reputation and ability of principals, marketability and competitive forces related to products, and so on.

Handling Orders from Established Customers

When an old, established account orders merchandise, credit department procedures are greatly simplified. The credit department refers to in-file information to determine whether the account is in good standing or not. Most commercial credit departments periodically accumulate credit information and revise credit limits on established accounts. Hence in-file data is usually reasonably current, leading to a rapid credit decision. If the

---

[3]This amount changes from time to time, depending on all the factors that affect company policy.

order is acceptable and within the assigned credit limit when added to any existing balances, it is approved and sent to the shipping department, where the order is filled and shipped to the customer.

However, if the account is not in good standing because previous balances remain unpaid or if filling the order would greatly exceed the account's credit limit, the order is sent to the credit manager for decision. With all in-file data available, the credit manager may revise the credit limit upward, seek additional credit information from external sources or, rather than assume greater risk from the customer, notify the customer of the negative decision. If the account is seriously overdue, the company may withhold shipment pending receipt of payment from the customer to defray the previous balance. In this event, the customer should be notified as to the reason for the shipping delay.

CREDIT LINES

The two terms *credit lines* and *credit limits* are often used interchangeably. Historically, the term *credit limit* has been in use for a longer time than the term *credit line*. This is truer in the commercial credit field than in the bank credit field, in which the term *credit line* or *line of credit* has always been common.

Some commercial credit managers interpret the two terms a little differently. Some companies view credit lines as the maximum amount of credit they are willing to accept from a customer. Viewed in this manner, the credit line becomes the credit limit.

In most instances a firm uses these two terms as a warning signal or as a red flag on the amount of credit to be approved. It does not mean that orders exceeding this limit are automatically refused but that the limit acts as a guide to force further analysis of the account and a decision on whether to accept or reject the larger order.

The credit manager is generally too involved with more pressing matters to have to give the final approval to every order. Thus the firm has to establish some procedure so the credit manager can delegate authority for credit approval and at the same time retain the degree of control necessary to protect the credit department from excessive bad debts. The use of credit lines or credit limits frees the credit manager for really important decisions and places routine where it rightly belongs in the departmental operation.

Advantages

The use of credit lines increases the efficiency of the credit department. If handled properly, they save the credit manager's time for really important decisions, permit delegation of authority but still allow the credit manager to retain control of the accounts, and place routine tasks in the hands of subordinate personnel. In addition, credit lines force overall consideration of the entire account, not merely consideration on a transaction-by-transaction basis. This should in turn lead to better decision making. Likewise, credit lines protect the buyer; they act as a check on reckless buyers who for the moment may be unduly optimistic and want to buy excessive amounts.

Limitations

Credit lines are involved in approximately two-thirds to three-fourths of all commercial credit approvals. However, use of credit lines has some problems and limitations.

Firms that establish lines of credit for their customer and then don't keep them up-to-date defeat the basic purpose of credit lines. Such revisions are time consuming and costly, but periodic review is necessary to establish the customer's current ability to pay.

Another limitation of credit lines is that approval of orders within the credit line is generally performed by clerical personnel and not by the credit manager. Thus the credit manager may lose contact with an account and not develop its full business potential.

Methods of Setting Credit Lines

The credit department is never in a better position to establish a credit line for a customer than when the credit investigation is completed. Generally, at this time the credit department examines the credit data more carefully, analyzes the account more completely, and gives more thought as to whether to accept future orders than at any other time in the life of the account. The question then arises—just how do credit managers set credit lines? Credit managers generally report that they follow certain techniques, but they are not sure these are the best methods possible.

Six methods are commonly used: (1) allow as much credit as the customer wishes as long as payment is made as agreed; (2) allow the customer as much as the other creditors are allowing; (3) allow a small dollar volume of purchases and raise the amount gradually as the customer proves to be a good risk; (4) allow purchases based on a time interval; (5) the basis-of-facts method (divide the number of creditors of the customer into net worth, current assets, net working capital, and inventory); and (6) the requirements (or pseudoscientific) method.

AS MUCH AS THE CUSTOMER WISHES. Some firms allow customers as much credit as they wish, as long as they pay as agreed. Such an arrangement stresses the "increasing sales volume" function of the credit department and does not create any real problems for the credit manager—unless the customer cannot or will not pay as agreed. As long as payment is prompt and automatic, this method is a highly desirable one.

On the other hand, some observers believe this procedure should not be regarded as a method of setting credit lines, since no definite line is established and the transaction is entirely flexible, depending on the wishes and actions of the customer.

AS MUCH AS OTHER CREDITORS ARE ALLOWING. This method is based on the premise that a firm can discover the amount of credit its competitors are allowing the customer in question. While exact figures may be hard to obtain, a firm can often acquire approximations through direct interchange of such information and from Dun & Bradstreet and National Business Credit Reports. Of course, the highest recent credit figure may exceed what the seller believes the limit should be. In certain cases, extenuating circumstances (such as a desire not to offend a long-time customer) may cause the figure to be excessive.

If a firm adopts this method, it should ask, "How did the competitors decide what the credit line should be?" Unfortunately, there is usually no good and dependable answer to this question. Many firms rely on their own analysis and interpretation of the credit information to set the credit line, using their competitors' experiences only as a guide in particular cases.

START LOW AND RAISE WITH EXPERIENCE. A very common and practical procedure is to start with a small dollar amount and raise it gradually as the customer proves to be a good risk. The credit department may start a customer with a low limit or with enough to take care of the first purchase. As experience with the account accumulates and the customer proves able to pay larger amounts, the credit department raises the limit to take care of larger purchases. If the customer proves incapable of paying, the credit department holds the limit to restrain the customer's purchases, or it even lowers it.

BASE PURCHASES ON A TIME INTERVAL. Some credit departments attempt to limit an account to a certain period such as a month's purchases, a week's purchases, or some other definite time. For example, a $5,000 per month line of credit means that during any one-month period a credit department clerk could approve orders totaling $5,000, without referral to the credit manager, regardless of the total amount outstanding and owing.

Credit lines stated in this manner are useful in companies that process orders at a number of locations but maintain more centralized accounts receivable. In such credit lines, the total credit involved is often larger than the amount of the line, because even prompt payment for all invoices billed is not necessarily received during that period.

BASIS OF FACTS. This method is based on certain financial data, such as net worth, current assets, net working capital, and inventory. The information is then related to the number of creditors the customer may have, by dividing the number of creditors into the financial figures chosen by the credit manager. For example, if a firm has a net worth figure of $100,000 and 10 creditors, then the line of credit may be established at $10,000.[4] If this firm has an inventory figure of $80,000, the credit line would be $8,000.

While figures for net worth, current assets, net working capital, and inventory generally are readily available from financial statements, it is difficult to accurately estimate the number of creditors. One method of obtaining this information is simply to ask the customer for a list of the names and addresses of all creditors. Sometimes, however, such lists are incomplete, either intentionally or unintentionally. As a check, some firms also obtain a Dun & Bradstreet report that shows a "now owes" column for the customer in question. A similar column appears in the Business Credit Reports. Generally, these reports do not list all of the creditors either, and some adjustment must be made to arrive at a fairly accurate estimate. One method of adjustment is illustrated as follows. The XYZ Retail Store is seeking to buy goods from the ABC Manufacturer. This is the initial order. XYZ furnishes a balance sheet showing accounts payable of $10,000. ABC receives a National Business Credit Report that lists eight creditors of XYZ with an indebtedness of $8,000. Thus, if 8 creditors account for $8,000 worth of debt, the $10,000 accounts payable total is probably owed to 10 creditors. Such estimates are quite rough. Critics of this method point out that one creditor may account for half of the accounts receivable; in such a situation any system of proportions would be misleading. The estimate of creditors is simply a guide, and the basis-of-fact methods should be supplemented with some of the other methods described.

REQUIREMENTS (PSEUDOSCIENTIFIC) METHOD. This method usually involves five basic steps in computing a line of credit.

1. Secure the customer's total annual sales volume. This figure can often be obtained directly from the customer, from financial statements if these are prepared for creditors' use or published to conform to security regulations, or from educated guesses of the customer's sales activity.

2. Find out what part of these sales is in the line of business covered by you, the seller. Often this type of information is difficult to obtain with accuracy, unless the customer is willing to cooperate. Otherwise, a "guesstimate" may have to prevail.

3. Decide what proportion of this business you, the seller, can hope to secure. This is perhaps the weakest link in the method because this figure

---

[4]Generally, a line of credit is not established on the basis of a single computation. Several of these methods may be averaged to arrive at the final credit line.

has to be an estimate. Often there is wide variation between the volume the seller actually furnishes the customer and the volume the seller hopes or thinks will be sold. The accuracy with which this third step is carried out is a determining factor in the accuracy of the credit limit itself.

4. Determine how many days you will allow the customer in your net credit period. This step is necessary because a customer generally doesn't buy only once a year. The line of credit usually relates to the total amount of indebtedness a firm plans to accept from a customer at any one time, not to the customer's yearly accumulation of orders.

5. Adjust the retail limit thus far determined to reflect the cost value of the order. This step is necessary because the customer's cost price is the seller's selling price. This last step requires that the seller be familiar with the customer's gross margin of profit on the goods involved.

To illustrate the five steps:

1. Customer's annual sales are $50,000.
2. Proportion in the seller's line is $10,000.
3. Proportion the seller hopes to obtain is one-fourth, or $2,500.
4. Terms of sale are net 60, which means the goods should turn six times a year; $2,500 ÷ 6 equals approximately $416.
5. Gross margin of the customer is 30 percent. Thus the limit of the seller may be estimated as between $290 and $300.

Credit managers should use this method cautiously because it really is an estimate. Most credit managers supplement this procedure with one or several of the other methods.

To Inform or Not to Inform Customers

There are different schools of thought as to whether customers should be advised of their credit limit as soon as it is established. Some executives claim that notification permits the seller to discuss the entire credit picture with the customer and to offer suggestions on improving the credit standing, if necessary. Likewise, customers know the amount of credit they can rely on from the seller.

On the other hand, some observers point out that notification may cause customers to restrict their buying to the dollar amount of the credit line; that is, customers may interpret the word *line* to mean an inflexible limit. Because such an interpretation may hurt goodwill and sales volume, some executives view the credit line only as an instrument of internal control.

There is a similar difference of opinion as to whether the seller's salespeople should be informed of credit limits on their customers. Unfortunately, there is no one correct answer to either of these problems.

Speed—Essential to Handling Orders

In the operation of a commercial credit department, *speed* in processing and acting on orders is imperative. Much of this speed is accomplished by routinizing the credit-decision task through the maintenance of the department's in-file information. Current in-file information on customers and credit limits safely permit automatic approval of a large volume of orders. New accounts on which no in-file data exists and revived old accounts must be processed quickly and the credit investigation started without delay.

Speed is necessitated by the strong competitive environment in which many companies operate. Speed is one of the most important considerations when customers have the alternative of purchasing elsewhere. Delays, withheld shipments, and unreasonable requests for credit information destroy the desirable customer relationships developed by the salespeople. Retaining present customers and gaining new ones depend as much on speed as they do on price, quality, service, personalities, and the like.

AUTOMATION IN THE COMMERCIAL CREDIT DEPARTMENT[5]

Credit departments have felt the impact of advanced automated processing systems for years. The commercial credit departments of virtually all major corporations use such systems.

A company adopts an automated and accounts receivable system for four basic reasons: to introduce more operations in the automated data information flow, to provide helpful information for financial planning and control, to reduce expenses through more expanded use of the computer, and to increase the turnover of the investment in receivables.

Over the past three decades, the quality of computers and the speed of processing information in commercial credit departments have increased significantly.

Before the advent of the computer, a company handled its accounts receivable manually. The technological changes of the 1960s made the computerized processing of accounts receivable possible.

The first computerized systems used punched tab cards. Figures 19–1 and 19–2 illustrate a punch card and the early generation International Business Machine computer that processed these cards.

In this system, a tab card represented a single invoice. Key punch operators in data processing departments would work on these invoices, or tab cards, a batch at a time. The holes punched in the cards represented information about the client.

---

[5]The author wishes to express his appreciation to Richard L. Cole for his assistance in preparing this section of Chapter 19.

FIGURE 19–1 **Punch Card**

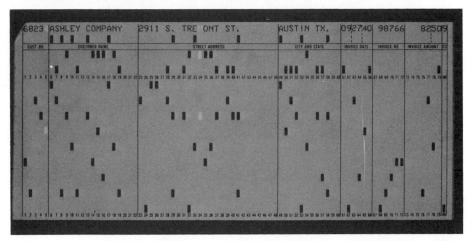

Courtesy of International Business Machines Corporation

FIGURE 19–2 **Early Generation IBM Computer**

Courtesy of International Business Machines Corporation

FIGURE 19-3 **Modern Mainframe Computer**

Courtesy of International Business Machines Corporation

Batches of these punched cards then were sent to the next stage where they were fed into the card reading machine to be processed.

It took at best 24 hours for management to get reports because of all the stages involved. This large number of stages also increased the potential for errors.

The tab card system gave way to on-line mainframes, minicomputers, and personal computers. Figure 19-3 shows a modern mainframe computer installation. Punched tab cards are no longer used; in their place are monitors and on-line terminals. These new on-line systems allow changes in a customer's account to be reflected immediately.

Today's system also allows instant access to databanks of information on customers, such as company name, address, phone numbers, and so on. The information could include the customer's Dun & Bradstreet rating, credit limit, and other special provisions pertinent to the account. It would also be possible to pull up the payment history for any time frame specified.

This speed and flexibility help credit departments make credit evaluations more quickly, identify problems before they arise, and ultimately reduce the number of questionable or high-risk clients in the system.

There have been other important recent developments in computers and software.

The development of packaged software has benefited all levels of commercial credit departments. While these packages have been most beneficial to small and medium-sized firms that could not afford programmers or expensive mainframes, they also have benefited large commercial credit departments because they have reduced the burden on in-house resources.

Large companies can customize the software rather than develop the software from scratch.

In addition, most vendors of these packages provide the initial setup and training, and they usually offer a maintenance option on a per month or per year basis. Companies also can upgrade the software as new versions are released. These new versions are usually priced one-fourth to one-half of the original cost, depending on the number of modifications.

Networking has increased the role of personal computers in commercial credit departments. Brenda Kelly, manager of marketing services for the Information Services Division of Lotus Development Corp., Cambridge, Massachusetts, in a recent article gives an excellent account of networking and its application in today's commercial credit department.

> Networking means sharing resources among several computers and peripherals that are cabled together, without necessarily drawing information from a corporate mainframe or minicomputer. Networking is key to a personal computer-based financial information center because it allows end users such as credit and finance departments to use state-of-the-art technology to perform their jobs more effectively, to access critical information in a timely fashion, and to share their results within their work groups. By joining personal computers in a network, finance departments can gain all the advantages of timesharing, particularly access to corporate financial information without the disadvantages associated with using larger machines.
>
> The biggest reason for the acceptance of the personal computer by corporate America was that it was easy to use. With the introduction of the personal computer, professionals could learn an application in hours rather than in days or even weeks.
>
> The second reason was the independence provided by the smaller machine. With a personal computer, a user could operate independently from the corporate management information systems (MIS) department. The user could choose software, develop proprietary applications. and operate daily without any interruptions from programmers. This new-found freedom encouraged finance departments to automate because it gave financial management more control over operations of the department.

* * * * *

Department Scenario

Here's what a contemporary department-level scenario might look like. Personal computers placed on the desktops of the entire department serve as the basis for a "financial workstation network." They are tied together in a local area network (LAN), which connects information among work groups.

Powerful spreadsheet, database, graphics, communications, and word processing software for business analysis and reporting are at the fingertips of individual users, while the financial data and analysis reports can be shared by the department through the network. The network acts as an information warehouse holding standard models and vast quantities of historical data. Central information is delivered throughout the network by a file server, which can either be a minicomputer or a personal computer.

* * * * *

When the network is operational, not only will the credit department be more efficient, but employees will be more productive and probably be more satisfied with their performance as well. At this point, it would be wise to hire a capable network administrator to keep the system operational and maximize return on the investment.

And then, it will be time for the credit manager to look at the next step: evaluating advances in data storage, operating systems, hardware, and applications software that will signal that is time to update the existing technology to realize even greater credit department productivity.[6]

Figure 19–4 shows an example of a network computer setup as mentioned in Brenda Kelly's article.

Another electronic or computer development used by commercial credit departments is electronic data interchange (EDI). EDI is defined as the business-to-business exchange of business documents, such as invoices, on an electronic basis.

The increased used of EDI has been driven by the move to other electronic business transactions, such as faxing. Faxing differs from EDI in that faxing transmits free-form rather than structured messages. In addition, faxed information must be transformed into a computer readable format, while the EDI transmission is already in a computer readable form.

While it is true that the number of commercial credit departments using EDI is low, this new technique is attracting increased attention. The automotive, chemical, and pharmaceutical industries use EDI extensively. Other industries increasing their use of EDI include the retail, electronic, and health care fields.

Surveys of companies using EDI show the main benefits of using EDI include the following:

- Cost efficiency.
- Faster response time.
- Potential increase in customer base.
- Convenience.

Companies mention some disadvantages of EDI:

- Initial setup cost.
- Lack of standardized formats.

---

[6]Brenda Kelly, "Networking," *Business Credit,* January 1988, pp. 22–23. Permission granted by National Association of Credit Management, *Business Credit.*

FIGURE 19–4 **IBM LAN Connectivity**

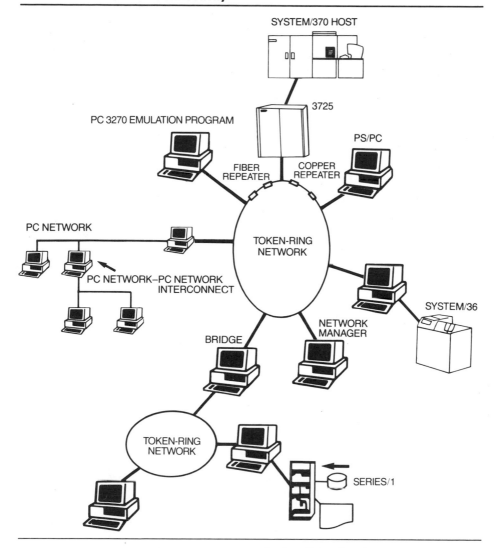

- Incompatibility between company computers and software.
- Lack of total management commitment.

Automation in commercial credit departments is constantly changing, and it is impossible to predict what the future holds.

REVIEW OF DECISIONS

Business conditions change. The credit standing of customers changes. The outlook of sellers changes. In fact, in credit operations change is a certainty, and successful credit managers recognize that decisions and credit lines must be regularly reviewed to bring them up-to-date. Otherwise, a company won't be able to increase sales volume, cut bad-debt losses, reduce the costs of credit administration, and efficiently manage the investment in receivables.

Unfortunately, despite all the safeguards of analyzing credit information from a number of sources, making careful and complete credit decisions, setting realistic lines of credit, and constantly reviewing all of these steps—not all credit accepted is repaid on time, and in some instances it is never repaid. For this reason, the next chapter discusses the policies and practices of commercial collection.

DISCUSSION QUESTIONS

1. Why should management furnish credit managers with a clearly defined and understood statement of what it desires of their departments?
2. How do various external factors influence a commercial creditor's house standard?
3. Discuss the controllable factors that influence a house standard.
4. What arrangements might be made to allow approval of orders from marginal and submarginal customers? Discuss these arrangements.
5. Why is it desirable as well as prudent business policy to provide a system for automatic approval of initial orders?
6. What are the advantages and disadvantages of developing a system of credit lines?
7. Describe how credit lines might be set. Can you suggest any methods other than those discussed in the text?
8. What provides the information needed to set limits on a customer's credit buying? Where can this be obtained?
9. Discuss the changes in the automation of the commercial credit department.
10. Explain what is meant by networking.

SUGGESTED READINGS

CLARK, GARY. "EDI: Where We've Been and Where We're Headed." *Business Credit,* December 1989, p. 20.

CLARK, WILLIAM M. "Controlled Architecture." *Business Credit,* May 1988, p. 23.

FARRAR, ROBERT L. "Cost-Benefit Analysis of an Automated System." *Business Credit,* May 1988, p. 28.

FERGUSON, DANIEL M., and NED C. HILL. "Missing the Boat." *Business Credit,* December 1988, p. 21.

HILL, NED C., and RUTH E. ANDERSEN. "EDI Gains Ground." *Business Credit,* December 1989, p. 18.

HOLT, RANDY B. "Instantaneous Information." *C&FM*, January 1987, p. 23.

KLEIN, FRANK. "Pluses and Pitfalls of Credit Office Automation." *Business Credit*, January 1990, p. 14.

ROBERTS, JULIE, and JACK SHAW. "Electronic Bridge." *Business Credit*, December 1987, p. 22.

SARGENT, JOHN S. "What's New in Pcs?" *Business Credit*, January 1989, p. 21.

SHAW, JACK. "Planning for EDI." *Business Credit*, December 1988, p. 18.

"Software: It's a New Game." *Business Week*, June 4, 1990, p. 102.

SOMERS, JOHN W. "The ACH Alternative." *Business Credit*, December 1987, p. 40.

WHITESIDE, BRYCE W. "Evaluation and Control." *C&FM*, November 1987, p. 39.

Collection Policies and Practices in Commercial Credit

The Objectives or Goals of Chapter 20 Are:

1. To discuss the factors affecting collection problems.
2. To set forth the preliminary steps in establishing a commercial collection system.
3. To distinguish between commercial credit insurance and consumer credit insurance.
4. To explain the basic features of commercial credit insurance.
5. To discuss the purposes of commercial credit insurance.
6. To illustrate the advantages and disadvantages of commercial credit insurance.
7. To discuss the collection actions available in commercial credit management.
8. To explain credit actions that may be taken by a single creditor.
9. To discuss credit actions that may be taken by a group of creditors.
10. To set forth the main provisions of a bankruptcy action.
11. To discuss third-party actions.

Collections are an inherent part of any commercial credit operation, just as they are an inherent part of any consumer credit operation. To be successful, a collection system must get the money. This objective becomes less obvious and much more difficult to attain when the creditor also must retain goodwill, rehabilitate the debtor, encourage prompt payment, and operate economically. If promptness is the major objective, it may be attained by handling all collections immediately. However, the methods selected and used may be very costly and may also lose goodwill. On the other hand, if retention of goodwill is the major objective, the appeals and techniques used will be very gentle, even delicate, and collections will tend to be slow in starting.

Thus the general purpose of a commercial collection system is twofold: maximization of collections and minimization of loss of future trade. Which segment of the purpose is emphasized depends on the aims and policies of the individual creditor firm.

FACTORS AFFECTING COLLECTION POLICY

Many factors influence a firm in its choice of a collection policy.[1] While the following factors are by no means a complete list, classification of debtors, capital, competition, type of business and type of goods, profit margin, credit policy followed, and type of records used are among the most important and influential factors. A brief discussion of each of these factors follows.

Classification of Debtors

Collection work would be less involved, time consuming, and headache producing if there were some magic formula by which each debtor firm could be immediately and accurately classified as to the reason for nonpayment of its account and as to the collection method or methods that would be most effective. Over the years, some firms have developed a classification of debtors similar to the following:

- Debtor misunderstood terms.
- Disputed amount.
- Careless or inefficient customer.
- Small amount involved, and customer therefore ignores.
- Slow by habit and by nature.
- Poor business management.
- Temporarily out of funds but good.
- Could pay but must be forced.
- Terms chiseler.
- A fraud.

The creditor may classify a past-due debtor into one or more of these categories and, from previous experience with similar customers, follow a predetermined policy to collect the amount due.

DEBTOR MISUNDERSTOOD TERMS. When this is the true situation, the solution is simple. Clarification of the credit terms and of what is ex-

---

[1]In recent years, many credit executives have been spending so much of their time with marginal customers and past-due accounts that they have forgotten the discount customers. There is a definite need to recognize and compliment these customers, since they are responsible for receivables turnover.

pected of the debtor should result in prompt payment. The word *should* is chosen because other reasons may be the true causes for nonpayment, and a professed misunderstanding of the terms may be merely an excuse. However, misunderstandings do occur, and businesses must take care to handle such cases in a manner that will maintain a maximum amount of goodwill. Sometimes salespeople, in an effort to make sales, assure customers that they can pay "whenever they wish to pay." This lack of coordination between sales and credit can make for customer ill will and may require reselling the customer when the true terms are spelled out.

DISPUTED AMOUNT. Disagreement between the seller and the buyer as to the quality and condition of the goods sold is to be expected from time to time. The buyer may withhold payment until some type of satisfactory agreement can be reached.

CARELESS OR INEFFICIENT CUSTOMER. Again, collecting from this customer should not be a major problem. Pressed with a variety of other problems and cares, this business executive has just overlooked making payment. The debtor may use an inefficient system to keep track of when bills are due or may just be careless or even forgetful. In most cases a simple reminder that the amount is due and immediately payable brings in payment with no loss of customer goodwill.

SMALL AMOUNT INVOLVED, AND CUSTOMER THEREFORE IGNORES. A small number of accounts payable personnel feel that if the indebtedness is small, they may ignore it for the time being, wait until the account becomes larger, and then write just one check to cover the entire amount. In such cases the debtor firm is making no attempt to escape payment; it is simply pursuing a delaying action that results in "future" payment to the creditor. In addition to the nuisance and trouble involved in having to start the collection procedure, there is always the problem that what is small to one firm may not be small to another.

SLOW BY HABIT AND BY NATURE. Some firms—and their accounts payable personnel—are notoriously slow in making payment. Payment is attained only after various types of collection devices are used and various degrees of persuasion applied. The firm that sells this type of customer, and knows beforehand that the customer is of this type, should carefully analyze the gross margin on any sale and compare it with the expenses involved in making the sale. Such expenses tend to be high because of the cost of the collection process. Even at the risk of losing a customer, the executive assigned the collection task should adopt a strict policy toward the firm that is slow by habit and nature. Such customers have a poor concept of responsibility and generally are undesirable and unprofitable accounts.

POOR BUSINESS MANAGEMENT. Firms falling into this category account for perhaps the largest number of difficulties for the collection manager. Often the operators of these firms are honest and optimistic but overbuy. Because of poor business management, they find they can't meet the terms to which they agreed. The creditor must decide whether there is any hope that such a business manager will learn to conduct buying activities profitably before determining whether to follow a strict or a lenient collection policy. Can the business manager be salvaged and made into a good customer? If the answer is no, the relationship should be terminated quickly.

TEMPORARILY OUT OF FUNDS BUT GOOD. This type of customer is usually delinquent because of conditions beyond his or her control, such as illness, business conditions, or other developments. The debtor is not actually attempting to avoid payment, and the delinquency should not be viewed as a reflection on the debtor's integrity, but this should not delay the collection action. An amicable adjustment or extension of the credit period should be made as quickly as possible, and the creditor should insist that the terms of the new agreement be carried out to the limit of the debtor's ability.

COULD PAY BUT MUST BE FORCED. This type of customer is somewhat similar to the customer that is slow by habit and by nature. However, in dealing with this group, more persuasion and even threats must be used to obtain payment. Most of the time, unless they are pursued vigorously, payment is unduly delayed or never occurs. Credit standing means very little to this customer who has become accustomed to severe collection methods. For this reason, in its dealings with these chronic delinquents the collection department should force the issue immediately and strongly, at the very moment when the account becomes past due. Less severe actions have little value, and the creditor will get no return for the expense involved.

TERMS CHISELER. At least two types of chiselers might be included in this classification. One is the type who regularly deducts cash discounts even when making payments after expiration of the cash discount period. Firms vary as to their policies in such a situation. Is it best to return the check and request full payment or to accept the check and bill the customer for the balance owing? Whichever procedure is followed, the action taken should be accompanied by a clear, concise statement that credit terms are being violated. How strong and threatening the statement should be largely depends on how profitable the customer is to the firm and on how much the customer's future business is desired.

Another type of chiseler is the customer who makes only a partial payment, sends a postdated check with deductions for cash discounts, or dates a check back so that the date is within the discount period. The chronic offender who operates this way should be told "the facts of credit" much more emphatically than the first-time offender who simply may have been careless.

A FRAUD. The creditor should show this dishonest debtor no consideration, nor should it make any effort to retain this debtor's goodwill or possible future business. Just as soon as the creditor firm is convinced that the debtor is dishonest and is engaged in fraudulent actions, the account should be turned over to an attorney, or possibly to a collection agency, with instructions to take legal action against the debtor. Time is of the essence in dealing with such offenders, and there is little reason to go through all the steps normally followed in a collection process.

Capital

The discussion that appeared under this topic in Chapter 11 applies equally well to commercial credit transactions and is repeated here. One of the most important factors affecting collection policy is the amount of capital the firm owns or has available. Regardless of how liberal a collection policy creditors may wish to follow, if they are operating within a limited capital structure, they usually have to adopt a strict collection policy in order to meet the demands of their own creditors. Most business firms are not blessed with an overabundance of working capital and are forced to depend on the turnover of their goods to provide the funds they need. A mere turnover of goods is not enough if these goods are sold on credit, as they usually are in commercial transactions. One step is added to the process—completing the credit transaction by receipt of cash payment. How quickly this last step must be completed depends on how badly the firm needs capital. Thus capital availability and need play a vital role in determining what type of collection policy a firm must adopt, despite the fact that a different policy might be more desirable in view of some of the other factors involved. Closely connected with the subject of capital availability is the question of whether a firm should charge its slow-paying customers interest for carrying their past-due accounts. There is no uniformity of opinion on this subject.

Competition

Modern businesses do not function in a vacuum or in the pure air of no competition. Rather, the firm attempting to sell its goods and services finds that the actions taken by its competitors have a great influence on the policies it establishes, including its collection policy. Thus, if an active competitor is "selling" its lenient credit and collection policy, a firm cannot simply ignore this policy and indiscriminately follow a strict credit and collection policy. That is, the firm cannot do so if it wants to obtain its share of the business. Thus, in deciding what type of collection policy to establish and follow, it must consider the competition.

Type of Business and Type of Goods

Collection methods and practices tend to vary with the type of business and method of operation of the selling firm and with the type of goods sold. As in consumer credit, the more perishable the product, the greater the need for prompt payment of the account, and thus the stricter the collection policy that should be followed.

Profit Margin

With any collection policy, the ultimate aim of the creditor firm is to collect the amount due and still have a net profit left after deducting all the expenses from the gross margin. Thus how wide this gross margin is influences the collection policy followed. The wider the profit margin a firm operates on, the more lenient its collection policy can be. On the other hand, narrow profit margins do not permit long delinquencies or extended and costly collection procedures. Thus both the risk and cost involved must be related to the creditor firm's profit margin. In addition, a collection policy must consider the profitableness of a particular debtor's business—some portions of a vendor's activities are more profitable than others. Not all lines carry the same profit margin; some sales carry higher selling, delivery, and service expenses than others. These differences need to be carefully analyzed.

Credit Policy Followed

The credit policy a firm establishes and follows has an important influence on the type of collection policy it adopts. Firms that follow a liberal credit approach usually have a strict collection policy, and firms with a strict credit approach usually have a liberal collection policy. To be liberal in both phases invites trouble; to be strict in both phases is to neglect the "increasing sales" aspect of credit activities. The creditor firm must recognize that as long as its customers regard credit solely as a service rather than a mutual privilege, its collection problems may be troublesome. When the customer thinks of credit as a joint business transaction, the collection problems of the creditor tend to become simpler, sentimentality lessens, and the creditor is less reluctant to insist on payment for fear of incurring customers' ill will. Terms established between the debtor and the creditor must be respected. Slow-paying customers not only cost additional money for collection efforts, but they also often are reluctant to return to the scene of their buying activities until they clear up their previous indebtedness.

Types of Records

While it is not possible to set up a record system that will fit all businesses, the type of record-keeping used directly affects the collection system introduced and the efficiency with which it operates. Each business should carefully study its own requirements and adopt a system to meet its needs. The credit and collection manager should carefully consider the numerous systems and the various kinds of equipment offered by the office equipment supply houses. These are being revised, modified, and improved constantly, with the aim of making information available faster. Before making any decision as to the system to introduce and to use, credit and collection managers should remind themselves that the system that *meets the needs* of their business at the *lowest relative cost* is the system they should adopt.

One of the essential features of an effective collection procedure is that it furnishes the first reminder notice promptly. If debtors receive this notice long after the due date has passed, they tend to feel that the credit is inefficient and indifferent. Collections may drop accordingly. Thus the system used should provide daily information on every overdue account.

PRELIMINARY STEPS IN ESTABLISHING A COMMERCIAL COLLECTION SYSTEM

Discussion of a general collection system that appears in Chapter 11 is pertinent here. While the material in that chapter is slanted toward collection problems and procedures in consumer credit transactions, many of the comments apply to commercial credit procedures and practices as well. The following comments are taken from that chapter.

Promptness and regularity of payment must be built into any system for the following reasons:

1. A lax collection policy often indicates an incompetent management. This in turn can affect the purchaser's attitude toward the firm's products.
2. Experience shows that there is a definite correlation between the length of time debts are unpaid and the volume of resulting bad-debt losses.
3. Slow collections tend to result in the loss of future sales to the slow-paying customers because of their reluctance to buy from creditors they've owed for some time. Of course, creditors may show an even stronger reluctance to sell to such customers.
4. Failure to enforce collection tends to encourage the imprudent purchaser. Thus foolhardy buyers may plunge headlong into unwise buying, knowing that the selling firm's collection department allows an excessively long time to pass before drastic legal action is taken, if it is ever taken.

To bring about prompt and regular payment, firms should take the following preliminary steps to establish a sound commercial collection system:

1. Determine the length of time for the collection process to run.
2. Select appropriate types of collection devices to use or actions to take.
3. Decide on the number of actions to be taken.
4. Arrange these actions in logical sequence.
5. Schedule the actions at appropriate intervals.

In the preliminary planning stage, the person responsible for collecting accounts receivable has to decide how long the entire collection process should run. Such a decision generally is controlled by circumstances other than the desires of the collection manager. For example, all the factors previously discussed (debtor classification, capital, competition, type of business, type of goods sold, profit margin, credit policy, and type of records) have an important bearing.

It is equally important—or possibly even more important—to select appropriate types of collection devices to use or actions to take.

The third step in establishing a sound commercial credit system is to decide on the number of these actions to be taken. In other words, once the credit manager has decided to use collection letters, for example, just how many of these letters will be included in any collection procedure? Undoubtedly, the more lenient the policy, the larger the number of such actions that will be included.

Step four involves arranging these actions in some logical sequence. Since collection efforts have the twofold objective of obtaining money and retaining goodwill, most successful collection managers use the milder methods first, following them with more intense actions, arranged in order of severity. Exceptions to this arrangement are appropriate when the debtor was a marginal risk to begin with and the collection manager knows that the milder methods would be a waste of time and money.

The last step is to determine the frequency with which the collection actions should be used or the time interval that should be allowed between each action taken. A lenient collection policy calls not only for a relatively large number of collection actions but also for a comparatively long lapse of time between different measures. In all instances, however, the time interval should become shorter as the stage of delinquency advances.

COLLECTION PRACTICES AVAILABLE[2]

Commercial collection actions can be divided into four categories: (1) use of commercial credit insurance, (2) actions between a single creditor and

---

[2]For articles on commercial collection practices, see the Suggested Readings at the end of the chapter.

a single debtor, (3) actions between a group of creditors and a single debtor, and (4) third-party actions between a creditor or group of creditors and a debtor. Which action proves most successful depends largely on the circumstances surrounding the particular account.

COMMERCIAL CREDIT INSURANCE

Commercial credit insurance is an arrangement between an insurance company and a business under which the insured firm is guaranteed payment against abnormal credit losses arising from the failure of business debtors to pay their obligations. In addition, the insured firm receives other services and benefits from the insurance company.

Life insurance certainly does not eliminate the need for doctors and attention to good health practices, and commercial credit insurance does not eliminate the need for credit departments and credit managers. But this type of insurance, which is still unused by a large segment of the business world, is a valuable management tool.

Commercial credit insurance is confined to manufacturers, wholesalers, and so forth; it is not available to firms selling goods and services or lending money to ultimate consumers. Transactions involving consumers are sometimes covered by credit life insurance or consumer credit insurance. This type of risk-sharing is predicated on the death or disability of the consumer. Commercial credit insurance is a different field of activity.

Some consider commercial credit insurance part of a firm's collection policy, whereas others consider it part of a firm's credit determination policy. From the first point of view, when an order is received, the creditor investigates the account through the accumulation of credit information from credit reporting agencies, decides to accept or reject the order, and, if accepted, determines a credit line to guide future orders. If all accounts paid as agreed, there would be no need to worry about collecting accounts receivable. Unfortunately, not every account pays as agreed. As a result some firms share part of the risk of noncollection with an insurance company and use commercial credit insurance as part of their collection policy. The other point of view is that commercial credit insurance should be used directly in connection with the formulation of credit decisions, as an aggressive weapon rather than a defensive one.

Basic Features of Commercial Credit Insurance

As previously pointed out, commercial credit insurance is used primarily to protect manufacturers, jobbers, wholesalers, and certain types of service organizations.

Since commercial credit insurance is offered in a wide variety of policy forms, endorsements, and stipulations, a commercial credit insurance policy can be virtually tailor-made to meet the needs of the policyholder. In the past, insurers wrote individual account policies, along with general coverage policies. The individual account policies covered only single accounts selected by the insured company. In recent years, very few individual account policies have been written because of the possible adverse selection of risk against the insurance company. Practically all policies now being written are of the general coverage type.

Policies may be written with or without a provision for the insurance company to handle all phases of the collection of past-due accounts. When the policy is written on an optional collection basis, the insured firm may turn over any past-due account for collection; no fees are charged on accounts collected within 10 days. The policy lists an agreed-on schedule of fees, usually based on Commercial Law League rates. Policies also may be written with no collection provision.

In a commercial credit insurance policy there may be two deductibles, coinsurance and primary loss. The amount of coinsurance (an arrangement by which an insured firm bears a specified percentage of its total losses on all insured accounts) is deducted from the invoiced price of the merchandise shipped. Coinsurance usually amounts to approximately 10 to 20 percent, although on many policies it can be waived. This amount usually is higher on customers who are not rated in the first or second credit appraisal category of recognized mercantile agencies or who carry no credit appraisal at all. Currently very few coinsurance policies are sold. Most policies today are written without coinsurance; this means there is only one deductible, and that is the primary loss.

The insurance company and the insured agree on a primary loss figure as a percentage of the insured's covered sales, with a definite minimum spelled out in the policy. This primary loss percentage varies with the risk covered, the size of the sales volume, and the insured's actual loss experience. If the applicant's loss experience is less than the national average for that line of business, the applicant is generally recognized as a better risk and the amount of primary loss is reduced.

In 1960 the American Credit Indemnity Company started offering a new standard policy available in either the back-coverage or the forward-coverage form. This new policy, which is in addition to the other standard policies offered, eliminates the coinsurance feature. Thus it is now possible for the insured to be reimbursed in excess of the primary loss for the full invoiced price of the shipped goods. The premium, of course, is higher than for policies with coinsurance.

Purpose of Commercial Credit Insurance

In Chapter 1 credit was defined as a medium of exchange of limited acceptance. It was further spelled out that credit is of limited acceptance because of two elements—time and risk. Thus in every credit transaction there is an element of risk, and the credit manager must decide whether to bear this risk alone or to share it with someone else. The firm that factors its accounts receivable has decided to let another institution bear the task of credit acceptance and credit collection without recourse. For this service, the firm pays a fee to the factor. Credit insurance is another method of sharing this risk with others—this time with an insurance institution rather than with a financial institution. For a charge, the risk accompanying the credit transaction is shared with a specialist, just as fire, theft, storm, and public liability dangers are passed on to other types of insurance companies. Credit insurance insures against unusual loss—it does not protect the insured against normal (or primary) loss.

With most firms, the extent of this unusual or abnormal loss depends on many factors. These include the highest credit accepted from any one customer, the type of business the seller is engaged in, the product or products sold (type, stability, diversification, seasonality, obsolescence), the quality and "freshness" of inventories, the geographic location of and competition in the buyer's markets, money supply in the economy, price-level fluctuations, the phase of the business cycle, and labor conditions. Some of these factors are within the seller's control; others are beyond the seller's control and depend on external circumstances.

Advantages of Commercial Credit Insurance

When a firm suffers an abnormal bad-debt loss, credit insurance has more to offer than just financial coverage.

BALANCE BETWEEN SALES AND PROFITS. Advocates of commercial credit insurance point out that users can have a clear idea in advance of what costs they will incur during the coming year in the form of excessive or abnormal credit losses. By combining normal losses with the premium cost paid for credit insurance, the credit manager can estimate the maximum cost fairly accurately. If a firm's expense control system is working properly and other expense items are subject to accurate prediction, the firm can then make a fairly good approximation of anticipated profits. This use of credit insurance depends on the type of policy written because some policies do not cover all possible losses on all classes of risks.

Credit insurance also works on the sales side of the credit manager's operations. Some credit managers believe that purchasing credit insurance makes them more careful about accepting credit. Care is necessary in order to stay within the provisions of the credit insurance policy. Other credit managers argue that the opposite effect results: By shifting extraordinary losses to the insurance company, the insured can afford to take greater risks in credit acceptance and thus can increase sales volume. Since the insurance company covers and the insured firm retains any increased profits, credit insurance may work for freer credit acceptance on the part of some companies.

IMPROVEMENTS IN COLLECTIONS. The longer an account remains unpaid, the more difficult it is to collect. The insurance company usually stipulates that to be proved as claims, delinquent accounts must be turned over to the company within 12 months of the shipping date or within 3 months of the due date, whichever is longer. The insurance company usually takes vigorous collection action, thus increasing the chances of early collection and greater return to the creditor company. The psychological impact of collection by a third party—when the third party is an insurance company—cannot be overlooked.

IMPROVEMENT IN BORROWING CAPACITY. Most firms have to borrow funds periodically to carry on their operations. Some of these loans are unsecured; some involve the assignment of accounts receivable as collateral. Credit insurance may help in the discounting of these accounts receivable with a commercial bank or a commercial finance company.

Disadvantages of Commercial Credit Insurance

Some credit executives believe the weaknesses connected with commercial credit insurance overshadow any benefits. Some even go so far as to say there is no legitimate place or need for credit insurance in an efficient and well-run credit department. Despite its widespread use, not all firms need commercial credit insurance. Some types of firms may find credit insurance unnecessary or of little or no advantage.

Some of the most important disadvantages generally listed are cost, a false sense of security, restrictions in placing accounts for collection, limiting features of the policy provisions, and need for credit insurance as opposed to other types of insurance.

COST. Premium payments on commercial credit insurance are an expense item for a business. Although credit insurance is designed to cover an abnormal or unusual credit loss, some firms find that amounts recovered from such accounts are frequently less than the premium cost over a number of years. Of course, a company cannot overlook the fact that it enjoyed *protection* from excess loss during the period and in one sense was fortunate that its bad debts stayed within a normal range. Similarly, individuals who buy health and accident insurance and are fortunate enough to stay well for five years may reason that they would have been ahead at the end of the five-year period if they had not taken out the insurance. Their reasoning would be very different, however, if they had required a month's hospital stay during the first year the policy was in effect. Even if no claim is made against the commercial credit insurance (or the health and accident insurance), remember that *protection* has been obtained for the premium paid.

FALSE SENSE OF SECURITY. Another important objection raised against commercial credit insurance is that it may cause some credit managers to rely more on insurance protection than on their own judgment. Credit insurance thus may give credit managers a false sense of security. Because excessive bad-debt losses are covered, credit managers may have less incentive to lower bad-debt losses and may exercise a freer hand in credit acceptance to receive a return from the credit insurance policies.

COLLECTION RESTRICTIONS. Under most commercial credit insurance policies, accounts that have gone unpaid are turned over to the insurance company within the stipulated period of 12 months from the shipment date. Previously, this period was only six months, which sometimes precluded a credit department from exploring all friendly means of collecting the entire amount or an acceptable and fair reduced amount (composition settlement as discussed later). Lengthening this period from 6 to 12 months recognized the facts that circumstances often prevent a firm from paying within the specified credit period and that a carefully worked out arrangement between seller and buyer may result in complete recovery of the indebtedness and the maintenance of goodwill.

LIMITING POLICY FEATURES. Commercial credit insurance does not cover all losses. Creditors must bear normal (or primary) bad-debt losses, and some criticism is leveled at the method by which this primary loss is computed.

Another debatable feature of credit insurance policies is that the insurable risk of any one customer may depend primarily on the ratings given by Dun & Bradstreet and by special mercantile agencies. To base credit decisions primarily on agency ratings fails to give due weight to all the other credit information normally available to the credit analyst. While the required limitation is justifiable from the insurance company's view, such a restriction seems to infringe on the credit manager's responsibility to weigh all the factors involved and analyze pertinent sources of information before arriving at a decision.

CREDIT VERSUS OTHER TYPES OF INSURANCE. Simply to say that a firm needs to protect its accounts receivable by insurance because insurance protects its inventory, building, and equipment against fire or "acts of God" fails to recognize the difference in the two needs. The company that has all of its inventory and equipment in one building faces the threat that a fire, flood, tornado, or windstorm could wipe out these assets in a short time. To protect against this calamity, companies carry insurance. There are companies, of course, whose plants are so widely scattered and whose danger of financial ruin because of fires and acts of God is so remote that they provide their own form of insurance through some system of reserves.

The chances that a firm's accounts receivable will be wiped out in a single disaster are very remote. Even though receivables are concentrated industrywide or geographically, it is hard to imagine a firm losing the major portion of its accounts in any one year. Nevertheless, protection against excessive loss in large accounts has proved a desirable activity for many firms.

The insurance company should never be considered as a replacement for the firm's credit department and credit manager. Commercial credit insurance is not intended to make credit executives careless in credit acceptance. Its primary purpose is to protect against the unexpected and unpreventable accidental losses that sometimes occur despite the precautions and safeguards taken by the insuring concern.

SINGLE CREDITOR AND SINGLE DEBTOR

Generally, the action between a single creditor and a single debtor occurs before a business makes any effort to use either of the other remaining types of action. Whether group action or third-party action occurs because single-party actions have not been successful depends on the circumstances.

The actions taken between a single creditor and a single debtor are practically the same in consumer credit and commercial credit. These devices, which generally are well known to both debtor and creditor, include:

Invoices.	Attorneys.
Statements.	Collection agencies (part
Reminders.	of the debtor company or
Telephone calls.	separate organizations).
Personal calls.	Replevin (repossession of
Personal letters.	merchandise).
Notes, drafts, and trade	Extension agreement.
acceptances.	Suit.
Assignment of accounts	
receivable.	

Chapter 11 contains a discussion of these devices.[3] However, the use of notes, drafts, and trade acceptances is common only in commercial credit transactions.

When the debtor firm does not meet its obligations on its indebtedness, the creditor may ask that a promissory note be signed. This usually takes place only after a predetermined extension has been worked out and a

---

[3]While the discussion in Chapter 11 is slanted toward consumer credit, the basic description of such actions applies equally well to commercial transactions.

definite date of repayment can be shown on the note. In addition to the stated repayment date, the parties may agree on an interest charge.

In other instances a sight draft may be used. The sight draft has declined in popularity in recent years; it is most commonly used today in connection with COD shipments. In brief, the creditor prepares the draft, which in effect requests the customer's bank to seek payment of the account. Perhaps moral pressure is the draft's greatest asset in that debtors want to maintain good working relations with their banks and have their bankers think highly of their credit responsibility.

The trade acceptance, likewise, is drawn up in connection with the shipment of goods from seller to buyer. The manufacturer prepares the trade acceptance at the time of shipment. On receiving the form, customers indicate their acceptance of the indebtedness by signing and dating the agreement and designate the bank at which they will make payment on the noted date. The manufacturer may hold the acceptance until collection time and then send it to the bank as a collection item, or it may discount the acceptance with the bank before the payment date.

Another action often taken by a single creditor is to delegate the early stages of the collection procedure to sales representatives. Just as sales representatives frequently do a nominal amount of investigative work on their customers, they may also be called on for collections. Sales representatives who call on smaller companies are in a good position to take collection action. Smaller companies have relatively simple organizational structures, and salespeople have easy access to the responsible parties. In fact, sales representatives can often discuss collection problems with the proprietor or partner personally. Furthermore, their closeness to the business and their observations and reasoning as to why a customer is delinquent may be particularly helpful to the collection department in plotting future actions. New orders from past-due and seriously delinquent accounts obviously will be rejected so sales representatives have a stake in prompt and effective collection procedures.

In 1984 the Western Union Telegraph Co. published its *8-Step Guide to More Effective Credit and Collections.* In this booklet, Western Union pointed out that it can help credit managers with communications, such as accepting or rejecting credit, requesting further information from a customer seeking credit, and collecting overdue accounts in various stages of delinquency. The help Western Union provides most often takes the form of Mailgram® messages (known for their high-priority look and overnight message delivery) and Computer Letter℠ Service (used for credit mailings that require enclosures, such as printed folders).

GROUP OF CREDITORS AND SINGLE DEBTOR

The most common types of action taken by a group of creditors against a single debtor are: extension agreement, composition settlement, assignment, bankruptcy, and arrangements.

Extension Agreement

An extension agreement, which may be either a single-creditor or a group-creditor action, is essentially a moratorium under which the debtor proposes to pay creditors in full at some future date. This agreement is binding only on those creditors who sign it, and no creditor is compelled to do so. For this reason, if larger creditors want to grant an extension to a debtor but some smaller creditors don't agree, the smaller creditors sometimes are paid in full by the other creditors to prevent them from filing involuntary bankruptcy proceedings. Credit managers have learned to be careful in estimating the extent of the debtor's difficulties, however, before granting an extension.

Composition Settlement

This settlement, either with or without an extension of time, is a contractual arrangement under which the creditors that sign the agreement offer to accept less than the full amount of their indebtedness and in turn agree to discharge the debtor from any future obligation to make full settlement.

Again, care should be taken to grant such settlements only to debtors who could probably operate profitably in the future if relieved of their present excessive debt burden. Also, evidence of fraud should cause any composition settlement to be set aside and the offender prosecuted to the limit.

Assignment

When an extension is not warranted and a composition settlement cannot be agreed on, "friendly" liquidation of the business and settlement of the indebtedness may come about through assignment proceedings.[4]

Assignment for the benefit of creditors is generally considered a voluntary, out-of-court action taken by debtors who usually are insolvent (liabilities exceed assets). The debtors transfer in trust some or all of their assets to a third party, an assignee, so that these assets or proceeds from their sale can be applied to pay their debts. Such an assignment may be made under either common law or state law—every state has some form of law that spells out the provisions for an assignment.

At first glance, it may appear that assignment prevents all the ills of bankruptcy (described in the subsequent section). Advocates of this method point out that it is fast, relatively inexpensive, free from court restraints, and private, and that it provides more money for distribution to the creditors. Critics of the plan point out that assignment constitutes

---

[4]Assignment as used here is entirely different from assignment of accounts receivable.

an act of bankruptcy, that debtors cannot be examined under oath, that recovery of preferential payments is not provided for, that debtors are not freed of their remaining indebtedness without the creditors' consent, that there is a lack of uniformity in state laws concerning the procedure,[5] and that there is little or no direct supervision over the assignee in estate administration.

Bankruptcy

Creditors have several duties and responsibilities in bankruptcy cases.[6] Credit managers handling bankruptcy matters should be familiar enough with the law to know the rights of their firms and to take the proper steps to protect these rights.

The most important responsibility of credit managers arises out of the fact that they often have the power to decide whether to place a debtor in bankruptcy or to attempt other means of working out a bad situation. Hastening to place every difficult collection into bankruptcy means overburdening the bankruptcy courts with unnecessary cases. Liquidation by bankruptcy may be more costly and less advantageous than liquidation by other means. The creditor, then, should consider carefully whether all other possible means of collecting the debt have been canvassed before consenting to be a party to a bankruptcy petition.

Another consideration is the debtor's attitude. If the debtor is giving preference to favored creditors or is dissipating the estate by conveyances, transferences, or concealment of property with the intent to hinder, delay, or defraud creditors, the estate must be put into bankruptcy to protect all creditors and to secure a fair and equitable distribution of the assets. If, however, the debtor is trying to be fair and is doing everything possible to protect the creditor's interests, intelligent creditors help the debtor avoid the stigma of bankruptcy and find some better way to work out the debtor's difficulties.

BANKRUPTCY LEGISLATION IN THE UNITED STATES. The Constitution of the United States provides in Article 1, Section 8, that: "The Congress shall have power . . . to establish . . . uniform laws on the subject of bankruptcies throughout the United States."

The grant of this power to the federal government was not subject to much discussion either in the Constitutional Convention or in the various ratifying conventions. Congress did not immediately exercise the power, and the first U.S. Bankruptcy Act was not passed until 1800. This act was

---

[5]This constitutes a problem when creditors in several states are involved with the delinquent debtor.

[6]For articles on bankruptcy, see the Suggested Readings at the end of the chapter.

repealed in 1803. A second, passed in 1841, was repealed in 1843. A third, passed in 1867, lasted until 1878. While there have been numerous amendments to the act, the most thorough revision was made in 1938.

Two important changes in the bankruptcy legislation took place in 1966. On July 6, 1966, the president signed bills H.R. 136 and H.R. 3438. These bills were enacted to provide fairer treatment of general creditors in bankruptcy and to establish a healthier climate for the future credit extensions necessary for an expanding economy.

An amendment to the Bankruptcy Act of 1938 was passed by the 91st Congress in mid-October 1970. It was designed

> to permit the discharge of debts in a subsequent proceeding after denial of discharge for specified reasons in an earlier proceeding, to authorize courts of bankruptcy to determine the dischargeability or nondischarge-ability of provable debts, and to provide additional grounds for the revocation of discharges.[7]

One of the amendment's most interesting provisions is that it prohibits creditors whose debts are discharged from instituting or continuing any action or employing any process to collect the debts as personal liabilities of the bankrupt. While this provision applies more directly to the field of consumer credit, it also is pertinent to the field of commercial credit, with all possible ramifications.

On November 6, 1978, the president signed the Bankruptcy Reform Act of 1978. This act repealed the Bankruptcy Act of 1898 and codified and enacted Title 11 of the United States Code. It became substantially effective on October 1, 1979, and applied to all cases filed after that date. Some of the most important provisions of the Bankruptcy Reform Act are explained in Chapter 11.

In July 1984, both houses of Congress passed and the president signed the long-awaited and controversial Bankruptcy Amendments and Federal Judgeship Act. While most of the provisions of the 1984 law pertained to consumer bankruptcy, proceedings relating to commercial bankruptcy were improved by the new arrangement in which bankruptcy judges reported to district courts. Additionally, the new law provided for the appointment of 85 new district and circuit court judges.

GENERAL PURPOSES OF BANKRUPTCY LEGISLATION. Legislation dealing with the relationship of debtors to their creditors has three general purposes.

The first and earliest purpose was to provide creditors with some legal means to obtain possession of the debtor's property and equitably distribute it among the claimants. In addition to possession of the debtor's

---

[7]Public Law 91-467, 91st Congress, S. 4247, October 19, 1970.

property, creditors frequently were given control of the debtor himself or herself to further enforce payment from a recalcitrant or unwilling debtor. Some severe penalties of early legislation had as their underlying motive the belief that treating the debtor severely would stir the debtor's relatives to renewed efforts to satisfy the debts or perhaps would dissuade the debtor from attempts to defraud creditors.

Later, creditors realized controlling the debtor's person served no useful purpose. Therefore, later bankruptcy acts attempted to provide merely for an equitable distribution of the debtor's property among the various creditors. Provisions for the distribution of property were needed to avoid an inequitable division of the debtor's estate that might result from permitting the debtor to make preferential payments after becoming insolvent. It also was necessary to prevent the estate from being apportioned exclusively to the more diligent creditors. The condition of insolvency means the debtor's equity in the estate is extinguished. Under this condition, the entire estate is used to satisfy the creditors' claims and thus may be said to belong to the creditors rather than to the debtor. Bankruptcy legislation provides a means whereby this property can be prorated among the creditors equitably and economically.

The second purpose of bankruptcy legislation was to relieve debtors from further demands after confessing their inability to satisfy claims against them. People now realize the folly and inhumanity of oppressing debtors by requiring them to continue the struggle to pay debts that are beyond their capacity. It is common decency to free debtors from an impossible burden and not to make them continually pay the penalty for past mistakes. The debtor is relieved of the legal necessity of paying debts by surrendering the entire estate. This does not necessarily relieve debtors from the moral obligation—they may still feel morally compelled to repay unsatisfied debts. The protection of the law, however, relieves them from the necessity of paying debts that are beyond their capacity.

The third purpose recognized that society had an interest in rehabilitating debtors. As long as debtors are oppressed by the results of past mistakes, they are lost to society as useful, active producers. Every effort they make to rehabilitate themselves may be defeated by the pressure of creditors, and they are forced to become drones or burdens on society. Furthermore, fear of the consequences of debt would inhibit ambitious people and stifle initiative. Thus economic development would be slower. Therefore, society should permit debtors to recover and provide an equitable process of so doing. However, this process should not go to the other extreme of unduly favoring debtors. When relief from debts is too easy and readily available, the fear of loss inhibits creditors from lending and slows down social and economic development. Thus the social good requires that laws provide full and equitable protection of creditors' rights and also relieve debtors from impossible burdens. But such controls should not enable fraudulent debtors to shield themselves from the consequences of their acts.

In general, bankruptcy legislation in the United States has attempted to strike a balance between the interests of debtors and the interests of creditors, while maintaining maximum social good. At times, changes designed to favor various groups have been proposed to Congress. Associations of creditors frequently agitate for "reforms" that would afford them more protection or prevent certain "abuses," while associations of debtors seek reforms that would provide them with more "relief."

WHAT IS BANKRUPTCY? According to the legal definition, bankruptcy exists when there is insolvency and legal and public recognition of the condition coupled with some specific act or acts on the part of the debtor or creditor or both. Moreover, not every firm can avail itself of the provisions of the Bankruptcy Act and become legally bankrupt.

KINDS OF BANKRUPTCY. Bankruptcy may be either voluntary or involuntary. As the terms imply, voluntary bankruptcy comes about through the conscious desire and initiative of the debtor. Involuntary bankruptcy is brought about through the conscious desire and initiative of the creditor(s).

WHAT FIRMS MAY BECOME BANKRUPT? Perhaps the easiest way to answer this question is to list the types or classes of firms that can neither voluntarily petition themselves into bankruptcy nor be forced into it. These are: municipalities, railroads, insurance companies, banking corporations, and building and loan associations.

RESPONSIBILITIES OF CREDIT MANAGERS IN REGARD TO BANK-RUPTCY. When becoming a party to an involuntary petition or when receiving notice of the filing of either a voluntary or an involuntary petition, credit managers should immediately take steps to protect their firms' interests. These necessary steps are as follows:

1. Stop all further credit. Mark all records to indicate that credit lines are suspended.
2. Recover as much as can be recovered. Hold up or stop payment on all checks and other remittances going to the bankrupt. Issue stoppage orders on goods in transit. Stop work on all goods in process or on order. File suit to recover goods already in the debtor's possession whenever there is a legal ground for doing so. Seize and hold all the debtor's property in your possession or that can be placed in your possession lawfully.
3. Start foreclosure proceedings on all secured claims, or take possession of all collateral or other property against which you have a lien claim; attempt possession wherever possible.
4. File proof of claim.
5. Attend creditors' meeting; cooperate in the election of a capable

trustee; and see, so far as is in your power, that the estate comes under the influence of a reputable lawyer.

    6. Whenever there is the slightest suspicion of fraud, assist other creditors by contributing to an investigation fund to expose further evidence of fraud. Postpone the examination of the bankrupt until the investigation is completed.

    7. Assist in the examination of the bankrupt, and help other creditors to set aside voidable preferences or conveyances where they are present in the case.

    8. Resist the final discharge whenever there are any grounds for opposing it; and if such grounds are present, assist in the criminal prosecution of the bankrupt.

Some of these duties are necessary to recover as much from the bankrupt's estate as is possible. Others pay benefits only over the long run. At times intelligent interest and cooperation in the correction of abuses seem thankless and profitless. They are, however, part of each citizen's social responsibility.

Arrangements—Chapter 11 of the Bankruptcy Act

Often a debtor can overcome many of the problems encountered in voluntary bankruptcy settlements by utilizing the arrangements proceedings in Chapter 11 of the Bankruptcy Act. An arrangement is defined as any plan of a debtor for the settlement, satisfaction, or extension of the time of payment of unsecured debts, on any terms.

    Chapter 11 proceedings became prominent in the mid-1980s when wage cuts became possible in bankruptcy court (only with the judge's prior approval). However, a landmark May 28, 1986, federal appeals court decision against Wheeling-Pittsburgh Steel Corp. made it much more difficult for companies to use bankruptcy to cut wage costs. The future of Chapter 11 cases is far from clear.

    The procedure followed in the Chapter 11 process is illustrated in Figure 20–1.

THIRD-PARTY ACTIONS

Recognizing the need to speed up the collection process, especially in cases of insolvent and embarrassed debtors, many industries have organized some form of adjustment bureau or agency to help their members, particularly those in the larger market centers, deal with their overdue accounts. The National Association of Credit Management has been an outstanding leader in the development and widespread use of such bureaus, through the establishment of local adjustment bureaus within its own organization.

FIGURE 20–1 **How Companies Reorganize under Chapter 11***

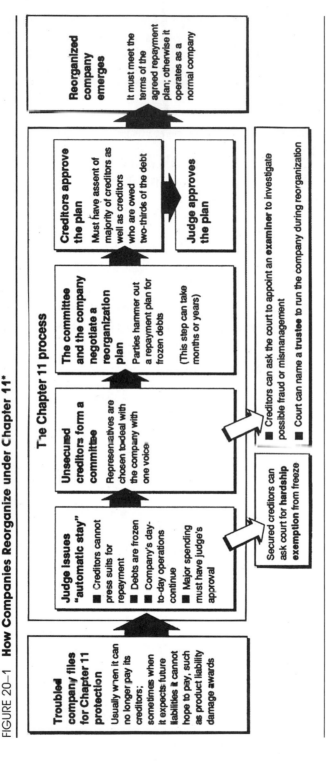

The Chapter 11 process

Troubled company files for Chapter 11 protection

Usually when it can no longer pay its creditors; sometimes when it expects future liabilities it cannot hope to pay, such as product liability damage awards

Judge issues "automatic stay"

■ Creditors cannot press suits for repayment
■ Debts are frozen
■ Company's day-to-day operations continue
■ Major spending must have judge's approval

Unsecured creditors form a committee

Representatives are chosen to deal with the company with one voice

The committee and the company negotiate a reorganization plan

Parties hammer out a repayment plan for frozen debts

(This step can take months or years)

Creditors approve the plan

Must have assent of majority of creditors as well as creditors who are owed two-thirds of the debt

Judge approves the plan

Reorganized company emerges

It must meet the terms of the agreed repayment plan; otherwise it operates as a normal company

Secured creditors can ask court for hardship exemption from freeze

■ Creditors can ask the court to appoint an examiner to investigate possible fraud or mismanagement
■ Court can name a trustee to run the company during reorganization

*Chapter 11 refers to the chapter in the Federal Bankruptcy Act that provides for court-supervised reorganization of debtor companies.
Source: *St. Petersburg Times,* January 16, 1990, p. 2A. Adapted with permission from AP/Times art.

Adjustment bureaus have a long history. The earliest known instance of merchants organizing to help solve the problems of distressed debtors occurred in 1868 in San Francisco. Since that time, other such organizations have evolved. There is a real need for adjustment bureau intervention in many cases. Adjustment bureau administration usually is less expensive than administration by the bankruptcy court; such administration gives creditors a more immediate sense of participation; and adjustment bureaus are often able to work out long-term solutions not readily achieved through the courts.

The National Collection Service was established in 1971 by the National Association of Credit Management and has as its primary goal the development of new collection business from national and regional companies. These companies' claims are forwarded to an approved National Collection Service Bureau nearest the debtor for action.

This section on group creditor action should also mention the bulk sales laws. While not strictly a collection device, state laws generally provide that prior to the sale of a business "in bulk,"[8] the seller must give the buyer a sworn list of creditors (names, addresses, and amounts owing), an inventory of the business must be taken, and the creditors must be notified that such a sale is scheduled to take place. These laws are designed to prevent debtors from selling out at so many cents on the dollar and leaving the creditors in a precarious position in trying to collect the full amount due them—a definite problem before the passage of such laws.

BETTER COLLECTIONS—IS THERE A SOLUTION?

Just as the conditions that lead to collections are caused by a number of factors, so the remedy or solution cannot be found in any one change in procedure or any one device.

Part of the remedy may be found in greater care on the part of creditors to accept credit only from debtors who have good credit to offer and only in amounts justified by the debtors' conditions. This would require creditors to make a more complete and careful investigation and a more penetrating and intensive analysis of the investigation's results.

Part of the remedy may be found in the greater care on the part of debtors in offering their credit. Debtors should regard credit as something they have in a limited stock. They should protect this stock carefully and replenish it frequently. They should recognize that credit is not granted indiscriminately, and therefore they should keep their reputation untarnished so they can offer good credit and be sure of its acceptance.

---

[8]What is meant by "in bulk" varies from state to state, depending on the provisions of the law in each state.

DISCUSSION QUESTIONS

1. Why are collections an inherent part of any commercial credit operation?
2. Discuss the twofold objectives of a commercial collection system.
3. Discuss why it is important to classify debtors in commercial collection operations.
4. Explain the 10 major classifications of debtors, as outlined in the text.
5. Which of these classifications would you say accounts for a major proportion of slow accounts? Why did you choose the one you did?
6. Under what circumstances and by what procedures can a credit manager advise and possibly help a debtor in overcoming a bad collection situation?
7. Discuss the importance of capital in establishing a collection policy.
8. What other factors must a commercial credit manager consider in establishing a collection policy? Discuss those you have listed.
9. What should a record-keeping system provide in the way of a "watching" device for a credit manager?
10. What are the possible consequences of a lax and ineffective collection policy? Discuss these consequences.
11. What are the usual preliminary steps in establishing a sound commercial collection system?
12. Explain why a firm might use commercial credit insurance. Why might it decide *not* to use commercial credit insurance?
13. Are collections stimulated by commercial credit insurance coverage?
14. Should commercial credit insurance be regarded as a substitute for the credit department and the credit manager of a manufacturing firm? Why or why not?
15. What is meant by the term *primary loss* in commercial credit insurance transactions?
16. Explain the categories into which collection actions may be divided.
17. Which of these actions do you regard as routine devices? Which have at least some aspect of pressure on the debtor? Explain.
18. Which collection actions do you find in the field of consumer credit but not in the field of commercial credit?
19. Which collection actions do you find in the field of commercial credit but not in the field of consumer credit?
20. Explain the essential characteristics of an extension agreement, a composition settlement, and an assignment for the benefit of creditors.
21. Explain how an extension agreement may be a single-creditor action or a group-creditor action.
22. Discuss how assignment in a commercial collection action differs from an assignment of accounts receivable in a consumer collection action.
23. How did the early bankruptcy legislation differ from the later acts?
24. How does society in general have an interest in rehabilitating the commercial debtor? Explain your answer.

25. What is the legal definition of bankruptcy?
26. What types of commercial enterprises may not declare themselves bankrupt?
27. Why do you believe that such enterprises may not take such an action?
28. What debts are not discharged by a bankruptcy action? Why?
29. Explain Chapter 11 of the Bankruptcy Act.
30. What do third-party collection actions attempt to accomplish?

SUGGESTED READINGS

Bankruptcy

BECKER, TIM. "Protecting Your Interests." *Business Credit,* March 1989, p. 21.

"Chapter 11 Isn't So Chic Anymore." *Business Week,* June 16, 1986, p. 35.

GROSS, KAREN. "Recent Bankruptcy Developments." *C&FM,* May 1986, p. 9.

MAPOTHER, WILLIAM R. "Bankruptcy Basics." *Business Credit,* January 1988, p. 61.

SWIECA, ROBERT W. "Bankruptcy Basics." *Business Credit,* September 1989, p. 14.

WOOD, DORMAN L. "Who Gets Hurt by Bankruptcy?" *Business Credit,* July–August 1990, p. 44.

Commercial Collection Practices

BERRY, STANLEY J. "Get That Payment in Full Today." *Business Credit,* October 1989, p. 12.

EMALFARB, HAL A. "How to Make Prompt Payment Work for You." *Business Credit,* September 1989, p. 32.

JORDAN, JAMES. "The Giant Step." *C&FM,* May 1987, p. 14.

McAULIFFE, ROBERT L. "Responsibilities of the Prepetition Creditor." *C&FM,* March 1987, p. 14.

MURRAY, J. WILLIAM, and MARK S. FURST. "Electronic Lockbox." *Business Credit,* December 1988, p. 35.

PATTIE, KENTON H. "New Prompt Pay Law Relieves Credit Headaches." *Business Credit,* September 1989, p. 28.

POWLEN, DAVID M., and ARNOLD H. WUHRMAN. "Good News, Bad News for Creditors." *ABA Banking Journal,* June 1988, p. 42.

ROLLINS, CATHY L. "Would a Bank Lockbox Make Sense for You?" *Business Credit,* December 1987, p. 32.

SIMMS, JOHN E. "Business Credit Insurance." *Business Credit,* July–August 1988, p. 39.

SWIECA, ROBERT W. "Enforcing Your Terms." *Business Credit,* January 1989, p. 33.

TATELBAUM, CHARLES M. "Passing Go: Collecting the Bad Check." *Business Credit,* April 1990, p. 21.

International Trade Credit

International Trade Credit*

The Objectives or Goals of Chapter 21 Are:
1. To explain the importance of credit in international trade.
2. To discuss the credit problems of export trade.
3. To point out the protection offered by the Federal Credit Insurance Association (FCIA).
4. To spell out the different terms of sale in export operations.
5. To discuss the sources of foreign credit information.

The United States is one of the world's leading exporters and importers of merchandise. However, the U.S. balance of payments has shown deficits for more than a decade, and this has caused the U.S. government to re-evaluate its foreign policy and to institute certain necessary adjustments to help reduce these deficits. As one adjustment, the government has enlarged its existing federal export expansion program to encourage exports by manufacturers not currently exporting and to expand sales among manufacturers currently exporting.

Commenting on the causes for an increased interest in export marketing, A. H. Kizilbash made the following observation:

> Certain other developments in the last two decades have also caused a resurgence of interest in export marketing. For instance, a closer exami-nation of the international economic picture will show that although the United States has remained a major producer and exporter of goods, its relative importance has diminished. Several Western European countries and Japan have regained some of their prewar markets as a result of post–World War II reconstruction. Their productive capacities have undergone both qualitative and quantitative improvement. They now are major competitors of American products in world markets. In addition to the problem of relatively diminishing exports due to the growth of these

---

*This chapter is not complete coverage of export trade credit. It is intended only to introduce the subject by surveying some of the major considerations of this important and growing area of credit. For a more complete treatment, see the Suggested Readings at the end of the chapter.

major competitors, the United States has become heavily committed in the task of economic and military assistance to many free world countries. These combined factors have contributed to the present unfavorable balance of payments position of this country. In addition they point up the need for improvement in export marketing skills of United States manufacturers.[1]

And of course these export marketing skills include skill in the use of credit. A company's credit policy, or lack of one, is vital to the success or failure of its international marketing program. The fact that a customer trading on credit is located in a foreign country does not alter the basic principles and procedures of sound credit management. Foreign customers must still be investigated, the risk carefully analyzed, logical credit limits imposed, and collections made. There are, however, some basic differences in practice and some problems not encountered in domestic credits and collections.

Most of the problems discussed in this chapter are encountered by firms that sell directly to foreign buyers. To market products directly to overseas buyers, manufacturers must possess the necessary capital, and deal with the organizational and personnel requirements. An export credit policy must be developed and capital must be sufficient to finance the slow turnover of receivables. A host of details and incidental problems create the need for qualified personnel who understand foreign trade credit.

The use of middlemen, or indirect marketing, may be plausible and advantageous in export trade, as it is in some domestic trade. In many instances varying export arrangements can be worked out with the export agency so that a major portion of the sales expenses can be shifted to it. Some of these agencies also assume all credit and exchange risks. The points to consider when deciding whether to market products overseas either directly or indirectly are: (1) the percentage of manufacturing output to be marketed for export, (2) the gross margin, (3) the personnel qualifications versus the personnel requirements, (4) the degree of control manufacturers desire over their product, (5) the need for service and product guarantee maintenance, and (6) financial requirements.

---

[1]Askari H. Kizilbash, "A Study of Export Marketing Objectives and Practices of Selected Small Manufacturers with Particular Reference to Their Use of Combination Export Management Firms" (Ph.D. diss., University of Nebraska, Lincoln, 1970), pp. 2–3.

Kizilbash divided combination export management firms (CEMs) into two categories: merchant and agent. "A merchant CEM is defined as one that takes title to the goods and handles all other aspects of export marketing. This allows the manufacturer to have minimal involvement with export trade. The manufacturer sells to the CEM in the same manner as it would to any other domestic account. An agent CEM is defined as one that does not take title to the goods and operates as the export department of the manufacturer. In this arrangement, the manufacturer has a greater involvement in export trade." Ibid., p. 10.

This publication is outdated, but it still gives a good picture of these firms in their export operations.

Changes are occurring in the international trade area, as evidenced by the enactment of the Export Trading Company Act of 1982, which permits and even encourages smaller companies to band together to sponsor export trading companies (ETCs). Bank holding companies, Edge Act or Agreement corporations, and bankers' banks can participate as lenders and equity investors in ETCs, subject to prior approval by the Federal Reserve Board.

Export trading companies can be the financing and services intermediary between American exporters and foreign markets. Or they can be the acquirers and subsequent exporters of goods and services. Financial institutions can use their ETCs to provide financing and other needed services, such as consulting, advertising, marketing research, insurance, legal help, and trade-documents processing.

CREDIT PROBLEMS OF EXPORT TRADE

The principal problem area for most credit managers stems from their need to judge the credit risk accurately. A foreign credit customer usually represents greater risk and is more difficult to evaluate. The increased degree of risk and difficulty in evaluation does not mean credit losses are higher on foreign customers than domestic customers. Risk and evaluation problems intensify, though, because of the following factors, which must be considered when judging the foreign credit risk: government, economic stability, currency and exchange, business practices, distance, the status of export credit insurance, and collections.

Government

Any nation's economy and business climate are directly influenced by the attitudes and policies of its government. A government's political orientation, whether right or left, also affects its economic policy and the degree to which it regulates both internal commerce and external trade. Textbook knowledge is not sufficient because conditions change constantly.

In deciding whether to sell to customers in a particular country, business executives have to consider the type of government involved. Although it is desirable to avoid politics in international business, American firms have found they cannot ignore local government because it influences so many phases of business activity. For example, the right to conduct business activities and the extent of foreign investment permitted are determined by government policy.

Economic Stability

Likewise, export credit executives must be alert to and understand the general economic situation in any foreign country in which they have customers. The efficient use of trade credit in a socioeconomic system can lead to further economic progress. Conversely, a poorly developed credit system limits economic progress. Thus American exporters should look for the prerequisites of a good credit system—that is, a system that can advance economic development—in the important country.

In addition, executives must note business cycles, crop failures, and many other factors able to cause fluctuations in a country's standard of living and in the demand for imports or the supply of goods for export.

Currency and Exchange

One of the inherent risks of export trade stems from the instability of some currencies. This risk must be assumed by one of the parties to the transaction. If the exporter bills the foreign customer in the native currency (pounds, pesos, francs, rupees, etc.), the exporter runs the risk that when the importer pays the bill, the exchange into dollars may yield a smaller amount than anticipated. If the foreign currency should drop in value, the seller will receive less as the foreign currency is converted into dollars. If, on the other hand, the exporter bills the foreign customer in dollars (this is more common), the risk of devaluation is placed on the importer.

Not only does risk surround the relative value of currencies, but each foreign country also rigidly enforces exchange regulations. In general, foreign money can be obtained only from designated exchange authorities usually controlled by the central banking system. Exchange regulations fluctuate with the country's political and economic conditions. In the past, importers in some countries have been prevented from remitting dollars to the United States; or, due to an unfavorable exchange situation, the foreign buyer may delay settlement of the account until more favorable exchange rates prevail.

A credit manager whose firm sells to foreign customers must be a student of international financial developments. The sufficiency of dollar reserves, the likelihood of foreign currency devaluation, and monetary restrictions all must be considered in evaluating the foreign credit risk.

Business Practices

Management techniques and the tools of efficient business management are not as advanced in most foreign countries as they are in the United States. This deficiency takes on particular significance in the area of accounting and preparation of financial statements. Foreign merchants, except for those in the largest trade centers, may not have trained accountants available. Furthermore, some foreign merchants still hold to the archaic view that their "names" and integrity are sufficient evidence on which to base credit appraisal. Foreign buyers are often highly irritated by what they think are unnecessary requests for credit information from U.S. sellers. Often these foreign firms have been in business many years and have done business with U.S. firms on an open account basis for fairly long periods. Unthoughtful actions in requesting certain information have proved distasteful to some foreign companies. Many are also reluctant to supply financial statements even though they have them, because they fear revealing business secrets. While these arguments have diminished in recent years as more firms adopt advanced business practices, gathering adequate financial information on foreign buyers still remains a problem.

The lack of, or the poor quality of, financial data is further complicated by language difficulties. Despite great emphasis on the foreign language requirement for those concerned with foreign trade, neither party is usually well versed in technical terms, commercial definitions, and trade names. Hence, there is a greater possibility of misunderstandings, disputes, and rejection of the shipment.

Business practices also are influenced by the diversity of commercial laws of foreign countries. Commonly, such things as import restrictions and licenses, laws of contract and title, bankruptcy, commercial arbitration, and patents are highly technical and complex. Because of the wide variety of such foreign regulations, most creditors should consult an attorney who is familiar with international law before getting involved for the first time with importers of a particular country.

Distance

The distance between the exporter and the importer compounds the problem of risk evaluation. If financial information on domestic customers is inadequate, the credit manager or a representative often can visit the prospective customer's place of business and make a judgment on nonfinancial factors. The opportunity for personal contact with foreign customers is limited, particularly where small accounts are involved. Consequently, the credit decision must be based almost entirely on data supplied by credit investigation agencies and other sources. In addition, good credit information cannot always be obtained on customers in other countries, even by well-known credit reporting agencies. Sufficient staff personnel are not always available in the foreign offices of these agencies, and access to important information is not always forthcoming.

Furthermore, the distance factor influences the terms of sale. Usually, there is a relatively long lapse of time between the purchase or shipment of goods and their receipt by the importer. Because of this, foreign terms of sale are often longer than domestic terms of sale, and hence accounts receivable remain unpaid for extended periods. Credit managers report that in recent years, as competition for foreign customers has increased, the demands of these customers for longer credit terms have also increased. Because the credit manager is not close to the foreign customer, it is extremely difficult to know whether the customer is actually playing one creditor against another or is taking advantage of a plausible situation. Whatever the circumstances, firms need greater financial capacity to carry foreign accounts than domestic accounts. The long lapse of time and longer terms granted to compete with other sellers aggravate exchange risks and risks created by the possibility of new import regulations.

Export Credit Insurance

Most of the major exporting nations have adopted either export credit insurance plans or guarantees that protect creditors against defaulting foreign customers. Great Britain, for example, has had such plans since 1920. Export credit insurance was first written in the United States in 1921 by a private insurance company. This company was liquidated in 1932 after a critical export credit situation arose when Great Britain abandoned the gold standard. Another private company succeeded this one, but it operated on a restricted basis until World War II, when the volume of export trade declined and the character of the available risks deteriorated.

The export credit insurance program of the federal government has been described as follows:

> In 1961 the U.S. government, through Eximbank—in conjunction with the U.S. private insurance industry—undertook the development of a program of export assistance which would place U.S. exporters on a basis of equality with their foreign competitors. The result was the Federal Credit Insurance Association (FCIA), which began operations in 1962. Although the services of FCIA are scarcely more than a decade old in the U.S., foreign exporters have long enjoyed similar programs of export credit assistance. The company's program has grown and by 1975 the association expects to be providing assistance for U.S. exports of approximately $10 billion per year. To accomplish this FCIA has to a large extent expanded and simplified its internal operations, and embarked on a large scale educational program for credit executives, bankers, and insurance agents and brokers.
>
> In addition, the company has recently inaugurated its Pre-Qualification (PQ) Program—a computerized service for exporters which offers immediate answers to telephone inquiries regarding coverage to specific foreign buyers. By means of this program FCIA is able to give the inquirer an on-the-spot commitment.
>
> * * * * *
>
> The protection offered by FCIA is a safeguard for international credit decisions. It is also a vital tool to obtain financing at lower interest rates. An association of 50 of the nation's leading capital stock and mutual property insurance companies, FCIA, in partnership with the Export-Import Bank of the U.S. (Eximbank), insures exporters—of goods and services—against the risk of nonpayment by foreign buyers for commercial or political reasons. FCIA's 50 member companies cover commercial credit risks, while Eximbank covers political risks and reinsures certain commercial risks. Both categories of risk are insured under a single comprehensive policy. As in domestic credit, commercial losses may be caused

by insolvency, but the company also pays claims on a doubtful account when a buyer is 180 days past due. Political risks include such hazards as transfer delays (the inability to convert the buyer's local currency into U.S. dollars); war, insurrection, hostilities; and cancellation or non-renewal of an export or import license. Other political risks difficult to foresee include confiscation or intervention in the business of the buyer by a government agency and unexpected transportation or insurance charges caused by interruption or diversion of voyage due to political action.[2]

The activities of the federal government in this area have been further explained:

> The Export-Import Bank of the United States (Eximbank) stands ready to work to provide the support needed for U.S. companies to sell effectively in the international marketplace.

* * * * *

> The Export-Import Bank Act instructs the bank to provide financing for U.S. exporters that is competitive with that offered to their foreign competitors by their governments, but in so doing to supplement, and not compete, with private financing.

* * * * *

> The bank's programs are divided into two functional categories: buyer credits and supplier credits. The buyer credit programs are comprised of direct loans from Eximbank to foreign buyers, and financial guarantees by Eximbank on financing provided by the private sector, generally commercial banks, for sales of equipment for large projects or products that require a repayment term of five or more years. The buyer credit area of the bank looks at big ticket items. In general, the minimum contract price eligible for buyer credit support is $10 million. Some examples are equipment for electric power generation, mining projects, and ground and air transportation.

> Eximbank offers several types of support to commercial banks and exporters to assist them in the export of medium-term U.S. goods and services. The area of Eximbank that has the responsibility for medium-term exports is the supplier credits division. By definition, medium-term exports refers to those products which quality for a repayment term of 181 days to five years. The supplier credit programs consist of the Working Capital Guarantee program, the Commercial Bank Guarantee program, the Small Business Credit program, and the Medium-Term Credit program.[3]

---

[2]A. Peter Costanzo, "FCIA: To Safeguard Your International Credit Decisions," *Credit & Financial Management,* May 1973, pp. 31–32.

[3]Kenneth M. Tinsley, "The Export-Import Bank," *Credit & Financial Management,* June 1986, p. 25. Reprinted with permission from *Credit & Financial Management,* Copyright 1986, published by the National Association of Credit Management, 520 Eighth Avenue, New York, NY 10018-6571.

In the late 1980s, the Export-Import Bank completed the most extensive overhaul of its programs since 1960. It now operates revised direct-loan and guarantee programs for medium- and long-term transactions. Under an intermediary funding program, Eximbank acts as a standby source of funds and, in some instances, even as a guarantor. A short-term insurance program continues through the Foreign Credit Insurance Association.

Information about Eximbank programs is available from several sources. Some banks have Eximbank-trained staff members, as do many regional offices of the Small Business Administration and the U.S. Commerce Department. Eximbank also has a business advisory hotline to assist exporters and bankers in determining which Eximbank or Foreign Credit Insurance Association programs best fit their needs. Eximbank has financial and credit information on some 100,000 foreign buyers the bank and FCIA have dealt with in the past. The Washington headquarters of Eximbank holds free monthly seminars on how to use its programs.

Collections

Another problem area of concern to the export credit manager is collections. As with domestic customers, the collection of foreign accounts is an inherent risk in the adoption of a credit policy. The cost of collecting overdue export accounts, the variance in commercial laws from one foreign country to another, and the factors already discussed compound the problem. Because of the greater collection problem, standards of acceptability are generally higher for foreign accounts than for domestic accounts. Despite the higher standards, creditors should expect to experience some difficulty with collections and some bad-debt losses.

The variety of reasons or conditions that cause export customers to become delinquent and the collection procedures and devices necessary to effect settlement are similar to those discussed in Chapter 20. Due to the conditions that influence the collection of foreign accounts, it is particularly important that the credit manager establish internal controls to detect overdue accounts at an early date. Prompt follow-up of the account by mail, telephone, or cable will usually elicit the reason for the delay. Once the specific reason is known, the credit manager can plan collection action more intelligently and can expect the actions taken to be more effective.

The credit manager confronts a particularly knotty problem when collection devices fail to bring results and the export account is eventually classified as "placed for collection" or "legal action." At this stage in the life of the account, the credit manager must decide whether it is worthwhile to proceed further. Litigation abroad is both costly and time consuming, and the effort outweighs the potential results. Obviously, only sizable accounts and large unpaid balances should be considered for legal action. If legal action is necessary, creditors should consult with their banks, their own legal counsel, or an export agency for advice on competent legal counsel in the foreign country. In some countries only nationals are permitted to practice law. American exporters' experiences with foreign lawyers have not all been positive; exporters frequently feel that their rights are not wholeheartedly enforced.

If a foreign account is to be placed for collection (as distinguished from collection by legal action), a number of well-known agencies may provide valuable help. Dun & Bradstreet and the FCIB of the National Association of Credit Management are two such agencies. Each of these services uses "moral suasion" letters that emphasize the importance of maintaining a good credit standing.

Commercial arbitration also is used to try to bring about speedy and inexpensive settlement of overdue accounts. A worldwide system of arbitration, organized by the American Arbitration Association and cooperating trade associations and chambers of commerce, has been in operation for many years.

EXPORT TERMS OF SALE

In recent years, competition for foreign customers has become particularly intense in a number of international markets. When this condition exists, importers do considerable bargaining for lenient credit terms. So prevalent is such bargaining today that credit managers believe the particular credit terms granted may be a deciding factor in making a sale. The export credit manager must, however, be careful to avoid those firms that take advantage of a competitive situation but still have a marginal or deteriorating financial condition. Even though the present-day competitive scene magnifies the exporter's credit problems, the future outlook is somewhat brighter. As competition improves, some international markets will have overcome their perplexing political and economic situations, and hence the risk of exchange and monetary restrictions is likely to decrease substantially.

Terms of sale used in export trade, to some extent at least, denote the quality of the risk, just as terms of sale in domestic trade classify commercial accounts by risk or unique circumstances. Export terms of sale may be classified in order of decreasing risk as follows:

1. Open account.
2. Consignment.
3. Draft drawn by the seller on the buyer.
4. Authority to purchase.
5. Export letter of credit.
6. Cash payment before delivery.

Open Account

The open account with terms to compensate for the distance factor and other normal delays is used in a minority of export credit transactions. Again the exporter must have the utmost confidence in the customer, and the exchange provisions must be favorable to the use of these terms. In some countries applications for exchange to settle dollar draft obligations receive priority over applications to settle open account obligations.

Consignment

Consignment sales are not widely used in export trade and are never used when exchange and monetary restrictions are not favorable to converting foreign currency into dollars. Laws on passing title to goods are not the same in all foreign countries, and such laws alone may preclude the use of this device. If, however, exporters are shipping to customers of long standing in whom they have the utmost confidence or to foreign subsidiaries and sales agents, consignment terms may be desirable. Customers of these types must be located in established foreign markets where the trade and banking facilities are capable of coping with the technicalities of consigned shipments.

Drafts

Time and sight drafts are widely used credit instruments in export credit sales. Drafts may be either *dollar* drafts or *foreign currency* drafts, depending on the arrangements previously made between the exporter and the buyer.

Usually, the drafts (whether time or sight) are *documentary* drafts as contrasted with *clean* drafts. The documentary draft is accompanied by all the title documents and papers essential to the shipment, such as bills of lading, insurance certificates, and shipping documents. The clean draft is free of these attachments. In this case the importer may have already received the shipment, and the exporter forwards the clean draft through banking channels to collect the amount due.

In using a draft to collect the credit accepted, the exporter should consult the *Credit Manual of Commercial Laws,* published annually by the National Association of Credit Management. This volume contains much helpful information on terms of sale, trade definitions, and the various documentary requirements. Furthermore, the instructions to the bank regarding collection of the draft, remittance of the funds by the foreign bank, the handling of collection charges and taxes, and other charges must be clearly set forth to avoid misunderstandings, delays, and more complicated collection procedures.

Authority to Purchase

Export sales may involve payment by documentary draft with authority to purchase, which is an authorization to a bank to purchase, on behalf of a foreign bank, the documentary draft drawn by the seller on the buyer. Such authority provides a place where the exporter may negotiate a draft with documents attached and thus obtain funds immediately.

Export Letter of Credit

The exporter who wants greater certainty of payment, other than cash before delivery, should request the importer to arrange for an export letter of credit.

On a sale that calls for payment by means of a letter of credit,[4] foreign importers arrange with their banks that a credit for the amount be established in favor of the exporter. Payment generally is made against documents evidencing shipment of the goods. Thus, under an export letter of credit, the importer's bank undertakes to pay the exporter.

A letter of credit issued by a foreign bank and accepted by an American bank is known as an *irrevocable* export letter of credit. An irrevocable letter of credit also may be issued by an American bank, or may be issued by a foreign bank but *unconfirmed* by an American bank. Drafts drawn under this type of letter of credit are paid by the foreign bank, not by the American bank. A *revocable* letter of export credit may be issued. Because this instrument may be revoked or amended at any time, the exporter has only day-to-day assurance that the issuing bank will accept sight drafts and time drafts drawn against it. Exporters much prefer the two former instruments, which are widely used.

The preference of export creditors for the irrevocable export letter of credit stems from their ability to convert accepted drafts into cash almost immediately. All the exporter must do is draw a draft, support it with the necessary shipping documents, and present it to the accepting bank. After verifying the exporter's claim, the bank accepts the draft. Once the bank accepts the draft on the irrevocable letter of credit, the exporter can in turn discount it on the open market and receive full payment for the shipment less the discount charge. For all practical purposes, then, the irrevocable letter of credit parallels a cash sale. If, however, the exporter wants to save the discount charge, the draft can be held until maturity.

The possible problems in using letters of credit are shown in Figure 21–1.

---

[4]Sidney S. Goldstein and Bruce S. Nathan, "How Strict Is Strict Compliance?" *Business Credit,* May–June 1990, p. 39.

FIGURE 21–1

Look for These L/C Red Flags:

DRAFTS

√ Amount in numbers and words do not agree with invoice amount.

√ Drawn to purchaser instead of issuing bank.

√ Letter of credit number and date of issuance are not shown or incorrectly shown.

√ Drawer's name does not agree with invoice name.

√ Draft is drawn to beneficiary and beneficiary's name is missing on reverse side.

√ Drafts are not presented even though it is required by letter of credit terms.

√ Tenor of draft differs from letter of credit.

√ Credit amount exceeded.

√ Amount disproportionate to quantity invoiced.

INVOICES

√ Invoice name and address do not agree with letter of credit.

√ Quantity does not agree with other supporting documents.

√ Unit price and extensions of unit price are incorrect.

√ Terms of sale omitted or incorrect (FOB, C&F, CIF, etc.).

√ Certification, which may be required by letter of credit terms, is missing.

√ Signatures, if required, are missing.

√ Marks and numbers differ from other documents.

√ Merchandise description is different from letter of credit.

√ Invoice shows excess shipment, short shipment, or partial shipment which may be prohibited by terms of the letter of credit.

√ Insufficient copies are presented.

√ Adjustments on previous shipments or charges are contained which are not allowed under the letter of credit terms (cable, airmail, storage, financing, or messenger fees).

BILLS OF LADING

√ Full set not presented, if required by letter of credit terms.

√ Unclean bills of lading (contains a notation as to a defect or qualification in packing or condition of merchandise).

√ Charter party bills of lading presented.

√ Does not show that the merchandise is actually "Shipped On-Board."

√ Shipments between ports differ from letter of credit terms.

√ Does not indicate whether freight is prepaid or not.

√ Shows that merchandise is shipped "On-Deck."

√ Indicates a later date than that allowed by letter of credit terms.

√ Not signed by carrier/agent/owner.

√ Merchandise description inconsistent with other documents.

INSURANCE DOCUMENTS

√ Coverage other than that required by letter of credit terms.

√ Claims payable in currency other than that of letter of credit.

√ Insurance policy/certificate not signed or properly endorsed.

√ Coverage effective after shipping date.

√ Amount of coverage insufficient.

√ Merchandise description inconsistent with other documents.

√ Incomplete sets presented.

√ Corrections not authenticated.

√ Not in negotiable form, unless letter of credit terms permit.

√ Not countersigned.

√ Transshipments not covered when bills of lading show it will take place.

√ Insurance certificate presented when policy is required.

OTHER DOCUMENTS

√ Certificates of origin should comply with importing country requirements.

√ Weight/packing/measurement list, analysis certificates, and inspection certificates, if required, must be fully detailed and conform strictly to the letter of credit terms.

√ Documents should be notarized, where required, as per letter of credit terms.

Source: Herman J. Ortmann, "The Pitfalls of Letters of Credit," *Business Credit*, November–December 1990, p. 24. Permission granted by the National Association of Credit Management, *Business Credit*.

Cash before Delivery Terms

The circumstances under which an exporter may demand CBD terms are much the same as those in domestic sales. When importers cannot qualify to meet the demand for a letter of credit or when their credit standing is clearly unsatisfactory, it is desirable to ask for cash before delivery. Not all circumstances that call for this arrangement are the importer's responsibility. Exporters may request these terms when the foreign country's exchange conditions are such that long delays are likely if more lenient terms are used. A few products have customarily been sold on CBD terms to domestic customers, and the same terms apply to foreign customers.

SOURCES OF FOREIGN CREDIT INFORMATION

The evaluation of the foreign credit customer is much the same as that for a domestic customer. The exception to this, of course, is the close evaluation of factors peculiar to export trade. Likewise, the sources of credit information and the content and format of credit reports are much the same as those frequently consulted in domestic credit analysis. However, as mentioned earlier, reasonably good credit information cannot always be obtained on customers in foreign countries. Foreign credit reporting offices are not always adequately staffed, nor do they always have access to all necessary information.

The sources of information on the foreign buyer can be classified as domestic and foreign. The domestic sources can be subdivided into commercial credit reporting agencies, the exporter's bank, the U.S. Department of Commerce, and foreign trade publications. The foreign sources include the buyer, the buyer's bank, and the exporter's foreign sales representatives.

Commercial Credit Reporting Agencies

Dun & Bradstreet and the FCIB of the National Association of Credit Management are two well-known sources of foreign credit information. Both agencies write credit reports on manufacturers, wholesalers, sales agents, and other commercial enterprises located in most of the free nations of the world. Dun & Bradstreet also supplies reports on companies located in the East bloc.

Dun & Bradstreet maintains offices in a large number of foreign countries, supplemented by an international network of credit correspondents. These Dun & Bradstreet facilities serve as a viable source of credit information for both domestic and foreign manufacturers, distributors, and bankers. Reports prepared on customers in foreign countries are of the same general type as those prepared for domestic use, except that more emphasis may be placed on background and reputation and less on financial standing. Most of the information shown in the credit reports and international publications (such as the *International Market Guide* for Latin America or continental Europe) is gathered through detailed investigations performed by credit reporters operating out of the Dun & Bradstreet foreign offices.

Dun & Bradstreet has a worldwide communication network that allows access to databases in Europe, North America, and the Pacific. Customers may gain access to these databases through their standard print terminals or personal computers. The European database offers summarized information in a choice of six languages.

Dun & Bradstreet publishes more than a dozen major international reference books and directories, including the *Exporters' Encyclopedia.* This encyclopedia can be a valuable aid for the credit executive, as it details the facts and rules needed to function effectively in over 220 world markets.

Other services of Dun & Bradstreet include: (1) worldwide commercial collection service through its network of offices and agents, (2) marketing research, (3) specialized investigations, (4) export support, (5) advertising, and (6) direct marketing.

The FCIB is the international arm of the National Association of Credit Management, serving those association members who are interested or engaged in international trade activities.[5]

Since 1919 the National Association of Credit Management has operated the member-owned FCIB-NACM Corporation in order to help exporters with the many credit problems inherent in international selling. Like its domestic counterpart, FCIB functions as a clearinghouse for payment experience, in this case, exporters' payment experiences with overseas customers. This information, rather than being historical and financial in character, is the actual ledger and credit experience of American export creditors. The body of the foreign report is essentially the same as the Business Credit Report. However, in the foreign report, each member who reports on a particular account also rates the customer as high, good, satisfactory, unsatisfactory, or undesirable by using the respective code letters Q, R, S, T, and U.

Other services of the NCIB include: (1) worldwide collection service; (2) free reciprocal copy of all foreign credit interchange reports to which the member contributes experience; (3) biweekly bulletins; (4) minutes of monthly roundtable conferences on foreign credit, collection, and exchange problems, with participation by either mail or attendance; and (5) consultation and market research service.

---

[5]Gerd-Peter E. Lota, "Foreign Trade and the FCIB," *Credit & Financial Management,* June 1986, p. 19.

Commercial Banks

Often the bank through which the exporter conducts international business has credit information on foreign customers. This is in direct contrast to the role of banks as a source of credit information for domestic customers. Banks accumulate a great deal of foreign information because they are often directly involved in export credit sales. Drafts and letters of credit are frequently used in export credit transactions, and hence banks have a great interest in the same types of credit information as do export credit managers.

The information contained in banks' extensive files may be available to clients who request it for credit purposes. In requesting such information, the creditor should completely reveal the details of the export credit transaction. Complete information on the transaction helps the bank make the most accurate and usable reply possible. Banks also write or cable for information not in their files. This is possible because their foreign offices and correspondent banks have firsthand experience with importers in the payment of their foreign trade obligations.

Bank information on foreign customers is highly regarded by export credit managers. The information that may be obtained from a bank includes the importer firm's history and antecedents; the importer firm's financial strength and capacity, when available; and the bank's record of the payment performance experienced by its overseas branches and correspondents. In general, this source of information has the advantages of completeness, high quality, and speed.

Other Sources

A number of other sources supply valuable information. Foreign trade publications, exporters' associations, and the importer's bank may provide supplemental information of value. An export credit manager closely associated with foreign trade groups has little difficulty picking up essential information on particular markets and on the exchange problems encountered by other members. Not to be overlooked are the exporter's salespeople, foreign representatives, and, of course, the customer.

The U.S. Department of Commerce supplies valuable facts about foreign firms; its *World Trade Data Reports* is also valuable to exporters. U.S. foreign service offices are in a position to secure information that may be valuable to an American exporter in making credit decisions.

The so-called Edge Law banks should be mentioned briefly. The Edge Law, passed in December 1919 as part of the Federal Reserve Act, provides for the federal incorporation of businesses to engage solely in international or foreign banking or in other types of foreign financial operations. These banks are an excellent source of valuable credit information.

DISCUSSION QUESTIONS

1. How do you account for the fact that the balance of payments of the United States has shown deficits for more than a decade?

2. How do you explain the increased interest in export marketing among U.S. manufacturers?

3. Why is a company's credit policy, or the lack of one, a vital factor in determining the success or failure of an international marketing program?

4. Explain what an export trading company (ETC) does.

5. What conditions magnify the problem of credit risk evaluation on foreign creditors? Explain each of the conditions you have listed.

6. What is the present status of export credit insurance?

7. What is the purpose of the Foreign Credit Insurance Association?

8. Under what conditions would you use consignment terms? Open account terms?

9. What is the difference between a time draft and a sight draft?

10. Discuss the statement, "For all practical purposes, an irrevocable letter of export credit results in a cash sale."

11. Do any American industries customarily sell on CBD terms? If so, which ones?

12. How do you account for the differences and similarities between domestic and foreign sources of credit information?

13. Why are commercial banks a source of information on foreign customers?

14. What is the FCIB? Explain what it attempts to accomplish.

SUGGESTED READINGS

BELCSAK, HANS P. "Global Mosiac." *C&FM,* June 1987, p. 21.

FAUST, JON. "U.S. Foreign Indebtedness: Are We Investing What We Borrow?" Federal Reserve Bank of Kansas City *Economic Review,* July–August 1989, p. 3.

GOMEZ, LUCAS. "Debt Plagues U.S.-Latin American Trade." *Business Credit,* November 1989, p. 13.

KING, A. S. "Government Publications Guide for International Business, Banking, Finance & International Trade." *C&FM,* June 1987, p. 27.

LOTA, GERD-PETER E. "Country Export Risk 1987–1988." *C&FM,* June 1987, p. 15.

―――. "International Freight Forwarders." *Business Credit,* June 1988, p. 29.

―――. "Unplugging Blocked Funds." *C&FM,* June 1987, p. 25.

OTT, MACK. "Have U.S. Exports Been Larger Than Reported?" Federal Reserve Bank of St. Louis *Review,* September–October 1988, p. 3.

SCHWEPPE, ELLEN. "Getting Export Financing." *Business Credit,* June 1989, p. 25.

SMITH, TIM R. "Foreign Direct Investment." Federal Reserve Bank of Kansas City *Economic Review,* July–August 1989, p. 21.

SWIECA, ROBERT W. "Balance of Trade." *Business Credit,* October 1989, p. 31.

————. "Fundamentals of International Credit." *Business Credit,* June 1989, p. 20.

TRUMAN, EDWIN M. "U.S. Policy on the Problems of International Debt." *Federal Reserve Bulletin,* November 1989, p. 727.

VALENTINE, CHARLES F. "The Art of International Competition." *Business Credit,* March 1988, p. 40.

Control of Credit Operations

Measuring Efficiency and Control of Credit Decisions

The Objectives or Goals of Chapter 22 Are:

1. To discuss the responsibility of credit department operations.
2. To explain the various tests of credit department operations.
3. To point out the difficulties in using the bad-debt loss index.
4. To discuss how new management tools can be adapted to testing credit department operations.
5. To point out how to present the test results.

Too often in the rush of getting the day's work done, credit managers lose themselves in the numerous details of their work and never stop to ask exactly what their objectives are or whether they still are on the right road to accomplishing them. Without clearly defined objectives and the means of measuring progress, credit executives may waste much precious time, effort, and money exploring side roads and bypaths that do not lead to the end desired. In fact, they may entirely lose sight of the destination and never arrive.

Credit executives should be prepared to answer the following questions:

1. What are the proper policies of my firm's credit department in view of current and anticipated conditions?
2. What measures can I use to determine whether these policies are reached?

Enlightened credit management should constantly follow clearly defined goals or aims. And success in reaching these goals increases when management can measure its progress toward the final objective—satisfying customers and making profits for the business.

Although credit managers are constantly engaged in testing the work of others, credit management has paid little attention to developing techniques to test its own work. It is not clear whether this situation is a result of the difficulty in measuring attainment, management indifference, failure to recognize the importance of evaluating credit operations, or some other reason.

Credit executives disagree as to *the* best method or technique for judging how efficiently a credit department operates. This lack of agreement is accounted for partially by variations in company size, credit policies, and organization. In addition, no statistical measure that attempts to show the results of credit and collection operations can actually measure how *effectively* these activities are performed. The person responsible for judging performance must have some predetermined standard to use as a basis of comparison. If this standard has been erroneously set or has not been adjusted to reflect changing conditions, the judgment will be wrong.

As credit executives well know, it is easier to voice the need for correct and proper standards than it is to establish them. One of the main reasons for this problem is that many organizations lack a meaningful, reasonably precise definition of top management's objectives. Until such a definition is given to the credit manager or is developed by the credit manager and approved by top management, it is difficult to clarify and answer the question of how to measure and appraise results.

In almost all instances, a business attempts to judge the effectiveness of its component parts by how much each part (department, etc.) contributes to the operation's net profit. This result is very difficult to isolate and measure, especially in the case of the credit department. As a result, efficiency is more often judged—when it *is* judged—on the basis of certain figures assumed to be closely correlated with the credit department's contribution to the firm's goals—when such goals have been spelled out.

RESPONSIBILITY OF THE CREDIT DEPARTMENT

In setting the proper objectives of the credit department, credit executives have an implied responsibility to three interests:

1. To the firms that employ them.
2. To the debtors whose credit they accept.
3. To the business and social community whose well-being may be—and undoubtedly will be—affected by their actions.

The responsibility to their own firms is the most direct and readily apparent. The main objective of business management is to make profits; the intermediate objective of the credit function is to achieve maximum sales and minimum losses. This is its contribution to the profit objective. At times the credit department emphasizes the sales portion of the task; at other times, the loss-avoidance portion. Most frequently, however, it keeps both objectives in mind. To accept this ideal, however, the phrase "minimum losses" must be interpreted in the widest possible sense. By a policy of careful and persistent collections, a firm can attain low bad-debt losses, but maximum profits may not result because of high collection costs and expenses and the high costs of carrying receivables. The final result may even be considerably less profit, and in times of stress such a policy may seriously handicap the firm's operations because capital is frozen in slow-moving receivables. Nor can the time element be ignored. Over what period shall the minimum of losses and the maximum of sales be calculated? Taking substandard business may mean some customers will cause losses, but some may become tomorrow's volume buyers. Perhaps a better statement of the ideal might be to seek minimum costs and maximum gains in both the present and the future.

Credit managers also serve the interests of the debtor. Credit managers have a responsibility to the debtor just as definite and exacting as their responsibility to their own firms. As enlightened sales departments have discovered that satisfaction is one of the most vital stages in a sale, so have credit departments recognized the need for customer satisfaction in every credit transaction. When customers are severely handicapped by heavy obligations, this final stage of satisfaction is not attained, and the credit department has not correctly handled its responsibility to the debtor.

The third interest involved is the interest of society at large. The economic community in general is not a party to the transaction arranged between debtor and creditor. It occupies the role of the innocent bystander. As such, society at large is frequently injured by the actions of the immediate participants, unless the debtor exercises care in seeking additional credit and the creditor exercises care in making sure acceptance of the additional amount benefits all concerned.

To some extent, credit management should be concerned with the social consequences of policy decisions or operating results. Overextension of credit is not good for the debtor, the creditor, or the business community. Excessive charges for the credit service not only impose excessive burdens on the debtor and interfere with the expansion of the creditor's market, but they also are socially undesirable. Excessive credit losses or long-delayed collections are costly to all the parties to a credit transaction and are damaging to the entire business community. They do not contribute to a healthy economic climate.

TESTS OF CREDIT DEPARTMENT OPERATIONS

Credit executives have been diligent in seeking and applying quality tests to the credit that they are asked to accept. They have discovered that their investigations must be sufficiently complete to uncover all unfavorable information and to permit proper analysis, must be reasonable from a cost point of view, and must be done with sufficient speed to enable a decision to be reached without causing customer dissatisfaction.

Credit management's responsibility to the firm, the debtor, and society having been recognized and the objectives of credit department operations having been clearly stated, the next step should be to measure the attainment of these objectives—to test the manner in which the credit department is meeting its responsibility. Some of the measuring devices used for this purpose are fairly well known to most credit personnel; some of them may be familiar only to credit management personnel who have studied this phase of credit work. Many credit departments operate without any checks on their operations other than the bad-debt loss index. The tools or indexes described in the following sections are designed to provide credit management with some means for testing the efficiency of its credit operations. These tools help credit managers determine whether their departments are bringing about maximum sales and minimum losses.

Certain tests of credit department operations have become conventional. Conventional tests that permit comparisons between the subject firm and similar firms are more useful because they have more meaning. Additional tests may be developed to meet the requirements of special situations or to explore some situations further. Some analysis of credit department operating results may be used to test closeness of fit between policies and actual operations or to see whether policy or operation is faulty. On occasion, an analysis of operations should be undertaken as a guide to the formation of new policies.

These tests are valuable in many important ways:

First, the periodic calculation of ratios, percentages, and other figures is necessary to measure credit and collection results. Unless this is done, you have no way of knowing just what has been accomplished and what changes have occurred in each of the various aspects of your firm's credit business.

Second, keeping these statistical records makes it possible to set up standards or goals to shoot at in each phase of your credit and collections activity. Without standards, you have no basis for judging accomplishments. Also, an important stimulus to efficiency will be lacking.

Third, the accumulation of records kept on the same basis from year to year enables you to compare current credit and collection performance with that of previous periods, and to determine the progress made. Credit-sales volume for the current month, for instance, may be compared with the figure for the same month last year, or the preceding month this year, to see whether there has been an increase or decrease.

Fourth, if your firm's credit business is large enough to require the time of more than one person, comparisons often may be made between different individuals. You can calculate separate collection percentages for each person having responsibility for a given section of the accounts. Separate rejection percentages may be computed wherever two or more persons are engaged in granting credit.

Fifth, you may compare results shown in your figures with those reported by other firms. Data for such comparisons are published by the National Retail Credit Association, the Credit Management Division of the National Retail Merchants Association, and many national trade associations in many specific lines of business, as well as by the Board of Governors of the Federal Reserve System.

Sixth, the records you maintain may be used in forecasting future trends in credit sales volume, collections, and other aspects of your credit business. These forecasts can be very helpful in revisions of your general budgets, and they often suggest changes in your credit and collection policies.[1]

Bad-Debt Loss

In the past, a credit department's efficiency has often been judged by rule of thumb. Successful operation was assumed to be evidenced by the manager's ability to reduce bad-debt losses to a minimum or to keep them at a minimum. Even now, some credit managers boast that their businesses have lost practically nothing during the year or that losses amounted to an insignificant fraction of credit sales or total sales. Such rule-of-thumb judgments are misleading although, unfortunately, they often appeal to certain segments of top management. An exceedingly small loss record alone is not indisputable evidence of efficient credit administration. In fact, it may be an inferior basis on which to judge performance efficiency because credit managers can easily accomplish such a feat by practicing conservatism and accepting only the best risks. Such a policy often diverts business to competitors and results in lost profits.

The bad-debt loss index was one of the first tests to be developed and still is one of the tests most generally used by credit managers. The relationship is generally shown by dividing bad debts incurred during a period by total credit sales during the same period, as follows:

$$\frac{\text{Bad-debt loss}}{\text{Total credit sales}} = \text{Bad-debt loss index}$$

However, there is little uniformity in calculating this proportion. Some firms calculate the percentage of bad debts to total sales; others calculate the percentage of bad debts to credit sales. There is no uniform practice as to the time when an account is classified as bad, and thus another variable is introduced into the calculation. Some firms leave it to an official's discretion to decide when to call an account bad; others so classify accounts after the passage of some definite time without payment; still others, after the occurrence of some definite act, such as the return of an unsatisfied judgment or a similar event. A big margin of error also exists because some accounts may be written off as bad debts shortly after they become overdue, while others may be carried for many months before they are eventually written off. Consequently, a substantial portion of the bad

---

[1]Clyde Williams Phelps, *Credit and Collections Controls for Small Marketers,* Small Marketers Aids No. 33 (Washington, D.C.: Small Business Administration, May 1958), p. 1. While this publication is out of date, the quotation is still applicable to present-day conditions.

debts recorded for a given year may have resulted from credit decisions or collection procedures in the preceding year. Yet they are compared with credit sales in the current year, and conclusions drawn from the ratio are applied to the current year's credit and collections policies. Furthermore, because of this lag in bad-debts recording, a substantial change in sales volume may introduce a misleading variation in the bad-debt ratio. Thus, when sales for credit are increasing while cash sales are remaining fairly stationary, the base on which the index is computed will increase and cause a more favorable showing than is justified.

Percentages of bad-debt losses naturally vary with different lines of business, competitive conditions, the month or season of the year, and general business conditions. Proper interpretation of bad-debt losses requires comparison between the current year's business, business for previous periods, and bad-debt losses by other firms operating under similar conditions. Data for comparison with other firms is increasingly available from various credit and trade associations and the federal government. However, credit managers should be cautious when using the bad-debt ratios of other sellers to determine a "sound" ratio for their own companies. The bad-debt ratio of any other business for a single year is of little value as a guide because of the lag factor just discussed. Furthermore, if the other company operates on a higher or lower profit margin, its "sound" bad-debt ratio should be smaller or larger. If the difference in profit margins is known, an adjustment should be made for it. Trend analysis of a company's bad-debt ratios over a few years does not, by itself, indicate whether its credit or collection policies are becoming more strict or more lax. General business fluctuation and particular regional and trade developments influence the bad-debt ratio more profoundly than changes in a firm's credit and collection policy.

Too great a reliance on the test of bad-debt losses is dangerous since it tends to overemphasize caution in accepting credit. The company's policy should be to hold the proportion within normal limits. And these normal limits should be determined, for each firm, on the basis of the profit margin it works on. To illustrate, the insurance field doesn't try to avoid all losses but to hold underwriting to the normal loss point so as to ensure that the profit margin is greater than the probability of loss.

If a firm's consumer credit plan includes several types of credit—such as open charge, installment, and revolving credit—it should keep separate data, if consistent with the accounting system used, on the bad-debt losses and credit sales in each.[2] Such a procedure helps the firm pinpoint any troublesome areas in each type of credit. In such instances, the additional indexes computed include:

---

[2]The increased use of credit cards, such as Visa, MasterCard, Discover, and so on, has reduced the importance of these ratios.

$$(1) \quad \frac{\text{Bad-debt losses from open charge sales}}{\text{Open charge sales}}$$

$$(2) \quad \frac{\text{Bad-debt losses from installment sales}}{\text{Installment sales}}$$

$$(3) \quad \frac{\text{Bad-debt losses from revolving credit sales}}{\text{Revolving credit sales}}$$

Credit Sales

In all business enterprises it is important to know what percentage of total sales is represented by credit transactions. This percentage or index is computed by dividing credit sales by total net sales:

$$\frac{\text{Credit sales}}{\text{Total net sales}} = \text{Credit sales index}$$

Generally, firms that deal with consumer credit should determine the percentage of business done on each type of credit (e.g., installment credit, charge account business, revolving charge account volume, CODs). When comparisons are made from month to month or over a period of years, the firm gets a valuable picture of its credit business and some effects of its credit policy. Comparisons with other firms operating under similar conditions indicate the success achieved in obtaining credit business.

Of perhaps more importance in commercial credit operations is a classification of accounts by risk categories. For example, the following type of breakdown can be carried out within the broader framework of an industry or product-line classification of accounts:

- *Government.*[3]
- *Prime*—large, well-established firms involving no real credit risk.
- *Good*—companies that can be expected to discount but lack the stature of prime accounts.
- *Limited*—companies that are suspect enough to be held within a definite credit line.
- *Marginal*—high-risk accounts that bear constant watching.

Such a classification has the advantage of enabling commercial credit analysts to determine more accurately whether the pattern of their company's credit decisions has changed significantly from period to period; whether the change will affect the timing of future collections, with an ensuing influence on cash needs; whether certain members of the credit department are doing a better job of accepting credit than others; and

---

[3]Certain governmental units are better credit risks than others. Some may pay eventually, but the time of payment depends on receipt of tax funds.

whether marginal accounts are really producing enough orders to make them worthwhile. All of these items, plus many others, may be valuable to credit analysts if they are willing to incur the expense of providing such detailed information.

Collection Percentage, Days to Collect, and Turnover of Receivables

These tests are included under one heading because they are simply different ways of stating a similar fundamental relationship. The collection percentage, which is one of the most commonly used credit control indexes, is determined by dividing the total amounts collected during a period (such as a month) by total receivables outstanding at the beginning of that period, as shown in the following formula:

$$\frac{\text{Collections made during period}}{\text{Receivables outstanding at beginning of period}} = \frac{\text{Collection}}{\text{index}}$$

A derivation of this index is an estimate of the average length of time that receivables are outstanding. If, for example, the net credit period in a particular line of business is 30 days and the collection index is 50 percent, indicating that only half of the outstanding receivables were collected during the month, receivables would "on the average" be outstanding 60 days. This estimate is made by using the following formula:

$$\frac{\text{Net credit period}}{\text{Collection index}} = \text{Average collection period}$$

$$\frac{30}{50\%} = 60$$

Another criterion of credit management efficiency is how it uses capital invested in accounts receivable. The rate of receivables turnover is found by dividing the total sales by the average receivables outstanding, as follows:

$$\frac{\text{Total credit sales}}{\text{Average receivables outstanding}} = \text{Receivables turnover rate}$$

The seasonality of the business is important in determining how to compute the average of the receivables outstanding. The activity of the investment in receivables may be expressed as a rate or in terms of the number of days required for one turn of the accounts. The latter can be computed by dividing 360 days by the receivables turnover rate, as shown below:

$$\frac{360 \text{ days}}{\text{Receivables turnover rate}} = \frac{\text{Number of days to}}{\text{collect credit accounts}}$$

These measures of credit management have an advantage over the bad-debt loss calculation; because they can often be figured earlier, they help forecast difficulties in collection far enough in advance for the company to take corrective measures. Collection percentages, when decreasing, show an accumulation of poor accounts or a slackening of collection efforts before the bad conditions become inevitable. These measures of credit activity should enable credit management to detect the effects of unsound policies. For example, a falling collection percentage indicates unduly lenient terms, solicitation of unsound classes of customers, and a yielding to competitive temptations to outdo others in credit. In addition, unduly stringent collection activity, overly conservative credit acceptance, and undue hesitation in taking risks can be detected earlier by studying the trend of collection percentages.

As with the other indexes, these figures should be compared with those for previous months and with those for the same month of as many preceding years as possible. Such an accumulation of figures over a period of years helps the credit manager to recognize seasonal trends that should be considered in any analysis. Likewise, comparisons with similar firms give some indication of the subject firm's relative standing. As with the other indexes, this information is valuable when broken down into the types of credit accepted.

These indexes reflect only averages; certain accounts may be falling behind in payments at the same time that overall collection tests disclose a favorable picture. Credit management personnel should recognize this situation and allow for it in any analysis based on averages.

Improvement in a firm's collection percentage may reflect improved economic conditions even before an increase in credit and cash sales. This situation arises because consumers tend to repay previously incurred debts before assuming new ones. Conversely, a decline in economic conditions is more likely to be reflected earlier in declining credit sales than in declining collection percentages. This results from the debtors' reluctance to make additional credit purchases until they are sure they can pay for them. Proper analysis of these pending changes should enable credit management to carry out its obligation to the firm, the firm's customers, and society.

Number of New Accounts Opened

The credit department's activity is reflected by the number of new accounts it opens during the period in question. This figure indicates the extent to which the business emphasizes credit service and whether or not it is alert to opportunities for attracting new trade. The number of new accounts opened may also measure the effectiveness of credit publicity. This figure, together with the acceptance percentage, measures the leniency or strictness of the business's credit policy.

Acceptance Index

The number of acceptances indicates the firm's attitude toward applications, the quality of the applicants, and the credit policy currently being followed. A measure of growing importance is the index or percentage showing the proportion of applications for credit that are accepted. This is computed as follows:

$$\frac{\text{Applications accepted}}{\text{Applications submitted}} = \text{Acceptance index}$$

This index varies considerably, depending on the firm's line of business, the leniency or strictness of its credit-granting policies, and the stage of the business cycle.

Past-Due Index

This test of credit management measures the proportion of all past-due accounts, in amount or in number.[4] It is computed by dividing the total past due by the total outstanding as follows:

$$\frac{\text{Total past due}}{\text{Total outstanding}} = \text{Past-due index}$$

When this index is computed for several successive periods, it serves as a barometer indicating whether the general trend of poor pay is up or down. If this percentage increases faster than it should at any given time, credit management can take steps to curb the trend or bring it back to its normal position (which can be ascertained from records maintained over a period of years).

Aging of Accounts

This test is a detailed analysis of accounts—such as not due, 30 days past due, 60 days past due, and over one year past due. It stems from the fact that there is a direct and important relationship between the length of time that an account has been outstanding, the rate of collection, and the probable net loss from bad debts.

Aging of accounts can be supplemented with a detailed itemized list of overdue accounts, showing both the name and present status of such accounts. A list of this kind is valuable in authorizing additional requests for credit. Computers help credit personnel make this type of analysis easily and quickly.

---

[4]This ratio should be figured in both number and dollars because computing both formulas could give a very different picture if one large account is severely past due versus several small accounts past due.

Slow accounts call for extra collection effort and expense, additional bookkeeping, extra interest costs in money tied up, and a higher cost of doing business. Early knowledge of such accounts usually leads to prompt remedial efforts.

Aging of consumer accounts is easier to accomplish if a firm uses only one billing date rather than a cycle billing system. Nevertheless, aging of accounts helps improve credit operations even under a cycle billing arrangement.

Cost Analysis

Any final summation of the results of credit department activities should include cost figures. Credit management can make sounder policy decisions if it has accurate knowledge about the cost of operating a credit service and carrying receivables. Bad debts give one such measure, but losses from bad debts are only one item in the credit department's operation. The expense of operating a credit department often exceeds all bad-debt losses. Wages and salaries of people employed in credit and collection activities are the most important single category of credit expense. Other expenses include interest on outstandings, fees and dues for credit information, rental or purchase of equipment, and charges for outside collection services. The costing of credit operations may seem needlessly complex and involve a detailed accumulation of data. At the same time, effective credit management cannot work blindly, nor can policies be intelligently decided without facts.

ADAPTATION OF NEW MANAGEMENT TOOLS TO TESTING CREDIT OPERATIONS

The tests of efficiency and control of credit decisions discussed thus far are generally measured against past results. This way of measuring actual results has been common for many years. More recently, truly professional commercial credit managers and a few industry representatives have been directing their attention toward (1) forecasting credit department performance activity, (2) measuring costs for various classifications of customers against sales and profitability, and (3) developing methods that explain why certain phenomena occur in credit department accounts or groupings of accounts. These techniques and the more revealing data they produce stem from the current emphasis on forecasting and budgeting procedures, cost and distribution analysis, statistical correlation analysis, and computer processing of masses of data. Although these approaches may appear sophisticated for the average credit executive, some large credit departments now use them to improve their contributions to total company objectives and to plan their operations on the basis of data not previously available. The rapid advancements in developing more modern management tools and the rapidity with which these tools are being accepted indicate that medium- and small-sized credit departments will soon be dealing with them too. Accordingly, students and practicing credit managers will have to be aware of these techniques and able to adapt to them as they pervade the economy.

Cost and distribution analysis is a research tool that can be useful in estimating probable costs, or cost savings, when a firm contemplates a change in its credit policy. For example, the functional expense statement (one of the accounting techniques used in cost and distribution analysis) helps plot costs of credit authorization, accounts receivable, invoicing, and the like against credit accounts classified by payment experiences and by sales volume of various classes of customers. Credit and collection costs, like all other marketing costs, enter in when determining the profitability of various types of customers. In other words, part of the answer to the question "Is this group of customers (classed by size of order, location, industry type, etc.) a profitable or potentially profitable class of customers in view of our costs of selling them?" can be obtained by employing today's superior measuring devices.

Similarly, some credit departments classify their customers according to credit risk and then, at later dates, measure the volume of business conducted, the volume of outstanding receivables, and the past collection efforts required for each category of risk. One of the most fruitful measures helps credit departments determine if rehabilitation efforts are helping a particular group of customers move from low to higher classifications. Most of the techniques suggested here are particularly significant when people realize that decisions in accepting credit are, for the most part, based on estimates of other future phenomena, such as changes in the nation's economy, trends in an industry, and changes in the individual firm.

Various regulatory agencies are changing their examination of financial institutions. With the new emphasis on the Community Reinvestment Act, for example, the question of how well the institution is meeting community needs has become a required concern of bank directors and bank officers and employees. Other required disclosures also help examiners determine how well the institution is performing.

PRESENTING THE MEASURED RESULTS

Justifying credit operations as an important division of the business is easier and more certain when the credit department can show the facts of its own operations. Charts may be used to present various measures of the department's success—or failure—to top management. For example, by using bar charts showing the aging of receivables and line charts illustrating the seasonal influence on collection ratios, the credit manager can give "the boss" much of the story at a glance and be better prepared to present information justifying the credit departments' operation and budget.

The foregoing discussion of techniques is not complete. This phase of credit calls for further refinement of concepts and greater skill in using the tests. As credit management becomes more conscious of the need to measure its own operations, it will make better credit decisions. Such an improvement will benefit the firm, the debtor, and society in general.

DISCUSSION QUESTIONS

1. Why should enlightened credit management constantly follow clearly defined goals or aims?

2. What two questions should the credit manager be prepared to answer?

3. It is said that the credit executive has an implied responsibility to three interests. What are these three interests?

4. Why is it necessary for a credit department to have certain tests by which to judge its operations?

5. What is "satisfaction" in a credit transaction?

6. Professor Phelps said tests of credit department operations were valuable in six important ways. Discuss each of the ways.

7. How would you define a bad-debt loss?

8. Why are bad-debt losses defined differently by credit managers?

9. How are the following indexes computed, and what do they show:
   a. Credit sales index?
   b. Collection index?
   c. Receivables turnover index?
   d. Acceptance index?
   e. Past-due index?

10. Why should a firm keep separate data of its bad-debt losses and credit sales in each type of consumer credit it accepts?

11. Discuss why accounts receivable should be aged.

12. How would you present to top management the measured results of your credit department operations?

GLOSSARY OF TERMS

adjusted balance method. Bases the finance charge on last month's ending balance less any payments or credits.

adverse opinion. The auditor states that as a whole the financial statements are not presented fairly in conformity with generally accepted accounting principles.

affinity credit cards. Marketing bank credit cards to organizations or looser groupings of people with common interests.

aging of accounts. A detailed analysis of accounts—such as, not due, 30 days past due, 60 days past due, and over one year past due.

annual percentage rate. Sometimes called true annual rate or simple annual rate.

ARMs (adjustable rate mortgages). Many loans have interest rates (and monthly payments) that can change from time to time.

ATMs (automated teller machines). Enable consumers to perform various banking transactions without the aid of a teller.

authorization. The control of the quantity of credit used by the customers.

average daily balance method. The charge varies according to the point in the billing cycle when payment is made.

balance sheet. A statement of the financial condition of a company as of a moment of time.

balloon mortgage. A type of loan that can be computed on a fixed rate for any number of years payback with a balloon payment for the remainder of the loan placed at any given year.

bankruptcy. In addition to the condition of insolvency, there must also be some legal and public recognition of the condition, coupled with some specific act or acts on the part of the debtor or creditor or both.

business credit. One of the principal means by which business executives can translate into reality their interpretation of the opportunities that exist to carry on productive ventures.

capacity. In a narrow sense, it may mean simply the ability to pay a specific dollar obligation when it is due.

capital. The financial strength of the risk that would be available in case of the inability or mere unwillingness of the individual to pay obligations when due.

cash discounts. This may be allowed for early payment of an account.

cash flow forecast. A planned procedure for estimating cash receipts and disbursements over a specified period of approximately 10 days from the date of invoice.

cash terms. Do not indicate the immediate payment of cash but the acceptance of credit for a period approximately 10 days from the date of invoice.

character. May be defined as an intangible sum of personal attributes, and these attributes are revealed indirectly rather than directly.

charge card. A card, plate, or any other single device that may be used from time to time to obtain credit that is not subject to a finance charge.

collateral. Takes the form of some tangible asset owned by the individual and offored as additional security to the loaning institution

compensating balances. A fraction of the line credit the borrower is expected not to withdraw.

conditions. Involves interpreting credit information in terms of the economic environment or conditions in which businesses and credit applicants exist.

consignment terms. Most often used for other than credit reasons.

consumer credit. The medium of exchange that an individual consumer may offer to a seller of goods or services or to a lender of money in order to obtain these items at the present moment on the promise to repay at some future time.

consumer finance companies. Make loans to consumers under regulations enacted by states.

credit. Medium of exchange of limited acceptance.

credit card. A card that is subject to a finance charge.

credit lines. In most instances a firm will use them to indicate the amount of credit to be approved, as a warning signal or as a red flag.

credit period. The length of time allowed the buyer before payment is considered past due.

credit scoring plan. A system assigning points to certain characteristics deemed an indication of creditworthiness.

credit union An association of people who decide to save their money together and in turn make loans to each other at relatively low interest rates.

cycle billing. The names in the credit files are divided systematically and statements are rendered to a different group of customers each working day of the month.

daily simple interest method. This is different from the add-on method in that it is figured on a daily interest rate—usually 1/365th of the annual finance charge—that is added to the daily outstanding balance of the cash loan.

debit card. Used to withdraw cash, to transfer funds from one account to another, and increasingly to pay bills at electronic money terminals.

descriptive billing. A machine-produced monthly statement showing various financial figures pertaining to a customer.

disclaimer of opinion. When an auditor is unable to form an opinion as to the fairness of the financial statements and thus disclaims an opinion.

factoring. Purchasing of accounts receivable from clients without recourse for credit losses and with the assumption of all credit losses involved.

falsification. Placing untrue conditions on a statement in order to deceive credit analysts.

FDIC (Federal Deposit Insurance Corporation). Provides protection of deposits in commercial banks.

FIRREA (Financial Institutions Reform, Recovery and Enforcement Act of 1989). Changed the savings and loan industry and its federal regulation.

fixed-rate mortgage. Home mortgage loan used by people who want to know exactly how much their monthly payments will be for the length of the loan.

full recourse. Dealers sell or sign over to the bank installment sale paper that they have originated, with their unconditional guarantee and with full responsibility for the paper should the purchaser become delinquent.

grading the credit. The examination of evidence and the recording of the quality judgment drawn from specific evidence bearing on specific factors in an orderly manner.

home equity line of credit. Form of revolving credit in which a consumer's home serves as collateral.

house standard. Guide by which credit managers may judge the pertinent qualities of credit risks seeking to purchase from their firms.

identification. The technique of making sure the person purchasing is the party who has an account and not an impostor.

income statement. Covers a period of time and reflects the sales, costs of goods sold, expenses, and net profit or loss during the interval covered.

independent sales organizations (ISOs). Provide banks with outside assistance in finding and signing up additional cardholders and retail and service concerns in order to expand their bank credit card programs.

industrial banks. Most complex types of consumer lending institutions because of the varied nature of their services.

IRAs (individual retirement accounts). First authorized in 1974, these are consumer retirement accounts, taking advantage of reductions in federal income taxes.

limited acceptance. It is because of two elements, risk and time, found in every credit transaction that credit has limited acceptance.

liquidity. This is concerned with a firm's ability to meet day-to-day current obligations.

liquidity ratios. Seven ratios that generally are considered significant in analyzing a firm's ability to meet its debts.

managerial efficiency. As revealed by financial statement analysis, this determines a firm's ability to operate profitably and successfully over a long period.

medium of exchange. Facilitates the passage of goods or services from seller to buyer.

nominal annual rate. The nominal rate must be converted to a nominal annual rate if the period involved is less than or more than one year.

nominal rate. Simply the dollar amount of interest charge divided by the dollar amount of credit desired by the customer.

nonbank banks. An innovative species allowed to offer checking accounts or make commercial loans but cannot do both.

nonrecourse. Under this plan, dealers are not contingently responsible for the customer's credit failure.

Optima credit card. A credit card plan launched by American Express in March 1987.

ordinary accounts receivable financing. An agreement under which a financing institution purchases the open accounts receivable of its customers, with recourse and without notice to trade debtors.

ordinary terms. Including two component parts—the net credit period and the cash discounts.

P.M.I. (private mortgage insurance). Guarantees conventional home mortgage loans, that is, nongovernment loans.

"point" system. A point is 1 percent of the face value of a mortgage, generally charged the home buyer rather than the seller.

prepayment terms. These reduce or eliminate the element of risk that is inherent in credit transactions.

prestige card. Both Visa and MasterCard have consolidated a wide array of bank products into a single prestige product.

previous or opening balance method. The finance charge is based on last month's balance without deducting the payments or credits during the month if the account is not paid in full.

public credit. Includes that credit used by all governmental bodies and units.

qualification as to scope. Accountants express this generally when they have not confirmed the accounts receivable and have not actually observed the taking of inventories.

qualified opinion. Accountants express this when they believe the statement is a generally fair presentation but they are not completely satisfied on some point.

ratio analysis. Certain fundamental relationships of items in a financial statement are emphasized by stating them in the form of ratios.

repurchase. In case of consumer default on the terms of the contract, dealers are responsible for buying back the property for the unpaid balance after it has been retaken from the installment buyer.

RTC (Resolution Trust Corporation). Established to dispose of thrift institutions that failed and were taken over by regulators after January 1, 1989.

sales finance company. A specialized type of institution that engages primarily in buying consumer installment contracts from retail dealers and in providing wholesale financing for these dealers.

savings and loan associations. The primary source of financial assistance for a large segment of American homeowners.

savings banks. Receive their charters from the state governments, and the regulations governing their operations have a wide range of variations.

secured-card programs. Some banks offer questionable consumer credit cards secured by a cardholder deposit.

service credit. The amount owed by individuals to professional practitioners and service establishments.

share draft. A unique type of financial instrument, payable by a credit union out of a member's share draft account.

single-payment terms. In reality a special form of dating, in which customers are allowed to accumulate their obligations over a short time.

smart card. Credit card-sized bank card with an embedded microprocessor.

solvency. Indicated by a concern's dependence on finance support from creditors as contrasted to the financial investment by its owners.

solvency ratios. Seven ratios that are generally accepted as capable of showing a firm's solvency condition.

special-datings terms. Adjusting terms to conditions peculiar to a trade or its customers.

terms chiseler. One who regularly deducts cash discounts even though payment is made after expiration of the cash discount period; one who makes only a partial payment.

terms of sale. An understanding between the buyer and the seller regarding the conditions for the payment for the goods and services.

trade discounts. Discounts allowed uniformly to all customers of the same class.

undue optimism. A reflection of a firm's natural hope that certain items on a financial statement will in time return to the value at which they are now being carried.

unqualified opinion. Expressed by accountants when satisfied that a financial statement presents fairly the financial position and the results of operation.

usury. A premium paid by a consumer for the loan of money.

window dressing. Presenting the various aspects of a business in as favorable a light as possible.

INDEX